ANDROID

from A *to* D

Second Edition

Scott L. Hecht

Table of Contents (Chapters)

Table of Contents (Details)

Preface to the Second Edition

In this edition of *Android from A to D*, I have made several minor as well as major changes throughout the book.

Be aware that I have reorganized and renumbered some of the chapters, updated some images, corrected some sepllnig...uh...spelling mistakes, and so on. For example, the chapter on distributing your app, which mysteriously appeared in the middle of the First Edition, now appears at the end of the book in this edition. I have also placed a text file containing all of the code used throughout the book on my personal, yet strangely named, website: www.sheepsqueezers.com.

The installation instructions have been updated and now outline how to install the Android Software Development Kit (SDK) using the Android Developer Tools (ADT) Bundle. This method of installing the SDK greatly simplifies getting the prospective Android developer *up-and-running* in the shortest period of time.

In the previous edition, I included a Java Quick Start Guide. In this edition, that chapter remains, but I have also included a chapter outlining several useful Java classes such as `Math`, `String`, `SimpleDateFormat`, `ArrayList`, and more.

I have included a chapter on the new Android Studio Integrated Development Environment (IDE). Note that this software is still in *early access preview* status and not recommended for production programming projects. With that said, I explain many of its features and attempt to compare them to similar features found in Eclipse, where possible.

In this edition, I have included a light-and-fluffy introduction to fragments, for those of you who are curious. Many Android apps now make use of fragments and an explanation of this functionality was missing from the previous edition...oops!...my bad.

Note that there are several Android programming books out there promising to make you an Android programming guru in a few days or weeks. With all due respect to the authors of those books, if you are determined to create Android apps be aware that it will take you months of study - not days, not weeks - to learn how to program for the Android platform. Sorry if I'm bursting your bubble, but it's better to tell you the truth rather than give you false expectations.

Finally, on a personal note, I'd like to thank all of you who have purchased either the Kindle or the paperback version of this book. I realize it's not easy to plunk down money for a book on a complicated topic written by an unknown author, so thank you very much for giving me a chance!

Good luck with your Android programming studies!

Thanks,
Scott L. Hecht
July 12, 2014

Preface to the First Edition

This book is a collection of notes I created while learning Android programming. While I am no Android programming genius (that much is certain!), I thought it would be a good idea to gather all of those tiny little programming tips and tricks I've found along the way and place them in one spot. I do not claim that everything in this book is 100% original and I fully admit to copy-and-pasting a few tidbits from the Android documentation and stackoverflow.com. (The money you are paying for this book is for the grueling six months it took me to learn basic Android programming, code the examples, test them all, research problems and, finally, write it all down in a pleasing and, hopefully, enlightening format.) With that said, all of the examples shown below, as well as the code, I created myself. Since I am an Android novice, whether you can actually learn Android programming by reading this collection of notes remains to be seen. I'm sure there are spots throughout this book in which you will say "What the heck are you talking about?". Please drop me an e-mail if this book has helped you out or you have suggestions to make it better (see my e-mail address below).

It is assumed that the reader has some knowledge of programming, but no knowledge of GUI or object-oriented programming is assumed.   Also, no knowledge of Java programming is assumed as one of the chapters is dedicated to introducing Java programming as well as object-oriented programming.

Whereas some authors take great pains in creating a full-blown example used throughout their book, I prefer to create smaller programs which aid in quickly understanding the topic being presented.   I assume that the reader can successfully expand these examples for use in his/her own programs without having to slog through someone else's huge, mostly incomprehensible, program.

While Android apps can be created on the Apple and Linux platforms, this book was written with the Android SDK installed on Windows Vista. Be aware, though, that after you have completed installing the Android SDK, Eclipse IDE, Java SDK, etc., on your chosen platform, the task of creating apps for Android is the same (or very similar).

If you believe you have found an error or disagree with one of my comments or explanations (very possible!), please feel free to drop me a note at comments@sheepsqueezers.com. Don't forget to stop by www.sheepsqueezers. com to get more documents and presentations on a variety of topics. Also, please see our YouTube channel: sheepsqueezersYT.

Note that I have removed Chapter 32, *Package and Class Parade* as well as all of the appendices from the book and have placed them in an Adobe Acrobat Reader file on my website www.sheepsqueezers.com.   This book has become too unwieldy with the added pages and, besides, they are not needed upon first read of the book.

Thanks,
Scott L. Hecht
July 27, 2012 - June 23, 2014

Chapter 1: Installing the Android SDK on Windows

Overview

At the time the previous edition of this book was published, there was only one way to install the Android Software Development Kit (SDK): the complicated way. Recently, though, Android has introduced the Android Developer Tools (ADT) Bundle which makes installing the SDK much easier. The ADT Bundle contains the latest Android Software Development Kit (SDK), a version of the Eclipse IDE, the ADT plugin for Eclipse, and much more.

If you already have the Java Development Kit (JDK) and Eclipse installed on your machine, you may want to fall back on that complicated method, but if you have neither installed, I recommend using the easy method.

This chapter outlines the easy installation method for Windows using the ADT Bundle. If you already have the JDK and Eclipse installed on your computer, you may wish to visit the Android developer's website and follow the directions presented under the Download section labeled *Setting Up an Existing IDE* under the Tools menu.

Overview of the Steps to Be Performed

This chapter outlines what software you will need in order to install the Android Software Development Kit (SDK) on Windows using the Android Developer Tools (ADT) Bundle.

In Pre-Step 1, we download and install the Android Developer Tools (ADT) Bundle.

In Pre-Step 2, we download and install the Java SE 8 Development Kit (JDK). This contains the Java Runtime Environment (JRE) which will allow our Android programs to run as well as allow the Eclipse Integrated Development Environment (IDE) software to execute.

In Step 1, we open Eclipse for Android to ensure that everything works, set up a project workspace and determine if we want to send usage statistics to Google.

In Step 2, we use the Android SDK Manager to download older versions of the Android SDK. Note that the ADT Bundle includes only the latest SDK version (for me, it's version 4.4.2/API 19), but you may want to install additional SDKs if you are targeting older versions of Android. See the image below for more detailed information. We also install the local version of the SDK documentation to make life easier.

Version	Codename	API	Distribution
2.2	Froyo	8	0.8%
2.3.3 - 2.3.7	Gingerbread	10	14.9%
4.0.3 - 4.0.4	Ice Cream Sandwich	15	12.3%
4.1.x	Jelly Bean	16	29.0%
4.2.x		17	19.1%
4.3		18	10.3%
4.4	KitKat	19	13.6%

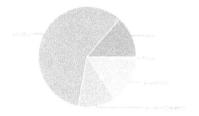

Data collected during a 7-day period ending on June 4, 2014.
Any versions with less than 0.1% distribution are not shown.

In Post-Step 1, we download and install the Eclipse Data Tools Platform (DTP). This will add in the Eclipse Database Perspective missing in the version of Eclipse included in the ADT Bundle. This perspective allows you to interact with SQLite databases from within Eclipse. We talk more about Eclipse as well as perspectives later in the book.

In Post-Step 2, we configure one or more *virtual devices*. You probably own an Android device such as a smart phone (e.g., Samsung Galaxy Nexus) or e-reader (e.g., Barnes and Noble Nook Color). These physical devices will run the software you create. But, you don't have to use your Android device while coding. You can create a *virtual* device which is an Android device emulator with specific settings that you choose (such as how much memory is available on the micro SD card, etc.). When you create an Android application, you can test and debug it using the emulator directly on your computer without attaching your Android device (via USB) to your computer. With that said, the development process seems to go much faster if you use a physical rather than virtual device.

Pre-Step 1 - Download and Install the Android Developer Tools (ADT) Bundle

1. Navigate your favorite browser to the Android developer website at
   http://developer.android.com/sdk/index.html. You will see a similar page to the
   one shown below:

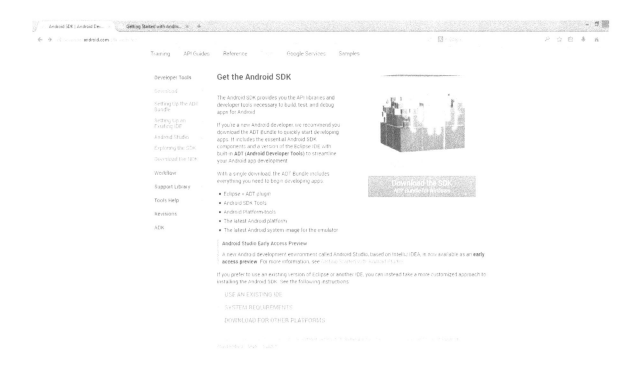

2. Click on the big button labeled *Download the SDK*.
3. Next, you will be presented with terms and conditions as well as a choice of 32-
   bit or 64-bit. Ensure that the checkbox to the left of the text *I have read and
   agree with the above terms and conditions* is checked. Select the radio button
   based on whether your system is 32- or 64-bit. Finally, click the button labeled
   Download the SDK ADT Bundle for Windows. Proceed with the normal
   download procedure for your particular browser.

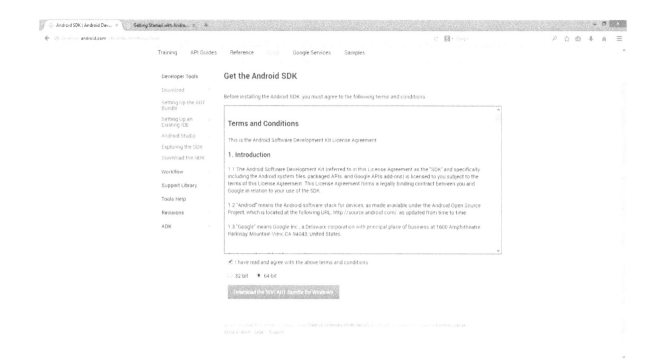

4. Unlike most software that requires you to execute installation software, the ADT Bundle is packaged as a zip file containing a single root folder. Open up this file with your favorite unzipping program (e.g., WinZip, PKZip, etc.) and copy the root folder to your desired location on disk. For me, the zip file contained the root folder labeled as `adt-bundle-windows-x86_64-20140321` (yours may be different) and I copied it over to my C-Drive renaming it to `androidSDK`.

5. Finally, I drilled down to the `eclipse` folder, and created a shortcut to the Eclipse application `eclipse.exe`. It is this shortcut that will start Eclipse and allow us to create Android programs. Huzzah!

Pre-Step 2 - Download and Install the Java SE 8 Development Kit (JDK)

1. Navigate your favorite browser to Oracle's website at
   http://www.oracle.com/technetwork/java/javase/downloads/index.html. You will
   see a similar web page to the one shown below:

2. Scroll down to the entry labeled `Java SE 8u5` (or later) and click on the JDK
   `DOWNLOAD` button.

3. On the `Java SE Development Kit 8 Downloads` webpage, click the
   radio button to the left of the text `Accept License Agreement`. (As soon as
   you do this, the radio buttons will disappear. Poof!)

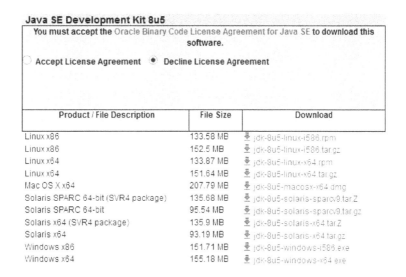

4. Based on your target platform, click the appropriate link under the column
   labeled `Download`. For the Windows platform, you will be asked to either run
   or save the file. Click on the Save File button to save the file to disk. Once the

download has completed, double-click on the executable to start the installation process.

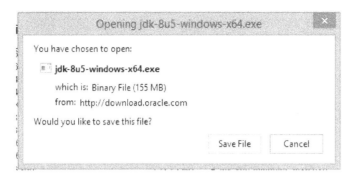

5. A User Account Control dialog box may appear asking you for permission to install the JDK. Click on the Yes button.
6. When the Setup dialog box appears, click on the Next button.

7. When the Custom Setup dialog box appears, click on each of the down arrows to the left of Development Tools, Source Code and Public JRE and select This feature, and all subfeatures, will be installed on local hard drive. Ensure that the *Install to:* location meets your approval (take note of this location as you will need it later on: _____). Click the Next button.

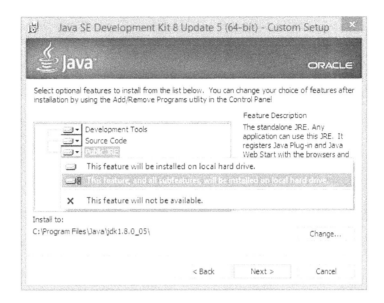

8. The `Progress` dialog box will appear indicating that the software is being installed.

9. The `Destination Folder` dialog box will appear showing you where the Java Runtime Environment (JRE) software will be installed. Click the Change... button to change this location (take note of the *Install to:* location as you may need it later on:_____). Click the Next button.

10. While the installation proceeds, you will be shown the following Progress dialog box:

11. Once the installation is completed, click the Next Steps button if you are so inclined. Click the Close button.

12. Next, you must update your Windows `Path` environment variable so that the Java SDK executables can be found:
   a. Depending on your version of Windows, click either START > Control Panel > System or right click START > Control Panel > System and Security > System. This will bring up the system window.
   b. Click on the Advanced system settings link. A User Account Control dialog box may appear; if so, click Continue.

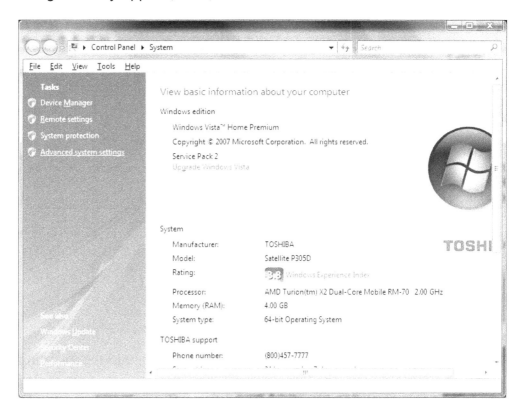

   c. Once the System Properties dialog box appears, click on the Advanced tab and then click on the Environment Variables... button at the bottom.

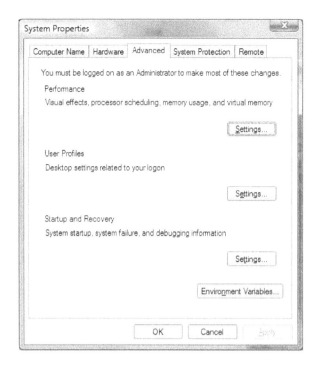

d. Once the Environment Variables dialog box appears, scroll to the Path variable located in the System Variables section at the bottom of the dialog, highlight the line and then click the Edit... button.

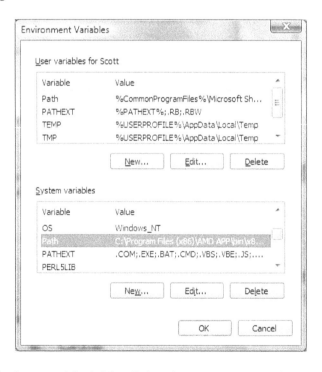

e. Once the Edit System Variable dialog box appears, add the following text to the end of the Variable Value input box: `;C:\Program Files\Java\jdk1.8.0_05\bin` (or the JDK-relevant version number for your download) as shown below:

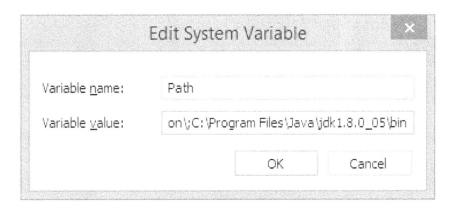

f. Click the OK button to save the change to the variable value.
g. Click the OK button to dismiss the Environment Variables dialog box.
h. Click the OK button to dismiss the System Properties dialog box.

13. In order to check that the Java executables can be found by the operating system, perform the following steps:
    a. Click START > Run... or right click START > Run...
    b. Enter the text `cmd` in the Open input box and click the OK button.

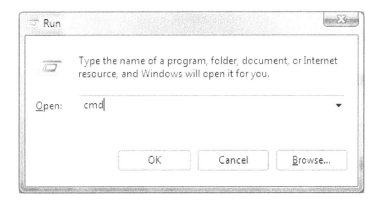

c. When the command prompt window appears, type in the text `javac -version` and hit the Enter key. If all goes well, you should see text similar to `javac 1.8.0_05` in the command window. If you do not see this, please check that the text you added to the Path variable is correct.

Step 1 - First Time Start up of Eclipse for Android

1. Locate the shortcut to Eclipse for Android and double-click it. If the installation of the JDK or the Path variable is faulty, you will be presented with a dialog box indicating that the JRE could not be found. Please repeat the steps in Pre-Step 2 to ensure that the JDK is installed properly and the Path variable is set correctly. If all goes well, you will be presented with the following startup screen:

2. Next, you will be asked to select a folder to serve as the workspace folder. A workspace is a location under which all of your projects are stored. You will be presented with the dialog box shown below.
   a. Note that I chose the folder `C:\temp\android_workspace` as my workspace folder, but the choice is yours.
   b. Ensure that the checkbox to the left of the text *Use this as the default and do not ask again* is checked.
   c. Click the OK button.

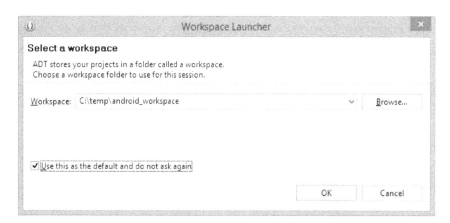

3. Next, you will be asked if you wish to contribute usage statistics to Google. Click Yes to help the cause...Power to the People! Click Finish to dismiss the dialog box.

4. Finally, you will be presented with the Eclipse IDE, as shown below.

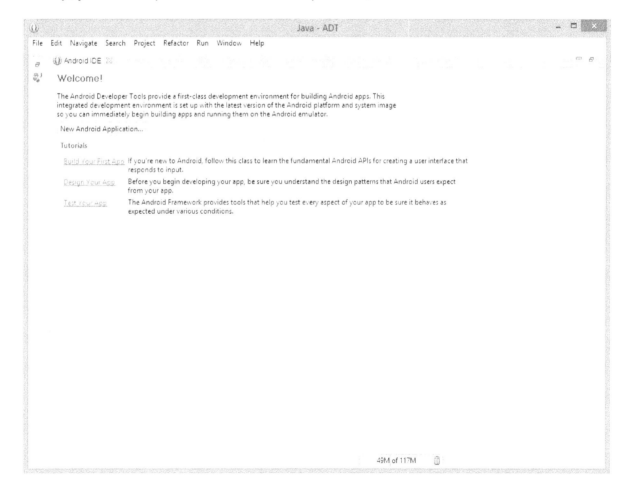

Step 2 - Installing SDKs with the Android SDK Manager

1. Ensure that you are in Eclipse for Android.
2. Click on the Android SDK Manager menu item under the Window menu.

3. You will initially be presented with a Progress Information dialog, as shown below.

4. Finally, the Android ADK Manager will appear, as shown (in part) below. Within the Packages window, select additional Android SDK versions, such as Android 2.3.3 (API 10), Documentation for Android SDK for one or more versions, and so on. Ensure that you have a representative selection in order to compile and test your applications for a variety of Android versions.

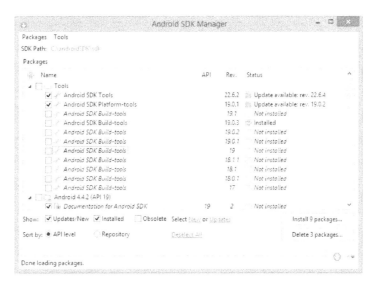

5. Click the Install # packages... button and the *Choose Packages to Install* dialog will appear. Ensure that you accept all licenses by clicking the Accept License radio button. Note that once you accept the licenses, most of the red Xs will disappear, as shown below. In order to remove any remaining red Xs, you will have to click on the items individually and accept each license.

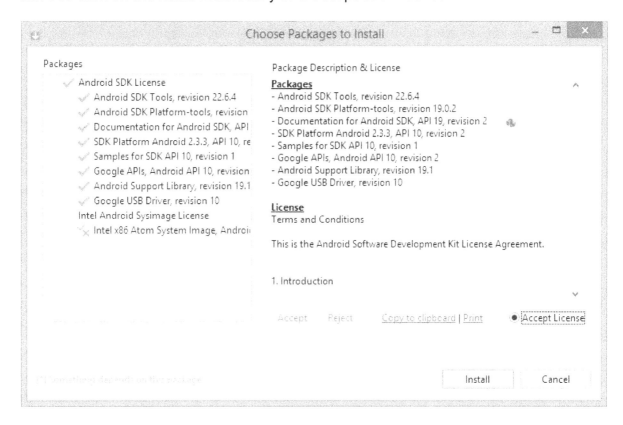

6. Finally, click on the Install button to download and install the software. You will see a progress bar at the bottom of the Android SDK Manager, as shown below:

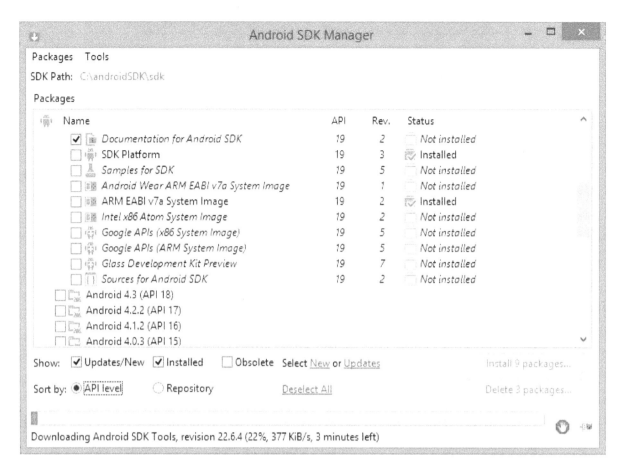

7. Once the installation is complete, you will be asked to restart Eclipse. Click OK.

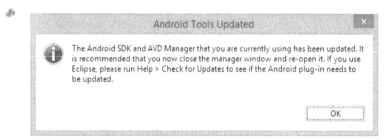

8. Occasionally, you will want to check for updates.
    a. Within Eclipse, click on the Check for Updates menu item on the Help menu.

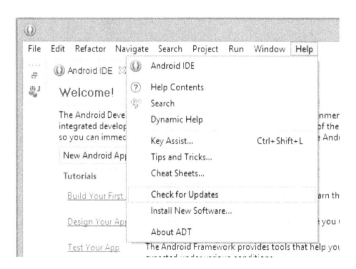

b. You will be presented with a Contacting Software Sites dialog box as well as a progress bar:

c. Since this is a new install, you are more than likely to be presented with this dialog box. Click OK to dismiss the dialog.

Post-Step 1 - Installing the Database Perspective with Eclipse DTP

1. Start Eclipse.
2. To install the Eclipse DTP plug-in, click on Help...Install New Software.

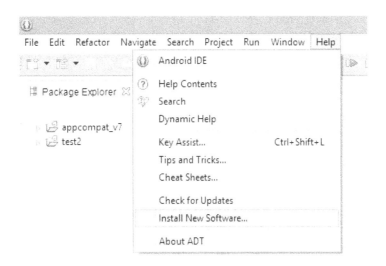

3. On the Install dialog, enter the following URL into the input box to the right of the text *Work with:* and then press the Enter key:

   ```
   http://download.eclipse.org/releases/kepler
   ```

   Alternatively, you can click the Add... button to add the URL above and give it a permanent name. Note that for my version of the ADT Bundle, Eclipse version 4.3 is installed. Eclipse version 4.3 is also known as Kepler. Please make sure that you are installing the correct DPT for your version of Eclipse. See Help > About ADT to determine the version of Eclipse you are running.
4. It will take a moment for the table to fill in, but when it does, check the checkbox to the left of the text *Database Development.*

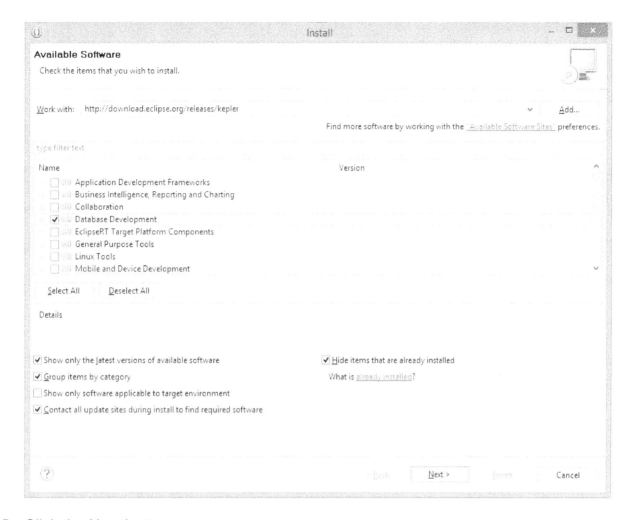

5. Click the Next button.
6. The software will compute space requirements as well as dependencies. Once this is complete, you will be presented with the Install Details dialog box. Click the Next button.
7. You will be presented with a dialog asking you to accept several license agreements. Ensure that the radio button to the left of the text *I accept the terms of the license agreement* is checked for each item listed in the Licenses: pane on the left of the dialog. Click the Finish button.
8. The Installing Software dialog will appear for a moment, as shown below:

9. A Security Warning pop-up dialog box may appear telling you that *You are installing software that contains unsigned content*. Click the OK button to continue the installation.
10. Finally, the Software Updates dialog will appear asking you if you'd like to restart ADT. Click on the Yes button.

31

Post-Step 2 - Setting Up Virtual Devices with Android Virtual Device (AVD) Manager

1. Start Eclipse for Android
2. Click the Android Virtual Device Manager menu item under the Window menu. This will start the Android Virtual Device Manager which will allow us to create virtual devices.

3. Initially, the list of existing Android virtual devices will be empty (as you see below...barren and sad!).

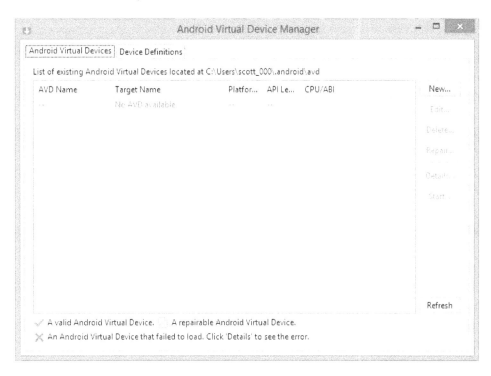

4. Click the New... button. The Create new Android Virtual Device (AVD) window will appear, as shown below.

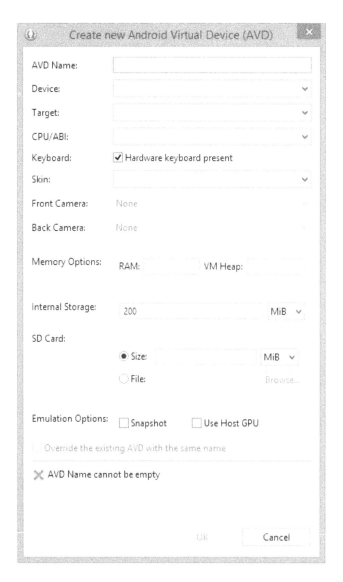

5. Give a name to your Android virtual device by filling in the AVD Name input box. I'll use the following name (and it'll become apparent by my selections below as to why I've chosen this rather long name): `AVD_233API10_SD2GB_WVGA800_MaxHeap32_Ram256`.

6. Select a default Android device. I choose the 4" WVGA (Nexus S) (480 x 800: hdpi) option.

7. Select a target Android from the Target drop-down box. I've chosen `Android 2.3.3 - API Level 10`.

8. The CPU/ABI field can be either ARM or Intel Atom. ARM is recommended.

9. Ensure that the checkbox to the left of the text *Hardware keyboard present* is checked.

10. For Skin, either select one of the built-in choices (`Default (WVGA800)`, `HVGA, QVGA, WQVGA400, WQVGA432, WVGA800, WVGA854`) or specify your own resolution (width first followed by height). I've selected `Default (WVGA800)`. Note that if you are targeting a specific device (such as if I were to create an application for my own Nook Color), you should probably change the resolution to match the specific device.

11. If available, select your front and back camera options.

12. For memory options, I've set RAM to 256 and VM Heap to 32.

13. For Internal Storage, I've selected 200 MiB.
14. Select the size of your desired SD Card. I've chosen 2 GiB, but you may want to throttle that back if you believe the devices that will be running your application will have less available memory on the SD Card.
15. Leave Snapshot Enabled and Use Host GPU both unchecked.

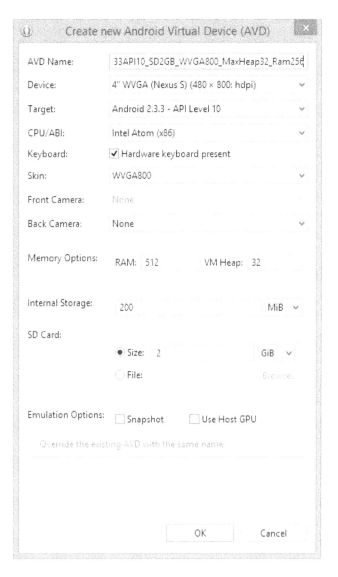

16. Click the OK button.
17. Once completed, you are brought back to the Android Virtual Device Manager window, shown below. Click the X-button to close it.

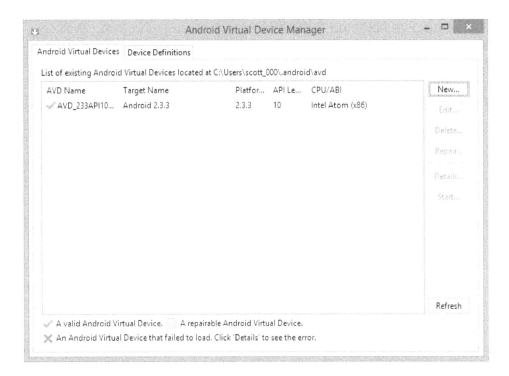

Be aware that, just like a physical Android device (like a cell phone or tablet), when you install software on the emulator, it will be there once the emulator is restarted. That is, the emulator is not a pristine copy each time it is started. This makes sense because that is how your own physical Android device (like that fancy phone or tablet) works!

Summary

In this chapter, we installed the software and tools needed to create an Android application. In the subsequent chapters, we will delve into these tools in more detail.

Note that we did not discuss the Android Native Development Kit (NDK). The NDK is used to create C/C++ code for use by your Android application, but this is usually not necessary to do.

Finally, note that the Eclipse for Android IDE appears slightly different from the Eclipse IDE shown in the remaining part of the book. Rather than replace each image in the book - which would have given me an aneurysm - I left the images as they were in the first edition. The main difference, though, is the appearance of the title bar between the two IDEs.

Chapter 2: Creating Our First Android Application

Hello, World!

In this chapter, we create our first Android application using Eclipse. This will be the traditional "Hello, World!" application, so it won't be so terrific, but it'll get you started.

1. Start Eclipse.
2. When Eclipse first starts, you will be shown the Welcome page containing links to an Overview, Tutorials, Samples, and What's New. To get to the IDE, you can either click on the X button to the right of the text Welcome on the Welcome tab, click on the Workbench icon on the upper-right corner or start a project. To start a new project, click on File...New...Project...
3. When the New Project wizard appears, expand the branch labeled Android. You will see the following four entries: Android Application Project, Android Project from Existing Code, Android Sample Project, and Android Test Project. Click on the Android Application Project and click the Next button.

4. When the New Android Application dialog box appears, fill in the following fields with the appropriate entries:
   a. Application Name: Fill in the friendly name of the application, such as `My First Android Application`.
   b. Project Name: This is the name of your project in computer gibberish, such as `andapp1`. Note that Project Name and Application Name can be the same.
   c. Package Name: This is a Java package name in reverse domain name form. When you fill in the Application Name and Project Name, this field is created using `com.example.`*`project_name`*`.` You can modify this

to reflect your own domain name. For us, let's use `com.example.andapp1`.

d. Build SDK: I've chosen `Android 2.3.3 (API 10)`.
e. Minimum Required SDK: I've chosen `API 10: Android 2.3.3 (Gingerbread)`.
f. Create custom launcher icon: Ensure that this is checked.
g. Mark this project as a library: Ensure that this is NOT checked.
h. Create project in Workspace: Ensure that this is checked.

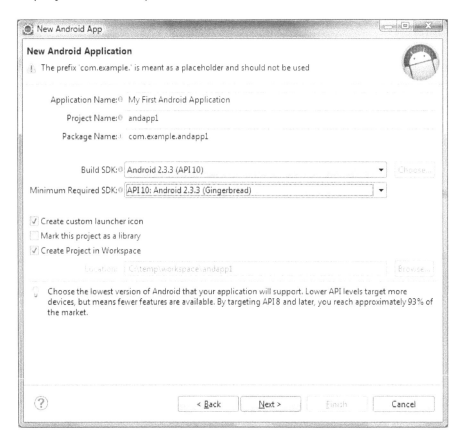

i. Click the Next button.
5. In the Configure Launcher Icon dialog box, select the icon you want associated with your application. By default, Clipart is selected, but you can select either Image or Text. Take note of the preview displayed on the right side of the dialog box. Click the Next button.

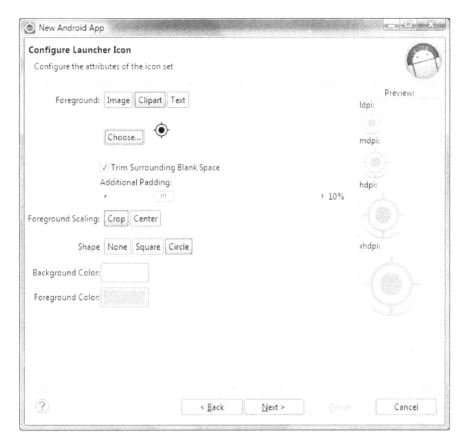

6. In the Create Activity dialog box, ensure that the checkbox to the left of the text Create Activity is checked and that BlankActivity is highlighted. Click the Next button.

7. In the New Blank Activity dialog box, fill in the fields as follows:

a. Activity Name: This is the name of the class to create. Leave this set to `MainActivity`.
b. Layout Name: This is the name of the layout with your activity. You can think of layout as being similar to HTML and the activity class as being the JavaScript that controls what happens when a use clicks or taps the layout. For each activity (which is just a fancy name for a dialog or screen), you can associate a layout responsible for placing your buttons, text boxes, etc. on the screen in the appropriate location. Leave this set to `activity_main`.
c. Navigation Type: Leave this set to None.
d. Hierarchical Parent: Leave this blank.
e. Title: This is the title that appears at the top of the device. Change this to `First Android App`.
f. Click the Finish button to generate the application.

Once Eclipse has completed generating the application from the information you placed in the wizard, you will see a screen similar to the following. Note that you will see a representation of an Android device (by default, a Nexus One) with the default screen generated by the Wizard. Note that the words `Hello world!` appear in the center of the screen. This text was generated automatically and we will talk about this in a moment.

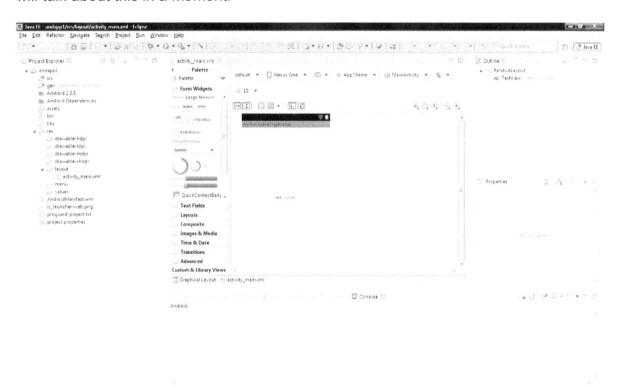

Running the Project Using an Android Virtual Device

Now, let's run the code in this project:

1. Click on Run...Run Configurations... This will bring up the Runs Configurations dialog box.
2. Click on the Android Application item on the left pane.

3. Either right-click and click New or click the New Launch Configuration icon on the upper left.
4. In the Name field, fill in the name of this configuration. I used Configuration1.
5. In the Android tab:
    a. Click the Browse... button and select the name of your application.
    b. In the Launch Action section, ensure that the radio button to the left of the text Launch Default Activity is selected.
    c. Click the Apply button.
6. In the Target tab:
    a. Ensure that the radio button for either Always prompt to pick device OR Automatically pick compatible device is selected. For the latter selection, choose the Android Virtual Device (AVD) we created earlier.
    b. Click Apply.
7. I made no changes to the Common tab.
8. Click the Run button.
9. When the Android Device Chooser dialog appears (as shown below), ensure that the radio button to the left of the text Launch a new Android Virtual Device is selected and that the sole entry is highlighted. Click the OK button. Note that clicking on the Details... button displays information about that virtual device. Also, clicking on the Start... button brings up the Launch Options dialog box. This allows you to set the screen size as well as previously stored user data. If you don't specify the screen size, it'll fill your computer screen vertically.

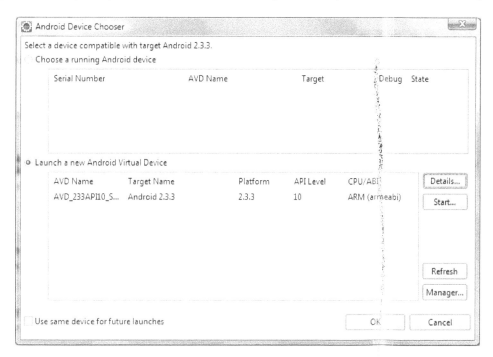

Now, it takes **quite a while** for the emulator to start up the first time. Initially, you will see the following screen.

You will then see the following screen. Again...you'll wait a few moments.

Then you will finally see the Android Home screen:

If you wait too long, then you will see the locked screen. Use your mouse pointer to swipe the icon of the unlocked lock to the right to get back to the home screen.

Normally, your application will start automatically. Here is what our Hello, World! application looks like:

Just like a real Android device, you can also click on the Launcher Icon to bring up the list of applications installed on the device. You will see our application, called MainActivity, in this list. Click on the icon (the blue bull's eye) and our application will run.

Now, you don't have to close the emulator window each time you make a change to the code. For example, if I change `Hello world!` to `HELLO, WORLD!!` and click Run...Run, the Android Device Chooser dialog appears with a selection in the

Choose a running Android device section where one was not there before. This selection is our currently running Android emulator. Select this and click OK. In the Eclipse IDE, you will see the following messages:

```
[2012-08-07 12:12:19 - andapp1] Android Launch!
[2012-08-07 12:12:19 - andapp1] adb is running normally.
[2012-08-07 12:12:19 - andapp1] Performing com.example.andapp1.MainActivity activity launch
[2012-08-07 12:13:42 - andapp1] Uploading andapp1.apk onto device 'emulator-5554'
[2012-08-07 12:13:44 - andapp1] Installing andapp1.apk...
[2012-08-07 12:13:56 - andapp1] Success!
[2012-08-07 12:13:56 - andapp1] Starting activity com.example.andapp1.MainActivity on
                                              device emulator-5554
[2012-08-07 12:13:59 - andapp1] ActivityManager: Starting: Intent {
                act=android.intent.action.MAIN cat=[android.intent.category.LAUNCHER]
                cmp=com.example.andapp1/.MainActivity }
```

And you will see the change reflected in the emulator:

Running the Project Using an Android Physical Device

Now, let's run our application using a physical Android device. Turn on your Android device and hook it up to your computer via the USB cable. Now, in this case, when you click on Run...Run, you will be presented with an entry for your physical device, as shown below (bn-nookcolor is my device, a Barnes & Noble Nook Color):

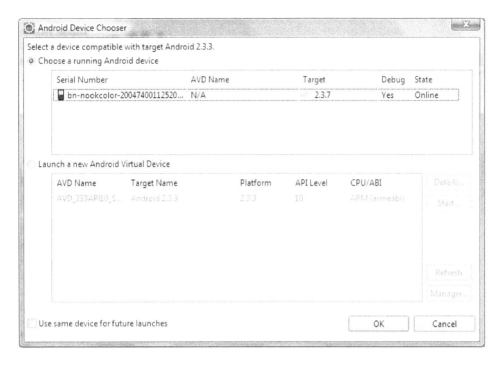

Select that device and click OK. You should see our application appear on the device's screen. Also, if you click on the Launcher icon, you will see our blue bull's eye icon in the list. Clicking on this icon starts the application

You can uninstall the application from your device by clicking on Settings...Applications...Manage Applications...All, scrolling down the list until you find the name of the application,   click on the application name and then click on the Uninstall button. This will remove your application from the device.

To remove the Android device from your computer, you perform the normal steps for removing any USB device. Note, though, that occasionally Windows will refuse to stop the ADB connection. To circumvent this, start Task Manager and kill the `adb.exe` process. This will then allow you to stop the ADB connection and remove the device safely from your computer.

When Things Go Wrong

1. Occasionally, a file named `activity_main.out.xml` (or `activity_main.out.out.xml`) appears in the layout folder. These files seem to cause issues when you go to re-run the application. You can delete these files by right-clicking on them and clicking on the Delete menu-item. See image below.
2. When you go to re-run the project, it's probably a good idea to clean the project first by clicking on Project...Clean..., selecting the appropriate project to clean and clicking the OK button.
3. It seems that hooking up your Android device via USB to your computer and testing your application on it rather than an emulator seems to be the faster way to go. The emulator seems to take some time to come up, but the physical device seems to be much faster.

A Quick Look into Our First Android Project

Each Android project contains a file called `AndroidManifest.xml` which holds application-specific information such as the package name, the application's version number and version name, the minimum SDK version and the target SDK version of the application, the location of the application's icon, the application's label, the application's theme (think CSS styles, in this case), and so on. Here is what the Wizard generated for us:

```
<manifest xmlns:android="http://schemas.android.com/apk/res/android"
    package="com.example.andapp1"
    android:versionCode="1"
    android:versionName="1.0" >

    <uses-sdk
        android:minSdkVersion="10"
        android:targetSdkVersion="15" />

    <application
        android:icon="@drawable/ic_launcher"
        android:label="@string/app_name"
        android:theme="@style/AppTheme" >
        <activity
            android:name=".MainActivity"
            android:label="@string/title_activity_main" >
            <intent-filter>
                <action android:name="android.intent.action.MAIN" />
                <category android:name="android.intent.category.LAUNCHER" />
            </intent-filter>
        </activity>
    </application>

</manifest>
```

Along with this XML file, there is an XML file which describes the layout (think HTML, in this case) of the screen (called an *activity*, in Android-speak) which displays the text `HELLO, WORLD!`. This XML file (located in the layout folder) is called `activity_main.xml` and is referenced in the Java code when the program is executed. Here is what this XML file looks like:

```
<RelativeLayout xmlns:android="http://schemas.android.com/apk/res/android"
    xmlns:tools="http://schemas.android.com/tools"
    android:layout_width="match_parent"
    android:layout_height="match_parent" >

    <TextView
        android:layout_width="wrap_content"
        android:layout_height="wrap_content"
        android:layout_centerHorizontal="true"
        android:layout_centerVertical="true"
        android:text="@string/hello_world"
        tools:context=".MainActivity" />

</RelativeLayout>
```

Note that there are several ways to create layout within Android. One way is to code every activity using Java. This seems like a lot of work to go through, but may be necessary in certain instances. Another way is to use the XML as shown above. Finally, you can use the Graphical Layout shown in Eclipse. This Graphical Layout is associated with the XML file.

Both the `AndroidManifest.xml` and `activity_main.xml` layout XML files reference variables defined in other XML files. For example, the code `android:text= "@string/hello_world"` indicates that the value associated with the variable `hello_world` located in the `strings.xml` file (which is in the values folder) is to be substituted at this point. Here is what `strings.xml` looks like:

```
<resources>

    <string name="app_name">My First Android Application</string>
    <string name="hello_world">HELLO, WORLD!!</string>
    <string name="menu_settings">Settings</string>
    <string name="title_activity_main">MainActivity</string>

</resources>
```

If you look at the bold code above, the XML `string` node contains the `hello_world` attribute and the value of this node is `HELLO, WORLD!`. This indicates that the text `HELLO, WORLD!` is to be substituted wherever `@string/hello_world` is used within other XML files.

When you place a text string directly in the XML of the view (i.e., control) itself, it is termed a *raw string*. Normally you want to place the string, as shown above, in `strings.xml` and reference the string using the @-sign notation. In some cases, raw strings are allowed, but in other cases, such as within certain attributes in the Android manifest, they are not allowed and you may see a caution icon alerting you to place your text in `strings.xml`. Also, note that the XML tag is named `string` whereas the associated XML file is named `strings.xml`.

Note that the `TextView` XML, located in `activity_main.xml`, is associated with a `TextView` widget which is responsible for displaying the text `HELLO,`

WORLD!. Here is the Java code which accesses the `activity_main.xml` file (see the bold code below):

```
package com.example.andapp1;

import android.os.Bundle;
import android.app.Activity;
import android.view.Menu;

public class MainActivity extends Activity {

  @Override
  public void onCreate(Bundle savedInstanceState) {
    super.onCreate(savedInstanceState);
    setContentView(R.layout.activity_main);
  }

  @Override
  public boolean onCreateOptionsMenu(Menu menu) {
    getMenuInflater().inflate(R.menu.activity_main, menu);
    return true;
  }

}
```

Note that Android creates the variable `R` which allows you to access the values stored within these XML files. For instance, `R.layout.activity_main` references the `activity_ main.xml` file located within the layout folder.

Now, in order for Android to know which activity (screen, form, GUI, etc.) is to be presented *when the application first starts up*, the `AndroidManifest.xml` file contains the `application` section which further contains the `activity` section. Within this section, the intent-filter section indicates that this activity is the MAIN activity and should be launched first:

```
<activity
  android:name=".MainActivity"
  android:label="@string/title_activity_main" >
  <intent-filter>
    <action android:name="android.intent.action.MAIN" />
    <category android:name="android.intent.category.LAUNCHER" />
  </intent-filter>
</activity>
```

Further, within this section, the `android:name=".MainActivity"` associates this activity with the Java class `MainActivity`. This class is the *code behind* the layout being displayed. If you are familiar with ASP.NET, you will find this very familiar. You can also think of this as the Model-View-Controller (MVC) design pattern.

A Quick Note about Debugging

Throughout this chapter, we have continually used the Run...Run menu item to run our application, but another way to run the application is by using Run...Debug. This method of executing your application will allow you to debug the application. One nice feature of using Run...Debug is that you can include logging methods that allow you to place your own debugging messages in your code using the `Log.d` method. Note that `Log.d` has no effect if run using Run...Run. When your code reaches the `Log.d` method, any message that you've placed in its parameters will be shown in the LogCat window (explained below). First, here is how you code the `Log.d` method in your code:

```
@Override
public void onCreate(Bundle savedInstanceState) {
 super.onCreate(savedInstanceState);
 setContentView(R.layout.activity_main);
 Log.d("MYAPPTAG","MY IMPORTANT MESSAGE GOES HERE!");
}
```

The first parameter of `Log.d` is a tag that is used to distinguish your logging messages from the systems logging messages (and, boy, there are a lot of system messages!). The second parameter is your message. To see your messages, in Eclipse, click on Window...Show View...Other... and double-click on the LogCat item under the Android node. This will add the LogCat tab to the list of other tabs such as Console, Properties, Snippets, etc. When you run your application, you will see an entry in the LogCat like the one shown below (see the first line):

Two important things to note:
1. `Log.d` outputs messages to the debug window of the LogCat, so ensure that the drop-down box is displaying the word debug (as shown above). There are additional methods such as `Log.i` (outputs to the info window), `Log.v` (outputs to the verbose window), `Log.e` (outputs to the error window) and `Log.w` (outputs to the warn window).
2. You can subset the output by placing your tag in the `Search for messages` input box directly to the left of the drop-down box. This will only show those messages associated with your tag (shown below). Note that when I entered my entire tag (`MYAPPTAG`), the debug window returned no results, but when I entered just the text `MY`, the debug window showed the desired logging message:

Finally, you can save your filter by clicking on the green plus-sign to the right of the text Saved Filters (see image above). By default, there are no filters, but by clicking on the green plus-sign, the Logcat Message Filter Settings dialog box appears. Below is an example of my tag:

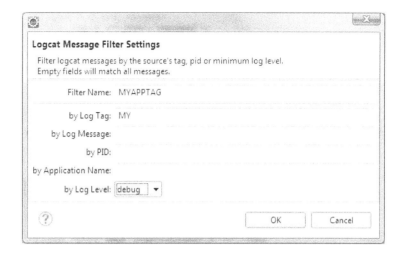

The `Filter Name` is set to MYAPPTAG is and is NOT used in the search. The `by Log Tag` text, MY in the input box above, *is* used in the search. When you click on the OK button, here is what the LogCat window looks like now with your own filter showing under Saved Filters:

Accessing the Internet from the Emulator

By default, the emulator is not given access to the internet. In order to allow the emulator to access the internet, you need to perform the following steps:

1. Determine your DNS Server IP Address.
   a. Start a Command Window by clicking on Start...Run and enter the text `cmd.exe` in the Open input box. Click OK.
   b. Enter the command `ipconfig/all` at the command line and hit the Enter key.
   c. Find the first occurrence of the text `DNS Servers` starting from the top of the output. Take note of the IP Address given.
2. In Eclipse, navigate to Window...Preferences...Android...Launch. Add the `-dns-server` option to the input box labeled Default emulator options followed by the IP Address in 1c (an example is shown below).
3. Click Apply then OK.

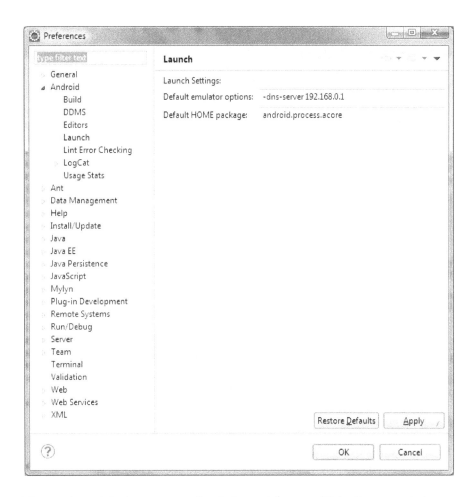

You should now be able to access the internet from within the emulator.

Note that this just gives you the ability to access the internet from within the emulator via the browser, but your application will still need the `<uses-permission android:name ="android.permission.INTERNET" />` line added to the Android Manifest to allow your software to access the internet. We talk more about the Android Manifest later in the book.

Summary

In this chapter, we created our first Android application and looked into the XML files and code more deeply. In subsequent chapters, we will look more deeply into the XML files as well as the Java code.

Chapter 3: Quick Start Guide to Java Programming

Java Type System

Each variable declared in Java must be associated with a particular data type. Java breaks up its data types into two distinct groups: *primitives* and *objects*. The primitive data types, such as integers and floating-point numbers, are probably familiar to you if you've been programming for any length of time. The full list of primitive data types is shown in the table below:

Data Type Keyword	Description	Size (in bits)	Range
boolean	The values true or false	N/A	true/false
byte	A 2's-complement integer	8 bits	-128 to +127
short	A 2's-complement integer	16 bits	-32768 to +32767
int	A 2's-complement integer	32 bits	-2,147,483,648 to +2,147,483,647
long	A 2's-complement integer	64 bits	-9223372036854775808 to +9223372036854775807
char	An unsigned integer representing a UTF-16 code unit	16 bits	N/A
float	An IEEE-754 floating-point number	32 bits	7 significant digits
double	An IEEE-754 floating-point number	64 bits	15 significant digits

Object data types are discussed later in this chapter.

You declare a variable by entering the data type followed by the name of the variable, such as:

```
int iCounter;
iCounter=1;
```

...or equivalently...

```
int iCounter = 1;
```

Java variable names can start with a letter, underscore (_) or dollar sign ($) followed by letters or numbers. Special symbols such as the @-sign are usually reserved for Java and should probably be avoided in your own variable names.

Making Comments

You should make comments in your code to remind you what you did or to aid the programmer who takes over your program. There are three types of comments in Java: single-line, multi-line and Javadoc comments.

A single line comment starts with a double-slash (//) followed by your comment. Java ignores everything else on the line following the double-slash:

```
int iCounter = 1; //My counter variable set to 1.
```

A multiline comment starts with /* and ends with */. Everything in between is ignored even if the comment spans multiple lines:

```
/* This program is used to do something
wonderful and people will be amazed at
how great it is! */ int iCounter=1;
```

The final type of comment is the Javadoc comment and is used to produce API documentation for each variable, method, class, etc. you define in your program. For example,

```
/**
 * iCounter keeps track of counting things.
 *
 */
int iCounter=1;
```

When the documentation is produced, the comment will be associated with the variable iCounter.

Conditional Execution

You can use the if-then-else or switch statements as well as the ternary operator to conditionally execute code based on a condition:

The syntax for a variety of if-then-else is as follows:

```
if (condition)
    statement;
```

...or...

```
if (condition)
    statement-1;
else
 statement-2;
```

...or...

```
if (condition) {
    statement-1;
    statement-2;
    ...
}
```

...or...

```
if (condition) {
    statement-1;
    statement-2;
    ...
}
else {
    statement-3;
    statement-4;
    ...
}
```

...or...

```
if (condition-1) {
    statement-1;
    statement-2;
    ...
}
else if (condition-2) {
    statement-3;
    statement-4;
    ...
}
else if (condition-3) {
    statement-3;
    statement-4;
    ...
}
```

...or...

```
if (condition-1) {
    statement-1;
    statement-2;
    ...
}
else if (condition-2) {
    statement-3;
    statement-4;
    ...
}
else if (condition-3) {
    statement-3;
    statement-4;
    ...
}
else {
    statement-5;
    statement-6;
    ...
}
```

The syntax for `switch` is as follows:

```
switch(expression) {
 case constant-1:
   statement-1;
   statement-2;
   ...
   break;
 case constant-2:
   statement-3;
   statement-4;
   ...
   break;
 ...
 default:
   statement-1;
   statement-2;
   ...
   break;
}
```

The ternary operator is just a short-and-sweet if-then-else statement:

```
conditional-true-false-test ? condition-is-true : condition-is-false;
```

For example,

```
int iMinLenWid = iLength < iWidth ? iLength : iWidth;
```

Looping Constructs

Java has the traditional looping constructs such as the for, while, and do-while loops.

The syntax for the for-loop is:

```
for (initialize; stopping-condition; increments) {
 statements;
}
```

For example,

```
for (int i=0; i<10; i++) {
 iTotal += i;
}
```

The syntax for the while-loop is:

```
while (condition) {
 statements;
}
```

For example,

```
while (i<10) {
 iTotal += i;
 i++;
}
```

The do-while loop is similar to the while-loop except that it will execute at least once. The while-loop, depending on its associated condition, may not execute at all. For syntax for the do-while loop is:

```
do {
 statements;
} while (condition);
```

For example,

```
do {
 iTotal += i;
 i++;
} while (i<10);
```

Note that all three of these constructs can make use of the break or continue statements. The break statement will stop a loop from executing immediately upon its being reached. The continue statement will force the code to start from the top of the loop skipping all of the code below it.

```
while (i<10) {
 iTotal += i;
```

```
i++;
if (i==5) {
  break;
}
}
```

Arithmetic Operators

Java has the traditional arithmetic operators such as + (addition), – (subtraction), *
(multiplication), / (division) and % (modulus). Be careful when performing division!
If the two operators are integers, then your result will be an integer with any
fractional part discarded.

Assignment Operators

Java has the traditional assignment operators such as +=, -=, *= and /=. You
can, of course, just use a single equal sign (=) to mean assignment. For example,

```
iCounter += x;
```

is equivalent to

```
iCounter = iCounter + x;
```

Note that you can also string together assignments, such as

```
iCounter = iCounter2 = iCounter3 = 0;
```

Java also has the traditional increment and decrement operators such as x++,
++x, x--, --x.

Comparison Operators

Java has the traditional comparison operators such as == (is equal to), != (is not
equal to), < (is less than), > (is greater than), <= (is less than or equal to), >= (is
greater than or equal to).

Logical Operators

Java has the traditional logical operators such as && (Logical AND), || (Logical
OR) and ! (negation). Note that these are not bitwise operators (we discuss those
next).

Bitwise Operators

Java has the traditional bitwise operators such as << (left shift), >> (right shift),
>>> (right shift, zero fill), ~ (complement), & (bitwise AND), | (bitwise OR), ^
(bitwise XOR).

Working with Strings

Besides the `char` data type, you can use the `String` data type (which is not primitive, but an object data type) to allow you to work with large strings of text. For example,

```
String sGreeting = "Bonjour";
String sTitle = "Monsieur";
```

You can concatenate two strings together using the + operator:

```
String sFullGreeting = sGreeting + " ," + sTitle;
```

Working with Arrays

Whereas a variable stores *one* piece of information of a specific data type, an array stores *several* pieces of information all with a specific data type. For example,

```
int[] aNums = new int[10];
```

The code above creates an array that will hold 10 integers. The empty brackets to the left indicate that `aNums` is an array of integers whereas the 10 on the right indicates how many items the array can hold in total.

You can read a specific array element by referring to the array name followed by the specific element you desire in brackets:

```
int X = aNums[5];
```

Arrays work well within for-loops:

```
for(i=0; i<10; i++) {
 iTotal += aNums[i];
}
```

Exceptions

Rather than using an if-then-else construct to catch an exception, you can use the more modern try-catch-finally block to handle exceptions. Here is what this looks like:

```
class jpgm6 {

 public static void main(String args[]) {

  try {

   //Divide by zero
   int iNum = 5/0;

  }
  catch(ArithmeticException e) {
   System.out.println("Arithmetic Exception Detected: " + e);
  }
```

```
  catch(Exception e) {
    System.out.println("Generic Exception Detected: " + e);
  }
  finally {
    System.out.println("Finally!");
  }

  }

}
```

As you see, you start off with the `try` block which is responsible for processing your desired code such as connecting to a database, downloading an HTML web page, computing a value, etc. Next, you provide one or more `catch` blocks whose argument is either the name of a specific exception (such as `ArithmeticException`) or a generic exception (such as `Exception`), and whose body either attempts a retry or notifies the user of the exception. Note that `Exception` should appear last in the list of `catch` blocks! The `finally` block will *always* be executed no matter if an error occurred or not. Below is a list of Java runtime exceptions you can catch:

```
AnnotationTypeMismatchException, ArithmeticException, ArrayStoreException,
BufferOverflowException, BufferUnderflowException, CannotRedoException,
CannotUndoException, ClassCastException, CMMException,
ConcurrentModificationException, DataBindingException, DOMException,
EmptyStackException, EnumConstantNotPresentException, EventException,
IllegalArgumentException, IllegalMonitorStateException,
IllegalPathStateException, IllegalStateException, ImagingOpException,
IncompleteAnnotationException, IndexOutOfBoundsException, JMRuntimeException,
LSException, MalformedParameterizedTypeException, MirroredTypeException,
MirroredTypesException, MissingResourceException, NegativeArraySizeException,
NoSuchElementException, NoSuchMechanismException, NullPointerException,
ProfileDataException, ProviderException, RasterFormatException,
RejectedExecutionException, SecurityException, SystemException,
TypeConstraintException, TypeNotPresentException, UndeclaredThrowableException,
UnknownAnnotationValueException, UnknownElementException, UnknownTypeException,
UnmodifiableSetException, UnsupportedOperationException, WebServiceException
```

Object-Oriented Programming Concepts

Primitive data types are nice, but they only get you so far. Java is an object-oriented language like C++ and C# and allows you to step up your programming to the next level.

When you program using *structured programming*, you create a series of functions, subroutines, global variables, local variables, etc. that will help you achieve your desired programming results.

With object-oriented programming (OOP), you create one or more classes (indicated by the `class` keyword) representing objects. Within each class, you have your functions/subroutines (called *methods* in OOP terminology) and variables (called *attributes* in OOP terminology).

For example, you can think of a generic car as an object. A car has attributes such as the exterior color name, the number of cylinders, and so on. A car has methods such as the `start_engine` method and the `turn_on_radio` method. Here is an example class for our car:

```
class Car {
 String exteriorColor;
 int numberOfCylinders;
 boolean start_engine() { ...code to start the engine... }
 boolean turn_on_radio() { ...code to turn on the radio... }
}
```

Now, the `Car` class is just a *definition*. Just like using primitive data types, you have to create a variable that uses the class. For example, to create a usable `Car`, we *instantiate* it using the `new` keyword:

```
Car MyCar = new Car();
```

The code above creates a usable `Car` object called `MyCar` from the `Car` class.

Now, our class, as defined, doesn't do much of anything. For example, we have no way to set the `exteriorColor` or `numberOfCylinders` for our car. We can change that by adding a *constructor*; that is, a method called whenever the `new` keyword is used to create an object. This constructor allows us to initialize our attributes at instantiation time. For example,

```
class Car {

 String exteriorColor;
 int numberOfCylinders;

 //Our constructor is below
 Car() {
  exteriorColor = "LimeGreen";
  numberOfCylinders = 5;
 }

 boolean start_engine() { ...code to start the engine... }
 boolean turn_on_radio() { ...code to turn on the radio... }
}
```

Now, a constructor MUST have the same name as the class. Note that the constructor above takes no parameters and we force our `exteriorColor` to LimeGreen and the `numberOfCylinders` to 5. However, if you want to pass in a different exterior color or number of cylinders into the constructor during object instantiation, you will have to add parameters to your constructor:

```
class Car {

 String exteriorColor;
 int numberOfCylinders;

 //Our constructor is below
 Car(String pExtClr,int pNumCyl) {
  exteriorColor = pExtClr;
  numberOfCylinders = pNumCyl;
 }

 boolean start_engine() { ...code to start the engine... }
 boolean turn_on_radio() { ...code to turn on the radio... }
}
```

Here is how we would instantiate our new car:

```
Car MyCar = new Car("LimeGreen",5);
```

60

Now, `MyCar` is an instantiated object of class `Car` that is LimeGreen and with a dubious number of cylinders. One small problem, we have no way of returning the exterior color or number of cylinders if you need to know them later on in the program. So, let's add to additional methods that will return these two attributes:

```
class Car {

 String exteriorColor;
 int numberOfCylinders;

 //Our constructor is below
 Car(String pExtClr,int pNumCyl) {
  exteriorColor = pExtClr;
  numberOfCylinders = pNumCyl;
 }

 public String getExteriorColor() {
  return(exteriorColor);
 }

 public int getNumberOfCylinders() {
  return(numberOfCylinders);
 }

 boolean start_engine() { ...code to start the engine... }
 boolean turn_on_radio() { ...code to turn on the radio... }
}
```

These two methods are known as *getters* because they return (or get) some piece of information held in the instantiated object. In our case, we are returning the name of the car's exterior color as well as the engine's number of cylinders.

Now, we can use `MyCar` to retrieve both the exterior color and number of cylinders by following the object name with a period and the name of the method:

```
Car MyCar = new Car("PurplePassion",4);
System.out.println(MyCar.getExteriorColor());
System.out.println(MyCar.getNumberOfCylinders());
```

Note that the function `System.out.println()` prints output to the console and is not very useful for an Android application running on someone's Android device. We'll look into this later on.

We can also create two methods that will allow us to update (or set) these two attributes. These methods are called *setters*:

```
public void setExteriorColor(String pExtClr) {
 exteriorColor = pExtClr;
}

public void setNumberOfCylinders(int pNumCyl) {
 numberOfCylinders = pNumCyl;
}
```

Notice that we made use of the keyword `public` for both the getters and the setters. This keyword indicates that, if you have access to the instantiated variable `MyCar`, the outside world can run these four methods. If these four methods used the keyword `private` instead of `public`, then the outside world would **not** be able to run these methods. For getters and setters, you most likely want the outside world to access them. But, some methods may be for internal use to the class only and should be set to `private`. Also, some attributes may be for internal use to the class only and should be set to `private` as well. For example, if your class makes use of the American Social Security Number (SSN), then you probably don't want the outside world accessing it! Thus, SSN would be private. Similar for any method that, say, validates the SSN within the class.

By default, if you do not use the `public` or `private` keywords, attributes and methods are considered `public`. This means that you can access `exteriorColor` by the following code:

```
System.out.println(MyCar.exteriorColor);
```

Since we created getters and setters to allow us to interact with the `exteriorColor` attribute, allowing direct access to the attributes within the class is probably not a good idea. Here is how we can rectify that situation using the `private` keyword:

```
private String exteriorColor;
private int numberOfCylinders;
```

At this point, the outside world can ONLY inquire or update the exterior color and/or the number of cylinders via their associated getters and setters.

Besides the keywords `public` and `private`, there is a third keyword: `protected`. We will talk about that keyword later on in this chapter.

Now, suppose you instantiate two objects from the class `Car`:

```
Car MyCar1 = new Car("PurplePassion",4);
Car MyCar2 = new Car("VomitYellow",8);
```

Be aware that the attributes associated with `MyCar1` do not affect those in `MyCar2`. That is, both objects are distinct.

However, suppose you want to keep track of the number of `Car` objects that have been instantiated (two in the example above). You can degrade yourself by keeping track on a piece of paper, but that's not going to cut it in the cut-throat world of object-oriented programming. A more appropriate way is to create a *static variable* in the `Car` class and update it within the constructor. A static variable (also known as a *class variable*) is shared across ALL instantiated objects from the same class. For example, if we add the following line to our `Car` class...

```
public static int objectCount = 0;
```

...we can go ahead and instantiate two cars as well as print out the value of `objectCount`...

```
Car MyCar1 = new Car("PurplePassion",4);
System.out.println("Number of Objects = " + MyCar1.objectCount);

Car MyCar2 = new Car("YellowVomit",8);
```

```
System.out.println("Number of Objects = " + MyCar2.objectCount);
```

Here is the output:

```
Number of Objects = 1
Number of Objects = 2
```

The keyword `static` on an attribute indicates that the variable is a static (or class) variable.

You can also have static *methods* within a class. This indicates that you do NOT have to instantiate the class in order to run the method. For example,

```
class NumberInfo {

 public static double PI = 3.1415;

 public static double SquareIt(double pNum) {
  return(pNum*pNum);
 }

}
```

```
System.out.println("Cheap PI = " + NumberInfo.PI);
System.out.println("Square of 5 = " + NumberInfo.SquareIt(5));
```

The results are:

```
Cheap PI = 3.1415
Square of 5 = 25.0
```

Now, suppose your project requires that you not only keep track of car-specific information, but truck-specific information as well. You can probably see that both cars and trucks have the attributes exterior color and number of cylinders in common. While you can blindly create a `Car` class and a `Truck` class, does this make sense especially in light of the fact that several attributes and methods will overlap? No, it doesn't. If, instead, you create a `Vehicle` class containing the common attributes and methods, you then can use the object-oriented concept of a *subclass* to create your `Car` and `Truck` classes. For example, let's create our `Vehicle` class:

```
class Vehicle {

 private String exteriorColor;
 private int numberOfCylinders;

 //Our constructor is below
 public Vehicle(String pExtClr,int pNumCyl) {
  exteriorColor = pExtClr;
  numberOfCylinders = pNumCyl;
 }

 //Getters
 public String getExteriorColor() {
  return(exteriorColor);
 }

 public int getNumberOfCylinders() {
  return(numberOfCylinders);
 }
```

```
//Setters
public void setExteriorColor(String pExtClr) {
 exteriorColor = pExtClr;
 }

public void setNumberOfCylinders(int pNumCyl) {
 numberOfCylinders = pNumCyl;
 }

}
```

Next, let's create a `Car` class that extends the functionality of the `Vehicle` class. Take note that I've added a car-specific attribute: `ipodCharger` which is true if the `Car` has a built-in IPod charger and false if not. Note that I've included both a getter and setter for this attribute within the `Car` class:

```
class Car extends Vehicle {

 private boolean ipodCharger;

 public Car(String pExtClr,int pNumCyl,boolean pIPC) {
  super(pExtClr,pNumCyl);
  ipodCharger = pIPC;
 }

 public boolean getIpodCharger() {
  return(ipodCharger);
 }

 public void setIpodCharger(boolean pIPC) {
  ipodCharger = pIPC;
 }

}
```

As you see above, you use the `extends` keyword to indicate that the `Car` class will contain everything in the `Vehicle` class *as well as* everything coded within the `Car` class. Here is similar code for the `Truck` class with its truck-specific getter and setter for Gross Vehicular Weight:

```
class Truck extends Vehicle {

 private double grossVehicularWeight;

 public Truck(String pExtClr,int pNumCyl,double pGVW) {
  super(pExtClr,pNumCyl);
  grossVehicularWeight = pGVW;
 }

 public Double getGrossVehicularWeight() {
  return(grossVehicularWeight);
 }

 public void setGrossVehicularWeight(double pGVW) {
  grossVehicularWeight = pGVW;
 }

}
```

If you look at the constructors for both the `Car` and `Truck` classes, you'll see the following line of code:

64

```
super(pExtClr,pNumCyl);
```

This indicates that the constructor in the *superclass* - in this case, the `Vehicle` class - should be called from within the `Car` constructor and `Truck` constructor. This allows the variables `exteriorColor` and `numberOfCylinders` to be initialized since they appear within the `Vehicle` class and not the `Car` or `Truck` classes. If you did not include this line of code, both of these variables would be initialized to their default values (0 for numbers and a blank for strings).

Subclassing is not an esoteric topic. The concept of extending a class is used quite a bit within the Android framework as we shall see in subsequent chapters.

Now, suppose that you are not happy with the way the superclass's `getExteriorColor` method works. Are you stuck with it? No! You can override this and other methods appearing in the superclass (`Vehicle`, in this example) and place the replacement code in your subclass (`Car` or `Truck`, in this example). For example, let's override the `getExteriorColor` method by placing the replacement code in our `Car` and `Truck` classes:

```java
class Car extends Vehicle {

 private boolean ipodCharger;

 public Car(String pExtClr,int pNumCyl,boolean pIPC) {
  super(pExtClr,pNumCyl);
  ipodCharger = pIPC;
 }

 public boolean getIpodCharger() {
  return(ipodCharger);
 }

 public void getIpodCharger(boolean pIPC) {
  ipodCharger = pIPC;
 }

 //Override the getExteriorColor method appearing
 // in the Vehicle class with my own method.
 @Override
 public String getExteriorColor() {
  return("The exterior color for this CAR is " + super.getExteriorColor());
 }

}

class Truck extends Vehicle {

 private double grossVehicularWeight;

 public Truck(String pExtClr,int pNumCyl,double pGVW) {
  super(pExtClr,pNumCyl);
  grossVehicularWeight = pGVW;
 }

 public Double getGrossVehicularWeight() {
  return(grossVehicularWeight);
 }

 public void getGrossVehicularWeight(double pGVW) {
  grossVehicularWeight = pGVW;
 }
```

65

```
//Override the getExteriorColor method appearing
// in the Vehicle class with my own method.
@Override
public String getExteriorColor() {
 return("The exterior color for this TRUCK is " + super.getExteriorColor());
 }

 }
```

Notice that in both the `Car` and `Truck` classes, we have overridden the `getExteriorColor` method with each class's own method. The keyword `@Override` is called an *annotation* and is used by the Java compiler to indicate that the current method is intended to override, or replace, the superclass's version of the method. The `@Override` annotation is not really needed and you can program without it, but its function is to tell the compiler to ensure that the superclass's method you are intending to override actually exists. That is, if you do NOT use `@Override` annotation and you misspell your method in the subclass, you will not receive a compiler error (because Java thinks you're creating a new method), but your program will not work as expected since you have not actually overridden the method you intended to. `@Override` will give you an error message like the one below:

```
C:\temp\javapgms>javac jpgm5.java
jpgm5.java:79: method does not override or implement a method from a supertype
 @Override
  ^
1 error
```

Overriding methods appears a lot when programming for Android especially working with the `Activity` class.

Interface

As shown in the examples above, a class can be extended by a single base class. Java only allows for single inheritance and does not allow multiple inheritance. That is, you cannot name more than one class after the `extends` keyword. To work around this, interfaces were created. Java allows you to define an *interface* as a set of method *signatures*. By signatures, we mean that you do not, in fact, create the code within the method, but just define the method name, parameters, return type, etc. This is similar to function prototypes in C.

One author refers to an interface as *...a scaled down mechanism to achieve multiple inheritance.* That is, a class can inherit from one or more interfaces (as well as a single base class, if needed). The class that inherits from an interface is responsible for defining the methods within that interface.

Another author states that *an interface specifies what a class must do, but not how to do it.*

Some authors state that an interface is a *contract between two pieces of code.* That is, once a class inherits from an interface, that class is *guaranteed* to implement the methods of the interface (i.e., the program won't compile otherwise).

66

Other authors say that *coding to an interface, rather than an implementation, makes your software easier to extend.*

Still other authors say that an interface describes *behavioral characteristics or abilities* that can be *applied to* classes regardless of the class hierarchy. They say that classes, on the other hand, are responsible for *actions*. Personally, I prefer this description of interfaces rather than the others.

Note that this is not a pie-in-the-sky programming construct; interfaces are used a lot in Android programming!

Now, to implement an interface, the programmer is responsible for implementing the classes defined in any pre-existing interface he is using. On the other hand, if the programmer creates his own interface, he is responsible for coding the methods within it (no duh!). Here is the syntax to define an interface:

```
access-modifier interface interface-name {

  //Define your attributes
  data-type var-name-1 = value-1;
  data-type var-name-2 = value-2;
  ...

  //Define your methods
  return-data-type method-name-1(parameter-list-1);
  return-data-type method-name-2(parameter-list-2);
  ...

}
```

where `access-modifier` can be `public` (which allows other packages to use the interface), or left off completely (which only allows the code within the package to access it). The remaining code should be apparent.

Note that some authors name their interfaces starting with a capital letter `I` followed by the rest of the interface name. This is not set in stone, so follow your heart. For example, `IColor`, `ISize`, `IRadio`, etc. are all names of interfaces.

For example, let's create an interface which defines the characteristics or behaviors of a car radio:

```
interface IRadio {
  public bool bOn=false;
  public String sBand="AM";
  public float fHertz=1060;

  public void turn_on_off(bool bOn);
  public void change_station(float fHertz);
  public void change_band(String sBand);
}
```

Any variables defined in an interface are implicitly `public` as well as `final` and `static`. All variable must be initialized within an interface's definition.

Now, to use your interface, you add the `implements` keyword followed by the name of the interface after the name of your class or after the `extends` keyword followed by the name of a base class:

```
class Car extends Vehicle implements IRadio {
  ...fill in the methods here...
}
```

It is within your class that you are responsible for implementing the methods defined in the interface.

Abstract

In the section above, the programmer is responsible for implementing all of the classes defined within the interface. While using interfaces is a perfectly reasonable way to go, all you may want to do is create a method in your class that the final programmer is responsible for implementing. You may define the method's signature, but due to not knowing how the target programmer will use the method, you may want to code the method yourself. This is where the `abstract` keyword comes in. By defining a method of your class as `abstract`, you are saying to the target programmer (that is, the programmer using your class): *I don't know in what context you will be using this method; all I know is that the rest of my code needs it and you have to implement this method yourself. So, get to work, buddy!*

Note that this differs from using `@Override` annotation shown previously. The `@Override` annotation indicates that your *fully-implemented-method* **will replace** their *fully-implemented-method*.

Note that if you have one abstract method in your class, the class itself must be defined as abstract. This does not mean that everything within your class must be implemented by the target programmer, and your class can contain fully implemented code within its method.

Note that *an abstract class cannot be instantiated*. Instead, you must place the name of the abstract class to the right of the `extends` keyword.

For example, in the code above, we could have defined the `Vehicle` class as abstract as well as its `getExteriorColor()` method.

```
abstract class Vehicle {

  private String exteriorColor;
  private int numberOfCylinders;

  //Our constructor is below
  public Vehicle(String pExtClr,int pNumCyl) {
    exteriorColor = pExtClr;
    numberOfCylinders = pNumCyl;
  }

  //Getters
  abstract public String getExteriorColor();

  public int getNumberOfCylinders() {
    return(numberOfCylinders);
```

```
  }

  //Setters
  public void setExteriorColor(String pExtClr) {
   exteriorColor = pExtClr;
  }

  public void setNumberOfCylinders(int pNumCyl) {
   numberOfCylinders = pNumCyl;
  }

}
```

Now, when extending the `Car` class with the `Vehicle` class, you must code the `getExteriorColor()` method yourself. Here is the full code:

```
import java.util.*;

abstract class Vehicle {

 private String exteriorColor;
 private int numberOfCylinders;

 //Our constructor is below
 public Vehicle(String pExtClr,int pNumCyl) {
  exteriorColor = pExtClr;
  numberOfCylinders = pNumCyl;
 }

 //Getters
 abstract public String getExteriorColor();

 public int getNumberOfCylinders() {
  return(numberOfCylinders);
 }

 public String getColor() {
  return(exteriorColor);
 }

 //Setters
 public void setExteriorColor(String pExtClr) {
  exteriorColor = pExtClr;
 }

 public void setNumberOfCylinders(int pNumCyl) {
  numberOfCylinders = pNumCyl;
 }

}

class Car extends Vehicle {

 private boolean ipodCharger;

 public Car(String pExtClr,int pNumCyl,boolean pIPC) {
  super(pExtClr,pNumCyl);
  ipodCharger = pIPC;
 }

 public boolean getIpodCharger() {
  return(ipodCharger);
 }

 public void getIpodCharger(boolean pIPC) {
  ipodCharger = pIPC;
 }
```

```
 //Create the code for the abstract method getExteriorColor.
 public String getExteriorColor() {
  return("The exterior color for this CAR is " + getColor());
 }

}

class Truck extends Vehicle {

 private double grossVehicularWeight;

 public Truck(String pExtClr,int pNumCyl,double pGVW) {
  super(pExtClr,pNumCyl);
  grossVehicularWeight = pGVW;
 }

 public Double getGrossVehicularWeight() {
  return(grossVehicularWeight);
 }

 public void getGrossVehicularWeight(double pGVW) {
  grossVehicularWeight = pGVW;
 }

 //Create the code for the abstract method getExteriorColor.
 public String getExteriorColor() {
  return("The exterior color for this TRUCK is " + getColor());
 }

}

class jpgm7 {

 public static void main(String args[]) {

  Car MyCar = new Car("PurplePassion",5,true);
  Truck MyTruck = new Truck("BisonBrown",5,56.7643);

  //Print out the exterior color of the car and truck.
  System.out.println(MyCar.getExteriorColor());
  System.out.println(MyTruck.getExteriorColor());

 }

}
```

The results are:

```
C:\temp\javapgms>java jpgm7
The exterior color for this CAR is PurplePassion
The exterior color for this TRUCK is BisonBrown
```

Variable-Length Arguments

In the methods shown above, there was exactly one parameter for each desired parameter. This makes complete sense! However, Java allows you to define a variable-length argument using the ellipsis notation. An ellipsis is just three periods following the data type but before the name of the parameter. For example, here is a method that sums up a series of numbers passed in via the variable-length argument:

```
public double SumTotal(double... nums) {

 double tot=0.0;
```

```
 for(int i=0;i<nums.length;i++) {
  tot += nums[i];
 }

 return(tot);
}
```

As you see above, an ellipsis follows the `double` data type. As shown above, you can access the individual elements of `nums` using the bracket notation, or you can use the following notation instead:

```
public double SumTotal(double... nums) {

 double tot=0.0;

 for(double anum : nums) {
  tot += anum;
 }

 return(tot);
}
```

To use this method, provide a comma-delimited list of values or variable to the method:

```
double GrandTotal_Qtr1 = SumTotal(Qtr1,Qtr2,Qtr3);
```

Note that if you have more than one argument on your method, the ellipsis must appear as the *last* parameter in the list! You cannot include it in the middle or the beginning. Naturally, this doesn't matter if you only have the one parameter, as shown in the example above.

Running Java Test Programs

While you are attempting to learn Java as detailed above, you may want to create a few test programs and then compile them using the Java compiler (`javac`). When I just want to create a quick Java test program, I open up a text editor (such as Notepad, TextPad, etc.), type in some code and then compile the program. In order to compile the Java test program, you will need to open up a command window, by clicking on START...Run... and entering the word `cmd` in the input box when the Run dialog box appears. Click on the OK button and your command window will appear, as shown below. Change directory to where your Java test programs are stored and type in `javac` *`your_test_program_name.java`*. Hit the enter key and your program will be compiled. The result of compiling a `.java` program is a `.class` Java class. If all went well, you can run your program by typing `java` *`your_test_program_name`* at the command line and hitting the Enter key. Your program will then execute.

Note that you can run test programs from within the Eclipse IDE (choose Java and not Android when you create your new project), but I find that using the command line removes all of the noise around me and I can concentrate on my test program. But, hey, that's probably just me! ☺

Summary

In this chapter, we learned how to write computer programs using the Java language. Traditional constructs, such as the if-then-else, for-loop, and so on, were discussed as well as object-oriented programming constructs.

Chapter 4: Exploring Useful Java Classes

Introduction

In this chapter, we'll explore several useful Java classes such as the `String` class, `Math` class, and so on. Although not every method in every class will be discussed, we do present enough information to justify why you should know about a particular class, show you basic examples to get you started, and point you in the right direction if further information is required.

If you would like to peruse a list of all of the classes available in Java 8, navigate your browser to http://docs.oracle.com/javase/8/docs/api/allclasses-noframe.html, but be aware that there are well over 4000 classes listed, so you might want to bring a change of clothes.

We will explore the following classes:

- Text-related Classes
  - `String` - this class contains methods used to manipulate strings.
  - `RegExp` - this class contains methods used to work with regular expressions.
- Mathematics-related Classes
  - `Math` - this class contains mathematical constants and methods used to work with numbers.
  - `Integer` - this class contains methods used to work with integers.
  - `Big Decimal` - this class contains methods used to work with integral values that exceed the minimum and maximum permitted values of the data types `int` and `long`.
  - `Random` - this class contains methods used to produce random numbers.
- Collections-Related Classes
  - `Arrays` - this class contains methods useful when working with arrays.
  - `ArrayList` - this class contains methods useful when you need to work with an unordered list.
  - `HashMap` - this class contains method useful when you need to work with a series of key/value pairs.
- Date- and Time-Related Classes
  - `Date` - this class contains methods useful when working with dates and times.
  - `SimpleDateFormat` - this class contains methods useful when working with and formatting dates and times.

While not strictly Android-specific, these classes can help you write useful and efficient code as well as prevent you from *reinventing the wheel*, something we've all done at least once in the past...heavy sigh...

Text-Related Classes

In this section, we explore the `String` and `RegExp` classes.

73

You can access these two classes by importing the Java packages `java.lang` and `java.util.regex` by placing the following two lines of code at the top of your Java program:

```
import java.lang.*;
import java.util.regex.*;
```

In the previous chapter, we worked with creating text strings using the `String` class in a limited way:

```
String sBand="AM";
```

...or...

```
String exteriorColor;
```

In both cases, `sBand` and `exteriorColor` are now `String` objects and have access to the myriad of methods available to that class.

Another way to instantiate a `String` object is to use one of the many constructors, although you may only ever use the following one to create an empty `String`:

```
String sBand = new String();
```

But, you are more likely to code this instead:

```
String sBand = "";
```

Now, the following methods of the `String` class are useful to know:

- `charAt(index)` - this method returns the character located at `index` in your `String`.
- `concat(addString)` - this method concatenates your `String` and `addString` together, similar to `String + addString`.
- `indexOf(char)` - this method returns the position of `char` within your `String`.
- `indexOf(search,index)` - this method, similar to the above, returns the position of the search term `search` starting at `index` within your `String`.
- `length()` - this method returns the length of your `String` as an `int`.
- `split(regexp)` - this method splits your `String` into an array of `String`s using the provided regular expression.
- `substring(start, end)` - this method returns a substring of your `String` starting at `start` (the offset of the first character) and ending at `end` (the offset one past the last character). A variation of this method, without the `end` argument, returns the substring from `start` to the end of the entire string.
- `toLowerCase()` - this method converts your `String` to lower case.
- `toUpperCase()` - this method converts your `String` to upper case.

- `trim()` - this method removes both leading and trailing whitespace characters from your `String`.

For example, given the following `String`:

```
String sSaying = "The quick brown fox jumps over the lazy dog.";
```

Let's create upper and lower case versions of it:

```
String sFiller_Upper = sFiller.toUpperCase();
String sFiller_Lower = sFiller.toLowerCase();
```

And the results, as you might expect, are:

```
THE QUICK BROWN FOX JUMPS OVER THE LAZY DOG.
the quick brown fox jumps over the lazy dog.
```

Now, let's substring `sFiller` so that we end just before the word *dog*. First, let's find the location of the letter *d*. First, create a string to hold our search term:

```
String sSearchTerm = "dog.";
```

Next, find the location of the start of this search term within `sFiller`:

```
int iSearchTermLocation = sFiller.indexOf(sSearchTerm);
```

Finally, take the substring from the beginning of `sFiller` (starting at zero) and ending at `iSearchTermLocation`:

```
String sFillerNoDog = sFiller.substring(0,iSearchTermLocation);
```

The results are predictable, but be aware that there is a blank space at the end of this string:

```
The quick brown fox jumps over the lazy
```

Next, let's concatenate the word moose to our new `String`, sFillerNoDog:

```
String sLargeAnimal = "moose.";
String sFillerWithMoose = sFillerNoDog.concat(sLargeAnimal);
```

And the results are:

```
The quick brown fox jumps over the lazy moose.
```

One nice method is the `split()` method which allows us to break apart a `String` using the provided regular expression as the argument. The result of `split()` is an array of `String`s containing substrings of the original `String`. For example, let's break apart `sFiller` at the blanks by creating a `String` to hold the desired regular expression. Note that we have to escape the first backslash!

```
String sRegExp = "\\s+";
```

Next, let's use the `split()` method to break apart `sFiller`:

```
String[] sFillerSplits = sFiller.split(sRegExp);
```

And, let's display each piece of the array `sFillerSplits`:

```
for(String s : sFillerSplits) {
 System.out.println(s);
}
```

And the results are as follows:

```
The
quick
brown
fox
jumps
over
the
lazy
dog.
```

You can perform more complicated regular expression tasks than the one shown above by using the classes and methods provided in the `java.util.regex` package.

In order to use regular expressions in Java, you first compile your regular expression and then you use the compiled regular expression for matches, replacements, and so on.

Now, by *compile* we don't mean you need to create a separate Java program, but just use the `compile()` method of the `Pattern` class along with your regular expression. You normally do this if you will be using a particular regular expression many times. For example, suppose you are trying to parse millions of addresses stored within individual text strings.

We won't go into the details of regular expressions themselves, so please peruse the InterWeb for more on regular expressions. (By the way, if you don't already know regular expressions, it is definitely worth spending some time learning about them...and the following example may convince you of this!)

For example, given this address,

```
123 NORTH MAIN STREET SOUTH SUITE A123
```

Let's use regular expressions to separate out each address component into indivual pieces using the following regular expression:

```
String sRE = "^(\\d+)
+(NORTH|NORHT|NRTH|SOUTH|SOUHT|SUOTH|EAST|EASST|WEST|WESST{1}) +(\\w+)
+(ST|STREET|STREE|STEET|STREEET|STRET{1})
+(NORTH|NORHT|NRTH|SOUTH|SOUHT|SUOTH|EAST|EASST|WEST|WESST{1})
+(SUITE|SUTIE|SUIT|SUI|STE{1}) +(\\w+) *$";
```

Now, this regular expression makes use of *alternation*, the vertical bars used to represent an or-condition, in order to capture misspellings. For example, the address below will also be captured by the regular expression above because we took into account possible misspellings:

```
123 NRTH MAIN ST SUOTH STE A123
```

We also make use of *capturing groups*, the left and right parentheses, in order to capture the individual pieces within the completely matched regular expression. Each capturing group is numbered starting from the left-most position in the regular expression. The first capturing group is numbered 1, the second is 2, and so on. This will come in handy when we use use the `groups()` method in order to work with each individual piece.

Now that we've created our regular expression, let's compile it:

```
Pattern oRE = Pattern.compile(sRE);
```

Next, let's search for matches using the `matcher()` method to return a `Matcher` object:

```
Matcher oMATCH = oRE.matcher(sAddress);
```

At this point, we can ask if there are any matches using the `matches()` method of the `Matcher` object, `oMATCH`:

```
if (oMATCH.matches()) {
```

And, if there are matches, we can pull the individual pieces using the `groups()` method of the `Matcher` object `oMATCH` providing the capturing group number:

```
if (oMATCH.matches()) {

 String sHOUSE_NUMBER = oMATCH.group(1);
 System.out.println(sHOUSE_NUMBER);

 String sDIR_PRE = oMATCH.group(2);
 System.out.println(sDIR_PRE);

 String sSTREET_NAME = oMATCH.group(3);
 System.out.println(sSTREET_NAME);

 String sSTREET_TYPE = oMATCH.group(4);
 System.out.println(sSTREET_TYPE);

 String sDIR_POST = oMATCH.group(5);
 System.out.println(sDIR_POST);

 String sSUITE_TYPE = oMATCH.group(6);
 System.out.println(sSUITE_TYPE);

 String sSUITE_NBR = oMATCH.group(7);
 System.out.println(sSUITE_NBR);

}
```

Here are the results:

```
123
NRTH
MAIN
```

```
ST
SUOTH
STE
A123
```

Now, regular expressions not need be as complex as the one shown above. If you just want to search for a particular pattern, say a series of three numbers, multiple times within a text string, you can use the `find()` method of the `Matcher` class to return each occurrence appearing within the matched string. For example, let's create a `String` with a series of three numbers:

```
String sCodeNumbers = "123 456 789 012";
```

Next, let's create the regular expression to search for sets of three numbers:

```
String sRE = "\\d{3}";
```

Next, let's compile it and create the `Matcher` object:

```
Pattern oRE = Pattern.compile(sRE);
Matcher oMATCH = oRE.matcher(sCodeNumbers);
```

And, finally, let's loop through all of the matches:

```
while (oMATCH.find()) {
  System.out.println("Code Number=" + oMATCH.group());
}
```

And here are the results:

```
Code Number=123
Code Number=456
Code Number=789
Code Number=012
```

Please see the documentation for more on regular expressions as well as the `Pattern` and `Matcher` classes.

Mathematics-Related Classes

In this section, we explore the `Math`, `Random`, `Integer` and `BigInteger` classes.

You can access these classes by importing the Java packages `java.util`, `java.math` and `java.lang` by placing the following lines of code at the top of your Java program:

```
import java.lang.*;
import java.math.*;
import java.util.*;
```

The `Math` class provides basic mathematical constants (such as `E` and `PI`) as well as a plethora of mathematical functions (such as `abs()`, `cos()`, and so on). For example, if you would like to use the value for pi in your Java program, you can code something like this:

78

```
double myPI = Math.PI;
```

But, you can just as easily refer to `Math.PI` within your program instead of creating an individual variable.

Now, the great thing about the `Math` class is that all of the methods are `static` meaning that you do not have to instantiate a `Math` object in order to use a particular method. For example, let's take the absolute value of a number:

```
double myDouble = -2.457584743638;
System.out.println(Math.abs(myDouble));
```

Since you are probably already familiar with many of the methods that make up the `Math` class, here is an abbreviated list of methods for you to peruse:

- `abs()`, - this method returns the absolute value.
- `acos()` - this method returns the arc cosine.
- `asin()` - this method returns the arc sine.
- `atan()` - this method returns the arc tangent.
- `atan2()` - this method returns the arc tangent.
- `ceil()` - this method returns the ceiling.
- `cos()` - this method returns the cosine.
- `cosh()` - this method returns the hyperbolic cosine.
- `exp()` - this method returns powers of e (=2.7182818...).
- `floor()` - this method returns the floor.
- `hypot()` - this method computes the hypotenuse.
- `log()` - this method returns the log (base e).
- `log10()` - this method returns the log (base 10).
- `max()` - this method returns the maximum.
- `min()` - this method returns the minimum.
- `pow()` - this method raises a number to a power.
- `random()` - this method returns a pseudo-random number.
- `round()` - this method rounds a number to a specifiec number of decimal places.
- `sin()` - this method returns the sine.
- `sinh()` - this method returns the hyperbolic sine.
- `sqrt()` - this method returns the square root.
- `tan()` - this method returns the tangent.
- `tanh()` - this method returns the hyperbolic tangent.
- `toDegrees()` - this method converts radians to degrees.
- `toRadians()` - this method converts degrees to radians.

Take note, though, of the method `random()`. This method returns a pseudo-random number (as a `Double`) between zero (inclusive) and one (exclusive). For example, let's produce several random numbers:

```
double myRandNbr;
for(int i=0;i<10;i++) {
```

```
System.out.println(Math.random());
}
```

And here are the results:

```
0.9937116662147903
0.8832714457691465
0.021470912780462093
0.06808048975506253
0.2272317374013757
0.4853108586915391
0.003877548002589437
0.04306726829210694
0.13320416155649084
0.9509692890645647
```

Note that each time you run the code you will receive different random numbers.

Now, if you would like more control over your random numbers, you can use the `Random` class instead of the `random()` method of the `Math` class. There are two constructors to the `Random` class:

- `Random()` - this constructor, according to the Android documentation, *constructs a random generator with an initial state that is unlikely to be duplicated by a subsequent instantiation*.
- `Random(seed)` - this constructor *creates a random generator using seed to as the initial state. Note that seed is a `long` data type.*

Now, the `Random` class contains several methods to generate random numbers of a specific data type. For example, you can use the `nextDouble()` method to generate random numbers between zero (inclusive) and one (exclusive) as a `double` data type. On the other hand, if you just want a series of random integers between zero (inclusive) and some number *n* (exclusive), you can use the `nextInt(n)` method instead.

For example, let's generate a series of random numbers using these two methods:

```
Random oRand = new Random();
int iRandomInteger;
double dRandomDouble;

for(int i=0; i<5; i++) {
 System.out.println(oRand.nextDouble());
 System.out.println(oRand.nextInt(100));
}
```

And the results are:

```
0.7262704595568443
96
0.7307144140023264
22
0.8026506976431572
98
0.8235707998746877
46
0.23907124476393293
2
```

Now, let's discuss the `Integer` class. Occasionally, you will want to convert an `int` value into a `String` and attempts to do the following will fail:

```
String sInteger = iInteger.toString(); //FAIL!!
```

In order to convert an `int` to a `String`, you must make use of the `toString()` method of the `Integer` class, like so:

```
int iInteger = 3;
String sInteger = Integer.toString(iInteger);
```

Now, there are many methods available in the `Integer` class and we discuss some of them below. When looking at the Android documentation, please take note that some of the methods are `static` and others are not. Recall that `static` methods don't need an instantiated class to function.

For example, you can compare two `int`s using the `static compare()` method to determine if the values are greater than, less than, or equal to each other.

```
int iInteger1 = 3;
int iInteger2 = 5;
int iReturnValue = Integer.compare(iInteger1,iInteger2);
System.out.println(Integer.toString(iReturnValue));
```

Now, if `iInteger1` is less than `iInteger2`, a negative number will be returned (usually a -1). If `iInteger1` is greater than `iInteger2`, a positive number will be returned (usually a +1). If both numbers are the same, then a zero will be returned. In this example, a -1 was returned.

Since *some* negative or positive value will be returned by the `compare()` method, we can use the `static` method `signum()` to force the return values of the `compare()` method to -1, +1 and 0:

```
int iReturnValue = Integer.signum(Integer.compare(iInteger1,iInteger2));
```

Another nice `static` method of the `Integer` class is the `bitCount()` method which returns the number of 1 bits within a given `int`. This is also known as the *population count*. For example, the integer `12893` is represented by the binary number `11001001011101`. Counting the number of 1s in the binary number yields 8, the population count. Let's see that in code:

```
int iInteger = 12893; /* 11001001011101 = 8 one bits in total */
int iPopCnt = Integer.bitCount(iInteger);
System.out.println(Integer.toString(iPopCnt));
```

The result is, of course, 8.

Although we only discussed the `Integer` class, please see the documentation for similar classes such as `Boolean`, `Byte`, `Double`, `Float`, `Long`, `Number` and `Short`.

Next, let's talk about the `BigInteger` class. Recall that the range for an integer is between $2^{31}-1=2,147,483,647$ and $-2^{31}=-2,147,483,648$. Let's see what happens if we attempt to set an `int` to `2147483648`:

```
int iBigNumber = 2147483648;
```

Unfortunately, you will receive the following error message:

```
programname.java:19: error: integer number too large: 2147483648
         int iBigNumber = 2147483648;
                          ^
1 error
```

Now, we could use a `long` data type, but that is limited to a maximum value of $9,223,372,036,854,775,807$ and, hence, the same potential problem.

Now, if you need arbitrary precision integer numbers, you can use the `BigInteger` class. For example, let's use one of the many constructors to take a `String` containing these two very large numbers and instantiate two `BigInteger`s:

```
BigInteger oBI_ExceedsINT = new BigInteger("2147483648");
BigInteger oBI_ExceedsLONG = new BigInteger("9223372036854775808");
```

Next, let's add these two numbers together using the `add()` method and print out the result:

```
BigInteger oBI_TOTAL = oBI_ExceedsINT.add(oBI_ExceedsLONG);
System.out.println(oBI_TOTAL.toString());
```

And, the results are: `9223372039002259456`.

If need be, we can create a `double` to represent our sum total:

```
double dBI_TOTAL = oBI_TOTAL.doubleValue();
```

Besides `BigInteger`, please see `BigDecimal` in the Android documentation.

Finally, if you need your mathematical constants and functions to return *exactly the same* values across all platforms, please see the `StrictMath` class in the `java.lang` package.

Collections-Related Classes

In this section, we explore the `Arrays`, `ArrayList` and `Hashmap` classes.

You can access these classes by importing the Java package `java.util` by placing the following line of code at the top of your Java program:

```
import java.util.*;
```

Recall that you can create an array by using the left and right bracket (`[]`) after the data type. For example, to create an array of integers from 1 to 10, you can code something like this:

```
int[] aiNumbers = {1,2,3,4,5,6,7,8,9,10};
```

Now, the `Arrays` class allows you to work with arrays more easily. For example, suppose you want to perform a binary search of the `aiNumbers` array above. The `Arrays` class contains several overrides of the `binarySearch()` method which returns the zero-based **index** of the desired value. For example, let's retrieve the index of the number 9 in the `aiNumbers` array:

```
int iIndex = Arrays.binarySearch(aiNumbers,9);
```

Since arrays are zero-based, the resulting index is 8.

Unfortunately, `binarySearch()` requires that the array be sorted. If your array is not sorted, you can use the `sort()` method:

```
Arrays.sort(aiNumbers);
```

Note that the return type for the `sort()` method is `void`, so you cannot just use it as the first argument of the `binarySearch()` method.

If you would like to copy a portion of your array out to another array, you can use the `copyOfRange()` method. For example, let's create a new array made up of the fourth through the seventh array elements (the numbers 4, 5, 6, and 7):

```
int[] aiNumbersSubset = Arrays.copyOfRange(aiNumbers,3,7);
```

Again, since arrays are zero-based, the beginning of the range (the second argument) is set to 3. Also, note that the end of the range (the third argument) is *one more than* what we need, 7 in this case.

Now, if you would like to work with a list instead of an array, you can use the `ArrayList` class. According to the Android documentation: *An `ArrayList` is an implementation of `List`, backed by an array. All optional operations including adding, removing, and replacing elements are supported. A `List` is a collection which maintains an ordering for its elements. Every element in the List has an index. Each element can thus be accessed by its index, with the first index being zero. Normally, Lists allow duplicate elements, as compared to Sets, where elements have to be unique.*

For example, let's create an `ArrayList` to hold the names of several US states:

```
ArrayList<String> oAL_STATES = new ArrayList<String>();
```

Take note of the word `String` within angled brackets (`<>`) above. This indicates to `ArrayList` which data type it should enforce when adding elements to the list. If you do not include this bracketed syntax (called *generics*), Java will bark at you with the following error message:

Note: *programname*.java uses unchecked or unsafe operations.

Next, let's add values to our `ArrayList`:

```
oAL_STATES.add("Ohio");
oAL_STATES.add("Wyoming");
oAL_STATES.add("California");
oAL_STATES.add("Alabama");
```

Now, let's print out the values in our `ArrayList`:

```
for(String sThisState : oAL_STATES) {
 System.out.println(sThisState);
}
```

The results are predictable:

```
Ohio
Wyoming
California
Alabama
```

Another way to produce the same result is by using the `get()` and `size()` methods to pull each individual `ArrayList` element:

```
for(int i=0; i<oAL_STATES.size(); i++) {
 String sThisState = oAL_STATES.get(i);
 System.out.println(sThisState);
}
```

Besides the `get()` method to retrieve an item, you can use the `remove()` method to remove an item and the `set()` method to replace an item. Please see the documentation for more.

So far we've worked with arrays, the `Arrays` class and the `ArrayList` class. If you would like to work with key/value pairs rather than just items in an array or list, you can use the `HashMap` class. According to the Android documentation: *HashMap is an implementation of Map. All elements are permitted as keys or values, including null. Note that the iteration order for HashMap is non-deterministic. If you want deterministic iteration, use LinkedHashMap. A Map is a data structure consisting of a set of keys and values in which each key is mapped to a single value. The class of the objects used as keys is declared when the Map is declared, as is the class of the corresponding values.*

For example, let's create a `HashMap` to hold the four state names shown above along with the corresponding state capitals. For example, the capital of *Wyoming* is the *W*. Ha! That's a little joke! Ahem. The capital of *Wyoming* is *Cheyenne*.

```
HashMap<String,String> oHM_STATES = new HashMap<String,String>();
```

Note that in the code above we specified the keyword `String` twice in the generics. The first `String` indicates the data type of the **key** and the second `String` indicates the data type of the **value**. Since state and capital names are text, we specified both positions in the generic as `String`.

84

Next, let's add some key/value pairs to our `HashMap` using the `put()` method:

```
oHM_STATES.put("Ohio","Columbus");
oHM_STATES.put("Wyoming","Cheyenne");
oHM_STATES.put("California","Sacramento");
oHM_STATES.put("Alabama","Montgomery");
```

Note that the first argument indicates the key and the second indicates the value.

Next, let's iterate through all of the keys. You can do this by using the `keySet()` method:

```
for(String sThisState : oHM_STATES.keySet()) {
 System.out.println(sThisState);
}
```

Similarly, you can iterate through the values using the `values()` method:

```
for(String sThisCapital : oHM_STATES.values()) {
 System.out.println(sThisCapital);
}
```

Next, let's retrieve the state capital of *Wyoming*. We do this using the `get()` method:

```
String sWyoming_Capital = oHM_STATES.get("Wyoming");
```

And the result is, of course, *Cheyenne* (and not *W*).

Please see the documentation for more on the `Arrays`, `ArrayList` and `HashMap` classes.

Date- and Time-Related Classes

In this section, we explore the `SimpleDateFormat` and `Date` classes.

You can access these two classes by importing the Java packages `java.util` and `java.text` by placing the following two lines of code at the top of your Java program:

```
import java.util.*;
import java.text.*;
```

The `Date` class, despite its name, is used to hold times as well as dates and is accurate to the millisecond. In order to initialize the `Date` object to the current date and time, just code:

```
Date oTodaysDateTime = new Date();
```

In order to see what date and time were returned, you can use the `toString()` method on `oTodaysDateTime`:

```
System.out.println("Today's Date and Time = " + oTodaysDateTime.toString());
```

85

Note that the results are printed in a specific format that looks like this:

```
Today's Date and Time = Thu Jul 10 09:48:19 EDT 2014
```

Now, this particular output format may not be to your liking, so you can use the `SimpleDateFormat` class to not only produce dates and times in a specific textual format, but you can also parse a `String` containing date/time information to create a `Date` object.

For example, let's create a `String` from today's date in the format `MM/dd/yyyy`, or two-digit month, two-digit day and four-digit year all separated by forward slashes. First, instantiate a `SimpleDateFormat` object telling it which format will be used to output today's date:

```
SimpleDateFormat oSDF1 = new SimpleDateFormat("MM/dd/yyyy");
```

Next, let's retrieve today's date:

```
Date oTodaysDate = new Date();
```

Now, let's create a `String` from today's date. Note that since we specified `MM/dd/yyyy` when instantiating the `SimpleDateFormat` class, the resulting output will be in that specific format. Here, we are using the `format()` method supplying it the desired date, `oTodaysDate`:

```
String sDateInMMDDYYYYFmt = oSDF1.format(oTodaysDate);
System.out.println("Today's date is " + sDateInMMDDYYYYFmt);
```

And, the results are shown below:

```
Today's date is 07/10/2014
```

Now, the formatting letters, `MM`, `dd`, `yyyy`, and so on are called the *Time Pattern Syntax*. Here are some of the more common patterns:

- `M` - month as a single digit (1=January...12=December)
- `MM` - month as two-digits (01=January...12=December)
- `MMM` - month as three-letters (Jan=January...Dec=December)
- `MMMM` - month as full text (January...December)
- `d` - day of month a single digit (1=1...31=31)
- `dd` - day of month as two-digits (1=01...31=31)
- `yy` - two-digit year (14 for 2014)
- `yyyy` - four-digit year (2014=2014)
- `H` - hours in 24-hour clock (0 to 23)
- `h` - hours in 12-hour clock (1 to 12)
- `m` - minutes (0 to 59)
- `s` - seconds (0 to 59)
- `a` - AM or PM indicator
- `EEE` - day of the week as three-letters (Mon=Monday...Sun=Sunday)

- EEEE - day of week as full text (Monday...Sunday)

For example, to specify today's date as `Thursday July 10, 2014 10:16:56 AM` we will use the pattern "`EEEE MMMM dd, yyyy @ hh:mm:ss a`":

```
Date oTodaysDateTime = new Date();
SimpleDateFormat oSDF = new SimpleDateFormat("EEEE MMMM dd, yyyy hh:mm:ss a");
String oMyDate = oSDF.format(oTodaysDateTime);
System.out.println("Today's Date and Time = " + oMyDate);
```

And the results are shown below:

```
Today's Date and Time = Thursday July 10, 2014 10:16:56 AM
```

Next, let's go the other way round: let's produce a `Date` object from a `String` containing a specific date (not necessarily today's date).

First create a `String` to hold the desired date: `04/25/1964`:

```
String sMyDate="04/25/1964";
```

Next, instantiate `SimpleDateFormat` specifying the format `MM/dd/yyyy` which will be used to input the date `04/25/1964`:

```
SimpleDateFormat oSDF = new SimpleDateFormat("MM/dd/yyyy");
```

Create a `ParsePosition` object and sets its argument to zero. This object is used for debugging if there is ever a problem with your time pattern syntax. We won't discuss this object here, so please see the documentation for more.

```
ParsePosition oParsePosition = new ParsePosition(0);
```

Finally, we call the `parse()` method to read in our textual date and produce a `Date` object:

```
Date oMyDate = oSDF.parse(sMyDate,oParsePosition);
System.out.println("04/25/1964 as a Date Object = " + oMyDate.toString());
```

The results are shown below using `Date`'s `toString()` method:

```
04/25/1964 as a Date Object = Sat Apr 25 00:00:00 EST 1964
```

Please see the documentation for `SimpleDateFormat, Date` as well as `ParsePosition` for learn more about these classes.

Chapter 5A: Exploring the Eclipse Integrated Development Environment

A First Look at the IDE

When you first open the Eclipse IDE, you will see something like the following:

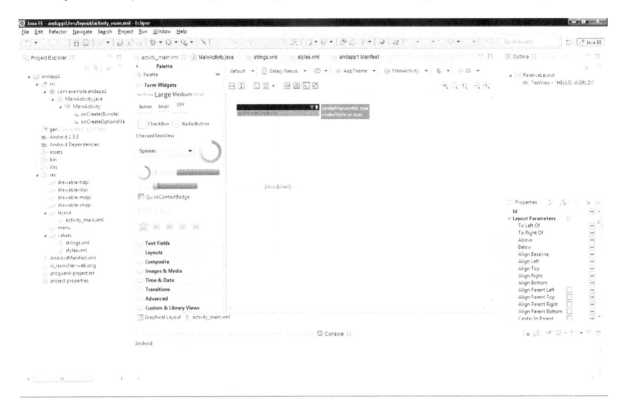

On the left side is the Project Explorer pane which shows you all of your project-specific code, resources, icons, Android manifest and more.

To the right of that is the Palette pane which is part of the Graphical Layout. The Graphical Layout allows you to create an activity (known as a *form* in other languages) by dragging-and-dropping widgets (also called *views*) from the Palette pane onto the Graphical Layout. Along with the Graphical Layout is its associated XML file called `activity_main.xml`.

Near the bottom of the IDE, you will see two tabs labeled Graphical Layout and `activity_main.xml`. If you click on the `activity_main.xml` tab, you will see the XML used to describe the layout of your activity.

Near the top of the IDE, you will see one or more tabs, the number of which depends on how many entries in the Project Explorer you've double-clicked. As you can see, my IDE is showing one tab for each of the following: `activity_main.xml` (which is currently displayed), `MainActivity.java` (the Java code behind this activity), `strings.xml` (the XML file containing variable names and associated values), `styles.xml` and the `andapp1` Manifest. By clicking on each tab, you will bring up the associated information. You can remove these tabs by clicking the X-button (displayed when you hover your mouse over each tab).

On the right side, you'll see the Outline and Task List panes (represented as tabs). If you double-click on `MainActivity.java` in the Project Explorer, the Outline pane will display the class as well as its members. If you click on one of the members in the Outline pane, such as `onCreate`, your cursor will be taken directly to the method definition and the code will appear in the center of the IDE.

Next to the Outline tab is the Task List tab. If you use bug tracking software such as Bugzilla or Mantis, you can link the Task List tab to one of those repositories. If you don't use those, you can create your own tasks locally by clicking on the New Task button (on the far left of the Task List tab) or you can click its down-arrow to reveal several options, as shown below, such as New Task...:

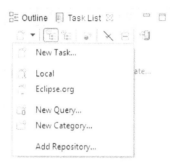

When you create a new task, the `Select a repository` dialog appears. Since we are working locally, click on the Local option and click the Finish button. A moment later, the Task dialog appears as the New Task tab in the main area of Eclipse, as shown below:

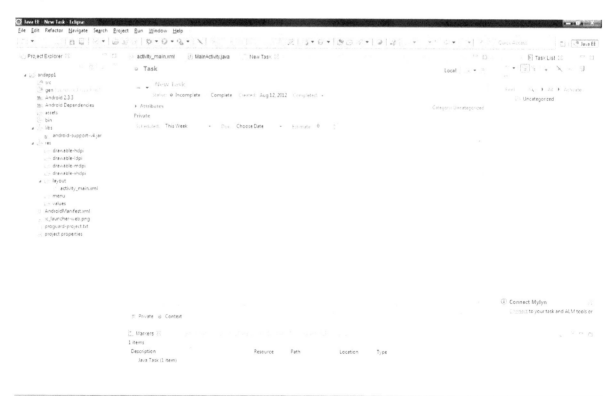

Fill in the task title where the text New Task appears, and fill in more detail in the large input box. Next, select a due date, etc. When you are done, click the X button on the New Task tab and click Yes when the Save Resource dialog box appears:

Finally, your task will appear in the Task List tab, as shown below:

At the bottom of the IDE, you will see the following tabs: Markers, Properties, Servers, Data Source Explorer, Snippets and Console. We explore each tab, in turn, next.

The Markers tab lists all of the places in your code where you have placed the task tags TODO or FIXME within comments. The TODO task tag indicates that the code directly below the comment needs to be created. The FIXME task tag indicates that the code directly below the comment needs to be reworked. For example, the comment in the code below contains the TODO task tag:

```
// TODO: Do it!
@Override
public boolean onCreateOptionsMenu(Menu menu) {
 getMenuInflater().inflate(R.menu.activity_main, menu);
 return true;
}
```

If you then click on the Markers tab, you will see the following:

If you double-click on the TODO: Do it! line above, you will be brought to the place in the code with the associated comment.

If TODO and FIXME are a little too non-descript for your tastes, you can add your own task tags by clicking on Window...Preferences. Expand the Java section and then expand the Compiler section. Finally, click on the Task Tags item. You will see something like the following:

You may want to turn off the `Case sensitive task tag names` check box. To add a new task tag, click on the New... button and fill in the Tag input box once the New Task Tag dialog box has appeared. Click on OK to save this task tag. You may be asked to rebuild the project in order for this to take effect. I've found that clicking the Save button forces Eclipse to search for all of the new tags and report them in the Markers tab.

The Properties tab is useful when you are working with views and widgets in the Graphical Layout editor. If you go into the Graphical Layout editor and you click on, say, the text box that holds the text `HELLO, WORLD!`, you will see a list of related properties displayed in the Properties tab. This is very similar in other IDEs like Visual Studio. For example, when I click on the textbox, the properties appear in the Properties tab. If you click on the Text Size property and enter the number 25dp in the second column (the column that contains the values of the properties which are listed in column one, the property names), then you will see that the text has increased its size (see below).

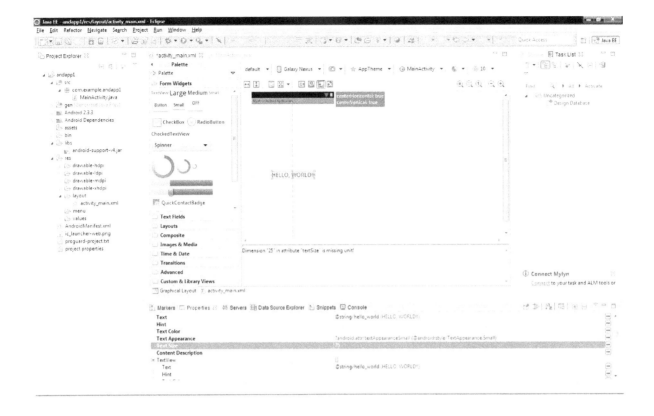

The Servers tab allows you to add, remove and edit one or more servers you are connected to from within Eclipse. We won't be using this feature in this book.

The Data Source Explorer tab allows you to add connections to databases such as Oracle, SQL Server, SQLite, and many more as well as flat files, XML Files and web services. We talk about databases later on in the book.

The Snippets tab is a great place to add all of those chunks of code you use repeatedly but have trouble finding when you need them. Instead of searching through your projects, you can place your code here. The Snippets tab contains one or more Snippet Drawers. By default, a snippet drawer is created for JSP (Java Server Pages). You can add more snippet drawers by right-clicking on a blank area within the Snippet section and clicking on Customize. When the Customize Palette dialog box appears, click on the New button to create a new category. By default, the new category is called Unnamed Category. Change this to a name you want and click the OK button. To add a snippet to this category, highlight and copy your code snippet, then right-click over the desired category name and click Paste as Snippet. The Customize Palette dialog box appears again. By default, the snippet is named Unnamed Template. Change this to your desired name. You can also enter in a full description of the code snippet in the Description section.

Now, you can create variables that can be used as placeholders in the code template. Click on the New button to create a new variable. Rename this variable to a more appropriate name, give it a description and a default value. Once you have one variable, the Insert Variable Placeholder... button becomes active. Move your cursor to the spot in the code template where you want the variable to be inserted. Click on the Insert Variable Placeholder... button which will bring up a dialog allowing you to select a variable. Do this for each placeholder you want to insert into the code template. Click the Apply button. Click the OK button to dismiss the dialog. See the image below for an example.

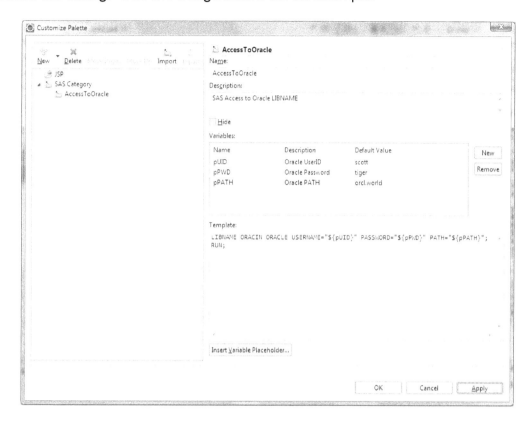

Now, move your cursor to a spot in your program where you want to insert your snippet. Double-click on the desired snippet in the Snippets tab and the Insert Template dialog box appears (as shown below).

If you are okay with the way the code appears in the Source section, click OK to insert the code into your program. Here is what the code looks like in the program:

```
LIBNAME ORACIN ORACLE USERNAME="scott" PASSWORD="tiger" PATH="orcl.world";
```

```
RUN;
```

Note that you can make use of Eclipse's code templates, which are a much more powerful feature than snippets. While we won't go into detail about templates, you can explore more about them by clicking on Windows...Preferences and expanding both the Code Style and Editor nodes within the Java root.

Code Templates contains two sections: Comments and Code. The Comments section contains predefined comment blocks for a variety of entities such as fields, constructors, etc. Similar for the Code section.

The Templates section, within the Editor node, contains drop-in code that prevents you from having to type it in by hand each time. For example, if you need a while-loop, type the word `while` in the code editor and click CTRL+SPACEBAR. A list of choices for a variety of while-loops appears, as shown below. Double-clicking on one of the selections drops in the while-loop template into the code editor. Note that you can add additional templates by clicking on the New... button and filling in the input boxes.

The Console tab allows you to see output from compiling and running your program.

Note that these tabs can be drag-and-dropped to another location in the IDE. For example, if you prefer to have your Markers to the right of the Project Explorer, you can drag the Markers tab just to the right of the Project Explorer tab. When you do this, you will either see two side-by-side green vertical rectangles (shown below) indicating that the Markers tab will be to one side of the Project Explorer tab, or you will see two horizontal green rectangles indicating that the Markers tab will be above or below the Project Explorer.

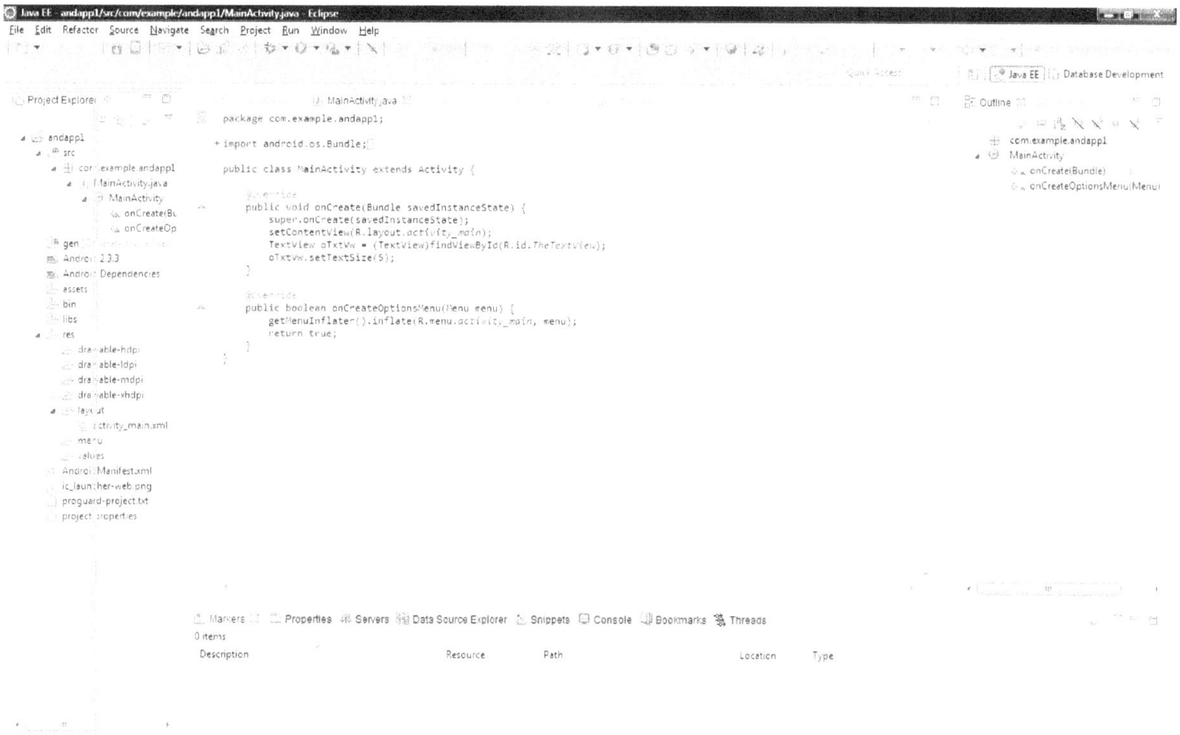

It may take some fiddling to get the tab placed exactly where you want it to be. Here is what the IDE looks like if you've chosen to place the Markers tab below the Project Explorer tab.

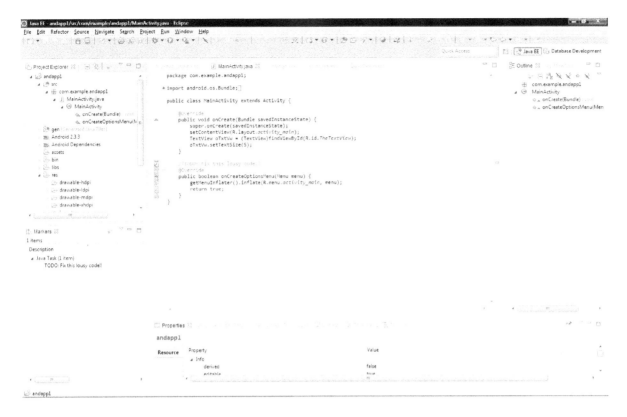

Perspectives

Like all software, Eclipse has its own set of terminology.

When we first started Eclipse, we had to set up a workspace. A *workspace* is the directory where all of your projects are stored. This includes your source code and Eclipse-specific settings.

After we set up the workspace directory, Eclipse presented us with the Welcome to Eclipse screen. On the top-right, there is a button for the Workbench. The *workbench* is just another name for the development environment we described in the last section. You can open up multiple workbenches by clicking on Window...New Window.

Within each workbench, the conglomeration of panes, editors, menus, toolbars, etc. is called a *perspective*. Each perspective is used for a specific task such as programming in a specific language such as Java or PHP, debugging your programs, etc. Eclipse is installed with a predefined list of perspectives, which you can switch to by clicking on Window...Open Perspective, shown below:

You can more quickly see the full list of perspectives by clicking on the Open Perspective button at the top-right of the IDE:

Here is a list of available perspectives when you click on this button:

For example, by clicking on the Database Development perspective in the list above, your workbench is rearranged slightly to look something like this (take note that a Database Development perspective button has been added to the right of the Open Perspective button):

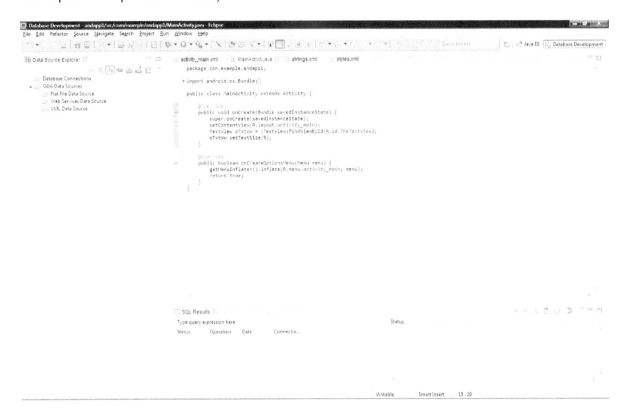

To switch between perspectives, you can click on the perspective buttons that appear to the right of the Open Perspective button. For example, to get back to the Java perspective, you can click on the Java EE perspective button (appearing directly to the left of the Database Development button shown above).

You can customize each perspective by first selecting the perspective you want to change either by clicking on one of the perspective buttons to the right of the Open Perspective button, or by clicking on the Open Perspective button itself and selecting the desired perspective. Next, click Window...Customize Perspective to bring up the Customize Perspective dialog box (as shown below). Take note that the title of the dialog box reflects which perspective you are modifying. For example, in the image below the title reads Customize Perspective - Java EE. From within this dialog box, you can make changes to the tool bar, the menus, the command groups and the shortcuts.

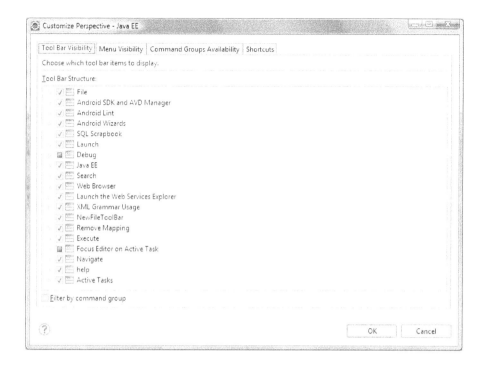

Note that a *checked* checkbox indicates that all of the sub-items have been selected whereas a *darkened* checkbox indicate that at least one sub-item has not been selected.

Views

Within each perspective is a series of *views*. Examples of views are the Project Hierarchy tab and the Markers tab. You can show additional views within your perspective by clicking on Window...Show View and either selecting a view from the list (as shown below), or clicking on the Other... menu item to bring up the Show View dialog.

The Show View dialog, as shown below, contains a folder for Android as well as other items. If you expand the Android folder, you will see additional views you can select and display.

For example, if I click on the Threads view, the Threads tab is added at the bottom of the Eclipse IDE.

Another nice view is the Bookmarks view. This view allows you to see each line of code you bookmarked. You can bookmark a line of code by right-clicking in the gutter (to the left of column one in the code window, as shown below) and clicking on Add Bookmark....

When the Add Bookmark dialog appears, enter a bookmark name or accept the default. Click the OK button.

After a moment, the new bookmark will appear in the Bookmarks tab and a small bookmark icon will appear to the left of the gutter on the line of code you just bookmarked. If you double-click on the description in the Bookmarks tab, your cursor will be brought to the corresponding line of code.

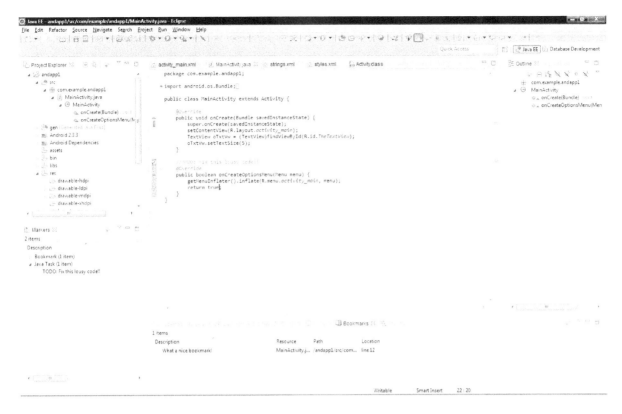

Note that bookmarks appear in the Markers tab along with any tasks, for some strange reason.

Menus

Nearly all software has one or more menus and Eclipse is no different. As you have discovered while reading this book, there is the File, Edit, Window, etc. menus. While we won't go into the detail of all of the menus, be aware that many of the panes contain a small white down-arrow - called the *View Menu* - which will display additional menu items for that particular pane. For example, on the Project Explorer pane, when the View Menu down-arrow is clicked, the following menu items are displayed:

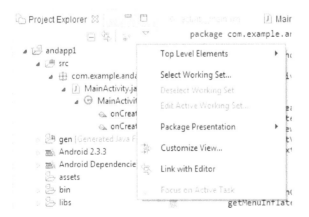

Also, you can right-click in several places in the IDE and a context-specific menu will appear. For example, if you right-click on the Android application name (`andapp1`, in this case), you will see the following pop-up menu:

Note that if you minimize a view by clicking on the minimize button, a toolbar will appear in its place. For example, when the Project Explorer is minimized, you will see the following:

There are two buttons on this toolbar. The top button is the restore button, which restores the pane to its standard position within the IDE. If you click the bottom button, Project Explorer will pop-up, as shown below. By clicking on a blank area of the IDE, this pop-up will disappear.

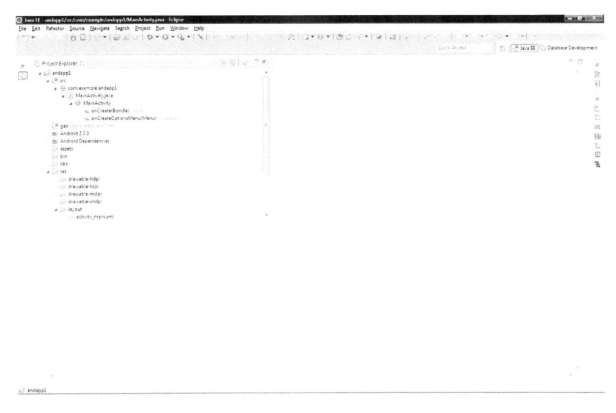

Take note that minimizing all of the panes gives you lots of room for coding, as shown below:

Search

There are so many different ways to search in Eclipse that there is a separate menu devoted just to searching:

By clicking on Search...Search... (or using its CTRL+H keyboard equivalent), you will bring up the Search dialog. This dialog has several tabs allowing you to search through files, tasks, your Java code, and more. If you just want to search within your code, click on the Java Search tab (shown below), fill in the Search string input box with the desired search term, select what to search for and where to search in, and click the OK button.

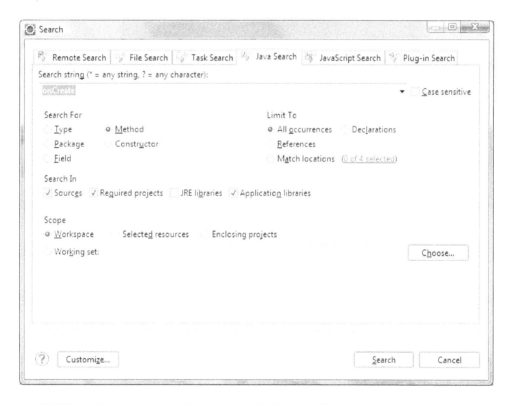

Eclipse will fill in the results of the search in the Search tab at the bottom of the IDE:

'onCreate' - 15 occurrences in workspace (no JRE) (0 matches filtered from view)
- android.support.v4.app - android-support-v4.jar - C:\temp\workspace\andapp1.libs - andapp1
- com.example.andapp1 - src - andapp1
  - MainActivity
    - onCreate(Bundle) (2 matches)
    - onCreateOptionsMenu(Menu)

Automatic Code Generation

We've already talked about using code snippets as well as templates to ease the burden of programming. To make programming even easier, Eclipse can generate a variety of code based on the state of the source code. For example, if a class called Stuff is created containing two attributes sStuff and iStuff, Eclipse can generate the getters and setters automatically. Ensure that your cursor is located somewhere within the class, then click on the Source menu and then click on the Generate Getters and Setters... menu item. The Generate Getters and Setters dialog box appears, as shown below.

Choose which attributes you would like getters and/or setters generated for and then click on the OK button. The code for the getters and/or setters is inserted into the code editor:

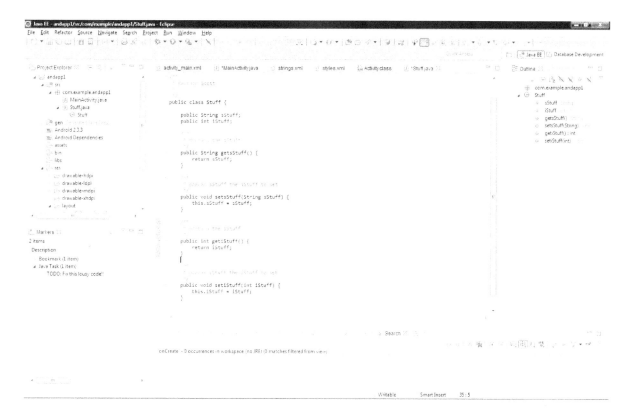

Note that the Source menu contains additional options for the beautification of your code. You can add/remove comments, add/remove indentation, format your code, etc. Below is the Source menu:

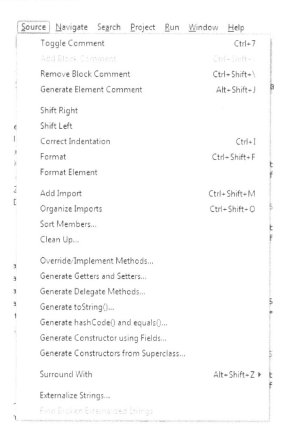

Using the Scrapbook

If you ever wanted to just test a piece of code without having to make a new project, it sounds like the Scrapbook is for you! The Scrapbook currently only works from within a Java project and not from within an Android project. Now, you can have multiple projects within Eclipse, so click on File...New...Project... and select Java Project within the Java node when the New Project dialog appears. Click the Next button. Fill in the name of the project (for example, ScrapbookProject) and click the Finish button.

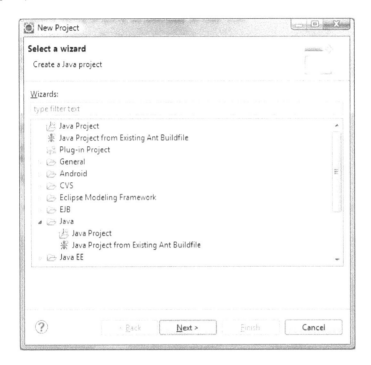

Now that an appropriate project has been created, we can setup the scrapbook. Click on File...New...Other.... Next, click on the Scrapbook Page node which appears within the Java Run/Debug node and then click the Next button. When the New Scrapbook Page dialog appears, click on the Scrapbook Project in the Enter or select the parent folder section, fill in the File Name input box with something like ScrapbookTests. Click the Finish button and the Scrapbook tab will appear. Naturally, you can move the tab anywhere you want within the IDE.

Now, in the Scrapbook tab, enter the following code:

```
String sTest = "ABC";
sTest
```

Highlight this code, right-click and click on the Display menu item. You should then see the results:

```
String sTest = "ABC";
sTest
(java.lang.String) ABC
```

If you receive the pop-up message *Unable to Launch Scrapbook VM*, then you may need to update the Java Runtime Environment location for the scrapbook. In Project Explorer, expand the ScrapbookProject root. Right-click the file called `ScrapbookTests.jpage` and click on the Properties menu item. When the Properties for `ScrapbookTests.jpage` dialog appears, click on the Scrapbook Runtime item on the left pane.

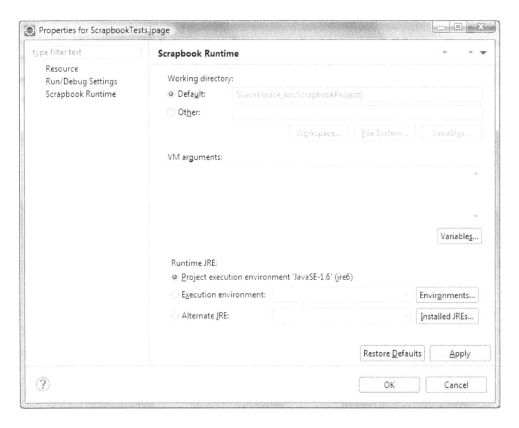

In the section labeled `Runtime JRE:` near the bottom of the dialog, click on the Installed JREs... button. You should see something like this:

If a JRE appears, ensure that its checkbox is checked. If a JRE does not appear, click on the Add... button and add a JRE. Click on the OK button. You should see something like this (jre6 appears in the Alternate JRE drop-down box):

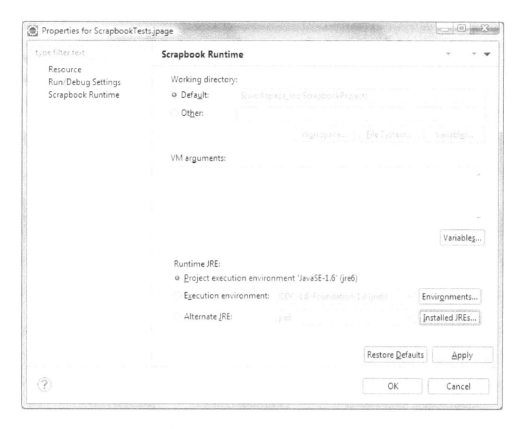

Next, ensure that the radio button to the left of the text Alternate JRE is checked. Click the Apply button and click the OK button. This should (hopefully) get your scrapbook to work.

Using Keyboard Short-Cuts

To make your programming life even easier, Eclipse has a lot of keyboard short-cuts. You can display them in a pop-up by clicking on CTRL+SHIFT+L (see below bottom right):

111

Below is a list of the keyboard short-cuts appearing in this pop-up:

Activate Editor	F12
Activate Task	Ctrl+F9
Add Artifact to Target Platform	Ctrl+Alt+Shift+A
Add Javadoc Comment	Alt+Shift+J
All Instances	Ctrl+Shift+N
Backward History	Alt+Left
Build All	Ctrl+B
Change Method Signature	Alt+Shift+C
Close	Ctrl+F4
Close All	Ctrl+Shift+F4
Collapse All	Ctrl+Shift+Numpad_Divide
Content Assist	Ctrl+Space
Context Information	Ctrl+Shift+Space
Copy	Ctrl+Insert
Cut	Shift+Delete
Deactivate Task	Ctrl+Shift+F9
Debug	F11
Debug Android Application	Alt+Shift+A, D
Debug Ant Build	Alt+Shift+D, Q
Debug Eclipse Application	Alt+Shift+D, E
Debug JUnit Plug-in Test	Alt+Shift+D, P
Debug JUnit Test	Alt+Shift+D, T
Debug Java Applet	Alt+Shift+D, A

Debug Java Application	Alt+Shift+D, J
Debug OSGi Framework	Alt+Shift+D, O
Debug on Server	Alt+Shift+D, R
Declaration in Workspace	Ctrl+G
Delete	Delete
Display	Ctrl+Shift+D
Execute	Ctrl+U
Exit	Ctrl+Q
Expand All	Ctrl+Shift+Numpad_Multiply
Extract Android String	Alt+Shift+A, S
Extract Local Variable	Alt+Shift+L
Extract Method	Alt+Shift+M
Find Text in Workspace	Ctrl+Alt+G
Find and Replace	Ctrl+F
Force Return	Alt+Shift+F
Forward History	Alt+Right
Generate Code	Alt+Shift+G
Inline	Alt+Shift+I
Inspect	Ctrl+Shift+I
Last Edit Location	Ctrl+Q
Make Landmark	Ctrl+Alt+Shift+Up
Make Less Interesting	Ctrl+Alt+Shift+Down
Maximize Active View or Editor	Ctrl+M

Plug-in Menu Spy	Alt+Shift+F2
Plug-in Selection Spy	Alt+Shift+F1
Previous	Ctrl+,
Previous Editor	Ctrl+Shift+F6
Previous Page	Alt+Shift+F7
Previous Perspective	Ctrl+Shift+F8
Previous Sub-Tab	Alt+PageUp
Previous View	Ctrl+Shift+F7
Print	Ctrl+P
Properties	Alt+Enter
Quick Access	Ctrl+3
Quick Fix	Ctrl+1
Quick Switch Editor	Ctrl+E
Redo	Ctrl+Y
References in Workspace	Ctrl+Shift+G
Refresh	F5
Remove All Visible Results	Shift+Delete
Remove Result	Ctrl+Delete
Rename	F2
Rename - Refactoring	Alt+Shift+R
Run	Ctrl+F11
Run Android Application	Alt+Shift+A, R
Run Ant Build	Alt+Shift+X, Q

Run Eclipse Application	Alt+Shift+X, E
Run JUnit Plug-in Test	Alt+Shift+X, P
Run JUnit Test	Alt+Shift+X, T
Run Java Applet	Alt+Shift+X, A
Run Java Application	Alt+Shift+X, J
Run OSGi Framework	Alt+Shift+X, O
Run on Server	Alt+Shift+X, R
Save	Ctrl+S
Save All	Ctrl+Shift+S
Search Repository for Task	Ctrl+Shift+F12
Select All	Ctrl+A
Show Context Quick View	Ctrl+Alt+Shift+Right
Show Contributing Plug-in	Alt+Shift+F3
Show In...	Alt+Shift+W
Show Key Assist	Ctrl+Shift+L
Show Occurrences in File Quick Menu	Ctrl+Shift+U
Show Refactor Quick Menu	Alt+Shift+T
Show Source Quick Menu	Alt+Shift+S
Show System Menu	Alt+-
Show View	Alt+Shift+Q, Q
Show View (Breakpoints)	Alt+Shift+Q, B
Show View (Cheat Sheets)	Alt+Shift+Q, H
Show View (Console)	Alt+Shift+Q, C

Move - Refactoring	Alt+Shift+V
New	Ctrl+N
New menu	Alt+Shift+N
Next	Ctrl+.
Next Editor	Ctrl+F6
Next Page	Alt+F7
Next Perspective	Ctrl+F8
Next Sub-Tab	Alt+PageDown
Next View	Ctrl+F7
Open Attached Javadoc	Shift+F2
Open Call Hierarchy	Ctrl+Alt+H
Open Declaration	F3
Open Manifest	Ctrl+Alt+Shift+M
Open Plug-in Artifact	Ctrl+Shift+A
Open Remote Task	Ctrl+Alt+Shift+F12
Open Resource	Ctrl+Shift+R
Open Search Dialog	Ctrl+H
Open Task	Ctrl+F12
Open Type	Ctrl+Shift+T
Open Type Hierarchy	F4
Open Type in Hierarchy	Ctrl+Shift+H
Organize Imports	Ctrl+Shift+O
Paste	Shift+Insert

Show View (Declaration)	Alt+Shift+Q, D
Show View (Error Log)	Alt+Shift+Q, L
Show View (History)	Alt+Shift+Q, Z
Show View (Javadoc)	Alt+Shift+Q, J
Show View (Outline)	Alt+Shift+Q, O
Show View (Package Explorer)	Alt+Shift+Q, P
Show View (Problems)	Alt+Shift+Q, X
Show View (Search)	Alt+Shift+Q, S
Show View (Synchronize)	Alt+Shift+Q, Y
Show View (Task List)	Alt+Shift+Q, K
Show View (Type Hierarchy)	Alt+Shift+Q, T
Show View (Variables)	Alt+Shift+Q, V
Show View Menu	Ctrl+F10
Surround With Quick Menu	Alt+Shift+Z
Switch to Editor	Ctrl+Shift+E
Terminate Result	Ctrl+Break
Toggle Breakpoint	Ctrl+Shift+B
Undo	Ctrl+Z
Use Step Filters	Shift+F5
Zoom In	Ctrl+=
Zoom Out	Ctrl+-

Note that you can add or edit keyboard short-cuts by clicking on Window...Preferences and clicking on the Keys node under the General node when the Preferences dialog appears.

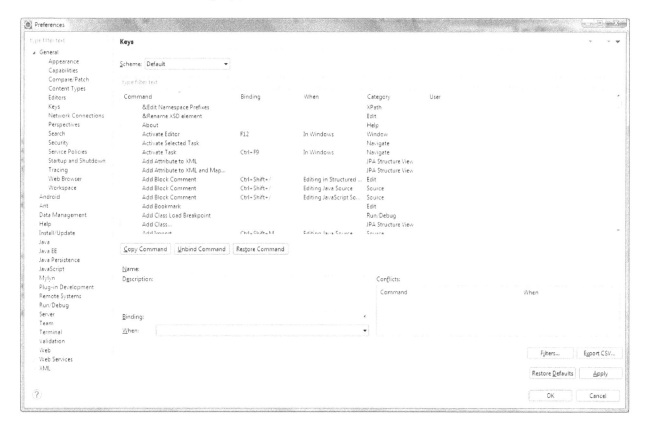

Summary

In this chapter, we learned how to use the Eclipse IDE to create programs more efficiently. While this chapter is definitely not the last word on Eclipse, it is a start. You can find out more about the Eclipse IDE by navigating your browser to http://www.eclipse.org.

Chapter 5B: Exploring Android Studio

Overview

Whereas Eclipse is a general-purpose integrated development environment (IDE) for developing in languages such as Java, Ruby, Perl, R, PHP and others, Android Studio is a development environment specifically for Android development. Android Studio is based on the Java integrated development environment IntelliJ IDEA rather than Eclipse.

Note that the download for Android Studio contains the Android SDK Tools, the latest Android SDK and the latest emulator used to test your applications when not using a connected device. This is similar to downloading the ADT Bundle.

As of the writing of this edition of the book, Android Studio is in *early access preview* and may still contain some bugs, so using Android Studio for a full-blown project may be unadvisable at this point. With that said, Android development *may* eventually move from an Eclipse-based to Android Studio-based solution entirely, so it's best to keep an eye on this new integrated development environment.

Downloading Android Studio

Android Studio is available as a separate download from the SDK and requires a Java Software Development Kit (JDK) to be installed on your machine. If you have followed the installation instructions outlined at the beginning of the book, you already have a version of the JDK installed along with an updated PATH environment variable.

To install Android Studio, perform the following instructions:
1. Navigate your browser to developer.android.com/sdk/installing/studio.html.
2. Click on the big button labeled *Download Android Studio v0.5.2* (your version number may be different).
3. A Terms and Conditions webpage appears. Ensure that the checkbox to the left of the text *I have read and agree with the above terms and conditions* is checked.
4. Click the button labeled *Download Android Studio v0.5.2 for Windows* which appears after you click the checkbox in Step #3.
5. Follow the download procedure for your browser. For me, the following dialog box appeared and I clicked the Save File button.

6. The download may take quite a while...yawn...

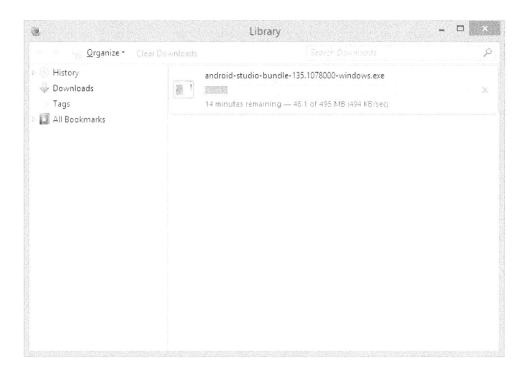

7. Once the download completes, double-click on the executable to start the installation process.
8. A User Account Control dialog box may appear. Click Yes to continue.
9. The Android Studio Setup dialog box should eventually appear. Click Next to continue.

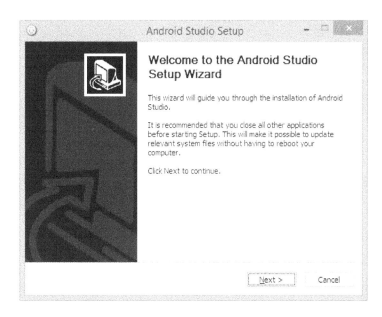

10. Ensure that the radio button to the left of the text *Install just for me* is checked.

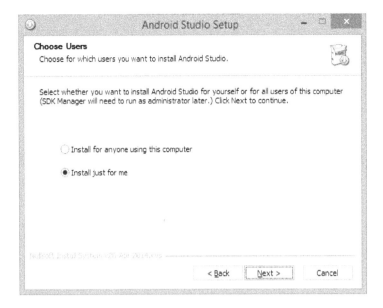

11. Ensure that the suggested destination folder is to your liking, and click Next.

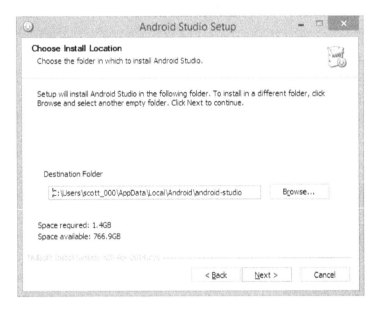

12. Select the desired start menu, and click Install.

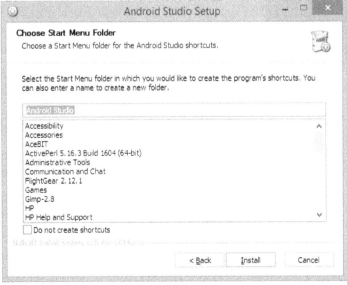

13. While the software is being installed, you will see the following dialog box:

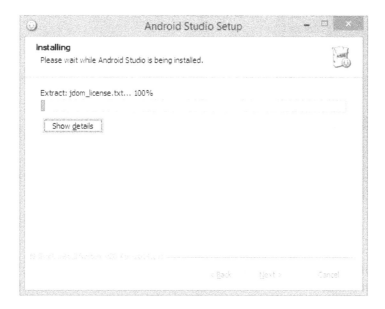

14. Once the installation completes, click the Next button.

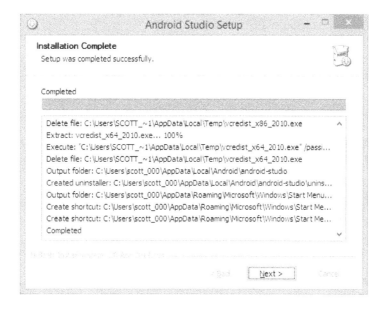

15. Finally, click the Finish button to complete the installation and start Android Studio.

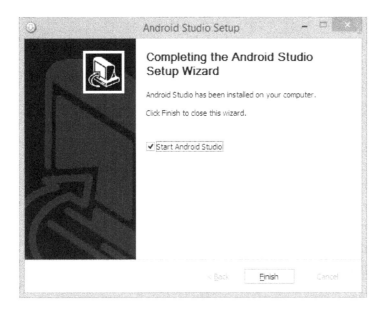

16. Once Android Studio starts, you may be greeted with the following nasty dialog box. Please ensure that the `JAVA_HOME` environment variable is defined.

Based on the installation instructions in Chapter 1, *Installing the Android SDK on Windows*, I set my `JAVA_HOME` environment variable as follows:

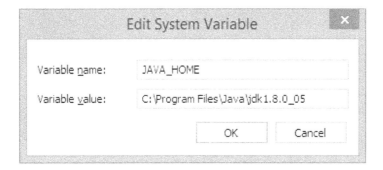

17. Restart Android Studio and the first time through you will be asked if you want to import settings from a previous version of Android Studio. Since this is a first time install, you can skip this.
18. Next, the following lovely start up screen will appear:

19. Finally, the *Welcome to Android Studio* dialog box appears, as shown below:

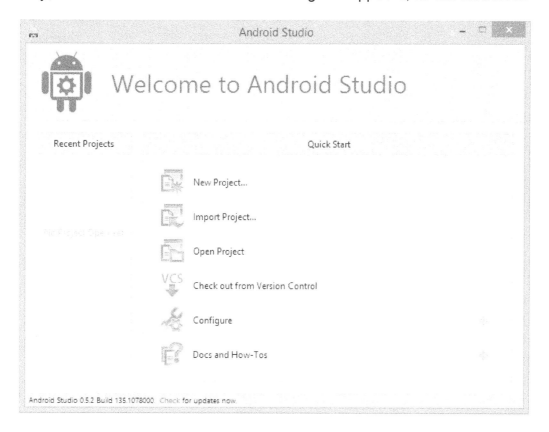

A First Look at the IDE

When you first open the Android Studio IDE, you will be shown the screen above. To create a new project, click on the New Project... link. To open an already existing project, either select it from the Recent Projects pane, or click on the Open Project link.

Let's create a new project by clicking the New Project... link. The New Project dialog box, shown below, will be displayed.

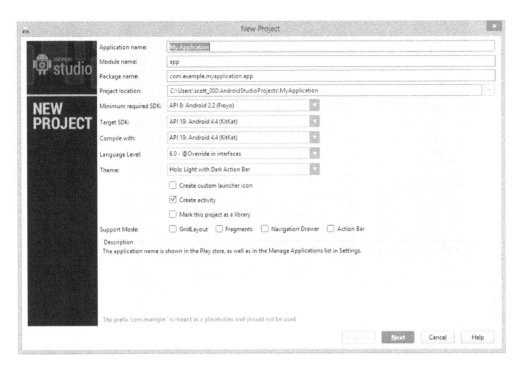

Fill in the input boxes shown above. For my test application, I filled in the input boxes as follows:

1. Application Name - this is the name of the application. The text you enter here will be displayed in the Play Store, so make sure the name is cool! I filled in `TestAndroidStudio` because, you know, that's cool!
2. Module Name - this is equivalent to the Project Name input box in the New Android App dialog box in Eclipse. Here I filled in `testas`.
3. Package name - this is the Java package name in reverse domain name form. For me, the following package name was filled in automatically: `com.example.testandroidstudio.testas`.
4. Minimum required SDK - this the minimum SDK version you want your Android app to support. Here, I selected API 10: Android 2.3.3 (Gingerbread).
5. Target SDK - this is the highest API your app can work with. Here, I've chosen API 19.
6. Compile with - this is the target API to compile your code against from all of the installed SDKs on your machine. This is equivalent to the Build SDK drop-down box in the New Android App dialog box in Eclipse. Here, I've chosen API 19.
7. Language Level - choose a language level. Here, option 6.0 is automatically chosen and I kept that option.
8. Theme - chose your theme. Here, I've selected Holo Light with Dark Action Bar.
9. Create custom launcher icon - check this box if you would like to select a custom launcher icon. Here, I have left it unchecked. If you do check this option, when you click the Next button, the Custom Launcher Icon dialog will be displayed similar to what we've seen in Eclipse.
10. Create activity - check this box if you would like the activity to be created for you. This is checked automatically, so I have left it checked.
11. Mark this project as a library - check this box if you would like your project to be marked as a library. Here, I have left it unchecked.
12. Support Mode - select one or more support options:
    a. GridLayout - check this if you are going to use the grid layout.

b. Fragments - check this if you are going to use fragments.
c. Navigation Drawer - check this if you are using the navigation drawer.
d. Action Bar - check this if you are using the action bar.

Here are my final choices:

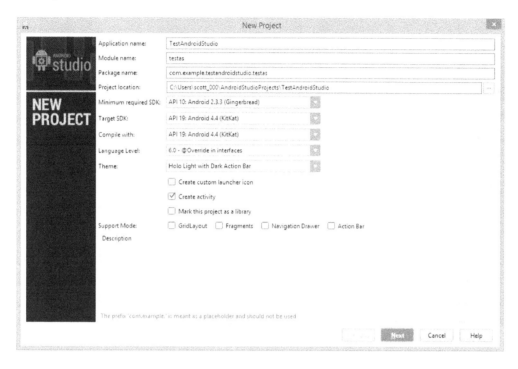

Click the Next button. Since I did not check the Create custom launcher icon checkbox, I am presented with a dialog box equivalent to the Create Activity dialog box in Eclipse.

I selected Blank Activity and clicked the Next button. The following dialog box asks you to input the following information:

1. Activity name - here I left it as `MainActivity`.
2. Layout name - here I left it as `activity_main`.
3. Additional Features - this drop-down box allows you to select additional features to add to your application such as including a blank fragment, navigation drawer, and so on. Here, I left it blank and clicked the Finish button.

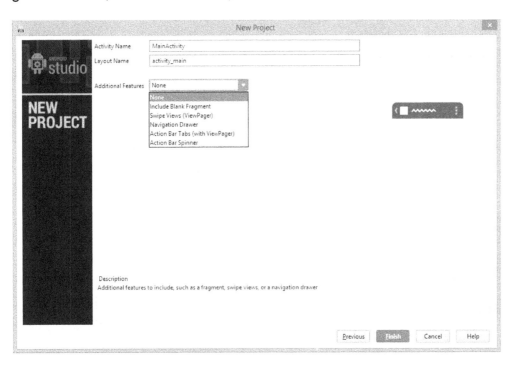

The creation of the project may take a while and you will be presented with the following dialog box:

When the application has been built, you may see the Tip of the Day dialog box. You can prevent it from appearing by unchecking the checkbox to the left of the text *Show Tips on Startup*. Click the Close button to dismiss the dialog box.

Finally, you will see the IDE, as shown below:

As you can see, the display is very similar to that of Eclipse. On the left side, you see the familiar Project Explorer, called Project in Android Studio. You may notice that the organization of an Android Studio project differs slightly from Eclipse with many of the folders now appearing under the `src` folder. In the center, you see the code for `MainActivity`. Now, don't be too disturbed by the vast amount of blank space on the right side, though. Open up the `res` folder in Project Explorer, then open up the `layout` folder. Next, double-click on the `activity_main.xml` file. The display is below. As you can see, the graphical user interface, labeled Design on the tab at the bottom, displays the default device as well as the default text string *Hello World!*. On the right, you will see the component tree which is equivalent the Outline tab in Eclipse. Further below, on the right, you will see the Properties for the component highlighted in the Component Tree. Below, the `RelativeLayout` is highlighted, so the properties displayed are for the `RelativeLayout`.

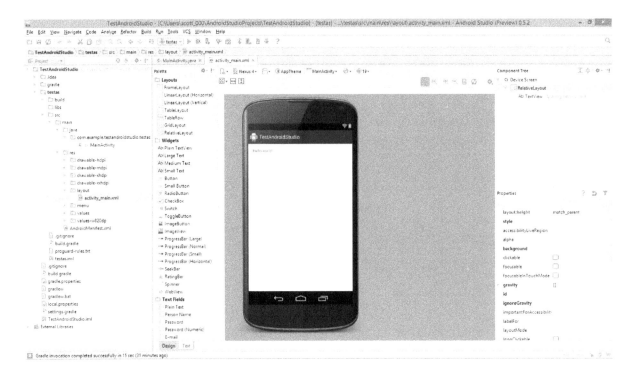

Running the Project using the Emulator

Now that we have a simple project set up, let's run this project using the emulator. On the toolbar, click on the green arrow to the right of the drop-down box containing the text `testas`. This will bring up the Choose Device dialog box. Take note that you can either choose a running device or launch the emulator. Since we already defined an emulator within the Android Virtual Device Manager within Eclipse, it is displayed as an option below. If you have not defined a virtual device, then click on the button displaying the ellipsis and follow the instructions for creating a virtual device in Chapter 2, *Creating Our First Android Application*.

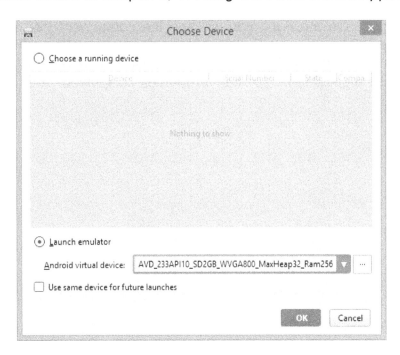

For now, ensure that the radio button to the left of the text *Launch emulator* is checked and click OK. It may take a while for the emulator to appear, and the bottom half of Android Studio will display some notes indicating what the IDE is doing. For me, the `emulator.exe` executable is started using my selected virtual device. You will eventually see the following familiar screen:

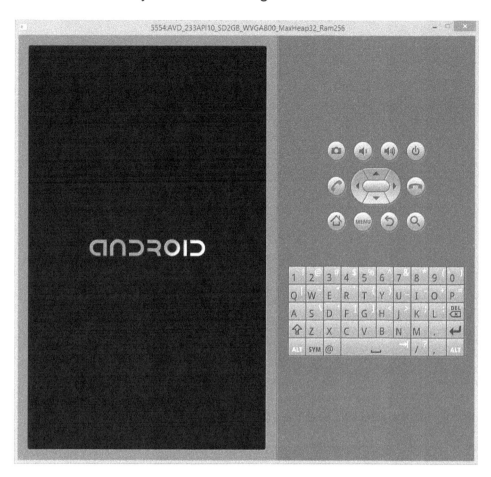

Note that you may see the following error message appear in the clipboard at the bottom of Android Studio: *Error: Could not access the Package Manager. Is the system running?*. This indicates that the emulator was not fully running when Android attempted to start your app. Please re-run the project and you should hopefully be presented with the following, or similar, screen below. Click the OK button to dismiss the less-than-helpful help screen (shown the first time the emulator is started) masking the home screen.

When the app finally starts, you will see the following:

Back in Android Studio, you will see the familiar Android DDMS display as well as the Logcat display.

Running the Project using a Physical Device

Let's rerun our application, but using a physical device instead of the virtual device. Plug in the physical device to your computer and click the green run button to bring up the Choose Device dialog box. Below, you will see my HTC device listed. Ensure that the radio button to the left of the text *Choose a running device* is selected and click OK.

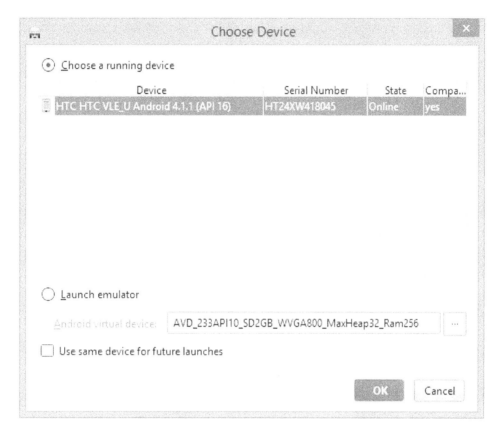

Once Android Studio connects to your device, the Android package for the project is uploaded, installed and started. You will see something like the following:

A Quick Note about Debugging

Similar to Eclipse, you can debug your application in Android Studio as well. Click the icon of the bug (Isn't that cute!) just to the right of the green run icon. First, though, let's add `Log.d()` to the `onCreate()` method, as shown below:

```
C MainActivity.java ×    activity_main.xml ×

import android.support.v7.app.ActionBarActivity;
import android.os.Bundle;
import android.util.Log;
import android.view.Menu;
import android.view.MenuItem;


public class MainActivity extends ActionBarActivity {

    @Override
    protected void onCreate(Bundle savedInstanceState) {
        super.onCreate(savedInstanceState);
        setContentView(R.layout.activity_main);
        Log.d("MYAPPTAG", "WE ARE IN THE ONCREATE METHOD!!");
    }
```

Don't forget the add an import for `android.util.Log`. If you do forget, Android Studio will remind you of this fact and tell you to hit Alt+Enter to add the appropriate import:

```
    @Override
    protected void onCreate(Bundle savedInstanceState) {
? android.util.Log? Alt+Enter e(savedInstanceState);
        setContentView(R.layout.activity_main);
        Log.d("MYAPPTAG", "WE ARE IN THE ONCREATE METHOD!!");
    }
```

Next, debug the application, choose the running device when the Choose Device dialog box appears, and click OK to run the app. Note that the debugger will take a while to attach to the device and you will see the following message **on your device**:

Back in Android Studio, you will see the log message we created, although you may have to scroll up the Logcat to see it:

```
logcat
06-26 11:49:35.563  25115-25115/com.example.testandroidstudio.testas I/System.out:  waiting for debugger to settle.
06-26 11:49:35.763  25115-25115/com.example.testandroidstudio.testas I/System.out:  waiting for debugger to settle.
06-26 11:49:35.963  25115-25115/com.example.testandroidstudio.testas I/System.out:  debugger has settled (1437)
06-26 11:49:37.064  25115-25115/com.example.testandroidstudio.testas D/MYAPPTAG:  WE ARE IN THE ONCREATE METHOD!!
06-26 11:49:37.335  25115-25115/com.example.testandroidstudio.testas I/Adreno200-EGL:  <qeglDrvAPI_eglInitialize:26!
     Build Date: 12/06/12 Thu
```

Note that you can search for your tag by entering it into the search box. Below, I entered the tag MYAPPTAG into the search box and only those lines containing that particular text are displayed in the logcat window, as shown below.

```
logcat
06-26 11:49:37.064  25115-25115/com.example.testandroidstudio.testas D/MYAPPTAG:  WE ARE IN THE ONCREATE METHOD!!
```

What about Perspectives and Views?

In the previous chapter, we learned that Eclipse has perspectives and views. Perspectives are just a conglomeration of panes, editors, menus, toolbars, etc. Android Studio doesn't have perspectives, but does have views called Tool Windows. By clicking on the Tool Windows menu item under the View menu, you will be shown a list of views such as Messages, Project, Android, and so on. By clicking on the Android menu item, you will bring up the familiar DDMS and Logcat windows. By clicking on the Project menu item, you toggle the display of the Project Explorer. And so on.

Bookmarks

Similar to Eclipse, you can bookmark a line of code. Move your cursor to the line of code you want bookmarked and click F11. This will display a checkmark within the gutter on the left side of the code window, as shown below. By clicking F11 again, you will toggle the bookmark feature and the checkmark will disappear.

```
        @Override
        protected void onCreate(Bundle savedInstanceState) {
            super.onCreate(savedInstanceState);
            setContentView(R.layout.activity_main);
            Log.d("MYAPPTAG", "WE ARE IN THE ONCREATE METHOD!!");
        }
```

To display a list of all of the bookmarks in your code window, click Navigate > Bookmarks > Show Bookmarks or click Shift+F11. A small window will appear, as shown below:

```
                                    Bookmarks                              x
  MainActivity.java:22      16    }
  MainActivity.java         17
                            18      @Override
                            19      public boolean onCreateOptionsMenu(Menu menu) {
                            20
                            21          // Inflate the menu; this adds items to the action bar i
                            22          getMenuInflater().inflate(R.menu.main, menu);
                            23          return true;
                            24      }
                            25
                            26      @Override
                            27      public boolean onOptionsItemSelected(MenuItem item) {
                            28          // Handle action bar item clicks here. The action bar wi
                            29          // automatically handle clicks on the Home/Up button, so
                            30          // as you specify a parent activity in AndroidManifest
                            31          int id = item.getItemId();
                            32          if (id == R.id.action_settings) {
                                                                    ..\MainActivity.java
```

You can navigate from bookmark to bookmark by clicking either the Navigate > Bookmarks > Next Bookmark or the Navigate > Bookmarks > Previous Bookmark menu items.

TODO, FIXME and Additional Comment Markers

Android Studio can also track comments containing the text TODO, FIXME, and other programmer-created comment markers. To use this feature, place a comment containing either TODO or FIXME in your code. Now, you will notice that these comments will be displayed in a different color from comments that do not contain comment markers. For example, the first comment below is a normal comment whereas the second comment contains the comment marker TODO. Note that the display of the comments is different.

```
    @Override
    protected void onCreate(Bundle savedInstanceState) {
        super.onCreate(savedInstanceState);

        //Set the content view here!!
        setContentView(R.layout.activity_main);
        //TODO: Remove this code!!
        Log.d("MYAPPTAG", "WE ARE IN THE ONCREATE METHOD!!");
    }
```

Now, in order to find all of your TODOs or FIXMEs, click on View > Tool Windows > TODO. This will bring up the TODO window at the bottom of the IDE, as shown below:

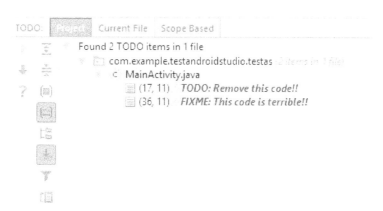

By double-clicking a comment line, such as those shown above, your cursor will be placed on the corresponding line of code.

Now, if you would like to add more comment markers, bring up the settings dialog by clicking on File > Settings... The Settings dialog allows you to change either project-related settings or IDE settings, as seen in the pane on the left of the Settings dialog (shown below).

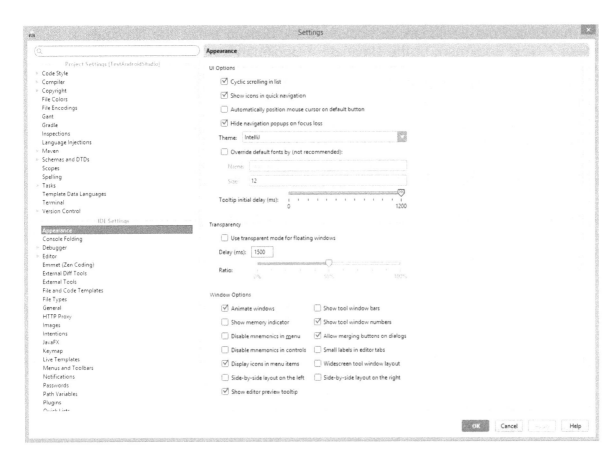

If you click on the TODO item listed under the IDE Settings section, you will be shown a list of currently available comment markers as regular expressions:

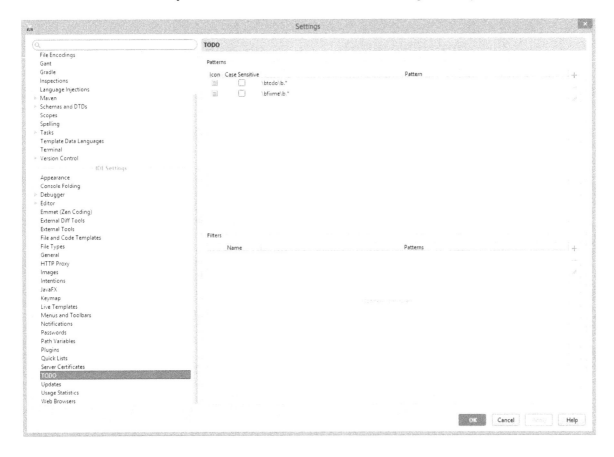

If you would like to add an additional comment marker, click on the green plus sign on the right side of the display and insert the appropriate regular expression for your comment marker in the input box to the right of the text *Pattern:*. For example, to add a BEER comment marker, you can use the regular expression `\bbeer\b.*` as shown below. Note that you can change the icon displayed in the TODO window as well as change the colors. Click OK to save your changes.

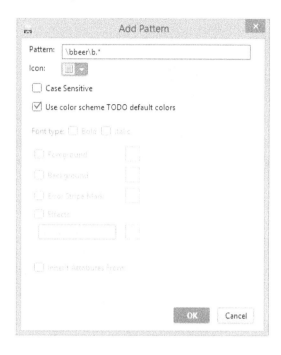

Finally, you will notice that colored marks appear on the far right of the code window. These indicate the location of bookmarks, comment markers, code that can be optimized, and so on. By hovering your mouse over the colored marks, an informative message will be displayed, as shown below. These messages can be very helpful in optimizing your code!

Search

Just like Eclipse, Android Studio has very rich searching capabilities. By clicking Edit > Find, several searching options are available to you. For example, Edit > Find > Find... will display the Find Toolbar within the code window, shown below the tabs in the image below:

```
  C MainActivity.java ×    B ActionBarActivity.class ×    Cᴀ FragmentActivity.java ×    activity_main.xml ×

Q setContentView                            ⬆ ⬇ ☐ ☐ ☐ Match Case ☐ Regex ☐ Words  1 match

   import android.view.Menu;
   import android.view.MenuItem;

   public class MainActivity extends ActionBarActivity {

       @Override
       protected void onCreate(Bundle savedInstanceState) {
           super.onCreate(savedInstanceState);

           //Set the content view here!!
           setContentView(R.layout.activity_main);
           // TODO: Remove this code!!
           Log.d("MYAPPTAG", "WE ARE IN THE ONCREATE METHOD!!");
       }
```

When you type in the search input box, the text is automatically searched for. By using the blue up and down arrows, you can search backwards or forwards in the code window.

Code Snippets

Recall that Eclipse has a very nice feature which allows you to save snippets of code that can easily be recalled later on. While Android Studio doesn't have a snippets feature per se, you can save snippets of code as Live Templates instead.

To save a piece of code as a Live Template, follow these steps:

1. Highlight the code you want to save.
2. Click on Tools > Save as Live Template... Note that this particular menu item won't appear if you don't perform Step #1. The Live Templates dialog box appears, as shown below, and is opened under the user folder ready for you to name your template.

3. In the Abbreviation input box, fill in a name for the template.
4. In the Description input box, fill in a description of the template.
5. Click OK to save the Live Template.

Before we move away from this dialog, you'll notice that there are several additional pre-existing folders such as *html/xml*, *other*, *output*, and so on. If you expand each folder, you will see the available code snippets you can use. For example, if you expand the *other* folder, you will see something like the following:

If you click on, say, *ifn*, the Template text input box will display the associated code snippet; here, an `if` statement comparing a variable against `null`. Note that the Template text contains two variables: `$VAR$` and `$END$`. `$VAR$` is a user-defined variable indicating to Android Studio to present you with a list of variables to choose from when you insert this particular Live Template into the editor.

Besides user-defined variables, Live Template has two built-in edit variables available for your use:

1. `$END$` - this edit variable indicates the desired location of the cursor *after* the Live Template code has been inserted into the editor. The text `$END$` will not appear in the editor because that would be silly!
2. `$SELECTION$` - this variable indicates that the highlighted text in the editor will be **surrounded by** the Live Template. For example, you may occasionally need to surround some XML with a CDATA section. Here is the pre-existing Live Template to do that, shown below:

Note that the edit variable $SELECTION$ appears within the CDATA section as shown in the Template text input box above.

Now, in order to actually use a Live Template, position your cursor in the appropriate place in your editor, and click Code > Insert Live Template... This will display a list of available Live Templates, as shown below:

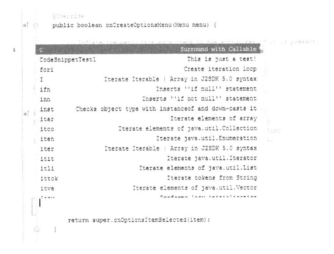

Take note that my own Live Template, CodeSnippetTest1, is shown in the list above. Click on the desired template and watch the fireworks!! For example, when I select the ifn Live Template, because the VAR user-defined variable appears in the template code, a popup window appears giving me a choice of variables to insert, as shown below. Once you select the desired variable, the code is inserted.

```
if (id == null) {
  V  o  id              int
  P  o  item      MenuItem
  f  o  iTest           int  };
}
```

Finally, Live Templates are context sensitive meaning that only those templates related to code are displayed when you are in the code editor, only those templates related to XML are displayed when you are in the layout XML editor, and so on.

Code Completion

As we mentioned above, if you attempt to use a class with no corresponding import, Android Studio will suggest a class to import and indicate that it can be added to the list of imports automatically by clicking the Alt+Enter key combination:

```
        @Override
        protected void onCreate(Bundle savedInstanceState) {
?  android.util.Log? Alt+Enter  e(savedInstanceState);
        setContentView(R.layout.activity_main);
        Log.d("MYAPPTAG", "WE ARE IN THE ONCREATE METHOD!!");
    }
```

Android Studio has a rich variety of code completion functionality such as displaying relevant methods, completing statements, and more. Please see the website   www.jetbrains.com/idea/webhelp/auto-completing-code.html   for   a complete list of code completion functionality.

For example, just like Microsoft's IntelliSense, Android Studio will display a list of methods based on the context. For example, below I entered the word `Toast` followed by a period. Android Studio followed up by displaying a list of methods I might want to use, as shown below:

```
    return true;
m  makeText(Context context, CharSequence text, int duration)   Toast
m  makeText(Context context, int resId, int duration)           Toast
   LENGTH_LONG                                                   int
   LENGTH_SHORT                                                  int
   class
   cast                                             ((SomeType) expr)
   field                                            myField = expr;
   instanceof    expr instanceof SomeType ? ((SomeType) expr) : null
   notnull                                          if (expr != null)
   null                                             if (expr == null)
   par                                              (expression)
   var                                              T name = expr;
Ctrl+Down and Ctrl+Up will move caret down and up in the editor  >>
Toast.
```

Another nice feature is the ability to suggest code based on the context. For example, as shown below, the third variable of the `makeText()` method requires an integer indicating how long to display the popup message. One way to easily see a list of pre-defined values is to either click Code > Completion > Basic or Code > Completion > SmartType. The latter will make suggestions based on the context whereas the former will potentially show much more than you need.   For example, below are the suggestions from Code > Completion > Basic.

137

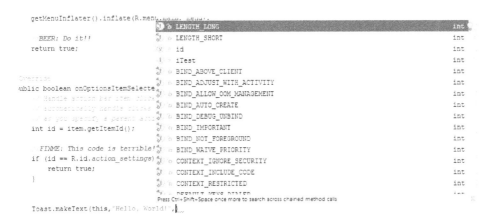

And below are the suggestions from Code > Completion > Smart Type.

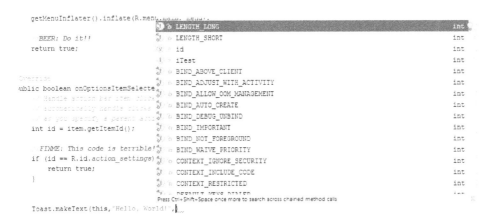

As you can see, there are more items listed in the former than the latter.

Automatic Code Generation

Just like with Eclipse, you can automatically generate code such as getters and setters, constructors, override methods and more. For example, to generate code automatically, make sure your cursor appears somewhere within the class and click on Code > Generate... and the following popup box will be displayed.

To generate a getter and setter, click on the *Getter and Setter* menu item and the Select Fields to Generate Getters and Setters dialog box appears, shown below.

Select the desired field, here I selected `iTestint`, click OK and one getter and one setter will be generated automatically for that variable.

Android Studio Plugins

Although Android Studio has a lot of built-in functionality straight of of the box, you may occasionally want to add additional features beyond what is included by default. One way to do this is by adding one or more plugins to Android Studio. First, in order to see which plugins are already installed on your machine, click File > Settings to bring up the Settings dialog box. Next, click on the Plugins entry under the IDE Settings section within the pane on the left. For me, I see the following:

Take note of the three buttons towards the bottom of the dialog box:

1. Install JetBrains plugin... - this will allow you to peruse the plugins available from the JetBrains repository. Recall that JetBrains is the creator of the IntelliJ IDEA integrated development environment which Android Studio is based on.

2. Browse repositories... - this allows you to browse plugins beyond those created by the vendor JetBrains.
3. Install plugin from disk... - this allows you to install a plugin that you have stored on disk.

For example, let's install the fun, but useless, Aquarium plugin created by LiquidArt:

1. Click on Browse repositories...
2. Scroll down to Aquarium.
3. Click on the Install plugin button in the right pane.
4. You will be asked if you want to download and install the plugin. Click Yes to continue.
5. Restart Android Studio for the plugin to take effect.

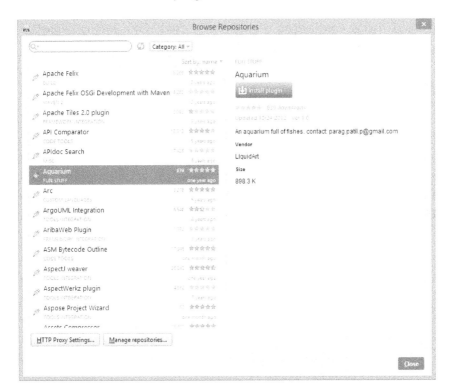

Now, in order to see the aquarium, bring up the Tool Buttons by clicking View > Tool Buttons. On the right side of Android Studio, you will see a button marked Aquarium. Click this button and you will see the aquarium, as shown below.

To disable or remove this plugin (which is highly recommended), go back into the Plugins page in Settings, click Aquarium and then click on Uninstall Plugin. To disable this plugin, uncheck the checkbox to the left of the text Aquarium and click the OK button.

There are other plugins out there and, although you may find this hard to believe, they are more useful than an aquarium.

Using Keyboard Short-Cuts

You can bring up a list of keyboard short-cuts by clicking on Help > Default Keymap Reference. This will display an Adobe Acrobat Reader (PDF) file, shown below in part:

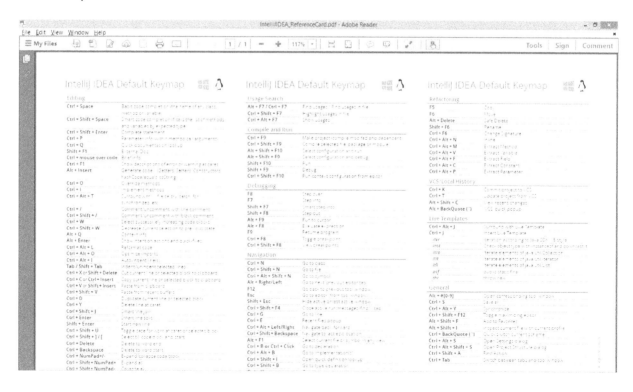

Version Control with Git

Android Studio comes with a plugin for the free and very popular version control software git. For those of you familiar with CVS, RCS, Subversion, Visual SourceSafe, and so on, git far surpasses these. According to Wikipedia,

> *Git is a distributed revision control and source code management (SCM) system with an emphasis on speed, data integrity, and support for distributed, non-linear workflows. Git was initially designed and developed by Linus Torvalds for Linux kernel development in 2005, and has since become the most widely adopted version control system for software development.*

> *As with most other distributed revision control systems, and unlike most client-server systems, every Git working directory is a full-fledged repository with complete history and full version tracking capabilities, independent of network access or a central server. Like the Linux kernel, Git is free software distributed under the terms of the GNU General Public License version 2.*

In order to use git with Android Studio, you first need to download and install the Git software. Follow these simple instructions:

1. Navigate your favorite browser to http://git-scm.com/downloads.
2. On the Downloads webpage, you will see a button indicating the suggested download for your operating system. For me, I see a big button labeled *Download for Windows*. Click on this button and perform the appropriate download procedure for your particular browser.

3. Once the software has been downloaded, double-click on the executable to launch the installation.
4. If a User Account Control dialog box appears, click Yes to continue the installation.
5. The Git Setup dialog box will appear. Click on Next to continue.
6. The GNU General Public License will be displayed. Spend as much time as you need reading through it, taking notes as necessary. Click on Next to continue.
7. The Select Destination Location dialog box will appear. Check that the suggested installation location is to your liking and click Next.
8. The Select Components dialog box will appear. Check any additional components you'd like installed. For me, I requested that an icon be placed on the desktop as well as use TrueType fonts in all console windows. Click Next.
9. The Select Start Menu Folder dialog box will appear. Click Next.

10. The Adjusting your PATH environment dialog box will appear giving you three options:
    a. Use Git from Git Bash only.
    b. Use Git from the Windows Command Prompt
    c. Use Git and optional Unix tools from the Windows Command Prompt

    For me, I chose (a) since Android Studio will interact with git itself. Click Next.

11. The Configuring the line ending conversions dialog box will appear giving you three options:
    a. Checkout Windows-style, commit Unix-style line endings
    b. Checkout as-is, commit Unix-style line endings
    c. Checkout as-is, commit as-is

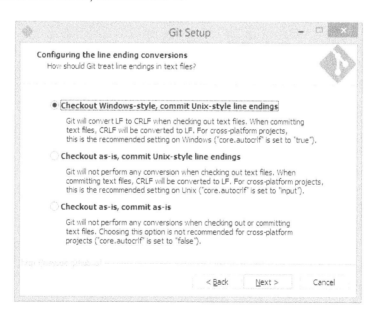

Some authors recommend using option (a), so let's go with that. Click Next to start the installation process which takes a while...you might want to get a sandwich or something...I'm just saying...

143

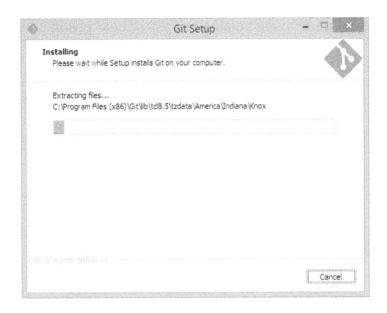

Once the Git installation process completes, click Finish to dismiss the Git Setup dialog box. You'll notice that an icon for Git Bash has been placed on your desktop. This will bring up the command line version of Git just in case you need it. Alternatively, you can right-click on a blank area of the desktop and you will see the following popup menu containing menu items for Git Init Here, Git Gui and Git Bash.

Now, in order to incorporate Git into Android Studio, you need to add the path to the Git executable in the Settings dialog within Android Studio:

1. Open Android Studio.
2. Click on File > Settings to bring up the Settings dialog box. On the left pane, click on the Version Control link, located under the Project Settings section, in order to display the list of version control software. Next, click on Git. Ensure that the path to the Git executable, `git.exe`, appears correctly in the *Path to Git executable:* input box.

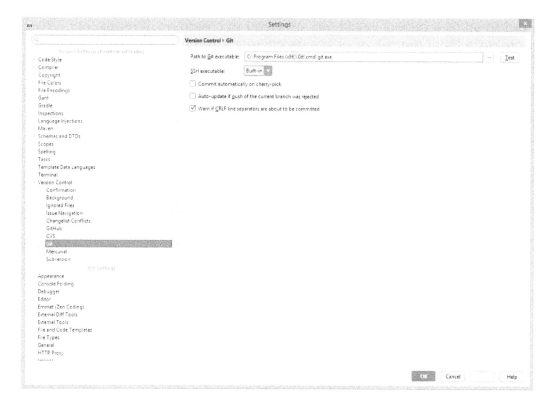

3. For the drop-down box to the right of the text *SSH executable:*, ensure that Built-in is selected. Note that selecting this option prevents us from installing Putty or other secure shell management software.
4. Leave *Commit automatically on cherry-pick* unchecked.
5. Leave *Auto-update if push of the current branch was rejected* unchecked.
6. Ensure that the checkbox to the left of the text *Warn if CRLF line separators are about to be committed* is checked.
7. Click the Test button to check if everything is working correctly. If everything goes well, you should see something like the following:

8. Click OK to save the settings.
9. Next, click on the Enable Version Control Integration... menu item under the VCS menu to display the Enable Version Control Integration dialog box. In the drop-down box, select Git and click OK.

Now, in order to store a project within Git, we need to create a Git repository. You can either create a local repository or create/access a remote repository. Below, we describe how to create a local Git repository.

1. Click on VCS > Import into Version Control > Create Git Repository... This will display the *Select directory for git init* dialog box which suggests a location for your Git repository. Click OK to accept the suggestion.

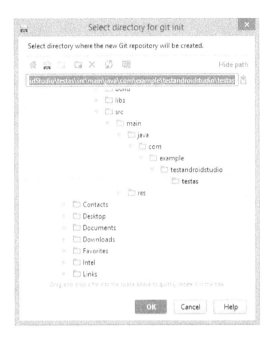

2. You will then be asked to approve the selected directory. Click Yes to continue.

3. Now, to add your project to the repository, follow these steps:
   a. Bring up the Changes Tool Window: View > Tool Windows > Changes.

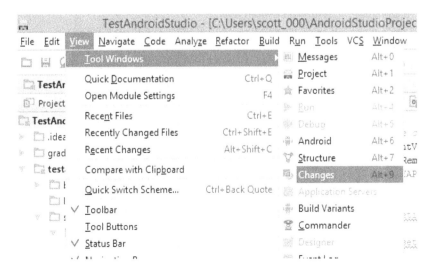

b. In the Changes window, right-click on the folder labeled Unversioned Files (# files) and click on the Add to VCS menu item.

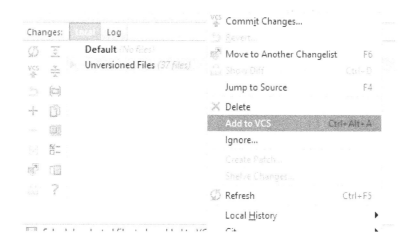

c. You will note that the number of files indicated on the Unversioned Files folder now appears on the Default folder.

To commit all changes to the respository for your project, perform the following steps:

1. Bring up the Changes Tool Window: View > Tool Windows > Changes.
2. Right-click on the Default folder and click the Commit Changes... menu item. The Commit Changes dialog box will appear, as shown below. Ensure that you enter your name in the *Author:* input box in the form `FirstName LastName <your@email.zz>`.

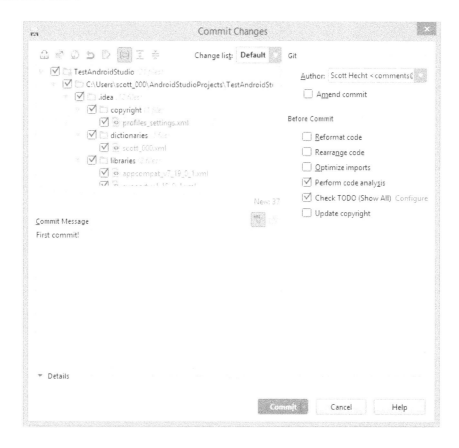

3. Enter a message in the *Commit Message:* input box explaining the reason for the commit.
4. Click on the Commit button to commit the changes to the respository. Note that you do not have to commit the entire project each time, but can commit a single file. To do this, expand the Default folder, right-click on the file you want to commit and select Commit Changes... Again, this will bring up the Commit Changes dialog box, as shown above, and you can commit the single file.

Note that since we left both *Perform code analysis* as well as *Check TODO* checked in the Commit Changes dialog box above, we will be shown several pieces of useful information. Finally, upon first time through this process, you'll be asked to specify your e-mail address for your user name. Don't worry, all of this is (mostly) harmless.

While we only scratched the surface of Git integration in Android Studio, you can read more about it at IntelliJ's website at `www.jetbrains.com/idea/webhelp/using-git-integration.html`. Also, Scott Chacon has written a very nice introduction to Git entitled *Pro Git* and is available for free download at `github.s3.amazonaws.com/media/progit.en.pdf`. This book is not geared towards Android Studio, but still gives you a lot of important insights into Git.

Finally, while we only discussed setting up a local Git repository, you can access a remote Git server, either one you've set up in your own shop or one available online (such as Unfuddle, GitHub, Bitbucket, etc.) although you may need an Android Studio plug-in to get it to work. Please see the *Pro Git* documentation for more on remote Git servers.

Summary

In this chapter, we briefly introduced some of the features of Android's new integrated development environment (IDE) Android Studio. Since Android Studio is still in *early access preview* status as of the writing of this book, we will use Eclipse throughout the remainder of this book.

Chapter 6: Introduction to the Android Platform

Overview

In this chapter, we describe many aspects of the Android platform. There are so many moving parts to Android that diving right in would confuse rather than clarify. In subsequent chapters, we explain all of the aspects touched on in this chapter in more detail. If something is not completely clear in this chapter, it will become much clearer in later chapters.

As you know, wacky terminology abounds in the computer industry and Android is no exception. For example, while you are probably used to talking about dialog boxes or GUI interfaces, Android calls them *activities*. An activity is similar to a Visual Basic form. When you need a form to appear, you *display* a *form*, but in Android you *inflate* an *activity*. The act of inflating an activity displays it on your smartphone or tablet.

Within a form, you place one or more controls such as a button, checkbox, and so on. In Android, a control is called a *view* and you place one or more views within a *view group* in an activity. (Don't confuse the word *view* within Android with the word *view* within the Eclipse IDE since they are different things.) The word view is synonymous with *widget*.

When a user clicks on a button control, an `onClick` event is fired and something wonderful happens such as a dialog box appears, etc. In Android, events are replaced by intents. An *intent* is a method of describing what needs to be performed when something happens, such as a user tapping on a button.

Android makes heavy use of XML files for everything from describing which intents map to which activities, mapping key/value pairs for use within your code, describing how an activity is layed out on the screen, and so on. These XML files allow you to separate your Java code from the GUI interface in a Model-View-Controller (MVC) design pattern.

The Android platform makes use of the Linux kernel as the operating system and it uses a Java virtual machine to execute applications. Note that Android uses the Dalvik Virtual Machine rather than the full-blown Java Virtual Machine (JVM) since a mobile platform has limited computing power as compared to a super-fast desktop computer.

As we've seen, the Java Virtual Machine produces a `.class` file from a `.java` program. On the other hand, the Dalvik Virtual Machine produces a `.dex` file from your Android project. A `.dex` file is a more compact way of storing a compiled Java application and is more appropriate for mobile platforms.

The Android platform executes each application within its own instance of the Dalvik Virtual Machine. This prevents one failing application from taking down the entire Android platform.

Android is also impatient. If an application does not respond within Android's five-second tolerance window, it will display the Force Close dialog box asking you if

149

you want to close the application or wait for it to respond. This occurs because each activity is run on a single thread. (It may seem strange to talk about threads when most smartphones have only one CPU onboard, although there are a few that are dual-core as of this writing.) When creating an Android application, you must remember that your code needs to run very quickly and any slow-running code should be placed on a thread separate from the activity's main thread.

Activities and Intents

An activity corresponds to a display screen. You application can have many activities, but only one is designated the main activity. This main activity is displayed when the application is started. As users click on the views (controls) within each activity (screen), an intent (event) is fired causing an action to occur. This action could be to display another of your activities; or this action could open a PDF file; or display your e-mail; or bring up your contacts list; and so on.

Note that the last three actions listed above - open a PDF, display e-mail, bring up contacts list - are not part of *your* application's code, but Android allows you to make use of *other* activities and this is performed through intents as well. That is, you can create an intent within your Android application which tells Android to display a PDF file (say) and Android will comply. This occurs because an application installed on the device tells Android that it has the ability to display a PDF file (say, Adobe PDF Reader). If there is more than one application capable of displaying a PDF file, Android will display a list of these applications and the user can then choose which one he wants to use to read the PDF file.

Since each running application can be killed and re-started at any time, each activity goes through a *lifecycle*. An activity's lifecycle is composed of a series of methods that are fired by Android when the activity is going through a change. For example, when a user moves from your application to another application, say, to check his e-mail, Android fires the `onPause` or `onStop` methods. We talk more about the activity lifecycle later on in the book.

Services

Just like other operating systems, services run in the background and are not, in general, visible to the user although the user can start an activity to control the service. Only one instance of a service can run at a time.

Note that there are several publicly available services that you can access from within your own application. For example, if the device is fitted with a Global Position System (GPS), you can use the GPS Service to determine the device's (and, hopefully, the user's) current coordinates.

Besides the GPS Service, the Download Service can be used from within your application if you need to download something off the internet. This service takes care of retrying failed downloads. Just imagine how much coding you'd have to do to re-create this service yourself!

Finally, the Notification Service allows you to alert the user of some action that has occurred within your application even if it's not currently visible. Notifications do not steal focus from what the user is currently doing by allowing you to display an icon on the Status Bar.

Just like activities, services go through their own lifecycle and we'll talk about that later on in the book.

Maintaining State

During the execution of your application, it may be advisable to save the user's current selections as well as access them later. There are several methods of doing this:

1. Writing data to and reading data from an external file, either in the device's memory or on the SDCard (assuming one is installed)
2. Using the `SharedPreferences` class, you can save key/value pairs for use later on. Note that only primitive data types - Boolean, float, integer, long, string - can be used with this method.
3. Extending the `PreferenceActivity` class to create a preferences dialog similar to Android's Settings dialog. Just like for activities, you layout your preference screen within an XML file, but be aware this is limited compared to the full layout in Android.
4. Using an activity's `Bundle` parameter for use when the activity is paused and then subsequently resumed. Just before the activity is paused, you save important information into the `Bundle` and, when Android resumes your activity, you can read in this information and take actions accordingly. Note that this is similar to Shared Preferences.
5. Using the SQLite database installed, by default, on Android to store and retrieve desired information in a SQL-like manner.

Content Providers

If you've done any programming with SQL databases, you know that you issue a SQL query against one or more database tables, your SQL is executed and the relevant data is returned.

If you've used ODBC or OLEDB from within, say, a Visual Basic, C#, PHP, etc. application, somewhere along the way a SQL query is formed, sent to the database, executed and the results are returned to your program.

In Android, a *content provider* is a method of retrieving information from a database without having to explicitly code a SQL query. Android performs this magic by matching a specific URL - similar to a website's URL - with code that issues SQL queries against a SQLite database. You generate this URL within your application's code.

With content providers, not only can you hide all of the SQL code from your own application, you can access data from other publicly available content providers on the device. For example, the Contacts List on Android has a publicly available content provider, which you can use within your own applications. This frees you up to worry about your own application and not how the Contacts database is structured, how the tables should be joined, etc.

Now, similar to accessing the Contacts database via a content provider within your own application, your own application can allow other programmers to access your data via a content provider that you make publicly available. So, if your Android application has a database of stock market information, you can allow other Android applications to access this data via your publicly available content provider.

Broadcast Receivers

Earlier in this chapter, we stated that intents are used to capture button clicks. But, you can use intents to interact with device events, not just your application's clicks. For example, you can set up your application to be notified when the device is, say, first turned on or when the phone rings. The device broadcasts these events and the intents within your application that are wired-up to hear these broadcasts are executed. Note that your application does not have to be currently executing for it to hear and respond to these broadcasts.

Layouts

As we mentioned earlier, you create the look of your GUI interface from within an XML file. Similar to the way you layout items within an HTML webpage, you use one or more layouts to design your interface. The layouts are:

1. Linear Layout - used to display views that follow one another either in a horizontal or vertical fashion.
2. Table Layout - uses rows and columns similar to the HTML TABLE tag to generate your interface. Note that rows within the table layout are specified using `TableRow` XML tags.
3. Frame Layout - used to display only one view which takes up the entire interface.
4. Relative Layout - allows views to be positioned relative to one another within the interface.
5. Scroll View Layout - can contain a layout itself and allows you to scroll up or down using the buttons or touch screen.
6. Horizontal Scroll View Layout - can contain a layout itself and allows you to scroll left or right using the buttons or touch screen.
7. Grid View Layout - creates a horizontally and vertically scrolling grid layout populated with entries via Java code.
8. List View Layout - similar to the scroll view layout but is optimized for large lists. This view takes care of its own scrolling so there is no need to place it in a `ScrollView` layout. It is populated with entries via Java code.

Note that you are allowed to create layouts from within code rather than from within the XML files. But, if you do that you are playing with the MVC design pattern, so think carefully if you want to do that. We discuss layouts in much more detail in the next chapter.

Alerting Users

You can alert users that something within your application has taken place by using the Notification Service, as described above, or via toasts. A *toast* is a transient, non-modal dialog box used to display information on the screen without taking focus from the active application.

Application

Hovering above all of the activities, intents, content providers, etc. lives the Application behaving much like an umbrella. One author states that subclassing the Application class is unnecessary, but another author states that subclassing the Application class can be used to:

1. Manage application state
2. Transfer objects between application components
3. Manage and maintain resources used by several application components.

Similar to the service and activity, the application has its own lifecycle. We talk more about application, service and activity lifecycles within their respective chapters. When interacting with the Application class, it is best to set it up as a singleton. We discuss this later on.

External Resources

As mentioned above, you can either create your layout using Java code or within an XML file. This XML file as well as other XML used by Android is called an *external resource*. Not only are external resources used to create layouts of views within an activity, external resources are used to hold color and style choices, initial drop-down box choices, key/value pairs, etc. With that said, there is one extremely important XML file called the *application manifest* - AndroidManifest.xml - containing information about your application's contents (i.e., activities, intents, etc.). For example, here are the contents of the AndroidManifest.xml file for our sample application:

```xml
<manifest xmlns:android="http://schemas.android.com/apk/res/android"
    package="com.example.andapp1"
    android:versionCode="1"
    android:versionName="1.0" >

    <uses-sdk
        android:minSdkVersion="10"
        android:targetSdkVersion="15" />

    <application
        android:icon="@drawable/ic_launcher"
        android:label="@string/app_name"
        android:theme="@style/AppTheme" >
        <activity
            android:name=".MainActivity"
            android:label="@string/title_activity_main" >
            <intent-filter>
                <action android:name="android.intent.action.MAIN" />
                <category android:name="android.intent.category.LAUNCHER" />
            </intent-filter>
        </activity>
    </application>
```

```
</manifest>
```

Since we only have one activity in our sample application, there is only one section in the XML file for that activity (see the highlighted code above).

Another XML file used very often is the `strings.xml` file. This file contains key/value pairs. Here is the `strings.xml` file for our sample application:

```
<resources>

    <string name="app_name">My First Android Application</string>
    <string name="hello_world">HELLO, WORLD!!</string>
    <string name="menu_settings">Settings</string>
    <string name="title_activity_main">MainActivity</string>

</resources>
```

This indicates that, for example, the key `app_name` is mapped to the value `My First Android Application`. Rather than hard-coding strings within your code, you can place them within this XML file and refer to them using the key within your code and the value will be returned.

The `ApplicationManifest.xml` file is located off the root of the application in the Eclipse IDE whereas other XML resource files are located within the `res` (**res**ource) node.

We talk more about this and other XML resource files later on in the book.

Android Platform Versions, API Levels and Version Code Names

Below is a chart mapping each Android platform version with its corresponding API Level and version code name. Note that the VERSION_CODEs ending in _MR# are maintenance releases.

Platform Version	API Level	VERSION_CODE	Notes
Android 4.4	19	KITKAT	Platform Highlights
Android 4.3	18	JELLY_BEAN_MR2	Platform Highlights
Android 4.2, 4.2.2	17	JELLY_BEAN_MR1	Platform Highlights
Android 4.1, 4.1.1	16	JELLY_BEAN	Platform Highlights
Android 4.0.3, 4.0.4	15	ICE_CREAM_SANDWICH_MR1	Platform Highlights
Android 4.0, 4.0.1, 4.0.2	14	ICE_CREAM_SANDWICH	
Android 3.2	13	HONEYCOMB_MR2	
Android 3.1.x	12	HONEYCOMB_MR1	Platform Highlights
Android 3.0.x	11	HONEYCOMB	Platform Highlights
Android 2.3.4 Android 2.3.3	10	GINGERBREAD_MR1	Platform Highlights
Android 2.3.2 Android 2.3.1 Android 2.3	9	GINGERBREAD	
Android 2.2.x	8	FROYO	Platform Highlights
Android 2.1.x	7	ECLAIR_MR1	Platform Highlights
Android 2.0.1	6	ECLAIR_0_1	
Android 2.0	5	ECLAIR	
Android 1.6	4	DONUT	Platform Highlights
Android 1.5	3	CUPCAKE	Platform Highlights
Android 1.1	2	BASE_1_1	
Android 1.0	1	BASE	

Summary

In this chapter, we briefly introduced the Android platform and the capabilities available to the programmer. In the next chapter, we start to delve more deeply into how Android lays out views (i.e., controls) on the interface.

Chapter 7: Android Layouts

Overview

As mentioned in the previous chapter, you use a layout to organize your views (i.e., controls) to be displayed on the screen. In this chapter, we will discuss each layout type in turn. Some authors introduce Android activity and views before this chapter, but I feel that the layout is so important that it should be taught first. Besides, if you've read the book up to this point, you understand that an activity is just a GUI interface and a view is just a control. We will discuss both activities and views later on in the book.

Note that you can generate layouts within code rather than the XML files. We will look at how to generate layouts within code later on in the book.

As mentioned in the previous chapter, there are several layouts:

1. Linear Layout - used to display views that follow one another either in a horizontal or vertical fashion.
2. Table Layout - uses rows and columns similar to the HTML TABLE tag to generate your interface. Note that rows within the table layout are specified using `TableRow` XML tags.
3. Frame Layout - used to display only one view which takes up the entire interface.
4. Relative Layout - allows views to be positioned relative to one another within the interface.
5. Scroll View Layout - can contain a layout itself and allows you to scroll up or down using the buttons or touch screen.
6. Horizontal Scroll View Layout - can contain a layout itself and allows you to scroll left or right using the buttons or touch screen.
7. Grid View Layout - creates a horizontally and vertically scrolling grid layout that is populated with entries via Java code.
8. List View Layout - similar to the scroll view layout but is optimized for large lists. This view takes care of its own scrolling so there is no need to place it in a `ScrollView` layout. Populated with entries via Java code.

Note that within the activity-specific XML file (i.e., `activity_main.xml`) the layout XML tags corresponding to the layouts listed above are as follows (I show mixed case below because that is what the Eclipse IDE generates although I've seen the XML tags in all uppercase as well):

1. Linear Layout - `LinearLayout`
2. Table Layout - `TableLayout`
3. Table Row - `TableRow`
4. Frame Layout - `FrameLayout`
5. Relative Layout - `RelativeLayout`
6. Scroll View Layout - `ScrollView`
7. Horizontal Scroll View Layout - `HorizontalScrollView`
8. Grid View Layout - `GridView`
9. List View Layout - `ListView`

Two Views - `TextView` and `Button`

In our example application, we opted for the default interface which features a `LinearLayout` with a single view called a `TextView` that contained the text `Hello, World!!`. For the examples in this chapter, we will make use of just two views, the `TextView` and the `Button`, although we may repeat them several times within an interface.

In the example, we generated the following XML for our main activity (`activity_main.xml`):

```
<RelativeLayout xmlns:android="http://schemas.android.com/apk/res/android"
    xmlns:tools="http://schemas.android.com/tools"
    android:layout_width="match_parent"
    android:layout_height="match_parent" >

    <TextView
        android:id="@+id/TheTextView"
        android:layout_width="wrap_content"
        android:layout_height="wrap_content"
        android:layout_centerHorizontal="true"
        android:layout_centerVertical="true"
        android:text="@string/hello_world"
        tools:context=".MainActivity" />

</RelativeLayout>
```

As you can see, there is a layout that surrounds the `TextView`. As a reminder, here is what this looks like:

Within the Eclipse IDE, if we drag a Button from the Form Widgets palette to just below the text `Hello, World!!`, you will see the following interface:

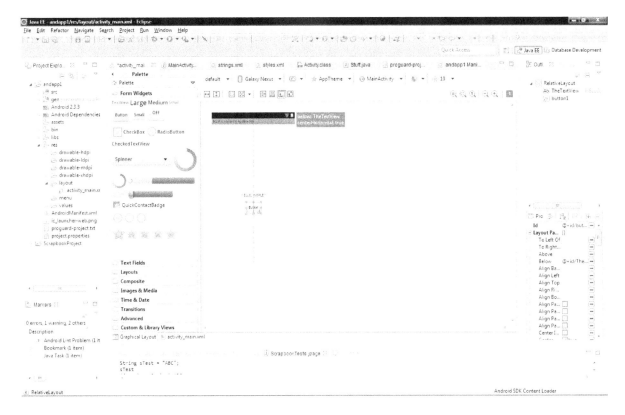

And here is the XML you generate:

```xml
<RelativeLayout xmlns:android="http://schemas.android.com/apk/res/android"
    xmlns:tools="http://schemas.android.com/tools"
    android:layout_width="match_parent"
    android:layout_height="match_parent" >

    <TextView
        android:id="@+id/TheTextView"
        android:layout_width="wrap_content"
        android:layout_height="wrap_content"
        android:layout_centerHorizontal="true"
        android:layout_centerVertical="true"
        android:text="@string/hello_world"
        tools:context=".MainActivity" />

    <Button
        android:id="@+id/button1"
        android:layout_width="wrap_content"
        android:layout_height="wrap_content"
        android:layout_below="@+id/TheTextView"
        android:layout_centerHorizontal="true"
        android:layout_marginTop="21dp"
        android:text="Button" />

</RelativeLayout>
```

Note that both the `TextView` and the `Button` views have an `android:id` attribute. This allows you to refer to that view within your Android programming code. Take note that within the double-quotes, you have a string in the following form: `@+id/name`. The name is any valid name you wish to use to refer to your view within the code later on. Here is a close-up of the interface now:

158

As you see, we have both a `TextView` containing the text `Hello, World!!` and a `Button` with the hard-coded text `Button` as the displayed text. The warning symbol indicates that you should place the hard-coded text `Button` within the `strings.xml` file and refer to it. If you take a look at the XML file shown above, you will see that the `android:text` attribute is hard-coded to "Button". To change this, open up the `strings.xml` file by expanding the values folder and double-clicking on the `strings.xml` node. Add a line similar to the last line shown below:

```
<resources>

 <string name="app_name">My First Android Application</string>
 <string name="hello_world">HELLO, WORLD!!</string>
 <string name="menu_settings">Settings</string>
 <string name="title_activity_main">MainActivity</string>
 <string name="button_text">Button</string>

</resources>
```

Now, go back to the `activity_main.xml` file and change this code...

```
android:text="Button"
```

...to this code...

```
android:text="@string/button_text"
```

If you receive either a warning or error symbol (or both), make sure to save your project first by clicking on the Save All button on the toolbar or by clicking Ctrl+Shift+S. Here is what you should see now:

My First Android Application

HELLO, WORLD!!

Button

Linear Layout

The `LinearLayout` comprises both a horizontal layout and a vertical layout distinguished by the XML attribute `android:orientation`. When `android:orientation` is set to `horizontal`, you have a horizontal linear layout in which each view (i.e., control) is displayed one to the right of the next. When `android:orientation` is set to `vertical`, you have a vertical linear layout in which each view (i.e., control) is displayed one below the next.

Note that when using the Eclipse GUI interface to drag either a horizontal or vertical linear layout to the graphical layout, the attribute `android:orientation` is not included and will have to be manually entered. For example, here is a horizontal layout (I repeated the text view and the button so that you can see the difference between horizontal and vertical),

```
<LinearLayout xmlns:android="http://schemas.android.com/apk/res/android"
        android:layout_width="fill_parent"
        android:layout_height="fill_parent"
        android:orientation="horizontal">

        <TextView
        android:id="@+id/TheTextView"
        android:layout_width="wrap_content"
        android:layout_height="wrap_content"
        android:layout_centerHorizontal="true"
        android:layout_centerVertical="true"
        android:text="@string/hello_world"
        tools:context=".MainActivity" />

    <Button
        android:id="@+id/button1"
        android:layout_width="wrap_content"
        android:layout_height="wrap_content"
        android:layout_below="@+id/TheTextView"
        android:layout_centerHorizontal="true"
        android:layout_marginTop="21dp"
        android:text="@string/button_text" />

        <TextView
```

160

```
        android:id="@+id/TheTextView"
        android:layout_width="wrap_content"
        android:layout_height="wrap_content"
        android:layout_centerHorizontal="true"
        android:layout_centerVertical="true"
        android:text="@string/hello_world"
        tools:context=".MainActivity" />

    <Button
        android:id="@+id/button1"
        android:layout_width="wrap_content"
        android:layout_height="wrap_content"
        android:layout_below="@+id/TheTextView"
        android:layout_centerHorizontal="true"
        android:layout_marginTop="21dp"
        android:text="@string/button_text" />

</LinearLayout>
```

By changing `android:orientation="horizontal"` to
`android:orientation="vertical"`, you will see the difference immediately:

161

Now, if we continue to add views to the vertical linear layout (as shown above), we will go off the displayable screen and the last few text views and buttons will not be displayed. Even if you run this on your touch screen device, you will not get the views to move up and down. In order to enable scrolling, you have to use a `ScrollView`, as described in the next section.

ScrollView Layout

The `ScrollView` allows you to scroll your views up and down using the buttons or touch screen of your device. Note that you are only allowed one layout within a single `ScrollView` layout. In this example, we used a `LinearLayout` within the `ScrollView`. Here is the XML code:

```
<ScrollView xmlns:android="http://schemas.android.com/apk/res/android"
        android:id="@+id/scrollView1"
        android:layout_width="fill_parent"
        android:layout_height="fill_parent" >

  <LinearLayout xmlns:android="http://schemas.android.com/apk/res/android"
        android:layout_width="fill_parent"
        android:layout_height="wrap_content"
        android:orientation="vertical">

    <TextView
        android:id="@+id/TheTextView"
        android:layout_width="wrap_content"
        android:layout_height="wrap_content"
        android:text="@string/hello_world" />

    <Button
        android:id="@+id/button1"
        android:layout_width="wrap_content"
        android:layout_height="wrap_content"
        android:layout_marginTop="21dp"
        android:text="@string/button_text" />

    <TextView
        android:id="@+id/TheTextView2"
        android:layout_width="wrap_content"
        android:layout_height="wrap_content"
        android:text="@string/hello_world" />

    <Button
        android:id="@+id/button2"
        android:layout_width="wrap_content"
        android:layout_height="wrap_content"
        android:layout_marginTop="21dp"
        android:text="@string/button_text" />

    <TextView
        android:id="@+id/TheTextView3"
        android:layout_width="wrap_content"
        android:layout_height="wrap_content"
        android:text="@string/hello_world" />

    <Button
        android:id="@+id/button3"
        android:layout_width="wrap_content"
        android:layout_height="wrap_content"
        android:layout_marginTop="21dp"
        android:text="@string/button_text" />

    <TextView
        android:id="@+id/TheTextView4"
        android:layout_width="wrap_content"
```

162

```xml
        android:layout_height="wrap_content"
        android:text="@string/hello_world" />

    <Button
        android:id="@+id/button4"
        android:layout_width="wrap_content"
        android:layout_height="wrap_content"
        android:layout_marginTop="21dp"
        android:text="@string/button_text" />

    <TextView
        android:id="@+id/TheTextView5"
        android:layout_width="wrap_content"
        android:layout_height="wrap_content"
        android:text="@string/hello_world" />

    <Button
        android:id="@+id/button5"
        android:layout_width="wrap_content"
        android:layout_height="wrap_content"
        android:layout_marginTop="21dp"
        android:text="@string/button_text" />

    <TextView
        android:id="@+id/TheTextView6"
        android:layout_width="wrap_content"
        android:layout_height="wrap_content"
        android:text="@string/hello_world" />

    <Button
        android:id="@+id/button6"
        android:layout_width="wrap_content"
        android:layout_height="wrap_content"
        android:layout_marginTop="21dp"
        android:text="@string/button_text" />

    <TextView
        android:id="@+id/TheTextView7"
        android:layout_width="wrap_content"
        android:layout_height="wrap_content"
        android:text="@string/hello_world" />

    <Button
        android:id="@+id/button7"
        android:layout_width="wrap_content"
        android:layout_height="wrap_content"
        android:layout_marginTop="21dp"
        android:text="@string/button_text" />

    <TextView
        android:id="@+id/TheTextView8"
        android:layout_width="wrap_content"
        android:layout_height="wrap_content"
        android:text="@string/hello_world" />

    <Button
        android:id="@+id/button8"
        android:layout_width="wrap_content"
        android:layout_height="wrap_content"
        android:layout_marginTop="21dp"
        android:text="@string/button_text" />

    <TextView
        android:id="@+id/TheTextView9"
        android:layout_width="wrap_content"
        android:layout_height="wrap_content"
        android:text="@string/hello_world" />

    <Button
        android:id="@+id/button9"
```

```
            android:layout_width="wrap_content"
            android:layout_height="wrap_content"
            android:layout_marginTop="21dp"
            android:text="@string/button_text" />

    </LinearLayout>

</ScrollView>
```

And here is what this looks like on the emulator (take note of the thin scrollbar on the right):

HorizontalScrollView Layout

The `HorizontalScrollView` allows you to scroll your views left and right using the buttons or touch screen on your device. In the example below, I've replaced the `ScrollView` with a `HorizontalScrollView` and I changed the `android:orientation` of the `LinearLayout` to `horizontal`. Here is the XML code:

```
<HorizontalScrollView xmlns:android="http://schemas.android.com/apk/res/android"
        android:id="@+id/scrollView1"
        android:layout_width="fill_parent"
        android:layout_height="fill_parent" >

    <LinearLayout xmlns:android="http://schemas.android.com/apk/res/android"
        android:layout_width="wrap_content"
        android:layout_height="fill_parent"
        android:orientation="horizontal">

    <TextView
        android:id="@+id/TheTextView"
        android:layout_width="wrap_content"
        android:layout_height="wrap_content"
        android:text="@string/hello_world" />

    <Button
        android:id="@+id/button1"
        android:layout_width="wrap_content"
        android:layout_height="wrap_content"
        android:layout_marginTop="21dp"
```

164

```xml
        android:text="@string/button_text" />

    <TextView
        android:id="@+id/TheTextView2"
        android:layout_width="wrap_content"
        android:layout_height="wrap_content"
        android:text="@string/hello_world" />

    <Button
        android:id="@+id/button2"
        android:layout_width="wrap_content"
        android:layout_height="wrap_content"
        android:layout_marginTop="21dp"
        android:text="@string/button_text" />

    <TextView
        android:id="@+id/TheTextView3"
        android:layout_width="wrap_content"
        android:layout_height="wrap_content"
        android:text="@string/hello_world" />

    <Button
        android:id="@+id/button3"
        android:layout_width="wrap_content"
        android:layout_height="wrap_content"
        android:layout_marginTop="21dp"
        android:text="@string/button_text" />

    <TextView
        android:id="@+id/TheTextView4"
        android:layout_width="wrap_content"
        android:layout_height="wrap_content"
        android:text="@string/hello_world" />

    <Button
        android:id="@+id/button4"
        android:layout_width="wrap_content"
        android:layout_height="wrap_content"
        android:layout_marginTop="21dp"
        android:text="@string/button_text" />

    <TextView
        android:id="@+id/TheTextView5"
        android:layout_width="wrap_content"
        android:layout_height="wrap_content"
        android:text="@string/hello_world" />

    <Button
        android:id="@+id/button5"
        android:layout_width="wrap_content"
        android:layout_height="wrap_content"
        android:layout_marginTop="21dp"
        android:text="@string/button_text" />

    <TextView
        android:id="@+id/TheTextView6"
        android:layout_width="wrap_content"
        android:layout_height="wrap_content"
        android:text="@string/hello_world" />

    <Button
        android:id="@+id/button6"
        android:layout_width="wrap_content"
        android:layout_height="wrap_content"
        android:layout_marginTop="21dp"
        android:text="@string/button_text" />
    <TextView
        android:id="@+id/TheTextView7"
        android:layout_width="wrap_content"
        android:layout_height="wrap_content"
```

```
            android:text="@string/hello_world" />

        <Button
            android:id="@+id/button7"
            android:layout_width="wrap_content"
            android:layout_height="wrap_content"
            android:layout_marginTop="21dp"
            android:text="@string/button_text" />

        <TextView
            android:id="@+id/TheTextView8"
            android:layout_width="wrap_content"
            android:layout_height="wrap_content"
            android:text="@string/hello_world" />

        <Button
            android:id="@+id/button8"
            android:layout_width="wrap_content"
            android:layout_height="wrap_content"
            android:layout_marginTop="21dp"
            android:text="@string/button_text" />

        <TextView
            android:id="@+id/TheTextView9"
            android:layout_width="wrap_content"
            android:layout_height="wrap_content"
            android:text="@string/hello_world" />

        <Button
            android:id="@+id/button9"
            android:layout_width="wrap_content"
            android:layout_height="wrap_content"
            android:layout_marginTop="21dp"
            android:text="@string/button_text" />

</LinearLayout>

</HorizontalScrollView>
```

And here is what this looks like on the emulator:

A Word about the Android Reference Manual

If you've installed the documentation as instructed during the installation of the Android SDK, you have the entire reference manual available locally. You can access this by navigating to the following URL (assuming you installed the SDK in `C:\android-sdk-windows`):

`C:\android-sdk-windows\docs\reference\packages.html`

Here is what you should see in the browser:

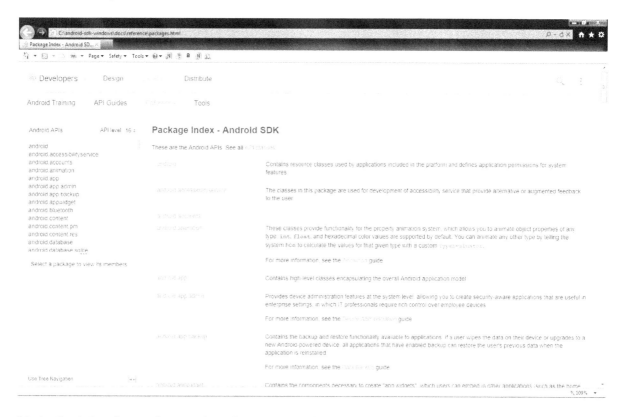

Note that the frame located at the upper-left contains a list of Android packages. If you click on a package in this frame, a list of interfaces, classes, enums and exceptions is shown in the frame on the lower left. Clicking on an entry within the frame on the lower left brings up an overview page in the main body of the web page on the right. For example, if you click on the `android.widget` package and then click on the `HorizontalScrollView` entry, information about the `HorizontalScrollView` will be displayed in the main body of the web page, as shown below:

In the next section, we look at the `Table` and `TableRow` layouts, so let's take a look at the `TableRow.LayoutParams` located in the frame on the lower-left. This will bring up information about the additional parameters related to the `TableRow`, as shown below:

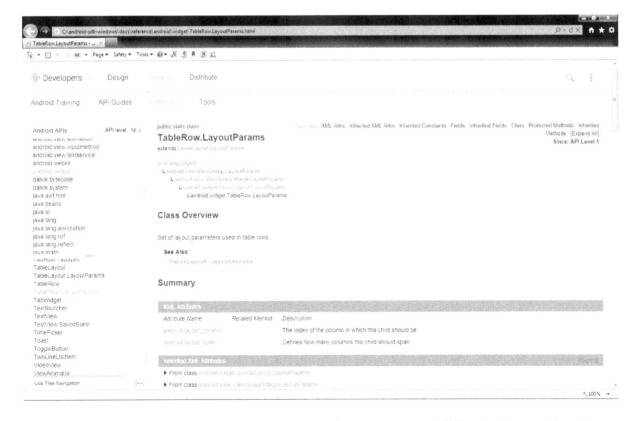

Note that in the Summary section above, there are two XML Attributes listed: `android:layout_column` and `android:layout_span`. Just like the cells on an HTML TABLE, you can force cells to span across multiple columns.

168

The `android:layout_span` attribute indicates how many columns the `TableLayout` will contain. This is similar to using a certain number of <TD> </TD> tags with the HTML TABLE tag. Note that this value must be greater than or equal to 1. For example, in the XML code below, I specify that the table itself will consist of three columns:

```
<TableLayout xmlns:android="http://schemas.android.com/apk/res/android"
        android:layout_width="fill_parent"
        android:layout_height="fill_parent"
        android:layout_span="3">
```

When used in a particular view's XML, the `android:layout_span` attribute indicates how many columns the **view** will span across the row. This is similar to using the `COLSPAN` attribute with the HTML TABLE tag. For example, in the XML below, I specify the the `TextView` will span across two columns (the `Button` will appear in the following column):

```
    <TableRow
        android:id="@+id/tableRow2"
        android:layout_width="wrap_content"
        android:layout_height="wrap_content" >

      <TextView
        android:id="@+id/TheTextView2"
        android:layout_width="wrap_content"
        android:layout_height="wrap_content"
        android:text="@string/hello_world"
        android:layout_span="2"/>

      <Button
        android:id="@+id/button2"
        android:layout_width="wrap_content"
        android:layout_height="wrap_content"
        android:layout_marginTop="21dp"
        android:text="@string/button_text" />

    </TableRow>
```

If you would like a particular view to be placed in a specific column rather than just having Android fill up the columns from left to right, use the `android:layout_column` attribute on that view. In the example below, I force the `Button` to appear in column three (`layout_column` is zero-based, so column three is set as two):

```
    <TableRow
        android:id="@+id/tableRow3"
        android:layout_width="wrap_content"
        android:layout_height="wrap_content" >

      <TextView
        android:id="@+id/TheTextView3"
        android:layout_width="wrap_content"
        android:layout_height="wrap_content"
        android:text="@string/hello_world" />

      <Button
        android:id="@+id/button4"
        android:layout_width="wrap_content"
        android:layout_height="wrap_content"
        android:layout_marginTop="21dp"
```

```
        android:text="@string/button_text"
        android:layout_column="2"/>

    </TableRow>
```

Here is what this looks like:

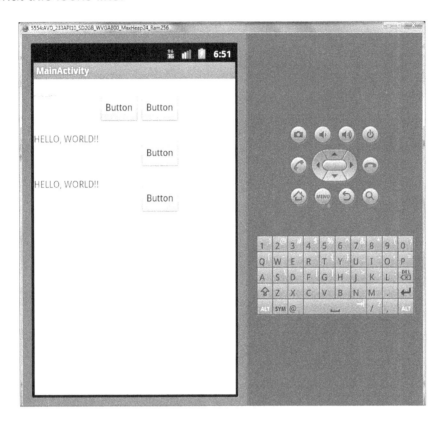

The Android reference manual is the ultimate place for Android information, so please have this opened in a browser when you are programming.

Table Layout

As alluded to in the previous section, the `TableLayout` is very similar to the HTML TABLE tag in that it creates a grid of rows and columns. Note that if you do not force a view into a specific column - using the `android:layout_column` attribute, as mentioned above - all views will be filled in from left to right.

For example, here is our code using the `TableLayout` as well as the `TableRow` tags:

```
<TableLayout xmlns:android="http://schemas.android.com/apk/res/android"
        android:layout_width="fill_parent"
        android:layout_height="fill_parent"
        android:layout_span="3">

    <TableRow
        android:id="@+id/tableRow1"
        android:layout_width="wrap_content"
        android:layout_height="wrap_content" >

    <TextView
        android:id="@+id/TheTextView"
        android:layout_width="wrap_content"
        android:layout_height="wrap_content"
```

170

```xml
            android:text="@string/hello_world" />

        <Button
            android:id="@+id/button1"
            android:layout_width="wrap_content"
            android:layout_height="wrap_content"
            android:layout_marginTop="21dp"
            android:text="@string/button_text" />

        <Button
            android:id="@+id/button3"
            android:layout_width="wrap_content"
            android:layout_height="wrap_content"
            android:layout_marginTop="21dp"
            android:text="@string/button_text" />

    </TableRow>

    <TableRow
        android:id="@+id/tableRow2"
        android:layout_width="wrap_content"
        android:layout_height="wrap_content" >

        <TextView
            android:id="@+id/TheTextView2"
            android:layout_width="wrap_content"
            android:layout_height="wrap_content"
            android:text="@string/hello_world"
            android:layout_span="2"/>

        <Button
            android:id="@+id/button2"
            android:layout_width="wrap_content"
            android:layout_height="wrap_content"
            android:layout_marginTop="21dp"
            android:text="@string/button_text" />

    </TableRow>

    <TableRow
        android:id="@+id/tableRow3"
        android:layout_width="wrap_content"
        android:layout_height="wrap_content" >

        <TextView
            android:id="@+id/TheTextView3"
            android:layout_width="wrap_content"
            android:layout_height="wrap_content"
            android:text="@string/hello_world" />

        <Button
            android:id="@+id/button4"
            android:layout_width="wrap_content"
            android:layout_height="wrap_content"
            android:layout_marginTop="21dp"
            android:text="@string/button_text"
            android:layout_column="2"/>

    </TableRow>
</TableLayout>
```

And, here is what this looks like:

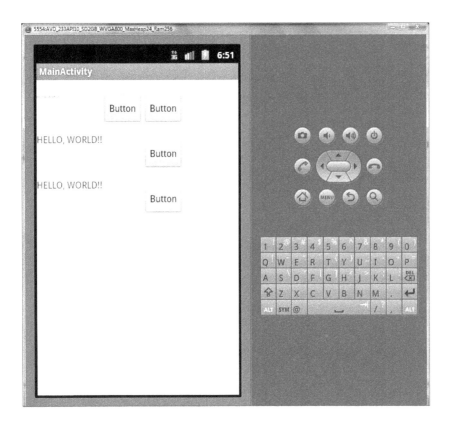

Relative Layout

The `RelativeLayout` layout allows you to specify the positions of views relative to each other or relative to a parent view. Our sample application was created using `RelativeLayout`:

```
<RelativeLayout xmlns:android="http://schemas.android.com/apk/res/android"
    xmlns:tools="http://schemas.android.com/tools"
    android:layout_width="match_parent"
    android:layout_height="match_parent" >

    <TextView
        android:id="@+id/TheTextView"
        android:layout_width="wrap_content"
        android:layout_height="wrap_content"
        android:layout_centerHorizontal="true"
        android:layout_centerVertical="true"
        android:text="@string/hello_world"
        tools:context=".MainActivity" />

    <Button
        android:id="@+id/button1"
        android:layout_width="wrap_content"
        android:layout_height="wrap_content"
        android:layout_below="@+id/TheTextView"
        android:layout_centerHorizontal="true"
        android:layout_marginTop="21dp"
        android:text="@string/button_text" />

</RelativeLayout>
```

If you take a look at the emboldened attribute above for the `Button` view, you will notice that it is defined using the `android:layout_below` attribute. This attribute positions the top edge of the `Button` view below the view specified as the value of the attribute, `TheTextView` in this case. There are several similar XML attributes you can use:

Attribute Name	Description
`android:layout_above`	Positions the bottom edge of this view above the given anchor view ID.
`android:layout_alignBaseline`	Positions the baseline of this view on the baseline of the given anchor view ID.
`android:layout_alignBottom`	Makes the bottom edge of this view match the bottom edge of the given anchor view ID.
`android:layout_alignLeft`	Makes the left edge of this view match the left edge of the given anchor view ID.
`android:layout_alignParentBottom`	If true, makes the bottom edge of this view match the bottom edge of the parent.
`android:layout_alignParentLeft`	If true, makes the left edge of this view match the left edge of the parent.
`android:layout_alignParentRight`	If true, makes the right edge of this view match the right edge of the parent.
`android:layout_alignParentTop`	If true, makes the top edge of this view match the top edge of the parent.
`android:layout_alignRight`	Makes the right edge of this view match the right edge of the given anchor view ID.
`android:layout_alignTop`	Makes the top edge of this view match the top edge of the given anchor view ID.
`android:layout_alignWithParentIfMissing`	If set to true, the parent will be used as the anchor when the anchor cannot be be found for layout_toLeftOf, layout_toRightOf, etc.
`android:layout_below`	Positions the top edge of this view below the given anchor view ID.
`android:layout_centerHorizontal`	If true, centers this child horizontally within its parent.
`android:layout_centerInParent`	If true, centers this child horizontally and vertically within its parent.
`android:layout_centerVertical`	If true, centers this child vertically within its parent.
`android:layout_toLeftOf`	Positions the right edge of this view to the left of the given anchor view ID.
`android:layout_toRightOf`	Positions the left edge of this view to the right of the given anchor view ID.

For example, if I include the `android:layout_toRightOf` and `android:layout_centerInParent` attributes on the Button and remove the `android:layout_below` attribute, then the `Button` will appear to the right of the `TextView`:

173

Frame Layout

The `FrameLayout` layout is used to display either a single view, or multiple views that overlap each other; that is, one on top of another. Note that the `ScrollView` and `HorizontalScrollView` layouts make use of the `FrameLayout`. According to the reference manual:

> *Generally, FrameLayout should be used to hold a single child view because it can be difficult to organize child views in a way that's scalable to different screen sizes without the children overlapping each other. You can, however, add multiple children to a FrameLayout and control their position within the FrameLayout by assigning gravity to each child, using the* `android:layout_gravity` *attribute.*

For example, given this XML layout,

```
<FrameLayout xmlns:android="http://schemas.android.com/apk/res/android"
        android:layout_width="fill_parent"
        android:layout_height="fill_parent" >

    <TextView
        android:id="@+id/TheTextView"
        android:layout_width="wrap_content"
        android:layout_height="wrap_content"
        android:layout_centerHorizontal="true"
        android:layout_centerVertical="true"
        android:text="@string/hello_world"
        tools:context=".MainActivity" />

    <Button
        android:id="@+id/button1"
        android:layout_width="wrap_content"
        android:layout_height="wrap_content"
        android:layout_centerHorizontal="true"
        android:layout_marginTop="21dp"
        android:text="@string/button_text" />

</FrameLayout>
```

...you will see this in the Graphical Layout window:

Now, if we change the `android:layout_gravity` for both the `TextView` and `Button,` as shown in the code below...

```xml
<FrameLayout xmlns:android="http://schemas.android.com/apk/res/android"
        android:layout_width="fill_parent"
        android:layout_height="fill_parent" >

    <TextView
        android:id="@+id/TheTextView"
        android:layout_width="wrap_content"
        android:layout_height="wrap_content"
        android:layout_centerHorizontal="true"
        android:layout_centerVertical="true"
        android:text="@string/hello_world"
        tools:context=".MainActivity"
        android:layout_gravity="top" />

    <Button
        android:id="@+id/button1"
        android:layout_width="wrap_content"
        android:layout_height="wrap_content"
        android:layout_centerHorizontal="true"
        android:layout_marginTop="21dp"
        android:text="@string/button_text"
        android:layout_gravity="bottom" />

</FrameLayout>
```

...you will see the following display in the Graphical Layout window:

My First Android Application
HELLO, WORLD!!

Button

ListView and GridView Layout

The `ListView` layout shows items in a vertically scrolling list. Note that there is no need to use the `ScrollView` around the `ListView` since it handles scrolling by itself. In addition, `ListView` is optimized to handle many entries, so use this whenever your number of entries is large.

The `GridView` layout shows items in both a vertically and horizontally scrolling list (or "grid").

Both the `ListView` and `GridView` layouts don't allow child entries such as `TextView` and `Button` views and are mainly populated via Java code. We will defer this topic until later in the book when we talk more about coding with Android.

With that said, you can use the `android:entries` attribute to indicate a list of hard-coded array values to be displayed. Here is an example of how to use hard-coded values with the `android:entries` attribute. In `activity_main.xml`, place the following XML code:

```
<ListView xmlns:android="http://schemas.android.com/apk/res/android"
    android:id="@+id/listView1"
    android:layout_width="fill_parent"
    android:layout_height="fill_parent"
    android:entries="@array/list_entries">
</ListView>
```

Take note that we refer to an array called `list_entries` in the `arrays.xml` file. Note that if the file `arrays.xml` does not exist, you will have to create it in the `res\values` folder. You do this by right-clicking on the folder name `values`, selecting the menu item New...File and filling out the New File dialog box. Next, in the `arrays.xml` file place the following XML:

```
<resources>
  <string-array name="list_entries">
    <item name="AGP">AMERIGROUP CORP</item>
    <item name="PVR">PENN VIRGINIA RESOURCE PARTN</item>
    <item name="CVG">CONVERGYS CORP</item>
```

176

```
        <item name="INGR">INGREDION INC</item>
        <item name="NCO">NUVEEN CAL MUNI MKT OPPOR FD</item>
        <item name="C_PRS">CITIGROUP CAPITAL IX, 6.00% TRUPS CAPITAL SEC</item>
        <item name="FST">FOREST OIL CORP</item>
        <item name="FLY">FLY LEASING LTD-ADR</item>
        <item name="MAC">MACERICH CO/THE</item>
        <item name="FCH">FELCOR LODGING TRUST INC</item>
        <item name="KRC">KILROY REALTY CORP</item>
        <item name="SEE">SEALED AIR CORP</item>
        <item name="MWR">MORGAN STANLEY CAPITAL TRUST III</item>
    </string-array>
</resources>
```

Click the Save All button (or click Ctrl+Shift+S) to save all of the modified files. When you run this program, you should see the following in the emulator:

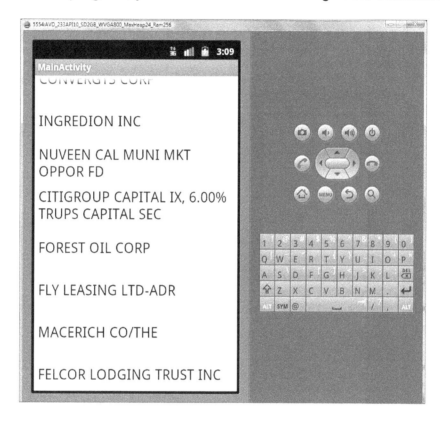

Note that you cannot control the text size within a `ListView` or `GridView`, which is why coding is needed. We will talk more about that later on in the book.

Also, note that the `android:entries` attribute is not available for a `GridView`. This means that you must use code to fill in the grid.

Note that when sub-classing the `ListActivity` class to create a simple `ListView`, you can easily provide an Android-provided layout on the fly for the list items. For just a single line of text, you can use `android.R.layout.simple_list_layout_1`. There are other Android-provided layouts or you can roll your own. We discuss this in more detail later on in the book.

Combining Layouts

As you've seen, you can add multiple views, such as a `TextView` and `Button`, to a single layout. But, you can also add multiple layouts to a single layout file as well as embed layouts within layouts (with the caveat that some layouts, like the `ListView` and `GridView`, do not allow this). Try to think how you would create a webpage from your intended interface and you're half way there.

For example, below is a **mock-up** of what I'd like to create. The first row contains the header with the words Symbol and Description. The following rows contain stock symbols as well as the description. These rows should scroll up and down. Finally, the last row, which is the footer, contains the copyright information.

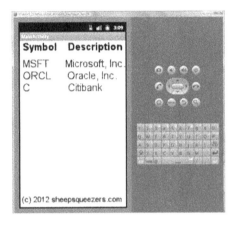

Here is what my XML file looks like (I removed several additional stocks just to keep the size down):

```
<LinearLayout xmlns:android="http://schemas.android.com/apk/res/android"
            android:layout_width="fill_parent"
            android:layout_height="fill_parent"
            android:orientation="vertical">

 <TableLayout xmlns:android=http://schemas.android.com/apk/res/android
            android:layout_width="fill_parent"
            android:layout_height="wrap_content"
            android:stretchColumns="*">

  <TableRow android:layout_width="fill_parent"
            android:layout_height="wrap_content" >

   <TextView android:layout_width="fill_parent"
            android:layout_height="wrap_content"
            android:text="SYMBOL" />
   <TextView android:layout_width="fill_parent"
            android:layout_height="wrap_content"
            android:text="DESCRIPTION" />

  </TableRow>

 </TableLayout>

 <ScrollView xmlns:android="http://schemas.android.com/apk/res/android"
            android:id="@+id/scrollView1"
            android:layout_width="fill_parent"
```

```
            android:layout_height="910dp"
            android:scrollbars="vertical" >

    <TableLayout xmlns:android=http://schemas.android.com/apk/res/android
            android:layout_width="fill_parent"
            android:layout_height="wrap_content"
            android:stretchColumns="*">

      <TableRow android:layout_width="fill_parent"
            android:layout_height="wrap_content" >

        <TextView android:layout_width="fill_parent"
            android:layout_height="wrap_content"
            android:text="MSFT" />
        <TextView android:layout_width="fill_parent"
            android:layout_height="wrap_content"
            android:text="Microsoft, Inc." />

      </TableRow>

      <TableRow android:layout_width="wrap_content"
            android:layout_height="wrap_content" >

        <TextView android:layout_width="wrap_content"
            android:layout_height="wrap_content"
            android:text="ORCL" />
        <TextView android:layout_width="wrap_content"
            android:layout_height="wrap_content"
            android:text="Oracle, Inc." />
      </TableRow>

      ...and so on...

    </TableLayout>

  </ScrollView>

  <TableLayout xmlns:android=http://schemas.android.com/apk/res/android
            android:layout_width="fill_parent"
            android:layout_height="wrap_content">

    <TableRow android:layout_width="wrap_content"
            android:layout_height="wrap_content" >

      <TextView android:layout_width="wrap_content"
            android:layout_height="wrap_content"
            android:text="" />

    </TableRow>

    <TableRow android:layout_width="fill_parent"
            android:layout_height="wrap_content" >

      <TextView android:layout_width="wrap_content"
            android:layout_height="wrap_content"
            android:text="©2012 sheepsqueezers.com" />

    </TableRow>

  </TableLayout>

</LinearLayout>
```

Here is what the screen on my Nook Color looks like:

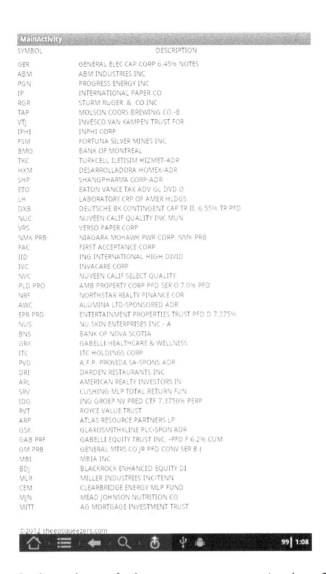

Note that I forced the size of the `ScrollView` to be 900dp instead of `fill_parent` so that the copyright line would appear. This doesn't work when you turn the device to landscape!

Note that you can capture your device's screen to an image from within Eclipse by clicking on Window...Show View...Other...Android...Devices. This will display the Devices tab. If you click on the device you are working with, the camera icon become active (as shown below):

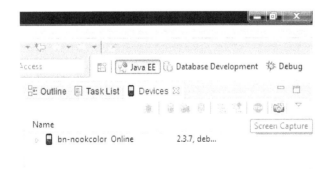

Clicking the camera icon brings up the Device Screen Capture window (as shown below):

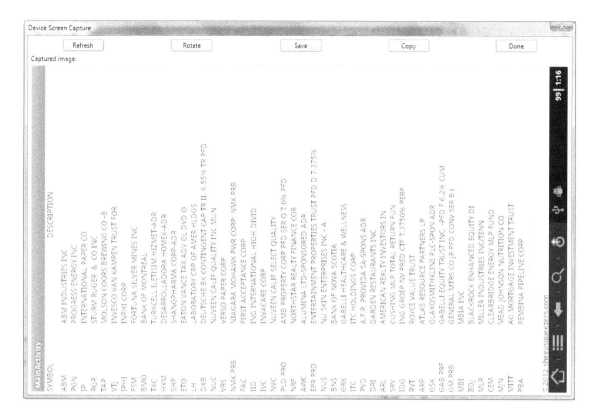

You can rotate the image using the Rotate button as well as copy the image to the clipboard by clicking on the Copy button.

Summary

In this chapter, we learned about the variety of layouts available to the programmer within Android. While it may seem strange that we did not write any Java code, we did take the time to learn how views can be displayed on a GUI interface using XML and Eclipse's Graphic Layout. In the next chapter, we avoid coding still further and talk about the views available to the programmer via Eclipse's Palette.

Chapter 8: Views Parade and the Eclipse Palette

Overview

In the last chapter, we looked into the variety of layouts available for the Android platform. In this chapter, we will look at the variety of *views* that can be placed on the layouts. Thanks to Eclipse's Palette pane, we can easily drag-and-drop views onto our layout.

As you can see to the left, Eclipse offers a Palette pane containing several panels each containing a different set of views. Naturally, you can expect to see buttons, input boxes, text boxes, check and radio buttons, etc. However, there are several non-standard views such as the rotating progress bar, the ratings bar and the zoom control.

It is the goal of this chapter to introduce each view in turn and say a few words about them. In the next chapter, we will begin learning how to code in Android and will use these controls.

Form Widgets

The Form Widgets panel in the Eclipse Graphical Layout Palette contains the following views:

- TextView - We've seen this view several times in the last chapter. This view displays text on the interface.
- Large - This view is just a TextView that has its `android:textAppearance` set to display a large-sized font.
- Medium - This view is just a TextView that has its `android:textAppearance` set to display a medium-sized font.
- Small - This view is just a TextView that has its `android:textAppearance` set to display a small-sized font.
- CheckedTextView - This view is an extension of the TextView that supports the Checkable interface. If this view is set to checked (`android:checked="true"`), then a programmer-selected checkmark image (`android:checkmark="@drawable/checkmark"`) will be displayed; otherwise, no image will be displayed.
- Button - This view is just a traditional button and we've seen it several times in the previous chapter.
- Small - This view is a Button with its style attribute set to `"?android:attr/buttonStyleSmall"`. That is, it's just a small button.
- ToggleButton - This view is an on/off toggle button where a green line is shown when the button is on; otherwise, no green line is shown. You can

also change the text displayed when the ToggleButton is on or off (see `android:textOn` and `android:textOff`).

- CheckBox - This view is a typical checkbox that can be set to checked (true) or unchecked (false).
- RadioButton - This view is a typical radio button that can be set to checked (true) or unchecked (false)
- RadioGroup - This view is a group of radio buttons (three, by default) that act as a group; that is, if one radio button is selected, the others are unselected. Note that a RadioGroup is created using the `<RadioGroup>` XML and contains one or more RadioButton views within.
- Spinner - This view is a drop-down box that contains a list of entries, for example, stock symbols. You can select one entry only. This view can be populated from a static array or from within code.
- RatingBar - This view displays five stars (although this can be altered) allowing you to set a rating from one to five using your cursor. Tapping on the third star sets the first three stars to green. Note that you can have fractional stars allowing for a rating of, say, 3.5.
- ProgressBar (large) - This view is a large-sized rotating progress bar. This view has its style attribute set to `"?android:attr/progressBarStyleLarge"`.
- Progress Bar (normal) - This view is a normal-sized rotating progress bar.
- Progress Bar (small) - This view is a small-sized rotating progress bar. This view has its style attribute set to `"?android:attr/progressBarStyleSmall"`.
- Progress Bar (horizontal) - This view is a traditional horizontal progress bar. This view has its style attribute set to `"?android:attr/progressBarStyleHorizontal"`. You can set this bar to have an initial progress set to, say, 25 (for 25%) and one-fourth of the bar appears green.
- SeekBar - This view is similar to a horizontal progress bar with the addition of a sliding button allowing the user to set the desired percentage. As the user slides the sliding button from left to right, the horizontal bar turns yellow indicating the selected percentage.
- QuickContactBadge - This view is used to show a list of contacts via e-mail, website addresses, phone numbers, etc. You can assign contacts via code.

Text Fields

With the exception of the `AutoCompleteTextView` and the `MultiAuto CompleteTextView`, all of the entries in the Text Fields panel are `<EditText>` input boxes. The differences between them are determined by the `android:inputType` attribute. If no `android:inputType` attribute appears, then any type of text can be placed within the input box. But, if there is a specific type of data you want to limit the user to entering, such as an e-mail address, you can specify this in `android:inputType` attribute.

A list of inputTypes appears below. Note that the keyboard that is displayed on the device's screen will be set to allow text or numbers depending on the choice(s) below. Attributes such as `textEMailAddress` will allow a user to enter characters, numbers and the at-sign, but will not force the user into the form `aaa@bbb.ccc.` The programmer will still have to check the input values for form correctness.

- none - the least restrictive indicating that any characters can be entered into the field.
- text - only text can be entered into the field, no numbers.
- textCapCharacters - text is capitalized in the field.
- textCapWords - the first letter of each word is capitalized in the field.
- textCapSentences - the first letter of each sentence is capitalized in the field.
- textAutoCorrect - the text has autocorrection applied to it.
- textAutoComplete - the text has autocomplete applied to it as the user types.
- textMultiline - allows for multiple lines of input in the field.
- textImeMultiline - allows for multiple lines of input in the field during fullscreen.
- textNoSuggestions - does not provide autocorrect choices.
- textUri - allows for a URI to be entered into the field.
- textEMailAddress - allows for an e-mail address to be entered into the field.
- textEMailSubject - allows for an e-mail subject line to be entered into the field.
- textShortMessage - allows for a short message line an instant message or text message.
- textLongMessage - allows for a long messge such as the body of an e-mail.
- textPersonName - allows for entering the name of a person.
- textPostalAddress - allows for entering an address.
- textPassword - allows for entering a password. Note that the field automatically hides the password with asterisks as it's typed, although each character is displayed briefly.
- textVisiblePassword - same as textPassword except the password is not hidden.
- textWebEditText - allows for entering text similar to that of a web form.
- textFilter - allows for entering text used to filter a list.
- textPhonetic - allows for entering text used for phonetic pronounciation.
- number - allows for entering numbers.
- numberSigned - allows for entering signed numbers.
- numberDecimal - allows for entering decimal digits.
- phone - allows for entering phone numbers.
- datetime - allows for entering datetimes.
- date - allows for entering dates only.
- time - allows for entering times only.

Note that you can select more than one inputType by selecting the checkboxes in the Eclipse GUI or by placing a vertical bar between attribute values: `textPassword|number`.

The remaining two views are:

- AutoCompleteTextView - allows you to enter text with auto-complete turned on. Note that you will have to enter a list of words to be used as auto-completion suggestions via code. With that said, if you do not suggest words, then the on-board dictionary is used.
- MultiAutoCompleteTextView - similar to the AutoCompleteTextView but allows for multiple lines.

Layouts

We've already discussed this panel extensively in the last chapter, so we will skip most of the entries. The only additional entries we did not touch on in the last chapter are:

- include - this layout allows you to include a pre-existing layout within the current layout. You can use this, for example, to include a header or footer common to all your activities. We discuss this topic in detail in Chapter 29, *Using <include>*.
- fragment - a piece of an application's user interface or behavior that can be placed in an activity. From the manual: *The Fragment class can be used many ways to achieve a wide variety of results. In its core, it represents a particular operation or interface that is running within a larger Activity. A Fragment is closely tied to the Activity it is in, and cannot be used apart from one. Though Fragment defines its own lifecycle, that lifecycle is dependent on its activity: if the activity is stopped, no fragments inside of it can be started; when the activity is destroyed, all fragments will be destroyed.*

Composites

We've already discussed some of the items in this panel such as the `ListView`, the `GridView`, the `ScrollView` and the `HorizontalScrollView`. Additional items are as follows:

- ExpandableList - the view is similar to a `ListView` except that it allows for children, which are displayed when the row is clicked. Unlike a `ListView`, you cannot use the `android:entries` attribute to specify a list of entries.
- SlidingDrawer - this is a container that is off-screen except for a handle image. When the user slides the handle, the content appears. From the manual: *SlidingDrawer hides content out of the screen and allows the user to drag a handle to bring the content on screen. SlidingDrawer can be used vertically or horizontally. A special widget composed of two children views: the handle that the user drags, and the content attached to the handle and dragged with it. SlidingDrawer should be used as an overlay inside layouts. This means SlidingDrawer should only be used inside of a FrameLayout or a RelativeLayout for instance. The size of the SlidingDrawer defines how much space the content will occupy once slid out, so SlidingDrawer should usually use `match_parent` for both its dimensions. Inside an XML layout, SlidingDrawer must define the id of the handle and of the content.*
- TabHost - this is a container for TabWidgets. From the manual (for TabHost): *Container for a tabbed window view. This object holds two children: a set of tab labels that the user clicks to select a specific tab, and a*

FrameLayout object that displays the contents of that page. The individual elements are typically controlled using this container object, rather than setting values on the child elements themselves. From the manual (for TabWidget): *Displays a list of tab labels representing each page in the parent's tab collection. The container object for this widget is TabHost. When the user selects a tab, this object sends a message to the parent container, TabHost, to tell it to switch the displayed page. You typically won't use many methods directly on this object. The container TabHost is used to add labels, add the callback handler, and manage callbacks. You might call this object to iterate the list of tabs, or to tweak the layout of the tab list, but most methods should be called on the containing TabHost object.*

- WebView - this displays a webpage on the screen. Note that, unlike the other views, the corresponding class can be found in `android.webkit` and not `android:widget`.

Images & Media

In this panel, we have image- and media-related views. This panel contains the following views:

- ImageView - this view displays a single image.
- ImageButton - this view combines a Button and ImageView to display an image on the button. You can select the desired image by changing the `android:src` attribute.
- Gallery - this view shows items in a center-locked, horizontally scrolling list. According to the manual, this is deprecated and the programmer should use HorizontalScrollView or ViewPager instead.
- MediaController - From the manual: *A view containing controls for a MediaPlayer. Typically contains the buttons like "Play/Pause", "Rewind", "Fast Forward" and a progress slider. It takes care of synchronizing the controls with the state of the MediaPlayer. The way to use this class is to instantiate it programatically. The MediaController will create a default set of controls and put them in a window floating above your application. Specifically, the controls will float above the view specified with setAnchorView(). The window will disappear if left idle for three seconds and reappear when the user touches the anchor view.*
- VideoView - this view displays a video file. You can set the video within code.

Time & Date

This panel contains time and date pickers as well as an analog and digital clock and chronometer. This panel contains the following views:

- TimePicker - this view allows the user to select a time as well as A.M. or P.M.
- DatePicker - this view allows the user to select a date (month, day, year).
- AnalogClock - this view displays an analog clock.
- DigitalClock - this view displays a digital clock.

- Chronometer - this view implements a timer. From the manual: *You can give it a start time in the elapsedRealtime() timebase, and it counts up from that, or if you don't give it a base time, it will use the time at which you call start(). By default it will display the current timer value in the form "MM:SS" or "H:MM:SS", or you can use setFormat(String) to format the timer value into an arbitrary string.*

Transitions

This panel contains views whose purpose is to switch between views, image, text, etc.

- ViewSwitcher - this view switches between two other views only one of which is shown at a time. Both the ImageSwitcher and the TextSwitcher are subclasses of this class.
- ImageSwitcher - this view is a subclass of the ViewSwitcher and is used to switch between two images.
- TextSwitcher - this view is a subclass of the ViewSwitcher and is used to animate a label on the screen.
- ViewAnimator - this view is a superclass of ViewSwitcher (which is the superclass of both ImageSwitcher and TextSwitcher). From the manual: *Base class for a FrameLayout container that will perform animations when switching between its views.*
- ViewFlipper - this view is a subclass of ViewAnimator. From the manual: *Simple ViewAnimator that will animate between two or more views that have been added to it. Only one child is shown at a time. If requested, can automatically flip between each child at a regular interval.* This may be useful for flipping between advertisements on an interface.

Advanced

This panel contains more advanced views serving a variety of purposes.

- ZoomControls - this view adds a plus and minus zoom control to the interface.
- ZoomButton - this view is a single circular button with a plus-sign for a button image. This is a subclass of the `ImageButton` class. You can change the image, though, by changing the `android1:src` attribute to your desired image.
- TwoLineListItem - From the manual: *A view group with two children intended for use in ListViews. This item has two TextViews elements (or subclasses) with the ID values text1 and text2. There is an optional third View element with the ID selectedIcon, which can be any View subclass (though it is typically a graphic View, such as ImageView) that can be displayed when a TwoLineListItem has focus. Android supplies a standard layout resource for TwoLineListView (which does not include a selected item icon), but you can design your own custom XML layout for this object.*
- GestureOverlayView (`android.gesture.GestureOverlayView`) - this view is a transparent overlay for gesture input that can be placed on top of other widgets or contain other widgets.

- SurfaceView - this view, which is in the `android.view` class, provides a dedicated drawing surface embedded inside of a view hierarchy. You can control the format of this surface and, if you like, its size; the SurfaceView takes care of placing the surface at the correct location on the screen. From the manual: *One of the purposes of this class is to provide a surface in which a secondary thread can render into the screen. If you are going to use it this way, you need to be aware of some threading semantics:*
  • All SurfaceView and SurfaceHolder.Callback methods will be called from the thread running the SurfaceView's window (typically the main thread of the application). They thus need to correctly synchronize with any state that is also touched by the drawing thread.
  • You must ensure that the drawing thread only touches the underlying Surface while it is valid -- between SurfaceHolder.Callback.surfaceCreated() and SurfaceHolder. Callback.surfaceDestroyed().
- View - This view is part of the `android.view` class. From the manual: *This class represents the basic building block for user interface components. A View occupies a rectangular area on the screen and is responsible for drawing and event handling. View is the base class for widgets, which are used to create interactive UI components (buttons, text fields, etc.). The ViewGroup subclass is the base class for layouts, which are invisible containers that hold other Views (or other ViewGroups) and define their layout properties.*
- DialerFilter - this view will be discussed later on.
- ViewStub - this view lets you include other XML layouts inside your application at runtime.
- requestFocus - Any element representing a View object can include this empty element, which gives its parent initial focus on the screen. You can have only one of these elements per file.

Custom & Library Views

This panel is initially empty, but the developer can add his/her own views to it.

Summary

In this chapter, we learned about the variety of views available to the Android programmer. Although, we did not do any coding, we will do so later on in the book.

Chapter 9: Activities

Overview

In this chapter, we begin to use code to manipulate our GUI interfaces, or Activities. We learn how to display - that is, *inflate* - an activity as well as how to manipulate the views within an activity. We talk about accessing resources that you've created and resources that are provided by the Android SDK.

Each GUI interface you add to your project is contained in a separate XML file located in the `res\layouts` subdirectory in Eclipse as well as on disk. Along with this XML file, a file (.java) contains the associated Java code, which controls the display and manipulation of the interface. This Java file is located in the `src` subdirectory in Eclipse and on disk. You can think of this separation of interface and code as the Model-View-Controller (MVC) design pattern. While you can generate your display in code, as alluded to in previous chapters, you are encouraged not to do that, but you may be forced to depending on your needs.

A Look at Our Simple Example

Below is the code that displays our `activity_main.xml` activity. The code is called `MainActivity.java` and displays (or *inflates*) this activity (see the bold line of code below). Each activity has an `onCreate` method which is called when the activity is about to be displayed. Note that each activity you create is a subclass of the `Activity` class, as you can see below.

```
package com.example.andapp1;

import android.os.Bundle;
import android.app.Activity;
import android.view.Menu;

public class MainActivity extends Activity {

 @Override
 public void onCreate(Bundle savedInstanceState) {
  super.onCreate(savedInstanceState);
  setContentView(R.layout.activity_main);
 }

}
```

Android knows that `activity_main.xml` is the first activity to be displayed when the application starts by an appropriate entry in the `AndroidManifest.xml` file. Within each `<application>` node, you have one or more `<activity>` nodes, one for each activity in your application. If an activity does not appear in the manifest, it cannot be displayed by your application. Below is a portion of our `AndroidManifest.xml` file. Pay particular attention to the emboldened code below because this is the entry for our activity in our application. Note that the `android:name` attribute is set to the name of our Java code (`MainActivity.java`), excluding the `.java` extension and with a period at the beginning. Also, note that the title of the application that appears below the application's icon on the device (on the Application Launcher page) is determined by the activity's `android:label` attribute. Here we point to a string resource called `title_activity_main`, which is located in the `strings.xml` resource file. The value of `title_activity_main` is the text `MainActivity`. The `action` and `category` XML nodes below indicate to Android that this activity is also the main program; that is, the activity that is to be displayed **first** when the application is started.

```
<application android:icon="@drawable/ic_launcher"
            android:label="@string/app_name"
            android:theme="@style/AppTheme" >
    <activity android:name=".MainActivity"
            android:label="@string/title_activity_main" >
        <intent-filter>
          <action android:name="android.intent.action.MAIN" />
          <category android:name="android.intent.category.LAUNCHER" />
        </intent-filter>
    </activity>
</application>
```

Note that the application's `android:label` attribute points to the resource `app_name` (also in `strings.xml`) which contains the application label. In this case, the application label is `My First Android Application`. This label will appear in the device's settings when you tap on the Manage Applications button.

The application icon is set using the `android:icon` attribute. In this case, we have an icon called `ic_launcher.png` appearing in more than one of the `drawable-*` folders. These folders are defined as follows:

- drawable-ldpi - images for low-density screens (approx. 120dpi) go here.
- drawable-mdpi - images for medium-density screens (approx. 160dpi) go here. Note that 160dpi is considered the *baseline* screen size.
- drawable-hdpi - images for high-density screens (approx. 240dpi) go here.
- drawable-xhdpi - images for extra-high density screens (approx. 320dpi) go here.

Each folder can contain one or more image files (preferably .png, but .jpg and .gif are accepted but slightly frowned upon), but you should ensure you have an image for at least the medium-density screens. The Android documentation suggests that you use the following multipliers:

- drawable-ldpi - 0.75
- drawable-mdpi - 1.00
- drawable-hdpi - 1.50
- drawable-xhdpi - 2.00

That is, if your image is 48x48 pixels, you can create an ldpi by multiplying by .75 (.75*48x48=36x36). For hdpi, 1.5*(48x48)=72x72. For xhdpi, 2.0*(48x48)=96x96. The mdpi image is just the original 48x48-pixel image.

If you are familiar with cascading style sheets (CSS) in HTML, you've probably used the `STYLE=` attribute before. This allows you to change the style of text to, say, bold. This is similar to what the `android:style` attribute does. You can apply a series of styles across an entire application using the `android:theme` attribute. We talk about styles and themes later on.

Looking at the XML code above again, you will see that for our activity, we have the following code:

```
<intent-filter>
 <action android:name="android.intent.action.MAIN" />
 <category android:name="android.intent.category.LAUNCHER" />
</intent-filter>
```

The `<action>` node specifies the `MAIN` action indicating that this particular activity is the first activity to be displayed. This is similar to how `main()` is the first function to execute in a C/C++ program.

The `<category>` node specifies the `LAUNCHER` category indicating that this application should be listed in Android's application launcher page. We go into more detail about the Android manifest later on in the book.

Referring to the Java code for our activity,

```
package com.example.andapp1;

import android.os.Bundle;
import android.app.Activity;
import android.view.Menu;

public class MainActivity extends Activity {

 @Override
 public void onCreate(Bundle savedInstanceState) {
  super.onCreate(savedInstanceState);
  setContentView(R.layout.activity_main);
 }

}
```

The first line of code, `package com.example.andapp1;` is the name of your *package*. This is made up of a reverse web address idea: `com` + `"."` + *your-company-name* + `"."` + *app_name*. Here, the word `example` is being used as the company name. Note that this is placed in your code automatically by Eclipse. You are prevented from uploading an application to the Marketplace when using `com.example`, so please use your own website address when creating a real application.

The next three lines are similar to C/C++ `#include` files specifying what packages and/or classes to include. Note that if you attempt to use a feature that is not located within the imported packages, you will not be able to compile your code, but Eclipse will suggest an appropriate package to import. Refer to the Android SDK to determine in which package/class the feature you are using is.

Next, we create a public class called `MainActivity`, which extends the Android `Activity` class. Within this class, you need to override one or more methods from the `Activity` class. These methods help to control the lifecycle of the activity; that is, what the activity does before it is displayed on the screen, after it is displayed on the screen, after it is killed, etc. We discuss the activity lifecycle later in the chapter.

When an activity is about to be displayed on the device, the `onCreate` method is executed. It is this method that tells Android which XML file contains the layout relevant to this activity. In the code above, the line...

```
setContentView(R.layout.activity_main);
```

...tells Android to display (or *inflate*) the `activity_main.xml` activity (without the `.xml` extension). We talk more about the `R` class later on in this chapter.

Finally, even though you are overriding a base class method (`onCreate`, in the code above), you should always call the base class's associated method using the `super` keyword...

```
super.onCreate(savedInstanceState);
```

This will allow the base class to perform any additional operations beyond those that you've already coded for in the overridden class.

Accessing *Programmer Created* Resources

As we've seen, you can quickly place text strings, arrays, styles, colors, booleans, etc. in individual XML Resource files instead of hard-coding them in your code. Each XML Resource file is located in the application's `res` folder. Located within the `res` folder are individual subfolders containing a particular type of data. For example, we've seen that strings are placed in the `strings.xml` file located in the `res\values` folder. There are two ways of accessing this data:

1. From within other XML Resource files, use the `@ + XML_node_name + "/" + desired_node` construct. For example, you can access the `app_name` located in the `strings.xml` file by the following construct: `@string/app_name`. Note that you can also include the package name if you are referring to a resource outside the current package: `@packagename:XML_node_name/desired_node`.
2. From within your code, use the `R` class. This class is created by Eclipse and the Android SDK automatically for you so you can easily access your resources from within your code. For example, to access the `app_name` (located in the `strings.xml` file) within your code, use the following construct: `R.string.app_name`.

Now, in both of the examples above, it may seem strange to use the word `string` when the XML Resource file is named `string**s**.xml`. Both the @-sign and the R class are referring to the XML node name *within* the XML Resource file itself. For example, here is our `strings.xml` file in its entirety:

```
<resources xmlns:android="http://schemas.android.com/apk/res/android">

  <string name="app_name">My First Android Application</string>
  <string name="hello_world">HELLO, WORLD!!</string>
  <string name="menu_settings">Settings</string>
  <string name="title_activity_main">MainActivity</string>
  <string name="button_text">Button</string>
```

```
</resources>
```

As you can see above, the XML node name is `string` and not strings. This is similar for other resources such as styles, bools, etc. Note that all of these resources can be accessed via the @-sign as well as the R construct as detailed in the following table:

Data Type	Resource XML File	Folder Location	R Class Access	@-Sign Access
layouts	*activity_name*.xml	res\layout	R.layout.*activity_name*	@layout/*activity_name*
menus	*activity_name*.xml	res\menu	R.menu.*activity_name*	@menu/*activity_name*
arrays	arrays.xml	res\values	R.array.*name*	@array/*name*
bools	bools.xml	res\values	R.bool.*name*	@bool/*name*
colors	colors.xml	res\values	R.color.*name*	@color/*name*
integers	integers.xml	res\values	R.integer.*name*	@integer/*name*
strings	strings.xml	res\values	R.string.*name*	@string/*name*
styles	styles.xml	res\values	R.style.*name*	@style/*name*

Note that there are several more data types that are available such as `anim`, `dimen`, etc., but those listed above are used most often. Also, note that for layouts and menus, the name of the file is the same as the name of the activity. With the exception of layouts and menus, all of the XML Resource files listed above should contain the following XML:

```
<resources xmlns:android="http://schemas.android.com/apk/res/android">

    ...additional XML...

</resources>
```

In addition, with the exception of layouts, menus and arrays, all of the XML Resource files contain additional XML nodes using a singular, rather than plural, form of the data type shown in the table above. For example, for integers, use `<integer name="">value</integer>`. For Booleans, use `<bool name="">value</bool>`.

Here is an example of `bools.xml`:

```
<resources xmlns:android="http://schemas.android.com/apk/res/android">
 <bool name="bTest">false</bool>
 <bool name="bTest2">true</bool>
</resources>
```

For arrays, use `<string-array name="">` and one or more `<item name="">value</item>` nodes. For example, here is an example `arrays.xml` file:

```
<resources xmlns:android="http://schemas.android.com/apk/res/android">
 <string-array name="stocks">
  <item name="AGP">AMERIGROUP CORP</item>
  <item name="PVR">PENN VIRGINIA RESOURCE PARTN</item>
  <item name="CVG">CONVERGYS CORP</item>
  <item name="INGR">INGREDION INC</item>
  <item name="NCO">NUVEEN CAL MUNI MKT OPPOR FD</item>
  <item name="C PRS">CITIGROUP CAPITAL IX, 6.00% TRUPS CAPITAL SEC</item>
```

```
<item name="FST">FOREST OIL CORP</item>
<item name="FLY">FLY LEASING LTD-ADR</item>
<item name="MAC">MACERICH CO/THE</item>
<item name="FCH">FELCOR LODGING TRUST INC</item>
<item name="KRC">KILROY REALTY CORP</item>
<item name="SEE">SEALED AIR CORP</item>
<item name="MWR">MORGAN STANLEY CAPITAL TRUST III</item>
</string-array>
</resources>
```

Note that you access an array within code by its string-array name (stocks, in the code above): R.array.*stocks*.

For layouts, the XML Resource file contains the XML for the specific layout you are using, such as LinearLayout, RelativeLayout, etc. For example,

```
<LinearLayout xmlns:android="http://schemas.android.com/apk/res/android"
    xmlns:android1="http://schemas.android.com/apk/res/android"
    android:layout_width="fill_parent"
    android:layout_height="fill_parent"
    android:orientation="vertical" >

    ...more layout goes here...

</LinearLayout>
```

Similar for menus,

```
<menu xmlns:android="http://schemas.android.com/apk/res/android">
  <item android:id="@+id/menu_settings"
        android:title="@string/menu_settings"
        android:orderInCategory="100" />
</menu>
```

Many Android views require the android:id attribute. This attribute contains a developer-chosen name for use later on in code. The way you specify an ID is in the form: @+id/your_id_name. For example, here is a TextView which uses the android:id attribute:

```
<TextView android:id="@+id/myTxtVw"
          android:layout_width="wrap_content"
          android:layout_height="wrap_content"
          android:layout_centerHorizontal="true"
          android:layout_centerVertical="true"
          android:text="@string/hello_world" />
```

Within your code, you can access the ID by using the code R.id.myTxtVw. Note that this code does **not** return an object reference! In order to access the corresponding object you must use the findViewById() method. For example,

```
TextView oTxtVw = (TextView) findViewById(R.id.myTxtVw);
```

At this point, the variable oTxtVw points to the TextView object and you then have access to all of the methods and attributes of a TextView object. For example, you can retrieve the text within your text box by using the getText() method: oTxtVw.getText().

Accessing *Android Provided* Resources

The Android SDK provides several resources for you to use in your programs and, just like for your own resources, are accessible by using the `R` class. You must prepend the keyword `android:` in XML files and `android.` in code. For example, the `R.color` class contains the following freely available colors for you to use in your applications:

- background_dark
- background_light
- black
- darker_gray
- holo_blue_bright - A really bright Holo shade of blue
- holo_blue_dark - A dark Holo shade of blue
- holo_blue_light - A light Holo shade of blue
- holo_green_dark - A dark Holo shade of green
- holo_green_light - A light Holo shade of green
- holo_orange_dark - A dark Holo shade of orange
- holo_orange_light - A light Holo shade of orange
- holo_purple - A Holo shade of purple
- holo_red_dark - A dark Holo shade of red
- holo_red_light - A light Holo shade of red
- primary_text_dark
- primary_text_dark_nodisable
- primary_text_light
- primary_text_light_nodisable
- secondary_text_dark
- secondary_text_dark_nodisable
- secondary_text_light
- secondary_text_light_nodisable
- tab_indicator_text
- tertiary_text_dark
- tertiary_text_light
- transparent
- white
- widget_edittext_dark

To refer to, say, `darker_gray` in code, specify `android.R.color.darker_gray`. In XML files, specify `@android:color/darker_gray`. Note that some of the colors listed above (which are from the Android SDK documentation) do not appear within the Eclipse IDE context help. Caution is advised!!

Colors are not the only Android-provided resources. The `R.style` class contains many themes available for use within the style attribute for your views. In addition, the `R.string` class contains many helpful text strings.

Now, you can refer to Android-provided themes in an XML Resource file by using the ?-sign: `?android:desired_theme`. For example, in our `TextView`, let's provide a theme for the text:

```
<TextView android:id="@+id/myTxtVw"
          android:textColor="?android:textColorSecondary"
          android:layout_width="wrap_content"
          android:layout_height="wrap_content"
          android:layout_centerHorizontal="true"
          android:layout_centerVertical="true"
          android:text="@android:string/emptyPhoneNumber" />
```

Notice that we also made use of the Android-provided `emptyPhoneNumber` string. This displays the text "`(No Phone Number)`" in the TextView on the device.

Finally, look at the `R.attr` class. This class provides many additional attributes available from Android.

The Activity Lifecycle

The `onCreate` method is one piece of each activity's birth, life and death. There are several additional methods called during an Activity's lifecycle and the application's developer should take into account those methods that he/she deems important. Naturally, the `onCreate` method is needed, since you will not be able to display the activity's associated layout without it.

Activities on an Android device are organized into a stack called the activity stack. Each running activity appears on the activity stack with the currently visible activity on the top of the stack obscuring the other activities. For example, if you were watching a video with the YouTube app and then switched to Yahoo! E-Mail app to get your e-mail, the Yahoo! E-Mail app moves to the top of the activity stack and the YouTube app is just below it. When you leave the Yahoo! E-Mail app, the YouTube app is again on the top of the stack.

All activities move through several states during their lifetime. From the Android SDK documentation:

An activity has essentially four states:

- *If an activity in the foreground of the screen (at the top of the stack), it is active or running.*
- *If an activity has lost focus but is still visible (that is, a new non-full-sized or transparent activity has focus on top of your activity), it is paused. A paused activity is completely alive (it maintains all state and member information and remains attached to the window manager), but can be killed by the system in extreme low memory situations.*
- *If an activity is completely obscured by another activity, it is stopped. It still retains all state and member information, however, it is no longer visible to the user so its window is hidden and it will often be killed by the system when memory is needed elsewhere.*
- *If an activity is paused or stopped, the system can drop the activity from memory by either asking it to finish, or simply killing its process. When it is*

displayed again to the user, it must be completely restarted and restored to its previous state.

There are three key loops you may be interested in monitoring within your activity:

- *The entire lifetime of an activity happens between the first call to onCreate(Bundle) through to a single final call to onDestroy(). An activity will do all setup of "global" state in onCreate(), and release all remaining resources in onDestroy(). For example, if it has a thread running in the background to download data from the network, it may create that thread in onCreate() and then stop the thread in onDestroy().*
- *The visible lifetime of an activity happens between a call to onStart() until a corresponding call to onStop(). During this time the user can see the activity on-screen, though it may not be in the foreground and interacting with the user. Between these two methods you can maintain resources that are needed to show the activity to the user. For example, you can register a BroadcastReceiver in onStart() to monitor for changes that impact your UI, and unregister it in onStop() when the user no longer sees what you are displaying. The onStart() and onStop() methods can be called multiple times, as the activity becomes visible and hidden to the user.*
- *The foreground lifetime of an activity happens between a call to onResume() until a corresponding call to onPause(). During this time the activity is in front of all other activities and interacting with the user. An activity can frequently go between the resumed and paused states -- for example when the device goes to sleep, when an activity result is delivered, when a new intent is delivered -- so the code in these methods should be fairly lightweight.*

The entire lifecycle of an activity is defined by the following Activity methods. All of these are hooks that you can override to do appropriate work when the activity changes state. All activities will implement onCreate(Bundle) to do their initial setup; many will also implement onPause() to commit changes to data and otherwise prepare to stop interacting with the user. You should always call up to your superclass when implementing these methods.

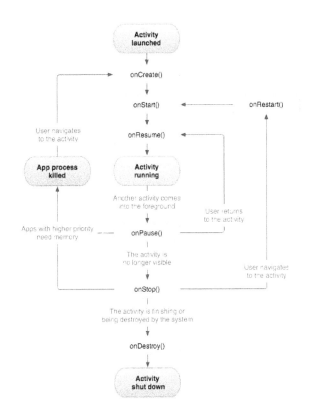

In general, the movement through an activity's lifecycle looks like this:

Method	Description	Killable?	Next
onCreate	Called when the activity is first created. This is where you should do all of your normal static set up: create views, bind data to lists, etc. This method also provides you with a Bundle containing the activity's previously frozen state, if there was one. Always followed by onStart().	No	onStart()
onRestart	Called after your activity has been stopped, prior to it being started again. Always followed by onStart()	No	onStart()
onStart	Called when the activity is becoming visible to the user. Followed by onResume() if the activity comes to the foreground, or onStop() if it becomes hidden.	No	onResume() or onStop()
onResume	Called when the activity will start interacting with the user. At this point your activity is at the top of the activity stack, with user input going to it. Always followed by onPause().	No	onPause()
onPause	Called when the system is about to start resuming a previous activity. This is typically used to commit unsaved changes to persistent data, stop animations and other things that may be consuming CPU, etc. Implementations of this method must be very quick because the next activity will not be resumed until this method returns. Followed by either onResume() if the activity returns back to the front, or onStop() if it becomes invisible to the user.	Pre-HONEYCOMB	onResume() or onStop()
onStop	Called when the activity is no longer visible to the user, because another activity has been resumed and is covering this one. This may happen either because a new activity is being started, an existing one is being brought in front of this one, or this one is being destroyed. Followed by either onRestart() if this activity is coming back to interact with the user, or onDestroy() if this activity is going away.	Yes	onRestart() or onDestroy()
onDestroy	The final call you receive before your activity is destroyed. This can happen either because the activity is finishing (someone called finish() on it, or because the system is temporarily destroying this instance of the activity to save space. You can distinguish between these two scenarios with the isFinishing() method.	Yes	nothing

Notifications

Occasionally, you will want your application (or service) to notify the user of something without losing focus on the currently displayed activity. To notify the user, you use the `Toast` Class to display a small message on the screen. Although you can change it, toasts normally display text messages centered near the bottom of the screen. The following is an example of how to create a toast notification:

```
@Override
public void onCreate(Bundle savedInstanceState) {
 super.onCreate(savedInstanceState);
 setContentView(R.layout.activity_main);

 String sText = "Now is the time...";
 Toast toast = Toast.makeText(getApplicationContext(), sText, Toast.LENGTH_LONG);
 toast.show();

}
```

Note that the constant `Toast.LENGTH_LONG` allows the toast notification to be displayed for about five seconds whereas `Toast.LENGTH_SHORT` will display the toast notification for about two seconds. You can change this by providing your own duration as the third parameter to the `makeText()` method. Note that the `Toast` class is located in `android.widget` package and you should add the code `import android.widget.Toast;` at the top of your activity's code.

Here is what the toast notification looks like:

199

If a toast notification, as defined above, is not to your liking, you can display your own customized layout by creating an XML Layout file and using Toast's `setView()` method to point to that layout. Here is an example,

```
import android.widget.Toast;
import android.view.LayoutInflater;
import android.view.View;
import android.view.ViewGroup;

public class MainActivity extends Activity {

 @Override
 public void onCreate(Bundle savedInstanceState) {
  super.onCreate(savedInstanceState);
  setContentView(R.layout.activity_main);

  LayoutInflater inflater = getLayoutInflater();
  View layout=inflater.inflate(R.layout.toast_layout,
                    (ViewGroup) findViewById(R.id.toast_layout_root));
  Toast toast = new Toast(getApplicationContext());
  toast.setGravity(Gravity.CENTER_VERTICAL, 0, 0);
  toast.setDuration(Toast.LENGTH_LONG);
  toast.setView(layout);
  toast.show();

 }
```

Here is the file `toast_layout.xml`:

```
<LinearLayout xmlns:android="http://schemas.android.com/apk/res/android"
    android:id="@+id/toast_layout_root"
    android:layout_width="fill_parent"
    android:layout_height="fill_parent"
    android:orientation="horizontal"
    android:background="#DAAA">

    <ImageView android:id="@+id/imageView1"
            android:layout_width="wrap_content"
            android:layout_height="fill_parent"
            android:background="#DAAA"
            android:contentDescription="Smile!!"
            android:src="@drawable/smiley_face" />

    <TextView android:id="@+id/textView1"
            android:layout_width="wrap_content"
            android:layout_height="fill_parent"
            android:text="Cities Destroyed By Nuclear Blast! News at 11!"
            android:textSize="14dp"
            android:textColor="#000000" />

</LinearLayout>
```

And here is what this looks like:

Note that, in this case, you do not need to add an entry for `toast_layout.xml` in the `AndroidManifest.xml` file since it is not a true activity.

Summary

In this chapter, we were introduced to Android activities and notifications. We did a little bit of coding and will continue to do more coding in subsequent chapters.

Chapter 10: Wiring-Up Event Handlers

Overview

In the previous few chapters, we saw how to create layouts, looked at a variety of views and even created some activities. Even with all of that information, our Android app doesn't really do much. In this chapter, we explain how to handle events, like the `onClick` event, to allow our applications to do something useful based on a user's interaction.

Ways to Wire-Up Event Handlers

There are several ways to wire-up an event handler to a view (i.e., `Button`, `TextView`, etc.) in Android:

1. In your activity's code, create a `public void` method that will perform some action. In your activity's XML layout file, locate the view (i.e., `Button`, `TextView`, etc.) you are interested in wiring-up an event handler to. For that view's properties in the Eclipse GUI, locate the desired event (such as `onClick`) and enter the name of the `public void` method, without parentheses, as the value of that event. When a user clicks on the view, your method will be called.
2. Similar to #1 above, but instead of using the GUI's properties, you can enter the event name directly in the XML for the view. For example, the `onClick` event is coded in XML as `android:onClick="method-name"` for, say, a `Button` view (do not enter in the parentheses). Note that Method #1 does this for you automatically, so Method #2 is equivalent to Method #1.
3. Create an *event listener* and then associate that listener with a particular view using the appropriate `set*Listener()` method. For example, if you want to wire-up an event handler for a `Button` view's `onClick` event, use the `onClickListener` method to establish the listener as well as code for the `onClick` event. Next, use `setOnClickListener` to establish a link between the listener and the view object. As you can see, this is a two-step process.
4. Similar to #3, but is a one-step process where `onClickListener`, `onClick` and `setOnClickListener` are handled at one time. This method is a bit more confusing, but is equivalent in functionality to Method #3.

We look into each of the methods in the next few sections.

Event Handler Method #1 & #2

Below is a `public void` method we added to our code. It changes the text appearing in a `TextView` view.

```
//Create a method used to handle the onClick for the Button
public void changeText(View view) {
 TextView oTxtVw = (TextView) findViewById(R.id.TheTextView);
 oTxtVw.setText("DISREGARD NUCLEAR WARNING!!");
}
```

Below is the XML layout. Take note of the bold text below. This is the `onClick` event along with the name of the method to be called. Note that you cannot pass in any parameters, as you see below, **but Android will automatically pass in a `View` as the sole parameter** to `changeText` which is why there is the single parameter `View view` associated with the `changeText` method. Note that the XML below is the same whether you coded `android:onClick` by hand or used the GUI interface.

```
<RelativeLayout xmlns:android="http://schemas.android.com/apk/res/android"
    xmlns:tools="http://schemas.android.com/tools"
    android:layout_width="match_parent"
    android:layout_height="match_parent" >

    <TextView
        android:id="@+id/TheTextView"
        android:layout_width="wrap_content"
        android:layout_height="wrap_content"
        android:layout_centerHorizontal="true"
        android:layout_centerVertical="true"
        android:text="@string/hello_world"
        tools:context=".MainActivity" />

    <Button
        android:id="@+id/button1"
        android:layout_width="wrap_content"
        android:layout_height="wrap_content"
        android:layout_below="@+id/TheTextView"
        android:layout_centerHorizontal="true"
        android:layout_marginTop="21dp"
        android:text="@string/button_text"
        android:onClick="changeText"/>

</RelativeLayout>
```

Now, when you click the Big Red Button, the text in the `TextView` will be changed:

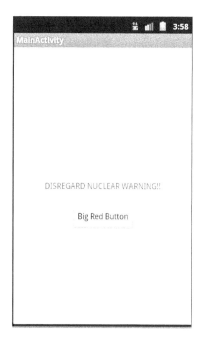

Event Handler Method #3

The XML is the same as above, but the `android:onClick` attribute has been removed:

```
<Button android:id="@+id/button1"
        android:layout_width="wrap_content"
        android:layout_height="wrap_content"
        android:layout_below="@+id/TheTextView"
        android:layout_centerHorizontal="true"
        android:layout_marginTop="21dp"
        android:text="@string/button_text" />
```

Below is the code:

```
public class MainActivity extends Activity {

 @Override
 public void onCreate(Bundle savedInstanceState) {
  super.onCreate(savedInstanceState);
  setContentView(R.layout.activity_main);

  //Step #1: Create an onClickListener
  View.OnClickListener listener = new View.OnClickListener() {
   public void onClick(View view) {
    changeText(view);
   }
  };

  //Step #2: Associate the listener with the button via setOnClickListener
  ((Button) findViewById(R.id.button1)).setOnClickListener(listener);

 }

 //Create a method used to handle the onClick for the Button
 public void changeText(View view) {
  TextView oTxtVw = (TextView) findViewById(R.id.TheTextView);
  oTxtVw.setText("DISREGARD NUCLEAR WARNING!!");
 }

}
```

In the code above, we are still calling the `changeText()` method. You could just as easily have placed the two lines of code from that method into the `onClick()` code in Step #1 and do away with the call to `changeText`.

Note that we are using `View.onClickListener` instead of `Button.onClickListener` because there is no `Button.onClickListener`. One author recommended the latter, but I could not get that to work, but the former does work!

Note that only one `onClickListener` can be associated per `View`. That is, if you subsequently associate a different listener with the button, it would overwrite the previous listener. Some languages allow you to add multiple listeners (i.e., C#) for an object, but not in Android.

Event Handler Method #4

The XML is the same as for Method #3 above:

```
<Button android:id="@+id/button1"
        android:layout_width="wrap_content"
        android:layout_height="wrap_content"
        android:layout_below="@+id/TheTextView"
        android:layout_centerHorizontal="true"
        android:layout_marginTop="21dp"
        android:text="@string/button_text" />
```

Below is the code:

```
public class MainActivity extends Activity {

 @Override
 public void onCreate(Bundle savedInstanceState) {
  super.onCreate(savedInstanceState);
  setContentView(R.layout.activity_main);

  //Create an onClickListener and associate it with the button
  ((Button) findViewById(R.id.button1)).setOnClickListener(

    new View.OnClickListener() {
     public void onClick(View view) {
      changeText(view);
     }
    }

  );

 }

 //Create a method used to handle the onClick for the Button
 public void changeText(View view) {
  TextView oTxtVw = (TextView) findViewById(R.id.TheTextView);
  oTxtVw.setText("DISREGARD NUCLEAR WARNING!!");
 }
}
```

In this case, the setOnClickListener contains the onClickListener and the onClick code. I find the code above to be a bit confusing, so I'm not in favor of it. In addition, if I create a listener, I may need to use it again, so I'm apt to create a listener variable anyway for potential use later on.

Discussion

Not every event is available from with the view's XML. For example, for a Button, the only event that can be referred to in XML is the onClick event via the XML android:onClick. That's it! Similar for a TextView. So, in order to handle other events, you need to use Method #3 or Method #4 above.

In order to find out the events available for the view you are working with, navigate to that page in the Android documentation. For example, if you are working with a Button view, then locate the Button documentation page within the android.widget package, shown below:

However, this may not always be enough to determine the associated events and you may need to traverse up the inheritance chain in order to find the event you are looking for. For example, the `Button` documentation page does not mention any events. However, if you look at the inheritance chain (shown below in detail), you will see that `Button` inherits from `TextEdit`, which inherits from `View` (everything inherits from `Object`, so I didn't mention it...until now...). Referring to `TextEdit` in the documentation, you will see that there is no list of events, not even `onClick`. This is because `onClick` is located in `android.view.View` class.

Note that, while you are looking at the `Button` documentation page, you can scroll down to the public methods section and look for the `set*Listener` method for the event you are interested in. Take note of the natural correspondence between: `set<event-name>Listener`, `<event-name>Listener`, and `<event-name>`.

Chapter 11: Intents

Overview

So far, we've seen how to create layouts, peeked at a variety of views, looked into activities and wired-up events to a view or two. However, an Android programmer won't go far without understanding *intents*. From the manual:

> *An intent is an abstract description of an operation to be performed. It can be used with startActivity to launch an Activity, broadcastIntent to send it to any interested BroadcastReceiver components, and startService(Intent) or bindService(Intent, ServiceConnection, int) to communicate with a background Service.*

> *An Intent provides a facility for performing late runtime binding between the code in different applications. Its most significant use is in the launching of activities, where it can be thought of as the glue between activities. It is basically a passive data structure holding an abstract description of an action to be performed.*

One common use of intents is to inflate an activity. That is, if a user clicks (or taps) a button in your application, another GUI interface (i.e., activity) can be displayed at that point. This allows your Android app to behave just like, say, desktop or web applications. The user can either click the back button to return to the previous activity or the programmer can forcibly close the current activity and the previous activity will be displayed.

There are several ways to display an activity and it depends if your activity needs to return data back to the calling activity. If no data needs to be returned, you can use the `startActivity` method. If you need to return data, you can use the `startActivityForResult` method along with its associated `setResults` method.

However, intents go beyond just the mere display of an interface. Have you ever downloaded, say, a PDF file to your Android device and tried to open it up? What does Android do? If you have more than one application with the ability to display a PDF file, Android presents you with a list of choices and each choice has, at the very least, the ability to display a PDF file. You then tap on the application you want to use to open up your PDF file. Here is what this looks like on my device:

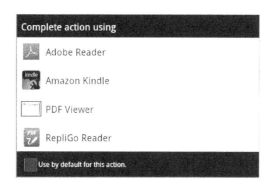

In this chapter, we will talk about *explicit intents* (using the `Intent` Class) and *implicit intents* (using Android's built-in intents).

Explicit Intents

In this section, we will learn how to display activities that *do not* return data - using the `startActivity` method - as well as activities that *do* return data - using the `startActivityForResult` method.

Recall that we talked about an activity's lifecycle. When an activity is displayed, such as the `MAIN` activity defined in the Android Manifest, it goes through a pre-determined lifecycle. This lifecycle is also used on any additional activities you display regardless if it's defined as the `MAIN` activity and displayed automatically when the application is started, or it is displayed programmatically using explicit intents. Thus, when you create any additional activities, they must also be a subclass of the `Activity` Class.

In Eclipse, you can add an additional activity to the `res\layout` folder by right-clicking on the layout folder and clicking on the New...Other... menu item. When the New dialog box appears, scroll to the Android folder and expand it (shown below).

Next, click on the Android Activity item and click Next. When the New Activity dialog box appears (see below), select BlankActivity and click on Next.

208

In the New Blank Activity dialog, fill in the input boxes like this:

- Activity Name - fill in the *name of the class* to generate from the Activity Class.
- Layout Name - fill in the *name of the XML file* to generate.
- Title - fill in the title for this activity.
- Navigation Type - None.

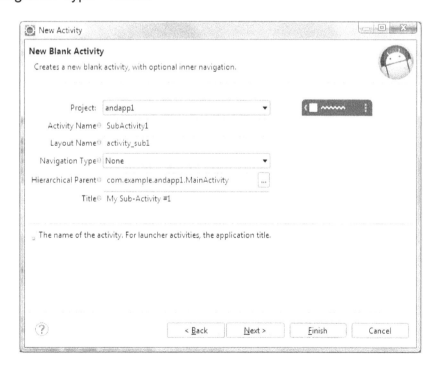

Next, click on the button to the right of the Hierarchical Parent input box and select `MainActivity` when the Choose Activity Class dialog box appears. This indicates that the new activity is a child of `MainActivity` and when the user clicks the back button while in the new activity, the main activity is re-displayed.

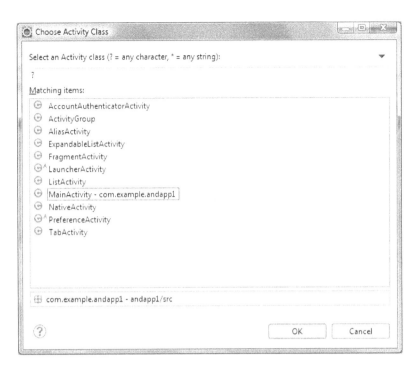

When the Preview dialog appears, look at the changes to the `AndroidManifest.xml` file it displays. The original is on the left and the modified version appears to the right.

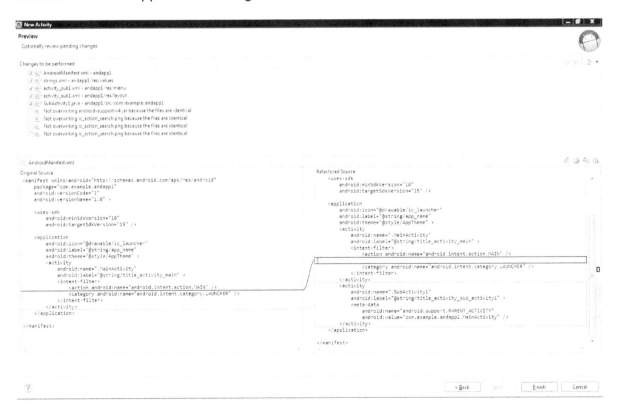

Click the Finish button to generate the new activity and automatically modify the manifest. At this point, you'll notice that there is a new Activity in the `res\layout` folder called `activity_sub1.xml`, and new Java code called `SubActivity.java` appears in the `src` folder.

If you look at the Java code, you'll notice that some additional code that isn't necessary (right now, at least) appears. Remove the additional code and you should be left with just the following `onCreate` method:

```
package com.example.andapp1;

import android.os.Bundle;
import android.app.Activity;

public class SubActivity1 extends Activity {

 @Override
 public void onCreate(Bundle savedInstanceState) {
  super.onCreate(savedInstanceState);
  setContentView(R.layout.activity_sub1);
 }

}
```

Finally, the wizard generates a default `activity_sub1.xml` code with `Hello World!` in it. You can change this to your own layout for the new activity.

Now, let's modify `MainActivity.java` to use intents to display the `activity_sub1.xml` when the button is clicked:

```
package com.example.andapp1;

import android.os.Bundle;
import android.app.Activity;
import android.view.Gravity;
import android.view.Menu;
import android.view.LayoutInflater;
import android.view.View;
import android.view.ViewGroup;
import android.widget.*;
import android.content.Intent;

public class MainActivity extends Activity {

 @Override
 public void onCreate(Bundle savedInstanceState) {
  super.onCreate(savedInstanceState);
  setContentView(R.layout.activity_main);

  //Create an onClickListener and associate it with the button
  //This will inflate activity_sub1.
  ((Button) findViewById(R.id.button1)).setOnClickListener(

    new View.OnClickListener() {
     public void onClick(View view) {
      Intent intent = new Intent(MainActivity.this,SubActivity1.class);
      startActivity(intent);
     }
    }

  );

 }

}
```

If you look at the bold code above, you'll notice that we are creating a new intent. The particular constructor I am using holds the class of the current activity

(`MainActivity.this`) as the first parameter, and the class of the activity to be displayed as the second parameter (`SubActivity1.class`). We then execute the `startActivity` method to display the sub-activity. Here is what this looks like:

When you click on the Big Red Button (which, by the way, isn't really red), the sub-activity is generated. Note that if you click on the back button, you will get back to the `MainActivity`.

Now, suppose that you want to return data from the sub-activity to the parent (`MainActivity`, in this case) activity. That is, you want to return data back to the point where you inflated the sub-activity in the parent activity. For our example, this is where we have coded the `startActivity` method. There are several additional steps we need to perform in order to return data from a sub-activity to a main activity:

1. In your sub-activity, add a `Button` that will create some data that will be returned. The code for the corresponding `onClick` event will then call the `setResult` method to add that data to a `null` intent (which is the object passed from the sub-activity to the main activity containing your data). Finally, the `onClick` code will call the `finish` method to close the sub-activity.
2. In your parent activity, add code for the `public void onActivityResult` method. This will be called once the sub-activity has closed. It is within this method that you will pull out the data you need from the passed in intent by using the `getStringExtra`, or related, methods.

Below is the modified XML for `activity_sub1.xml`:

```
<RelativeLayout xmlns:android="http://schemas.android.com/apk/res/android"
    xmlns:tools="http://schemas.android.com/tools"
    android:layout_width="match_parent"
    android:layout_height="match_parent" >

    <TextView
        android:id="@+id/textView1"
```

```
            android:layout_width="wrap_content"
            android:layout_height="wrap_content"
            android:layout_centerHorizontal="true"
            android:layout_centerVertical="true"
            android:text="THIS IS YOUR SUB-ACTIVITY SPEAKING!!"
            tools:context=".SubActivity1" />

    <Button
            android:id="@+id/btnSubAct"
            android:layout_width="wrap_content"
            android:layout_height="wrap_content"
            android:layout_below="@+id/textView1"
            android:layout_centerHorizontal="true"
            android:text="Close!" />

</RelativeLayout>
```

Below is the modified code for `SubActivity1.java`:

```
package com.example.andapp1;

import android.widget.Button;
import android.os.Bundle;
import android.app.Activity;
import android.view.Gravity;
import android.view.Menu;
import android.view.LayoutInflater;
import android.view.View;
import android.view.ViewGroup;
import android.widget.*;
import android.content.Intent;


public class SubActivity1 extends Activity {

 @Override
 public void onCreate(Bundle savedInstanceState) {
  super.onCreate(savedInstanceState);
  setContentView(R.layout.activity_sub1);

  //Create an onClickListener and associate it with the button
  //This will create the data, insert it into the intent and close
  //the sub-activity returning us back to the main activity.
  ((Button) findViewById(R.id.btnSubAct)).setOnClickListener(

    new View.OnClickListener() {
     public void onClick(View view) {
      String sText="Now is the time...";
      Intent results = new Intent(); //null Intent created here!
      results.putExtra("RETURNED_TEXT",sText); //insert key/value pair.
      setResult(RESULT_OK,results); //set results for return to main
      finish(); //close this activity
     }

  });

 };

}
```

Take note of how to create a new blank intent, place data into it and close the sub-activity.

The `putExtra` method takes two parameters. The first parameter is the name, or *key*, of the data (`RETURNED_TEXT`, in the example above). The second parameter is the *value* of that key (`"Now is the time..."`, in the example above).

213

The `setResult` method takes two parameters as well. The first is `RESULT_OK` and is the `resultCode` returned to the method `onActivityResult`. If things did not go well, use `RESULT_CANCELED` and this will be the `resultCode`. If the user clicked the back button instead of clicking the button, `RESULT_CANCELED` is returned by default.

Finally, we close the sub-activity by using the `finish()` method.

Below is the code in `MainActivity.java`:

```
package com.example.andapp1;

import android.os.Bundle;
import android.app.Activity;
import android.view.Gravity;
import android.view.Menu;
import android.view.LayoutInflater;
import android.view.View;
import android.view.ViewGroup;
import android.widget.*;
import android.content.Intent;

public class MainActivity extends Activity {

 private static final int SUBACTIVITY_ID=1000; //ID number for activity_sub1.

 @Override
 public void onCreate(Bundle savedInstanceState) {
  super.onCreate(savedInstanceState);
  setContentView(R.layout.activity_main);

  //Create an onClickListener and associate it with the button
  //This will inflate activity_sub1.
  ((Button) findViewById(R.id.button1)).setOnClickListener(

    new View.OnClickListener() {
    public void onClick(View view) {
     Intent intent = new Intent(MainActivity.this,SubActivity1.class);
     startActivityForResult(intent,SUBACTIVITY_ID);
    }
   }

  );

 }

 @Override
 public void onActivityResult(int requestCode,int resultCode,Intent data) {
  super.onActivityResult(requestCode, resultCode, data);

  //Based on the sub-activity returning here, pull out their data.
  switch(requestCode) {

   //Pull in the data coming from activity_sub1 (ID # 1000)
   case (SUBACTIVITY_ID): {
    if (resultCode == Activity.RESULT_OK) {

     //Here is where we pull the string data based on the key RETURNED_TEXT.
     String sTextFromSubAct1 = data.getStringExtra("RETURNED_TEXT");

     //Place the returned text into the text view @+id/TheTextView.
     TextView oTxtVw = (TextView) findViewById(R.id.TheTextView);
     oTxtVw.setText(sTextFromSubAct1);
```

```
        }
        else {

         //Oops...things didn't go well...RESULT_CANCELED was returned!!

         //Place the returned text into the text view @+id/TheTextView.
         TextView oTxtVw = (TextView) findViewById(R.id.TheTextView);
         oTxtVw.setText("NO DATA RETURNED");

        }

       break;

      }
    }
  }

}
```

The emboldened code above is just the creation of an integer value to identify our sub-activity (SUBACTIVITY_ID). It is this value that is used in the onActivityResult method to determine what to do based on which activity triggered the onActivityResult method. This integer value is used above in the startActivityForResult method.

Finally, onActivityResult is called when either the sub-activity issued the finish method or the user clicked the back button. It is the responsibility of this code to pull out any data, if any, returned by a sub-activity. We are using a switch statement based on the SUBACTIVITY_ ID to determine what to do.

Below is what this looks like. The first row of images represents what occurs when the user clicks the Close button on the sub-activity (RESULT_OK), while the second row of images represents what happens when the user clicks the back button (RESULT_CANCELED).

Notice that when the user clicks the back button, the default text of NO DATA RETURNED is displayed.

Implicit Intents

In this section, we use implicit intents to request Android to perform a specific action based on the data passed to it. For example, if you pass a telephone number to an intent, it makes sense for Android to dial that number. If you pass a PDF file name to an intent, it makes sense for Android to open up the PDF file, or at least allow you to choose your favorite PDF application installed on the device which will then be used to open up the PDF file.

We will modify our SubActivity1 from the last section to include a second button. This button will open up a PDF file when pressed, or display a list of appropriate applications. Here is what that looks like on my device. My device gives me a choice, as shown below.

Here is what the code in SubActivity.java looks like:

```
//Create an onClickListener and associate it with the button
//This will open up a pdf file.
((Button) findViewById(R.id.btnPDF)).setOnClickListener(
  new View.OnClickListener() {
   public void onClick(View view) {

     //Set up a path to the pdf file ON THE DEVICE
     //You wouldn't necessarily hard-code this!
     String path = "/mnt/sdcard/download/Reporting_Suite_Highlights.pdf";
     File targetFile = new File(path);
     Uri targetUri = Uri.fromFile(targetFile);

     //Set up the intent with a default action of ACTION_VIEW.
     Intent intent = new Intent(Intent.ACTION_VIEW);
     intent.setDataAndType(targetUri, "application/pdf");

     //start the activity...even though it isn't an activity we created!
     startActivity(intent);

   }
});
```

Note that I added an additional button, called `btnPDF`, in `activity_sub1.xml` file, which is not shown here.

There are many more actions besides `ACTION_VIEW`. Below is a list of the Standard Activity Actions:

- `ACTION_MAIN` - Start as a main entry point, does not expect to receive data. Constant Value: "android.intent.action.MAIN". Note that this constant is used in the `AndroidManifest.xml` file for the activity considered the main activity.
- `ACTION_VIEW` - Display the data to the user. This is the most common action performed on data - it is the generic action you can use on a piece of data to get the most reasonable thing to occur. For example, when used on a contacts entry it will view the entry; when used on a `mailto:` URI it will bring up a compose window filled with the information supplied by the URI; when used with a `tel:` URI it will invoke the dialer. Constant Value: "android.intent.action.VIEW". Note that action is used in our example above.
- `ACTION_ATTACH_DATA` - Used to indicate that some piece of data should be attached to some other place. For example, image data could be attached to a contact. It is up to the recipient to decide where the data should be attached; the intent does not specify the ultimate destination. `getData()` is URI of data to be attached. Constant Value: "android.intent.action.ATTACH_DATA".
- `ACTION_EDIT` - Provide explicit editable access to the given data. `getData()` is URI of data to be edited. Constant Value: "android.intent.action.EDIT".
- `ACTION_PICK` - Pick an item from the data, returning what was selected. Input: `getData()` is URI containing a directory of data (vnd.android.cursor.dir/*) from which to pick an item. Output: The URI of the item that was picked. Constant Value: "android.intent.action.PICK".

- `ACTION_CHOOSER` - Display an activity chooser, allowing the user to pick what they want to before proceeding. This can be used as an alternative to the standard activity picker that is displayed by the system when you try to start an activity with multiple possible matches (see my PDF file example above), with these differences in behavior: (1) You can specify the title that will appear in the activity chooser; (2) The user does not have the option to make one of the matching activities a preferred activity, and all possible activities will always be shown even if one of them is currently marked as the preferred activity. This action should be used when the user will naturally expect to select an activity in order to proceed. An example of when not to use it is when the user clicks on a "mailto:" link. They would naturally expect to go directly to their mail app, so startActivity() should be called directly: it will either launch the current preferred app, or put up a dialog allowing the user to pick an app to use and optionally marking that as preferred. In contrast, if the user is selecting a menu item to send a picture they are viewing to someone else, there are many different things they may want to do at this point: send it through e-mail, upload it to a web service, etc. In this case the CHOOSER action should be used, to always present to the user a list of the things they can do, with a nice title given by the caller such as "Send this photo with:". If you need to grant URI permissions through a chooser, you must specify the permissions to be granted on the ACTION_CHOOSER Intent in addition to the EXTRA_INTENT inside. This means using setClipData(ClipData) to specify the URIs to be granted as well as FLAG_GRANT_READ_URI_PERMISSION and/or FLAG_GRANT_WRITE_URI_PERMISSION as appropriate. As a convenience, an Intent of this form can be created with the createChooser(Intent, CharSequence) function. Input: No data should be specified. get*Extra must have a EXTRA_INTENT field containing the Intent being executed, and can optionally have a EXTRA_TITLE field containing the title text to display in the chooser. Output: Depends on the protocol of EXTRA_INTENT. Constant Value: "android.intent.action.CHOOSER".
- `ACTION_GET_CONTENT` - Allow the user to select a particular kind of data and return it. This is different than ACTION_PICK in that here we just say what kind of data is desired, not a URI of existing data from which the user can pick. A ACTION_GET_CONTENT could allow the user to create the data as it runs (for example taking a picture or recording a sound), let them browse over the web and download the desired data, etc. There are two main ways to use this action: if you want a specific kind of data, such as a person contact, you set the MIME type to the kind of data you want and launch it with startActivity(Intent). The system will then launch the best application to select that kind of data for you. You may also be interested in any of a set of types of content the user can pick. For example, an e-mail application that wants to allow the user to add an attachment to an e-mail message can use this action to bring up a list of all of the types of content the user can attach. In this case, you should wrap the GET_CONTENT intent with a chooser (through createChooser(Intent, CharSequence)), which will give the proper interface for the user to pick how to send your data and allow you to specify a prompt indicating what they are doing. You will usually specify a broad MIME type (such as image/* or */*), resulting in a broad range of content types the user can select from. When using such a broad GET_CONTENT action, it is often desirable to only pick from data

that can be represented as a stream. This is accomplished by requiring the CATEGORY_OPENABLE in the Intent. Callers can optionally specify EXTRA_LOCAL_ONLY to request that the launched content chooser only returns results representing data that is locally available on the device. For example, if this extra is set to true then an image picker should not show any pictures that are available from a remote server but not already on the local device (thus requiring they be downloaded when opened). Input: getType() is the desired MIME type to retrieve. Note that no URI is supplied in the intent, as there are no constraints on where the returned data originally comes from. You may also include the CATEGORY_OPENABLE if you can only accept data that can be opened as a stream. You may use EXTRA_LOCAL_ONLY to limit content selection to local data. Output: The URI of the item that was picked. This must be a content: URI so that any receiver can access it. Constant Value: "android.intent.action.GET_CONTENT".

- ACTION_DIAL - Activity Action: Dial a number as specified by the data. This shows a UI with the number being dialed, allowing the user to explicitly initiate the call. Input: If nothing, an empty dialer is started; else getData() is URI of a phone number to be dialed or a tel: URI of an explicit phone number. Output: nothing. Constant Value: "android.intent.action.DIAL".

- ACTION_CALL - Perform a call to someone specified by the data. Input: If nothing, an empty dialer is started; else getData() is URI of a phone number to be dialed or a tel: URI of an explicit phone number. Output: nothing. Note: there will be restrictions on which applications can initiate a call; most applications should use the ACTION_DIAL. Note: this Intent cannot be used to call emergency numbers. Applications can dial emergency numbers using ACTION_DIAL, however. Constant Value: "android.intent.action.CALL".

- ACTION_SEND - Deliver some data to someone else. Who the data is being delivered to is not specified; it is up to the receiver of this action to ask the user where the data should be sent. When launching a SEND intent, you should usually wrap it in a chooser (through createChooser(Intent, CharSequence)), which will give the proper interface for the user to pick how to send your data and allow you to specify a prompt indicating what they are doing. Input: getType() is the MIME type of the data being sent. get*Extra can have either a EXTRA_TEXT or EXTRA_STREAM field, containing the data to be sent. If using EXTRA_TEXT, the MIME type should be "text/plain"; otherwise it should be the MIME type of the data in EXTRA_STREAM. Use */* if the MIME type is unknown (this will only allow senders that can handle generic data streams). If using EXTRA_TEXT, you can also optionally supply EXTRA_HTML_TEXT for clients to retrieve your text with HTML formatting. As of JELLY_BEAN, the data being sent can be supplied through setClipData(ClipData). This allows you to use FLAG_GRANT_READ_URI_PERMISSION when sharing content: URIs and other advanced features of ClipData. If using this approach, you still must supply the same data through the EXTRA_TEXT or EXTRA_STREAM fields described below for compatibility with old applications. If you don't set a ClipData, it will be copied there for you when calling startActivity(Intent). Optional standard extras, which may be interpreted by some recipients as appropriate, are: EXTRA_EMAIL, EXTRA_CC, EXTRA_BCC, EXTRA_SUBJECT. Output: nothing. Constant Value: "android.intent.action.SEND".

- `ACTION_SENDTO` - Send a message to someone specified by the data. Input: `getData()` is URI describing the target. Output: nothing. Constant Value: "android.intent.action.SENDTO".
- `ACTION_ANSWER` - Handle an incoming phone call. Input: nothing. Output: nothing. Constant Value: "android.intent.action.ANSWER".
- `ACTION_INSERT` - Insert an empty item into the given container. Input: `getData()` is URI of the directory (vnd.android.cursor.dir/*) in which to place the data. Output: URI of the new data that was created. Constant Value: "android.intent.action.INSERT".
- `ACTION_DELETE` - Delete the given data from its container. Input: `getData()` is URI of data to be deleted. Output: nothing. Constant Value: "android.intent.action.DELETE"
- `ACTION_RUN` - Run the data, whatever that means. Input: ? (Note: this is currently specific to the test harness.) Output: nothing. Constant Value: "android.intent.action.RUN".
- `ACTION_SYNC` - Perform a data synchronization. Input: ? Output: ? Constant Value: "android.intent.action.SYNC".
- `ACTION_PICK_ACTIVITY` - Pick an activity given an intent, returning the class selected. Input: get*Extra field EXTRA_INTENT is an Intent used with queryIntentActivities(Intent, int) to determine the set of activities from which to pick. Output: Class name of the activity that was selected. Constant Value: "android.intent.action.PICK_ACTIVITY".
- `ACTION_SEARCH` - Perform a search. Input: `getStringExtra(SearchManager. QUERY)` is the text to search for. If empty, simply enter your search results Activity with the search UI activated. Output: nothing. Constant Value: "android.intent.action.SEARCH".
- `ACTION_WEB_SEARCH` - Perform a web search. Input: `getStringExtra(SearchManager.QUERY)` is the text to search for. If it is a url that starts with `http` or `https`, the site will be opened. If it is plain text, Google search will be applied. Output: nothing. Constant Value: "android.intent.action.WEB_SEARCH".
- `ACTION_FACTORY_TEST` - Main entry point for factory tests. Only used when the device is booting in factory test node. The implementing package must be installed in the system image. Input: nothing Output: nothing Constant Value: "android.intent.action.FACTORY_TEST".

For example, we can use the action `ACTION_WEB_SEARCH` to search Google based on the text `minestrone`.

```
//Create an onClickListener and associate it with the button
//This will search Google based on the word minestrone.
((Button) findViewById(R.id.btnSEARCH)).setOnClickListener(

  new View.OnClickListener() {

  public void onClick(View view) {

    //Set up your search term
    String search_term = "minestrone";

    //Set up the intent with a default action of ACTION_WEB_SEARCH.
    //Insert the search term into the intent
    Intent intent = new Intent(Intent.ACTION_WEB_SEARCH);
    intent.putExtra(SearchManager.QUERY,search_term);

    //start the activity...even though it isn't an activity we created!
    startActivity(intent);

  }

});
```

Note that each action will require you to learn its foibles. For example, we needed to use the key `SearchManager.QUERY` in the `putExtra` method as the first parameter above. The second parameter just contains our search term (*"minestrone"*). It is the combination of the action (`ACTION_WEB_SEARCH`) and the extra data that tells Android to open up the browser and search for `minestrone` on Google.

Discussion

In the previous two sections, we learned about explicit intents - that is, intents you code to display an activity - and implicit intents - that is, intents offered by Android to perform an action based on the data passed to it (like a PDF file, telephone number, search term, etc.). However, that's not the whole story when it comes to intents. You can use intents to create *services* as well as *broadcast receivers*.

Services, similar to services or processes on a desktop computer, are interface-less programs that run in the background. The user does not normally interact with a service (although he/she could). We talk about services later in the book.

Broadcast receivers allow you to capture and take action on events triggered by either the Android system or other applications. For example, when the phone rings, Android sends out a broadcast to all applications interested in knowing when the phone rings. If your application contains a *broadcast receiver* for when the phone rings, your application will be notified and it can perform some action whenever the phone rings. We talk about broadcast receivers later in the book.

There is another subtle thing going on with intents. Recall from the previous section on implicit intents that we wrote some code to open up a PDF file. However, instead of displaying the PDF file right off the bat, Android displayed a list of applications with the ability to display a PDF file. However, how did Android know that those applications had the ability to display a PDF file? An alternate, but equivalent, question might be: *How do **you** tell Android that **your** application can display a PDF?* You do this by using *Intent Filters*, the subject of our next section.

221

Intent Filters

As described in the previous section, we want to tell Android that our application can perform some functionality (say, display a PDF file) and that our application should be added to the list of possible applications (those that display PDFs) listed by Android when a user attempts to open up a file (say, PDF file). To do this, you use an intent filter in your `AndroidManifest.xml` file. From the documentation: *Each filter describes a capability of the component, a set of intents that the component is willing to receive. It, in effect, filters in intents of a desired type, while filtering out unwanted intents - but only unwanted implicit intents (those that don't name a target class). A component has separate filters for each job it can do, [that is] each face it can present to the user. An intent filter is an instance of the IntentFilter class (android.content.IntentFilter).* **However, since the Android system must know about the capabilities of a component BEFORE it can launch that component, intent filters are generally not set up in Java code, but in the application's manifest file as `<intent-filter>` elements.** *A filter has fields that parallel the action, data and category fields of an Intent object. An implicit intent is tested against the filter in all three areas. In order to be delivered to the component that owns the filter, it must pass all three tests.*

Recall that our `AndroidManifest.xml` already has an `<intent-filter>` section in it:

```
<activity android:name=".MainActivity"
          android:label="@string/title_activity_main" >
 <intent-filter>
   <action android:name="android.intent.action.MAIN" />
   <category android:name="android.intent.category.LAUNCHER" />
 </intent-filter>
</activity>
```

This allows our application to be launched as well as be placed on the Application Launcher page. Note that when your application is installed, it is this intent-filter that is analyzed to determine that your application can be executed (`android.intent.action.MAIN`) as well as be placed on the Application Launcher page (`android.intent.category.LAUNCHER`). This analysis is performed for any other `<intent-filters>` appearing in your `Android Manifest.xml` file.

Within the `<intent-filter>` node, you can specify `<action android:name="">`, `<category android:name="">` and `<data>`.

Referring to the XML above, for the `<action>` node, `android:name` uses the long form `android.intent.action.MAIN` instead of shorter form `ACTION_MAIN`. This is true for all actions used as values to attributes within XML.

Again, referring to the XML above, for the `<category>` node, `android:name` uses the long form `android.intent.category.LAUNCHER` instead of the shorter form `CATEGORY_LAUNCHER`. This is true for all categories used as values to attributes within XML.

Please see the list of *Standard Activity Actions* a few pages back to determine the long form and short form for *actions*.

The list of *categories* along with their short and long forms is listed below:

- `CATEGORY_DEFAULT` - Set if the activity should be an option for the default action (center press) to perform on a piece of data. Setting this will hide from the user any activities without it set when performing an action on some data. Note that this is normal -not- set in the Intent when initiating an action -- it is for use in intent filters specified in packages. Constant Value: "android.intent.category.DEFAULT".

- `CATEGORY_BROWSABLE` - Activities that can be safely invoked from a browser must support this category. For example, if the user is viewing a web page or an e-mail and clicks on a link in the text, the Intent generated execute that link will require the BROWSABLE category, so that only activities supporting this category will be considered as possible actions. By supporting this category, you are promising that there is nothing damaging (without user intervention) that can happen by invoking any matching Intent. Constant Value: "android.intent.category.BROWSABLE".

- `CATEGORY_TAB` - Intended to be used as a tab inside of a containing TabActivity. Constant Value: "android.intent.category.TAB".

- `CATEGORY_ALTERNATIVE` - Set if the activity should be considered as an alternative action to the data the user is currently viewing. See also `CATEGORY_SELECTED_ ALTERNATIVE` for an alternative action that applies to the selection in a list of items. Supporting this category means that you would like your activity to be displayed in the set of alternative things the user can do, usually as part of the current activity's options menu. You will usually want to include a specific label in the <intent-filter> of this action describing to the user what it does. The action of IntentFilter with this category is important in that it describes the specific action the target will perform. This generally should not be a generic action (such as ACTION_VIEW, but rather a specific name such as "com.android.camera.action.CROP. Only one alternative of any particular action will be shown to the user, so using a specific action like this makes sure that your alternative will be displayed while also allowing other applications to provide their own overrides of that particular action. Constant Value: "android.intent.category. ALTERNATIVE".

- `CATEGORY_SELECTED_ALTERNATIVE` - Set if the activity should be considered as an alternative selection action to the data the user has currently selected. This is like `CATEGORY_ALTERNATIVE`, but is used in activities showing a list of items from which the user can select, giving them alternatives to the default action that will be performed on it. Constant Value: "android.intent.category.SELECTED_ALTERNATIVE".

- `CATEGORY_LAUNCHER` - Should be displayed in the top-level launcher. Constant Value: "android.intent.category.LAUNCHER".

- `CATEGORY_INFO` - Provides information about the package it is in; typically used if a package does not contain a CATEGORY_LAUNCHER to provide a front-door to the user without having to be shown in the all apps list. Constant Value: "android.intent.category.INFO".

- `CATEGORY_HOME` - This is the home activity, that is the first activity that is displayed when the device boots. Constant Value: "android.intent.category.HOME".
- `CATEGORY_PREFERENCE` - This activity is a preference panel. Constant Value: "android.intent.category.PREFERENCE".
- `CATEGORY_TEST` - To be used as a test (not part of the normal user experience). Constant Value: "android.intent.category.TEST".
- `CATEGORY_CAR_DOCK` - An activity to run when device is inserted into a car dock. Used with ACTION_MAIN to launch an activity. For more information, see UiModeManager. Constant Value: "android.intent.category.CAR_DOCK".
- `CATEGORY_DESK_DOCK` - An activity to run when device is inserted into a desk dock. Used with ACTION_MAIN to launch an activity. For more information, see UiModeManager. Constant Value: "android.intent.category.DESK_DOCK".
- `CATEGORY_LE_DESK_DOCK` - An activity to run when device is inserted into an analog (low end) dock. Used with ACTION_MAIN to launch an activity. For more information, see UiModeManager. Constant Value: "android.intent.category.LE_DESK_DOCK".
- `CATEGORY_HE_DESK_DOCK` - An activity to run when device is inserted into a digital (high end) dock. Used with ACTION_MAIN to launch an activity. For more information, see UiModeManager. Constant Value: "android.intent.category.HE_DESK_DOCK".
- `CATEGORY_CAR_MODE` - Used to indicate that the activity can be used in a car environment. Constant Value: "android.intent.category.CAR_MODE".
- `CATEGORY_APP_MARKET` - This activity allows the user to browse and download new applications. Constant Value: "android.intent.category.APP_MARKET".

By creating an activity and specifying an `<intent-filter>` in the `AndroidManifest.xml` specifically for this activity, the Android system will then know what this activity is capable of doing. When an activity is associated with an action (like displaying a PDF file), Android inflates that activity and passes in the data associated with the action. In the case of a PDF file, the location and file name is passed in. The activity, just like all other activities, goes through the normal lifecycle including calling `onCreate`.

For example, let's update our sample application so that if a user attempts to open up a PDF file, the Android system will display a list of appropriate applications including ours. Note that our application won't actually display the PDF file (since it can't actually do that!), but it will display an activity with the name of the PDF file to be opened. I added an additional activity (see the beginning of this chapter for instructions on how to do that) with a layout file called `activity_intent_example.xml` which contains a `TextView` with an id of `txtIntTxtVw`. Below is the XML:

```
<RelativeLayout xmlns:android="http://schemas.android.com/apk/res/android"
    xmlns:tools="http://schemas.android.com/tools"
    android:layout_width="match_parent"
    android:layout_height="match_parent" >
```

```xml
    <TextView
        android:id="@+id/txtIntTxtVw"
        android:layout_width="wrap_content"
        android:layout_height="wrap_content"
        android:layout_centerHorizontal="true"
        android:layout_centerVertical="true"
        android:text="LET'S DISPLAY THE WONDERFUL PDF!!"
        tools:context=".IntentExampleActivity" />

</RelativeLayout>
```

The associated Java code, called `IntentExampleActivity.java`, contains the code which pulls in the PDF filename and updates the `TextView` with this name. Here is the Java code:

```java
package com.example.andapp1;

import android.os.Bundle;
import android.app.Activity;
import android.content.Intent;
import android.widget.TextView;

public class IntentExampleActivity extends Activity {

 @Override
 public void onCreate(Bundle savedInstanceState) {
  super.onCreate(savedInstanceState);
  setContentView(R.layout.activity_intent_example);

  //Get the intent and data
  Intent intent = getIntent();
  String data = intent.getData().toString();

  //Replace the data in the text view (txtIntTxtVw) with the data.
  TextView oTxtVw = (TextView) findViewById(R.id.txtIntTxtVw);
  oTxtVw.setText(data);

 }


}
```

The emboldened code above is responsible for pulling in the data associated with the action that fired the intent. In this case, by clicking (or tapping) on a PDF file, the Android system passes the name of the file into the intent where it is pulled out by using the `getData` method. The code following the emboldened code just places the filename into the `TextView`. Normally, you would display the PDF file at this point assuming your application can do that!

Below is the part of the `AndroidManifest.xml` for the `IntentExampleActivity`:

```xml
<activity android:name=".IntentExampleActivity"
          android:label="@string/title_activity_intent_example" >

 <intent-filter>

  <action android:name="android.intent.action.VIEW"></action>
  <category android:name="android.intent.category.DEFAULT"></category>
  <data android:mimeType="application/pdf"
        android:scheme="file"
        android:pathPattern=".*\.[pP][dD][fF]"></data>
```

```
    </intent-filter>
```
```
</activity>
```

You notice that there is no mention of the MAIN action or the LAUNCHER category in the XML shown above. This is because IntentExampleActivity is not the "main program", but just another activity. You will notice that we have specified the VIEW action and the DEFAULT category. The VIEW action displays the data to the user and is the most common action performed on data. The DEFAULT category is required for all intent filters. The <data> node specifies the PDF mimeType (application/pdf), the scheme (file) and the filename/extension as a regular expression in android:pathPattern (*.pdf, *.PDF, etc.).

Now, when you run the application, the main screen will still appear, but back out of the program and go into File Explorer. If you click on a PDF file, you will be given a list of applications, as shown below, and you will see our application in the list (displayed as Intent Example Activity):

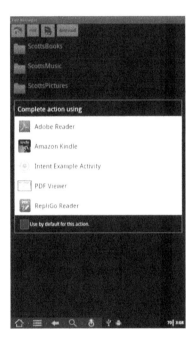

When you tap on Intent Example Activity, you will see something like the following screen:

You will also notice that, in File Manager, all of the PDF icons now reflect the icon for our application. This change is due to the `DEFAULT` category.

If you uninstall the application, the previous application's icon will be displayed.

Determining Applications Providing a Specific Intent Filter

As shown in the previous section, you can use Intent Filters to make Android aware that your application can perform a certain action such as display a PDF file. You may occasionally want to know which applications can perform a specific intent filter. Unfortunately, as of 2012, you cannot obtain the intent filters of a component. You can, though, get a list of all of the packages installed on the device by using the `PackageManager` class. When you instantiate that class, you can gain access to the list of installed packages by using the `getInstalledPackages()` method to get back a `List` of `PackageInfo`

227

objects. To show this list of packages, I used a `ListView`. Although you can skip this on first read, here is the Java code specifically for this `ListView` (called `AppListActivity.java`):

```java
package com.example.andapp1;

import java.util.ArrayList;
import java.util.Comparator;
import java.util.List;
import android.os.Bundle;
import android.app.Activity;
import android.view.Menu;
import android.view.MenuItem;
import android.widget.ArrayAdapter;
import android.support.v4.app.NavUtils;
import android.app.ListActivity;
import android.content.Context;
import android.content.pm.*;

public class AppListActivity extends ListActivity {

 ArrayList<String> listItems = new ArrayList<String>();
 ArrayAdapter<String> adapter;

 @Override
 public void onCreate(Bundle savedInstanceState) {
  super.onCreate(savedInstanceState);
  setContentView(R.layout.activity_app_list);

  //Package info
  PackageManager oPackMan = getPackageManager();
  List<PackageInfo> oPackInfoList = oPackMan.getInstalledPackages(
                                       PackageManager.GET_ACTIVITIES |
                                       PackageManager.GET_GIDS |
                                       PackageManager.GET_CONFIGURATIONS |
                                       PackageManager.GET_INSTRUMENTATION |
                                       PackageManager.GET_PERMISSIONS |
                                       PackageManager.GET_PROVIDERS |
                                       PackageManager.GET_RECEIVERS |
                                       PackageManager.GET_SERVICES |
                                       PackageManager.GET_SIGNATURES |
                                       PackageManager.GET_UNINSTALLED_PACKAGES
                              );

  String sTextPackageName = "";
  for(int i=0; i < oPackInfoList.size(); i++) {
   sTextPackageName = oPackInfoList.get(i).packageName;
   listItems.add(sTextPackageName);
  }

  //Associate the listItems with the adapter.
  //Note that we specify simple_list_item_1 as the layout.
  //See the image below.
  adapter = new ArrayAdapter<String>(this,
                              android.R.layout.simple_list_item_1,
                              listItems);
  //Sort the list
  adapter.sort(new Comparator<String>() {

   public int compare(String object1, String object2) {
     return object1.compareTo(object2);
   };

  });

  setListAdapter(adapter);
```

```
//Un-comment the line below if your listItems is updated occasionally.
//adapter.notifyDataSetChanged();

}

}
```

Here is the associated activity (`activity_app_list.xml`):

```xml
<LinearLayout xmlns:android="http://schemas.android.com/apk/res/android"
    xmlns:tools="http://schemas.android.com/tools"
    android:layout_width="match_parent"
    android:layout_height="match_parent"
    android:paddingLeft="8dp"
    android:paddingRight="8dp">

    <ListView
        android:id="@android:id/list"
        android:layout_width="match_parent"
        android:layout_height="wrap_content"
        android:background="#666666"
        android:layout_weight="1"
        android:drawSelectorOnTop="false">
    </ListView>

</LinearLayout>
```

If you take a look at the emboldened attribute above, you'll see that we labeled the `ListView` as `@android:id/list`. This name is required when you extend the `ListActivity` class (as we've done in the Java code above). This makes creating lists a little easier.

Here is what this looks like (this is what `simple_list_item_1` displays):

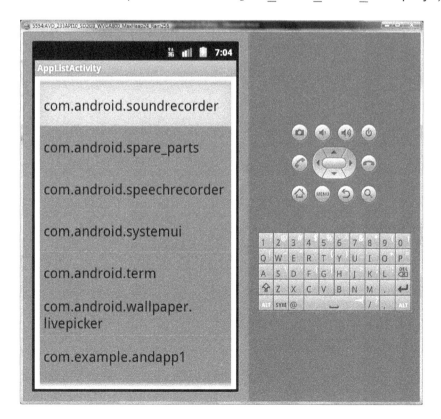

Summary

In this chapter, we looked at intents in detail. In later chapters, we will see how intents are used in content providers as well as broadcast receivers.

Chapter 12: The Android Manifest

Overview

In this chapter, we look into the Android manifest file, `AndroidManifest.xml`. This file contains some extremely important information such as the name of your package, the name of the application as well as its associated icon and theme, a list of all of the activities in the application along with their associated code and title, etc. However, without the Android manifest, your Android application won't get too far. Note that this chapter can be skimmed upon first read of the book.

There are two ways to modify your application's `AndroidManifest.xml` file:

1. By hand, by entering information into the `AndroidManifest.xml` file directly
2. By using the Eclipse ADT GUI interface to update the `AndroidManifest.xml` file for you

We show both methods later on in this chapter. First, though, let's go through what tags are allowed in the `AndroidManifest.xml` file.

Structure of the `AndroidManifest.xml` File

Based on the Android manual, the `AndroidManifest.xml` file has the following structure. Note that not all of the elements shown below are necessary.

```
<?xml version="1.0" encoding="utf-8"?>

<manifest>

    <uses-permission />
    <permission />
    <permission-tree />
    <permission-group />
    <instrumentation />
    <uses-sdk />
    <uses-configuration />
    <uses-feature />
    <supports-screens />
    <compatible-screens />
    <supports-gl-texture />

    <application>

        <activity>
            <intent-filter>
                <action />
                <category />
                <data />
            </intent-filter>
            <meta-data />
        </activity>

        <activity-alias>
            <intent-filter> . . . </intent-filter>
            <meta-data />
        </activity-alias>

        <service>
            <intent-filter> . . . </intent-filter>
            <meta-data/>
```

```
        </service>

        <receiver>
            <intent-filter> . . . </intent-filter>
            <meta-data />
        </receiver>

        <provider>
            <grant-uri-permission />
            <meta-data />
        </provider>

        <uses-library />

    </application>

</manifest>
```

We will describe each of the following tags in turn in this chapter:
<manifest>, <uses-sdk>, <application>, <activity>, <activity-alias>, <meta-data>, <intent-filter>, <action>, <category>, <data>, <provider>, <receiver>, <service>, <grant-uri-permission>, <instrumentation>, <permission>, <permission-group>, <permission-tree>, <supports-screens>, <uses-configuration>, <uses-feature>, <uses-library>, <uses-permission>.

The <manifest> Tag

```
<manifest xmlns:android="http://schemas.android.com/apk/res/android"
          package="string"
          android:sharedUserId="string"
          android:sharedUserLabel="string resource"
          android:versionCode="integer"
          android:versionName="string"
          android:installLocation=["auto" | "internalOnly" | "preferExternal"] >
    . . .
</manifest>
```

The <manifest> tag is the top-level tag for the entire ApplicationManifest.xml file and it must contain the <application> tag. Within the <manifest> tag, but outside the <application> tag, you can place the following tags: <instrumentation>, <permission>, <permission-group>, <permission-tree>, <uses-configuration> and <uses-permission>. We talk about these tags later on in the chapter.

The attributes are defined as follows:

- package - this attribute contains the package name for the application. As explained in a previous chapter, this attribute should be a reverse-domain name such as com.example.andapp1. This must be unique and you cannot change this name after you've published your application.
- android:sharedUserId - Normally, when your application is installed on an Android device, which is running a variant of the Linux operating system, it is automatically given a unique Linux user ID. However, if you have more than one application and they need to access each other's data, you can choose to force all of your application to have the user ID be the value of

this attribute effectively forcing the user ID to be the same for all of your applications.

- `android:sharedUserLabel` - a user-readable label associated with `android:sharedUserid`.
- `android:versionCode` - this is your internal version number of your application as an integer (no decimal places!). This is internal and is not shown to the users. If you've updated your app and want to load it to Google Play, you must up this number as well as modify the `android:versionName`.
- `android:versionName` - this is the version number shown to users. Since this is a string, it can contain periods to reflect, say, `major.minor.build.revision`.
- `android:installLocation` - this value can be set to one of the following values indicating where your application is installed on the device:
  - `internalOnly` - install the application on the internal storage only. Installation fails if there is not enough storage for the application. This is the default.
  - `auto` - similar to `internalOnly`, but will install on external storage if internal storage is full.
  - `preferExternal` - install application on external storage only. This may not be honored depending on the availability or amount of storage on the SDcard. Note that application databases are still installed on internal storage even if the application is installed on the external storage device!!

The `<uses-sdk>` Tag

```
<uses-sdk android:minSdkVersion="integer"
          android:targetSdkVersion="integer"
          android:maxSdkVersion="integer" />
```

The `<uses-sdk>` tag, contained within the `<manifest>` tag, allows you to indicate your application's compatibility with one or more versions of the Android platform as indicated by the Android API Level number. Note that, despite its name, it has nothing to do with the Android Software Development Kit (SDK)! Here is a list of the API Levels and Android Platform Version numbers:

Platform Version	API Level	VERSION_CODE	Notes
Android 4.0.3	16	ICE_CREAM_SANDWICH_MR1	Platform Highlights
Android 4.0, 4.0.1, 4.0.2	14	ICE_CREAM_SANDWICH	
Android 3.2	13	HONEYCOMB_MR2	
Android 3.1.x	12	HONEYCOMB_MR1	Platform Highlights
Android 3.0.x	11	HONEYCOMB	Platform Highlights
Android 2.3.4 Android 2.3.3	10	GINGERBREAD_MR1	Platform Highlights
Android 2.3.2 Android 2.3.1 Android 2.3	9	GINGERBREAD	
Android 2.2.x	8	FROYO	Platform Highlights
Android 2.1.x	7	ECLAIR_MR1	Platform Highlights
Android 2.0.1	6	ECLAIR_0_1	
Android 2.0	5	ECLAIR	
Android 1.6	4	DONUT	Platform Highlights
Android 1.5	3	CUPCAKE	Platform Highlights
Android 1.1	2	BASE_1_1	
Android 1.0	1	BASE	

The attributes are defined as follows:

- `android:minSdkVersion` - this attribute contains the minimum API Level that your application can run under. If you do not specify this, Android assumes API Level 1. If the user's device meets this minimum level, then your application will be installed on the device; otherwise, it will not be installed. Be forewarned that if you specify a lower API Level than your application can run under, your application may crash when executed! Always specify this attribute!!
- `android:targetSdkVersion` - this attribute designates the API Level that your application targets. This will default to `android:minSdkVersion` if not specified.
- `android:maxSdkVersion` - this attribute designated the maximum API Level that your application can run on. Note that this attribute is not recommended since higher API Levels are fully backward compatible.

The `<application>` Tag

```
<application android:allowTaskReparenting=["true" | "false"]
             android:backupAgent="string"
             android:debuggable=["true" | "false"]
             android:description="string resource"
             android:enabled=["true" | "false"]
             android:hasCode=["true" | "false"]
             android:hardwareAccelerated=["true" | "false"]
             android:icon="drawable resource"
             android:killAfterRestore=["true" | "false"]
             android:largeHeap=["true" | "false"]
             android:label="string resource"
             android:logo="drawable resource"
             android:manageSpaceActivity="string"
             android:name="string"
             android:permission="string"
             android:persistent=["true" | "false"]
             android:process="string"
             android:restoreAnyVersion=["true" | "false"]
             android:taskAffinity="string"
             android:theme="resource or theme"
             android:uiOptions=["none" | "splitActionBarWhenNarrow"] >
    . . .
</application>
```

The `<application>` tag, contained within the `<manifest>` tag, contains XML tags describing your activities, services, content providers, intents, and so on. The attributes in the `<application>` tag affect all of the items contained within it.

The attributes are defined as follows:

- `android:allowTaskReparenting` - this attribute is set to `false` by default indicating that activities can **NOT** move from the task that started them to the task they have an affinity for when the task is next brought to the front. Set to `true` if you would like to allow this.
- `android:backupAgent` - the name of the class that implements the application's backup agent (a subclass of the `BackupAgent` class). The value must be a fully qualified class name (such as `com.example.andapp1.MyBackupAgent`).

- `android:debuggable` - if set to `true`, indicates that the application can be debugged. This is set to `false` by default.
- `android:description` - User-readable text about the application, longer and more descriptive than the application label.
- `android:enabled` - indicates whether the Android system can instantiate components of the application. This is set to `true` by default.
- `android:hasCode` - indicates whether your application has any code or not. This is set to `true` by default. An application can safely set this value to `false` if it does not contain any code and only uses built-in component classes.
- `android:hardwareAccelerated` - indicates whether hardware-accelerated rendering is enabled for all activities and views within your application. This is set to `false` by default.
- `android:icon` - indicates the icon to use across the application (although, as you will see below, individual components can defined their own icon which overrides the application icon). This is not set by default, although you can reference a drawable such as `@drawable/icon`.
- `android:killAfterRestore` - indicates that the application should be killed after a full system restore has occurred. This is a rare event and most likely won't be needed by your application.
- `android:largeHeap` - indicates that your application's process should be created with a large Dalvik heap. Most likely, your application won't need this attribute.
- `android:label` - a user-readable label for the application (although, as you will see below, individual components can defined their own label which overrides the application label).
- `android:logo` - specifies a logo for the application and must be set as a reference to a drawable. The difference between `android:icon` and `android:logo` is the icon is used by the Launcher whereas the logo is used by the Action Bar.
- `android:manageSpaceActivity` - a fully qualified name of an `Activity` subclass that the system can launch to let users manage the memory occupied by the application on the device. This activity must have its own `<activity>` tag in the manifest.
- `android:name` - the fully qualified name of the `Application` subclass implemented for the application. This is most likely not needed and Android will instantiate the base `Application` class by default.
- `android:permission` - the name of a permission that clients must have in order to interact with the application. Applies to all of the application's components.
- `android:persistent` - indicates whether the application should remain running at all times. This is set to `false` by default and, most likely, should not be changed.
- `android:process` - Assuming that the `android:sharedUserId` is the same for two or more of your own applications, the value of this attribute is the name of the process under which your applications will run. By default, this is set to the value of the `package` attribute defined in the `<manifest>` tag.

235

- `android:restoreAnyVersion` - indicates whether the application's Backup Manager can restore old data even if supplanted by newer data. This is set to `false` by default.
- `android:taskAffinity` - By default, all activities within an application share the same affinity and is set to the value of the `package` attribute defined in the `<manifest>` tag.
- `android:theme` - a reference to a style resource defining a default theme for all activities in the application.
- `android:uiOptions` - indicates whether there are extra options for an activity's user-interface. Options are "`none`" or "`splitActionBarWhenNarrow`". The latter option adds a bar at the bottom of the screen to display action items in the ActionBar when constrained for horizontal space.

The `<activity>` Tag

```
<activity android:allowTaskReparenting=["true" | "false"]
          android:alwaysRetainTaskState=["true" | "false"]
          android:clearTaskOnLaunch=["true" | "false"]
          android:configChanges=["mcc", "mnc", "locale",
                              "touchscreen", "keyboard", "keyboardHidden",
                              "navigation", "screenLayout", "fontScale",
                              "uiMode","orientation", "screenSize",
                              "smallestScreenSize"]
          android:enabled=["true" | "false"]
          android:excludeFromRecents=["true" | "false"]
          android:exported=["true" | "false"]
          android:finishOnTaskLaunch=["true" | "false"]
          android:hardwareAccelerated=["true" | "false"]
          android:icon="drawable resource"
          android:label="string resource"
          android:launchMode=["multiple" | "singleTop" |
                              "singleTask" | "singleInstance"]
          android:multiprocess=["true" | "false"]
          android:name="string"
          android:noHistory=["true" | "false"]
          android:parentActivityName="string"
          android:permission="string"
          android:process="string"
          android:screenOrientation=["unspecified" | "user" | "behind" |
                              "landscape" | "portrait" |
                              "reverseLandscape" | "reversePortrait" |
                              "sensorLandscape" | "sensorPortrait" |
                              "sensor" | "fullSensor" | "nosensor"]
          android:stateNotNeeded=["true" | "false"]
          android:taskAffinity="string"
          android:theme="resource or theme"
          android:uiOptions=["none" | "splitActionBarWhenNarrow"]
          android:windowSoftInputMode=["stateUnspecified",
                              "stateUnchanged", "stateHidden",
                              "stateAlwaysHidden", "stateVisible",
                              "stateAlwaysVisible", "adjustUnspecified",
                              "adjustResize", "adjustPan"] >
    . . .
</activity>
```

The `<activity>` tag, contained within the `<application>` tag, contains XML tag describing an individual activity. If you do not define an activity within the manifest, then it will never be displayed by the application.

The attributes are defined as follows:

- `android:allowTaskReparenting` - this attribute is set to `false` by default indicating that activities can **NOT** move from the task that started them to the task they have an affinity for when the task is next brought to the front. Set to `true` if you would like to allow this.
- `android:alwaysRetainTaskState` - indicates whether the Android system can reset the task to its initial state. This is set to `false` by default. If set to true, Android will maintain the state and the user will be brought back into the application as if he never left it.
- `android:clearTaskOnLaunch` - all activities will be removed from the task if set to `true`. If set to `false`, the default value, the tasks will remain intact and the user is brought back to that activity when the application is brought to the front rather than being sent directly to the root activity.
- `android:configChanges` - this attribute takes a list of those configuration changes that the application will handle itself, such as the `orientation` configuration change which indicates that the device's orientation has changed. Normally, when a configuration change occurs, the activity is shutdown and restarted, but if specified in this attribute, the activity will not be shutdown and the `onConfigurationChanged()` method is called. More than one configuration can be handled and are separated by a vertical bar. For example, `android:configChanges="orientation|locale"`. Below is a list of accepted configuration changes:
  - "mcc" -- The IMSI mobile country code (MCC) has changed — a SIM has been detected and updated the MCC.
  - "mnc" -- The IMSI mobile network code (MNC) has changed — a SIM has been detected and updated the MNC.
  - "locale" -- The locale has changed — the user has selected a new language that text should be displayed in.
  - "touchscreen" -- The touchscreen has changed. (This should never normally happen.)
  - "keyboard" -- The keyboard type has changed — for example, the user has plugged in an external keyboard.
  - "keyboardHidden" -- The keyboard accessibility has changed — for example, the user has revealed the hardware keyboard.
  - "navigation" -- The navigation type (trackball/dpad) has changed. (This should never normally happen.)
  - "screenLayout" -- The screen layout has changed — this might be caused by a different display being activated.
  - "fontScale" -- The font scaling factor has changed — the user has selected a new global font size.
  - "uiMode" -- The user interface mode has changed — this can be caused when the user places the device into a desk/car dock or when the the night mode changes. See UiModeManager. Introduced in API Level 8.
  - "orientation" -- The screen orientation has changed — the user has rotated the device. Note: If your application targets API level 13 or higher (as declared by the minSdkVersion and targetSdkVersion attributes), then you should also declare the "screenSize"

237

configuration, because it also changes when a device switches between portrait and landscape orientations.

- "screenSize" -- The current available screen size has changed. This represents a change in the currently available size, relative to the current aspect ratio, so will change when the user switches between landscape and portrait. However, if your application targets API level 12 or lower, then your activity always handles this configuration change itself (this configuration change does not restart your activity, even when running on an Android 3.2 or higher device). Added in API level 13.
- "smallestScreenSize" -- The physical screen size has changed. This represents a change in size regardless of orientation, so will only change when the actual physical screen size has changed such as switching to an external display. A change to this configuration corresponds to a change in the smallestWidth configuration. However, if your application targets API level 12 or lower, then your activity always handles this configuration change itself (this configuration change does not restart your activity, even when running on an Android 3.2 or higher device). Added in API level 13.

- android:enabled - Set to true if the activity can be instantiated; otherwise, false.
- android:excludeFromRecents - Set this to true if you want the activity to be excluded from this list of recent applications. This is set to false by default.
- android:exported - Determines whether or not the activity can be launched by components of other applications. Set to true if it can be. If set to false, only the same application or application with the same user ID can launch the activity. The default value is determined if there is an intent-filter for the activity. If there is an intent-filter, the default is true; otherwise, false.
- android:finishOnTaskLaunch - If set to true, when the user re-launches the activity, the previous one is shutdown (finished). This is set to false by default.
- android:hardwareAccelerated - indicates whether hardware-accelerated rendering is enabled for all activities and views within your application. This is set to false by default.
- android:icon - indicates the icon to use for the activity. If this is not set by default, although you can reference a drawable such as @drawable/icon. If not set, then the application's icon is used instead.
- android:label - a user-readable label for the activity. If not set, the application's label is used instead.
- android:launchMode - contains one of four launch modes indicating to Android how the activity is to be launched. These modes are: standard, singleTop, singleTask, and singleInstance. Of the four, singleTask and single Instance are not recommended for general use. This is set to standard by default.

Use Cases	Launch Mode	Multiple Instances?	Comments
Normal launches for most activities	"standard"	Yes	Default. The system always creates a new instance of the activity in the target task and routes the intent to it.
	"singleTop"	Conditionally	If an instance of the activity already exists at the top of the target task, the system routes the intent to that instance through a call to its onNewIntent() method, rather than creating a new instance of the activity.
Specialized launches (not recommended for general use)	"singleTask"	No	The system creates the activity at the root of a new task and routes the intent to it. However, if an instance of the activity already exists, the system routes the intent to existing instance through a call to its onNewIntent() method, rather than creating a new one.
	"singleInstance"	No	Same as "singleTask", except that the system doesn't launch any other activities into the task holding the instance. The activity is always the single and only member of its task.

- `android:multiprocess` - Set to `true` if an instance of an activity can be launched into the process of the component that started it. This is set to `false` by default.
- `android:name` - the fully qualified name of the `Activity` subclass implemented for the activity. Normally, this should be a fully qualified name, but if it starts with a period, the value of the package attribute from the `<manifest>` tag is automatically prepended to this name to create the fully qualified name.
- `android:noHistory` - If set to `true`, the activity will be removed from the activity stack and finished when the user navigates away from it and it is no longer visible on the screen. Thus, the user will not be able to return to it, but will have to re-start the application. This is set to `false` by default.
- `android:parentActivityName` - indicates the class name of the logical parent of the activity. This helps to determines where to navigate to when the user presses the Up button on the Action Bar. When the programmer creates a new activity from within Eclipse, the hierarchical parent selection is used to set this attribute. Note, though, that this does not show up in the activity's XML.
- `android:permission` - the name of the permission that clients must have to launch the activity. If a caller of `startActivity()` or `startActivityForResult()` has not been granted the specified permission, its intent will not be delivered to the activity. If this is not set, the permission from the application is used instead.
- `android:process` - the name of the process in which the activity should run. Normally, all components of an application run in the default process created for the application. It has the same name as the application package. The `<application>` element's process attribute can set a different default for all components. But each component can override the

239

default, allowing you to spread your application across multiple processes. If the name assigned to this attribute begins with a colon (':'), a new process, private to the application, is created when it's needed and the activity runs in that process. If the process name begins with a lowercase character, the activity will run in a global process of that name, provided that it has permission to do so. This allows components in different applications to share a process, reducing resource usage.

- `android:screenOrientation` - specifies the orientation of the activity's display on the screen. See the `<uses-feature>` tag for additional information. The allowed options are:
    - "unspecified" - The default value. The system chooses the orientation. The policy it uses, and therefore the choices made in specific contexts, may differ from device to device.
    - "user" - The user's current preferred orientation.
    - "behind" - The same orientation as the activity that's immediately beneath it in the activity stack.
    - "landscape" - Landscape orientation (the display is wider than it is tall).
    - "portrait" - Portrait orientation (the display is taller than it is wide).
    - "reverseLandscape" - Landscape orientation in the opposite direction from normal landscape. Added in API level 9.
    - "reversePortrait" - Portrait orientation in the opposite direction from normal portrait. Added in API level 9.
    - "sensorLandscape" - Landscape orientation, but can be either normal or reverse landscape based on the device sensor. Added in API level 9.
    - "sensorPortrait" - Portrait orientation, but can be either normal or reverse portrait based on the device sensor. Added in API level 9.
    - "sensor" - The orientation is determined by the device orientation sensor. The orientation of the display depends on how the user is holding the device; it changes when the user rotates the device. Some devices, though, will not rotate to all four possible orientations, by default. To allow all four orientations, use "fullSensor".
    - "fullSensor" - The orientation is determined by the device orientation sensor for any of the 4 orientations. This is similar to "sensor" except this allows any of the 4 possible screen orientations, regardless of what the device will normally do (for example, some devices won't normally use reverse portrait or reverse landscape, but this enables those). Added in API level 9.
    - "nosensor" - The orientation is determined without reference to a physical orientation sensor. The sensor is ignored, so the display will not rotate based on how the user moves the device. Except for this distinction, the system chooses the orientation using the same policy as for the "unspecified" setting.
- `android:stateNotNeeded` - If `true`, the activity can be killed and restarted without the reference to its previous state. This is set to `false` by default. Normally, an activity's `onSaveInstanceState()` method is called in order to store the activity's state in a `Bundle` object which is subsequently passed into the `onCreate()` method when the activity is restarted.

- `android:taskAffinity` - See the `<application>` tag for more on this attribute.
- `android:theme` - See the `<application>` tag for more on this attribute.
- `android:uiOptions` - See the `<application>` tag for more on this attribute.
- `android:windowSoftInputMode` - this attribute indicates how the activity reacts when the on-screen soft keyboard is displayed:
  - "stateUnspecified" - The state of the soft keyboard (whether it is hidden or visible) is not specified. The system will choose an appropriate state or rely on the setting in the theme. This is the default setting for the behavior of the soft keyboard.
  - "stateUnchanged" - The soft keyboard is kept in whatever state it was last in, whether visible or hidden, when the activity comes to the fore.
  - "stateHidden" - The soft keyboard is hidden when the user chooses the activity — that is, when the user affirmatively navigates forward to the activity, rather than backs into it because of leaving another activity.
  - "stateAlwaysHidden" - The soft keyboard is always hidden when the activity's main window has input focus.
  - "stateVisible" - The soft keyboard is visible when that's normally appropriate (when the user is navigating forward to the activity's main window).
  - "stateAlwaysVisible" - The soft keyboard is made visible when the user chooses the activity — that is, when the user affirmatively navigates forward to the activity, rather than backs into it because of leaving another activity.
  - "adjustUnspecified" - It is unspecified whether the activity's main window resizes to make room for the soft keyboard, or whether the contents of the window pan to make the currentfocus visible on-screen. The system will automatically select one of these modes depending on whether the content of the window has any layout views that can scroll their contents. If there is such a view, the window will be resized, on the assumption that scrolling can make all of the window's contents visible within a smaller area. This is the default setting for the behavior of the main window.
  - "adjustResize" - The activity's main window is always resized to make room for the soft keyboard on screen.
  - "adjustPan" - The activity's main window is not resized to make room for the soft keyboard. Rather, the contents of the window are automatically panned so that the current focus is never obscured by the keyboard and users can always see what they are typing. This is generally less desirable than resizing, because the user may need to close the soft keyboard to get at and interact with obscured parts of the window.

The `<activity-alias>` Tag

```
<activity-alias android:enabled=["true" | "false"]
                android:exported=["true" | "false"]
                android:icon="drawable resource"
                android:label="string resource"
```

```
                android:name="string"
                android:permission="string"
                android:targetActivity="string" >
    . . .
</activity-alias>
```

The `<activity-alias>` tag, contained within the `<application>` tag, holds an alias for an activity, named by the `targetActivity` attribute. The target must be in the same application as the alias and it must be declared before the alias in the manifest. The alias presents the target activity as an independent entity. It can have its own set of intent filters, and they, rather than the intent filters on the target activity itself, determine which intents can activate the target through the alias and how the system treats the alias. For example, the intent filters on the alias may specify the "`android.intent.action.MAIN`" and "`android.intent.category.LAUNCHER`" flags, causing it to be represented in the application launcher, even though none of the filters on the target activity itself set these flags. With the exception of targetActivity, `<activity-alias>` attributes are a subset of `<activity>` attributes. For attributes in the subset, none of the values set for the target carry over to the alias. However, for attributes not in the subset, the values set for the target activity also apply to the alias.

The attributes for `<activity-alias>` are a subset of the `<activity>` tag, so we do not relist them here. The subset of the attributes is: `android:enabled`, `android:exported`, `android:icon`, `android:label`, `android:name`, `android:permission`, and `android:targetActivity`.

The `<meta-data>` Tag

```
<meta-data android:name="string"
           android:resource="resource specification"
           android:value="string" />
```

The `<meta-data>` tag, contained within one or more of the `<activity>`, `<activity-alias>`, `<service>` or `<receiver>` tags, contains a name-value pair for an item of additional, arbitrary data that can be supplied to the parent component. A component element can contain any number of `<meta-data>` subelements. The values from all of them are collected in a single `Bundle` object and made available to the component as the `PackageItemInfo.metaData` field. Ordinary values are specified through the `value` attribute. However, to assign a resource ID as the value, use the `resource` attribute instead. It is highly recommended that you avoid supplying related data as multiple separate `<meta-data>` entries. Instead, if you have complex data to associate with a component, store it as a resource and use the resource attribute to inform the component of its ID.

The attributes are defined as follows:

- `android:name` - this is a unique name for the item. To ensure its uniqueness, use a Java-style naming convention: "`com.example.andapp1.myactivity.MyName`".

- `android:value` - this is the value for `android:name`. You can retrieve the name/value pairs using the appropriate `Bundle` method: `getString()`, `getInt()`, `getBoolean()`, or `getFloat()`.
- `android:resource` - this is the a reference to a resource and the ID of the resource is assigned to the item. The ID can be retrieved by using `Bundle.getInt()`.

The `<intent-filter>` Tag

```
<intent-filter android:icon="drawable resource"
               android:label="string resource"
               android:priority="integer" >
    . . .
</intent-filter>
```

The `<intent-filter>` tag, contained within one or more of the `<activity>`, `<activity-alias>`, `<service>` or `<receiver>` tags, specifies the types of intents that an activity, service or broadcast receiver respond to. The subelements of the `<intent-filter>` are `<action>`, `<category>` and `<data>`. An intent filter declares the capabilities of its parent component — what an activity or service can do and what types of broadcasts a receiver can handle. It opens the component to receiving intents of the advertised type, while filtering out those that are not meaningful for the component.

We talk about `<action>`, `<category>` and `<data>` on subsequent pages.

The attributes are defined as follows:

- `android:icon` - an icon that represents the parent activity, service, or broadcast receiver when that component is presented to the user as having the capability described by the filter. Must be specified as a drawable and the default icon is pulled from the `<application>` tag.
- `android:label` - a user-readable label for the parent component. The default value is pulled from the `<application>` tag.
- `android:priority` - a priority number, higher numbers indicate higher priorities.
  - When an intent could be handled by multiple activities, Android considers only those with the highest priorities as potential targets for the intent.
  - The order in which broadcast receivers are executed, higher priorities are called first.

The `<action>` Tag

```
<action android:name="string" />
```

The `<action>` tag, contained in the `<intent-filter>` tag, specifies an action to an intent filter. This tag is required!!

The attributes are defined as follows:

- `android:name` - the name of the action beginning with
  `"android.intent.action."` and followed by the desired action such as
  `MAIN, WEB_SEARCH`, etc.

The `<category>` Tag

```
<category android:name="string" />
```

The `<category>` tag, contained in the `<intent-filter>` tag, specifies a category name to the intent filter. Unlike the `<action>` tag, this tag is not required.

The attributes are defined as follows:

- `android:name` - the name of the action beginning with
  `"android.intent.category."` and followed by the desired category such as `LAUNCHER`.

The `<data>` Tag

```
<data android:host="string"
      android:mimeType="string"
      android:path="string"
      android:pathPattern="string"
      android:pathPrefix="string"
      android:port="string"
      android:scheme="string" />
```

The `<data>` tag, contained in the `<intent-filter>` tag, adds a data specification to the intent filter. Unlike the `<action>` tag, this tag is not required. **You can have multiple `<data>` tags within a single `<intent-filter>`, but they all act on the single intent filter.** There are no default values to the attributes listed above.

The attributes are defined as follows:

- `android:host` - the host part of the URI authority. If you specify this attribute, you must also specify the `android:scheme` attribute.
- `android:mimeType` - the MIME media type such as `application/pdf`, `image/jpeg`, etc. You can specify an asterisk (*) for the sub-type: `image/*` indicating all image types.
- `android:path, android:pathPrefix, android:pathPattern` - indicates the path portion of the URI. The `path` attribute specifies a complete path that is matched against the complete path in an Intent object. The `pathPrefix` attribute specifies a partial path that is matched against only the initial part of the path in the Intent object. The `pathPattern` attribute specifies a complete path that is matched against the complete path in the Intent object, but it can contain the following wildcards:
  - An asterisk ('*') matches a sequence of 0 to many occurrences of the immediately preceding character

244

- A period followed by an asterisk (".*") matches any sequence of 0 to many characters.
- `android:port` - the port part of a URI authority. This attribute is meaningful only if the `android:scheme` and `android:host` attributes are also specified for the filter.
- `android:scheme` - The scheme part of a URI. This is the minimal essential attribute for specifying a URI; at least one scheme attribute must be set for the filter, or none of the other URI attributes are meaningful. A scheme is specified without the trailing colon (for example, `http` rather than `http:`). If the filter has a data type set (the `mimeType` attribute) but no `scheme`, the `content:` and `file:` schemes are assumed.

The `<provider>` Tag

```
<provider android:authorities="list"
          android:enabled=["true" | "false"]
          android:exported=["true" | "false"]
          android:grantUriPermissions=["true" | "false"]
          android:icon="drawable resource"
          android:initOrder="integer"
          android:label="string resource"
          android:multiprocess=["true" | "false"]
          android:name="string"
          android:permission="string"
          android:process="string"
          android:readPermission="string"
          android:syncable=["true" | "false"]
          android:writePermission="string" >
    . . .
</provider>
```

The `<provider>` tag, contained in the `<application>` tag, declares a content provider. You need to declare only those content providers that you develop as part of your application, not those developed by others that your application uses. Note that content providers use the `content://` scheme. We discuss content providers later in the book.

The attributes are defined as follows:

- `android:authorities` - A list of one or more URI authorities that identify data under the purview of the content provider. Multiple authorities are listed by separating their names with a semicolon. To avoid conflicts, authority names should use a Java-style naming convention (such as `com.example.provider.cartoonprovider`). Typically, it's the name of the `ContentProvider` subclass.
- `android:enabled` - If set to `true`, indicates that the content provider can be instantiated. If set to `false`, it cannot be instantiated. This is set to `true` by default.
- `android:exported` - if set to `true`, the content provider can be used by components of other applications. If set to `false`, the content provider is available only to the same application or applications with the same user ID. This is set to `true` by default.
- `android:grantUriPermissions` - whether or not those who ordinarily would not have permission to access the content provider's data can be

granted permission to do so, temporarily overcoming the restriction imposed by the `readPermission, writePermission,` and `permission` attributes — `true` if permission can be granted, and `false` if not. If `true`, permission can be granted to any of the content provider's data. If `false`, permission can be granted only to the data subsets listed in `<grant-uri-permission>` subelements, if any. The default value is `false`.

- `android:icon` - an icon representing the content provider. This must be a reference to a drawable. By default, the `<application>` icon is used.
- `android:initOrder` - the order in which the content provider should be instantiated, relative to other content providers hosted by the same process. When there are dependencies among content providers, setting this attribute for each of them ensures that they are created in the order required by those dependencies. The value is a simple integer, with higher numbers being initialized first.
- `android:label` - a user-readable label for the content provider. By default, the `<application>` label is used.
- `android:multiprocess` - Whether or not an instance of the content provider can be created in every client process — `true` if instances can run in multiple processes, and "false" if not. The default value is `false`. Normally, a content provider is instantiated in the process of the application that defined it. However, if this flag is set to `true`, the system can create an instance in every process where there's a client that wants to interact with it, thus avoiding the overhead of interprocess communication.
- `android:name` - the name of the class that implements the content provider. This must be a fully qualified name. However, if the name begins with a period, the value of the package attribute from the `<manifest>` tag is prepended to it.
- `android:permission` - the name of the permission that clients must have to read or write the content provider's data.
- `android:process` - See the `<application>` tag for more on this attribute.
- `android:readPermission` - a permission that clients must have to query the content provider.
- `android:syncable` - set to `true` if the data under the content provider's control is to be synchronized with data on a server.
- `android:writePermission` - a permission that clients must have to make changes to the data controlled by the content provider.

The **<receiver>** Tag

```
<receiver android:enabled=["true" | "false"]
          android:exported=["true" | "false"]
          android:icon="drawable resource"
          android:label="string resource"
          android:name="string"
          android:permission="string"
          android:process="string" >
    . . .
</receiver>
```

The `<receiver>` tag, contained in the `<application>` tag, declares a broadcast receiver, a subclass of `BroadcastReceiver` class, as one of the application's components. Broadcast receivers enable applications to receive intents that are broadcast by the system or by other applications, even when other components of the application are not running.

The attributes are defined as follows:

- `android:enabled` - If set to `true`, indicates that the broadcast receiver can be instantiated. If set to `false`, it cannot be instantiated. This is set to `true` by default. This attribute must be set to true in **both** the `<application>` and `<receiver>` tag in order for the broadcast receiver to be instantiated.
- `android:exported` - if set to `true`, the broadcast receiver can be used by components of other applications. If set to `false`, the broadcast receiver is available only to the same application or applications with the same user ID. This is set to `true` by default.
- `android:icon` - an icon representing the broadcast receiver. This must be a reference to a drawable. By default, the `<application>` icon is used.
- `android:label` - a user-readable label for the broadcast receiver. By default, the `<application>` label is used.
- `android:name` - the name of the class that implements the broadcast receiver. This must be a fully qualified name. However, if the name begins with a period, the value of the package attribute from the `<manifest>` tag is prepended to it.
- `android:permission` - the name of a permission that broadcasters must have to send a message to the broadcast receiver. If this attribute is not set, the permission set by the `<application>` element's permission attribute applies to the broadcast receiver. If neither attribute is set, the receiver is not protected by a permission.
- `android:process` - See the `<application>` tag for more on this attribute.

The `<service>` Tag

```
<service android:enabled=["true" | "false"]
      android:exported=["true" | "false"]
      android:icon="drawable resource"
      android:isolatedProcess=["true" | "false"]
      android:label="string resource"
      android:name="string"
      android:permission="string"
      android:process="string" >
   . . .
</service>
```

The `<service>` tag, contained in the `<application>` tag, declares a service, a subclass of `Service` class, as one of the application's components. Unlike activities, services lack a visual user interface. They're used to implement long-running background operations or a rich communications API that can be called by other applications. All services must be represented by `<service>` elements in the manifest file. Any that are not declared there will not be seen by the system and will never be run.

The attributes are defined as follows:

- `android:enabled` - If set to `true`, indicates that the service can be instantiated. If set to `false`, it cannot be instantiated. This is set to `true` by default. This attribute must be set to true in **both** the `<application>` and `<service>` tag in order for the service to be instantiated.
- `android:exported` - if set to `true`, the service can be used by components of other applications. If set to `false`, the service is available only to the same application or applications with the same user ID. This is set to `true` by default.
- `android:icon` - an icon representing the service. This must be a reference to a drawable. By default, the `<application>` icon is used.
- `android:isolatedProcess` - if set to `true`, this service will run under a special process that is isolated from the rest of the system and has no permissions of its own. The only communication with it is through the Service API (binding and starting).
- `android:label` - a user-readable label for the service. By default, the `<application>` label is used.
- `android:name` - the name of the class that implements the service. This must be a fully qualified name. However, if the name begins with a period, the value of the package attribute from the `<manifest>` tag is prepended to it.
- `android:permission` - The name of a permission that that an entity must have in order to launch the service or bind to it. If a caller of `startService()`, `bindService()`, or `stopService()`, has not been granted this permission, the method will not work and the Intent object will not be delivered to the service. If this attribute is not set, the permission set by the `<application>` element's permission attribute applies to the service. If neither attribute is set, the service is not protected by a permission.
- `android:process` - See the `<application>` tag for more on this attribute.

The `<grant-uri-permission>` Tag

```
<grant-uri-permission android:path="string"
                      android:pathPattern="string"
                      android:pathPrefix="string" />
```

The `<grant-uri-permission>` tag, contained in the `<provider>` tag, specifies which data subsets of the parent content provider permission can be granted for. Data subsets are indicated by the path part of a `content:` URI. (The authority part of the URI identifies the content provider.) Granting permission is a

248

way of enabling clients of the provider that don't normally have permission to access its data to overcome that restriction on a one-time basis. If a content provider's `grantUriPermissions` attribute is `true`, permission can be granted for any the data under the provider's purview. However, if that attribute is `false`, permission can be granted only to data subsets that are specified by this element. A provider can contain any number of `<grant-uri-permission>` elements. Each one can specify only one path (only one of the three possible attributes).

The attributes are defined as follows:

- `android:path`, `android:pathPrefix`, `android:pathPattern` - A path identifying the data subset or subsets that permission can be granted for. The `path` attribute specifies a complete path; permission can be granted only to the particular data subset identified by that path. The `pathPrefix` attribute specifies the initial part of a path; permission can be granted to all data subsets with paths that share that initial part. Because '\' is used as an escape character when the string is read from XML (before it is parsed as a pattern), you will need to double-escape: For example, a literal '*' would be written as "*" and a literal '\' would be written as "\\\\". This is basically the same as what you would need to write if constructing the string in Java code. The `pathPattern` attribute specifies a complete path, but one that can contain the following wildcards:
  - An asterisk ('*') matches a sequence of 0 to many occurrences of the immediately preceding character.
  - A period followed by an asterisk (".*") matches any sequence of 0 to many characters.

The `<instrumentation>` Tag

```
<instrumentation android:functionalTest=["true" | "false"]
                 android:handleProfiling=["true" | "false"]
                 android:icon="drawable resource"
                 android:label="string resource"
                 android:name="string"
                 android:targetPackage="string" />
```

The `<instrumentation>` tag, contained in the `<manifest>` tag, declares an `Instrumentation` class that enables you to monitor an application's interaction with the system. The instrumentation object is instantiated before any of the application's components.

The attributes are defined as follows:

- `android:functionalTest` - If set to `true`, indicates that the instrumentation class should run as a functional test. This is set to `false` by default.
- `android:handleProfiling` - whether or not the Instrumentation object will turn profiling on and off — `true` if it determines when profiling starts and stops, and `false` if profiling continues the entire time it is running. A value of `true` enables the object to target profiling at a specific set of operations. The default value is `false`.

- `android:icon` - an icon representing the `Instrumementation` class. This must be a reference to a drawable.
- `android:label` - a user-readable label for the `Instrumentation` class.
- `android:name` - the name of the `Instrumentation` subclass. This must be a fully qualified name. However, if the name begins with a period, the value of the package attribute from the `<manifest>` tag is prepended to it.
- `android:targetPackage` - specifies the application that the `Instrumentation` object will run against. An application is identified by the package name assigned in its manifest file by the `<manifest>` element.

The `<permission>` Tag

```
<permission android:description="string resource"
            android:icon="drawable resource"
            android:label="string resource"
            android:name="string"
            android:permissionGroup="string"
            android:protectionLevel=["normal" | "dangerous" |
                            "signature" | "signatureOrSystem"] />
```

The `<permission>` tag, contained in the `<manifest>` tag, declares a security permission that can be used to limit access to specific components or features of this or other applications.

The attributes are defined as follows:

- `android:description` - A user-readable description of the permission, longer and more informative than the label. It may be displayed to explain the permission to the user — for example, when the user is asked whether to grant the permission to another application. This attribute must be set as a reference to a string resource; unlike the label attribute, it cannot be a raw string.
- `android:icon` - an icon representing the permission. This must be a reference to a drawable.
- `android:label` - a user-readable label for the permission.
- `android:name` - the name of the permission. This must be a fully qualified name. However, if the name begins with a period, the value of the package attribute from the `<manifest>` tag is prepended to it.
- `android:permissionGroup` - assigns this permission to a group. The value of this attribute is the name of the group, which must be declared with the `<permission-group>` element in this or another application. If this attribute is not set, the permission does not belong to a group.
- `android:protectionLevel` - characterizes the potential risk implied in the permission and indicates the procedure the system should follow when determining whether or not to grant the permission to an application requesting it. The value can be set to one of the following strings:
    - "normal" - The default value. A lower-risk permission that gives requesting applications access to isolated application-level features, with minimal risk to other applications, the system, or the user. The system automatically grants this type of permission to a requesting

250

application at installation, without asking for the user's explicit approval (though the user always has the option to review these permissions before installing).

- "dangerous" - A higher-risk permission that would give a requesting application access to private user data or control over the device that can negatively impact the user. Because this type of permission introduces potential risk, the system may not automatically grant it to the requesting application. For example, any dangerous permissions requested by an application may be displayed to the user and require confirmation before proceeding, or some other approach may be taken to avoid the user automatically allowing the use of such facilities.
- "signature" - A permission that the system grants only if the requesting application is signed with the same certificate as the application that declared the permission. If the certificates match, the system automatically grants the permission without notifying the user or asking for the user's explicit approval.
- "signatureOrSystem" - A permission that the system grants only to applications that are in the Android system image or that are signed with the same certificates as those in the system image. Please avoid using this option, as the signature protection level should be sufficient for most needs and works regardless of exactly where applications are installed. The "signatureOrSystem" permission is used for certain special situations where multiple vendors have applications built into a system image and need to share specific features explicitly because they are being built together.

The `<permission-group>` Tag

```
<permission-group android:description="string resource"
                  android:icon="drawable resource"
                  android:label="string resource"
                  android:name="string" />
```

The `<permission-group>` tag, contained in the `<manifest>` tag, declares a name for a logical grouping of related permissions. Individual permissions join the group through the `permissionGroup` attribute of the `<permission>` element. Members of a group are presented together in the user interface. Note that this element does not declare a permission itself, only a category in which permissions can be placed. See the `<permission>` element for element for information on declaring permissions and assigning them to groups.

The attributes are defined as follows:

- `android:description` - A user-readable text that describes the group. The text should be longer and more explanatory than the label. This attribute must be set as a reference to a string resource. Unlike the label attribute, it cannot be a raw string.
- `android:icon` - an icon representing the permission. This must be a reference to a drawable.
- `android:label` - a user-readable label for the group.

- `android:name` - the name of the group. This is the name that can be assigned to a `<permission>` element's `<permissionGroup>` attribute.

The `<permission-tree>` Tag

```
<permission-tree android:icon="drawable resource"
                 android:label="string resource" ]
                 android:name="string" />
```

The `<permission-tree>` tag, contained in the `<manifest>` tag, declares the base name for a tree of permissions. The application takes ownership of all names within the tree. It can dynamically add new permissions to the tree by calling PackageManager.addPermission(). Names within the tree are separated by periods ('.'). For example, if the base name is `com.example.project.taxes`, permissions like the following might be added: `com.example.project.taxes.CALCULATE`, `com.example.project.taxes.deductions.MAKE_SOME_UP`, `com.example.project.taxes.deductions.EXAGGERATE`. Note that this element does not declare a permission itself, only a namespace in which further permissions can be placed. See the `<permission>` element for information on declaring permissions.

The attributes are defined as follows:

- `android:icon` - an icon representing all the permissions in the tree. This must be a reference to a drawable.
- `android:label` - a user-readable label for the group.
- `android:name` - specifies the name that's at the base of the permission tree. It serves as a prefix to all permission names in the tree. Java-style scoping should be used to ensure that the name is unique. The name must have more than two period-separated segments in its path — for example, `com.example.base` is OK, but `com.example` is not.

The `<compatible-screens>` Tag

```
<compatible-screens>
    <screen android:screenSize=["small" | "normal" | "large" | "xlarge"]
            android:screenDensity=["ldpi" | "mdpi" | "hdpi" | "xhdpi"] />
    ...
</compatible-screens>
```

The `<compatible-screens>` tag, contained in the `<manifest>` tag, specifies each screen configuration with which the application is compatible. Only one instance of the `<compatible-screens>` element is allowed in the manifest, but it can contain multiple `<screen>` elements. Each `<screen>` element specifies a specific screen size-density combination with which the application is compatible. The Android system does not read the `<compatible-screens>` manifest element (neither at install-time nor at runtime). This element is informational only and may be used by external services (such as Google Play) to better understand the application's compatibility with specific screen configurations and enable filtering for users. Any screen configuration that is not declared in this element is a screen with which the application is not compatible. Thus, external services (such as Google Play) should not provide the application to devices with such screens. You should not normally need to provide this tag. If you want to set only a minimum screen size for your application, then you should use the `<supports-screens>` element. For example, if you want your application to be available only for large and xlarge screen devices, the `<supports-screens>` element allows you to declare that your application does not support small and normal screen sizes. External services (such as Google Play) will filter your application accordingly. You can also use the `<supports-screens>` element to declare whether the system should resize your application for different screen sizes. See the Android documentation for more on this tag.

The `<supports-screens>` Tag

```
<supports-screens android:resizeable=["true"| "false"]
                  android:smallScreens=["true" | "false"]
                  android:normalScreens=["true" | "false"]
                  android:largeScreens=["true" | "false"]
                  android:xlargeScreens=["true" | "false"]
                  android:anyDensity=["true" | "false"]
                  android:requiresSmallestWidthDp="integer"
                  android:compatibleWidthLimitDp="integer"
                  android:largestWidthLimitDp="integer"/>
```

The `<supports-screens>` tag, contained in the `<manifest>` tag, lets you specify the screen sizes your application supports and enable screen compatibility mode for screens larger than what your application supports. It's important that you always use this element in your application to specify the screen sizes your application supports.

The attributes are defined as follows:

- `android:resizeable` - **(deprecated)** indicates whether the application is resizeable for different screen sizes. This attribute is true, by default. If set false, the system will run your application in screen compatibility mode on large screens.
- `android:smallScreens` - indicates whether the application supports smaller screen form-factors. A small screen is defined as one with a smaller aspect ratio than the "normal" (traditional HVGA) screen. An application that does not support small screens will not be available for small screen devices from external services (such as Google Play), because there is little the platform can do to make such an application work on a smaller screen. This is `true` by default.
- `android:normalScreens` - indicates whether an application supports the "normal" screen form-factors. Traditionally this is an HVGA medium density screen, but WQVGA low density and WVGA high density are also considered to be normal. This attribute is `true` by default.
- `android:largeScreens` - indicates whether the application supports larger screen form-factors. A large screen is defined as a screen that is significantly larger than a "normal" handset screen, and thus might require some special care on the application's part to make good use of it, though it may rely on resizing by the system to fill the screen. The default value for this actually varies between some versions, so it's better if you explicitly

declare this attribute at all times. Beware that setting it `false` will generally enable screen compatibility mode.

- `android:xlargeScreens` - indicates whether the application supports extra large screen form-factors. An xlarge screen is defined as a screen that is significantly larger than a "large" screen, such as a tablet (or something larger) and may require special care on the application's part to make good use of it, though it may rely on resizing by the system to fill the screen. The default value for this actually varies between some versions, so it's better if you explicitly declare this attribute at all times. Beware that setting it `false` will generally enable screen compatibility mode.

- `android:anyDensity` - indicates whether the application includes resources to accommodate any screen density. For applications that support Android 1.6 (API level 4) and higher, this is `true` by default and you should not set it `false` unless you're absolutely certain that it's necessary for your application to work. The only time it might be necessary to disable this is if your app directly manipulates bitmaps (see the Supporting Multiple Screens document for more information).

- `android:requiresSmallestWidthDp` - specifies the minimum smallestWidth required. This attribute is not used by the Android system. See the documentation for more on this attribute.

- `android:compatibleWidthLimitDp` - This attribute allows you to enable screen compatibility mode as a user-optional feature by specifying the maximum "smallest screen width" for which your application is designed. If the smallest side of a device's available screen is greater than your value here, users can still install your application, but are offered to run it in screen compatibility mode. By default, screen compatibility mode is disabled and your layout is resized to fit the screen as usual, but a button is available in the system bar that allows the user to toggle screen compatibility mode on and off.

- `android:largestWidthLimitDp` - This attribute allows you to force-enable screen compatibility mode by specifying the maximum "smallest screen width" for which your application is designed. If the smallest side of a device's available screen is greater than your value here, the application runs in screen compatibility mode with no way for the user to disable it. If your application is compatible with all screen sizes and its layout properly resizes, you do not need to use this attribute. Otherwise, you should first consider using the `android:compatibleWidthLimitDp` attribute. You should use the `android:largestWidthLimitDp` attribute only when your application is functionally broken when resized for larger screens and screen compatibility mode is the only way that users should use your application.

The `<supports-gl-texture>` Tag

```
<supports-gl-texture android:name="string" />
```

The `<supports-gl-texture>` tag, contained in the `<manifest>` tag, declares a single GL texture compression format that is supported by the application. An application "supports" a GL texture compression format if it is capable of providing texture assets that are compressed in that format, once the application is installed on a device. The application can provide the compressed assets locally, from inside the .apk, or it can download them from a server at runtime. See the documentation for more on this attribute.

The attributes are defined as follows:

- `android:name` - specifies a single GL texture compression format supported by the application, as a descriptor string. Common descriptor values are listed in the table below:
    - GL_OES_compressed_ETC1_RGB8_texture - Ericsson texture compression. Specified in OpenGL ES 2.0 and available in all Android-powered devices that support OpenGL ES 2.0.
    - GL_OES_compressed_paletted_texture - Generic paletted texture compression.
    - GL_AMD_compressed_3DC_texture - ATI 3Dc texture compression.
    - GL_AMD_compressed_ATC_texture - ATI texture compression. Available on devices running Adreno GPU, including HTC Nexus One, Droid Incredible, EVO, and others. For widest compatibility, devices may also declare a <supports-gl-texture> element with the descriptor GL_ATI_texture_compression_atitc.
    - GL_EXT_texture_compression_latc - Luminance alpha texture compression.
    - GL_EXT_texture_compression_dxt1 - S3 DXT1 texture compression. Supported on devices running Nvidia Tegra2 platform, including Motorala Xoom, Motorola Atrix, Droid Bionic, and others.
    - GL_EXT_texture_compression_s3tc - S3 texture compression, nonspecific to DXT variant. Supported on devices running Nvidia Tegra2 platform, including Motorala Xoom, Motorola Atrix, Droid Bionic, and others. If your application requires a specific DXT variant, declare that descriptor instead of this one.
    - GL_IMG_texture_compression_pvrtc - PowerVR texture compression. Available in devices running PowerVR SGX530/540 GPU, such as Motorola DROID series; Samsung Galaxy S, Nexus S, and Galaxy Tab; and others.

The `<uses-configuration>` Tag

```
<uses-configuration android:reqFiveWayNav=["true" | "false"]
                 android:reqHardKeyboard=["true" | "false"]
                 android:reqKeyboardType=["undefined" | "nokeys" | "qwerty" |
                                    "twelvekey"]
                 android:reqNavigation=["undefined" | "nonav" | "dpad" |
                                    "trackball" | "wheel"]
                 android:reqTouchScreen=["undefined" | "notouch" | "stylus" |
                                    "finger"] />
```

The <uses-configuration> tag, contained in the <manifest> tag, indicates what hardware and software features the application requires. For example, an application might specify that it requires a physical keyboard or a particular navigation device, like a trackball. The specification is used to avoid installing the application on devices where it will not work.

The attributes are defined as follows:

- `android:reqFiveWayNav` - whether or not the application requires a five-way navigation control — "true" if it does, and "false" if not. A five-way control is one that can move the selection up, down, right, or left, and also provides a way of invoking the current selection. It could be a D-pad (directional pad), trackball, or other device.
- `android:reqHardKeyboard` - whether or not the application requires a hardware keyboard — "true" if it does, and "false" if not.
- `android:reqKeyboardType` - the type of keyboard the application requires, if any at all. This attribute does not distinguish between hardware and software keyboards. If a hardware keyboard of a certain type is required, specify the type here and also set the `reqHardKeyboard` attribute to "true". It must be one of the following:
  - "undefined" - The application does not require a keyboard. (A keyboard requirement is not defined.) This is the default value.
  - "nokeys" - The application does not require a keyboard.
  - "qwerty" - The application requires a standard QWERTY keyboard.
  - "twelvekey" - The application requires a twelve-key keypad, like those on most phones — with keys for the digits from 0 through 9 plus star (*) and pound (#) keys.
- `android:reqNavigation` - the navigation device required by the application, if any. The value must be one of the following strings:
  - "undefined" - The application does not require any type of navigation control. (The navigation requirement is not defined.) This is the default value.
  - "nonav" - The application does not require a navigation control.
  - "dpad" - The application requires a D-pad (directional pad) for navigation.
  - "trackball" - The application requires a trackball for navigation.
  - "wheel" - The application requires a navigation wheel.
- `android:reqTouchScreen` - the type of touch screen the application requires, if any at all. The value must be one of the following strings:
  - "undefined" - The application doesn't require a touch screen. (The touch screen requirement is undefined.) This is the default value.
  - "notouch" - The application doesn't require a touch screen.
  - "stylus" - The application requires a touch screen that's operated with a stylus.
  - "finger" - The application requires a touch screen that can be operated with a finger.

The `<uses-feature>` Tag

```
<uses-feature android:name="string"
              android:required=["true" | "false"]
```

```
android:glEsVersion="integer" />
```

The `<uses-feature>` tag, contained in the `<manifest>` tag, declares a single hardware or software feature that is used by the application. The purpose of a `<uses-feature>` declaration is to inform any external entity of the set of hardware and software features on which your application depends. The element offers a required attribute that lets you specify whether your application requires. You must specify each feature in a separate `<uses-feature>` element.

The attributes are defined as follows:

- `android:name` - specifies a single hardware or software feature used by the application, as a descriptor string. See the documentation for more on this attribute.
- `android:required` - boolean value that indicates whether the application requires the feature specified in `android:name`.
  - When you declare `android:required="true"` for a feature, you are specifying that the application cannot function, or is not designed to function, when the specified feature is not present on the device.
  - When you declare `android:required="false"` for a feature, it means that the application prefers to use the feature if present on the device, but that it is designed to function without the specified feature, if necessary.
- `android:glEsVersion` - The OpenGL ES version required by the application. The higher 16 bits represent the major number and the lower 16 bits represent the minor number. For example, to specify OpenGL ES version 2.0, you would set the value as "0x00020000". To specify OpenGL ES 2.1, if/when such a version were made available, you would set the value as "0x00020001". An application should specify at most one `android:glEsVersion` attribute in its manifest. If it specifies more than one, the `android:glEsVersion` with the numerically highest value is used and any other values are ignored. If an application does not specify an `android:glEsVersion` attribute, then it is assumed that the application requires only OpenGL ES 1.0, which is supported by all Android-powered devices. An application can assume that if a platform supports a given OpenGL ES version, it also supports all numerically lower OpenGL ES versions. Therefore, an application that requires both OpenGL ES 1.0 and OpenGL ES 2.0 must specify that it requires OpenGL ES 2.0. An application that can work with any of several OpenGL ES versions should only specify the numerically lowest version of OpenGL ES that it requires. (It can check at run-time whether a higher level of OpenGL ES is available.)

The **`<uses-library>`** Tag

```
<uses-library android:name="string"
              android:required=["true" | "false"] />
```

The `<uses-library>` tag, contained in the `<application>` tag, specifies a shared library that the application must be linked against. This element tells the system to include the library's code in the class loader for the package. All of the android packages (such as `android.app`, `android.content`, `android.view`,

257

and `android.widget`) are in the default library that all applications are automatically linked against. However, some packages (such as `maps`) are in separate libraries that are not automatically linked. Consult the documentation for the packages you're using to determine which library contains the package code.

The attributes are defined as follows:

- `android:name` - the name of the library. The name is provided by the documentation for the package you are using. An example of this is "android.test.runner", a package that contains Android test classes.
- `android:required` - boolean value that indicates whether the application requires the library specified by `android:name`. To check for a library, you can use reflection to determine if a particular class is available. The default is `true`.
    - "true": The application does not function without this library. The system will not allow the application on a device that does not have the library.
    - "false": The application can use the library if present, but is designed to function without it if necessary. The system will allow the application to be installed, even if the library is not present. If you use "false", you are responsible for checking at runtime that the library is available.

The `<uses-permission>` Tag

```
<uses-permission android:name="string" />
```

The `<uses-permission>` tag, contained in the `<manifest>` tag, requests a permission that the application must be granted in order for it to operate correctly. **Permissions are granted by the user when the application is installed, not while it's running.** A list of permissions defined by the base platform can be found in the documentation for `android.Manifest.permission`.

The attributes are defined as follows:

- `android:name` - the name of the permission. It can be a permission defined by the application with the `<permission>` element, a permission defined by another application, or one of the standard system permissions, such as "`android.permission.CAMERA`" or "`android.permission.READ_CONTACTS`". As these examples show, a permission name typically includes the package name as a prefix.

Using the Android Manifest GUI Interface

Rather than editing the `AndroidManifest.xml` file directly, you can use the manifest GUI interface from within Eclipse. Below is a screenshot of the GUI interface:

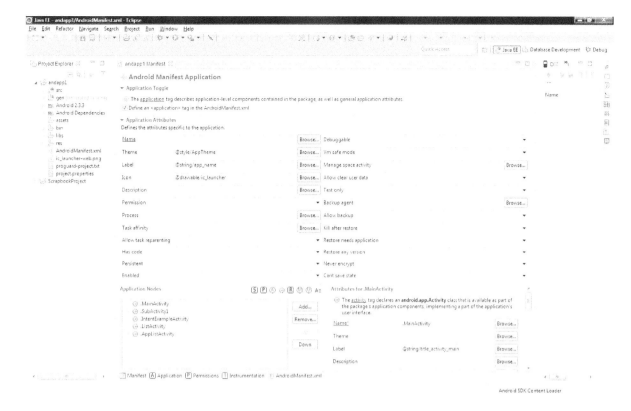

As you can see, there are several tabs at the bottom of the screen: Manifest, Application, Permissions, Instrumentation and AndroidManifest.xml. The last tab is just the XML file itself and not the GUI interface.

In the screenshot above, we are working on the Application tab and you will see the familiar attributes such as name, theme, label, etc. At the bottom left, you will see a list of your classes such as `MainActivity`, `SubActivity1`, etc. When you click on each of these classes, the bottom right displays a list of attributes associated with each class such as name, theme, label, description, etc.

As you can guess, each possible entry in the `AndroidManifest.xml` file can be inserted via the GUI interface. For myself, I prefer to enter the XML in the manifest by hand.

Summary

In this chapter, we introduced the many tags and attributes available to the application manifest. Either you can enter these in the `AndroidManifest.xml` file by hand, or you can use the GUI interface available from Eclipse.

Chapter 13: Android Menus

Overview

In this chapter, we learn how to create menus in Android. There are two varieties of menu *display* depending on the version of Android running on the device. For Android 3.0/API Level 11 or higher, your menu items appear within the Action Bar at the top of the device's screen. Prior to Android 3.0, your menus appear on the bottom of the device's screen and are shown via pushing the menu button. The display type is handled by the Android system.

Regardless of how the menu is displayed, there are three *types* of menus in Android:

1. Options Menus - these menus are the primary collection of menu items for an activity. If you think of an entire desktop application's user interface as an activity, the collection of menus (File, Edit, ...) constitutes the options menus. For Android 3.0/API Level 11 or higher, these menus are displayed in the Action Bar. Prior to Android 3.0, your menus appear on the bottom of the device's screen and are shown via pushing the menu button.
2. Context Menus - these menus appear when the user long-clicks (or long-touches) the screen, view or widget. For example, if you long-click (or long-touch) on the Android Home screen, the Add to Home Screen menu appears. Whereas an *options menu* appears at the bottom of the device's screen or on the Action Bar, a *context menu* appears as a floating menu.
3. Popup Menus - these menus display a list of items in a vertical list that's anchored to the view that invoked the menu.

Finally, you can create menus either using XML or via code. You'll notice that when you create a new activity from the Eclipse GUI, an XML file appears in the `res\menu` folder with the same name as that appearing in the `res\layout` folder. Also, additional menu-specific code appears in your activity's code. For example,

```
@Override
public boolean onCreateOptionsMenu(Menu menu) {
 getMenuInflater().inflate(R.menu.activity_main, menu);
 return true;
}
```

Here is the XML file (`res\menu\activity_main.xml`) for the menu:

```
<menu xmlns:android="http://schemas.android.com/apk/res/android">
    <item android:id="@+id/menu_settings"
          android:title="@string/menu_settings"
          android:orderInCategory="100" />
</menu>
```

We discuss how to create menus using menu resource XML files, how to handle the click event for menu items and, finally, how to change menus programmatically.

The Menu Resource XML File

As stated above, when you add a new layout (located in the `res\layout` folder) a menu resource XML file is automatically created in the `res\menu` folder with the same name. Setting up a menu using the menu resource file allows you to display options menus, context menus and popup menus as described in the last section.

Just like the Android manifest, there are several XML tags and attributes associated with the menu resource file. We describe these below:

The **`<menu>`** Tag

```
<menu xmlns:android="http://schemas.android.com/apk/res/android">
```

The `<menu>` tag, the root node, defines an application menu (options, context or submenu). Each `<menu>` tag can contain one or more `<item>` and `<group>` tags as described below.

The attributes are defined as follows:

- `xmlns:android` - the XML namespace which must be set as shown above.

The **`<item>`** Tag

```
<item android:id="@[+][package:]id/resource_name"
      android:title="string"
      android:titleCondensed="string"
      android:icon="@[package:]drawable/drawable_resource_name"
      android:onClick="method name"
      android:showAsAction=["ifRoom" | "never" | "withText" | "always" |
                           "collapseActionView"]
      android:actionLayout="@[package:]layout/layout_resource_name"
      android:actionViewClass="class name"
      android:actionProviderClass="class name"
      android:alphabeticShortcut="string"
      android:numericShortcut="string"
      android:checkable=["true" | "false"]
      android:checked=["true" | "false"]
      android:visible=["true" | "false"]
      android:enabled=["true" | "false"]
      android:menuCategory=["container" | "system" | "secondary" |
                           "alternative"]
      android:orderInCategory="integer" />
```

The `<item>` tag, contained in the `<menu>` tag, defines the menu items to appear in the menu. You can have any number of `<item>` tags. You can create a submenu by inserting a `<menu>` tag within an `<item>` tag, but you are only permitted one submenu; that is, you **cannot** have submenus of submenus.

The attributes are defined as follows:

- `android:id` - a unique resource id in the typical form of `@+id/name`.
- `android:title` - the menu title

- `android:titleCondensed` - when `android:title` is too long, the value of this attribute is used instead.
- `android:icon` - a drawable image to be used as the menu icon. Note that not every situation allows an icon to be displayed.
- `android:onClick` - the name of the method in code to be called when the item is clicked. Note that your method must accept a single parameter of type `MenuItem`. This method takes precedence over the `onOptionsItemSelected` method which is called when the `android:onClick` attribute is not defined for this menu item. Note that this attribute is available as of Android 3.0 and forward!
- `android:showAsAction` - determines how the menu item is displayed in an Action Bar. This attribute takes on one of the following values:
  - "ifRoom" - Only place this item in the Action Bar if there is room for it.
  - "withText" - Also include the title text (defined by `android:title`) with the action item. You can include this value along with one of the others as a flag set, by separating them with a pipe |.
  - "never" - Never place this item in the Action Bar.
  - "always" - Always place this item in the Action Bar. Avoid using this unless it's critical that the item always appear in the action bar. Setting multiple items to always appear as action items can result in them overlapping with other UI in the action bar.
  - "collapseActionView" - The action view associated with this action item (as declared by `android:actionLayout` or `android:actionViewClass`) is collapsible.
- `android:actionLayout` - a layout to use as the Action view.
- `android:actionViewClass` - a fully-qualified class name for the `View` to use as the action view.
- `android:actionProviderClass` - a fully-qualified class name for the `ActionProvider` to use as the action view.
- `android:alphabeticShortcut` - a character for the alphabetic shortcut key
- `android:numericShortcut` - a number for the numeric shortcut key
- `android:checkable` - set to true if the item is checkable; false, otherwise
- `android:checked` - set to true if the item is checked; false, otherwise
- `android:visible` - set to true if the item is visible; false, otherwise
- `android:enabled` - set to true if the item is enabled; false, otherwise
- `android:menuCategory` - a value corresponding to the `Menu`'s `CATEGORY_*` constants which defines the item's priority. Valid values are:
  - "container" - For items that are part of a container.
  - "system" - For items that are provided by the system.
  - "secondary" - For items that are user-supplied secondary (infrequently used) options.
  - "alternative" - For items that are alternative actions on the data that is currently displayed.
- `android:orderInCategory` - an integer representing the importance of the menu item within a group.

The `<group>` Tag

```
<group android:id="@[+][package:]id/resource name"
       android:checkableBehavior=["none" | "all" | "single"]
       android:visible=["true" | "false"]
       android:enabled=["true" | "false"]
       android:menuCategory=["container" | "system" | "secondary" |
                             "alternative"]
       android:orderInCategory="integer" >
```

The `<group>` tag, contained in the `<menu>` tag, defines a group of menu items that share a particular trait. This tag contains one or more `<item>` tags.

The attributes are defined as follows:

- `android:id` - a unique resource id in the typical form of `@+id/name`.
- `android:checkableBehavior` - the type of checkable behavior for the group. Valid values are:
    - "none" - not checkable
    - "all" - all items can be checked (using checkboxes)
    - "single" - only one item can be checked (using radio buttons)
- `android:visible` - set to true if the group is visible; false, otherwise
- `android:enabled` - set to true if the group is enabled; false, otherwise
- `android:menuCategory` - a value corresponding to the `Menu`'s `CATEGORY_*` constants which defines the group's priority. Valid values are:
    - "container" - For items that are part of a container.
    - "system" - For items that are provided by the system.
    - "secondary" - For items that are user-supplied secondary (infrequently used) options.
    - "alternative" - For items that are alternative actions on the data that is currently displayed.
- `android:orderInCategory` - the default order of the items within the category.

Creating an Options Menu using a Menu Resource XML File

Let's create a menu for our `MainActivity`. Recall that the layout is located in `res\layout\activity_main.xml` and the Eclipse-generated menu is located in `res\menu\activity_main.xml`. Here is what this menu resource looks like now:

```
<menu xmlns:android="http://schemas.android.com/apk/res/android">
    <item android:id="@+id/menu_settings"
          android:title="@string/menu_settings"
          android:orderInCategory="100" />
</menu>
```

Note that this menu contains a single item with the menu title set to Settings (in the `strings.xml` file). Here is what this looks like when we click on the menu button when our application is running:

263

As you see, the single menu item Settings appears...how lonely...let's add some more menu items to our menu resource. Note that I downloaded the icons from the website `www.dryicons.com`. These icons are displayed using `android:icon` which accepts the name of a drawable. We discuss drawables later in the book.

```xml
<menu xmlns:android="http://schemas.android.com/apk/res/android">

    <item android:id="@+id/menu_import"
        android:title="@string/menu_import"
        android:titleCondensed="@string/menu_import_tc"
        android:icon="@drawable/up_arrow"
        android:orderInCategory="100" />

    <item android:id="@+id/menu_settings"
        android:title="@string/menu_settings"
        android:titleCondensed="@string/menu_settings_tc"
        android:icon="@drawable/settings"
        android:orderInCategory="200" />

    <item android:id="@+id/menu_rateus"
        android:title="@string/menu_rateus"
        android:titleCondensed="@string/menu_rateus_tc"
        android:icon="@drawable/star"
        android:orderInCategory="300" />

    <item android:id="@+id/menu_help"
        android:title="@string/menu_help"
        android:titleCondensed="@string/menu_help_tc"
        android:icon="@drawable/help"
        android:orderInCategory="400" />

    <item android:id="@+id/menu_about"
        android:title="@string/menu_about"
        android:titleCondensed="@string/menu_about_tc"
        android:icon="@drawable/light_bulb"
        android:orderInCategory="500" />

    <item android:id="@+id/menu_contact"
```

264

```
        android:title="@string/menu_contact"
        android:titleCondensed="@string/menu_contact_tc"
        android:icon="@drawable/edit"
        android:orderInCategory="600" />

    <item android:id="@+id/menu_showManual"
        android:title="@string/menu_showManual"
        android:titleCondensed="@string/menu_showManual_tc"
        android:icon="@drawable/pages"
        android:orderInCategory="700" />

    <item android:id="@+id/menu_search"
        android:title="@string/menu_search"
        android:titleCondensed="@string/menu_search_tc"
        android:icon="@drawable/magic_wand"
        android:orderInCategory="800" />

    <item android:id="@+id/menu_goToWebsite"
        android:title="@string/menu_goToWebsite"
        android:titleCondensed="@string/menu_goToWebsite_tc"
        android:icon="@drawable/world"
        android:orderInCategory="900" />

</menu>
```

Here is what this looks like in the emulator:

Note that some of the menu items are not shown because Android only displays the first five and then adds a More button. When you click the More button, this is what will be displayed:

As you can see, the remaining items are displayed. Note that the `android:title` is displayed above, but the `android:titleCondensed` is displayed in the previous image.

Next, let's make a submenu and see what that looks like. Let's change the "Go to Our Website" to a submenu with different selections. Here is what that XML looks like now (note that the title was changed to "Go To Sites" in `strings.xml`):

```
<item android:id="@+id/submenu_goToWebsite"
      android:title="@string/submenu_goTo"
      android:titleCondensed="@string/submenu_goTo_tc"
      android:icon="@drawable/world"
      android:orderInCategory="900">
 <menu>
  <item android:id="@+id/menu_goToGoogle"
        android:title="@string/submenu_google"
        android:titleCondensed="@string/submenu_google_tc"
        android:icon="@drawable/world"
        android:orderInCategory="910" />
  <item android:id="@+id/menu_goToYahoo"
        android:title="@string/submenu_yahoo"
        android:titleCondensed="@string/submenu_yahoo_tc"
        android:icon="@drawable/world"
        android:orderInCategory="920" />
  <item android:id="@+id/menu_goToOurSite"
        android:title="@string/submenu_goToOurWebsite"
        android:titleCondensed="@string/submenu_goToOurWebsite_tc"
        android:icon="@drawable/world"
        android:orderInCategory="930" />
 </menu>
</item>
```

Looking at the emboldened XML above, you see that we include the `<menu>` tag again. This signals that we want a submenu to appear. Within the `<menu>` tag, we include three submenu items using the `<item>` tag. As you can see below,

266

when you click on the *Go to Sites* menu item, the submenu appears with the title *Go To Sites* and our three menu items listed below it.

Next, let's add a checkbox to our menu. Note that when you click on the Menu button, no checkboxes or radio buttons will be displayed there, but they will be when you click on More or use a submenu. Here is the XML code with an additional `<item>` for our menu that includes the `android:checkable` attribute:

```
<item android:id="@+id/menu_checkbox"
    android:title="@string/menu_checkbox"
    android:titleCondensed="@string/menu_checkbox_tc"
    android:icon="@drawable/magic_wand"
    android:checkable="true"
    android:orderInCategory="1000" />
```

Here is what the checkbox looks like on our menu item:

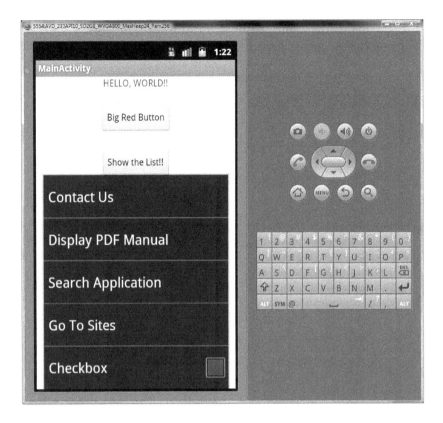

Note that if you want to have the checkbox checked, include the attribute `android:checked="true"` in the XML. One issue is that, if you click the Checkbox menu item, the checkbox indicator never changes state. You can handle this in code, as we will see later on in this chapter.

Next, to create a series of radio buttons, add the following XML to the submenu:

```
<group android:id="@+id/radiobuttons"
       android:checkableBehavior="single"
       android:orderInCategory="850">
  <item android:id="@+id/chocolate"
        android:title="@string/chocolate" />
  <item android:id="@+id/vanilla"
        android:title="@string/vanilla" />
  <item android:id="@+id/strawberry"
        android:title="@string/strawberry" />
</group>
```

Handling Item Clicks in Code

You can handle click events in code by either using the `android:onClick` attribute (for Android 3.0 or higher) or by overriding the `onOptionsItemSelected` method in your activity. To use the `android:onClick` attribute, place the attribute in your XML as shown below:

```
<item android:id="@+id/menu_checkbox"
      android:title="@string/menu_checkbox"
      android:titleCondensed="@string/menu_checkbox_tc"
      android:icon="@drawable/magic_wand"
      android:checkable="true"
      android:onClick="myClickHandler"
      android:orderInCategory="1000" />
```

268

In your activity's code, code `myClickHandler` with a `MenuItem` as the sole parameter:

```
public void myClickHandler(MenuItem item) {

 if (item.isChecked()) {
  item.setChecked(false);
 }
 else {
  item.setChecked(true);
 }

}
```

If you are using a version of Android prior to Android 3.0, then you cannot use `android:onClick` attribute (it won't appear in the tips in Eclipse). Regardless of what version of Android you are targeting, you can use the `onOptionsItemSelected` method with a `MenuItem` as the sole parameter:

```
@Override
public boolean onOptionsItemSelected(MenuItem item) {

 switch(item.getItemId()) {

  case R.id.menu_checkbox:
   Log.d("APP_MSGS","checkbox");
   if (item.isChecked()) {
    item.setChecked(false);
   }
   else {
    item.setChecked(true);
   }
   return true;

  case R.id.chocolate:
   Log.d("APP_MSGS","chocolate");
   if (item.isChecked()) {
    item.setChecked(false);
   }
   else {
    item.setChecked(true);
   }
   return true;

  default:
   return super.onOptionsItemSelected(item);

 }

}
```

Take note of the switch statement in the code above. This allows you to target multiple clicks as opposed to a single click when using the `android:onClick` attribute. Also, make sure that you execute the superclass's `onOptionsItem Selected` method when there is no matching switch statement. If you don't want to include a default in your switch statement, then place the code `return super.onOptionsItemSelected(item);` at the end of the code block.

269

Creating a Context Menu

A context menu is a small menu that appears when you long-click over a view such as a `ListView` or `GridView`, but you are not limited to those two views. For example, when you long-click on the Calculator, a content menu appears, as shown below, with the menu items Edit text, Select word, Select all and Input method.

There are two display types for context menus:
1. A *Floating context menu* is similar to the menu shown in the image above.
2. A *Contextual action bar*, appearing in Android 3.0 or greater, is a rectangular bar shown at the top of the device's screen. This rectangular bar contains one or more icons representing the desired actions, such as those shown in the floating context menu above.

In the example below, we create a floating context menu for a `TextView` (with an ID of `textView1`) appearing in our activity. Here is what our activity looks like now with the `TextView` appearing in the middle of the screen:

We register the view in the `onCreate` method by using the `registerForContextView` method to indicate that the TextView can display a context menu:

```
TextView oTxtVw = (TextView) findViewById(R.id.textView1);
registerForContextMenu(oTxtVw);
```

Next, we override the `onCreateContextMenu` method which is responsible for inflating our context menu (here, located in the XML file `res\menu\txtvw1_context_menu`):

```
@Override
public void onCreateContextMenu(ContextMenu menu,
                                View v,
                                ContextMenuInfo menuInfo) {
  super.onCreateContextMenu(menu, v, menuInfo);
  MenuInflater inflater = getMenuInflater();
  inflater.inflate(R.menu.txtvw1_context_menu, menu);
}
```

Here is what `res\menu\txtvw1_context_menu` looks like:

```
<?xml version="1.0" encoding="utf-8"?>
<menu xmlns:android="http://schemas.android.com/apk/res/android" >

 <item android:id="@+id/txtvw1cmClear"
       android:title="@string/txtvw1cmClear"
       android:icon="@drawable/magic_wand"
       android:orderInCategory="100" />

 <item android:id="@+id/txtvw1cmReset"
       android:title="@string/txtvw1cmReset"
       android:icon="@drawable/light_bulb"
       android:orderInCategory="200" />
```

```
</menu>
```

Finally, here is the context menu looks like when we long-click over the `TextView` view:

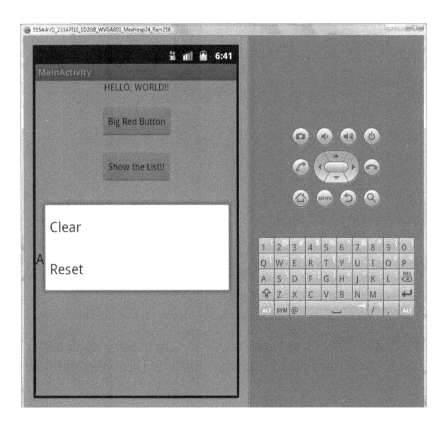

Next, we have to add click events so that when a user clicks either `Clear` or `Reset`, an action occurs. Note that this is very similar to handling click events for the options menu, but instead of coding for the `onOptionsItemSelected` method, you code for the `onContextItemSelected` for each of the items in the context menu:

```
@Override
public boolean onContextItemSelected(MenuItem item) {

 TextView oTxtVw = (TextView) findViewById(R.id.textView1);

 switch (item.getItemId()) {

  case R.id.txtvw1cmClear:
   oTxtVw.setText("");
   return true;

  case R.id.txtvw1cmReset:
   oTxtVw.setText("Sometown, Somestate USA");
   return true;

   default:
    return super.onContextItemSelected(item);

 }

}
```

When you click on `Reset`, the `TextView` is set to *Sometown, Somestate USA* whereas clicking on `Clear` will clear the `TextView`.

Creating a Popup Menu

A popup menu is a similar to a context menu except that it is anchored to a View and displays either above or below the anchor. As we've seen, floating context menus just appear in the middle of the screen. Popup menus are available as of Android 3.0 or greater.

Summary

In this chapter, we discussed how to create a variety of menus for your activities.

Chapter 14: Saving State: Bundle, SharedPreference and PreferenceActivity

Overview

In this chapter, we learn how to save the state of your application or activity including any user-modifiable preferences.

By using SharedPreferences, you can save several pieces of information in a key-value pair and then recall them when you wish. SharedPreferences can act across an entire application or a particular activity.

The `Bundle` is similar to SharedPreferences in that it saves key-value pairs, but it is normally used when your application is paused and then subsequently resumed. The `Bundle` parameter is passed by the Android System into the `onCreate` method where you can pull out the key-value pairs and programmatically restore the application's state to how it looked before the application was paused.

If your application has several options, you may want to create a *settings* page to allow the user to modify these options. You do this by creating a PreferenceActivity which is designed in a similar fashion to an activity's layout.

Although we don't talk about them in this chapter, two additional ways for you to store information is in a SQLite database or on the device's storage media (in internal memory or the external SD card) via file access.

Using the `Bundle` Parameter

When an application is about to be killed by the Android system, the method `onSaveInstanceState()` is called being passed a `Bundle` parameter. This method gives you time to save important data into the `Bundle` before the application is killed. When the application is started again, the `onCreate()` method is called being passed the `Bundle` parameter that was passed to `onSaveInstanceState()`. It's at this point you can pull out the data from the `Bundle` and restore your application to an appropriate state. Note that you should check if the `Bundle` is `null` before attempting to pull out data from it.

Now, a `Bundle` is an object in its own right and has several methods associated with it. For example, if you want to store an integer into the `Bundle`, you use the `putInt()` method; if you want to store a text string, you use the `putString()` method; and so on. When you subsequently want to pull the data back, you use the `getInt()` and `getString()` methods, respectively.

Note that a `Bundle` can handle only primitive (i.e., non-object) data types such as integers, strings, floating point numbers, etc. as well as arrays of primitives.

As mentioned in the Overview, a `Bundle` saves data in key-value pairs; that is, you must give a name to the value you want to save, and that name is the key. For example, to save the value of Pi as well as a stock symbol the user was viewing before the application was killed, store it in the `Bundle` with code similar to this:

```
@Override
protected void onSaveInstanceState(Bundle outState) {

 //Send debugging info to the LogCat
 Log.d("MYAPPTAG","IN ONSAVEINSTANCESTATE!");

 //Save the value of PI to the Bundle
 outState.putDouble("PI", Math.PI);

 //Save the Stock Symbol the user was perusing
 outState.putString("SYMBOL", "GOOG");

 //Call the superclass!
 super.onSaveInstanceState(outState);

}
```

Don't forget to include a call to the superclass in `onSaveInstanceState()` as shown above. The superclass is responsible for saving the appearance of each view (i.e., control) so that you don't have to.

When it's time to retrieve the data from the `Bundle`, you can code for it like this:

```
@Override
public void onCreate(Bundle savedInstanceState) {
 super.onCreate(savedInstanceState);
 setContentView(R.layout.activity_main);

 //Retrieve data from a non-null Bundle
 if (savedInstanceState != null) {

   //Send debugging info to the LogCat
   Log.d("MYAPPTAG","IN IF STATEMENT IN ONCREATE!");

   double PI_SAVED = savedInstanceState.getDouble("PI ");
   String SYMBOL_SAVED = savedInstanceState.getString("SYMBOL ");

   //Substitute the SYMBOL_SAVED for the text in textView1
   TextView oTxtVw = (TextView) findViewById(R.id.textView1);
   oTxtVw.setText(SYMBOL_SAVED);

 }
 ...snip...
```

Notice that, for debugging purposes, I placed a `Log.d()` method in both the `onSaveInstanceState()` and `onCreate()` methods in order to ensure that both methods are being called. Recall from the last chapter that output from `Log.d()` goes into the LogCat.

Now, when you run your application in debug mode, you'll notice that you never see the debugging message `IN IF STATEMENT IN ONCREATE!` in the LogCat. This is because your activity is not truly being killed by the Android system. Therefore, the `Bundle` is always `null` when `onCreate()` is called.

One way to work around this is to use the Android *Dev Tools App* installed by default on the device (whether a physical device or on an emulator). Among other things, the Dev Tools App allows you to tell the Android system to destroy an activity once it is stopped. This is very useful to help check if the `Bundle` is working as you expect it to.

275

To start the Dev Tools App on the device, click on the Application Launcher, and then click on the Dev Tools icon, as shown below:

Once the Dev Tools app starts, you will see the following screen:

Click on Development Settings, and the following screen will appear:

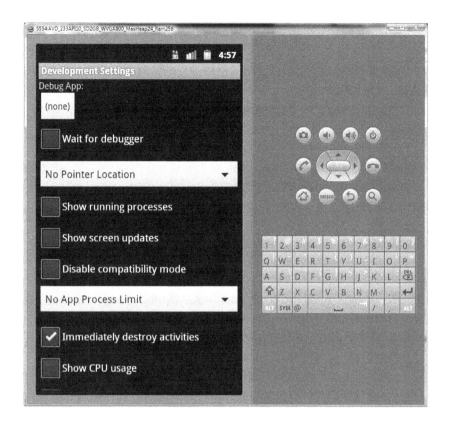

In order test the `Bundle`, ensure that the checkbox to the left of the text *Immediately destroy activities* is checked (by default, it is not checked). Next, to test if the `Bundle` is working properly, go back and start your application. When you move to another activity in your application, you should see the LogCat message `IN ONSAVEINSTANCESTATE!`. Navigate back to the original activity by clicking the Back button, you will see the LogCat message `IN IF STATEMENT IN ONCREATE!`. Below is an image of my LogCat:

You'll notice that in the code for `onCreate()`, I included code to update the `TextView` appearing in the activity with the stock symbol I've chosen.

To sum up, in order to test the `Bundle`, make sure to use the Dev Tools App installed on the device and ensure that you are running in debug mode to capture any output from the `Log.d()` method to the LogCat. Since the setting *Immediately destroy activities* remains checked even across emulator sessions, it's probably a good idea to uncheck it when you are done debugging!

Using `SharedPreferences`

As a programmer, it may seem like the `Bundle` is an excellent way to save user preferences or settings. Unfortunately, a `Bundle` is only a short-term solution. If the user forcibly kills the application or restarts the device, the `Bundle` is set to `null` and all of your key-value pairs are lost.

SharedPreferences allows you to save key-value pairs which persist across user sessions (even if the application is killed). SharedPreferences are available in the `SharedPreferences` class in the `android.content` package.

There are two methods you can call to return a `SharedPreferences` object to your code:

1. If you only need preferences specific to a *particular activity*, you can use the `getPreferences()` method (part of the `android.app.Activity` class).
2. If you need preferences for your *entire application*, you can use the `getSharedPreferences()` method (part of the `android.content.Context` class). This method allows you to pass a group name of the preferences such as StockSelections, FriendNames, etc. Multiple key-value pairs can then be stored within the group allowing you to keep one logical grouping of preferences separate from another logical grouping of preferences.

Regardless of the method you choose, you will have to pass the desired mode into the method:

1. `Context.MODE_PRIVATE` - the shared preferences file can only be accessed by your application (or applications sharing the same user ID). This is the default mode.
2. `Context.MODE_WORLD_READABLE` - all applications, not just yours, are allowed to read from your shared preferences.
3. `Context.MODE_WORLD_WRITABLE` - all applications, not just yours, are allowed to write to your shared preferences.

Normally, you will choose `Context.MODE_PRIVATE`. Below, I've created a method called `SaveSettings()` which writes out a stock symbol to the activity's shared preferences:

```
private void SaveSettings() {

  //Start editing mode on the SharedPreferences object.
  SharedPreferences.Editor oSPEditor =
                        getPreferences(Context.MODE_PRIVATE).edit();


  //Add in a key-value pair using the appropriate put* method.
  oSPEditor.putString("SYMBOL_SAVED", "MSFT");

  //Commit the changes to the SharedPreferences object.
  oSPEditor.commit();

}
```

Note that the first step is to return a `SharedPreferences.Editor` object by using the `edit()` method on the `SharedPreferences` object returned by the `getPreferences()` method. Note that in the code above I did not create a variable to hold the `SharedPreferences` object since it is not used by itself, but only in conjunction with the `SharedPreferences.Editor` object. Be aware that it is the `edit()` method that allows you to add in key-value pairs. Next, we use the `putString()` method to add in the key `SYMBOL_SAVED` along with its value `MSFT`. Finally, we use the `commit()` method to save the shared preferences. This is similar to using COMMIT when updating a database with changes.

Although not shown, we call the `SaveSettings()` method above from within the `onStop()` activity lifecycle method for our activity.

Next, below is how we read back our shared preferences when the application starts:

```
@Override
public void onCreate(Bundle savedInstanceState) {

  super.onCreate(savedInstanceState);
  setContentView(R.layout.activity_main);

  //Retrieve the SharedPreferences
  String SYMBOL_SAVED =
          getPreferences(Context.MODE_PRIVATE).getString("SYMBOL_SAVED","????");

  //Update the text view.
  TextView oTxtVw = (TextView) findViewById(R.id.textView1);
  oTxtVw.setText(SYMBOL_SAVED);
  ...snip...
```

The bold code above is responsible for reading in the value associated with the `SYMBOL_SAVED` key. Note that if the key `SYMBOL_SAVED` is not found, the value will default to `????`, but you can set that to whatever makes sense for your application.

I run my test application and then I forcibly kill it from the Android Settings app. When I restart the application, the `TextView` is filled in with MSFT indicating that the shared preferences worked correctly.

Finally, if you decide to use the `getSharedPreferences()` method instead of the `getPreferences()` method, you must pass the preferences group name to it first. For example, `SaveSetting()` now looks like this:

```
private void SaveSettings() {

  //Start editing mode on the SharedPreferences object.
  SharedPreferences.Editor oSPEditor =
                  getPreferences("MY_PREF_GROUP",Context.MODE_PRIVATE).edit();

  //Add in a key-value pair using the appropriate put* method.
  oSPEditor.putString("SYMBOL_SAVED", "MSFT");

  //Commit the changes to the SharedPreferences object.
  oSPEditor.commit();

}
```

Retrieving the shared preferences looks like this:

```
String SYMBOL_SAVED =
    getSharedPreferences("MY_PREF_GROUP",
                    Context.MODE_PRIVATE).getString("SYMBOL_SAVED", "????");
```

A list of the `put*` methods can be found in the `SharedPreferences.Editor` documentation page while a list of the `get*` methods can be found in `SharedPreferences` documentation page.

Using `Map<K,V>` with SharedPreferences

Now, if you would like to store your `SharedPreferences` key/value pairs in a `Map<>` construct for use later on, you can use the `getAll()` method on the `SharedPreferences` object (**not** the editor!) to do this. Here is an example:

```
//Get the SharedPreferences object
SharedPreferences oSP =
                getSharedPreferences("EQUITYYO_PORTFOLIO",Context.MODE_PRIVATE);

//When using Map<>, place the SuppressWarnings "unchecked" annotation
//to tell Java that the generic Map will work with no problems.
@SuppressWarnings("unchecked")
Map<String, String> oSP_ALL = (Map<String, String>) oSP.getAll();

//Initialize the final String
String sAllKeys = "Symbols: ";

//Loop for each element in the Map to get the keys using the keyset() method.
for(String sKey : oSP_ALL.keySet()) {
 sAllKeys = sAllKeys + "-" + sKey;
}
```

In the code above, we are using the `Map<K,V>` generic class. This requires two generic parameters:

1. K - the datatype for the Keys.
2. V - the datatype for the Values.

In our case, K would be set to `String` since our `SharedPreferences` keys are Strings. Similar for the values.

Note that we are using the `@SuppressWarnings("unchecked")` Java annotation. As explained by Jon Skeet on StackOverflow.com: *Sometimes Java generics just doesn't let you do what you want to, and you need to effectively tell the compiler that what you're doing really will be legal at execution time.*

Please see the `values()` method to retrieve the values instead of the keys as shown above using the `keySet()` method.

Using `PreferenceActivity`

So far, we've talked about the `Bundle` and `SharedPreferences`. Recall that the key-value pairs in a `Bundle` are only available for the duration of the application

280

and are destroyed once your application is killed. On the other hand, `SharedPreferences` remain around even after your application is killed, but `SharedPreferences` are used by the programmer and are not usually accessed by a user during his/her interaction with the application.

In order to allow your application's users to change application settings, you can create an activity specifically designed for that purpose. Instead of subclassing the `Activity` class, you subclass the `PreferenceActivity` class. If you've ever seen the Settings page for the Android Browser (shown below), you've seen an example of a `PreferenceActivity`.

Preference activities allow for a *subset* of the views available to activities and are limited to checkboxes (`CheckBoxPreference` class), input/edit text boxes (`EditTextPreference` class), spinners (`ListPreference` class), multiple selection (`MultiSelectListPreference` class) and two-state toggles (`SwitchPreference` class). Note that `SharedPreferences`, humorously enough, is the method a `PreferenceActivity` uses to store its data. Note that the `MultiSelectListPreference` and `SwitchPreference` classes are not available until Android 3.0.

Just like activities, you will need to create an XML file containing the layout of your preferences. In order to do this, you'll need a class that is a subclass of the `PreferenceActivity` class, and you'll need a way to display your preference activity (e.g. menu item, button, etc.). Unlike activities, you need to place your preference activity layout file in the `res\xml` folder in your application. Note that the `xml` folder does not appear under `res` by default, so you'll have to create it by right-clicking on the `res` folder and clicking New...Folder.

Recall that for activities, you can create your layout in XML and preview it in the Graphical Layout in Eclipse. Unfortunately, there is no equivalent graphical interface for preference activities.

Here is an example XML file (called `res\xml\preferences.xml`) which contains a checkbox, spinner and input box:

```xml
<?xml version="1.0" encoding="utf-8"?>
<PreferenceScreen xmlns:android="http://schemas.android.com/apk/res/android">
 <PreferenceCategory android:title="Internet Protocol Preferences">
    <CheckBoxPreference android:key="PREF_FTP_HTTP"
                        android:title="FTP or HTTP?"
                        android:summaryOn="HTTP Protocol will be used"
                        android:summaryOff="FTP Protocol will be used"
                        android:defaultValue="true"/>
 </PreferenceCategory>

 <PreferenceCategory android:title="Sign-On Preferences">
    <EditTextPreference android:key="PREF_UID"
                        android:title="System Userid"
                        android:summary="Enter your System password"
                        android:defaultValue=""/>

    <EditTextPreference android:key="PREF_PWD"
                        android:title="System Password"
                        android:summary="Enter your System password"
                        android:defaultValue=""/>
 </PreferenceCategory>

 <PreferenceCategory android:title="Threading Preference">
    <ListPreference android:key="PREF_NTHREADS"
                        android:title="Single- or Multi-Threaded"
                        android:summary="Select your desired threading option"
                        android:entries="@array/thread_entries"
                        android:entryValues="@array/thread_values"
                        android:defaultValue="1"/>
 </PreferenceCategory>

</PreferenceScreen>
```

Note that the XML file starts with the traditional `<?xml version="1.0" encoding="utf-8" ?>` tag.

Next, an entire PreferenceActivity begins with the `<PreferenceScreen>` tag and ends with the `</PreferenceScreen>` tag.

Next, there are a series of `<PreferenceCategory>` tags, one for each logical grouping of user-modifiable settings. Take note that each `<PreferenceCategory>` tag has the `android:title` attribute. It is the value of this attribute that is displayed across the width of the device's screen indicating that one or more related preferences are to follow.

Within each `<PreferenceCategory>` tag, you have one or more preference-related views (such as the checkbox, etc.). Take note that `<CheckBoxPreference>`, `<EditText Preference>` and `<ListPreference>` all contain the attributes `android:title`, `android:summary`, and `android:key`. The `android:title` is displayed in a large font whereas the `android:summary` is displayed in a small font. The `android:key` is used as the key into the `SharedPreferences`.

282

Note that the `<CheckboxPreference>` has two additional attributes: `android:summaryOn` and `android:summaryOff`. Both of these allow you to specify summary text (the small font) but when the checkbox is checked, `android:summaryOn` is displayed and when the checkbox is not checked, `android:summaryOff` is displayed instead. If you don't wish to use these two attributes, you can use `android:summary` instead.

In order to display your preferences on the device's screen, you need to modify the subclass of the `PreferenceActivity` class. One way to create this class is to add a new activity as describe earlier in the book. You will have to delete the associated layout file since you won't need it. Another way is to add just the class is to right-click over the package name (in our example, `com.example.andapp1`) and click on New...Class.

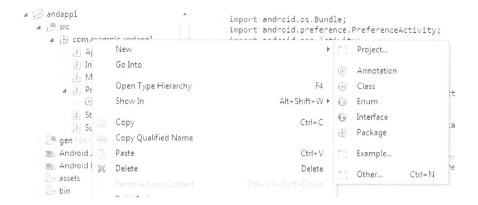

Once the New Java Class dialog appears, fill in the name of the class and the superclass (as shown below). Click Finish to create the class. Note that you will still need to create the associated XML file (`res\xml\preferences.xml`) containing the layout of the preferences (as shown in the XML above).

Within the new class, you should code something similar to this:

```
package com.example.andapp1;

import android.os.Bundle;
import android.preference.PreferenceActivity;

public class PrefsActivity extends PreferenceActivity {

 @Override
 public void onCreate(Bundle savedInstanceState) {
  super.onCreate(savedInstanceState);

  //Add the preferences located in the preferences.xml file.
  addPreferencesFromResource(R.xml.preferences);

 }

}
```

Next, you will need a way to inflate the preferences. A nice way to do this is via our menu item labeled *Settings*. In the `MainActivity` class, within the `onOptionsItemSelected()` method, I added a CASE Statement for the `menu_settings` from the menu we created previously. In that CASE Statement, I added a `startActivity()` line to display the PreferenceActivity:

```
@Override
public boolean onOptionsItemSelected(MenuItem item) {

 switch(item.getItemId()) {

  case R.id.menu_settings:
    startActivity(new Intent(MainActivity.this,PrefsActivity.class));
  return true;

  default:
```

```
    return super.onOptionsItemSelected(item);

  }

}
```

In the code above, we inflate the preferences by using the `startActivity()` method.

Here is what this preference activity looks like once it is displayed on the device:

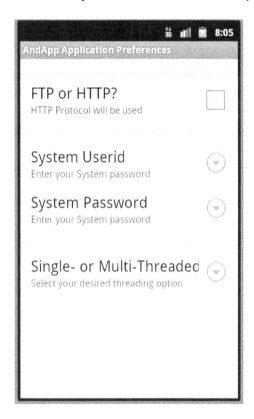

The first `<PreferenceCategory>` contains a single checkbox. The `android:title`, Internet Protocol Preferences, is displayed across the width of the device's screen. As you see, there is a single checkbox presented by the `<CheckBoxPreference>` tag. The `android:title` within the `<CheckBoxPreference>` tag is displayed in a larger font (FTP or HTTP?) whereas the `android:summaryOn`/`android:summaryOff` attributes are displayed just below the `android:title` and are in a smaller font (`HTTP Protocol will be used` is displayed above).

The second `<PreferenceCategory>` contains two `<EditTextPreference>` tags, one for the userid and the other for the password. By clicking the down-arrow, an input box appears and the keyboard is displayed:

The third `<PreferenceCategory>` contains a `<ListPreference>` tag.   There are two additional attributes for this preference: `android:entries` and `android:entryValues`.   These attributes take references to arrays located in the `res\values\arrays.xml` file.   The first attribute, `android:entries`, displays the human-readable values whereas the second attribute, `android:entryValues` contains the values that will be stored in the `SharedPreferences`. Here is what our arrays look like:

```
<string-array name="thread_entries">
 <item>Single-Threaded</item>
 <item>Multi-Threaded</item>
</string-array>
<string-array name="thread_values">
 <item>1</item>
 <item>2</item>
</string-array>
```

Your desired default value is specified in the `android:defaultValue` attribute (see the <ListPreference> XML a few pages back) and the value of which is taken from the array specified in the `android:entryValues` attribute (called `thread_values` in the XML directly above).   Here, we specify `android:defaultValue="1"` and the Single-Threaded option is selected by default. *Note that when attempting to use "S" and "M" instead of "1" and "2", the default value of* `android:defaultValue="S"` *did not work and no radio button was selected. It's probably a good idea to stick with numbers here!*

When you click on the down-arrow for a `<ListPreference>`, you are shown a series of radio buttons each with an entry from the `android:entries` array, as shown below:

286

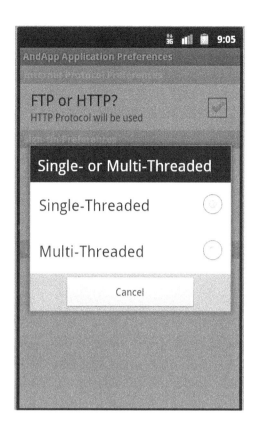

Now, when your application starts, you may want to read in the key/value pairs from the `SharedPreferences` object associated with the `PreferenceActivity`. Note that the `SharedPreferences` key/value pairs are **stored against the context of the application rather than a specific activity**. This makes sense since user-modifiable settings are usually application-wide. Here is the code that I placed in the `onCreate()` method of the `MainActivity.class` to send debugging messages to the LogCat:

```
//Retrieve the key/value pairs from the PreferenceActivity for
//this application.
Context oCtx = getApplicationContext();
SharedPreferences oAppPrefs =
                      PreferenceManager.getDefaultSharedPreferences(oCtx);

//Display the key/value pairs to the LogCat
Boolean bFTPVal = oAppPrefs.getBoolean("PREF_FTP_HTTP", false);
String sFTPVal = Boolean.toString(bFTPVal);

Log.d("MYAPPTAG","PREF_FTP_HTTP=" + sFTPVal);
Log.d("MYAPPTAG","PREF_UID=" + oAppPrefs.getString("PREF_UID", "UNKNOWN"));
Log.d("MYAPPTAG","PREF_PWD=" + oAppPrefs.getString("PREF_PWD", "UNKNOWN"));

String sTHREADSVal = oAppPrefs.getString("PREF_NTHREADS", "UNKNOWN");

Log.d("MYAPPTAG","PREF_NTHREADS=" + sTHREADSVal);
```

The first two lines get the application context as well as the associated `SharedPreferences` object. The next series of lines pulls data from the application's `SharedPreferences` and writes them out to the LogCat. Take care to use the correct `get*` method or your application will crash. Note that for checkboxes, you must use `getBoolean()`; for input boxes, you must use `getString();` and for lists, you must use `getString()` as well (I tried to use `getInt()`, but my application crashed),

Here is what the LogCat looks like once the application starts. Note that the very first time you run your application, you may receive the defaults specified in the `get*` methods because the shared preferences hasn't been created and updated.

So far, we've created a PreferenceActivity, populated it with settings, changed our code to display it, and read those settings back in using the appropriate `get*` methods. But, what happens if our user changes a setting during the execution of the application? How will our application know if a setting has changed?

The interface `onSharedPreferenceChangeListener` (located in the `android.content.SharedPreferences` class) is implemented on a class that you wish to have the `onSharedPreferenceChanged()` method called whenever a shared preference has changed. This interface is not specific to the application context's shared preferences (those used for settings within a `PreferenceActivity`), but for any shared preference. Since this section deals with the `PreferenceActivity` class, we will restrict the interface to our application context.

When the `onSharedPreferenceChanged()` method is called, it is passed two parameters:

1. `SharedPreferences sharedPreferences`
2. `String key`

It is the `key` parameter that tells you which setting was changed and, based on that, you can update your interface accordingly. There are three modifications you need to make to your code to allow the onSharedPreferenceChangeListener interface to work:

1. Modify the class to implement `onSharedPreferenceChangeListener`.

```
public class MainActivity extends Activity implements
                                    OnSharedPreferenceChangeListener
{
```

2. Add the `registerOnSharedPreferenceChangeListener()` method to the `onCreate()` method to allow the `SharedPreferences` to know that the

class is supposed to listen for changes (note the first two lines below already appeared in our code above):

```
//Retrieve the key/value pairs from the PreferenceActivity for this
application.
Context oCtx = getApplicationContext();
SharedPreferences oAppPrefs =
                    PreferenceManager.getDefaultSharedPreferences(oCtx);

//Register the onSharedPreferenceChangeListener
oAppPrefs.registerOnSharedPreferenceChangeListener(this);
```

3. Finally, implement the `onSharedPreferenceChanged()` method (does not require the `@Override` keyword):

```
public void onSharedPreferenceChanged(SharedPreferences prefs,String key) {

  if (key.contentEquals("PREF_FTP_HTTP")) {
   Log.d("MYAPPTAG","PREF_FTP_HTTP WAS CHANGED!!");
  }
  else if (key.contentEquals("PREF_UID")) {
   Log.d("MYAPPTAG","PREF_UID WAS CHANGED!!");
  }
  else if (key.contentEquals("PREF_PWD")) {
   Log.d("MYAPPTAG","PREF_PWD WAS CHANGED!!");
  }
  else if (key.contentEquals("PREF_NTHREADS")) {
   Log.d("MYAPPTAG","PREF_NTHREADS WAS CHANGED!!");
  }

}
```

In the code in #3 above, you can implement changes to the application based on new settings.

Here is what the LogCat looks like when I change some of the settings:

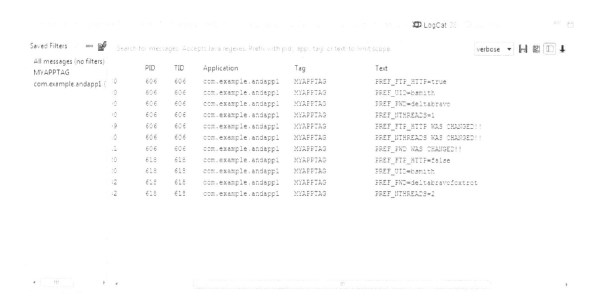

The first four lines report the current settings. The next three lines indicate that I changed those settings. I then killed the application and restarted it allowing the last four lines to be reported. This indicates that the changes I made were successfully stored in the `Shared Preferences` for the application as well as persist across application sessions.

Summary

In this chapter, we talked about a variety of ways to store your application's data, either temporarily or permanently.

Chapter 15: Working with the SQLite Database

Overview

In this chapter, we learn how to use the SQLite (http://www.sqlite.org) database, the default installed database available on all Android devices. Unlike SharedPreferences, discussed in the previous chapter, SQLite allows you to use the power of a database to load and query data more complex than just simple key/value pairs.

Based on the Android documentation, the version of SQLite installed with Android is 3.4.0, although newer releases of Android, or newer smartphones, may have a later version installed. As of this writing, the currently available version of SQLite is 3.8.5. Unfortunately, the SQLite website does not give you an easy method of downloading an older version of the database. This may seem like a problem if you are programming with a later version of the database while the device is running an earlier version, but according to their website:

> *Single-file Cross-platform Database*
>
> *A database in SQLite is a single disk file. Furthermore, the file format is cross-platform. A database that is created on one machine can be copied and used on a different machine with a different architecture. SQLite databases are portable across 32-bit and 64-bit machines and between big-endian and little-endian architectures.*
>
> *The SQLite database file format is also stable. All releases of of SQLite version 3 can read and write database files created by the very first SQLite 3 release (version 3.0.0) going back to 2004-06-18. This is "backwards compatibility". The developers promise to maintain backwards compatibility of the database file format for all future releases of SQLite 3. **"Forwards compatibility" means that older releases of SQLite can also read and write databases created by newer releases. SQLite is usually, but not completely forwards compatible.***
>
> *The stability of the SQLite database file format and the fact that the file format is cross-platform combine to make SQLite database files an excellent choice as an Application File Format.*

So, earlier versions of SQLite can *most likely* read in databases created by later versions. With that said, you probably want to test on several Android devices before releasing your application to the world.

Installing SQLite on Windows

In order to interact with a SQLite database on your personal computer, you need to download and install the SQLite software by following these instructions:

1. Navigate your browser to http://www.sqlite.org/download.html.
2. Scroll down to the section labeled *Precompiled Binaries for Windows*.
3. Download the file sqlite-shell-win32-x86-3071400.zip to your hard drive. This file contains the SQLite command line shell.

4. Download the file `sqlite-dll-win32-x86-3071400.zip` to your hard drive. This file contains the appropriate DLL for Windows.
5. Unzip both files into the same folder, say `C:\SQLite3`, by using your favorite decompression software such as WinZip, PKZip, WinRAR, etc.
6. Test the installation by performing the following:
    a. Open up a Windows Command Prompt (Start...Run...`cmd.exe`...OK...)
    b. Change directory to `C:\SQLite3` (or your folder) using the command: `cd C:\SQLite3`.
    c. Enter in the command `sqlite3 --version` and hit the Enter key. You should see something like the following:

```
3.7.13 2012-06-11 02:05:22 f5b5a13f7394dc143aa136f1d4faba6839eaa6dc
```

At this point, you have completed the installation of SQLite. That was easy!

Installing the SQLite Expert Personal Edition Software

Rather than use the SQLite command line to interact with the database on your Windows machine, you can use a GUI interface such as the free personal edition of SQLite Expert. Download and install the software by following these instructions:

1. Navigate your browser to `http://www.sqliteexpert.com`.
2. Click on the Download link.
3. Click the large green Download button to the right of the text SQLite Expert Personal. This will download the free version of the software (named `SQLiteExpertPersSetup.exe`), but if your Android application starts to make oodles of money, please consider purchasing the Professional edition for US$59.
4. Double-click on `SQLiteExpertPersSetup.exe` to start the setup process. Follow the on-screen instructions.

To start using SQLite Expert, click on Start...All Programs...SQLite Expert...Personal 3... SQLite Expert Personal. Once the application starts, click on File...Open Database to open your desired database file or click on File...New Database to create a blank database. Here is a screenshot showing SQLite Expert connected to my test database:

In order to set up a database connection from within Eclipse, you will need to have, at the very least, a blank database available on disk. To create a new database, click on File...New Database and fill in the Database Creation Properties dialog box as shown below:

At this point, SQLite Expert has created a file called `MySQLite3TestDB.db3` on the hard drive connected to your Windows computer. The GUI will refer to it by its alias (see the Database Alias input box in the image above) `MySQLite3TestDB`.

Read-Only or Read-Write SQLite Database

As mentioned above, a SQLite database is stored within a single file which, for an Android application developer, will either be created on, or eventually be transferred to, an Android device. There are several ways you can generate this file depending on how you will use the database in your application. If your goal is to create a read-only database, you can initialize it by loading your data into a database by using the SQLite database software downloaded from their website and installed on your personal computer (as in the steps we performed above). By installing the software on your personal computer, you can create and load your database via a GUI interface such as SQLite Expert which allows you to interact with the database from something other than the SQLite's command line interface. An example of a read-only database would be a list of stock symbols and historical prices which will either not be updated (making for a rather boring application), updated by using the Download Manager (we talk about this later in the book), or updated using some other method.

On the other hand, if your goal is to collect and maintain a database of ever-changing data, you can create a blank read/write database when your application is first started on the Android device. This does not require that you initialize a database and transfer it onto the device as described above, you just create it on the fly and your code will maintain the database as the user works with your application.

Note that you are not limited to a single database on a device. If your application calls for a read-only database of, say, historical stock prices as well as a read/write database of stock symbols chosen by the user and maintained by your application, you can have both.

Storage Location of the SQLite Database

No matter if you've created a database up-front or generated it on the Android device on the fly from code, it is placed in the appropriate application-specific directory on the Android device. The application-specific directory is located in the `/data/data/app-package-name/` folder, where `app-package-name` is, for our sample program, `com.example.andapp1`. You *may be able to* transfer the database to the device by using Eclipse's File Explorer tab in conjunction with the Devices tab (we discuss the *may be able to* remark in the next section). The Devices tab shows you a list of the physical and virtual devices accessible from Eclipse. By clicking on one of these devices, File Explorer will then be populated with the files and folders for that device. As you can see in the image below, the folder `/data/data/com.example.andapp1` is open and contains two folders.

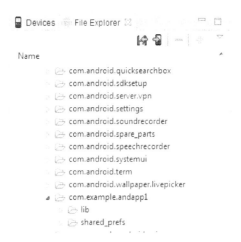

If you want to transfer a file such as a SQLite database *to* the device, click on the icon second from the left (the image of a cell phone with a red arrow pointed to it). If you want to transfer a file *from* the device to your personal computer, click on the icon on the left (the image of a floppy disk with a red arrow pointed to it). Both icons display the File dialog allowing you to either select a file to transfer to the device or a location to store the file onto your hard drive. To delete a file from the device, highlight it and click on the third icon from the left (the grey dash that will turn red when you click on a file).

Be aware that the application-specific directory resides on the device's on-board memory and not the SD card. Please be cognizant of the size of your database and its potential growth since you don't want to cause the device to run out of storage space.

Besides the application-specific directory, you can create a database on the SD card as well. However, be aware that the SD card is publicly accessible meaning that anyone can look at what's stored on it and can delete anything at anytime. This differs from the application-specific directory, which can only be accessed by your application. Your application software should check for the existence of the SD card, check whether it is mounted as read or write, check for the existence of your database, etc.

Be aware that if you've rooted your device, you may not see any entries in File Explorer even though you have clicked on the device's name in the Devices tab. Please see Appendix A (in the external document) for instructions on how to rectify that problem.

Transferring Your SQLite Database to the Device

As mentioned above, and alluded to in the remaining sections of this chapter, you may be able to copy your SQLite database directly to the device by using the File Explorer in Eclipse.

Unless you've rooted your device, this is most likely not possible; so, for the remainder of this chapter, when I tell you to copy your database to the device, you should probably perform the actions described below instead.

For example, on my *rooted* Barnes & Noble Nook Color, I am able to successfully copy my SQLite database over to the `/data/data/com.example.andapp1` folder. On the other hand, I cannot do that using my stock HTC One S device because of security reasons.

Now, it may seem like a show-stopper, but you should not be copying over your SQLite database by hand anyway, but storing it within your app's file structure and allowing Android to copy it over. I found a VERY nice piece of code from ReadyState Software called the Android `SQLiteAssetHelper` class. This is located at https://github.com/jgilfelt/android-sqlite-asset-helper. Please follow the instructions contained within the Zip File.

I won't go through the entire program, but the gist of it is that you place your SQLite database in the \assets\databases folder as a zip file, and when you need to access the database, you instantiate the class which unzips the database and copies it over to a private location for your app. At this point, you can query your database normally.

Interacting with a SQLite Database

There are several ways to access a SQLite database:

1. You can use Eclipse's Database Development Perspective to view, load and browse the data in a database located on either a physical or a virtual device. Note that this requires that you download a SQLite JDBC driver. We talk more about this in the next section.
2. You can use your favorite SQLite GUI program, such as SQLite Expert Personal Edition (`http://www.sqliteexpert.com`), to interact with SQLite on your desktop. You cannot use this method to interact with a SQLite database stored directly on a physical or virtual device.
3. You can use the Android Debug Bridge (`adb.exe`) to interact with SQLite on either a physical or a virtual device from the Windows command line. This method is the only way you can submit SQL code directly to a SQLite database on either a physical or a virtual device. We talk more about this later on in the chapter.

Installing a SQLite JDBC Driver and Using the Eclipse Database Perspective

In order to use Eclipse's Database Development Perspective, you must download and install a SQLite JDBC Driver by following these instructions:

1. Navigate your browser to
   `http://www.xerial.org/maven/repository/artifact/`
   `org/xerial/sqlite-jdbc/`.
2. Scroll down to the bottom of the page to find the highest numbered folder. As of this writing, it is 3.7.2. Click on the 3.7.2 folder.
3. Locate the file `sqlite-jdbc-3.7.2.jar` and click on the link. The Save bar should appear at the bottom of your screen. Click on the down arrow to the right of the word Save and click on the Save As... popup menu item. Save the jar file to your hard drive.
4. In order to determine where the `.jar` file should be moved to, go into Eclipse and click on Window...Preferences...Java...Installed JREs. On the right side of the dialog, you will see something like the following image. Take note of the directory specified in the Location column. For me, my Java jar files are stored in the `lib` folder within `C:\Program Files\Java\jre6`. Move the `sqlite-jdbc-3.7.2.jar` to this location.

5. In Eclipse, change to the Database Development Perspective by either clicking on the Database Development button on the upper right of the interface, or by clicking on Window...Open Perspective and clicking on the Database Development item when the Open Perspective dialog box appears. You should see something like the image below:

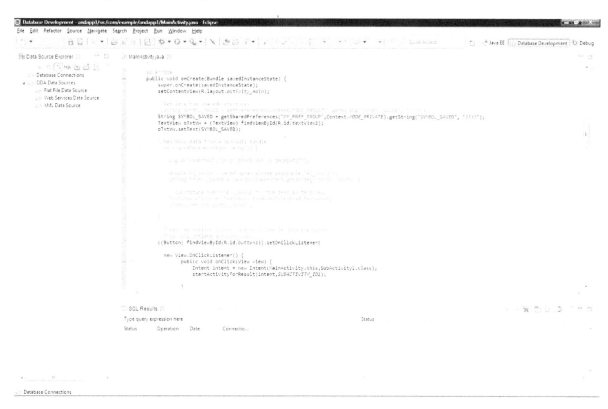

6. As you see in the image above, the folder labeled Database Connections is empty. We will now create a new database connection to a specific SQLite database. The following instructions assume that you already have a SQLite database called `MySQLite3TestDB.db3`, so make sure that you create an

empty database by following the instructions in the section *Installing the SQLite Expert Personal Edition Software* above.

7. Right-click on the Database Connections folder and click on New... from the popup menu.

8. In the New Connection Profile dialog, scroll down until you see the entry for SQLite in Connection Profile Types. Click on SQLite once to highlight it.

9. In the Name input box, enter the name of the profile for the specific database you are connecting to: `MySQLite3TestDB Profile`.

10. In the optional Description input box, fill in a description.

11. Click the Next button.

12. On the Specify a Driver and Connection Details dialog, despite the driver entry of SQLite JDBC Driver, you will have to create a new driver connection to point to the SQLite JDBC Driver you downloaded and placed in the `C:\Program Files\Java\jre6\lib` (or similar) folder. To do this, perform the following:

   a. Click on the New Driver Definition icon to the right of the drop-down box containing the text SQLite JDBC Driver. The New Driver Definition dialog will appear.

   b. On the Name/Type tab:

      i. Click once on the sole entry in the Available driver templates grid to highlight it.

      ii. In the Driver name input box, enter the text `SQLite JDBC Driver 3.7.2.`

   c. On the JAR List tab:

      i. Highlight the driver labeled `sqlitejdbc-v051.jar` and click on the Remove JAR/Zip button.

      ii. Click on the Add JAR/Zip... button. The Select the file dialog will appear.

      iii. **Navigate to** `C:\Program Files\Java\jre6\lib`, **locate the file** `sqlite-jdbc-3.7.2.jar` **and double-click on it.**

   d. On the Properties tab:

    i. In the Value column to the right of the text Connection URL, enter `jdbc:sqlite:C:\TEMP\MySQLite3TestDB.db3`.

    ii. In the Value column to the right of the text Database Name, enter `MySQLite3TestDB`.

  e. Click the OK button.

13. At this point, the New Driver Definition dialog will disappear and you will be returned to the Specify a Driver and Connection Details dialog. You should see the text `SQLite JDBC Driver 3.7.2` in the drop-down box to the right of the text Drivers.

14. On the General tab, fill in the following fields:

  a. Database: `MySQLite3TestDB`

  b. Database Location: `C:\TEMP\MySQLite3TestDB.db3`

  c. URL: `jdbc:sqlite:C:\TEMP\MySQLite3TestDB.db3`

15. Click the Test Connection button to test the connection to your database. If all goes well, a dialog box with the words `Ping Succeeded!` should appear.

16. Click the Finish button.

At this point, you should see a single entry in the Database Connections folder labeled `MySQLite3TestDB`. If you expand the `MySQLite3TestDB` folder, you will see two folders: Authorization IDs and Schemas. Expanding the folder Schemas will reveal the schema DEFAULT. Expanding this folder will reveal the folders Dependencies, Stored Procedures, Tables, User-Defined Functions and Views. The Tables folder contains all of the tables appearing in the database. Since we created a blank database, the Tables folder is empty.

Using SQLite from the Command Line

Although you can use Eclipse's Database Perspective and SQLite Expert Personal Edition to interact with a SQLite database located on your personal computer, this is not an option when interacting with a SQLite database stored on a physical or virtual device such as an Android Emulator or smartphone. In these cases, you must use SQLite from the command line. In this section, we show you how to use SQLite from the command line on both your Windows machine and on an Android device (physical or virtual).

Whether you are using SQLite from a Windows or Linux command line, the commands are the same. To start a Windows command line, click on Start...Run...`cmd.exe`...OK. The following window will appear:

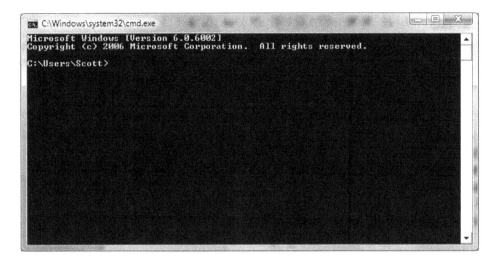

Next, change to the directory where you installed the two SQLite executable (.exe and .dll) files by entering the command `cd C:\TEMP\SQLITE` and hitting the Enter key. At this point, you can enter `sqlite3` and hit the Enter key to start SQLite. Note that this method creates a blank database for you to use.

If you want to open up an existing database, enter the location and name of it after the `sqlite3` command: `sqlite3 c:\temp\MySQLite3TestDB.db3`. You should see something similar to the image below:

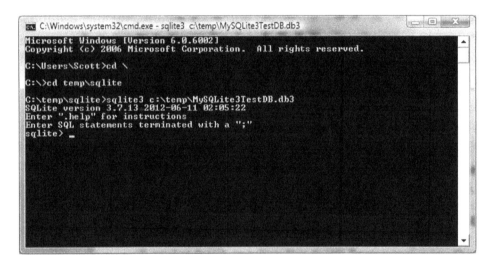

At this point, you are able to enter SQL query commands (described in the next section). If you want to exit out of SQLite, enter `.quit` and hit the Enter key. This will bring you back to the Windows command line. Here is a list of SQLite commands, such as `.quit`, you can enter on the SQLite command line:

SQLite Command Line	Description
.backup ?DB? FILE	Backup DB (default "main") to FILE
.bail ON|OFF	Stop after hitting an error. Default: OFF
.databases	List names and files of attached databases
.dump ?TABLE? ...	Dump the database in an SQL text format. If TABLE specified, only dump tables matching LIKE pattern TABLE.
.echo ON|OFF	Turn command echo on or off
.exit	Exit this program
.explain ?ON|OFF?	Turn output mode suitable for EXPLAIN on or off. With no args, it turns EXPLAIN on.
.header(s) ON|OFF	Turn display of headers on or off

300

`.help`	Show this message
`.import FILE TABLE`	Import data from FILE into TABLE
`.indices ?TABLE?`	Show names of all indices. If TABLE specified, only show indices for tables matching LIKE pattern TABLE.
`.load FILE ?ENTRY?`	Load an extension library
`.log FILE|off`	Turn logging on or off. FILE can be stderr/stdout
`.mode MODE ?TABLE?`	Set output mode where MODE is one of:
	csv - comma-separated values
	column - Left-aligned columns. (See .width)
	html - HTML <table> code
	insert - SQL insert statements for TABLE
	line - One value per line
	list - Values delimited by .separator string
	tabs - Tab-separated values
	tcl - TCL list elements
`.nullvalue STRING`	Print STRING in place of NULL values
`.output FILENAME`	Send output to FILENAME
`.output stdout`	Send output to the screen
`.prompt MAIN CONTINUE`	Replace the standard prompts
`.quit`	Exit this program
`.read FILENAME`	Execute SQL in FILENAME
`.restore ?DB? FILE`	Restore content of DB (default "main") from FILE
`.schema ?TABLE?`	Show the CREATE statements. If TABLE specified, only show tables matching LIKE pattern TABLE.
`.separator STRING`	Change separator used by output mode and .import
`.show`	Show the current values for various settings
`.stats ON|OFF`	Turn stats on or off
`.tables ?TABLE?`	List names of tables. If TABLE specified, only list tables matching LIKE pattern TABLE.
`.timeout MS`	Try opening locked tables for MS milliseconds
`.trace FILE|off`	Output each SQL statement as it is run
`.vfsname ?AUX?`	Print the name of the VFS stack
`.width NUM1 NUM2 ...`	Set column widths for "column" mode
`.timer ON|OFF`	Turn the CPU timer measurement on or off
`.backup ?DB? FILE`	Backup DB (default "main") to FILE

Make sure that you do **not** place a semi-colon at the end of the line when using the commands above. If you do, you will receive no output and no warning!

Take note that you can easily retrieve a list of tables in your database by using the `.tables` command. By using the `.schema` *table_name* command, you will be shown the `CREATE TABLE` statement used to create the table. We talk more about the `CREATE TABLE` command later on in this chapter.

Now, if you want to modify the SQLite database *on either a physical or virtual device*, you will have to use the Android Debug Bridge (`adb.exe`) to access the database. You do this by opening up a shell, Linux's version of a command window, starting SQLite and issuing your SQL commands. For example, to open up a shell on the emulator you issue the command `adb -e shell` at the Windows command prompt. To open up a shell on your physical device you issue the command `adb -d shell`. If you have multiple virtual and physical devices, then use the `-s` option followed by the name of the device: `adb -s *device-name* shell`.

Once at the shell, you can issue the command `sqlite3` to start SQLite. At this point, the discussion above applies. Since you did not specify a database, SQLite opens up a blank one for you.

If you want to open up an existing database, you have to place the name of it on the command line: `sqlite3 MySQLite3TestDB.db3`. See the image below for an example.

To exit SQLite, type `.quit` and hit the Enter key. To exit the shell, type `exit` and hit the Enter key.

In the next section, we introduce the Structured Query Language (SQL) and show you how to query tables, create tables, populate them with data, and much more.

Introduction to the Structured Query Language (SQL)

If you've been reading this book from page one, the last thing you probably want to do is stop and learn yet another programming language. The Structured Query Language, or SQL, is a very simple, yet very powerful, language to learn since there are only a few keywords. Here they are:

```
SELECT
 FROM
 WHERE
 GROUP BY
 HAVING
 ORDER BY
```

Learning SQL is like learning to use the `vi` editor: you know that every Unix/Linux operating comes with it, so it's better to learn it than not. The same goes for SQL: every database uses SQL as its query language, so it's better to learn it than not.

Now, except for a few additional keywords used to join two or more tables together, the list of keywords shown above is all there is to the query language. And to make the language even simpler, the order of the keywords listed above is the order in which they **must** appear in your SQL queries. That is, the order above is immutable, so the `SELECT` keyword **must** appear before the `FROM` keyword which itself **must** appear before the `WHERE` keyword, and so on. The collection of these keywords is referred to as the *Data Manipulation Language* (DML).

A *database* is a container for one or more tables. You can think of a database as being similar to an Excel Workbook which is itself a container for one or more Excel Spreadsheets. You can think of a table as being similar to an Excel Spreadsheet; that is, a *table* has rows and columns of data similar to an Excel Spreadsheet.

Unlike an Excel Spreadsheet, you must define up front the *names* of the columns as well as the *data type* that will be contained within each column of your table.

The names of the columns are up to you and should reflect the data contained within the table. For example, if a column contains stock price data, then call the column `STOCK_PRICE`. Usually, programmers use alphabetic characters (A to Z), numbers (0 to 9) and the underscore (_) to form the column names with the restriction that they must begin with an alphabetic character (A to Z). You may want to restrict the length of your column names to 30 characters or less. I am suggesting this in the off-chance that you'll need to load your SQLite table into another database, such as Oracle, which limits its column names to 30 characters. This will prevent you from having to perform the annoying task of renaming the columns.

You are also in control of the *data type* for each of the columns. That is, if one column will contain integers, and another will contain floating point numbers, and yet another will contain text, then you tell the database all of this information when you create your table. There is a set of keywords, distinct from those listed above, which is used to define tables and columns, and the collection of these keywords is referred to as the *Data Definition Language* (DDL). Some of these keywords are `CREATE TABLE`, `INSERT INTO`, `DROP TABLE`, `CREATE INDEX`, `DROP INDEX`, etc. We talk more about DDL later in the chapter.

The type of data within each column is defined by specifying the appropriate *data type* on that column. SQLite has only a few data types:

1. `INTEGER` - the column will contains integer numbers (such as 1, 2, 101, etc.)
2. `REAL` - the column will contain floating-point numbers (such as 3.1415, 2.1828, etc.)
3. `TEXT` - the column will contain text (such as "Donut", "Baked Good", etc.)
4. `BLOB` - the column will contain a Binary Large Object (such as a JPEG or PNG image file, a PDF file, an MP3 file, etc.)

Note that this is a subset of the available data types (storage classes) in SQLite, so please view the document *Datatypes in SQLite Version 3* available on the SQLite website.

Finally, it is possible for the intersection of a column and row of a table to contain no data. In Excel, this is represented by a blank cell. In a database table, it is represented by a `NULL` value. Note that a `NULL` value is very different from the values "None" or "Unknown" appearing in a cell. Both of those are valid values. You cannot make any judgement as to what `NULL` means except that there is no data in that cell.

The Data Manipulation Language (DML)

In this section, we explain each of the DML keywords listed above.

- The `SELECT` keyword indicates which columns you are interested in returning from the query. For example, if you have several columns in your table and you only want to return two of them, you specify those two columns on the `SELECT` line: `SELECT STOCK_SYMBOL,STOCK_PRICE`. If you wish to receive a distinct (de-duplicated) set of data from your query, place the keyword `DISTINCT` directly after the `SELECT` keyword and before the list of columns.
- The `FROM` keyword indicates the table from which your desired data will be pulled. For example, if the table is called `HISTORICAL_STOCK_PRICES`, then you code: `FROM HISTORICAL_STOCK_PRICES`. Note that you can join two or more tables together as we show below in the section labeled *Joining Tables Together*.
- The `WHERE` keyword specifies the criteria for subsetting the data to be pulled from the table listed on the `FROM` keyword. That is, if you want to select a specific stock symbol, say `GOOG`, then you code:

```
SELECT STOCK_SYMBOL,STOCK_PRICE
 FROM HISTORICAL_STOCK_PRICES
 WHERE STOCK_SYMBOL="GOOG";
```

  Take note that you use double-quotes around text strings, but not around numbers. You can add additional constraints using the optional keywords `AND`, `OR` and `NOT`. For example, to pull data for stock symbol `MSFT` as well as `GOOG`, you would code:

```
SELECT STOCK_SYMBOL,AVG(STOCK_PRICE) AS AVERAGE_STOCK_PRICE
 FROM HISTORICAL_STOCK_PRICES
 WHERE STOCK_SYMBOL="GOOG" OR STOCK_SYMBOL="MSFT";
```

  Note that if you wish to query for NULLs in a column then you have to use the special syntax `WHERE column_name  IS NULL`. If you wish to skip passed the NULLs, you use the syntax `WHERE column_name IS NOT NULL`.
- The `GROUP BY` keyword indicates that you want the data to be aggregated down to a specific level. For example, to summarize the

`HISTORICAL_STOCK_PRICES` table down to the `STOCK_SYMBOL` level while finding the average `STOCK_PRICE`, you would code the following:

```
SELECT STOCK_SYMBOL,AVG(STOCK_PRICE) AS AVERAGE_STOCK_PRICE
 FROM HISTORICAL_STOCK_PRICES
 WHERE STOCK_SYMBOL="GOOG" OR STOCK_SYMBOL="MSFT"
 GROUP BY STOCK_SYMBOL;
```

Note that we need to place the same column(s) appearing on the `GROUP BY` line on the `SELECT` line which is why `STOCK_SYMBOL` appears there. In order to compute the average `STOCK_PRICE`, we use one of SQLite's Aggregate Functions, `AVG()` which computes the average of the `STOCK_PRICE` within each `STOCK_SYMBOL`. There are several more aggregate functions:

- `COUNT(column_name)` - this aggregate function counts the number of times `column_name` is not a `NULL` value. If you specify `COUNT(*)` instead, this returns the count of the number of rows (including those rows that may contain a `NULL` value in one or more of the columns).
- `MAX(column_name)` - this aggregate function returns the maximum value of `column_name` within the data.
- `MIN(column_name)` - this aggregate function returns the minimum value of `column_name` within the data.
- `SUM(column_name)` - this aggregate function returns the sum of `column_name` within the data. This function returns an integer value if all values appearing in `column_name` are integer values.
- `TOTAL(column_name)` - this aggregate function is the same as the `SUM()` aggregate function except it returns a floating point value instead of an integer.

Note that in the SQL query above we used the `AS` keyword to give a useful new name (`AVERAGE_STOCK_PRICE`) to the results of the aggregate function `AVG(STOCK_PRICE)`. This is called an *alias* and, as you'll see below, you can use it on tables as well as columns.

- The `HAVING` keyword is similar to the `WHERE` keyword except that, instead of subsetting the data pulled from the table, it subsets the data generated by the SQL query. For example, if you want to limit the resulting data to those stocks that have an average price greater than 100, you would code:

```
SELECT STOCK_SYMBOL,AVG(STOCK_PRICE) AS AVERAGE_STOCK_PRICE
 FROM HISTORICAL_STOCK_PRICES
 WHERE STOCK_SYMBOL="GOOG" OR STOCK_SYMBOL="MSFT"
 GROUP BY STOCK_SYMBOL
 HAVING AVERAGE_STOCK_PRICE > 100;
```

You should think of the `HAVING` line as being performed **after** the rest of the SQL query has been executed.

- The `ORDER BY` keyword indicates that you want the resulting data to be sorted in a specific order rather than the default order. For example, if you want to sort the `HISTORICAL_STOCK_PRICES` data by `STOCK_SYMBOL` as well as `PRICE_DATE`, then you would code:

```
SELECT STOCK_SYMBOL,PRICE_DATE,STOCK_PRICE
 FROM HISTORICAL_STOCK_PRICES
 WHERE STOCK_SYMBOL="GOOG" OR STOCK_SYMBOL="MSFT"
 ORDER BY STOCK_SYMBOL,PRICE_DATE;
```

Note that the default sort ordering when using `ORDER BY` is ascending, but you can force a descending sort order by using the keyword `DESC` after the column name. For example, if you want the data sorted by ascending `STOCK_SYMBOL`, but descending `PRICE_DATE`, then you would code:

```
SELECT STOCK_SYMBOL,PRICE_DATE,STOCK_PRICE
 FROM HISTORICAL_STOCK_PRICES
 WHERE STOCK_SYMBOL="GOOG" OR STOCK_SYMBOL="MSFT"
 ORDER BY STOCK_SYMBOL,PRICE_DATE DESC;
```

There is more to querying SQLite than what we've shown, so please peruse the SQLite documentation on the SQLite website.

Limiting the Number of Rows Returned from a Query

In the SQL queries shown above, every row of data selected by the query is returned to you. Usually, this is exactly what you want, but there may be times when you want to limit the number of rows returned. To do this, you can use the `LIMIT` statement following the entire SQL query. For example, to limit the number of rows returned from your query to 10, you would code something like this:

```
SELECT STOCK_SYMBOL,PRICE_DATE,STOCK_PRICE
 FROM HISTORICAL_STOCK_PRICES
 WHERE STOCK_SYMBOL="GOOG" OR STOCK_SYMBOL="MSFT"
 ORDER BY STOCK_SYMBOL,PRICE_DATE DESC
 LIMIT 10;
```

If the SQL query without the `LIMIT` statement actually returned less than 10 rows, say 8 rows, the `LIMIT 10` statement would still return just 8 rows. The syntax is:

```
LIMIT max-rows-returned
```

If you've ever shopped online - and I suspect that you have - you'll recall that the website presented you with a few items per page, say 10, numbered from 1 to 10. You then clicked the Next button and the website displayed the next 10 items numbered from 11 to 20. And so on. There is an additional option to the `LIMIT` statement, called `OFFSET`, which will let you specify an offset from the beginning of the query. The syntax is:

```
LIMIT max-rows-returned OFFSET offset-value
```

For example, to return the first 10 rows of data starting at item number 1, you would code:

```
SELECT STOCK_SYMBOL,PRICE_DATE,STOCK_PRICE
 FROM HISTORICAL_STOCK_PRICES
 WHERE STOCK_SYMBOL="GOOG" OR STOCK_SYMBOL="MSFT"
 ORDER BY STOCK_SYMBOL,PRICE_DATE DESC
 LIMIT 10 OFFSET 0;
```

Note that the value specified after the `OFFSET` keyword is zero; that is, there is no offset. Next, if you want to return the next 10 items (11 to 20), you would code:

```
SELECT STOCK_SYMBOL,PRICE_DATE,STOCK_PRICE
 FROM HISTORICAL_STOCK_PRICES
 WHERE STOCK_SYMBOL="GOOG" OR STOCK_SYMBOL="MSFT"
 ORDER BY STOCK_SYMBOL,PRICE_DATE DESC
 LIMIT 10 OFFSET 10;
```

An alternate syntax for `LIMIT` *max-rows-returned* `OFFSET` *offset-value* is:

```
LIMIT offset-value,max-rows-returned
```

Note that this syntax may be initially confusing because the *offset-value* now appears *first* whereas it appears last in the previous syntax. Caution is advised!

Joining Tables Together

If you have more than one table in your database, chances are you will eventually need to join two of them together. For example, say you have one table that contains a distinct list of stock symbols and company names, and another table that contains stock symbols along with the market capitalization and the price/earnings ratio. If you want to join these two tables together, you can use an *inner join* to join the two tables by the stock symbol:

```
SELECT A.STOCK_SYMBOL,B.MARKETCAP,B.PERATIO
 FROM STOCK_SYMBOLS A INNER JOIN STOCK_STATS B
 ON A.STOCK_SYMBOL=B.STOCK_SYMBOL;
```

The keywords `INNER JOIN` on the `FROM` line indicate that we are joining two tables together in a one-to-one fashion. Note that to the left of `INNER JOIN` is the name of one table and to the right is the name of the other table.

Each table is given a *table alias*, A or B here, useful in quickly referring to the columns from each table. Without the alias, you would have to use the table name instead; that is, `A.STOCK_SYMBOL` becomes `STOCK_SYMBOLS.STOCK_SYMBOL` and `B.PERATIO` becomes `STOCK_STATS.PERATIO`. That's just way too much typing!

The `ON` keyword specifies the join criteria and, in this case, indicates the two tables are to be joined by the `STOCK_SYMBOL`. Remember, `ON` is used for joins whereas `WHERE` is used for subsetting the data. Occasionally, you'll see some programmers use the `WHERE` keyword to join tables together, but that is not recommended.

Now, an inner join will only return data appearing in both tables. For example, if the stock symbol `GOOG` appears in the `STOCK_SYMBOLS` table, but does **not**

307

appear in the STOCK_STATS table, GOOG will not appear when performing an inner join.

If you *do* want GOOG to appear, even though no data for MARKETCAP and PERATIO exists, you can use a left join instead of an inner join. A *left join* is just an inner join with the unmatched rows from the table to the left of the keywords LEFT JOIN appended to it. Here is the syntax:

```
SELECT A.STOCK_SYMBOL,B.MARKETCAP,B.PERATIO
 FROM STOCK_SYMBOLS A LEFT JOIN STOCK_STATS B
 ON A.STOCK_SYMBOL=B.STOCK_SYMBOL;
```

In this case, a line for GOOG will appear, but both the MARKETCAP and PERATIO will be automatically set to NULL.

There is more to joining tables together in SQLite than what we've shown, so please peruse the SQLite documentation on their website.

Using the `sqlite_master` Table

SQLite keeps track of all the tables, indexes and views created by you in the system-maintained table sqlite_master. You can query this table if you'd like to enumerate, say, all of the tables in the database. This table has the following columns:

1. RecNo - the record number
2. type - the type of the record. This field contains values such as "table", "view", "index", etc.
3. name - the name of the table, index, view, etc.
4. tbl_name - the name of the associated table. For a type of table and view, name and tbl_name are the same. For a type of index, name is the name of the index and tbl_name is underlying table.
5. rootpage - ignore
6. sql - this is the SQL used to create the table, view or index.

For example, to enumerate all of the tables in the database, you can code something like this:

```
SELECT DISTINCT name
 FROM sqlite_master
 WHERE type="table"
 ORDER BY name;
```

1	HISTORICAL_STOCK_PRICES
2	STOCK_STATS
3	STOCK_SYMBOLS
4	TEST1
5	sqlite_stat1

And, to see the SQL used to create the view vwSTOCKSTATSMATCH (described in the next section):

```
SELECT sql
 FROM sqlite_master
```

308

```
WHERE type="view"
      AND name="vwSTOCKSTATSMATCH";
```

```
CREATE VIEW vwSTOCKSTATSMATCH AS
SELECT A.STOCK_SYMBOL,B.MARKETCAP,B.PERATIO
 FROM STOCK_SYMBOLS A LEFT JOIN STOCK_STATS B
 ON A.STOCK_SYMBOL=B.STOCK_SYMBOL
```

Using Views

Occasionally, your queries will become so large that building and managing a string containing the SQL will become a nightmare. One way around this is to create a database view. A *view* is a named query which you define up-front and call later on. A view name can be placed wherever you'd put a table name. For example, let's create a view from a complicated query:

```
CREATE VIEW vwSTOCKSTATSMATCH AS
 SELECT A.STOCK_SYMBOL,B.MARKETCAP,B.PERATIO
  FROM STOCK_SYMBOLS A LEFT JOIN STOCK_STATS B
  ON A.STOCK_SYMBOL=B.STOCK_SYMBOL;
```

Note that the view name vwSTOCKSTATSMATCH is just a LEFT JOIN query with no WHERE statement. You can add a WHERE statement, if desired, when you use the view in a query:

```
SELECT *
 FROM vwSTOCKSTATSMATCH
 WHERE STOCK_SYMBOL='MSFT';
```

If you want to delete the view, use the DROP VIEW statement:

```
DROP VIEW vwSTOCKSTATSMATCH;
```

The Data Definition Language (DDL)

In this section, we explain some of the more important DDL keywords. This is not an exhaustive list, so please visit the SQLite website and peruse their documentation.

- CREATE TABLE table_name(column_name1 data_type,...);
  This command creates a blank table called table_name with one or more columns. Each column name must be followed by its associated data type. Note that the name of the table should be restricted to the characters A to Z, numbers 0 to 9, underscore (_) and be limited to 30 characters or less.

- DROP TABLE table_name;
  This command deletes a table called table_name along with any data that is stored within it.

- ALTER TABLE table_name RENAME TO new_table_name;
  ALTER TABLE table_name ADD COLUMN new_column_name data_type ...;
  The ALTER TABLE command makes a modification to an existing table. In the first form, it allows you to rename an existing table. In the second form, it allows you to add a new column to an existing table.

309

- `DELETE FROM` *`table_name`*`;`
  This command deletes all of the data within *`table_name`*, but does **not** drop the table.

- `DELETE FROM` *`table_name`* `WHERE` *`...`*`;`
  This command deletes data from *`table_name`* that satisfies the `WHERE` statement.

- `INSERT INTO` *`table_name`* `VALUES(`*`val1`*`,`*`val2`*`,...);`
  This command inserts data into *`table_name`* with the values following the `VALUES` keyword. Note that *`val1`*, *`val2`*, and so on, must be in the **same** order as the columns are. If you created the table, refer to the `CREATE TABLE` command you used to see the order of the columns. If you are working at the SQLite command line, you can issue the command `.schema` *`table_name`* and SQLite will return the `CREATE TABLE` command used to generate the table. If you are working in the Database Perspective in Eclipse, expand the Columns folder under the relevant table (which appears in the Tables folder, shown below). If you are using SQLite Expert, click on the relevant table, and then click on the Design tab.

- `UPDATE` *`table_name`* `SET` *`column_name1=value1`*`,`*`column_name2=value2`*`,...`
  `WHERE` *`expr`*`;`
  The `UPDATE` command updates data in selected columns and can also update specific rows if the `WHERE` command is also included.

- `CREATE INDEX` *`index_name`* `ON`
  `table_name(column_name1,column_name2,...);`
  Please see the section labeled *Working with SQLite Indexes* below for more information.

- `DROP INDEX` *`index_name`*`;`
  This command drops the index called *`index_name`* on the appropriate table.

310

- `ANALYZE table_name;`
  `ANALYZE database_name;`

  The `ANALYZE` command computes important statistics for the table `table_name` and any associated indexes. These statistics are used by the SQLite optimizer to ensure that your SQL query is executed in the fastest possible manner. **If you go through the trouble of creating indexes on your table, make sure to run this command!!** Note that if you have several tables in your database, rather than running the `ANALYZE` command on each table, you can run it on the entire database using the second form of the command. This will run an `ANALYZE` on all tables and indexes within the database in one fell swoop.

A Discussion on Indexes

Indexes are similar in concept to an index found in the back of a book. If you want to search for a specific topic, you would turn to the index, look up the topic, get the topic's page number and then turn directly to that page. Would it make sense to start on page one and proceed page by page until you found that topic? Of course not! Using the index is faster than paging through an entire book!

This is true for indexes placed on a table. The SQLite query optimizer will attempt to use an appropriate index to find data quickly instead of searching through the entire table one row at a time. Unfortunately, programmers unfamiliar with how an index works have a tendency to create too many indexes.

To confuse the situation even more, you can create an index on several columns at once. This is called a *multi-column index* as opposed to a *single-column index* created on one column.

Note that you can have several single- and multi-column indexes on a table.

Here are a few tips on when to create indexes:

1. Create single-column or multi-column indexes based on the variety of `WHERE` statements you are planning to use against your tables. For example, if one of your SQL queries uses a `WHERE` statement such as `WHERE STOCK_SYMBOL="xxxx"` then it makes sense to create a single-column index on the column `STOCK_SYMBOL`. If one of your SQL queries uses a `WHERE` statement such as `WHERE STOCK_SYMBOL="xxxx" AND PRICE_DATE ="yyyy"` then it makes sense to create a multi-column index on `STOCK_SYMBOL` and `PRICE_DATE`.
2. It is usually, but not always, unnecessary to create an index on columns that are floating-point values such as `STOCK_PRICE`, `SALARY`, and so on because you most likely won't include those as a subsetting criteria in the `WHERE` statement. On the other hand, if you plan to subset a table based on a floating-point column, then you should create an index on that column.
3. The SQLite query optimizer will decide whether to use an index or not. As a very general rule of thumb, if your query pulls back 15% of the data or less from the table, you have more of a chance that the index will be used. Any more

than 15%, the query optimizer may just scan the entire table. If that's the case, just don't create the index since it won't be used anyway.

4. If all of your SQL queries traverse the entire table, don't bother creating any indexes on it. Indexes are used to subset data and if your queries aren't doing that, then indexes are unnecessary. An example of this is a table of stock symbols you plan on inserting into a `ListView`. Your query in this case will traverse the entire stock symbol table and not subset it, so there is no need for an index.

5. Always remember that indexes takes up additional space in the database file. Creating unnecessary or useless indexes is just a waste of space. This is all the more important on handheld devices due to the limited space available.

6. If you create a multi-column index on, say, columns A and B, it is unnecessary to then create an additional single-column index on column A. See Example #1 and #2 below. It is unnecessary to create a single-column index on `STOCK_SYMBOL` in Example #1 since the database can make use of it in the multi-column index generated in Example #2.

7. Finally, always remember to use the `ANALYZE` command (described in the previous section) to gather important statistics for the tables and indexes in the database. If you don't, SQLite's query optimizer will not be able to optimize your SQL code.

With that said, here are a few examples of how to create single- and multi-column indexes on a table:

1. Let's create a *single-column index*, called `INDX_HSP_SS`, on the `STOCK_SYMBOL` column:

```
CREATE INDEX INDX_HSP_SS ON HISTORICAL_STOCK_PRICES(STOCK_SYMBOL);
```

2. Let's create a *multi-column index*, called `INDX_HSP_SS_PD`, on the `STOCK_SYMBOL` and `PRICE_DATE` columns:

```
CREATE INDEX INDX_HSP_SS_PD ON
                    HISTORICAL_STOCK_PRICES(STOCK_SYMBOL,PRICE_DATE);
```

3. Finally, issue the `ANALYZE` command to gather table and index statistics:

```
ANALYZE HISTORICAL_STOCK_PRICES;
```

Alternately, you can analyze the entire database:

```
ANALYZE EQUITY_DATABASE;
```

Using EXPLAIN QUERY PLAN

In the previous section, we described how to speed up your SQL queries using indexes. In order to determine if SQLite is using the indexes you took so much time to create, you can use the `EXPLAIN QUERY PLAN` statement followed by a single SQL query. Given the `HISTORICAL_STOCK_PRICE` table, I created a single index on the `STOCK_SYMBOL` column and now I'd like to know if my queries are using it. Here are two examples:

```
sqlite> EXPLAIN QUERY PLAN
   ...>   SELECT *
   ...>    FROM HISTORICAL_STOCK_PRICES;
0|0|0|SCAN TABLE HISTORICAL_STOCK_PRICES (~2 rows)

sqlite> EXPLAIN QUERY PLAN
   ...>   SELECT *
   ...>    FROM HISTORICAL_STOCK_PRICES
   ...>    WHERE STOCK_SYMBOL='MSFT';
0|0|0|SEARCH TABLE HISTORICAL_STOCK_PRICES USING INDEX ix_hsp_ss (STOCK_SYMBOL=?)
(~1 rows)
```

In the first example, the output of EXPLAIN QUERY PLAN shows that a full scan on the table HISTORICAL_STOCK_PRICES is what SQLite will do when that query is submitted.

In the second example, I am subsetting the data by selecting a specific stock symbol. EXPLAIN QUERY PLAN, in this case, indicates that it will be using the index ix_hsp_ss.

If you test all of your queries in this manner, you may determine that one or more indexes are not being used, so you are probably justified in dropping them.

There is much more to EXPLAIN QUERY PLAN, so please peruse the documentation on SQLite's website.

Column Constraints

As described above, when you create a table, you name the columns as well as indicate the data type associated with each column. Besides the data type, you can add additional keywords to indicate *constraints* on the columns. Constraints force a column to have certain attributes.

One column constraint is the NULL/NOT NULL constraint. Specifying one of these constraints after the data type indicates that the column either accepts NULLs or does not accept NULLs. If you attempt to load NULL data into a column that is specified as NOT NULL, you will receive an error message and the load will abort. For example, here is a brief SQLite session:

```
C:\temp>sqlite3 MySQLite3TestDB
SQLite version 3.7.4
Enter ".help" for instructions
Enter SQL statements terminated with a ";"
sqlite> .tables
sqlite> create table test1(col1 text NOT NULL);
sqlite> insert into test1 values("ABC");
sqlite> insert into test1 values("");
sqlite> insert into test1 values(NULL);
Error: test1.col1 may not be NULL
```

Note that when you attempt to insert a NULL into COL1, you receive an error message. Also note that a zero-length string is not considered a NULL but just an empty string.

Another important constraint is the PRIMARY KEY constraint. This constraint indicates to the database that the column must contain unique values. If a value repeats, you will receive an error message. Here is a brief SQL session:

```
C:\temp>sqlite3 MySQLite3TestDB
SQLite version 3.7.4
Enter ".help" for instructions
Enter SQL statements terminated with a ";"
sqlite> .tables
sqlite> create table test1(col1 text primary key);
sqlite> insert into test1 values("ABC");
sqlite> insert into test1 values("DEF");
sqlite> insert into test1 values("ABC");
Error: column col1 is not unique
```

As you see above, attempting to re-enter the data "ABC" for COL1 yields an error message. Note that NULL values are the exception to this, but you'll most likely want to use the NOT NULL constraint on a column that specifies PRIMARY KEY. Primary key constraints are used when accessing data from a SQLite database via content providers. We talk about content providers in the next chapter.

One other important constraint is the AUTOINCREMENT constraint. This indicates that, as data is added to the table, this column is automatically incremented by one for each row added to it. The first row starts off at 1, the second row becomes 2, and so on. For example,

```
C:\temp>sqlite3 MySQLite3TestDB
SQLite version 3.7.4
Enter ".help" for instructions
Enter SQL statements terminated with a ";"
sqlite> create table test1(_id integer primary key autoincrement,
   ...>                     col1 stock_symbol text not null);
sqlite> insert into test1 values(NULL,"MSFT");
sqlite> insert into test1 values(NULL,"GOOG");
sqlite> insert into test1 values(NULL,"INTL");
sqlite> select * from test1;
1|MSFT
2|GOOG
3|INTL
```

In order to insert data into a table that contains an AUTOINCREMENT column, you must place the keyword NULL in the appropriate position in the VALUES statement (as shown above). While this may not make logical sense, the results shown above indicate that it does work.

Note that due to an oversight with SQLite, you should probably add the NOT NULL constraint to the PRIMARY KEY AUTOINCREMENT constraints so that NULL values will not be allowed into the column. This will ensure that the column will **only** have integer values from 1 on up.

Programming with the SQLite Database

With that teensy-weensy introduction complete, let's move on to how you can program an application to access a SQLite database from Java code.

If you've created a database (for test or production), don't forget to transfer it to either the emulator or the device.

314

Now, there are several Java packages listed in the Android documentation containing the word *database*:

1. `android.database.*` - this package is used with Content Providers and is not needed when accessing a SQLite database directly as we will be doing for the remainder of this chapter (although see #3 below). We discuss Content Providers in the next chapter.
2. `android.database.sqlite.*` - this package contains classes used to manage application-specific SQLite databases. This is the package you should import for use with the code shown in the remainder of this chapter.
3. `android.database.Cursor` - despite what we mentioned in #1 above, some of the classes in `android.database.sqlite` contain methods which return a `Cursor` object. This `Cursor` object is located in `android.database.Cursor`, so you will need to import this into your program as well.

There are several classes that you will be using during the remainder of this chapter, so we introduce them now:

1. `SQLiteDatabase` - this class exposes several methods used to interact with a SQLite database. The more important methods allow you to open an existing database, create a blank database, query a given table without using SQL, query the database by supplying a SQL query, and so on.
2. `SQLiteQueryBuilder` - this class contains methods which allow you to build a SQL query by describing the desired columns, the table name, how the data is to be subsetted, the sort order, etc. without creating the SQL query yourself.
3. `SQLiteStatement` - this class contains methods which allow you to execute a SQL query which returns a *single column and row of data* from the database. Note that the method used to compile the SQL query is located in the `SQLiteDatabase` class, but the methods used to execute them are located in this class. Crazy!
4. `SQLiteCursor` - this class exposes methods useful when working with cursors. A cursor is an object containing the results of your query. Note that you will often see the `Cursor` class used with SQLite instead of the `SQLiteCursor` class.
5. `SQLiteOpenHelper` - this class helps manage the opening, creation and/or upgrading of a database.

Besides the classes shown above, `android.database.sqlite` also contains the following exceptions you may want to use in your code:

```
SQLiteAbortException, SQLiteAccessPermException,
SQLiteBindOrColumnIndexOutOfRangeException, SQLiteBlobTooBigException,
SQLiteCantOpenDatabaseException, SQLiteConstraintException,
SQLiteDatabaseCorruptException, SQLiteDatabaseLockedException,
SQLiteDatatypeMismatchException, SQLiteDiskIOException, SQLiteDoneException,
SQLiteException, SQLiteFullException, SQLiteMisuseException,
SQLiteOutOfMemoryException, SQLiteReadOnlyDatabaseException and
SQLiteTableLockedException
```

Quick Start Guide

In this section, we present several examples to help you ramp up querying your SQLite database as quickly as possible.

First, you need to create a variable to hold a `SQLiteDatabase` object. You can either provide this within your own method...

```
SQLiteDatabase oSQLiteDB;
```

...or you can create a private variable at the top of your class...

```
private static SQLiteDatabase oSQLiteDB;
```

Next, you need to connect to your database located on the device. Below, let's open the database in read/write mode:

```
//Open the database in read/write mode
oSQLiteDB =
SQLiteDatabase.openDatabase("/data/data/com.example.andapp1/MySQLite3TestDB.db3",
                            null,
                            SQLiteDatabase.OPEN_READWRITE);
```

If you wish to open the database in read-only mode, use `SQLiteDatabase.OPEN_READONLY` instead of `SQLiteDatabase.OPEN_READWRITE`. Take note that the first parameter of the `openDatabase()` method is the location and name of the SQLite database. (When using ReadyState's `SQLiteAssetHelper` class, you won't have to do this.) If you want to create a database with the location and name given in the first parameter, then replace the third parameter with `SQLiteDatabase.CREATE_IF_NECESSARY`. This will create a blank database for you. The second parameter is set to a non-null value if you want to supply your own cursor factory. Here we set it to `null` to force the method to use the default cursor factory. We talk about cursor factories later in the chapter.

Now, the `openDatabase()` method returns a `SQLiteDatabase` object. Please refer to the documentation on this class for the list of features available. Note that you can pass the special SQLite database name ":memory:" as the first parameter to the `openDatabase()` method and you will be using a purely *in-memory* database rather than a physical file. Be aware that as soon as you close the connection to the database, the in-memory database will cease to exist.

Now, skipping a bit, when you are done using the database, you should close it:

```
//Close the database
if (oSQLiteDB != null) {
    oSQLiteDB.close();
}
```

In between opening the database and closing it, you can interact with the database in a variety of ways. For example, let's pull in a distinct list of stock symbols from our stock table, create a text string from them and display the results with a `Toast`. The first thing we need to do is create a string to hold our SQL query:

```
//Create the SQL string
String sSQL = "SELECT DISTINCT STOCK_SYMBOL FROM HISTORICAL_STOCK_PRICES";
```

Next, let's submit the query to the database using the `rawQuery()` method. This method's first parameter is the SQL query string and the second is set to a null value. (If your SQL query contains one or more question marks, each question mark is replaced by the corresponding value in a string array - specified in the second parameter - before the query is submitted to the database. We talk more about this later on, but let's leave this second parameter null for now.) The `rawQuery()` method returns a `Cursor` object, so please peruse the documentation on the `Cursor` class for a list of methods available.

```
//Get a cursor to the returned data
Cursor oCSR = oSQLiteDB.rawQuery(sSQL,null);
oCSR.moveToFirst(); //Moves to the first row returned from the Cursor.
```

Next, we initialize a string to hold the stock symbols. Note that I am using the `getCount()` method to retrieve the total number of rows the query has pulled back through the cursor. The string `sAllStockSymbols` is initialized with the row count followed by a colon.

```
//Initialize the sAllStockSymbols variable with the number of rows pulled back.
String sAllStockSymbols = Integer.toString(oCSR.getCount()) + ": ";
```

Checking that our query pulled back at least one row of data, we then perform a `while` loop to populate the `sAllStockSymbols` variable with the stock symbols. The `moveToNext()` method returns `true` as long as there are rows of data to process. On the last row, `moveToNext()` still returns `true`. But after that, `moveToNext()` returns `false` forcing the `while` loop to end. The `getColumnIndex()` method takes the name of the column you want to retrieve data for and returns an integer position index. In the code below, we pass "STOCK_SYMBOL" to the `getColumnIndex()` method and are given an index number. It is this number which is passed into the `getString()` method which retrieves the appropriate data (the stock symbol).

```
//Loop for each row in the cursor to create a large string of stock symbols
if (oCSR.getCount() > 0) {
 while(oCSR.moveToNext()) {
   sAllStockSymbols +=
         oCSR.getString(oCSR.getColumnIndex("STOCK_SYMBOL")) + " ";
 }
}
```

Finally, we display the list of stock symbols on the screen:

```
//Let's display the stock symbols using a Toast
Toast toast = Toast.makeText(getApplicationContext(), sAllStockSymbols,
Toast.LENGTH_LONG);
toast.show();
```

2: GOOG MSFT

Next, let's insert two additional rows of data into the table HISTORICAL_STOCK_PRICES. The first method uses the `execSQL()` method to pass a non-SELECT statement to the database; for example, these are some of the statements you can execute using execSQL(): INSERT, UPDATE, DELETE, ALTER TABLE, CREATE INDEX, ANALYZE, etc., but not the SELECT statement!

```
//Let's insert a new row into the database using execSQL
String sSQL_INSERT="INSERT INTO HISTORICAL_STOCK_PRICES " +
                   "VALUES('INTC',julianday('now','0 seconds'),22.81);";
oSQLiteDB.execSQL(sSQL_INSERT);
```

The next method of inserting data is the insert() method. This method's first parameter is the name of the table you are inserting into. The second parameter is set to null. The third parameter is the name of a ContentValues object containing your columns as well as their associated values. ContentValues is similar to Bundle or SharedPreferences in that it can hold several key/value pairs:

```
//Create a ContentValues object to hold key-value pairs
//ContentValues is located in android.content.
ContentValues oCV = new ContentValues();

//Put the key/value pairs into oCV
oCV.put("STOCK_SYMBOL", "CSCO");
oCV.put("PRICE_DATE", "2456196");
oCV.put("STOCK_PRICE", "18.65");

//Insert the row of data into the table.
long lRowID = oSQLiteDB.insert("HISTORICAL_STOCK_PRICES", null, oCV);
```

Note that the insert() method returns the row ID of the newly created row or -1 if an error occurred.

Next, let's repeat the query above by using the query() method instead of the rawquery() method. The query() method has several parameters each of which is associated with, for the most part, a separate SQL clause. This method is great for those of you whose eyes glazed over when I was explaining SQL DDL and DML above! This method, unlike the rawquery() method, does not require you to form a SQL query!

```
//Let's query the database using query() instead of rawquery()
Cursor oCSR2 = oSQLiteDB.query(true,
                    "HISTORICAL_STOCK_PRICES",
                    new String[] {"STOCK_SYMBOL"},
                    null,
                    null,
                    null,
                    null,
                    "STOCK_SYMBOL",
                    null);
```

1. boolean distinct: The first parameter determines if your query is to return distinct data. If set to true, this mimics the DISTINCT keyword on the SELECT statement.
2. String table: The second parameter indicates the table you want to pull data from. Note that query() method does not allow for joins.

3. `String[] columns`: The third parameter is a `String` array containing the names of the desired columns to retrieve. Here I am only interested in one column, `STOCK_SYMBOL`, but I still need to create an array.
4. `String selection`: The fourth parameter is a `String` which mimics the `WHERE` statement. Here it is set to `null` indicating that all rows of data are to be returned. Note that you do not insert the word `WHERE` in this string!
5. `String[] selectionArgs`: The fifth parameter is a `String` array whose values will replace the question marks (?) placed in the fourth parameter. This is set to `null` indicating that there are no question marks in the fourth parameter's string. See below for an example of this.
6. `String groupBy`: The sixth parameter is a `String` containing a comma-delimited list of columns used on the `GROUP BY` statement. Here it is set to `null` indicating that the query will not group the rows. Note that you do not insert the word `GROUP BY` in this string.
7. `String having`: The seventh parameter is a `String` which mimics the `HAVING` statement. Here it is set to `null` indicating that all rows post-`GROUP BY` will be returned. Note that you do not insert the word `HAVING` in this string.
8. `String orderBy`: The eighth parameter is a `String` which mimics the `ORDER BY` statement. Here is it set to `STOCK_SYMBOL` indicating that the data will be sorted in ascending order on `STOCK_SYMBOL`. Note that you do not insert the words `ORDER BY` in this string. Use `null` if you do not require sorting.
9. `String limit`: The ninth parameter is a `String` which mimics the `LIMIT` statement. Here it is set to `null` indicating that all rows will be returned. Note that you do not insert the word `LIMIT` in this string.

At this point, the if statement and while loop are the same as the code for the `rawquery()` method:

```
String sAllStockSymbols2 = Integer.toString(oCSR2.getCount()) + ": ";
if (oCSR2.getCount() > 0) {
 while(oCSR2.moveToNext()) {
  sAllStockSymbols2 +=
             oCSR2.getString(oCSR2.getColumnIndex("STOCK_SYMBOL")) + " ";
 }
}

Toast toast2 = Toast.makeText(getApplicationContext(), sAllStockSymbols2,
Toast.LENGTH_LONG);
toast2.show();
```

4: CSCO GOOG INTC MSFT

There are many times when you just want to retrieve a single row and column containing a pertinent value such as the row count of a table, or the existence of a value, etc. In these cases, you don't have to use `query()` or `rawquery()`, but you can use `simpleQueryForLong()` or `simpleQueryForString()` on a compiled SQL statement. Now, it may seem strange, but you compile your SQL using the `compileStatement()` method located in the `SQLiteDatabase` class, but you execute the compiled SQL statement using methods found in the `SQLiteStatement` class. Go figure! In any case, here is an example of how to retrieve the row count from a table using compiled statements:

```
//Let's get back the count of the number of row in the table using
// compiled statement
String sSQL_ROWCOUNT = "SELECT COUNT(*) AS ROWCNT FROM HISTORICAL_STOCK_PRICES";

//Generate a compiled SQL statement using the compileStatement() method.
SQLiteStatement oSLS_RC = oSQLiteDB.compileStatement(sSQL_ROWCOUNT);

//Retrieve the row count into the long variable lRowCount.
long lRowCount = oSLS_RC.simpleQueryForLong();

Toast toast3 = Toast.makeText(getApplicationContext(), "Number of Rows=" +
Long.toString(lRowCount), Toast.LENGTH_LONG);
toast3.show();
```

Number of Rows=4

Finally, here is an example of using the question mark substitution in a `WHERE` statement when using the `query()` method:

```
Cursor oCSR2 = oSQLiteDB.query(true,
                    "HISTORICAL_STOCK_PRICES",
                    new String[] {"STOCK_SYMBOL"},
                    "STOCK_SYMBOL=? OR STOCK_SYMBOL=?",
                    new String[] {"MSFT","CSCO"},
                    null,
                    null,
                    "STOCK_SYMBOL",
                    null);
```

There is no need to surround the question marks in the `WHERE` statement with apostrophes or double quotes since that is taken care of for you. The first question mark is replaced with the first entry in the `String` array (`MSFT`) and the second question mark with the second entry (`CSCO`).

2: CSCO MSFT

If you need to delete all or some of the rows in a table, you can either use the `execSQL()` method with the appropriate SQL code, or you can use the `delete()` method. For example, to delete the rows containing the stock symbols `INTC` or `CSCO`, you can code something like this:

```
//Delete INTC and CSCO
int iNbrRowsDel = oSQLiteDB.delete("HISTORICAL_STOCK_PRICES",
                    "STOCK_SYMBOL IN (?,?)",
                    new String[] {"INTC","CSCO"});
```

Number of Rows Deleted=2

320

Take note that the `delete()` method returns the number of rows deleted. If you set the second and third parameters to `null`, all rows in the table will be deleted, but you will receive zero instead of the actual number of rows deleted. If you want to receive the actual number of rows deleted when deleting all rows, pass in a simple true statement as the *second* parameter, such as "1=1".

If you need to update all or some of the rows in a table, you can either use the `execSQL()` method with the appropriate SQL code, or you can use the `update()` method. For example, to change the `STOCK_PRICE` for `MSFT` from 4.12 to 2.56, you can code something like this:

```
//Update MSFT's stock price
ContentValues oCV_UPDATE = new ContentValues();
oCV_UPDATE.put("STOCK_PRICE", 2.56);
int iNbrRowsUpdated = oSQLiteDB.update("HISTORICAL_STOCK_PRICES",
                                oCV_UPDATE,
                                "STOCK_SYMBOL=?",
                                new String[] {"MSFT"});
```

Number of Rows Updated=1

Note that you have to pass a `ContentValue` object as the second parameter. The third parameter contains the `WHERE` statement indicating which row(s) should be updated. The fourth parameter contains the list of values that will replace each question mark in the `WHERE` statement.

As mentioned above, if you are not very familiar with SQL, you can use the `query()` method to build a SQL query behind the scenes by passing the appropriate text into its parameters. Unfortunately, this method does not show you the SQL that was constructed. If you do want to see the SQL, use the `SQLiteQueryBuilder` class to construct the SQL query as a `String`. You can look at this string to ensure that the query being built is correct. Finally, you can use the `rawQuery()` method to execute the query on the database. For example, let's build a complicated SQL query using `SQLiteQueryBuilder`'s `buildQuery String()` method:

```
String sBuiltSQL = SQLiteQueryBuilder.buildQueryString(
                                false,
                                "HISTORICAL_STOCK_PRICES",
                                new String[] {"STOCK_SYMBOL","STOCK_PRICE"},
                                "STOCK_SYMBOL IN ('MSFT','GOOG')",
                                null,
                                null,
                                "STOCK_SYMBOL,STOCK_PRICE DESC",
                                "2");
```

Note that the order of the parameters is the same for the `query()` method. Below is the SQL that it constructed:

```
SQL Query=SELECT STOCK_SYMBOL,
STOCK_PRICE FROM
HISTORICAL_STOCK_PRICES WHERE
STOCK_SYMBOL IN ('MSFT','GOOG')
ORDER BY STOCK_SYMBOL,STOCK_PRICE
DESC LIMIT 2
```

Recall that at the beginning of this section, we mentioned to close the database when you are done with it by using the `close()` method. Another way of handling this is to call the `startManagingCursor()` method which handles the close for you. If you use this method, do not call the `close()` method.

Occasionally, your database-driven app will crash with the LogCat error message `CursorIndexOutOfBoundsException: Index -1 requested, with a size of #`. I've solved this particular error by placing the `moveToFirst()` method on the cursor just after the call to `rawQuery()`:

```
//Get a cursor to the returned data
Cursor oCSR = oSQLiteDB.rawQuery(sSQL,null);
oCSR.moveToFirst(); //Moves to the first row returned from the Cursor.
```

So Why Use Anything Else? The `SQLiteOpenHelper` Class

The previous section outlined several classes and methods you can use to read from and write to your SQLite database. Although the code shown above allows you to query and modify your tables, it lacks any cohesive method of upgrading your database when the latest version of your application is released to the world. This is where the `SQLiteOpenHelper` class and its methods come in handy. Not only does it allow you to open, close, and upgrade your database, the subclass you create can serve as a general database access class containing your own methods.

Before we get to that, the following methods are available in the `SQLiteOpen Helper` class:

- `SQLiteOpenHelper(Context context,String db-name, SQLiteDatabase. CursorFactory factory, int version)` - this method is the constructor for the `SQLiteOpenHelper` class and returns a `SQLiteOpenHelper` object. You can pass a `null` for factory in order to use the default cursor factory. We discuss cursor factories later in this chapter. If you set `db-name` to `null`, then an in-memory database will be used instead of a physical db.
- `onConfigure(SQLiteDatabase db)` - this method allows you to configure your database before `onCreate()`, `onUpgrade()` or `onDowngrade()` is called. Use this method to call `SQLiteDatabase` methods such as `setLocale()` and so on. (See the section labeled *A Comment about Database Locale* below for more on `setLocale()`.)
- `onCreate(SQLiteDatabase db)` - this method is called when the database is created for the first time. If you have decided not to generate a

database up-front, then use this method to generate your tables and initialize them.

- onUpgrade(SQLiteDatabase db,int oldVersion,int newVersion) - this method is responsible for upgrading the database, if necessary.
- onDowngrade(SQLiteDatabase db,int oldVersion,int newVersion) - this method is responsible for downgrading the database, if necessary.
- onOpen(SQLiteDatabase db) - this method is called when the database is opened.
- getReadableDatabase() - this method creates and/or opens the database in read-only mode. It returns a SQLiteDatabase object.
- getWritableDatabase() - this method creates and/or opens the database in read-write mode. It returns a SQLiteDatabase object. Note that when this method is called for the first time, the database is opened and onCreate(), onUpgrade() and/or onOpen() will be called.
- close() - this method closes the database.

Since both getReadableDatabase() and getWritableDatabase() return a SQLite Database object, you can use the methods (i.e., query(), rawquery(), execSQL(), etc.) we discussed in the previous section.

Now, to use the SQLiteOpenHelper class, you must subclass this in your own class. Here is an example. Not only have I included overrides to the methods in SQLiteOpenHelper, but I have included additional methods (i.e., insertStock(), enumerateStocks(), etc.) I need during my own database processing.

```
package com.example.andapp1;

import android.content.Context;
import android.database.sqlite.*;
import android.database.sqlite.SQLiteDatabase.CursorFactory;
import android.database.*;
import android.database.sqlite.SQLiteOpenHelper;
import android.util.Log;
import android.content.ContentValues;

public class MySQLiteOpenHelper extends SQLiteOpenHelper {

 private SQLiteDatabase oDB;

 //public constructor
 public MySQLiteOpenHelper(Context context,
                           String sDBName,
                           CursorFactory factory,
                           int iDBVersion) {
  super(context,sDBName,null,iDBVersion);
 }

 //onCreate - called when the database is created for the first time
 @Override
 public void onCreate(SQLiteDatabase db) {
  Log.d("MYSQLTAG","IN ONCREATE!!");
 }

 //onUpgrade
```

```java
@Override
public void onUpgrade(SQLiteDatabase db,int oldVersion,int newVersion) {
 Log.d("MYSQLTAG","IN ONUPGRADE!!");
}

//onOpen
@Override
public void onOpen(SQLiteDatabase db) {
 super.onOpen(db);
 oDB=db;
 Log.d("MYSQLTAG","IN ONOPEN==>" + oDB.getPath());
}

//getReadableDatabase
@Override
public SQLiteDatabase getReadableDatabase() {
 Log.d("MYSQLTAG","IN GETREADABLEDATABASE!!");
 return super.getReadableDatabase();
}

//getWriteableDatabase
@Override
public SQLiteDatabase getWritableDatabase() {
 Log.d("MYSQLTAG","IN GETWRITABLEDATABASE!!");
 return super.getWritableDatabase();
}

//enumerateTables
public String enumerateTables() {

 //use oDB since the database is already opened.
 String sTables = "";

 //Using the SQLite sqlite_master table to get a list of tables in the database.
 //Note that we exclude sqlite_stat1 and android_metadata from the list.
 String sSQL = "SELECT name" +
               " FROM sqlite_master" +
               " WHERE type='table'" +
               "       and name not in ('sqlite_stat1','android_metadata')" +
                                               "ORDER BY name";

 //Get a cursor
 Cursor oCSR = oDB.rawQuery(sSQL,null);

 //Loop for each row in the cursor to create a large string of stock symbols
 if (oCSR.getCount() > 0) {
  while(oCSR.moveToNext()) {
   sTables += oCSR.getString(oCSR.getColumnIndex("name")) + " ";
  }
 }

 return sTables;
}

//getDB - returns the oDB object if you need it.
public SQLiteDatabase getDB() {
 return oDB;
}

//insertStock
public long insertStock(String sSymbol) {

 ContentValues oCV = new ContentValues();
 oCV.put("STOCK_SYMBOL", sSymbol);
 oCV.put("PRICE_DATE", "2456197");
 oCV.put("STOCK_PRICE", "12.34");
 long lRowID = oDB.insert("HISTORICAL_STOCK_PRICES", null, oCV);

 return lRowID;
```

324

```
    }

  //enumerateStocks
  public String enumerateStocks() {

    //use oDB since the database is already opened.
    String sStocks = "";
    String sSQL = "SELECT DISTINCT STOCK_SYMBOL" +
                  " FROM HISTORICAL_STOCK_PRICES" +
                  " ORDER BY STOCK_SYMBOL";


    //Get a cursor
    Cursor oCSR = oDB.rawQuery(sSQL,null);

    //Loop for each row in the cursor to create a large string of stock symbols
    if (oCSR.getCount() > 0) {
      while(oCSR.moveToNext()) {
        sStocks += oCSR.getString(oCSR.getColumnIndex("STOCK_SYMBOL")) + " ";
      }
    }

    return sStocks;
  }

  //close
  @Override
  public void close() {
    oDB.close();
    super.close();
  }

}
```

Here is an example of how I use this class:

```
//Instantiate the MySQLiteOpenHelper class
MySQLiteOpenHelper oMSOH =
    new MySQLiteOpenHelper(this,
                           "/data/data/com.example.andapp1/MySQLite3TestDB2.db3",
                           null,
                           1);

//Open the database in read/write mode.
oMSOH.getWritableDatabase();

//Get a list of tables in the database and display them.
String sTables = oMSOH.enumerateTables();
Toast toast=Toast.makeText(getApplicationContext(),"SQL Tables="+sTables,
Toast.LENGTH_LONG);
toast.show();
```

> SQL Tables=HISTORICAL_STOCK_PRICES
> TEST1

```
//insert a stock symbol into HISTORICAL_STOCK_PRICES
oMSOH.insertStock("YYYY");

//Get a list of stocks in the HISTORICAL_STOCK_PRICES table and display them.
String sStocks = oMSOH.enumerateStocks();
toast=Toast.makeText(getApplicationContext(),"Stock Symbols="+sStocks,
Toast.LENGTH_LONG);
toast.show();
```

```
//close the database
oMSOH.close();
```

Note that `SQLiteOpenHelper` is responsible for calling the `openDatabase()` method to get a `SQLiteDatabase` object. You don't have to call this method. But, in the code above, I do create a private variable to the `SQLiteDatabase` object when the `onOpen()` method is called. It is this private variable that is used in `enumerateTables()` and `enumerateStocks()`. As you see, I have included the method `getDB()` which returns a `SQLite Database` object associated with our open database. This is not strictly necessary since you can also obtain the equivalent object by using the instantiated variable along with `getWritableDatabase()` or `getReadableDatabase()`. Here we call `execSQL()`, but you can call whatever you like once you have a `SQLiteDatabase` object:

```
oMSOH.getWritableDatabase().execSQL(sql);
```

What is a Cursor Factory?

In the previous sections, you may have noticed that several of the methods require a cursor factory as a parameter, although we passed in a `null` instead in all cases. By passing in a `null`, we effectively tell Android that we want the default cursor factory. A *cursor factory* is a mechanism for handling cursor operations such as returning column values, moving to the next or previous row in the resultset, closing the cursor, etc. Now, for the most part, you will want to use the default cursor factory provided by Android, but you have the option of creating your own cursor factory by implementing the `SQLiteDatabase.CursorFactory` interface. We won't do that.

A Comment about Database Locale

If you create your own database using the methods described at the beginning of this chapter and then transfer it to either the emulator or device, when you open the database using the `openDatabase()` method you may be greeted with the following messages:

```
I/Database(622): sqlite returned: error code = 1, msg = no such table:
android_metadata
E/Database(622): SELECT locale FROM android_metadata failed
```

This error message indicates that the table `android_metadata` does not exist. This table contains a single `Text` column named `locale` and contains the two-letter language code, followed by a dash followed by the capitalized two-letter country code. For me, it's `en-US`. You can create this table in your database before you transfer it over, as shown below.

```
//MUST ADD android_metadata table into database!
CREATE TABLE android_metadata (locale TEXT);
```

326

```
INSERT INTO android_metadata VALUES('en_US');
```

An alternative method is to use the `NO_LOCALIZED_COLLATORS` flag when calling the `openDatabase()` method:

```
oSQLiteDB = SQLiteDatabase.openDatabase("/data/data/pkg-name/dbname",
                                        null,
                                        SQLiteDatabase.NO_LOCALIZED_COLLATORS);
```

Both methods prevent the error messages from occurring. If you want to have multiple flags set, use a vertical bar between each one of them:

```
oSQLiteDB = SQLiteDatabase.openDatabase("/data/data/pkg-name/dbname",
                                        null,
                                        SQLiteDatabase.NO_LOCALIZED_COLLATORS |
                                        SQLiteDatabase.OPEN_READONLY);
```

A Comment about SQLite Sort-Order Problems

Occasionally, the SQL `ORDER BY` Clause may not appear to be sorting your data appropriately. This may be caused by a feature in SQLite which allows you to insert any type of data within a column despite the column's original data type. That is, if a column is defined as being `REAL`, you can insert characters into that column and SQLite will not argue with you. Unfortunately, this feature changes the natural sort order from numeric-based to character-based, which may not be what you want. If the sort order for your numeric columns is not appropriate, try to use the SQLite `CAST()` function to re-cast the column back to `REAL`: `UPDATE MYTABLE SET MYCOLUMN = CAST(MYCOLUMN AS REAL);`. Hopefully, this will solve the sorting problem.

Summary

In this tiny chapter, we introduced the SQL language as well as described how to read from and write to a SQLite database. In the next chapter, we talk about Content Providers which, if desired, can allow public access to the data stored in your SQLite database.

Chapter 16: Content Providers

Overview

In this chapter, we discuss content providers. A *content provider* allows developers to easily access your application's data without having to worry about the underlying database structure. Any new application you (or another developer) create can use your application's content provider to access the underlying data. **Generally, your own application should not use its own content provider since access via the cursor mechanism (see previous chapter) is usually faster than access via the content provider mechanism!**

To convince you that this is not an esoteric programming topic and that you shouldn't skip this chapter, you must understand that the Android system comes with several built-in content providers which you can access from within your own applications:

1. `Contacts/ContactsContract` - this provider allows you to query the user's contacts data
2. `CalendarContract` - this provider allows you to query the user's calendar
3. `UserDictionary` - this provider allows you to query the user's dictionary
4. `MediaStore` - this provider allows you to query the user's media store which may contain albums, images, videos, etc.

You can learn more about these content providers by visiting the following website: `http://developer.android.com/reference/android/provider/package-summary.html`.

Access to the data provided through the `ContentProvider` class is through the `ContentResolver` class. We show you how to use this class later on in this chapter.

You can think of a content provider as a web server and a content resolver as a web browser. A content provider, like a web server, sends out information requested of it. A content resolver, like a web browser, makes use of that information. Here, *information* is not just a web page, but can be an image, a video, tabular data, an MP3 file, etc. and is as true of a content provider/content resolver as it is for a web server/web browser.

When you request a web page, you usually type in a web address - typically beginning with `http://` - into your web browser's address bar. It is this address that directs the web browser to a website, image, PDF file, etc., which is then displayed by the web browser. For content providers, you define a *content URI* which is the address of the content provider's data. Instead of using `http://`, though, content providers use `content://` followed by the address of the desired content provider's data. There are two forms of address for content providers:

1. `content://<package-name>.provider/<table-name>`
2. `content://<package-name>.provider/<table-name>/#`

The first form of address retrieves the data from a specific table. The second form retrieves a specific row - the # sign is replaced by the desired row number - within the table. It is for this reason, as well as a few others, that your tables should contain a column named `_id` that is defined as `INTEGER PRIMARY KEY AUTOINCREMENT`. For example, our test application has content providers similar to the following:

```
content://com.example.andapp1.provider/stocksymbols
content://com.example.andapp1.provider/stocksymbols/#
```

Continuing the analogy, when a web server sends data back to the web browser, the MIME type is part of the delivery. A *MIME type* answers the browser's question, "What is this stuff the web server just sent me?" For example, web pages have a MIME type of `text/html`; Adobe Acrobat Reader PDF files have a MIME type of `application/pdf`; image files have a MIME type of `image/jpeg`, `image/gif` or `image/png`. A MIME type is made up of a *type* and a *subtype*: `type/subtype`. A content provider also has a MIME type in the form of `type/subtype`. Content providers have two types:

1. `vnd.android.cursor.`**`dir`** - indicates there are multiple rows of data coming back
2. `vnd.android.cursor.`**`item`** - indicates there is one row of data coming back

Yes, those `type` names are very long, but serve a similar purpose to the types: `text`, `application`, `image`, etc. shown above. Remember: it's not the size, but what you do with it!

The `subtype` is generated by the developer of the content provider and is typically in the form: `vnd.com.<package-name>.provider.<table-name>`. For example, for our test program, the MIME types to access the `STOCK_SYMBOLS` table for both multiple and single rows of data are:

```
vnd.android.cursor.dir/vnd.com.example.andapp1.provider.stocksymbols
vnd.android.cursor.item/vnd.com.example.andapp1.provider.stocksymbols
```

Note that the `table-name` is arbitrary, but usually reflects the table the content provider is pulling from. Note that you can make use of an underlying database *view* instead of a physical table which allows you to create complex joins from two or more tables.

Occasionally, a website will ask you for a username and password in order to view its content; that is, you need permission to access the data. The same is true for data served up from a content provider. When creating a content provider, you place a `<permission>` tag in the `ApplicationManifest.xml` file. When a developer creates an application that wants access to your content provider, he has no choice but to place the appropriate permission(s) into his own `ApplicationManifest.xml` file. When his application is installed on the user's device, the user is asked if he/she allows the application to have that permission. For example, when you install an application that wants access to the `Contacts` content provider, you are asked if you want to allow that permission. If you agree, then the application is installed. If you disagree, the application is not installed and the developer is sacrificed.

Permissions, whether read or write, take the form `<package-name>.permission.<permission-type>`.

In our example, `com.example.andapp1.permission.READ_PERMISSION`. Similar for `WRITE_PERMISSION`.

Finally, how does the world find out about a particular website? Well, for the most part, people do a Google search and *voila!* publicly available websites appear. Now, for content providers, the developer creates a *contract class* that contains all of the relevant information the content resolver needs to pull data from the content provider: content URIs for table and individual row selection, names of the columns in the table, etc. The programmer of the content resolver makes use of these contract classes in order to access the data available through the content provider. We talk more about contract classes later on in the chapter.

The next few sections go through in more detail what was discussed above. First, though, since a content URI is used to specify the address of the content provider, the `Uri`, `Uri.Builder`, `ContentUris` and `UriMatcher` classes are used to parse this address, which is why the next section is dedicated to these classes. It is this parsed address that is used by the code in the content provider to determine which data and how much of it to return.

The `Uri`, `Uri.Builder`, `ContentUris` and `UriMatcher` Classes

As mentioned in the Overview, content providers assign a content URI which points to a content provider's data (i.e., table, view, etc.). The content resolver then uses this URI to pull the desired data. Since the URI is such an integral part of this process, there are several classes that you can use to make working with URIs a little simpler. Both the `Uri` and `Uri.Builder` classes are generic classes whereas `ContentUris` and `UriMatcher` are specific to working with URIs related to content providers:

1. `android.net.Uri` - use this class to parse a generic URI
2. `android.net.Uri.Builder` - use this class to build a generic URI
3. `android.content.ContentUris` - use this class when working with `Uri` or `Uri.Builder` objects that are content provider-specific and you either need to append an id number to the end of a URI or retrieve the id number from the end of a URI
4. `android.content.UriMatcher` - use this class to determine if the requested content URI contains a request for data - either a specific table or row - that is allowed by your content provider

As mentioned in the previous section, content URIs take on two forms:

1. `content://<package-name>.provider/<table-name>`
2. `content://<package-name>.provider/<table-name>/#`

330

In general, though, URIs take the following *generic* form which you will see in some of the documentation as well as some upscale pornographic magazines:

scheme://*authority*/*path*?*query*#*fragment*

In order to create a `Uri` object, you can use the `parse()` method passing in a string containing your URI:

```
Uri uContentUri =
            Uri.parse("content://com.example.andapp1.provider/stocksymbols");
```

You can pull apart the URI into its constituent parts such as scheme, authority and path by using the relevant methods:

```
// content://com.example.andapp1.provider/stocksymbols
String sContentUri = uContentUri.toString();

// content
String sScheme= uContentUri.getScheme();

// com.example.andapp1.provider
String sAuthority = uContentUri.getAuthority();

// /stocksymbols
String sPath = uContentUri.getPath();

// stocksymbols
String sLastPath = uContentUri.getLastPathSegment();
```

Note that the `getPath()` method returns the leading slash. If you use the `getLastPathSegment()` method instead, it will return the last path without the leading slash. If you have more than one path, you can use the `getPathSegments()` method to pull out all of them into a `List<String>` array:

```
Uri uContentUri =
         Uri.parse("content://com.example.andapp1.provider/stocksymbols/amex");
List<String> lPaths = uContentUri.getPathSegments();

//process each path segment using a for loop
for(String sThisPath : lPaths) {
 //Process code using sThisPath
 //First time through loop, sThisPath=stocksymbols
 //Second time through loop, sThisPath=amex
}
```

Once you have a `Uri` object, you can add additional paths to it using the `withAppendedPath()` method. For example, let's add `nyse` to the end of our content URI:

```
Uri uContentUri_ExchangeSpecific = Uri.withAppendedPath(uContentUri, "nyse");
```

This returns the following:

```
content://com.example.andapp1.provider/stocksymbols/nyse
```

Now, given strings containing the scheme, authority, path, etc., you can use the `Uri.Builder` class to generate a `Uri` from these pieces:

First, we instantiate a new `Uri.Builder`:

```
Uri.Builder ubContentUriBuilder = new Uri.Builder();
```

Next, we set the scheme, authority and path:

```
// content
ubContentUriBuilder.scheme(sScheme);

// com.example.andapp1.provider
ubContentUriBuilder.authority(sAuthority);

// stocksymbols
ubContentUriBuilder.path(sLastPath);
```

Finally, we generate a `Uri` by using the `build()` method:

```
ubContentUriBuilder.build();
```

This is the result if you use the `toString()` method on `ubContentUriBuilder`:

```
content://com.example.andapp1.provider/stocksymbols
```

Now, if you already have a `Uri`, you can create a `Uri.Builder` by using the `buildUpon()` method of the `Uri`:

```
Uri.Builder ubContentFromUri = uContentUri.buildUpon();
```

Next, let's add the `nyse` path to the end of the content provider:

```
ubContentFromUri.appendPath("nyse");
```

This is the result if you use the `toString()` method on `ubContentFromUri`:

```
content://com.example.andapp1.provider/stocksymbols/nyse
```

Now, there are many methods available in the `Uri` and `Uri.Builder` classes that we did not cover, so please check the documentation for more on these classes.

Now, the two classes we just described are *generic* classes for working with URIs. The `ContentUris` class is used more often when the scheme is `content`. There are three static methods in this class:

1. `appendId(Uri.Builder builder,long id)` - this method takes a `Uri.Builder` and `long` and returns a `Uri.Builder` with the id appended to the end of the URI.
2. `parseId(Uri contentUri)` - this method takes a `Uri`, pulls out the last path segment - which is a row number if the MIME type is `vnd.android.cursor.item` - converts it to `long` and returns it. Use this method to get the ID number.
3. `withAppendedId(Uri contentUri, long id)` - this method is similar to `appendId()` except it returns a `Uri` instead of `Uri.Builder`.

For example, let's create a `Uri` containing our example content URI and then use the `withAppendId()` method to add a row number to it:

```
Uri uContentUri =
                Uri.parse("content://com.example.andapp1.provider/stocksymbols");
Uri uContentUriWithID = ContentUris.withAppendedId(uContentUri, 4);
```

This is the result if you use the `toString()` method on `ubContentUriWithID`:

```
content://com.example.andapp1.provider/stocksymbols/4
```

We can also pull the ID number from the end of a content URI using the `parseId()` method:

```
long lID = ContentUris.parseId(uContentUriWithID);
```

The result is predictable: `4`.

The `UriMatcher` class is used to easily determine which content URI was requested from the content resolver. The usefulness of this class will become more apparent later on in this chapter when we explain how to code a content provider. When instantiating the `UriMatcher()`, you initially pass the static constant `UriMatcher.NO_MATCH`. You then add each content URI using the `addURI()` method. Finally, you use the `match()` method to determine which URI matches the URI passed to the content provider. For example, let's set up a series of static constants, one for each possible request from the content resolver:

```
//All stock symbols from all exchanges
private static final int STOCK_SYMBOLS_ALL = 1;

//All stock symbols for stock symbol _ID
private static final int STOCK_SYMBOLS_ALL_ID = 2;

//NYSE stock symbols only
private static final int STOCK_SYMBOLS_NYSE = 3;

//NYSE for stock symbol _ID
private static final int STOCK_SYMBOLS_NYSE_ID = 4;

//NASDAQ stock symbols only
private static final int STOCK_SYMBOLS_NASDAQ = 5;

//NASDAQ  for stock symbol _ID
private static final int STOCK_SYMBOLS_NASDAQ_ID = 6;

//AMEX stock symbols only
private static final int STOCK_SYMBOLS_AMEX = 7;

//AMEX for stock symbol _ID
private static final int STOCK_SYMBOLS_AMEX_ID = 8;
```

Next, let's create a `UriMatcher` and add the authority and path associated with each one of the constants above by using the `addURI()` method. The first parameter is the authority, the second parameter is the path and the third parameter is the return value:

```
//Initial by passing NO_MATCH
UriMatcher umStock = new UriMatcher(UriMatcher.NO_MATCH);

umStock.addURI("com.example.andapp1.provider",
               "stocksymbols",
               STOCK_SYMBOLS_ALL);

umStock.addURI("com.example.andapp1.provider",
               "stocksymbols/nyse",
               STOCK_SYMBOLS_NYSE);

umStock.addURI("com.example.andapp1.provider",
               "stocksymbols/nasdaq",
               STOCK_SYMBOLS_NASDAQ);

umStock.addURI("com.example.andapp1.provider",
               "stocksymbols/amex",
               STOCK_SYMBOLS_AMEX);

umStock.addURI("com.example.andapp1.provider",
               "stocksymbols/#",
               STOCK_SYMBOLS_ALL_ID);

umStock.addURI("com.example.andapp1.provider",
               "stocksymbols/nyse/#",
               STOCK_SYMBOLS_NYSE_ID);

umStock.addURI("com.example.andapp1.provider",
               "stocksymbols/nasdaq/#",
               STOCK_SYMBOLS_NASDAQ_ID);

umStock.addURI("com.example.andapp1.provider",
               "stocksymbols/amex/#",
               STOCK_SYMBOLS_AMEX_ID);
```

Next, let's create a content URI to use in the test code below:

```
Uri uContentUri =
        Uri.parse("content://com.example.andapp1.provider/stocksymbols/amex/5");
```

Finally, let's create a `switch` statement that will use the `match()` method to determine if the test content URI (above) matches any of those we defined by using the `addURI()` method:

```
String sType = "";
switch(umStock.match(uContentUri)) {

 case STOCK_SYMBOLS_ALL:
  sType="vnd.android.cursor.dir/stocksymbol";
  break;

 case STOCK_SYMBOLS_NYSE:
  sType="vnd.android.cursor.dir/stocksymbol/nyse";
  break;

 case STOCK_SYMBOLS_NASDAQ:
  sType="vnd.android.cursor.dir/stocksymbol/nasdaq";
  break;

 case STOCK_SYMBOLS_AMEX:
  sType="vnd.android.cursor.dir/stocksymbol/amex";
  break;

 case STOCK_SYMBOLS_ALL_ID:
  sType="vnd.android.cursor.item/stocksymbol/#";
  break;
```

334

```
case STOCK_SYMBOLS_NYSE_ID:
  sType="vnd.android.cursor.item/stocksymbol/nyse/#";
  break;

case STOCK_SYMBOLS_NASDAQ_ID:
  sType="vnd.android.cursor.item/stocksymbol/nasdaq/#";
  break;

case STOCK_SYMBOLS_AMEX_ID:
  sType="vnd.android.cursor.item/stocksymbol/amex/#";
  break;

default:
  sType = "???";
  break;

}
```

As you can guess, `sType` is set to `vnd.android.cursor.item/stocksymbol/amex/#`. Note that it is the *form* of the string that is being matched and not the exact string!

Note this concept will help us when we learn how to create the `getType()` method for our content provider.

Steps Involved in Creating a Content Provider: Overview

There are several steps involved in creating a content provider:

1. Create a SQLite database containing the data for your application. Note that not all of the data in your database needs to be world-accessible since you can tell the content provider exactly what data other applications can access. Don't forget to include a column named `_id` defined as `INTEGER PRIMARY KEY AUTOINCREMENT` in each of your world-accessible tables. Also, don't forget to create appropriate indexes and use the `ANALYZE` command after you've loaded the tables with data.
2. Create content URIs used to access your table's data, either entirely or for a specific row number, or both. For example,

   ```
   content://com.example.andapp1.provider/stocksymbols
   content://com.example.andapp1.provider/stocksymbols/#
   ```

3. Create the MIME types associated with the tables. This also includes creating our static variables associating an integer with each MIME type. This will be used in the `getType()` method below. See the previous section for an example of this.
4. Create one contract class for each table. This public class must contain public static final variables mapping the Java variable names to the table column names as well as the content URIs. For example, if your table `STOCK_SYMBOLS` contains the stock symbol column `STK_SYM`, you might code the following in the contract class associated with the `STOCK_SYMBOLS` table (the Java variable `STOCKSYMBOL` below refers to the *column* and not the *table*):

   ```
   public static final string STOCKSYMBOL = "STK_SYM";
   ```

5. Create the content provider by subclassing the `ContentProvider` class (`android. content.ContentProvider`). This involves overriding several methods such as `delete()`, `insert()`, `update()`, `query()`, `getType()` and `onCreate()`. The `getType()` method will contain code suspiciously similar to the `switch` statement in the previous section.
6. Create one or more permissions to allow external access to your data via the content provider. These permissions will be used by another application using a content resolver to access your content provider.
7. Update the `AndroidManifest.xml` file with `<provider>` tags within the `<application>` tag. Without the `<provider>` tags, other applications won't be able to access your data. You will also need to add the `<permission>` tag based on the results of Step #6.

We go through each of the steps outlined above in much more detail below. Hold on to your hat, folks, it's gonna be a bumpy ride!

Step #1: Creating the SQLite Database

Although we discussed creating a SQLite database in the previous chapter, including adding tables and populating them with data, the tables used with a content provider have some additional requirements that we will outline here.

For our example, let's create the `STOCK_SYMBOLS` table containing the stocks that make up the Dow Jones Industrial Average, and the `STOCK_STATS` table containing the symbol as well as several financial statistics. Below is the SQL code I used to generate these two tables. Take note that both tables have a column named `_ID` that is defined as `INTEGER PRIMARY KEY AUTOINCREMENT`. Also, when using the `VALUES` statement, setting that column to `NULL` will force SQLite to generate a new integer for that row automatically. The database is called `EQUITY_DATABASE`.

```
DROP TABLE STOCK_SYMBOLS;
CREATE TABLE STOCK_SYMBOLS(_ID INTEGER PRIMARY KEY AUTOINCREMENT,
                           STOCK_SYMBOL TEXT,
                           COMPANY_NAME TEXT);
INSERT INTO STOCK_SYMBOLS VALUES(NULL,'MMM','3M');
INSERT INTO STOCK_SYMBOLS VALUES(NULL,'AA','ALCOA');
INSERT INTO STOCK_SYMBOLS VALUES(NULL,'AXP','AMERICAN EXPRESS');
INSERT INTO STOCK_SYMBOLS VALUES(NULL,'T','AT&T');
INSERT INTO STOCK_SYMBOLS VALUES(NULL,'BAC','BANK OF AMERICA');
INSERT INTO STOCK_SYMBOLS VALUES(NULL,'BA','BOEING');
INSERT INTO STOCK_SYMBOLS VALUES(NULL,'CAT','CATERPILLAR');
INSERT INTO STOCK_SYMBOLS VALUES(NULL,'CVX','CHEVRON');
INSERT INTO STOCK_SYMBOLS VALUES(NULL,'KO','COCA-COLA');
INSERT INTO STOCK_SYMBOLS VALUES(NULL,'CSCO','CISCO SYSTEMS');
INSERT INTO STOCK_SYMBOLS VALUES(NULL,'DIS','DISNEY');
INSERT INTO STOCK_SYMBOLS VALUES(NULL,'DD','DU PONT');
INSERT INTO STOCK_SYMBOLS VALUES(NULL,'XOM','EXXON MOBIL');
INSERT INTO STOCK_SYMBOLS VALUES(NULL,'GE','GENERAL ELECTRIC');
INSERT INTO STOCK_SYMBOLS VALUES(NULL,'HPQ','HEWLETT-PACKARD');
INSERT INTO STOCK_SYMBOLS VALUES(NULL,'HD','HOME DEPOT');
INSERT INTO STOCK_SYMBOLS VALUES(NULL,'IBM','IBM');
INSERT INTO STOCK_SYMBOLS VALUES(NULL,'INTC','INTEL');
INSERT INTO STOCK_SYMBOLS VALUES(NULL,'JNJ','JOHNSON & JOHNSON');
INSERT INTO STOCK_SYMBOLS VALUES(NULL,'JPM','JP MORGAN CHASE');
INSERT INTO STOCK_SYMBOLS VALUES(NULL,'UNH','UNITEDHEALTH GROUP');
INSERT INTO STOCK_SYMBOLS VALUES(NULL,'MCD','MCDONALDS');
```

```
INSERT INTO STOCK_SYMBOLS VALUES(NULL,'MRK','MERCK');
INSERT INTO STOCK_SYMBOLS VALUES(NULL,'MSFT','MICROSOFT');
INSERT INTO STOCK_SYMBOLS VALUES(NULL,'PFE','PFIZER');
INSERT INTO STOCK_SYMBOLS VALUES(NULL,'PG','PROCTER & GAMBLE');
INSERT INTO STOCK_SYMBOLS VALUES(NULL,'TRV','TRAVELERS');
INSERT INTO STOCK_SYMBOLS VALUES(NULL,'UTX','UNITED TECH');
INSERT INTO STOCK_SYMBOLS VALUES(NULL,'VZ','VERIZON COMMUNICATIONS');
INSERT INTO STOCK_SYMBOLS VALUES(NULL,'WMT','WAL-MART');

CREATE INDEX IX_STKSYMS_STKSYM ON STOCK_SYMBOLS(STOCK_SYMBOL);
ANALYZE STOCK_SYMBOLS;

DROP TABLE STOCK_STATS;
CREATE TABLE STOCK_STATS(_ID INTEGER PRIMARY KEY AUTOINCREMENT,
                         STOCK_SYMBOL TEXT,
                         LAST_TRADE_DATE INTEGER,
                         LAST_PRICE REAL,
                         VOLUME INTEGER,
                         MARKETCAP REAL,
                         PERATIO REAL,
                         EPS REAL,
                         YIELD REAL);
INSERT INTO STOCK_STATS VALUES(NULL,'AA',ROUND(JULIANDAY('2012-10-
06')+0.5),9.09,19298836,9.70,131.74,0.07,1.30);
INSERT INTO STOCK_STATS VALUES(NULL,'AXP',ROUND(JULIANDAY('2012-10-
06')+0.5),58.56,4761539,66.39,13.72,4.27,1.40);
...and so on...

CREATE INDEX IX_STKSTATS_STKSYM ON STOCK_STATS(STOCK_SYMBOL);
ANALYZE STOCK_STATS;

DROP VIEW vwSTOCKSTATSMATCH;
CREATE VIEW vwSTOCKSTATSMATCH AS
 SELECT A.STOCK_SYMBOL,
        A.COMPANY_NAME,
        B.LAST_TRADE_DATE,
        B.LAST_PRICE,
        B.VOLUME,
        B.MARKETCAP,
        B.PERATIO,
        B.EPS,
        B.YIELD
  FROM STOCK_SYMBOLS A LEFT JOIN STOCK_STATS B
  ON A.STOCK_SYMBOL=B.STOCK_SYMBOL;
```

Note that I don't create an index on the `_ID` column because the keyword `PRIMARY KEY` indicates that an index will be created automatically behind the scenes.

Finally, I created a view that merges both tables together. Transfer this SQLite database to the device by directly copying it over (if permissions allow), using ReadyState's `SQLiteAssetHelper` class, or choosing another method.

Step #2: Create the Content URIs

Now that we have our database set up and the tables populated, we have a better idea as to which tables we want other programmers to be able to access. In this case, we will allow the two tables `STOCK_SYMBOLS` and `STOCK_STATS` as well as the view, `vwSTOCKSTATSMATCH` to be accessible via content resolvers (which we discuss later on in the chapter). Thus, we set up our content URIs as follows:

1. `content://com.example.andapp1.provider/stocksymbols`

2. `content://com.example.andapp1.provider/stocksymbols/#`
3. `content://com.example.andapp1.provider/stockstats`
4. `content://com.example.andapp1.provider/stockstats/#`
5. `content://com.example.andapp1.provider/stockalldata`

Notice that we created two content URIs for each table: one will be used to pull all of the data and the other will be used to pull a single row of data (the #-sign content URI). The view, on the other hand, only has one content URI used to pull all of the data. This is because a view does not have a row number associated with it.

Step #3: Create the MIME Types

Now that we have the content URIs defined, let's create a MIME type associated with each one:

1. `vnd.android.cursor.dir/stocksymbols`
2. `vnd.android.cursor.item/stocksymbols`
3. `vnd.android.cursor.dir/stockstats`
4. `vnd.android.cursor.item/stockstats`
5. `vnd.android.cursor.dir/stockalldata`

Along with this, let's create our associated integers for use in matching:

1. `private static final int STOCKSYMBOLS_ALL=1; //All stock symbols`
2. `private static final int STOCKSYMBOLS_ID = 2; //All stock symbols specific _ID`
3. `private static final int STOCKSTATS_ALL = 3; //All stock stats`
4. `private static final int STOCKSTATS_ID = 4; //All stock stats for specific _ID`
5. `private static final int STOCKALLDATA = 5; //All view data`

Step #4: Create the Contract Classes

Now, let's define three contract classes, one for each table and one for the view. These classes will contain:

1. Mappings between the SQLite table columns to Java variables which is used to give another name to your columns.
2. Content URIs
3. MIME Types
4. Additional information you feel is necessary

Usually, the contract class implements the `BaseColumns` interface (located in the `android.provider` package). This interface contains two public static Strings:

1. `_ID` - this variable holds the column name associated with the _ID column. This is set to "_id" by default and, if you created your SQLite database as I did in Step #1, is the same as in your tables.
2. `_COUNT` - this variable holds the column name associated with the _COUNT column. This is set to "_count" by default. We don't have an _count column in our tables and that's okay.

While you are not required to implement the `BaseColumns` interface, we will do so. Here are our three contract classes. Note that each one has to be in its own `.java` file. Take note that the contract classes contain both the variables CONTENT_TYPE and CONTENT_ITEM_TYPE. CONTENT_TYPE contains the MIME Type which allows for all the table's data to be pulled back whereas CONTENT_ITEM_TYPE contains the MIME Type which allows only a specific row to be pulled back.

```java
//ContractClassSTOCKSYMBOLS
package com.example.andapp1;

import android.provider.BaseColumns;
import android.net.Uri;

public final class ContractClassSTOCKSYMBOLS implements BaseColumns {

 //This class should not be instantiated
 private ContractClassSTOCKSYMBOLS() {
 }

 //Define CONTENT_AUTHORITY
 public static final String CONTENT_AUTHORITY = "com.example.andapp1.provider";

 //Define BASE_CONTENT_URI as a Uri object
 public static final Uri BASE_CONTENT_URI = Uri.parse("content://" +
                                                       CONTENT_AUTHORITY);

 //Define CONTENT_URI as a Uri object
 public static final Uri CONTENT_URI = Uri.parse("content://" +
                                       CONTENT_AUTHORITY + "/stocksymbols");

 //Define CONTENT_TYPE to represent the MIME Type for all rows in the table
 public static final String CONTENT_TYPE = "vnd.android.cursor.dir/stocksymbols";

 //Define CONTENT_ITEM_TYPE to represent the MIME Type for an individual row
 // in the table
 public static final String CONTENT_ITEM_TYPE =
                                       "vnd.android.cursor.item/stocksymbols";

 //TABLE COLUMN DEFINITIONS:

 //_ID: Note that BaseColumns automatically brings in _ID set to "_id",
 // so we don't have to do that!

 //STOCK_SYMBOL
 public static final String STOCKSYMBOL = "STOCK_SYMBOL";

 //COMPANY_NAME
 public static final String COMPANYNAME = "COMPANY_NAME";

}

//ContractClassSTOCKSTATS
package com.example.andapp1;

import android.provider.BaseColumns;
import android.net.Uri;

public final class ContractClassSTOCKSTATS implements BaseColumns {

 //This class should not be instantiated
 private ContractClassSTOCKSTATS() {
 }

 //Define CONTENT_AUTHORITY
 public static final String CONTENT_AUTHORITY = "com.example.andapp1.provider";
```

339

```java
//Define BASE_CONTENT_URI as a Uri object
public static final Uri BASE_CONTENT_URI = Uri.parse("content://" +
                                                 CONTENT_AUTHORITY);

//Define CONTENT_URI as a Uri object
public static final Uri CONTENT_URI = Uri.parse("content://" +
                                      CONTENT_AUTHORITY + "/stockstats");

//Define CONTENT_TYPE to represent the MIME Type for all rows in the table
public static final String CONTENT_TYPE = "vnd.android.cursor.dir/stockstats";

//Define CONTENT_ITEM_TYPE to represent the MIME Type for an individual row
// in the table
public static final String CONTENT_ITEM_TYPE =
                                "vnd.android.cursor.item/stockstats";

//TABLE COLUMN DEFINITIONS

//_ID: Note that BaseColumns automatically brings in _ID set to "_id",
// so we don't have to do that!

//STOCK_SYMBOL
public static final String STOCKSYMBOL = "STOCK_SYMBOL";

//LAST_TRADE_DATE
public static final String LASTTRADEDATE = "LAST_TRADE_DATE";

//LAST_PRICE
public static final String LASTPRICE = "LAST_PRICE";

//VOLUME
public static final String VOLUME = "VOLUME";

//MARKETCAP (in billions)
public static final String MARKETCAP = "MARKETCAP";

//PERATIO
public static final String PERATIO = "PERATIO";

//EPS
public static final String EPS = "EPS";

//YIELD (as a percent)
public static final String YIELD = "YIELD";

}
```

//ContractClassSTOCKALLDATA
```java
package com.example.andapp1;

import android.provider.BaseColumns;
import android.net.Uri;

public final class ContractClassSTOCKALLDATA implements BaseColumns {

 //This class should not be instantiated
 private ContractClassSTOCKALLDATA() {
 }

 //Define CONTENT_AUTHORITY
 public static final String CONTENT_AUTHORITY = "com.example.andapp1.provider";

 //Define BASE_CONTENT_URI as a Uri object
 public static final Uri BASE_CONTENT_URI = Uri.parse("content://" +
                                                 CONTENT_AUTHORITY);

 //Define CONTENT_URI as a Uri object
 public static final Uri CONTENT_URI = Uri.parse("content://" +
                                    CONTENT_AUTHORITY + "/stockalldata");
```

```
//Define CONTENT_TYPE to represent the MIME Type for all rows in the table
public static final String CONTENT_TYPE = "vnd.android.cursor.dir/stockalldata";

//Define CONTENT_ITEM_TYPE to represent the MIME Type for an individual row
// in the table
public static final String CONTENT_ITEM_TYPE =
                                    "vnd.android.cursor.item/stockalldata";

//TABLE COLUMN DEFINITIONS

//_ID: Note that BaseColumns automatically brings in _ID set to "_id",
// so we don't have to do that!

//STOCK_SYMBOL
public static final String STOCKSYMBOL = "STOCK_SYMBOL";

//COMPANY_NAME
public static final String COMPANYNAME = "COMPANY_NAME";

//LAST_TRADE_DATE
public static final String LASTTRADEDATE = "LAST_TRADE_DATE";

//LAST_PRICE
public static final String LASTPRICE = "LAST_PRICE";

//VOLUME
public static final String VOLUME = "VOLUME";

//MARKETCAP (in billions)
public static final String MARKETCAP = "MARKETCAP";

//PERATIO
public static final String PERATIO = "PERATIO";

//EPS
public static final String EPS = "EPS";

//YIELD (as a percent)
public static final String YIELD = "YIELD";

}
```

Step #5: Create the Content Provider

Next, create the code associated with the content provider by subclassing the `ContentProvider` class (`android.content.ContentProvider`). This involves overriding several methods such as:

1. `int delete(Uri uri, String selection, String[] selectionArgs)` - this method allows you to delete a row from a table based on the content URI passed into its first parameter. This method should return the number of rows deleted (it may not just be one row). The `selection` parameter is an optional `WHERE` statement that may contain questions marks to be replaced by the data in `selectionArgs`.
2. `Uri insert(Uri uri, ContentValues values)` - this method allows you to insert a new row using the `ContentValues` object. This method should return the `Uri` of the new row. If you want to insert more than one row, use the `bulkInsert()` method instead.
3. `int update(Uri uri, ContentValues values, String selection, String[] selectionArgs)` - this method allows you to

update one or more rows of data. This method should return the number of rows updated.

4. `Cursor query(Uri uri, String[] projection, String selection, String[] selectionArgs, String sortOrder)` - this method allows you to query the database and return a Cursor.

5. `String getType(Uri uri)` - this method compares the parameter against the `UriMatcher` object to see if there is a match. If so, return the MIME type; otherwise, return `null`.

6. `boolean onCreate()` - normally a constructor is used to initialize variables, but for content providers, use this method instead. Return `true` if all went well; otherwise, return `false`.

The `getType()` method will contain code suspiciously similar to the `switch` statement in the previous section. Note that you do not have to implement all methods, so if you don't wish to allow deleting from your table, then don't code anything in the `delete()` method.

Now, at the top of the class, you will need to include the `private static final int` variables we created in Step #3:

```
//All stock symbols
private static final int STOCKSYMBOLS_ALL=1;

//All stock symbols specific _ID
private static final int STOCKSYMBOLS_ID = 2;

//All stock stats
private static final int STOCKSTATS_ALL = 3;

//All stock stats for specific _ID
private static final int STOCKSTATS_ID = 4;

//All view data
private static final int STOCKALLDATA = 5;
```

You should also create the following two attributes as well:

1. `DATABASE_NAME` - this is the name of the SQLite database as a `String`, `"EQUITY_ DATABASE.db3"` in our example.
2. `DATABASE_VERSION` - this is the version number of the database as an `int`. It is set to 1 for our example.

Here is the entire class:

```
package com.example.andapp1;

import android.content.ContentProvider;
import android.content.ContentValues;
import android.content.UriMatcher;
import android.database.Cursor;
import android.net.Uri;
import android.database.sqlite.*;
import android.database.*;
import android.content.ContentUris;

public class MyContentProviderClass extends ContentProvider {

  //Database Object
```

```
    private SQLiteDatabase oSQLiteDB;

    //Mappings used by the addURI() method
    //All stock symbols
    private static final int STOCKSYMBOLS_ALL=1;

    //All stock symbols specific _ID
    private static final int STOCKSYMBOLS_ID = 2;

    //All stock stats
    private static final int STOCKSTATS_ALL = 3;

    //All stock stats for specific _ID
    private static final int STOCKSTATS_ID = 4;

    //All view data
    private static final int STOCKALLDATA = 5;

    //PACKAGE_NAME
    private static final String PACKAGE_NAME = "com.example.andapp1";

    //CONTENT_AUTHORITY
    private static final String CONTENT_AUTHORITY = "com.example.andapp1.provider";

    //Database information
    private static final String DATABASE_NAME = "EQUITY_DATABASE.db3";
    private static final int DATABASE_VERSION = 1;

    //UriMatcher used to compare requested content URI with those that are
    // allowed by this content provider.
    UriMatcher umStock = new UriMatcher(UriMatcher.NO_MATCH);

    public MyContentProviderClass() {
    }

    @Override
    public String getType(Uri uri) {

     String sType = "";
     switch(umStock.match(uri)) {

      case STOCKSYMBOLS_ALL:
       sType="vnd.android.cursor.dir/stocksymbol";
      break;

      case STOCKSYMBOLS_ID:
       sType="vnd.android.cursor.item/stocksymbol/#";
      break;

      case STOCKSTATS_ALL:
       sType="vnd.android.cursor.dir/stockstats";
      break;

      case STOCKSTATS_ID:
       sType="vnd.android.cursor.item/stockstats/#";
      break;

      case STOCKALLDATA:
       sType="vnd.android.cursor.dir/stockalldata";
      break;

      default:
       sType = null;
      break;

     }

     return sType;
    }
```

```java
@Override
public boolean onCreate() {

  //Add content URIs to the UriMatcher object
  umStock.addURI(CONTENT_AUTHORITY, "stocksymbols", STOCKSYMBOLS_ALL);
  umStock.addURI(CONTENT_AUTHORITY, "stocksymbols/#", STOCKSYMBOLS_ID);
  umStock.addURI(CONTENT_AUTHORITY, "stockstats", STOCKSTATS_ALL);
  umStock.addURI(CONTENT_AUTHORITY, "stockstats/#", STOCKSTATS_ID);
  umStock.addURI(CONTENT_AUTHORITY, "stockalldata", STOCKALLDATA);

  //Open the database.   YOU MAY NEED TO MODIFY THE FIRST PARAMETER!!
  oSQLiteDB = SQLiteDatabase.openDatabase(
                          "/data/data/" + PACKAGE_NAME + "/" + DATABASE_NAME,
                          null,
                          SQLiteDatabase.OPEN_READONLY);

  return true;
}

public Cursor query(Uri uri, String[] projection,
                    String selection,
                    String[] selectionArgs,
                    String sortOrder) {

  String sSQL = "";
  String sID = "";
  Cursor oCSR = null;

  switch(umStock.match(uri)) {

    case STOCKSYMBOLS_ALL:
      sSQL = "SELECT STOCK_SYMBOL,COMPANY_NAME FROM STOCK_SYMBOLS";
      if (selection != null) {
        sSQL += " WHERE " + selection;
      }
      oCSR = oSQLiteDB.rawQuery(sSQL,null);
      break;

    case STOCKSYMBOLS_ID:
      sID = uri.getLastPathSegment();
      sSQL = "SELECT STOCK_SYMBOL,COMPANY_NAME FROM STOCK_SYMBOLS WHERE _ID= " +
                                                                          sID;
      oCSR = oSQLiteDB.rawQuery(sSQL,null);
      break;

    case STOCKSTATS_ALL:
      sSQL = "SELECT STOCK_SYMBOL,LAST_TRADE_DATE,LAST_PRICE,VOLUME,MARKETCAP," +
                                  "PERATIO, EPS, YIELD FROM STOCK_STATS";
      if (selection != null) {
        sSQL += " WHERE STOCK_SYMBOL='" + selection + "'";
      }
      oCSR = oSQLiteDB.rawQuery(sSQL,null);
      break;

    case STOCKSTATS_ID:
      sID = uri.getLastPathSegment();
      sSQL = "SELECT STOCK_SYMBOL,LAST_TRADE_DATE,LAST_PRICE,VOLUME,MARKETCAP," +
                      "PERATIO,EPS,YIELD FROM STOCK_STATS WHERE _ID=" + sID;
      oCSR = oSQLiteDB.rawQuery(sSQL,null);
      break;

    case STOCKALLDATA:
      sSQL = "SELECT STOCK_SYMBOL,COMPANY_NAME,LAST_TRADE_DATE,LAST_PRICE," +
                  "VOLUME,MARKETCAP,PERATIO,EPS,YIELD FROM vwSTOCKSTATSMATCH";
      oCSR = oSQLiteDB.rawQuery(sSQL,null);
      break;

  }
```

```
 //Ensure that if there is a change in the database, then the content
 // resolver is notified!!
 if (oCSR != null) {
  oCSR.setNotificationUri(getContext().getContentResolver(), uri);
 }

 return oCSR;
}

//These methods are not implemented in our test program!
@Override
public int delete(Uri uri, String selection, String[] selectionArgs) {
 return 0;
}

@Override
public Uri insert(Uri uri, ContentValues values) {
 return null;
}

@Override
public int update(Uri uri,
                  ContentValues values,
                  String selection,
                  String[] selectionArgs) {
 return 0;
}

}
```

Step #6: Determine Content Provider Permission(s)

If you do not provide permissions for your content provider, they are consider world-readable and world-writable. You probably don't want this, so let's create a permission that will allow other applications to read our data. Permissions take on a form similar to the following:

```
<package-name>.provider.permission.<permission>
```

where `<permission>` is any name we want to use to indicate the type of permission we are creating. For example, let's create a read-only permission for our example application:

```
com.example.andapp1.provider.permission.READ_PROVIDER
```

Note that you will need to add this to the `AndroidManifest.xml` file which we describe in the next step. If you would like a write permission, you can create that as well.

Step #7: Update `AndroidManifest.xml`

The next step is to update your `AndroidManifest.xml` file with `<provider>` tags within the `<application>` tag. Without the `<provider>` tags, other applications won't be able to access your data. Here is how I modified the example application's `AndroidManifest.xml`:

1. Add the following XML below `<uses-sdk>` but above `<application>`:

```
<permission android:description="@string/perm_desc"
            android:label="Equity Database Read-Only"
```

345

```
          android:name=
                  "com.example.andapp1.provider.permission.READ_PROVIDER"
          android:protectionLevel="normal"/>
```

2. Add the following XML within the `<application>` section just above `</application>` tag:

```
<provider android:name=".MyContentProviderClass"
          android:label="Equity Database Content Provider"
          android:authorities="com.example.andapp1.provider"
          android:readPermission=
                  "com.example.andapp1.provider.permission.READ_PROVIDER"
          android:syncable="false"/>
```

Note that the exact placement within the manifest is up to you and the instructions above are just suggestions. If you created a write permission in Step #6, add an additional line `android:writePermission="<your-write-permission>"` in the XML above.

Note that any application that wants to use your content provider must contain the corresponding permission(s) within its own `AndroidManifest.xml`. We explain this in detail in the next section.

Steps Involved in Using a Content Resolver

Now that you are finished creating your content provider and its permission(s), you can create a test application that will attempt to access the data provided by your content provider. There are several steps involved in using a content provider through the content resolver interface:

1. Compile your application with the content provider and install it on the target device or emulator.
2. Obtain the contract class(es) for the content provider you want to use. You can include this class in your own application in order to make use of the static attributes. Obtain the URI for the application whose data you want to access. Usually this is furnished by the developer of the application within the content contract class.
3. Create a test application in Eclipse. Don't forget to add the `<uses-permission>` tag to the `AndroidManifest.xml` in this test application!
4. Use the `ContentResolver` class to pull data (or insert, update, delete, etc.) from the content provider.

Step #1: Compile and Install Your Application

Before you attempt to pull data via the Content Resolver, you must compile and install the application that contains the content provider. Don't forget to copy over your SQLite database.

Step #2: Obtain the Contract Class(es)

Obtain the contract class(es) or, at the very least, documentation with the relevant information you need to access the content provider: content URI, column names, etc. This should be provided by the developer of the content provider.

Step #3: Create a Test Application

In order to test my content provider, I created a new Android application (still within Eclipse) by right-clicking in Eclipse's Project Explorer and selecting New...Project. Here is how I filled in the New Android App dialog box:

Note that you don't necessarily have to create a "test" application, but can just go forth and use the content resolver in your actual application. Although this is not the fastest way to access your own data, it does have the benefit that you can tell your friends and family that you created a content provider as well as content resolver! They'll love you even more!

Since my original application is still within my open Eclipse window, I copied the three contract classes from my content provider app into my content resolver test app.

In the `AndroidManifest.xml` for andapp2, I added the following XML after `<uses-sdk>` but before `<application>`:

```
<uses-permission
        android:name="com.example.andapp1.provider.permission.READ_PROVIDER"/>
```

This will allow our test application read-only access to the Equity Database.

Step #4: Using the `ContentResolver` Class

Finally, we use the `ContentResolver` class to pull the data from the Equity Database via its content provider. Note that a `ContentResolver` is **not** a

347

Cursor and you must use the query() method to generate the cursor. Here is the content resolver test app code I used to create one toast per stock. Take note of how I access the static variables of the contract class in the code below.

```
package com.example.andapp2;

import android.os.Bundle;
import android.app.Activity;
import android.view.Menu;
import android.view.View;
import android.widget.Button;
import android.content.ContentResolver;
import android.database.Cursor;
import android.widget.Toast;

public class MainActivity extends Activity {

 @Override
 public void onCreate(Bundle savedInstanceState) {
  super.onCreate(savedInstanceState);
  setContentView(R.layout.activity_main);

  //Add a listener for the click event of button1.
  ((Button) findViewById(R.id.button1)).setOnClickListener(

    new View.OnClickListener() {
     public void onClick(View view) {

      Toast toast;
      String sStockSymbol;
      String sStockName;
      String sStock;

      //content resolver code goes here
      ContentResolver oCR_EQDB = getContentResolver();

      //Create a cursor to the data
      Cursor oCSR = oCR_EQDB.query(
                      ContractClassSTOCKSYMBOLS.CONTENT_URI,
                      new String[] {ContractClassSTOCKSYMBOLS.STOCKSYMBOL,
                            ContractClassSTOCKSYMBOLS.COMPANYNAME},
                      null,
                      null,
                      null);

      //Show toasts for each of the entries
      if (oCSR.getCount() > 0) {
       while(oCSR.moveToNext()) {
        sStockSymbol = oCSR.getString(
                oCSR.getColumnIndex(ContractClassSTOCKSYMBOLS.STOCKSYMBOL));
        sStockName = oCSR.getString(
                oCSR.getColumnIndex(ContractClassSTOCKSYMBOLS.COMPANYNAME));
        sStock = sStockSymbol + "/" + sStockName;
        toast = Toast.makeText(getApplicationContext(),
                      sStock,
                      Toast.LENGTH_SHORT);
        toast.show();
       }
      }
     }
    }
  );
 }

 @Override
 public boolean onCreateOptionsMenu(Menu menu) {
  getMenuInflater().inflate(R.menu.activity_main, menu);
  return true;
```

```
    }
  }
```

Here is what I see on my screen (at least in part):

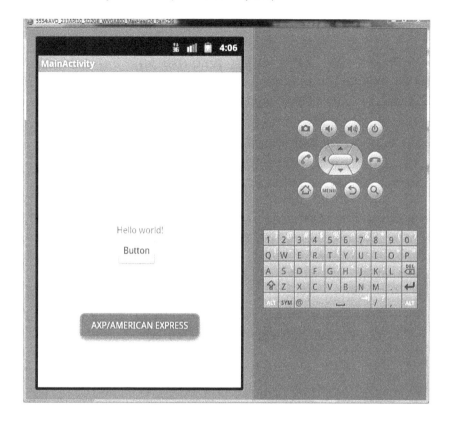

Note that you can include a subsetting criteria in the third parameter to the `query()` method, but you must have taken this into account in your content provider's `query()` method. If you ignored the `selection` (as well as `selectionArgs` and `sortOrder`) parameter, then the content resolver will not be able to subset the data or sort the output.

Using an Adapter to Populate the `ListView`

Toasts are great for debugging (`Log.d()` is better!), but let's try to populate a `ListView` with the data from the `STOCK_SYMBOLS` table. In addition, when a user clicks on a specific stock, that stock's statistics (i.e., `PERATIO`, `EPS`, etc.) are displayed in a popup dialog box.

Now, there are several ways to load data into a ListView:

1. Use XML via the `android:entries` attribute as we showed earlier in the book.
2. Load the data programmatically by extending your class with the `ListActivity` class. Then, load your data into an `ArrayList` and use the `setListAdapter()` method to associate the array with the list. This involves using an `ArrayAdapter`. Note that this method does not require you to insert a `ListView` widget into the layout. In fact, the `setContentView()` method is not needed because the `ListActivity` takes care of this for you automatically.

3. Load the data programmatically by extending your class with the `ListActivity` class. In this case, you can use the `SimpleCursorAdapter` to pull data from a database (either directly or via a content provider) and then populate the `ListView`. Note that this method does not require you to insert a `ListView` widget into the layout. In fact, the `setContentView()` method is not needed because the `ListActivity` takes care of this for you automatically.

4. Unlike #2 and #3, this time you place a `ListView` widget in your layout and you populate it with or without the use of the `ListActivity` class. If you use `ListActivity`, then the name of your `ListView` must be `@android:id/list`. Any text appearing in your TextViews must be named `@android:id/text1` depending on the layout you've specified in the `SimpleCursorAdapter` constructor.

We already showed an example of #1 previously in the book. We will defer #2 until the chapter on Adapters. We discuss #3 below.

When extending your class using the `ListActivity` class, you are telling Android to take care of handling the `ListView` as well as the text that it displays (using a `TextView`). Because of this, there is no need for you to place a `ListView` widget onto your layout. However, with this convenience come some restrictions:

1. The `ListView`'s id is named by Android and is `@android:id/list`.
2. The layout specified in the `SimpleCursorAdapter` constructor can be one of the following (or one of your own):
   a. `android.R.layout.simple_list_item_1` - this represents a single-line `TextView` with an id of `android.R.id.text1`.
   b. `android.R.layout.simple_list_item_2` - this represents a two-line textual display (two TextViews) with an id of `android.R.id.text1` for the upper (larger font) text and an id of `android.R.id.text2` for the lower (smaller font) text.

Note that `simple_list_item_1` and `simple_list_item_2`, which are just XML layouts, can be found in the following directory:

```
C:\android-sdk-windows\platforms\android##\data\res\layout\simple_list_item_1.xml
```

where **##** is the API Level (`android-10` for Android 2.3.3, etc.). The file `simple_list_item_1.xml` looks like this:

```
<?xml version="1.0" encoding="utf-8"?>
<!-- Copyright (C) 2006 The Android Open Source Project

     Licensed under the Apache License, Version 2.0 (the "License");
     you may not use this file except in compliance with the License.
     You may obtain a copy of the License at

          http://www.apache.org/licenses/LICENSE-2.0

     Unless required by applicable law or agreed to in writing, software
     distributed under the License is distributed on an "AS IS" BASIS,
     WITHOUT WARRANTIES OR CONDITIONS OF ANY KIND, either express or implied.
```

```
<TextView xmlns:android="http://schemas.android.com/apk/res/android"
    android:id="@android:id/text1"
    android:layout_width="match_parent"
    android:layout_height="wrap_content"
    android:textAppearance="?android:attr/textAppearanceLarge"
    android:gravity="center_vertical"
    android:paddingLeft="6dip"
    android:minHeight="?android:attr/listPreferredItemHeight"
/>
```

This is just a simple `TextView` with an id of `@android:id/text1`. Here is what `simple_list_item_2.xml` looks like:

```
<?xml version="1.0" encoding="utf-8"?>
<!-- Copyright (C) 2006 The Android Open Source Project
```

```
<TwoLineListItem xmlns:android="http://schemas.android.com/apk/res/android"
    android:paddingTop="2dip"
    android:paddingBottom="2dip"
    android:layout_width="match_parent"
    android:layout_height="wrap_content"
    android:minHeight="?android:attr/listPreferredItemHeight"
    android:mode="twoLine">

 <TextView android:id="@android:id/text1"
     android:layout_width="match_parent"
     android:layout_height="wrap_content"
     android:layout_marginLeft="6dip"
     android:layout_marginTop="6dip"
     android:textAppearance="?android:attr/textAppearanceLarge"/>

 <TextView android:id="@android:id/text2"
     android:layout_width="match_parent"
     android:layout_height="wrap_content"
     android:layout_below="@android:id/text1"
     android:layout_alignLeft="@android:id/text1"
     android:textAppearance="?android:attr/textAppearanceSmall"/>

</TwoLineListItem>
```

When extending with `ListActivity`, the XML file `list_content.xml` is used. Here is what this file looks like:

```
<?xml version="1.0" encoding="utf-8"?>
<!--
/* //device/apps/common/assets/res/layout/list_content.xml
**
** Copyright 2006, The Android Open Source Project
**
```

```
** Licensed under the Apache License, Version 2.0 (the "License");
** you may not use this file except in compliance with the License.
** You may obtain a copy of the License at
**
**      http://www.apache.org/licenses/LICENSE-2.0
**
** Unless required by applicable law or agreed to in writing, software
** distributed under the License is distributed on an "AS IS" BASIS,
** WITHOUT WARRANTIES OR CONDITIONS OF ANY KIND, either express or implied.
** See the License for the specific language governing permissions and
** limitations under the License.
*/
-->
<ListView xmlns:android="http://schemas.android.com/apk/res/android"
    android:id="@android:id/list"
    android:layout_width="match_parent"
    android:layout_height="match_parent"
    android:drawSelectorOnTop="false"/>
```

Take note that you do not need to generate these three XML files since they come with Android! Also, you don't need to place them in the res\layout folder of your application since they will be found automatically by the `ListActivity` class.

Just for fun, here is a complete list of XML files in the `\data\res\layout` folder:

```
activity_list.xml, activity_list_item.xml, activity_list_item_2.xml,
alert_dialog.xml, alert_dialog_progress.xml, always_use_checkbox.xml,
app_permission_item.xml, app_perms_summary.xml, auto_complete_list.xml,
browser_link_context_header.xml, character_picker.xml,
character_picker_button.xml, contact_header.xml, date_picker.xml,
date_picker_dialog.xml, dialog_custom_title.xml, dialog_title.xml,
dialog_title_icons.xml, expandable_list_content.xml, expanded_menu_layout.xml,
global_actions_item.xml, grant_credentials_permission.xml,
heavy_weight_switcher.xml, icon_menu_item_layout.xml, input_method.xml,
input_method_extract_view.xml, js_prompt.xml, keyboard_key_preview.xml,
keyboard_popup_keyboard.xml, keyguard.xml, keyguard_screen_glogin_unlock.xml,
keyguard_screen_lock.xml, keyguard_screen_password_landscape.xml,
keyguard_screen_password_portrait.xml, keyguard_screen_sim_pin_landscape.xml,
keyguard_screen_sim_pin_portrait.xml, keyguard_screen_tab_unlock.xml,
keyguard_screen_tab_unlock_land.xml, keyguard_screen_unlock_landscape.xml,
keyguard_screen_unlock_portrait.xml, launch_warning.xml, list_content.xml,
list_gestures_overlay.xml, list_menu_item_checkbox.xml, list_menu_item_icon.xml,
list_menu_item_layout.xml, list_menu_item_radio.xml, media_controller.xml,
menu_item.xml, number_picker.xml, permissions_account_and_authtokentype.xml,
permissions_package_list_item.xml, power_dialog.xml, preference.xml,
preferences.xml, preference_category.xml, preference_child.xml,
preference_dialog.xml, preference_dialog_edittext.xml,
preference_information.xml, preference_list_content.xml,
preference_widget_checkbox.xml, progress_dialog.xml, recent_apps_dialog.xml,
recent_apps_icon.xml, resolve_list_item.xml, safe_mode.xml, screen.xml,
screen_custom_title.xml, screen_progress.xml, screen_simple.xml,
screen_title.xml, screen_title_icons.xml, search_bar.xml,
search_dropdown_item_1line.xml, search_dropdown_item_icons_2line.xml,
seekbar_dialog.xml, select_dialog.xml, select_dialog_item.xml,
select_dialog_multichoice.xml, select_dialog_singlechoice.xml,
simple_dropdown_hint.xml, simple_dropdown_item_1line.xml,
simple_dropdown_item_2line.xml, simple_expandable_list_item_1.xml,
simple_expandable_list_item_2.xml, simple_gallery_item.xml,
simple_list_item_1.xml, simple_list_item_2.xml, simple_list_item_checked.xml,
simple_list_item_multiple_choice.xml, simple_list_item_single_choice.xml,
simple_spinner_dropdown_item.xml, simple_spinner_item.xml,
status_bar_latest_event_content.xml, tab_content.xml, tab_indicator.xml,
test_list_item.xml, textview_hint.xml, time_picker.xml, time_picker_dialog.xml,
transient_notification.xml, twelve_key_entry.xml, two_line_list_item.xml,
typing_filter.xml, usb_storage_activity.xml, volume_adjust.xml,
zoom_browser_accessory_buttons.xml, zoom_container.xml, zoom_controls.xml,
zoom_magnify.xml
```

Now, just to be clear, when you extend your class using the `ListActivity` class, the `list_content.xml` layout containing a `ListView` with an id of `@android:id/list` is used. Within each row of that `ListView`, you can use `simple_list_item_1.xml` to display a single line of text in a `TextView` with an id of `@android:id/text1`. If you decide that you need two lines of text rather than one, you can try `simple_list_item_2.xml` which displays two TextViews, one with an id of `@android:id/text1` and the other an id of `@android:id/text2`. Note that `text1` is displayed in a large font whereas `text2` is displayed in a smaller font. Here is what this looks like once the `ListView` is populated with data:

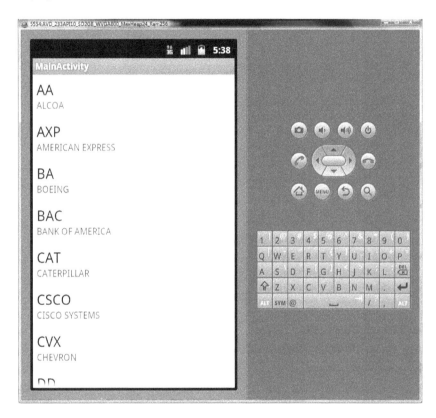

Note that using `simple_list_item_1.xml` will yield a single line of stock symbols. Here is the code associated with the image above:

```
public class MainActivity extends ListActivity {

 @Override
 public void onCreate(Bundle savedInstanceState) {

  super.onCreate(savedInstanceState);

  //Get a cursor to the stock symbol/company name in STOCK_SYMBOLS
  ContentResolver oCR_EQDB = getContentResolver();
  Cursor oCSR = oCR_EQDB.query(
              ContractClassSTOCKSYMBOLS.CONTENT_URI,
              new String[] {ContractClassSTOCKSYMBOLS._ID,
                         ContractClassSTOCKSYMBOLS.STOCKSYMBOL,
                         ContractClassSTOCKSYMBOLS.COMPANYNAME},
              null, null, null);

  //Manage the cursor
  startManagingCursor(oCSR);
```

```
//List of columns to be displayed in the List View
String[] sDisplayColumns = new String[] {ContractClassSTOCKSYMBOLS.STOCKSYMBOL,
                                ContractClassSTOCKSYMBOLS.COMPANYNAME};

//Create an integer array to hold the IDs of android.R.id.text1
// and android.R.id.text2. Note that they are in the same order as
// the columns that appear in sDisplayColumns.
int[] iLayoutIDs = new int[] {android.R.id.text1,android.R.id.text2};

//Set up a cursor adapter for the ListView using oCSR
SimpleCursorAdapter oSCAdapter = new SimpleCursorAdapter(
                                    this,
                                    android.R.layout.simple_list_item_2,
                                    oCSR,
                                    sDisplayColumns,
                                    iLayoutIDs);

//Set the list adapter to our simple cursor adapter oSCAdapter.
setListAdapter(oSCAdapter);

}

@Override
public boolean onCreateOptionsMenu(Menu menu) {
 getMenuInflater().inflate(R.menu.activity_main, menu);
 return true;
}

@Override
public void onListItemClick(ListView l, View v, int position, long id) {
 String sID = Long.toString(id);
 Toast toast = Toast.makeText(getApplicationContext(),
                        "_ID=" + sID,
                        Toast.LENGTH_SHORT);
 toast.show();
 }

}
```

If you would prefer to display an `ExpandableListView` rather than just a `ListView`, you can extend your class using the `ExpandableListActivity` class which makes use of `expandable_list_content.xml` containing an `ExpandableListView` with an id of `@android:id/list`. There are two associated XML files: `simple_expandable_ list_item_1.xml` which contains a single `TextView` with an id of `@android:id:/text1` and `simple_expandable_list_item_2.xml` which contains two `TextView`s with ids of `@android:id:/text1` and `@android:id:/text2`.

As you can see, there is a correspondence between `simple_list_item_#.xml` and `simple_expandable_list_item_#.xml`. Where the correspondence breaks down is how cursors are used. In the previous code, you create a simple cursor, pass it to the `SimpleCursorAdapter` and away you go. For an `ExpandableListView`, you need a parent cursor to populate the list initially, but you also need a child cursor to populate what is displayed when the down-arrow is clicked. To do this, you need to create a subclass of the `SimpleCursorTreeAdapter`. (We talk more about adapters later in the book.) Here is the code:

```
public class MainActivity extends ExpandableListActivity {

 @Override
```

```java
public void onCreate(Bundle savedInstanceState) {

  super.onCreate(savedInstanceState);

  //Get a cursor to the stock symbol/company name in STOCK_SYMBOLS
  Cursor parentCursor = getContentResolver().query(
                        ContractClassSTOCKSYMBOLS.CONTENT_URI,
                        new String[] {ContractClassSTOCKSYMBOLS._ID,
                                ContractClassSTOCKSYMBOLS.STOCKSYMBOL,
                                ContractClassSTOCKSYMBOLS.COMPANYNAME},
                        null, null, null);

  //Manage the cursor
  startManagingCursor(parentCursor);

  //PARENT: List of columns to be displayed in the List View
  String[] sGroupFrom = new String[] {ContractClassSTOCKSYMBOLS.STOCKSYMBOL};

  //PARENT: Create an integer array to hold the IDs of android.R.id.text1
  // and android.R.id.text2.  Note that they are in the same order as the
  // columns that appear in sDisplayColumns.
  int[] iGroupTo = new int[] {android.R.id.text1};

  //CHILD: List of columns to be displayed in the List View
  String[] sChildFrom = new String[] {ContractClassSTOCKSTATS.LASTPRICE,
                              ContractClassSTOCKSTATS.VOLUME};

  //CHILD: Create an integer array to hold the IDs of android.R.id.text1
  // and android.R.id.text2. Note that they are in the same order as the
  // columns that appear in sDisplayColumns.
  int[] iChildTo = new int[] {android.R.id.text1,android.R.id.text2};

  //Set up a cursor tree adapter for the ExpanableListView
  MySimpleCursorTreeAdapter oExpandableListAdapter =
          new MySimpleCursorTreeAdapter(
                              this,
                              parentCursor,
                              android.R.layout.simple_expandable_list_item_1,
                              sGroupFrom,
                              iGroupTo,
                              android.R.layout.simple_expandable_list_item_2,
                              sChildFrom,
                              iChildTo);

  //Set the list adapter to our simple cursor adapter oSCAdapter.
  setListAdapter(oExpandableListAdapter);

}

//Create my own subclass of the SimpleCursorTreeAdapter.
//At a minimum, you need to have the constructor super to the base and
//the method called getChildrenCursor which returns a cursor to the child's data
//based on the parent parameter passed into it.
//Note that SimpleCursorTreeAdapter implements ExpandableListAdapter, so the
//code above will work.
public class MySimpleCursorTreeAdapter extends SimpleCursorTreeAdapter {

  //Constructor passes onto base constructor
  public MySimpleCursorTreeAdapter(Context context,
                              Cursor cursor,
                              int groupLayout,
                              String[] groupFrom,
                              int[] groupTo,
                              int childLayout,
                              String[] childFrom,int[] childto) {

    super(context,cursor,groupLayout,groupFrom,
          groupTo,childLayout,childFrom,childto);

  }
```

```
//getChildrenCursor
@Override
protected Cursor getChildrenCursor(Cursor parentCursor) {

  //Get the _ID from the parentCursor (the STOCK_SYMBOLS table)
  long parentID = parentCursor.getLong(
                    parentCursor.getColumnIndex(ContractClassSTOCKSYMBOLS._ID));

  //Get a cursor for the child's data based on the parent's _ID. Note that there
  // must be a correspondence of the _ID's between the STOCK_SYMBOLS table and
  // the STOCK_STATS table.  I ensured that there was, but that might not always
  // be the case. If not, then pull the child's data based on the stock symbol
  // instead.

  //Create a new Uri from the CONTENT_URI for the STOCK_STATS table by appending
  // the parent _ID to it.
  Uri uriWithParentID =
                  Uri.withAppendedPath(ContractClassSTOCKSTATS.CONTENT_URI,
                                    Long.toString(parentID));

  //Query the table STOCK_STATS
  Cursor childCursor = getContentResolver().query(
                    uriWithParentID,
                    new String[] {ContractClassSTOCKSTATS._ID,
                                    ContractClassSTOCKSTATS.STOCKSYMBOL,
                                    ContractClassSTOCKSTATS.LASTTRADEDATE,
                                    ContractClassSTOCKSTATS.VOLUME},
                    null, null, null);

  //Manage the cursor
  startManagingCursor(childCursor);

  //return the child cursor
  return childCursor;
  }

 }

}
```

Here is what an `ExpandableListView` looks like when one of the stocks, AA, is expanded:

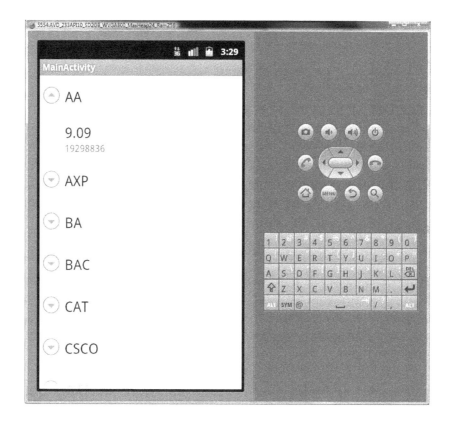

Summary

In this chapter, we learned about content providers and showed how other applications can make use of the data your application contains. We then applied that data to a `ListView` and `ExpandableListView`.

Chapter 17: Adapters

Overview

In this chapter, we learn about the variety of adapters available in Android. Recall that in *Chapter 16, Content Providers*, we created a content provider which pulled data from a SQLite database. We then proceeded to test our content provider by populating a `ListView` and `ExpandableListView` with the data in that database. Populating these two views required us to make use of two *adapters*: the `SimpleCursorAdapter`, which allowed us to populate a `ListView`; and the `SimpleCursorTreeAdapter`, which allowed us to populate the `Expandable ListView`.

An adapter in Android is similar to a power plug adapter used when visiting a foreign country. It is the job of the adapter to convert that country's voltage into something that your, say, electric toothbrush can use without bursting into flames. That is, an adapter is the intermediary between the electricity coming from the wall and the electric toothbrush itself.

This is similar to an adapter in Android, which acts as an intermediary between your data, and how that data appears in a `View` (such as a `ListView`). Beyond that task, an adapter in Android also has the added responsibility of generating the views (`TextView`s, for instance) which appear in, say, a `ListView`. It is these views that contain your data. For example, each row appearing in a `ListView` is a separate `TextView` that contains one row of data (a single stock symbol, in the case of our content provider). It is the adapter's responsibility to place that row of data into a `TextView` and ship that code out to the `ListView` for display. This occurs for each row appearing in the database table. According to the Android documentation: *An Adapter object acts as a bridge between an AdapterView and the underlying data for the view. The Adapter provides access to the data items. The Adapter is also responsible for making a View for each item in the data set.*

Now, in our content provider example, we pulled data from a SQLite database table using adapters, which work with cursors. It is the responsibility of the cursor to pull the data from the database and the adapter's responsibility to generate the view. Not all adapters are designed to work with cursors, but rather with arrays.

To make matters even more confusing, some of the adapters are interfaces, some are abstract classes and, finally, some are plain vanilla classes. Recall that you cannot instantiate an abstract class. Recall, also, that in order to implement an interface you must use the `implements` keyword. In many cases, you will be using the classes such as `ArrayAdapter` and `SimpleCursorAdapter`, but there are times when you will need to use an interface such as the `SimpleCursorTreeAdapter` we used to populate the `ExpandableListView` in Chapter 17, *Adapters*.

What about `ListActivity` and `ExpandableListActivity`?

To make matters even worse, there are several subclasses of the `Activity` class which are used to simplify the population of the view by hosting the layout for you.

For example, in Chapter 17, *Adapters*, we extended our activity by using the `ListActivity` class which allowed us to more easily add data into our `ListView`. Similarly, we extended our activity using the `ExpandableListActivity` class which allowed us to more easily add data into our `ExpandableListActivity`. Note that in the case of the `ExpandableListActivity`, we had to make use of the `SimpleCursorTreeAdapter` in order to populate both the parent and the child views. You are not required to use the `ListActivity` or `ExpandableList Activity` classes, but they do help. Note that not all views have a corresponding host activity. For example, there is **no** `GridActivity` for the `GridView`.

Be on the Lookout for the Elusive `TextView`

When reading the remainder of this chapter, take note that some of the adapters will generate `TextView`s. This does **not** mean that the adapter can only be used with `TextView`s, but can be used with any view that has a `TextView` as part of its guts. For example, the `ListView` and the `ExpandableListView` both display `TextView`s. So, when using a particular view, determine if it's just a wrapper for a `TextView` and then use the appropriate adapter.

Android-Provided Layouts or My Own?

As we saw previously, you can use Android-provided layouts to generate a `ListView`, `ExpandableListView`, etc. These layouts come with IDs such as `@android:id/list`, `@android:id/text1`, `@android:id/text2`, etc. You can use adapters with Android-provided layouts as well as your own layouts; you just have to be aware of the IDs when you provide them to the adapter.

Simple Data Display - No Need for an Adapter

Not all views require you to *wire them up* to an adapter. For example, if you have an individual `TextView` in your activity's layout which is used to display a stock symbol, then you can just set that text either within the XML for the `TextView` or within code using the `setText()` method of the object itself, as shown below:

```
<TextView
    android:id="@+id/myTxtVw"
    android:layout_width="wrap_content"
    android:layout_height="wrap_content"
    android:layout_centerHorizontal="true"
    android:layout_centerVertical="true"
    android:text="text-or-resource-goes-here" />

TextView oTxtVw = (TextView) findViewById(R.id.text-view-id);
oTxtVw.setText("your-text-goes-here");
```

This is also true of the `ListView`. Recall that we used the `android:entries` attribute along with an array to populate the `ListView` itself. In this case, there was no need to use an adapter:

```
<ListView xmlns:android="http://schemas.android.com/apk/res/android"
    android:id="@+id/listView1"
    android:layout_width="fill_parent"
```

```
    android:layout_height="fill_parent"
    android:entries="array-resource-goes-here">
</ListView>
```

Less Simple Data Display #1 - Using `ArrayAdapter`

In the previous section, we talked about inserting hard-coded data into a view. In this section, we complicate things a bit by assuming that our data is stored in a `String` array.

The `ArrayAdapter` is used to pull data from an array and generate one `TextView` for each array element. For example, given the following `String` array...

```
String[] sArray = {"INTC","MSFT","GOOG","CSCO","FB"};
```

...let's populate a `ListView` with the stock symbols above. Here is the code to do that:

```
//Create an array to hold all of the stocks.
//These are entered in by hand.
String[] sArray = {"INTC","MSFT","GOOG","CSCO","FB"};

//Set up an object to the ListView
ListView oLV = (ListView) findViewById(R.id.lvSS);

//Set up the ArrayAdapter
ArrayAdapter<String> adapter = new ArrayAdapter<String>(this,
                                   android.R.layout.simple_list_item_1,
                                   sArray);

//Load the array data into the ListView
oLV.setAdapter(adapter);
```

Take note of the emboldened line of code. This creates a new `ArrayAdapter` object which will generate `TextView`s using the Android-provided `android.R.layout.simple_list_item_1` definition along with the array of stock symbols provided to it from the array, `sArray`.

Note that you can also pull array entries from an XML resource instead of hard coding them:

```
String[] sArray = getResources().getStringArray(R.array.your-array-name);
```

Now, the code above relies on the Android-provided layout `android.R.layout.simple_list_item_1` that contains (as we saw) a single `TextView`. If you want to use your own, you have to create a layout containing a single `TextView` called, say, res\layout**mytextview.xml**:

```
<TextView xmlns:android="http://schemas.android.com/apk/res/android"
    android:id="@+id/tvSS"
    android:layout_width="match_parent"
    android:layout_height="match_parent"
    android:typeface="monospace"
    android:textSize="8dp"
    android:textColor="#FF00FF">
</TextView>
```

When you instantiate the `ArrayAdapter`, pass it the layout name of your layout:

```
//Set up the ArrayAdapter
ArrayAdapter<String> adapter = new ArrayAdapter<String>(this,
                                            R.layout.mytextview,
                                            sArray);
```

In either case, you get a `ListView` populated with stock symbols.

Now, you can intercept the normal flow of data from the array to the `TextView` by overriding the `toString()` method. This will allow you to modify your data *before* it is added to the `TextView`. But, it's not always convenient (or simple) to override the `toString()` method of a currently existing class. For example, the `String` class is marked as `final` which means that you cannot extend it...this makes us sad! But, one simple workaround is to create your own class and override the `toString()` method within it. For example, here is our new class:

```
public class MyClass {

 String sText = "";

 public MyClass(String pText) {
  sText = pText;
 }

 @Override
 public String toString() {
  return "New York Stock Exchange: " + sText;
 }

}
```

Our `toString()` method above takes the text data `sText` and fiddles with it by prepending the text "New York Stock Exchange: " to it.

This class is very simple because all it does is hold a string variable, `sText`, and overrides the default `toString()` class. Here is our activity's code now:

```
@Override
public void onCreate(Bundle savedInstanceState) {
 super.onCreate(savedInstanceState);
 setContentView(R.layout.activity_main);

 //Create an array to hold all of the stocks.
 MyClass[] sArray = new MyClass[5];
 sArray[0] = new MyClass("INTC");
 sArray[1] = new MyClass("MSFT");
 sArray[2] = new MyClass("GOOG");
 sArray[3] = new MyClass("CSCO");
 sArray[4] = new MyClass("FB");

 //Set up an object to the ListView
 ListView oLV = (ListView) findViewById(R.id.lvSS);

 //Set up the ArrayAdapter
 ArrayAdapter<MyClass> adapter = new
                    ArrayAdapter<MyClass>(this,R.layout.mytextview,sArray);

 //Load the array data into the ListView
 oLV.setAdapter(adapter);

}
```

361

As you can see above, instead of using `<String>` we use `<MyClass>` to indicate to the `ArrayAdapter` to use `MyClass`. By doing this, the `toString()` method within `MyClass` will be used instead of the one in the `String` class.

Besides overriding the `toString()` method, you can subclass the `ArrayAdapter` class and override its `getView()` method all within your own class. The `getView()` method is responsible for generating the `TextView` code and is a place you can fiddle with the incoming textual data as well as the view that is returned. Here is an example:

```java
import android.content.Context;
import android.view.LayoutInflater;
import android.view.View;
import android.view.ViewGroup;
import android.widget.ArrayAdapter;
import android.widget.TextView;

public class StockAdapter extends ArrayAdapter<String> {

  private String[] sArray;
  private Context context;

  public StockAdapter(Context context, int textViewResourceId, String[] objects) {
    super(context, textViewResourceId, objects);
    this.sArray = objects;
    this.context = context;
  }

  public int getCount() {
    return sArray.length;
  }

  @Override
  public String getItem(int position) {
    return sArray[position];
  }

  @Override
  public View getView(int position, View convertView, ViewGroup parent) {

    View view = convertView;

    //If convertView is null, inflate it with mytextview.
    if (view == null) {
      LayoutInflater inflater = (LayoutInflater)
                      context.getSystemService(Context.LAYOUT_INFLATER_SERVICE);
      //Inflate the layout.
      view = inflater.inflate(R.layout.mytextview, null);
    }

    //Get the current item based on the position passed in
    String sItem = sArray[position];

    //Create a variable to point to our TextView tvSS.
    TextView oTVSS = (TextView) view.findViewById(R.id.tvSS);

    //Set the text to whatever you want in mytextview
    oTVSS.setText("Nasdaq Stock Exchange Symbol: " + sItem);

    return view;
  }
}
```

The emboldened text `R.layout.mytextview` is a pointer to the layout file `mytextview` and **not** the id of the `TextView` itself! The second emboldened text, `R.id.tvSS`, **is** the id of the `TextView`. Note that, near the end, we modify the text by using the `setText()` method. Here is the modified code in the activity's `onCreate` method:

```
@Override
public void onCreate(Bundle savedInstanceState) {
 super.onCreate(savedInstanceState);
 setContentView(R.layout.activity_main);

 //Create an array to hold all of the stocks.
 //These are entered in by hand.
 String[] sArray = {"AAAA","BBBB","CCCC","DDDD","EEEE","FFFF","GGGG","HHHH"};

 //Set up an object to the ListView
 ListView oLV = (ListView) findViewById(R.id.lvSS);

 //Set up the ArrayAdapter using our StockAdapter class instead
 StockAdapter adapter = new StockAdapter(this,R.layout.mytextview,sArray);

 //Load the array data into the ListView
 oLV.setAdapter(adapter);

}
```

As you can see, we are using our `StockAdapter` class and not the `ArrayAdapter` class as before.

Less Simple Data Display #2 - Using `SimpleCursorAdapter`

In the previous section, we used an `ArrayAdapter` to display data held in an array. In this section, we talk about the `SimpleCursorAdapter` which can display data held in a database and accessed via an underlying `Cursor`. `SimpleCursorAdapter` is located in the `android.widget` class.

We learned a little about the `SimpleCursorAdapter` in *Chapter 16, Content Providers* so we won't go into a protracted explanation again. Below is code that makes use of a `SimpleCursorAdapter` to pull in data from a SQLite database.

```
//Get a cursor to the stock symbol/company name in STOCK_SYMBOLS
ContentResolver oCR_EQDB = getContentResolver();
Cursor oCSR = oCR_EQDB.query(
                    ContractClassSTOCKSYMBOLS.CONTENT_URI,
                    new String[] {ContractClassSTOCKSYMBOLS._ID,
                            ContractClassSTOCKSYMBOLS.STOCKSYMBOL,
                            ContractClassSTOCKSYMBOLS.COMPANYNAME},
                    null, null, null);

//Manage the cursor
startManagingCursor(oCSR);

//List of columns to be displayed in the List View
String[] sDisplayColumns = new String[] {ContractClassSTOCKSYMBOLS.STOCKSYMBOL,
                            ContractClassSTOCKSYMBOLS.COMPANYNAME};

//Create an integer array to hold the IDs of android.R.id.text1 and
// android.R.id.text2. Note that they are in the same order as the columns
// that appear in sDisplayColumns.
int[] iLayoutIDs = new int[] {android.R.id.text1,android.R.id.text2};
```

```
//Set up a cursor adapter for the ListView using oCSR
SimpleCursorAdapter oSCAdapter = new SimpleCursorAdapter(
                                    this,
                                    android.R.layout.simple_list_item_2,
                                    oCSR,
                                    sDisplayColumns,
                                    iLayoutIDs);

//Set the list adapter to our simple cursor adapter oSCAdapter.
setListAdapter(oSCAdapter);
```

While not strictly needed outside of a Content Provider, we call the `getContentResolver()` method and then go on to instantiate a cursor using the `query()` method. We call `startManagingCursor()` to have Android manage the cursor which allows us to avoid programmatically closing the cursor. Next, we create a `String` array containing the column names we want to pull from the database table. Next, we create an `int` array containing a list of IDs to views we want to hold each row and column of data. Next, we instantiate a `SimpleCursorAdapter` by passing in the current context, the name of the layout, the cursor, the array of display columns and the array of IDs. Finally, we use the `setListAdapter()` method to force the data into our `ListView` (the code above is part of a `ListActivity` class extension).

Less Simple Data Display #3 - Using `SimpleCursorTreeAdapter`

Recall that in *Chapter 16, Content Providers* we used a `SimpleCursorTree Adapter` along with an `ExpandableListActivity` to display an `ExpandableListView`. This view contains a list of *parent* items along with a down-arrow (for example, stock symbols are displayed along with a down-arrow icon). When the down-arrow icon is pressed, the *child* data is displayed just below the parent. It is the responsibility of the `SimpleCursorTreeAdapter` to return the child data for the specific parent. The code to do this is below. Be aware the code below is specific to a `ContentResolver`, but can be used outside of that context.

```
public class MainActivity extends ExpandableListActivity {

 @Override
 public void onCreate(Bundle savedInstanceState) {

  super.onCreate(savedInstanceState);

  //Get a cursor to the stock symbol/company name in STOCK_SYMBOLS
  Cursor parentCursor = getContentResolver().query(
                    ContractClassSTOCKSYMBOLS.CONTENT_URI,
                    new String[] {ContractClassSTOCKSYMBOLS._ID,
                            ContractClassSTOCKSYMBOLS.STOCKSYMBOL,
                            ContractClassSTOCKSYMBOLS.COMPANYNAME},
                null, null, null);

  //Manage the cursor
  startManagingCursor(parentCursor);

  //PARENT: List of columns to be displayed in the List View
  String[] sGroupFrom = new String[] {ContractClassSTOCKSYMBOLS.STOCKSYMBOL};

  //PARENT:Create an integer array to hold the IDs of android.R.id.text1 and
  // android.R.id.text2. Note that they are in the same order as the columns
  // that appear in sDisplayColumns.
  int[] iGroupTo = new int[] {android.R.id.text1};
```

```
//CHILD: List of columns to be displayed in the List View
String[] sChildFrom = new String[] {ContractClassSTOCKSTATS.LASTPRICE,
                                    ContractClassSTOCKSTATS.VOLUME};

//CHILD:Create an integer array to hold the IDs of android.R.id.text1 and
// android.R.id.text2. Note that they are in the same order as the columns
// that appear in sDisplayColumns.
int[] iChildTo = new int[] {android.R.id.text1,android.R.id.text2};

//Set up a cursor tree adapter for the ExpandableListView
MySimpleCursorTreeAdapter oExpandableListAdapter = new
     MySimpleCursorTreeAdapter(this,
                               parentCursor,
                               android.R.layout.simple_expandable_list_item_1,
                               sGroupFrom,
                               iGroupTo,
                               android.R.layout.simple_expandable_list_item_2,
                               sChildFrom,
                               iChildTo);

//Set the list adapter to our simple cursor adapter oSCAdapter.
setListAdapter(oExpandableListAdapter);

}

//Create my own subclass of the SimpleCursorTreeAdapter.
//At a minimum, you need to have the constructor super to the base and
//the method called getChildrenCursor which returns a cursor to the child's data
//based on the parent parameter passed into it.
//Note that SimpleCursorTreeAdapter implements ExpandableListAdapter, so the
//code above will work.
public class MySimpleCursorTreeAdapter extends SimpleCursorTreeAdapter {

//Constructor passes onto base constructor
public MySimpleCursorTreeAdapter(Context context,
                                 Cursor cursor,
                                 int groupLayout,
                                 String[] groupFrom,
                                 int[] groupTo,
                                 int childLayout,
                                 String[] childFrom,
                                 int[] childto) {

  super(context,cursor,groupLayout,groupFrom,groupTo,
        childLayout,childFrom,childto);

}

//getChildrenCursor
@Override
protected Cursor getChildrenCursor(Cursor parentCursor) {

 //Get the _ID from the parentCursor (the STOCK_SYMBOLS table)
 long parentID = parentCursor.getLong(
                 parentCursor.getColumnIndex(ContractClassSTOCKSYMBOLS._ID));

 //Get a cursor for the child's data based on the parent's _ID. Note that there
 // must be a correspondence of the _ID's between the STOCK_SYMBOLS table and
 // the STOCK_STATS table. I ensured that there was, but that might not always
 // be the case. If not, then pull the child's data based on the stock
 // symbol instead.

 //Create a new Uri from the CONTENT_URI for the STOCK_STATS table by appending
 // the parent _ID to it.
 Uri uriWithParentID = Uri.withAppendedPath(
                                ContractClassSTOCKSTATS.CONTENT_URI,
                                Long.toString(parentID));

 //Query the table STOCK_STATS
```

```
Cursor childCursor = getContentResolver().query(
                        uriWithParentID,
                        new String[] {ContractClassSTOCKSTATS._ID,
                            ContractClassSTOCKSTATS.STOCKSYMBOL,
                            ContractClassSTOCKSTATS.LASTTRADEDATE,
                            ContractClassSTOCKSTATS.VOLUME},
                        null, null, null);

    //Manage the cursor
    startManagingCursor(childCursor);

    //return the child cursor
    return childCursor;

  }

 }

}
```

Less Simple Data Display #4 - Using `ResourceCursorTreeAdapter`

Keeping with the `ExpandableListView` theme for a moment, you can use the `ResourceCursorTreeAdapter` class to display an `ExpandableListView` containing views located in XML files.

Since this class is marked as `abstract`, you will have to extend this class and fill in the methods that you need. Also, since `ResourceCursorTreeAdapter` extends `CursorTreeAdapter` which extends `BaseExpandableListAdapter`, you may need to override one or more methods in those classes as well in order to get your `ExpandableListView` to function properly.

First, let's create a class that extends the `ResourceCursorTreeAdapter`. In this class, you gain control over the text in the TextViews by overriding the `bindGroupView` and the `bindChildView` methods.

The `bindGroupView` method is responsible for displaying the text initially shown in the `ExpandableListView`. In our example above, it is just a list of stock symbols. As you will see in the code below, I pull in the text and manipulate it a bit. The `TextView` shown in this case is just the single `TextView text1` from `android.R.layout.simple_expandable_list_item_1`.

The `bindChildView` method is responsible for showing the text whenever the drop-down icon is clicked. In our case, it shows two `TextView`s, one for the Last Price and one for the Volume. The `TextView`s shown in this case are the `TextView`s `text1` and `text2` from the Android-provided layout `android.R.layout.simple_expandable_list_item_2`.

As we did above, you need to also override the `getChildrenCursor()` method which is passed the `parentCursor`. You can pull out the appropriate ID (usually, _ID) and then pull the child data from the appropriate database table.

Note that I was not able to get the content resolver concept to work in this context which is why I opted to pull data via the `rawQuery()` method along with SQL in a string.

366

Here is the code for this first part:

```
import java.text.DecimalFormat;
import android.content.Context;
import android.database.Cursor;
import android.database.sqlite.SQLiteDatabase;
import android.view.View;
import android.widget.ResourceCursorTreeAdapter;
import android.widget.TextView;

public class MyResourceCursorTreeAdapter extends ResourceCursorTreeAdapter {

  //Create a private variable for a SQLite Database
  private SQLiteDatabase oSQLiteDB;

  public MyResourceCursorTreeAdapter(SQLiteDatabase pSQLiteDB,
                         Context context, Cursor cursor,
                         int igroupLayout,
                         int ichildLayout) {

  super(context, cursor, igroupLayout, ichildLayout);

  //Set the SQLiteDB object to the open database from the main activity.
  oSQLiteDB = pSQLiteDB;

  }

  @Override
  protected void bindChildView(View view,
                         Context context,
                         Cursor childCursor,
                         boolean isLastChild) {

  //Retrieve the last trade date and volume from the cursor
  String sLastPrice = "Last Price: " + childCursor.getString(
                             childCursor.getColumnIndex("LAST_PRICE"));
  int iVolume = childCursor.getInt(childCursor.getColumnIndex("VOLUME"));

  //Format the volume to be comma-delimited.
  DecimalFormat oNF = new DecimalFormat("###,###,###,###");
  String sVolume = "Volume: " + oNF.format(iVolume);

  //Gain access to the two text views for the child
  TextView oLastPrice = (TextView) view.findViewById(android.R.id.text1);
  TextView oVolume = (TextView) view.findViewById(android.R.id.text2);

  //Change the font size
  oLastPrice.setTextSize(10);
  oVolume.setTextSize(10);

  //Set the two text views to the last trade date and the volume
  oLastPrice.setText(sLastPrice);
  oVolume.setText(sVolume);

  }

  @Override
  protected void bindGroupView(View view,
                         Context context,
                         Cursor parentCursor,
                         boolean isExpanded) {

  //Get the stock symbol from the parent cursor
  String sStockSymbol = "Symbol: " + parentCursor.getString(
                             parentCursor.getColumnIndex("STOCK_SYMBOL"));

  //Gain access to the single TextView that displays the stock symbol
```

367

```java
    TextView oStockSymbol = (TextView) view.findViewById(android.R.id.text1);

    //Set the text in the TextView.
    oStockSymbol.setText(sStockSymbol);

  }

  @Override
  protected Cursor getChildrenCursor(Cursor parentCursor) {

    //Get the _ID from the parentCursor (the STOCK_SYMBOLS table)
    long parentID = parentCursor.getLong(parentCursor.getColumnIndex("_id"));

    //Create the SQL string to pull data from the database for this parent _ID.
    String sSQL = "SELECT _id,STOCK_SYMBOL,LAST_PRICE,VOLUME FROM STOCK_STATS " +
                  " WHERE _ID=" + Long.toString(parentID);

    //Pull the data from the database into a cursor
    Cursor childCursor = oSQLiteDB.rawQuery(sSQL,null);

    //return the child cursor
    return childCursor;

  }

}
```

Note that I am formatting the Volume by using the `DecimalFormat` class's `format()` method.

Second, we have to modify the `onCreate()` method our `MainActivity` class to access the database, query the appropriate table for stock symbols, and instantiate our new class:

```java
package com.example.andapp6;

import android.os.Bundle;
import android.app.ExpandableListActivity;
import android.database.Cursor;
import android.database.sqlite.SQLiteDatabase;

public class MainActivity extends ExpandableListActivity {

  private SQLiteDatabase oSQLiteDB;

  @Override
  public void onCreate(Bundle savedInstanceState) {

    super.onCreate(savedInstanceState);

    //Open up the database
    oSQLiteDB = SQLiteDatabase.openDatabase(
                       "/data/data/com.example.andapp6/EQUITY_DATABASE.db3",
                       null,
                       SQLiteDatabase.OPEN_READONLY);

    //Get a cursor to the stock symbol/company name in STOCK_SYMBOLS
    String sSQL = "SELECT _id,STOCK_SYMBOL FROM STOCK_SYMBOLS";
    Cursor parentCursor = oSQLiteDB.rawQuery(sSQL,null);

    //Manage the cursor
    startManagingCursor(parentCursor);

    //Instantiate the class MyResourceCursorTreeAdapter
    MyResourceCursorTreeAdapter oExpandableListAdapter =
       new MyResourceCursorTreeAdapter(
```

```
                              oSQLiteDB,
                              this,
                              parentCursor,
                              android.R.layout.simple_expandable_list_item_1,
                              android.R.layout.simple_expandable_list_item_2);

    //Set the expandable list adapter to our resource cursor tree adapter.
    setListAdapter(oExpandableListAdapter);

  }

}
```

Here is what this looks like:

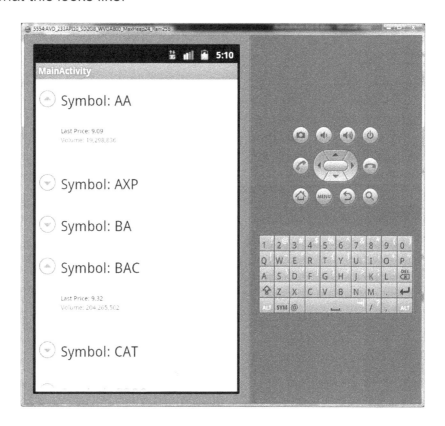

Less Simple Data Display #5 - Using `SpinnerAdapter`

If you would like to populate a spinner view with data, you can use the `SpinnerAdapter` interface. Now, this interface allows you to display one view when the drop-down list is shown and another view when it is not shown. Since `SpinnerAdapter` is an interface, you will have to use the `implements` keyword when creating your class, but you don't normally have to go that far.

One way to populate a `Spinner` is to create an array containing the desired data, create an adapter to that data, and then associate the adapter with the `Spinner`. For example, given a Spinner called `spinner1` and an array called DJIA (`R.array.DJIA`) which contains the stock symbols of the Dow Jones Industrial Average, here is the code to populate the `Spinner`:

```
@Override
public void onCreate(Bundle savedInstanceState) {

  super.onCreate(savedInstanceState);
```

369

```
setContentView(R.layout.activity_main);

//Instantiate the Spinner as an object
Spinner oSP = (Spinner) findViewById(R.id.spinner1);

//Set up an ArrayAdapter from the array to the spinner.  The layout
// simple_spinner_item is used to display a single item in the spinner.
// This has nothing to do with how the spinner displays multiple items
// when the drop-down arrow is clicked.  See below.
ArrayAdapter<CharSequence> adapter =
        ArrayAdapter.createFromResource(this,
                                        R.array.DJIA,
                                        android.R.layout.simple_spinner_item);

//Indicate which layout to use when the drop-down arrow is clicked.
adapter.setDropDownViewResource(android.R.layout.simple_spinner_dropdown_item);

//Assign adapter as the adapter to the spinner.
oSP.setAdapter(adapter);

}
```

Note that `ArrayAdapter<CharSequence>` produces a `SpinnerAdapter` which is then used in the `setAdapter()` method. Here is what the Spinner looks like when the down-arrow has **not** been clicked:

And here is what the `Spinner` displays when then down-arrow is clicked:

Note that the text "DJIA Stocks" is displayed by adding `android:prompt` in the XML for the Spinner:

```
<Spinner android:id="@+id/spinner1"
        android:layout_width="wrap_content"
        android:layout_height="wrap_content"
        android:layout_alignParentLeft="true"
        android:layout_alignParentTop="true"
        android:prompt="@string/prmpt"/>
```

Now, if you have data loaded into a database table, you can use a `SimpleCursorAdapter` as shown above. Here is an example for the `Spinner`:

```
private SQLiteDatabase oSQLiteDB;

@Override
public void onCreate(Bundle savedInstanceState) {
    super.onCreate(savedInstanceState);
    setContentView(R.layout.activity_main);

    //Open up the database...YOU MAY HAVE TO CHANGE THE FIRST PARAMETER!!
    oSQLiteDB = SQLiteDatabase.openDatabase(
                        "/data/data/com.example.andapp7/EQUITY_DATABASE.db3",
                        null,
                        SQLiteDatabase.OPEN_READONLY);

    //Set up SQL query and query the database.
    String sSQL = "SELECT _id,STOCK_SYMBOL FROM STOCK_SYMBOLS " +
                "ORDER BY STOCK_SYMBOL DESC";
    Cursor cursorStocks = oSQLiteDB.rawQuery(sSQL,null);

    //Manage the cursor
    startManagingCursor(cursorStocks);

    //Instantiate the Spinner as an object
    Spinner oSP = (Spinner) findViewById(R.id.spinner1);
```

371

```
//Set up a cursor adapter for the ListView using oCSR
SimpleCursorAdapter adapter =
                new SimpleCursorAdapter(this,
                                        android.R.layout.simple_spinner_item,
                                        cursorStocks,
                                        new String[] {"STOCK_SYMBOL"},
                                        new int[] {android.R.id.text1},0);

//Indicate which layout to use when the drop-down arrow is clicked.
adapter.setDropDownViewResource(
                            android.R.layout.simple_spinner_dropdown_item);

//Assign adapter as the adapter to the spinner.
oSP.setAdapter(adapter);

}
```

Note that in the constructor for SimpleCursorAdapter, we are passing in the android.R.layout.simple_spinner_item which shows the spinner item, the cursor to the list of stocks pulled from the database, an array of Strings containing the items to be displayed in the Spinner and the appropriate ID of the TextView, android.R.id.text1.

Summary

In this chapter, we learned about various adapters used to populate several views such as the ListView, ExpandableListView and Spinner. This chapter is certainly not the last word on adapters, so please peruse the Android SDK documentation to learn more.

Chapter 18: Broadcasting Events

Overview

In this chapter, we look into how your application can make a system-wide broadcast allowing other applications set up to receive your broadcast and perform some useful action. For example, if your application has downloaded an updated database, you can broadcast this fact to other applications that depend upon your database. They can, in turn, perform some action based on that fact.

On the other side of the broadcasting coin, you can also set up your own applications to receive broadcasts from either your own or a third-party's application.

Finally, Android broadcasts its own information such as battery level, screen on, etc. At the end of the chapter, we look into how you can wire your own application up to receive these system broadcasts.

Recall that we used intents to start new activities as well as applications such as Adobe Reader or the Browser. In all of the cases listed above, intents are used in the process to broadcast events. By using intents, you can also add, if desired, additional information to the broadcast using the `putExtra()` method as described in *Chapter 11, Intents*. The receiver of your broadcast can pull out this extra information and use it how it likes. For example, if you broadcast that your database has been updated, you may want to pass the location and file name of the new database (even if it's supposed to never change).

At the end of this chapter, we discuss how to use the `DownloadManager` service to download files from the Internet. The `DownloadManager` service requires a broadcast to indicate when the file has completed downloading.

Broadcasting an Event

Broadcasting an event using intents from within your own application is straightforward:

1. Create a `String` containing an event identifier of your own choosing such as `com.example.action.DATABASE_UPDATED`
2. Create a new intent by instantiating the `Intent` class
3. Insert additional data via the `putExtra()` method
4. Execute the `sendBroadcast()` method by passing in the event

Note that there is no need for the broadcaster to modify its `AndroidManifest.xml` file. As we shall see, it is the responsibility of the broadcast *receiver* to modify its own `Android Manifest.xml` file.

For example, here is our string:

```
//Create our broadcast event string
public static final String DATABASE_UPDATED_ACTION =
                              "com.example.action.DATABASE_UPDATED";
```

In our example activity, I've added an additional button that will broadcast the event when pushed. I've modified the `onCreate()` method to set up an `onClickListener` for the button:

```
//Create an onClickListener and associate it with the button
//that will send the updated database broadcast event.
((Button) findViewById(R.id.button3)).setOnClickListener(

  new View.OnClickListener() {
   public void onClick(View view) {

     //Set up a new Intent and load it with useful information for the broadcast.
     Intent oBC_EVT = new Intent(DATABASE_UPDATED_ACTION);
     oBC_EVT.putExtra("UPDATED_DATABASE_LOCATION",
                      "/data/data/com.example.andapp1");
     oBC_EVT.putExtra("UPDATED_DATABASE_FILENAME","EQUITY_DATABASE_v2.db3");

     //Initiate the broadcast
     sendBroadcast(oBC_EVT);

   }
  }
);
```

Receiving a Broadcasted Event

Receiving a broadcasted event within your application allows you to be notified when the broadcasted event has been triggered. This allows your application, whether currently running or not, to take some action based on the event triggered and the data passed along with the intent (if any).

To receive broadcasts, you must perform the following steps within a separate application from the application that broadcasts the event:

1. Modify your `AndroidManifest.xml` file to include the `<receiver>`, `<intent-filter>` and `<action>` tags. The receiver tag's `name` attribute indicates the class involved in the reception of the broadcast event. The action tag's `name` attribute contains the action string indicating which broadcast event to listen for (see the previous section).
2. Add a new class file to your project and extend the `BroadcastReceiver` class. Override the `onReceive()` method. This method is called when a broadcast named in the `AndroidManifest.xml` file is captured. One of the paramters of the `onReceive()` method is the intent which you can use with the `get*()` methods to pull out any additional data.

Here is the code we placed in our `AndroidManifest.xml` file:

```
<receiver android:name=".DatabaseUpdatedBroadcastReceiver">
 <intent-filter>
  <action android:name="com.example.action.DATABASE_UPDATED"/>
 </intent-filter>
</receiver>
```

Here is the code for our class `DatabaseUpdatedBroadcastReceiver`:

```
package com.example.andapp7;
```

374

```
import android.content.BroadcastReceiver;
import android.content.Context;
import android.content.Intent;
import android.widget.Toast;

public class DatabaseUpdatedBroadcastReceiver extends BroadcastReceiver {

 @Override
 public void onReceive(Context context, Intent intent) {

  //If this method is executed, then the database has been updated.
  //Take some useful action, buddy.
  String sUPDATED_DATABASE_LOCATION =
                      intent.getStringExtra("UPDATED_DATABASE_LOCATION");
  String sUPDATED_DATABASE_FILENAME =
                      intent.getStringExtra("UPDATED_DATABASE_FILENAME");

  //Use a toast to show this new file on the screen.
  Toast toast = Toast.makeText(context,
                      "New Database=" + sUPDATED_DATABASE_LOCATION
                                     + "/"
                                     + sUPDATED_DATABASE_FILENAME,
                      Toast.LENGTH_LONG);
  toast.show();

 }

}
```

Now, when you press the *Broadcast Database Update Event* button in the first app, the event is received by the second app and a toast appears on the screen. Make sure that you pass the correct context, as shown above, into the `makeText()` method.

Note that although we chose to alert Android that we are listening for a broadcast event by placing the `<receiver>` tag in the `AndroidManifest.xml` file, we can program the same thing by using the `Context.registerReceiver()` method. By using this method, your application **must be running** in order to receive the broadcast. This is not the case when using the `<receiver>` tag. Be aware that if the receiving application is not running, it will be started and will appear in Settings...Applications...Manage Applications...All/Downloaded among the list of running applications.

Note that instead of creating a separate class file containing our extension to the `BroadcastReceiver` class, you can instantiate a `BroadcastReceiver` class within, say, the `onCreate()` method of your Activity. Please see the example for `DownloadManager` later in the chapter.

Can I Send and Receive My Own Broadcasts?

Your application can be both a *broadcaster* and *broadcast receiver* of your own broadcasts. That is, much like shown above, one of your applications can be a broadcaster and another of your applications can be a receiver.

Now, if you would like to send and receive broadcasts within a *single* application, you should consider using the `LocalBroadcastManager` class instead of the `BroadcastReceiver` class. This allows the data you send to be intercepted solely by your own application and won't pose a security risk if you are sending sensitive data.

Please peruse the `LocalBroadcastManager` documentation for more on this functionality.

Receiving Android System Broadcasts

You can receive system-related broadcasts by supplying a desired *standard broadcast action* rather than your own. You can find a list of these actions in the section labeled Standard Broadcast Actions in the documentation on the `Intent` class. They are reproduced here:

1. `ACTION_TIME_TICK` - The current time has changed. Sent every minute. You cannot receive this through components declared in manifests, only by explicitly registering for it with `Context.registerReceiver()`. This is a protected intent that can only be sent by the system. Constant Value: "android.intent.action.TIME_TICK".
2. `ACTION_TIME_CHANGED` - The time was set. Constant Value: "android.intent.action.TIME_SET".
3. `ACTION_TIMEZONE_CHANGED` - The timezone has changed. The intent will have the following extra values: time-zone (the java.util.TimeZone.getID() value identifying the new time zone.) This is a protected intent that can only be sent by the system. Constant Value: "android.intent.action.TIMEZONE_CHANGED".
4. `ACTION_BOOT_COMPLETED` - This is broadcast once, after the system has finished booting. It can be used to perform application-specific initialization, such as installing alarms. You must hold the `RECEIVE_BOOT_COMPLETED` permission in order to receive this broadcast. This is a protected intent that can only be sent by the system. Constant Value: "android.intent.action.BOOT_COMPLETED".
5. `ACTION_PACKAGE_ADDED` - A new application package has been installed on the device. The data contains the name of the package. Note that the newly installed package does not receive this broadcast. My include the following extras: EXTRA_UID (containing the integer uid assigned to the new package), EXTRA_REPLACING (set to true if this is following an ACTION_PACKAGE_REMOVED broadcast for the same package.). This is a protected intent that can only be sent by the system. Constant Value: "android.intent.action.PACKAGE_ADDED".
6. `ACTION_PACKAGE_CHANGED` - An existing application package has been changed (e.g. a component has been enabled or disabled). The data contains the name of the package. EXTRA_UID (containing the integer uid assigned to the package), EXTRA_CHANGED_COMPONENT_NAME_LIST (containing the class name of the changed components), EXTRA_DONT_KILL_APP (containing boolean field to override the default action of restarting the application). This is a protected intent that can only be sent by the system. Constant Value: "android.intent.action.PACKAGE_CHANGED".
7. `ACTION_PACKAGE_REMOVED` - An existing application package has been removed from the device. The data contains the name of the package. The

package that is being installed does not receive this Intent. EXTRA_UID (containing the integer uid previously assigned to the package), EXTRA_DATA_REMOVED (set to true if the entire application -- data and code -- is being removed), EXTRA_REPLACING (set to true if this will be followed by an ACTION_PACKAGE_ADDED broadcast for the same package). This is a protected intent that can only be sent by the system. Constant Value: "android.intent.action.PACKAGE_REMOVED".

8. `ACTION_PACKAGE_RESTARTED` - The user has restarted a package, and all of its processes have been killed. All runtime state associated with it (processes, alarms, notifications, etc) should be removed. Note that the restarted package does not receive this broadcast. The data contains the name of the package. EXTRA_UID (containing the integer uid assigned to the package). This is a protected intent that can only be sent by the system. Constant Value: "android.intent.action.PACKAGE_RESTARTED".

9. `ACTION_PACKAGE_DATA_CLEARED` - The user has cleared the data of a package. This should be preceded by ACTION_PACKAGE_RESTARTED, after which all of its persistent data is erased and this broadcast sent. Note that the cleared package does not receive this broadcast. The data contains the name of the package. EXTRA_UID (containing the integer uid assigned to the package). This is a protected intent that can only be sent by the system. Constant Value: "android.intent.action.PACKAGE_DATA_CLEARED".

10. `ACTION_UID_REMOVED` - A user ID has been removed from the system. The user ID number is stored in the extra data under EXTRA_UID. This is a protected intent that can only be sent by the system. Constant Value: "android.intent.action.UID_REMOVED".

11. `ACTION_BATTERY_CHANGED` - This is a sticky broadcast containing the charging state, level, and other information about the battery. See `BatteryManager` for documentation on the contents of the Intent. You cannot receive this through components declared in manifests, only by explicitly registering for it with `Context.registerReceiver()`. See ACTION_BATTERY_LOW, ACTION_BATTERY_OKAY, ACTION_POWER_CONNECTED, and ACTION_POWER_DISCONNECTED for distinct battery-related broadcasts that are sent and can be received through manifest receivers. This is a protected intent that can only be sent by the system. Constant Value: "android.intent.action.BATTERY_CHANGED".

12. `ACTION_POWER_CONNECTED` - External power has been connected to the device. This is intended for applications that wish to register specifically to this notification. Unlike ACTION_BATTERY_CHANGED, applications will be woken for this and so do not have to stay active to receive this notification. This action can be used to implement actions that wait until power is available to trigger. This is a protected intent that can only be sent by the system. Constant Value: "android.intent.action.ACTION_POWER_CONNECTED".

13. `ACTION_POWER_DISCONNECTED` - External power has been removed from the device. This is intended for applications that wish to register specifically to this notification. Unlike ACTION_BATTERY_CHANGED, applications will be woken for this and so do not have to stay active to receive this notification. This action can be used to implement actions that wait until power is available to trigger. This is a protected intent that can only be sent

by the system. Constant Value: "android.intent.action.ACTION_POWER_DISCONNECTED".

14. ACTION_SHUTDOWN - Device is shutting down. This is broadcast when the device is being shut down (completely turned off, not sleeping). Once the broadcast is complete, the final shutdown will proceed and all unsaved data lost. Apps will not normally need to handle this, since the foreground activity will be paused as well. This is a protected intent that can only be sent by the system. Constant Value: "android.intent.action.ACTION_SHUTDOWN".

Besides the standard broadcast actions, please peruse the Intent Constants section for additional actions marked as broadcast actions.

For example, to receive the ACTION_SHUTDOWN broadcast, you would modify the AndroidManifest.xml file by adding the following XML:

```
<receiver android:name=".SystemShutdownBroadcastReceiver">
 <intent-filter>
  <action android:name="android.intent.action.ACTION_SHUTDOWN"/>
 </intent-filter>
</receiver>
```

You would then create a subclass called SystemShutdownBroadcastReceiver of the BroadcastReceiver class and override the onReceive() method in a similar manner to our DatabaseUpdateBroadcastReceiver subclass above.

Using the DownloadManager Service

In this section, we discuss how to download files from the Internet via the DownloadManager service. This service requires a broadcast receiver so that when the file has completed downloading, the broadcast is triggered.

Don't forget to add your broadcast receiver to the AndroidManifest.xml file! Also, in order to download files from the Internet, you need to add the INTERNET permission to the AndroidManifest.xml file within the <manifest> section:

```
<uses-permission android:name="android.permission.INTERNET" />
```

You will also need to have write permission to the external storage device, if you plan to download the file to the SDcard:

```
<uses-permission android:name="android.permission.WRITE_EXTERNAL_STORAGE" />
```

Now, you must create a method that is responsible for starting the download. Here is some example code:

```
//Method to start the downloading of the file
public void StartDownload(View view) {

 //Get an instance of the DownloadManager Service using getSystemService()
 oDM = (DownloadManager) getSystemService(Context.DOWNLOAD_SERVICE);

 //Ensure that the external folder exists
 Boolean bRC = Environment.getExternalStoragePublicDirectory(
                            Environment.DIRECTORY_DOWNLOADS).mkdirs();
```

```
//Set up a download request to our file to download (stored in sFileToDownload)
DownloadManager.Request oDMReq = new DownloadManager.Request(
                                          Uri.parse(sFileToDownload));

//Set preferred options for the DownloadManager.Request object
// Take note of the vertical bar at the end of the first line of code below!
oDMReq.setAllowedNetworkTypes(DownloadManager.Request.NETWORK_WIFI |
                           DownloadManager.Request.NETWORK_MOBILE)
 .setAllowedOverRoaming(false)
 .setTitle("Download Updated Database")
 .setDescription("Downloading latest updated database...")
 .setDestinationInExternalPublicDir(Environment.DIRECTORY_DOWNLOADS,
                               "download_file.pdf");

//Add this download to the queue.  When the download is complete, the
// BroadcastReceiver will be fired.
lEnqueueID = oDM.enqueue(oDMReq);

}
```

The key code above is the `setDestinationInExternalPublicDir` which is set to the directory download location on the SDcard along with the name of the file (`download_file.pdf`).

Note that the attributes `oDM` (the `DownloadManager` object), `lEnqueueID` (the ID of the enqueued download) and `sFileToDownload` (a `String` containing the URL of the file to download) are created at the top of the class:

```
//String to hold the file to download
private String sFileToDownload = "http://www.example.com/joomla/media/documents/"
                            + "InstallingUnixODBCLinux.pdf";

//DownloadManager object
private DownloadManager oDM;

//The ID of the enqueued file to download
private long lEnqueueID;
```

Next, in the `onCreate()` method of the `Activity`, we create a `BroadcastReceiver` that will do something wonderful when the download is complete. Note that we are instantiating the `BroadcastReceiver` rather than creating a separate class (which is another way to go):

```
//Instantiate the BroadcastReceiver and override the onReceive method
BroadcastReceiver oBR = new BroadcastReceiver() {

 @Override
 public void onReceive(Context context, Intent intent) {

  //Get a string of the action from the intent
  String sAction = intent.getAction();

  //If the download has been completed, then open up the PDF file
  if (DownloadManager.ACTION_DOWNLOAD_COMPLETE.equals(sAction)) {

   //Get the location of the PDF file on disk by querying
   //the DownloadManager database table
   Query oQuery = new Query();
   oQuery.setFilterById(lEnqueueID);
   Cursor oCSR = oDM.query(oQuery);
   oCSR.moveToFirst();

   //Get the download ID
   long lDownloadId = intent.getLongExtra(DownloadManager.EXTRA_DOWNLOAD_ID, 0);
```

```
    //Get the index within the cursor of the DownloadManager's
    // COLUMN_STATUS column.
    int iIndxColumnStatus = oCSR.getColumnIndex(DownloadManager.COLUMN_STATUS);

    //If the download was successful, then pull the file location and
    // display the file
    if (oCSR.getInt(iIndxColumnStatus) == DownloadManager.STATUS_SUCCESSFUL) {

      String uriString = oCSR.getString(
                          oCSR.getColumnIndex(DownloadManager.COLUMN_LOCAL_URI));
      Log.d("MYAPPTAG",uriString);

      //Set up the intent with a default action of ACTION_VIEW.
      Intent intentShowPDF = new Intent(Intent.ACTION_VIEW);
      intentShowPDF.setDataAndType(Uri.parse(uriString), "application/pdf");

      //Display the PDF.
      startActivity(intentShowPDF);

    }

  }

 }

};
```

Finally, right after the code above, we wire up our new broadcast receiver and the `DownloadManager`'s completion intent:

```
//Register our BroadcastReceiver to be fired when the download has completed.
registerReceiver(oBR,
             new IntentFilter(DownloadManager.ACTION_DOWNLOAD_COMPLETE));
```

Once the file is downloaded, the location and name of the file are determined with the following code:

```
String uriString =
         oCSR.getString(oCSR.getColumnIndex(DownloadManager.COLUMN_LOCAL_URI));
```

and the PDF file is displayed on the device. Note that `uriString` looks like this for the example above:

```
file:///mnt/sdcard/Download/download_file.pdf
```

Attempts to use `/mnt/sdcard/download/download_file.pdf` did not work, so include the scheme as well! Also, take note of the spelling of `Download`...it is not `download` despite what you may see in the File Manager.

Also, when the file already exists, `DownloadManager` does not overwrite the file. You can query `DownloadManager.COLUMN_REASON` to see if the value is `ERROR_FILE_ALREADY_EXISTS`. If so, the file already existed and was not overwritten. You can delete a file by using the `delete()` method of the `File` object.

Here is the full code from the activity. Note that there is a button on the interface with its onClick set to `android:onClick="StartDownload"`.

```
package com.example.andappA;

import java.io.File;
import java.io.FileNotFoundException;
import android.net.Uri;
import android.os.Bundle;
import android.os.Environment;
import android.os.ParcelFileDescriptor;
import android.app.Activity;
import android.app.DownloadManager;
import android.app.DownloadManager.Query;
import android.content.BroadcastReceiver;
import android.content.Context;
import android.content.Intent;
import android.content.IntentFilter;
import android.database.Cursor;
import android.util.Log;
import android.view.Menu;
import android.view.View;
import android.widget.TextView;

public class MainActivity extends Activity {

 //String to hold the file to download
 private String sFileToDownload="http://www.example.com/joomla/media/documents/"
                                 + "InstallingUnixODBCLinux.pdf";

 //DownloadManager object
 private DownloadManager oDM;

 //The ID of the enqueued file to download
 private long lEnqueueID;

 @Override
 public void onCreate(Bundle savedInstanceState) {
  super.onCreate(savedInstanceState);
  setContentView(R.layout.activity_main);

  //Update txtFileToDownload to display the file we will download
  TextView oTV = (TextView) findViewById(R.id.txtFileToDownload);
  oTV.setText(sFileToDownload);

  //Instantiate the BroadcastReceiver and override the onReceive method
  BroadcastReceiver oBR = new BroadcastReceiver() {

   @Override
   public void onReceive(Context context, Intent intent) {

    //Get a string of the action from the intent
    String sAction = intent.getAction();

    //If the download has been completed, then open up the PDF file
    if (DownloadManager.ACTION_DOWNLOAD_COMPLETE.equals(sAction)) {

     //Get the location of the PDF file on disk by querying
     //the DownloadManager database table
     Query oQuery = new Query();
     oQuery.setFilterById(lEnqueueID);
     Cursor oCSR = oDM.query(oQuery);
     oCSR.moveToFirst();

     //Get the download ID
     long lDownloadId = intent.getLongExtra(DownloadManager.EXTRA_DOWNLOAD_ID,0);

     //Get the index within the cursor of the DownloadManager's
     // COLUMN_STATUS column.
     int iIndxColumnStatus = oCSR.getColumnIndex(DownloadManager.COLUMN_STATUS);

     //If the download was successful, then pull the file location and
     // display the file
```

```
    if (oCSR.getInt(iIndxColumnStatus) == DownloadManager.STATUS_SUCCESSFUL) {

      String uriString = oCSR.getString(
                           oCSR.getColumnIndex(DownloadManager.COLUMN_LOCAL_URI));
      Log.d("MYAPPTAG",uriString);

      //Set up the intent with a default action of ACTION_VIEW.
      Intent intentShowPDF = new Intent(Intent.ACTION_VIEW);
      intentShowPDF.setDataAndType(Uri.parse(uriString), "application/pdf");

      //Display the PDF.
      startActivity(intentShowPDF);

    }
   }
  }
};

//Register our BroadcastReceiver to be fired when the download has completed.
registerReceiver(oBR,
             new IntentFilter(DownloadManager.ACTION_DOWNLOAD_COMPLETE));

}

//Method to start the downloading of the file
public void StartDownload(View view) {

 //Get an instance of the DownloadManager Service using getSystemService()
 oDM = (DownloadManager) getSystemService(Context.DOWNLOAD_SERVICE);

 //Ensure that the folder exists
 Boolean bRC = Environment.getExternalStoragePublicDirectory(
                             Environment.DIRECTORY_DOWNLOADS).mkdirs();

 //Set up a download request to our file to download
 DownloadManager.Request oDMReq = new DownloadManager.Request(
                                     Uri.parse(sFileToDownload));

 //Set preferred options for the DownloadManager.Request object
 oDMReq.setAllowedNetworkTypes(DownloadManager.Request.NETWORK_WIFI |
                          DownloadManager.Request.NETWORK_MOBILE)
  .setAllowedOverRoaming(false)
  .setTitle("Download Updated Database")
  .setDescription("Downloading latest updated database...")
  .setDestinationInExternalPublicDir(Environment.DIRECTORY_DOWNLOADS,
                                "download_file.pdf");

 //Add this download to the queue. When the download is complete the
 // BroadcastReceiver will be fired.
 lEnqueueID = oDM.enqueue(oDMReq);

 }

}
```

Summary

In this chapter, we learned about how to send and receive broadcasts as well as use the `DownloadManager` service.

Chapter 19: Services

Overview

In this chapter, we look at how to create a service that runs without a GUI interface and in the background. This allows your application to continue to respond to events even when the application is not being used actively in the foreground. Services are used by applications such as an MP3 player which plays music even if the user is not actively interacting with the GUI interface.

Another benefit of services is that they are given a higher priority than inactive Activities from Android's point of view. That is, there is less of a chance that your service will be killed when the system comes under resource pressure. As one author mentioned: *If your application performs actions that don't depend directly on user input, Services may be the answer.*

Note that up to this point in the book we have not discussed using background processing. Everything we've done up to now - opening a SQLite database, processing broadcasts via receivers, etc. - has been executed within the main thread of the application. This is dangerous since Android requires that the main thread return fairly quickly otherwise an Application Not Responding (ANR) or Force Close dialog box will appear which is not something you want displayed to your users. This is true of services which are, by default, executed off of the main thread. This is something you want to avoid. Since we will discuss threading later on in the book, we'll just focus on handling services in this chapter.

Similar to broadcast intents, your service needs to appear in the `AndroidManifest.xml` file. In this case, you use the `<service>` tag.

Note that the `Service` class is located in `android.app.Service` and you will have to include an import line at the top of your program when coding a service.

Creating a Service

In order to create a service, you must subclass the `Service` class and override the appropriate methods:

1. `public void onCreate()` - this method is called when the service is first created. Consider this method an initialization of the service, but not the actual meat of the service.
2. `public void onDestroy()` - this method is called by the system to let the service know that it is no longer needed and that it should clean up after itself. For example, connections to a database should be closed, open files should be closed, etc.
3. `public int onStartCommand(Intent intent,int flags, int startId)` - this method is called each time the method `startService(Intent)` is called. This is where the meat of the service should go and not in `onCreate()`. This method should return one of the three following constants:

a. `Service.START_STICKY` - indicates that if the service is killed while executing, the system should restart the service automatically by passing in a `null Intent` instead of the originating intent. The `null Intent` is an indication that the service has been restarted, so your `onStartCommand()` should take this into account.

b. `Service.START_NOT_STICKY` - indicates that if the service is killed while executing, the system should not automatically restart the service. The only way the service will be started is if a call to `startService(Intent)` is called.

c. `Service.START_REDELIVER_INTENT` - this constant is a combination of the previous two constants. If the service is killed while executing, the system will restart the service automatically but it will pass in the previous `Intent` instead of a `null`.

The `flags` parameter takes on two values:

a. `START_FLAG_REDELIVER` - indicates that the call to `onStartCommand()` was due to a restart and the `Intent` passed in is a redelivery of the previous `Intent` that started the service originally.

b. `START_FLAG_RETRY` - indicates that the `Intent` is a retry because the original attempt never got to `onStartCommand()` or returned from `onStartCommand()`. (...sounds like me in the morning...tee-hee!...)

The `startId` parameter is the identification number of the started service. You use this id when you want to stop a particular service with `stopSelf(startId)` or `stopSelfResult(startId)`.

4. `public IBinder onBind(Intent intent)` - this method returns the communication channel to the service. If this method returns `null`, clients cannot bind to the service. We discuss binding later on in the chapter.

5. `public void onTrimMemory(int level)` - this method is called when the operating system is coming under resource pressure and needs every application and service to reduce its memory usage. The `level` parameter indicates the desperation the system is under: `TRIM_MEMORY_COMPLETE`, `TRIM_MEMORY_MODERATE`, `TRIM_MEMORY_ BACKGROUND`, `TRIM_MEMORY_UI_HIDDEN`, `TRIM_MEMORY_RUNNING_CRITICAL`, `TRIM_MEMORY_RUNNING_LOW`, `TRIM_MEMORY_RUNNING_MODERATE`, `TRIM_MEMORY_BLOODY_HELL`. (Okay, okay, that last one's a joke and not real!)

6. `public void onLowMemory()` - this method is called when the operating system is coming under resource pressure and needs every application and service to reduce its memory usage. Unlike `onTrimMemory()`, there is no desperation parameter, so trim as much memory as you like within this method.

Once you create the subclass, you must do the following to start the service:

1. Instantiate the class. 'Nuf said.
2. Add an entry for `<service>` tag in the `AndroidManifest.xml` file.

3. Use the `startService()` method passing in an `Intent` to start the service. Don't forget that you can add additional information using the `putExtra()` method.

For example, let's create a service that will start displaying random toasts to the screen. Here is the code to do that:

```
package com.example.andapp1;

import java.util.Random;
import android.app.Service;
import android.content.Intent;
import android.os.IBinder;
import android.widget.Toast;

public class MyServiceClass extends Service {

  private String[] saMsgs = {"RED ALERT!","YELLOW ALERT!",
                             "BLUE ALERT!","ORANGE ALERT!","MAUVE ALERT!"};
  private Toast toast;
  private int iRndNbr;
  private Random oRandom;
  private int iStartID;

  @Override
  public void onCreate() {

    //Initialize the random number
    oRandom = new Random();
    iRndNbr = oRandom.nextInt(5);

  }

  @Override
  public void onDestroy() {

    saMsgs = null;
    toast = null;
    oRandom = null;

  }

  @Override
  public int onStartCommand(Intent intent,int flags, int startId) {

    //Save the startId for this service
    iStartID = startId;

    //Get a random number from 0 to 4 for use in deciding which message to toast.
    iRndNbr = oRandom.nextInt(5);

    //Show a random toast
    toast = Toast.makeText(this, saMsgs[iRndNbr], Toast.LENGTH_SHORT);
    toast.show();

    return Service.START_STICKY;
  }


  public void onTrimMemory(int level) {

    //Reduce memory usage, if possible.

  }


  @Override
```

385

```
public void onLowMemory() {

  //Reduce memory usage, if possible.

}

@Override
public IBinder onBind(Intent arg0) {
  return null;
}

}
```

Here is the entry I added within the `<application>` tag in the `Android Manifest.xml` file:

```
<service android:name=".MyServiceClass" android:enabled="true" />
```

In order to start the service, I added a button (called `btnStartService`) labeled Start Service to the interface and wired up an `onClick` event to it like this:

```
//Create an intent to our service
final Intent intent = new Intent(this,MyServiceClass.class);

//Create an onClickListener to start the service
((Button) findViewById(R.id.btnStartService)).setOnClickListener(

 new View.OnClickListener() {
  public void onClick(View view) {

    startService(intent);

  }
 }

);
```

Note that I create a `final Intent` variable called `intent` which initializes a new `Intent` with the context and `MyServiceClass.class`. I then call the `startService()` method passing in `intent`. When the service runs, it display a single random toast containing one of five messages from *Red Alert!* to *Mauve Alert!*. Note that the service does not continue to display toasts to the screen since we are asking it to just generate a single toast.

If the service you've created does continue to run and you want to stop it, call the `stopService()` by passing in the `intent` you stored when you started the service:

```
stopService(intent);
```

Now, if you were to click the Start Service button several times, you'd notice that one random toast after another is displayed on the screen. It's as if each service request is queued to run. But, once you stop the service, any pending requests will not execute.

Be aware that the code within the `onCreate()` as well as `onStartCommand()` methods must run quickly or the Force Close dialog box will be displayed. This is due to the fact that the code is running in the main application thread and is why, in

386

general, it is recommended that you create a separate thread for the code within the `onStartCommand()`. Creating a separate thread frees up the main application thread to respond to user events. We talk more about threading later on in the book.

For example, if I modified the code within `onStartCommand()` to contain a for-loop that just continually displays randoms toasts, you might think that the Force Close dialog box will be displayed since we are blocking the main application thread. But calls to the `startService()` method are asynchronous and won't block the client. Regardless, the code within `onStartCommand()` should be placed within a separate thread. Attempting to stop the code within the for-loop does not halt the execution of the service until `onStartCommand()` returns.

Alternate Ways to Stop a Service

In the previous section, we mentioned that you can use the `stopService(Intent)` command to stop an executing service. The `stopService(Intent)` command is used externally from the service, but if you wish to stop a service from within the service itself, you use the `stopSelf()` command with or without the ID of the service:

```
stopSelf(iStartID);
```

If you require an indication of whether the service was stopped, you can use `stopSelfResult(int started)` which returns true if the `startId` matches that last start request and the service will be stopped; otherwise, false.

Using `IntentService` instead of Handling Threading Yourself

Although we discuss threading later on in the book, you can avoid that topic (somewhat) by extending the `IntentService` class instead of the `Service` class. The `IntentService` class will run your `onStartCommand()` code within a thread and it will take care of starting the thread when needed and killing it when not needed.

When using the `IntentService` class, you do NOT override the `onStartCommand()` method with your own code, but instead you place your code in the `onHandleIntent(Intent)` method.

Make sure that you call the `super`'s for the appropriate methods, as shown in the code below. For example,

```
import java.util.Random;
import android.app.IntentService;
import android.app.Service;
import android.content.Context;
import android.content.Intent;
import android.util.Log;
import android.widget.Toast;

public class MyIntentServiceClass extends IntentService {

  private String[] saMsgs = {"RED ALERT!","YELLOW ALERT!",
                    "BLUE ALERT!","ORANGE ALERT!","MAUVE ALERT!"};
```

387

```java
private Toast toast;
private int iRndNbr;
private Random oRandom;
private Context cntx;

public MyIntentServiceClass() {
  super("MyWorkerThreadName");
}

@Override
public void onCreate() {

  super.onCreate();

  //Initialize the random number
  oRandom = new Random();
  iRndNbr = oRandom.nextInt(5);

  Log.d("MYAPPTAG","In onCreate!");

}

@Override
public void onDestroy() {

  saMsgs = null;
  toast = null;
  oRandom = null;

  super.onDestroy();

}

@Override
public int onStartCommand(Intent intent,int flags, int startId) {

  Log.d("MYAPPTAG","In onStartCommand!");
  return super.onStartCommand(intent, flags, startId);

}

@Override
protected void onHandleIntent(Intent intent) {

  Log.d("MYAPPTAG","In onHandleIntent!");
  ShowToasties();

}

private void ShowToasties() {

  for(int i=0;i<5;i++) {

    //Get a random number from 0 to 4 for use in deciding which message to toast.
    iRndNbr = oRandom.nextInt(5);

    //Show a random toast
    Log.d("MYAPPTAG",saMsgs[iRndNbr]);

  }

 }

}
```

Note that to start an `IntentService`, you still call the `startService(Intent)` method:

```
final Intent intent = new Intent(this,MyIntentServiceClass.class);
startService(intent);
```

Note that the string returned in the constructor above is arbitrary. Also, despite the fact that there is a constructor, you do not have to physically instantiate your subclass.

Also, take note that we do not display the toasts from the `ShowToasties()` method, but show them using `Log.d()` method. This is because, at this point in the process, we are in a thread which cannot show toasts (although you may be able to pass it a `Context` and show the toasts that way...let me know if you got that to work!)

Binding a Client to a Service

In the previous sections, we executed a service that did something wonderful, but you are probably wondering how you can get a result back from the method run by our service. For example, if our service performed some long-running computation, how can our client retrieve the results performed by this computation? Here, the word *client* can mean a request within our own application's code, or a request from another application using the public methods coded in our service. In this section, we only discuss how to bind to a service within our own application.

In order to return a result from a public method running within a service, the client needs to bind to the service using the `bindService()` method. There are several moving parts to using binding, so pay close attention to the code below.

According to the Android SDK: *A service is bound when an application component binds to it by calling* `bindService()`. *A bound service offers a client-server interface that allows components to interact with the service, send requests, get results and even do so across processes with interprocess communication (IPC). A bound service runs only as long as another application component is bound to it. Multiple components can bind to the service once, but when all of them unbind, the service is destroyed.*

Recall that, in the previous section, we returned a `null` in the `onBind()` method. In this chapter, we do not return a `null`, but instead return an `IBinder` object which, as the Android SDK states, *defines the programming interface that clients can use to interact with the service*.

There are several ways to define the interface that a client can use to interact with a service:

1. Extending the `Binder` class
2. Using a Messenger
3. Using AIDL

In this chapter, we only discuss Method #1.

The steps to create a binding to a service using the `Binder` class are as follows:

1. Create your own subclass, called `MyBindService`, of the `Service` class and include the usual suspects: `onCreate()`, `onStartCommand()`, `onDestroy()`, `onBind()`, etc.
2. Within `MyBindService`, create a subclass, called `MyBinder`, of the `Binder` class that contains a single method: `getService()`. This method returns `MyBindService.this`.
3. Within `MyBindService`, create one or more public methods and/or attributes that are useful. These will be accessible from another part of your application.
4. At the top of `MyBindService`, create a single `private final` attribute instantiating `MyBinder`:

   ```
   private final IBinder oBinder = new MyBinder();
   ```

5. In the `onBind()` method in `MyService` return `oBinder` instead of `null`.
6. Update the `AndroidManifest.xml` file with the additional `<service>` tag for the `MyBindService`.

For example, here is our `Service` subclass `MyBindService` along with the `MyBinder` subclass within and the public method `LengthOfHypotenuse`:

```java
import android.app.Service;
import android.content.Intent;
import android.os.Binder;
import android.os.IBinder;

public class MyBindService extends Service {

  private final IBinder oBinder = new MyBinder();

  //BELOW ARE THE OVERRIDDEN METHODS OF THE SERVICE CLASS
  @Override
  public void onCreate() {

  }

  @Override
  public void onDestroy() {

  }

  @Override
  public int onStartCommand(Intent intent,int flags, int startId) {
   return Service.START_STICKY;
  }

  @Override
  public IBinder onBind(Intent intent) {
   return oBinder;
  }

  //BELOW IS THE BINDER SUBCLASS
  public class MyBinder extends Binder {

   MyBindService getService() {
    return MyBindService.this;
   }

  }
  //ABOVE IS THE BINDER SUBCLASS
```

```
//BELOW ARE THE PUBLIC METHODS AVAILABLE TO THE BOUND SERVICE
public double LengthOfHypotenuse(double x,double y) {
  return Math.sqrt(x*x + y*y);
 }

}
```

Within our main activity, create a button with an `onClick` event that triggers the method `ShowLength` that makes use of our public method `LengthOf Hypotenuse`:

```
public void ShowLength(View v) {
 if (bIsBound) {
  double len = oMyBindService.LengthOfHypotenuse(3, 4);
  Toast.makeText(getApplicationContext(),
            "Length of Hypotenuse with sides 3 and 4=" +
                                    Double.toString(len),
            Toast.LENGTH_LONG).show();
 }
}
```

Below is the code for the entire activity:

```
public class MainActivity extends Activity {

 //Attributes used with a bound service
 MyBindService oMyBindService;
 boolean bIsBound = false;

 // Defines callback for service binding, passed to bindService()
 public ServiceConnection mConnection = new ServiceConnection() {

  public void onServiceConnected(ComponentName className, IBinder service) {

    //We've bound to LocalService, cast the IBinder and get
    // LocalService instance
    MyBinder binder = (MyBinder) service;
    oMyBindService = binder.getService();
    bIsBound = true;
  }

  public void onServiceDisconnected(ComponentName className) {
    bIsBound = false;
  }

 };

 @Override
 public void onStop() {
  super.onStop();

  //For bound service
  if (bIsBound) {
   unbindService(mConnection);
   bIsBound = false;
  }

 }

 @Override
 protected void onStart() {
  super.onStart();
  // Bind to LocalService
  Intent intent = new Intent(this, MyBindService.class);
  bindService(intent, mConnection, Context.BIND_AUTO_CREATE);
 }
```

```
@Override
public void onCreate(Bundle savedInstanceState) {
 super.onCreate(savedInstanceState);
 setContentView(R.layout.activity_main);
}

public void ShowLength(View v) {
 if (bIsBound) {
  double len = oMyBindService.LengthOfHypotenuse(3, 4);
  Toast.makeText(getApplicationContext(),
              "Length of Hypotenuse with sides 3 and 4=" +
                                          Double.toString(len),
              Toast.LENGTH_LONG).show();
 }
}

}
```

Note that the starting and stopping of the service occurs within `onStart()` and `onStop()` and not `onCreate()` as you'd think. Also, the variable `mConnection` is a `ServiceConnection` object that contains the following two methods: `onServiceConnected()` and `onServiceDisconnected()`. These two methods are called when the service connects and disconnects.

When the button is clicked, the length of a 3x4 right triangle is displayed: 5.0.

Summary

In this chapter, we learned about how to program services.

Chapter 20: The `Application` Class

Overview

In this chapter, we look at the `Application` class. As we've learned throughout the book, the `Activity` class is the GUI interface that allows your app's users to see and respond to the information presented. However, above all of the activities, services, broadcasts, etc. is the `Application`. In addition, just like the `Activity` class, the `Application` class has its own lifecycle albeit much less complicated than the lifecycle for the `Activity` class.

Most of the time you won't need to subclass the `Application` class because Android does that automatically, but there are times where you may need to (as one author suggests):

1. Maintain application state
2. Transfer objects between application components
3. Manage and maintain resources used by several application components

Once you have subclassed the `Application` class, you will need to add it to the application tag's `android:name` attribute in the `AndroidManifest.xml` file. For example, assuming our subclass is called `MyApplication`, add the bold line to the application tag in the `AndroidManifest.xml` file:

```
<application android:name=".MyApplication"
            android:icon="@drawable/ic_launcher"
            android:label="@string/app_name"
            android:theme="@style/AppTheme" >
```

Below are the methods that you can override and how to implement the `Application` class. Note that this class is implemented as a singleton design pattern which will be explained in a moment:

```
import android.app.Application;
import android.content.res.Configuration;

public class MyApplication extends Application {

 public static MyApplication singleton;
 public String sStockPick = "????";

 //Returns the application instance
 public static MyApplication getInstance() {
  return singleton;
 }

 //onCreate
 @Override
 public final void onCreate() {
  super.onCreate();
  singleton=this;
 }

 //onTerminate
 @Override
 public final void onTerminate() {
  super.onTerminate();
 }
```

```
//onLowMemory
@Override
public final void onLowMemory() {
  super.onLowMemory();
}

//onConfigurationChanged
@Override
public final void onConfigurationChanged(Configuration newConfig) {
  super.onConfigurationChanged(newConfig);
}

}
```

The singleton design pattern only allows one instance of a class to be created. The static variable `singleton` does just this.

For example, if you look at the `String` attribute `sStockPick` above, you will be able to access this attribute from within each activity's own code. Thus, this variable is shared across the **entire** application. Note that you can also store this variable using `SharedPreferences`, but if this information is not something that should be stored for a long time, then you can use the method described here.

For example, in my main (first) activity, I have the following widgets:
1. an `EditText` box with an id of `editText1`
2. a `Button` with an id of `btnSave` which allows the user to save the text in `editText1` to the `Application`'s `sStockPick` variable
3. a `Button` with an id of `btnOpenActivity2` which opens up the second activity (called `activity_activity2`).

In my second activity, I have a single `TextView` box with an id of `TextView1` which pulls in the stock pick in the `Application`'s `sStockPick` variable and displays it.

```
//Reset the stock choice
MyApplication.singleton.sStockPick="MSFT";

//Set editText1 to the sStockPick
EditText oET = (EditText) findViewById(R.id.editText1);
oET.setText(MyApplication.singleton.sStockPick);

//Create an onClickListener to save the text to the application
//variable sStockPick
((Button) findViewById(R.id.btnSave)).setOnClickListener(

  new View.OnClickListener() {
    public void onClick(View view) {

      //Set editText1 to the sStockPick
      EditText oET = (EditText) findViewById(R.id.editText1);
      Editable sEditText = oET.getText();
      MyApplication.singleton.sStockPick = sEditText.toString();

    }
  }

);

//Create an onClickListener to open activity_activity2
((Button) findViewById(R.id.btnOpenActivity2)).setOnClickListener(
```

```
  new View.OnClickListener() {
    public void onClick(View view) {

      //Open the activity_activity2 layout
      Intent intent = new Intent(MainActivity.this,Activity2.class);
      startActivity(intent);

    }
  }

);
```

As you can see, it is easy to access shared variables from the `Application` object within any activity across the entire application.

Summary

In this chapter, we learned about how to create and modify our own `Application` object for use with sharing data between all of our application components.

Chapter 21: Status Notifications

Overview

In *Chapter 9, Activities*, we discussed the `Toast` class which notifies users by displaying a transient piece of text near the bottom of the screen. Unfortunately, toasts disappear as fast as they appear and aren't useful in getting the attention of the user especially when the phone, tablet, or user himself is turned off.

In this chapter, we discuss Status Notifications which are displayed in the Status Bar until the user clears them out. When the user clicks on a particular notification, an `Activity` is started, via a `Pending Intent`, allowing the user to perform some task such as update a database, or take other actions.

A `Notification` can be started via an `Activity` or a `Service`, but usually a `Service`. Once the `Service` has completed its task (say, downloading a file), it can fire the `Notification` and the user will see it in the status bar when the user wakes up from a restful night's sleep.

There are two major classes that are used to generate a Status Notification: `Notification` and `NotificationManager`. It's the `Notification` class that is instantiated and its attributes and methods are used to fill in the information you want to convey to the user. The `NotificationManager` is responsible for displaying the notification as well as other housekeeping.

Steps to Generate a Notification

Below are the steps used to generate a typical `Notification` to the user:

1. Create a unique ID for the notification.
2. Get a reference to the `NotificationManager` using the `getSystemService()` method.
3. Instantiate the `Notification` class in one of two ways:
    a. Using the `Notification` constructor, pass in a desired icon, text, and when to display the notification (usually set to the current time). This method is deprecated and you should probably use (b) below.
    b. Using the `Notification.Builder` class to set the desired icon, text, etc. Note that this is available starting API Level 11 so use (a) above if targeting an Android platform lower than this level.
4. Create a `PendingIntent` and pass it in using one of two methods:
    a. If using 2a, use the `setLatestEventInfo()` method of the instantiated `Notification`
    b. If using 2b, use the `setContentIntent(PendingIntent)` method
5. Pass the instantiated `Notification` to the `NotificationManager` for display on the Status Bar.

Example Code

Below is some simple code which generates a notification when the user clicks the *Display Notification!* button on the main activity. When the user clicks on the

396

notification on the Status Bar, a second activity (called `NotificationActivity`) is displayed.

```
//1. Create a unique ID for the notification
public static final int NOTIFICATION_ID_DATABASE_UPDATE_AVAIALBLE = 1;

//Generate a Status Bar Notification
public void GenerateNotification(View view) {

  //2. Get a pointer to the NotificationManager
  NotificationManager oNM =
    (NotificationManager) getSystemService(Context.NOTIFICATION_SERVICE);

  //3a. Instantiate a Notification object
  int icon = R.drawable.ic_launcher;
  CharSequence tickerText = "New Database Available!";
  long when = System.currentTimeMillis();
  Notification notification = new Notification(icon, tickerText, when);

  //4a. Update the notification and define the PendingIntent
  Context context = getApplicationContext();
  CharSequence contentTitle = "MyApplication Title";
  CharSequence contentText =
                      "New database downloaded and available for installation!";

  Intent notificationIntent = new Intent(this, NotificationActivity.class);
  PendingIntent contentIntent = PendingIntent.getActivity(this,
                                                0,
                                                notificationIntent,
                                                0);
  notification.setLatestEventInfo(context,
                              contentTitle,
                              contentText,
                              contentIntent);

  //5. Send the Notification to the NotificationManager
  oNM.notify(NOTIFICATION_ID_DATABASE_UPDATE_AVAIALBLE, notification);

}
```

Once the *Notify!* button is clicked, a message briefly appears on the Status Bar (as you can see below at the top of the screen, `New Database Available!`).

Once the message disappears, the icon will remain as a reminder that there is a notification available. If you click on the Status Bar and drag down, you will see the full message:

If you then click on the notification, your `Activity` as described by the `PendingIntent` will be displayed. Here, the activity `NotificationActivity` will be inflated.

There are additional features that you can set for your notification. We won't go over these features here, so please check the manual if you want to annoy the hell outta your users by blinking lights and vibrating the phone until it smokes.

Additions to the `AndroidManifest.xml` File

Recall that when activities are displayed, you can hit the Back Button to go back through the interfaces, much like hitting the Back Button in a browser. The documentation states that if you **don't** want the activity to be a part of that, you can add the following attributes to the `<activity>` referred to by the `PendingIntent`:

1. `android:launchMode="singleTask"` - creates a new root for the task
2. `android:taskAffinity=" "` - set this to blank to remove any affinity for the activity (normally, it's the package)
3. `android:excludeFromRecents="true"` - set this to true to exclude the activity from the back button history

You may want to consider using these with the notification activity displayed by the pending intent. This will prevent the user from seeing the screen while hitting the Back Button.

Summary

In this chapter, we learned about using notifications to alert the user that something has occurred.

Chapter 22: Thread Programming in Android

Overview

In this chapter, we will discuss how to make your application multi-tasking using the variety of threading methods available in Android. Up to this point in the book, all of the code you have written has been executed on the main GUI application thread. If a piece of code takes too much time, Android will display an Application Not Responding (ANR) dialog which is something you don't want to happen. Using threading in key areas in your code can prevent this from occurring giving the user a serene, life-altering experience.

There are several classes available to execute code on a separate thread:

1. `AsyncTask` Class - you extend this class and override the following methods:
   a. `doInBackground()` - this method contains the code you want executed in a separate thread. The code within this method does not, and should not, interact with the GUI interface. Instead, within this code, you may call the `publishProgress()` method which will call the code within the `onProgressUpdate()` method (described below) which can interact with the GUI interface. Once complete, this method returns the result of, say, your computation.
   b. `onProgressUpdate()` - this method, which is executed in the main (GUI) thread, can update the GUI interface such as moving a progress bar, etc.
   c. `onPreExecute()` - this method is executed on the GUI thread before `doInBackground()` is executed.
   d. `onPostExecute()` - this method is executed on the GUI thread after `doInBackground()` completes. The result of, say, the computation, performed within `doInBackground()` is passed as a parameter to this method. You can then do what you want with that value.
   e. `execute()` - this method is called in the GUI thread to start executing the code in `doInBackground()` in a separate thread. The parameters of this method are passed into `doInBackground()` and can be used how you see fit.
   f. `get()` - this method should probably be avoided since it will cause the GUI thread to block which is exactly the opposite of what you are using the `AsyncTask` class for. You'll have to fight the overwhelming urge to this method because it returns the resulting value produced by `doInBackground()` effectively making it look like a function. As Obi-wan Kenobi would say, "You don't need to use this method! And those aren't the damn droids you're looking for!".
2. `Thread` Class - this is more complex to use than using `AsyncTask`, but it has the benefit of allowing you to avoid the whole overriding methods lark for `AsyncTask`. The `Thread` class works with `Runnable` objects which is just a fancy name for the code you want executed in a separate thread.
3. `Handler` Class - this class works in conjunction with the `Thread` class allowing you *to send and process* `Message` *and* `Runnable` *objects associated with a thread's* `MessageQueue.` According to the Android SDK: *There are two*

main uses for a `Handler`*: (1) to schedule messages and runnables to be executed at some point in the future; and (2) to enqueue an action to be performed on a different thread than your own.*

4. `FutureTask` and `Executor` - we won't discuss these in this book

Using the `AsyncTask` Class

In this section, we describe the `AsyncTask` class with an example. This example mimics downloading a file in ten segments and update a progress bar 10% at a time. Since the simulated download is being done in a separate thread from the GUI thread, your GUI thread can respond to user events.

The GUI has two views on it:
1. `Button` - the button, named `btnDownload`, will start the simulated download when clicked. The `onClick` attribute is set to call the `downloadFile` method.
2. `ProgressBar` (horizontal) - the horizontal progress bar, named `progressBar`, will be filled in 10% at a time simulating a download in ten pieces.

Here is the code. You'll note that I've placed my extension of the `AsyncTask` class, called `DownloadAsyncClass`, within the `Activity` class in order for the `findViewById()` method to be found. (When I created my class in a separate class file, this method is not found, even when importing `android.app.Activity`! Very strange!!)

Take note that I am instantiating the `DownloadAsyncClass` within the `downloadNow` method and I follow up by calling the `execute()` method to start the background process.

```
package com.example.andappb;

import android.os.AsyncTask;
import android.os.Bundle;
import android.app.Activity;
import android.view.Menu;
import android.view.View;
import android.widget.ProgressBar;
import android.widget.Toast;

public class MainActivity extends Activity {

@Override
public void onCreate(Bundle savedInstanceState) {
  super.onCreate(savedInstanceState);
  setContentView(R.layout.activity_main);

  //Ensure that the progressBar is initialized to [0,100].
  ProgressBar oPB = (ProgressBar) findViewById(R.id.progressBar);
  oPB.setMax(100);
  oPB.setProgress(0);

}

//This method starts the simulated download
public void downloadFile(View view) {
```

```
   //Instantiate the class and execute the download in the background
   DownloadAsyncClass oDAC = new DownloadAsyncClass();
   oDAC.execute("http://www.microsoft.com/stuff.pdf");


}

//The Generics are as follows:
// 1.String (Params type) - this is the parameter passed in (the http://
//                          URL of the file to download)
// 2.int (Progess type) - the progress increment
// 3.String (Result type) - the post-download file location on the
//                          device's storage media
public class DownloadAsyncClass extends AsyncTask<String, Integer, String> {

  //doInBackground
  @Override
  protected String doInBackground(String... params) {

   String result = "";

   //Simulate the download of a file in ten pieces
   for(int i=0;i<10;i++) {

    //Similate download
    try {
      Thread.sleep(2000);
    } catch (InterruptedException e) {
      e.printStackTrace();
    }

    //Update the progressBar in the user interface
    publishProgress( (int) (100*(i+1)/10) );

   }

   result="myfile.pdf";

   return result;
  }

  //onPreExecute
  @Override
  protected void onPreExecute() {
   super.onPreExecute();
  }

  //onPostExecute
  @Override
  protected void onPostExecute(String result) {
   super.onPostExecute(result);
   Toast.makeText(getApplicationContext(), result, Toast.LENGTH_LONG).show();
  }

  //onProgressUpdate
  @Override
  protected void onProgressUpdate(Integer... values) {
   super.onProgressUpdate(values);

   //Get pointer to progressBar
   ProgressBar oPB = (ProgressBar) findViewById(R.id.progressBar);

   //Set the progress to the parameter which is the percentage of completion.
   oPB.setProgress(values[0]);

  }

 }

}
```

An important piece of code is the extends line above:

```
public class DownloadAsyncClass extends AsyncTask<String, Integer, String> {
```

Specifically, look at the data types within the less than and greater than symbols (this programming construct is known as *generics*). In order, they are:

1. The data type for the parameters passed to `doInBackground()`.
2. The data type for the progress information and passed to `onProgressUpdate()` and passed into `publishProgress()`.
3. The data type for the results.

Each of these three data types must match the data types for the input/output for the overridden methods. If you do not need a data type, use `Void`. That is, if you will not be using the progress information, then code this instead of what you see above:

```
public class DownloadAsyncClass extends AsyncTask<String, Void, String> {
```

In any case, here is what the GUI looks like *during* the simulated download:

And here is what the GUI looks like when the file has *completed* its download:

Using the `Thread` Class

In this section, we describe the `Thread` class when it is used with a `Runnable`. You can very easily execute some code within a separate thread by using the following construct:

```
new Thread(new Runnable() {

 public void run() {
   //your code goes here!!

 }

}).start();
```

Alternatively, you can break this apart and code it like this:

```
Thread oThread = new Thread(doInBackground);
oThread.start();

private Runnable doInBackground = new Runnable() {

 public void run() {
   //your code goes here!!
 }

};
```

Discussion

Don't forget that the whole reason to use threading is to prevent the dreaded Application Not Responding dialog box from appearing. So, any long-running pieces of code, services, etc. should be placed within a thread using one of the methods described here. This will prevent the user-interface from being blocked and keep the ANR from appearing.

Displaying a Progress Bar When Using the `AsyncTask` Class

Now, if you believe that your code will run for a while, then you can display a rotating progress bar (the spinning round thingy) while your code is running in a thread. To do this, you instantiate a `ProgressDialog` in the constructor of your class that subclasses the `AsyncTask`, like this:

```
public class SQLQueryAsyncClass extends AsyncTask<String, Integer, Cursor> {

private Context context;
ProgressDialog oPD;

public SQLQueryAsyncClass(Context ctx) {
 context = ctx;

 //Set up the progress dialog to display while the SQL Query is running.
 oPD = new ProgressDialog(context);
 oPD.setMessage("Please wait...");
 oPD.setIndeterminate(true);
 oPD.setCancelable(false);

}
```

Take note that the variable `oPD` is available across the entire class. Next, to display the progress dialog, you use the `show()` method within the `onPreExecute()` method:

```
//onPreExecute
@Override
protected void onPreExecute() {
 super.onPreExecute();

 //Display the ProgressDialog.
 oPD.show();

}
```

Now, once your code has finished running in the background, you have to hide the progress dialog using the `dismiss()` method from within the `onPostExecute()` method:

```
//onPostExecute
@Override
protected void onPostExecute(Cursor result) {
 super.onPostExecute(result);

 // ... code goes here ...

 //Dismiss the ProgressDialog at this point.
 oPD.dismiss();

 // ... more code goes here ...

}
```

Summary

In this chapter, we learned about threading using the `AsyncClass` as well as the `Thread` class. This is certainly not the last word on threading, so please check out the Android documentation to find out more.

Chapter 23: Graphics

Overview

In this chapter, we will discuss the variety of graphics capabilities available to the Android programmer.

Now, I know that you've done some graphics in your programming life. You know how it goes: you draw points, lines, circles, etc. on a blank area of the screen, add in some text, and *voila!* you have a graph. In Android, you can do the same thing, but Android gives you several graphics options you can use *before* you get to that stage. Specifically,

1. Graphics via XML Resources
   a. Animation - You can define a complete animation by specifying individual frames within an XML Resource file. You can think of this as an *animated GIF* that has been broken apart into its individual frames which are then defined as individual items within XML. Android is responsible for displaying each frame in turn.
   b. Transitions - You can define a transition between two images indicated in XML where the first image cross-fades to the second image. Think of a closed folder image that fades into an open folder image and you'll get the idea.
   c. Level List - You can define several images indicated in XML such that given a programmatically assigned level number, say 4, indicates that the fourth image should be drawn. Several uses of this are the battery level indicator and the WIFI power indicator images. By specifying a level of 1, an image of a battery (say) with one bar is shown, but by specifying a level of 4, an image of a battery with four bars is shown. You still have to create those images and programmatically request which one to display, but managing them is easy with the Level List.
   d. ...and so many more... - we talk about the others later in this chapter.

2. View Animation - You can use this to create a cheapy animation by using *tweening*. For example, given starting coordinates and ending coordinates, the view will be moved be*tween* (hence, *tween*) the two coordinates. This is similar to how Adobe Flash cartoons work.

3. Property Animation - Similar to View Animation, but allows you to animate properties of any object including those that do not actually render to the screen. This was introduced in Android 3.0 (ATI Level 11).

4. 2D Graphics - You can create two-dimensional graphics using the `Canvas` and `SurfaceView` classes. The `Canvas` class is used to generate a static image whereas the `SurfaceView` class is used to create an animation or 2D video game. You can also manipulate the look-and-feel of widgets like the `Button` by overriding the `onDraw()` method.

5. 3D Graphics - You can create three-dimensional graphics for use in, say, video games. This is accomplished by using OpenGL ES which defines a 3D graphics language. Note that OpenGL is not Android- or Java-specific, but a

general framework available on many platforms prior to the release of Android. Android can run OpenGL ES 1.0/1.1 and OpenGL ES 2.0. We will not discuss OpenGL ES in this book, but I refer you to the humorous book *Pro OpenGL ES for Android (Professional APress)* by Smithwick and Verma and *OpenGL ES2 for Android:A Quick Start Guide (Pragmatic Bookshelf)* by Kevin Brothaler.

We will discuss each of these in turn below.

What is a Drawable?

Before we talk about using XML Resources to create animations, we need to chat about the `Drawable` class.

According to the Android SDK: *A `Drawable` is a general abstraction for "something that can be drawn." Most often you will deal with `Drawable` as the type of resource retrieved for drawing things to the screen; the `Drawable` class provides a generic API for dealing with an underlying visual resource that may take a variety of forms. Unlike a `View`, a `Drawable` does not have any facility to receive events or otherwise interact with the user.*

A drawable resource is a general concept for a graphic that can be drawn to the screen and which you can retrieve with APIs such as `getDrawable(int)` or apply to another XML resource with attributes such as `android:drawable` and `android:icon`.

As we've seen earlier in the book, we have defined drawables in the `res\drawable` folder in Eclipse. We gained access to these drawables by referring to them within the `AndroidManifest.xml` file as, for example, `android:icon="@drawable/ic_launcher"`, or within code by using `R.drawable.ic_launcher`.

If you want to retrieve a resource as a `Drawable`, you can use this code:

```
Resources res = getResources(); //may need to prefix with "this."
//Replace R.drawable.ic_launcher below with your own drawable image
Drawable oDraw = res.getDrawable(R.drawable.ic_launcher);
```

Graphics via XML Resources - An Overview

In this section, we discuss the variety of graphics and animations available to the Android programmer when using nothing but XML Resources files and graphic images you've loaded into your project.

There are two packages containing the classes that we will discuss in this section:

1. `android.graphics.drawable` - this package contains the following classes related to graphics defined, for the most part, via an XML Resource file. We outline each item in more detail starting in the next section.
    a. `AnimationDrawable` - An object used to create frame-by-frame animations, defined by a series of `Drawable` objects, which can be used as a `View` object's background.

b. `BitmapDrawable` - A `Drawable` that wraps a bitmap and can be tiled, stretched, or aligned.
c. `ClipDrawable` - A `Drawable` that clips another `Drawable` based on this `Drawable`'s current level value.
d. `ColorDrawable` - A specialized `Drawable` that fills the `Canvas` with a specified color.
e. `GradientDrawable` - A `Drawable` with a color gradient for buttons, backgrounds, etc.
f. `InsetDrawable` - A `Drawable` that insets another `Drawable` by a specified distance.
g. `LayerDrawable` - A `Drawable` that manages an array of other `Drawables`.
h. `LevelListDrawable` - A resource that manages a number of alternate `Drawables`, each assigned a numerical value (or level number).
i. `NinePatchDrawable` - A resizeable bitmap, with stretchable areas that you define.
j. `PaintDrawable` - `Drawable` that draws its bounds in the given paint, with optional rounded corners.
k. `PictureDrawable` - `Drawable` subclass that wraps a Picture, allowing the picture to be used wherever a `Drawable` is supported.
l. `RotateDrawable` - A `Drawable` that can rotate another `Drawable` based on the current level value.
m. `ScaleDrawable` - A `Drawable` that changes the size of another `Drawable` based on its current level value.
n. `ShapeDrawable` - A `Drawable` object that draws primitive shapes.
o. `StateListDrawable` - Lets you assign a number of graphic images to a single `Drawable` and swap out the visible item by a string ID value.
p. `TransitionDrawable` - An extension of `LayerDrawables` that is intended to cross-fade between the first and second layer.

2. `android.graphics.drawable.shapes` - this package contains the following classes related to drawable shapes. Note that the classes listed below are only available via code and not XML. The exception is the generic `<shape>` tag used to display shapes such as a rectangle, an oval, a line and a ring.
   a. `ArcShape` - Creates an arc shape.
   b. `OvalShape` - Defines an oval shape.
   c. `PathShape` - Creates geometric paths, utilizing the `Path` class.
   d. `RectShape` - Defines a rectangle shape.
   e. `RoundRectShape` - Creates a rounded-corner rectangle.
   f. `Shape` - Defines a generic graphical "shape." Any `Shape` can be drawn to a `Canvas` with its own `draw()` method, but more graphical control is available if you instead pass it to a `ShapeDrawable`.

Note that the XML Resource files you create for the classes listed above should be placed in the `res\drawable` folder. If that folder does not exist, you can right-click over the `res` folder, select New...Folder and specify `drawable` as the name of the new folder. Once the `drawable` folder has been created, you can insert an Android XML Resource file in it by right-clicking over the `drawable` folder, selecting New...Other, then selecting Android XML File, then selecting the root element of the XML to be auto-generated (here, I selected shape):

Here, Eclipse inserted myshape.xml into my project. Note that, as I started to add the android:shape= attribute, Eclipse displayed a selection of shapes for me to choose from:

Graphics via XML Resources - Animations using `<animation-list>` XML Tag

Recall we mentioned above that you can create an *animated GIF*-style animation by defining each frame. In order to do this, you create an XML Resource file containing the `<animation-list>` XML tag containing `<item>` tags, one for each frame in your animation.

Below is an example XML Resource file, called `animated_banana.xml`, containing 8 frames of a dancing banana. Note that each image is stored in the `res\drawable` folder and named `banana#.png`.

```
<animation-list xmlns:android="http://schemas.android.com/apk/res/android"
                android:id="@+id/banana"
                android:oneshot="false" >
 <item android:drawable="@drawable/banana1" android:duration="50" />
 <item android:drawable="@drawable/banana2" android:duration="50" />
 <item android:drawable="@drawable/banana3" android:duration="50" />
 <item android:drawable="@drawable/banana4" android:duration="50" />
 <item android:drawable="@drawable/banana5" android:duration="50" />
 <item android:drawable="@drawable/banana6" android:duration="50" />
 <item android:drawable="@drawable/banana7" android:duration="50" />
 <item android:drawable="@drawable/banana8" android:duration="50" />
</animation-list>
```

Note that each frame of the animation is entered in an individual `<item>` tag and is referenced as `@drawable/banana#` within the `android:drawable` attribute. The attribute `android:duration` is the amount of time, in milliseconds, to display the frame. The attribute `android:oneshot` is set to `false` indicating that the animation will continue to play indefinitely.

Now, we use an `ImageView`'s background to house this animation. Unfortunately, you cannot just specify the background to be `@drawable/animated_banana` and expect the animation to start automatically. You must do that in code:

1. Create a private class attribute called `oBananaAnimation`:

   ```
   private AnimationDrawable oBananaAnimation;
   ```

2. In the `onCreate()` method, initialize the `ImageView` and `oBananaAnimation`:

   ```
   ImageView oImageView = (ImageView) findViewById(R.id.imageView1);
   oImageView.setBackgroundResource(R.drawable.animated_banana);
   oBananaAnimation = (AnimationDrawable) oImageView.getBackground();
   ```

3. You cannot start the animation from within the `onCreate()` method since, according to the Android SDK, *the AnimationDrawable is not yet fully attached to the window.* To start the animation, override the `onWindowFocusChanged()` method to call the `start()` method for the animation variable `oBananaAnimation`:

   ```
   @Override
   public void onWindowFocusChanged(boolean hasWindowFocus) {
    super.onWindowFocusChanged(hasWindowFocus);
    oBananaAnimation.start();
   }
   ```

Here is what that looks like (in a static sense):

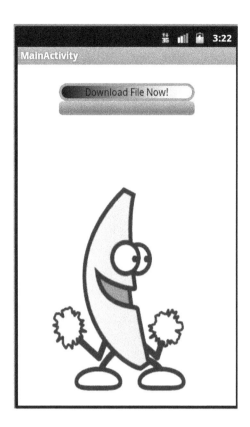

Referencing the instructions above, you can alternately specify the background within the XML using `@drawable/animated_banana` and avoid setting the background programatically to the `ImageView`:

```
oBananaAnimation = (AnimationDrawable) ((ImageView)
                            findViewById(R.id.imageView1)).getBackground();
```

Here is the syntax for `<animation-list>`:

```
<?xml version="1.0" encoding="utf-8"?>
<animation-list xmlns:android="http://schemas.android.com/apk/res/android"
                android:id="@[+][package:]id/resource_name"
                android:oneshot=["true" | "false"]
                android:visible=["true" | "false"]
                android:variablePadding=["true" | "false"]>
  <item android:drawable="@drawable/drawable_resource"
        android:duration="duration-in-milliseconds" />
</animation-list>
```

Note that the `<animation-list>` tag is related to the `AnimationDrawable` class, but the class gives you many more options than the tag itself.

Graphics via XML Resources - Handling Bitmaps using the `<bitmap>` XML Tag

Recall that, if you have an image located in the `drawable` folder, you can access it via the resource reference `R.drawable.name-of-image` within your code and `@drawable/name-of-image` within your XML Resources. Similar to how we changed the background in the previous section, you can do the same with an image. But, when you use the `<bitmap>` XML tag, you can specify additional options, such as dithering and antialiasing, that you cannot specify when using the

412

resource references. Note that when using `<bitmap>` you use the `android:src` attribute to refer to a pre-existing image.

For example, given an image of a financial graph called finance (that is, `finance.png` located in the `drawable` folder), let's see what happens when we use it as the background to a button:

As you see at the top of the image above, the background of the button now contains the image, and the image has been stretched to fit the size of the button.

Now, let's create an XML Resource file containing the `<bitmap>` tag and referencing the finance image:

```
<bitmap xmlns:android="http://schemas.android.com/apk/res/android"
        android:src="@drawable/finance"
        android:antialias="true"
        android:dither="true"
        android:gravity="center"
        android:tileMode="disabled"/>
```

Note that we are referencing the source by using `@drawable/finance`. We are also specifying the `android:gravity` which indicates what Android should do if the image is smaller than the container (in this case, the button's rectangle). Here, we specified "center" indicating that we want the image to be in the center of the button. Here is what this looks like now:

Here is the syntax for `<bitmap>`:

```
<?xml version="1.0" encoding="utf-8"?>
<bitmap
    xmlns:android="http://schemas.android.com/apk/res/android"
    android:src="@[package:]drawable/drawable_resource"
    android:antialias=["true" | "false"]
    android:dither=["true" | "false"]
    android:filter=["true" | "false"]
    android:gravity=["top" | "bottom" | "left" | "right" | "center_vertical" |
```

413

```
                    "fill_vertical" | "center_horizontal" | "fill_horizontal" |
                    "center" | "fill" | "clip_vertical" | "clip_horizontal"]
    android:tileMode=["disabled" | "clamp" | "repeat" | "mirror"] />
```

Note that the `<bitmap>` tag is related to the `BitmapDrawable` class, but the class gives you many more options than the tag itself.

Graphics via XML Resources - Clipping Images using the `<clip>` XML Tag

I'm sure during your many years of programming, you've created a faux progress bar by overlaying two images and slowly varying the size of the top image to reveal the bottom image. This concept is similar in functionality to the `<clip>` XML tag.

Now, in order to "reveal" the clipped drawable, you need to modify the `level` value by using the `setLevel()` method passing in the new level number. The level number ranges from 0, indicating the image is totally invisible, to 10000, indicating the image is completely visible.

For example, let's use the `<clip>` feature to reveal an image from the left. Here is the XML code for the clip, called myclip.xml (`@drawable/myclip`), which points to the finance image (`@drawable/finance`):

```
<clip xmlns:android="http://schemas.android.com/apk/res/android"
      android:drawable="@drawable/finance"
      android:clipOrientation="horizontal"
      android:gravity="left" />
```

It's important to note that the `android:gravity` indicates which direction the "reveal" will occur. If "left" is specified, as it is above, the image will reveal from left to right. If "center" is used instead, the reveal is similar to how curtains opening on a stage (from the center on out).

Next, the `ImageView`, called `imageView1`, has its background set to the clip:

```
<ImageView android:id="@+id/imageView1"
        android:layout_width="wrap_content"
        android:layout_height="wrap_content"
        android:layout_below="@+id/progressBar"
        android:layout_centerHorizontal="true"
        android:layout_marginTop="45dp"
        android:background="@drawable/myclip"
        android:visibility="visible" />
```

Next, the reveal occurs within code. First, initialize the level to zero in the `onCreate()` method:

```
ImageView oImageView = (ImageView) findViewById(R.id.imageView1);
oImageView.getBackground().setLevel(0);
```

To change the level from zero to a higher number, I placed the following code within a Button event, but you can place your code wherever is appropriate:

```
ImageView oImageView = (ImageView) findViewById(R.id.imageView1);
oImageView.getBackground().setLevel(
                        oImageView.getBackground().getLevel() + 1000);
```

414

The second line above just increases the clipping by an additional 1000. Here is what the finance image looks like when it is partially revealed:

Here is the syntax for `<clip>`:

```xml
<?xml version="1.0" encoding="utf-8"?>
<clip
    xmlns:android="http://schemas.android.com/apk/res/android"
    android:drawable="@drawable/drawable_resource"
    android:clipOrientation=["horizontal" | "vertical"]
    android:gravity=["top" | "bottom" | "left" | "right" | "center_vertical" |
                    "fill_vertical" | "center_horizontal" | "fill_horizontal" |
                    "center" | "fill" | "clip_vertical" | "clip_horizontal"] />
```

Note that the `<clip>` tag is related to the `ClipDrawable` class, but the class gives you many more options than the tag itself.

Graphics via XML Resources - Colors using the `<color>` XML Tag

While not strictly a graphic or animation, you can use the `<color>` XML tag as if it were a `Drawable` and use it as a background. You specify the `android:color` attribute using the typical RGB color format `#RRGGBB`. If you would like to include an alpha value, use the form `#AARRGGBB`. When AA is set to 00, the color is completely transparent and when AA is set to FF, the color is opaque.

For example, to create a color in an XML file (called `mycolor.xml`) that is blue (the 0000FF part) and is semi-transparent (the 80 part), you specify:

```xml
<color xmlns:android="http://schemas.android.com/apk/res/android"
       android:color="#800000FF"/>
```

415

Note that you can access this via `@drawable/mycolor`.

Note that the `<color>` tag is related to the `ColorDrawable` class, but the class gives you many more options than the tag itself.

Graphics via XML Resources - Gradients using the `<shape>` XML Tag

In order to create gradients, please refer to the section *Graphics via XML Resources - Shapes using the `<shape>` XML Tag* below.

Note that creating gradients using the `<shape>` tag is related to the `GradientDrawable` class, but the class gives you many more options than the tag itself.

Graphics via XML Resources - Insets using the `<inset>` XML Tag

An inset is a `Drawable` that overlays another `Drawable`. For example, given an `ImageView` that contains a background image, you can overlay another image somewhere on top of the background image.

One familiar example is the little arrow image at the bottom left of a Microsoft Windows shortcut.

For example, here is our XML code for our inset (called `myinset.xml`). Note that we specify that the image should be located at 25dp from the top of the `ImageView` and 25dp from the left of the `ImageView`.

```
<inset xmlns:android="http://schemas.android.com/apk/res/android"
       android:drawable="@drawable/finance"
       android:insetTop="25dp"
       android:insetLeft="25dp"/>
```

In the graphic below, the inset is shown at the right on top of the background. (The image on the left is just the background image with no inset.)

Note that changing the `android:insetTop`, `android:insertBottom`, `android:insetLeft`, and `android:insetRight` attributes will squeeze the image into position and not just shift it around. That is, the image will not be "cut off".

Here is the syntax for `<inset>`:

```
<?xml version="1.0" encoding="utf-8"?>
<inset
    xmlns:android="http://schemas.android.com/apk/res/android"
    android:drawable="@drawable/drawable_resource"
    android:insetTop="dimension"
    android:insetRight="dimension"
```

```
        android:insetBottom="dimension"
        android:insetLeft="dimension" />
```

Note that the `<inset>` tag is related to the `InsetDrawable` class, but the class gives you many more options than the tag itself.

Graphics via XML Resources - Layers using the `<layer-list>` XML Tag

A layer list, according to the Android SDK, *is a `Drawable` object that manages an array of other `Drawable`s. Each `Drawable` in the list is drawn in the order of the list - the last `Drawable` in the list is drawn on top.*

Although I'm not sure how to use this tag 100%, one crazy idea is to overlay several images and then programmatically change which is visible by altering which image is on top. For example, given two images of a traffic light, one green, the other red, let's create some code to change the light. Here is the `<layer-list>` for this:

```
<layer-list xmlns:android="http://schemas.android.com/apk/res/android" >
 <item android:id="@+id/green"
       android:drawable="@drawable/trafficlightgreen"
       android:top="0dp" android:left="0dp" />
 <item android:id="@+id/red"
       android:drawable="@drawable/trafficlightred"
       android:top="0dp" android:left="0dp" />
</layer-list>
```

Since the red image is listed last, it will be shown on top.

I created a method that responds to an onClick event which will change the light from red to green:

```
 public void changeLightToGreen(View view) {

   ImageView oImageView = (ImageView) findViewById(R.id.ivTrafficLight);
   LayerDrawable oLayerDrawable = (LayerDrawable)
                         getResources().getDrawable(R.drawable.mylayerlist);
   Drawable oGreen = oLayerDrawable.getDrawable(0);
   Drawable oRed = oLayerDrawable.getDrawable(1);
   oImageView.setBackgroundDrawable(oGreen);

 }
```

Here is the syntax for `<layer-list>`:

```
<?xml version="1.0" encoding="utf-8"?>
<layer-list
    xmlns:android="http://schemas.android.com/apk/res/android" >
    <item
        android:drawable="@[package:]drawable/drawable_resource"
        android:id="@[+][package:]id/resource_name"
        android:top="dimension"
        android:right="dimension"
        android:bottom="dimension"
        android:left="dimension" />
</layer-list>
```

Note that the `<layer-list>` tag is related to the `LayerDrawable` class, but the class gives you many more options than the tag itself.

Graphics via XML Resources - Levels using the `<level-list>` XML Tag

A level list, according to the Android SDK, *is a `Drawable` that manages a number of alternative Drawables, each assigned a maximum numerical value. Setting the level value of the drawable with `setLevel()` or `setImageLevel()` loads the drawable resource in the level list that has an `android:maxLevel` value greater than or equal to the value passed to the method.*

For example, given images for a red, yellow and green traffic light, let's create a `<level-list>`:

```
<level-list xmlns:android="http://schemas.android.com/apk/res/android">
  <item android:drawable="@drawable/trafficlightred" android:maxLevel="1" />
  <item android:drawable="@drawable/trafficlightyellow" android:maxLevel="2" />
  <item android:drawable="@drawable/trafficlightgreen" android:maxLevel="3" />
</level-list>
```

Next, in our code, we can change the light from red to green:

```
ImageView oImageView = (ImageView) findViewById(R.id.ivTrafficLight);
oImageView.setImageLevel(3);
```

Note the it seems that the default level is set to 1 which is why the red traffic light shows up when the test application starts.

Here is the syntax for `<level-list>` is:

```
<?xml version="1.0" encoding="utf-8"?>
<level-list
    xmlns:android="http://schemas.android.com/apk/res/android" >
    <item
        android:drawable="@drawable/drawable_resource"
        android:maxLevel="integer"
        android:minLevel="integer" />
</level-list>
```

Note that the `<level-list>` tag is related to the `LevelListDrawable` class, but the class gives you many more options than the tag itself.

Graphics via XML Resources - Nine-Patch Images using `<nine-patch>` XML Tag

A NinePatch, according to the Android SDK, *is a PNG image in which you can define stretchable regions that Android scales when content within the View exceeds the normal image bounds. You typically assign this type of image as the background of a View that has at least one dimension set to "wrap_content", and when the View grows to accomodate the content, the Nine-Patch image is also scaled to match the size of the View. An example use of a Nine-Patch image is the background used by Android's standard Button widget, which must stretch to accommodate the text (or image) inside the button.*

A NinePatch drawable is a standard PNG image that includes an extra 1-pixel-wide border. It must be saved with the extension .9.png, and saved into the res/drawable/ directory of your project.

418

The border is used to define the stretchable and static areas of the image. You indicate a stretchable section by drawing one (or more) **1-pixel-wide black line(s)** *in the left and top part of the border (the other border pixels should be fully transparent or white). You can have as many stretchable sections as you want: their relative size stays the same, so the largest sections always remain the largest.*

You can also define an optional drawable section of the image (effectively, the padding lines) by drawing a line on the right and bottom lines. If a View object sets the NinePatch as its background and then specifies the View's text, it will stretch itself so that all the text fits inside only the area designated by the right and bottom lines (if included). If the padding lines are not included, Android uses the left and top lines to define this drawable area.

To clarify the difference between the different lines, the left and top lines define which pixels of the image are allowed to be replicated in order to stretch the image. The bottom and right lines define the relative area within the image that the contents of the View are allowed to lie within.

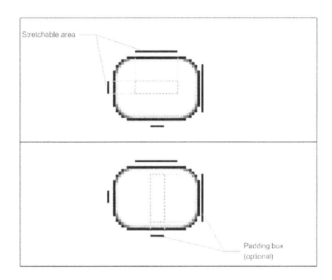

Here is the syntax for `<nine-patch>` is:

```
<?xml version="1.0" encoding="utf-8"?>
<nine-patch xmlns:android="http://schemas.android.com/apk/res/android"
        android:src="@[package:]drawable/drawable_resource"
        android:dither=["true" | "false"] />
```

Note that once a nine patch image has been created, with the required `.9.png` extension, you can refer to it anywhere an image or drawable would normally go.

Note that the `<nine-patch>` tag is related to the `NinePatchDrawable` class, but the class gives you many more options than the tag itself.

Graphics via XML Resources - PaintDrawable using the `<shape>` XML Tag

A `PaintDrawable` is a `Drawable` that draws its bounding box in the specified color with optional rounded corners. Please see the radius-related options of the `<shape>` XML tag below. There is **no** separate `<paint>` XML tag!

Graphics via XML Resources - PictureDrawable

A `PictureDrawable` wraps a `Picture` object so that it can be used wherever a `Drawable` can be used. A `Picture` object, according to the Android SDK, *records drawing calls (via the canvas returned by `beginRecording`) and can then play them back (via `picture.draw(canvas)` or `canvas.drawPicture`). The picture's contents can also be written to a stream, and then later restored to a new picture (via `writeToStream` / `createFromStream`). For most content (esp. text, lines, rectangles), drawing a sequence from a picture can be faster than the equivalent API calls, since the picture performs its playback without incurring any java-call overhead.*

There is **no** separate `<picture>` XML tag!

Graphics via XML Resources - RotateDrawable using the `<rotate>` XML Element

The `<rotate>` XML element is used with tweening in `View` animations. We talk about this tag later in the chapter.

Graphics via XML Resources - Scaling using the `<scale>` XML Tag

A `ScaleDrawable` is *a `Drawable` defined in XML that changes the size of another drawable based on its current level.*

For example, the traffic lights used in the previous few sections are rather large images. Let's use the `<scale>` tag to cut them down to size (the file is called `myscale.xml`):

```xml
<?xml version="1.0" encoding="utf-8"?>
<scale xmlns:android="http://schemas.android.com/apk/res/android"
       android:drawable="@drawable/trafficlightgreen"
       android:scaleGravity="center"
       android:scaleHeight="80%"
       android:scaleWidth="80%" />
```

Now, this particular XML tag does not behave like the other tags described above. When using the XML tags, Eclipse's Graphical Layout will display the results. This is not the case for the `<scale>` XML tag. You must use code to set the level, using the `setLevel()` method, in order for anything to show up on the screen. Here is the code I used:

```java
@Override
public void onCreate(Bundle savedInstanceState) {
  super.onCreate(savedInstanceState);
  setContentView(R.layout.activity_main);

  //ScaleDrawable from our XML file: myscale.xml
  ScaleDrawable oSD = (ScaleDrawable) getResources().getDrawable(
                                              R.drawable.myscale);

  //Set the level
  oSD.getDrawable().setLevel(1);

  //Apply the ScaleDrawable to the ImageView
```

420

```
    ImageView oIV = (ImageView) findViewById(R.id.imageView1);
    oIV.setImageDrawable(oSD);
  }
```

Note that the `ImageView` (`R.id.imageView1`) has its `android:src` set to `R.drawable.myscale`.

The syntax for `<scale>` is as follows:

```
<?xml version="1.0" encoding="utf-8"?>
<scale
    xmlns:android="http://schemas.android.com/apk/res/android"
    android:drawable="@drawable/drawable_resource"
    android:scaleGravity=["top" | "bottom" | "left" | "right" | "center_vertical"
                    | "fill_vertical" | "center_horizontal" | "fill_horizontal"
                    | "center" | "fill" | "clip_vertical" | "clip_horizontal"]
    android:scaleHeight="percentage"
    android:scaleWidth="percentage" />
```

Note that both `scaleHeight` and `scaleWidth` take a percentage along with the percent sign (%)! Also, the larger `scaleHeight` and `scaleWidth` are set to, the smaller the image will be! That is, 80% yields a smaller image than 10%!!

Note that the `<scale>` tag is related to the `ScalePatchDrawable` class, but the class gives you many more options than the tag itself.

Graphics via XML Resources - State Lists using the `<selector>` XML Tag

According to the Android SDK: *A `StateListDrawable` is a drawable object defined in XML that uses several different images to represent the same graphic, depending on the state of the object. For example, a `Button` widget can exist in one of several different states (pressed, focused, or neither) and, using a state list drawable, you can provide a different background image for each state.*

You can describe the state list in an XML file. Each graphic is represented by an <item> element inside a single <selector> element. Each <item> uses various attributes to describe the state in which it should be used as the graphic for the drawable.

During each state change, the state list is traversed top to bottom and the first item that matches the current state is used—the selection is not based on the "best match," but simply the first item that meets the minimum criteria of the state.

For example, you can apply the `<selector>` XML file you create to a `Button`'s background. Based on the focus of the button, a different background is displayed. In the example below, we set up several `<color>` tags to be used as Drawables for the `<selector>`'s `<item>` tag:

`color_default.xml` (green):

```
<?xml version="1.0" encoding="utf-8"?>
<color xmlns:android="http://schemas.android.com/apk/res/android"
      android:color="#FF00FF00" />
```

`color_focus.xml` (blue):

```xml
<?xml version="1.0" encoding="utf-8"?>
<color xmlns:android="http://schemas.android.com/apk/res/android"
        android:color="#FF0000FF" />
```

`color_pressed.xml` (red):

```xml
<?xml version="1.0" encoding="utf-8"?>
<color xmlns:android="http://schemas.android.com/apk/res/android"
        android:color="#FFFF0000" />
```

Next, we set up the `<selector>` XML file, called `mystatelist.xml`:

```xml
<?xml version="1.0" encoding="utf-8"?>
<selector xmlns:android="http://schemas.android.com/apk/res/android">
 <item android:state_pressed="true" android:drawable="@drawable/color_pressed" />
 <item android:state_focused="true" android:drawable="@drawable/color_focus" />
 <item                              android:drawable="@drawable/color_default" />
</selector>
```

Next, we place a Button on the screen and set the Button's background to `mystatelist`.

Here is what you see, by default (button is colored green):

Here is what you see when the button has focus (blue, use the arrows to move down to the button to get focus):

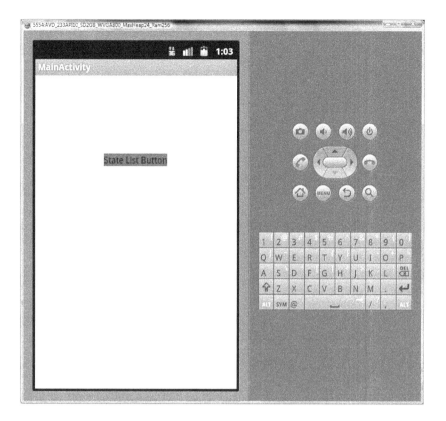

Finally, here is what you see when you press and hold the button (red, you can press and hold down your mouse button or press and hold the center button):

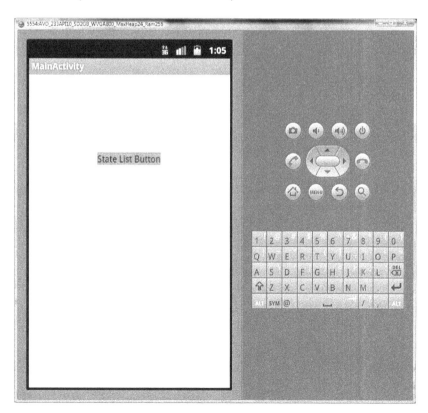

The syntax for `<selector>` is as follows:

```xml
<?xml version="1.0" encoding="utf-8"?>
<selector xmlns:android="http://schemas.android.com/apk/res/android"
    android:constantSize=["true" | "false"]
    android:dither=["true" | "false"]
```

423

```
        android:variablePadding=["true" | "false"] >
    <item
        android:drawable="@[package:]drawable/drawable_resource"
        android:state_pressed=["true" | "false"]
        android:state_focused=["true" | "false"]
        android:state_hovered=["true" | "false"]
        android:state_selected=["true" | "false"]
        android:state_checkable=["true" | "false"]
        android:state_checked=["true" | "false"]
        android:state_enabled=["true" | "false"]
        android:state_activated=["true" | "false"]
        android:state_window_focused=["true" | "false"] />
</selector>
```

Note that the `<selector>` tag is related to the `StateListDrawable` class, but the class gives you many more options than the tag itself.

Graphics via XML Resources - Shapes using the `<shape>` XML Tag

As mentioned in the previous section, you can create an XML Resource file to contain the shape you want to create. These shapes can be used as backgrounds to existing views by using the `android:background="@drawable/`*name-of-drawable*`"` syntax.

Alternatively, you can use the following syntax within your code to use a pre-defined `<shape>` as a background to a `Button`:

```
Resources res = getResources();
Drawable oDraw = res.getDrawable(R.drawable.name-of-drawable);
Button oBTN = (Button) findViewById(R.id.name-of-button);
oBTN.setBackgroundDrawable(oDraw);
```

You can also set an `ImageView` with the `Drawable` via code similar to the following:

```
ImageView oIV = (ImageView) findViewById(R.id.name-of-ImageView);
oIV.setImageResource(R.drawable.name-of-drawable);
```

An `ImageView` also takes the `android:src` attribute which allows you to specify the shape you created when using the `<shape>` tag.

The following is the valid XML you can use within the `<shape>` tag:

```
<shape
    xmlns:android="http://schemas.android.com/apk/res/android"
    android:shape=["rectangle" | "oval" | "line" | "ring"] >
    <corners
        android:radius="integer"
        android:topLeftRadius="integer"
        android:topRightRadius="integer"
        android:bottomLeftRadius="integer"
        android:bottomRightRadius="integer" />
    <gradient
        android:angle="integer"
        android:centerX="integer"
        android:centerY="integer"
        android:centerColor="integer"
        android:endColor="color"
        android:gradientRadius="integer"
        android:startColor="color"
```

```
            android:type=["linear" | "radial" | "sweep"]
            android:useLevel=["true" | "false"] />
      <padding
            android:left="integer"
            android:top="integer"
            android:right="integer"
            android:bottom="integer" />
      <size
            android:width="integer"
            android:height="integer" />
      <solid
            android:color="color" />
      <stroke
            android:width="integer"
            android:color="color"
            android:dashWidth="integer"
            android:dashGap="integer" />
</shape>
```

Please see the Drawable Resources documentation for more on this XML tag. Note that when specifying `android:shape="ring"`, there are additional attributes. See the documentation for more.

For example, to specify a rectangle 100x100 pixels wide with curved edges stroked in red and filled with yellow, you can use the following code:

```
<shape xmlns:android="http://schemas.android.com/apk/res/android"
      android:shape="rectangle">
 <size android:width="100dp"
      android:height="100dp"/>
 <corners android:radius="20dp" />
 <solid android:color="#FFFFFF00"/>
 <stroke android:width="4dp"
      android:color="#FFFF0000"/>
</shape>
```

Now, below is an example with the normal background for a `Button` replaced with the shape as defined above. Note that the `Button` has expanded in size based on the shape and does not retain its default size. At the bottom of the image is an `ImageView` with its `android:src` attribute set to the shape defined above as well:

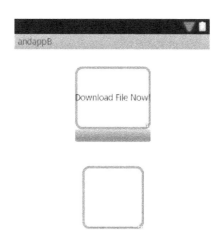

425

Note that you can also specify a gradient when using the `<shape>`. Here is an example of how to use a gradient with a `Button`. I've set the starting color to black and the ending color to white. The gradient is linear and, since I've set the angle to zero degrees, the color will vary moving left to right in a linear fashion. The centerX and centerY attributes indicate where the middle value between the starting and ending color will be. Here I've set it exactly in the center on both axes. Note that I've also expanded the `Button` just for fun!

```
<shape xmlns:android="http://schemas.android.com/apk/res/android"
       android:shape="rectangle">
 <size android:width="200dp"
       android:height="25dp"/>
 <corners android:radius="20dp" />
 <solid android:color="#FFFFFF00"/>
 <stroke android:width="4dp"
         android:color="#FFFF0000"/>
 <gradient android:angle="0"
           android:centerX="0.5"
           android:centerY="0.5"
           android:startColor="#FF000000"
           android:endColor="#FFFFFFFF"
           android:type="linear"/>
</shape>
```

Note that the `<shape>` tag is related to the `ShapeDrawable` class, but the class gives you many more options than the tag itself.

Graphics via XML Resources - Transitions using the `<transition>` XML Tag

A `TransitionDrawable` is a drawable object that can cross-fade between the two drawable resources. Each drawable is represented by an `<item>` element inside a single `<transition>` element. No more than two items are supported. To transition forward, call `startTransition()`. To transition backward, call `reverseTransition()`.

For example, let's transition between a closed folder to an open folder when a button is pressed. Here is my transition XML file (`mytransition.xml`):

```
<?xml version="1.0" encoding="utf-8"?>
<transition xmlns:android="http://schemas.android.com/apk/res/android">
  <item android:drawable="@drawable/close_folder" />
```

426

```
    <item android:drawable="@drawable/open_folder" />
</transition>
```

Next, I noticed that if you specify a source or background image to the `ImageView` (`imageView1`, here), when the transition runs, the image seems to move slightly. So, in order to avoid that, I set the source image to the `close_folder.png` file. First, place the following two lines of code as class variables:

```
TransitionDrawable oTransDraw;
ImageView oIV;
```

Next, in the `onCreate()` method, place the following code which is responsible for initializing the image to the closed folder:

```
//Get the TransitionDrawable from mytransition.xml
oTransDraw = (TransitionDrawable)
                    getResources().getDrawable(R.drawable.mytransition);

//Enable cross-fading
oTransDraw.setCrossFadeEnabled(true);

//Set the ImageView to imageView1
oIV = (ImageView) findViewById(R.id.imageView1);

//Set the image in the imageView1 to the TransitionDrawable, oTransDraw.
oIV.setImageDrawable(oTransDraw);
```

Next, in an `onClick` event of a button, place the following line:

```
//Run the transition showing the closed folder opening up in 1000
//milliseconds (1 second).
oTransDraw.startTransition(1000);
```

Here is the syntax:

```
<?xml version="1.0" encoding="utf-8"?>
<transition
xmlns:android="http://schemas.android.com/apk/res/android" >
    <item
        android:drawable="@[package:]drawable/drawable_resource"
        android:id="@[+][package:]id/resource_name"
        android:top="dimension"
        android:right="dimension"
        android:bottom="dimension"
        android:left="dimension" />
</transition>
```

Note that the `<transition>` tag is related to the `TransitionDrawable` class, but the class gives you many more options than the tag itself.

Static Graphics in Two-Dimensions - An Overview

In this section, we describe how to generate 2D static (not animated) graphics using the `Canvas` class. We discuss tweened animation later in this chapter.

Recall that we discussed how to create Adobe Flash-type graphics using the `<animated-list>` and `<transition>` XML tags in the previous section

According to the Android SDK, *the Canvas class holds the draw calls*. To draw something, you need four basic components:

1. a `Bitmap` to hold the pixels
2. a `Canvas` to host the draw calls (writing into the `Bitmap`)
3. a drawing primitive (e.g., `Rect`, `Path`, text, ...)
4. a `Paint` object (to describe the colors/styles for the drawing)

In other words, a `Canvas` is a *logical* entity that holds the result of calling several drawing methods (such as, drawing a line or rectangle). Just like an artist painting on an actual canvas, he may paint over what already exists either to enhance a portion of the artwork or to cover up a mistake. We, the skeptical viewing public, see only the top (final) layer when the artist has finished; we do not see the layers that have been covered over.

In Android, you create a graphic by calling one or more drawing methods on the `Canvas`. It is possible that several of the methods may lay on top of some of the previous methods obscuring them. That's just as okay as it is for the artist.

Now, during the process of drawing on the `Canvas`, you will make use of several additional classes such as `Path`, `Region`, `Rect`/`RectF`, `Paint`, and so on. Each class is used to modify a specific aspect of the graphic such as the color, style, font, line dashing, image size, etc.

When you are done creating your graphic on the `Canvas`, you generate a `Bitmap` that holds the *physical* result of those drawing methods you executed on the `Canvas`. It is this bitmap which is displayed to the unsuspecting public.

Before we talk about the details of creating a two-dimensional graphic, let's explore the relevant classes first.

Static Graphics in Two-Dimensions - Relevant Classes and Enums - An Overview

In this section, we describe the classes and enums used during the creation of a two-dimensional graphic on the Canvas. We cannot go into extreme detail here because that would be another book, so please peruse the documentation for much more detail than is presented here.

Below are the relevant classes:

- `Canvas` - this class holds the draw calls. To draw something, you need four basic components: a Bitmap to hold the pixels (that is, the results of all of the draw calls on the Canvas); a Canvas to host the draw calls (which are written into the Bitmap), one or more drawing primitives such as a Rect, Path, text, etc.; and a Paint used to describe the colors and styles for the drawing. The Canvas class contains several useful methods some of which are listed below:
  - drawArc/drawCircle/drawOval/drawRect/drawRoundRect - draws an arc, circle, oval, rectangle or rounded rectangle on the Canvas
  - drawBitmap - draws a pre-existing Bitmap on the Canvas

- drawLine/drawLines - draws a single or multiple lines on the Canvas
- drawPoint/drawPoints - draws a single or multiple points on the Canvas
- drawPosText/drawText/drawTextOnPath - places text on the Canvas
- drawVertices - draws an array of vertices interpreted as triangles
- save/restore - these methods save the state of the Canvas allowing you to make modifications anew and then restore the state back to the original
- setBitmap - this methods sets the Bitmap that will be drawn into if you did not specify one in the Canvas' constructor.
- ...and many more...
- `Bitmap` - this class allows you to create, configure and inquire about a Bitmap. Note that you do not "draw" onto a Bitmap, but a Canvas. It is the responsibility of the Canvas to draw into the Bitmap, not you, buddy!
    - createBitmap - several methods allowing you to create a blank Bitmap with a specific height and width
    - getHeight/getWidth - returns the height and width of the bitmap
    - getPixel/setPixel - returns or sets the color at a specific coordinate in the Bitmap
    - IsMutable - returns true if the Bitmap is mutable (that is, you are allowed to modify its contents); otherwise, false
- `Paint` - this class holds the style and color information about how to draw geometric shapes, text, etc. Note that several methods of Canvas allow for a Paint object as a parameter.
    - Paint()/Paint(int)/Paint(Paint) - several constructors allowing you to instantiate a Paint object, a Paint object with specific flags set (such as ANTI_ALIAS_FLAG, DITHER_FLAG, etc.), or a Paint object created from another Paint object.
    - setColor - sets the color of the Paint object
    - getPathEffect/setPathEffect - gets or sets the path effect object
    - getShader/setShader - gets or sets the shader object
    - getStrokeCap/setStrokeCap - gets or sets the stroke cap
    - getStrokeJoin/setStrokeJoin - gets or sets the stroke join
    - getStrokeMiter/setStrokeMiter - gets or sets the stroke miter value
    - getStrokeWidth/setStrokeWidth - gets or sets the stroke width
    - getStyle/setStyle - gets or sets the stroke style
    - getTextAlign/setTextAlign - gets or sets the text alignment
    - getTextSize/setTextSize - gets or sets the text size
    - getTextSkewX/setTextSkewX - gets or sets the text's horizontal skew
    - getTypeface/setTypeface - gets or sets the text's typeface
    - setUnderlineText - sets the text to be or not be underlined
- `Paint.FontMetrics/Paint.FontMetricsInt` - these classes describe the various metrics for a font's given text size. Note that Y values increase going down, so those values will be positive and values that measure distances going up will be negative. These classes are returned by Paint.getFontMetrics() and Paint.getFontMetricsInt().
- `RectF/Rect` - these classes (the first for floating point values, the second for integer values) hold four coordinates specifying a rectangle. You can use one of the constructors to specify each coordinate or use the set()

429

method to do so instead. Both of these classes contain the following four public fields:

- bottom - the Y coordinate of the bottom of the rectangle
- left - the X coordinate of the left side of the rectangle
- right - the X coordinate of the right side of the rectangle
- top - the Y coordinate of the top side of the rectangle

These classes also contain a few nice methods as well:

- centerX/exactCenterX - returns the horizontal center of the rectangle as int/float
- centerY/exactCenterY - returns the vertical center of the rectangle as int/float
- contains(x,y) - tests if the coordinate (x,y) lies within the rectangle

- `Path` - this class encapsulates compound (multiple contour) geometric paths consisting of straight line segments, quadratic curves and cubic curves. To be clear, there are methods of the Canvas class, such as drawArc, etc. which may seem similar to the methods of the Path class. But, a Path can be used for more things than just drawing a bunch of lines. A Path can be drawn with Canvas.drawPath() method, either filled or stroked (based on the setting of Paint.Style), or can be used for clipping or to draw text upon (that is, the text will follow the path and not just be appear to be on a straight line). This class contains the following methods, in part:

  - addArc/addCircle/addOval/addRect/addRoundedRect - adds an arc/circle/oval/ rectangle/rounded rectangle to the path
  - arcTo/lineTo/quadTo/cubicTo - adds (or appends) an arc/line/quadratic/cubic to an existing path
  - moveTo/rMoveTo - sets the beginning of the next contour to the point (x,y). This means that a Path does not have to be continuous, but can have breaks to it. rMoveTo moves relative to the previous point.
  - rLineTo/rCubicTo/rQuadTo - adds a line/cubic/quad relative to the previous point. For example, given a set of points that make up a line, you can lineTo the first point and then rLineTo each subsequent point without having to retain the previous coordinate
  - close - this method closes the contour and should probably be used when you are done creating your path.

- `DashPathEffect` - this class allows you to define the skip pattern for dashed lines (by that I mean *lines with small breaks in them* and not *bloody damn lines!*). In the constructor you provide an array of floating point values where the even values represent the "dash on length" and the odd values represent the "dash off length".

- `Region` - this class creates a region of a certain size. This region can make use of the Region.Op operators described in the enums section below.

- `Picture` - A Picture records drawing calls (via the canvas returned by beginRecording) and can then play them back (via Picture.draw(Canvas) or Canvas.drawPicture). The picture's contents can also be written to a stream and then later restored to a new picture (via writeToStream/createFromStream). For most content, drawing a sequence from a picture can be faster than the equivalent API calls since the picture performs its playback without incurring any Java-call overhead.

  - beginRecording/endRecording - begins/ends recording a picture
  - draw(Canvas) - draws the picture into the Canvas

- writeToStream/createFromStream - writes/reads the Picture to/from a stream
- `DrawFilter` - A DrawFilter subclass can be installed in a Canvas. When it is present, it can temporarily modify the paint that is used to draw. With this, a file can disable/enable antialiasing or change the color for everything that is drawn.
- `Matrix` - This class holds a 3x3 matrix for transforming coordinates. This class does not have a constructor so it must be explicitly initialized using either reset (to construct an identity matrix), or one of the set* methods such as setTranslate, setRotate, etc. See the Android SDK for more on this class.
- `Shader` - Shader is the base class for objects that return horizontal spans of colors during drawing. A subclass of Shader is installed in a Paint object by calling Paint.setShader(Shader). After that, any object (except a Bitmap) that is drawn with that Paint will get its color(s) from the Shader. Please see the Android SDK for more on this class.
- `PathDashPathEffect` - this class places a shape along a Path. The shape is first created by using the Path class and its methods. The shape is then strewn along another pre-defined Path similar to how dashes are strewn along a dashed line (by that I mean *lines with small breaks in them* and not *bloody damn lines!*).

Below are the relevant enums:

- `Bitmap.CompressFormat` - specifies the known formats a bitmap can be compressed into:
    - Bitmap.CompressFormat.JPEG - the JPEG format
    - Bitmap.CompressFormat.PNG - the Portable Network Graphics format
    - Bitmap.CompressFormat.WEBP - the WEBP format
- `Bitmap.Config` - this enumerator describes how the pixels of a bitmap are stored and affects the quality (i.e., color depth) as well as the ability to display transparent or translucent colors:
    - Bitmap.Config.ALPHA_8 - each pixel is stored as a single alpha channel
    - Bitmap.Config.ARGB_4444 - deprecated...do not use...
    - Bitmap.Config.ARGB_8888 - each pixel is stored on 4 bytes
    - Bitmap.Config.RGB_565 - each pixel is stored on 2 bytes with no alpha channel. Red is stored with 5 bits, Green is stored with 6 bits and Blue is stored with 5 bits
- `Canvas.EdgeType` - the edge type:
    - Canvas.EdgeType.AA - anti-alias edges by rounding-out
    - Canvas.EdgeType.BW - round edges to nearest pixel boundary
- `Canvas.VertexMode` - vertex mode enumerator is made up of the following:
    - Canvas.VertexMode.TRIANGLES
    - Canvas.VertexMode.TRIANGLE_FAN
    - Canvas.VertexMode.TRIANGLE_STRIP

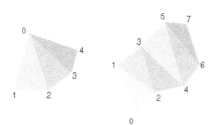

- `Interpolator.Result` - interpolator result enumerator is made up of the following:
  - Interpolator.Result.FREEZE_END
  - Interpolator.Result.FREEZE_START
  - Interpolator.Result.NORMAL
- `Matrix.ScaleToFit` - controls how the source rectangle should align itself into the destination rectangle and is made up of the following:
  - Matrix.ScaleToFit.CENTER - compute a scale that will maintain the original source aspect ratio, but will also ensure that source fits entirely into destination. At least one axis (X or Y) will fit exactly. The result is centered inside destination.
  - Matrix.ScaleToFit.END - Compute a scale that will maintain the original source aspect ratio, but will also ensure that source fits entirely inside destination. At least one axis (X or Y) will fit exactly. END aligns the result to the right and bottom edges of destination.
  - Matrix.ScaleToFit.FILL - Scale in X and Y independently, so that source matches destination exactly. This may change the aspect ratio of the source.
  - Matrix.ScaleToFit.START - Compute a scale that will maintain the original source aspect ratio, but will also ensure that source fits entirely inside destination. At least one axis (X or Y) will fit exactly. START aligns the result to the left and top edges of destination.
- `Paint.Align` - specifies how text is aligned relative to the (x,y)-coordinates and is made up of the following:
  - Paint.Align.CENTER - text is drawn centered horizontally on the (x,y) origin.
  - Paint.Align.LEFT - text is drawn to the **right** of the (x,y) origin. This is the default.
  - Paint.Align.RIGHT - text is drawn to the **left** of the (x,y) origin.
- `Paint.Cap` - specifies how the beginning and ending of stroked lines and paths appear and is made up of the following:
  - Paint.Cap.BUTT - the stroke ends with the path and does not project beyond it. This is the default.
  - Paint.Cap.ROUND - the stroke projects out as a semi-circle with the center at the end of the path.
  - Paint.Cap.SQUARE - the stroke projects out as a square with the center at the end of the path.

butt round square

- `Paint.Join` - specifies how lines and curves join on a stroked path and is made up of the following:
    - Paint.Join.BEVEL - the outer edges of a join meet with a straight line
    - Paint.Join.MITER - the outer edges of a join meet at a sharp angle
    - Paint.Join.ROUND - the outer edges of a join meet in a circular arc

'miter' join   'round' join   'bevel' join

- `Paint.Style` - specifies if the primitive that is being drawn is filled in, stroked only, or both. This enumerator takes on the following:
    - Paint.Style.STROKE - strokes only (image on the left)
    - Paint.Style.FILL - fills in only (image in the center)
    - Paint.Style.FILL_AND_STROKE - fills and strokes (image on the right, despite what the image shows below, there will be no white stripe between the stroke and the fill)

- `PathDashPathEffect.Style` - enumerator contains the following:
    - PathDashPathEffect.Style.MORPH
    - PathDashPathEffect.Style.ROTATE
    - PathDashPathEffect.Style.TRANSLATE
- `Path.Direction` - specifies how closed shapes are oriented when they are added to a path and contains the following:
    - Path.Direction.CCW - counter-clockwise
    - Path.Direction.CW - clockwise
- `PorterDuff.Mode` - given two images, src and dst, determines how the two image interact with each other. This enumerator takes on the following values:
    - PorterDuff.Mode.ADD
    - PorterDuff.Mode.CLEAR
    - PorterDuff.Mode.DARKEN
    - PorterDuff.Mode.DST
    - PorterDuff.Mode.DST_ATOP
    - PorterDuff.Mode.DST_IN

- PorterDuff.Mode.DST_OUT
- PorterDuff.Mode.DST_OVER
- PorterDuff.Mode.LIGHTEN
- PorterDuff.Mode.MULTIPLY
- PorterDuff.Mode.OVERLAY
- PorterDuff.Mode.SCREEN
- PorterDuff.Mode.SRC
- PorterDuff.Mode.SRC_ATOP
- PorterDuff.Mode.SRC_IN
- PorterDuff.Mode.SRC_OUT
- PorterDuff.Mode.SRC_OVER
- PorterDuff.Mode.XOR

Below is an image containing an example of nearly each mode. For example, given two images, src and dst, the SRC_IN Porter-Duff mode will display that portion of the src image that intersects the dst image (see src-in below).

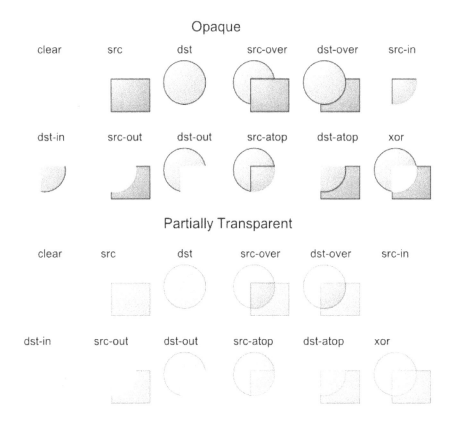

- `Region.Op` - this enumerator contains the following:
  - Region.Op.DIFFERENCE
  - Region.Op.INTERSECT
  - Region.Op.REPLACE
  - Region.Op.REVERSE_DIFFERENCE
  - Region.Op.XOR
- `Shader.TileMode` - this enumerator contains the following:
  - Shader.TileMode.CLAMP - replicate the edge color if the shader draws outside of its original bounds

- Shader.TileMode.MIRROR - repeat the shader's image horizontally and vertically, alternating mirror images so that adjacent image always seam
- Shader.TileMode.REPEAT - repeat the shader's image horizontally and vertically

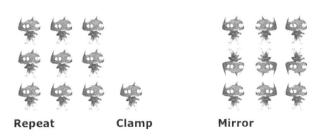

Repeat   **Clamp**   **Mirror**

In addition, several of the following will be useful when using the classes and enumerators listed above:

- `Typeface` - this class specifies the font family as well as the font style and is used with the `Paint` class. Note that methods such as `measureText()` use this information to compute the appropriate return value. Besides containing a series of constants and static variables related to the base fonts (`Typeface.MONOSPACE`, `Typeface.SANS_ SERIF`, `Typeface.SERIF`, `Typeface.DEFAULT`, `Typeface.DEFAULT_BOLD`), you can use your own font if you wish. Note that there are plenty of free fonts available on the web (for example, see `creativebloq.com`), but please install the font on your computer and try it out first before committing to it in your Android application.
  - `createFromAsset()` - this method creates a font from a font stored as an asset. Note that you will need to use the `getAssets()` method of the `android.Content.ContextWrapper` class. You can use the code `getContext().getAssets()` to return an `AssetManager` for use with this method.
  - `createFromFile()` - this method create a font from a font stored in a file
- `Color` - this class contains several color-related constants such as `Color.BLACK`, `Color.BLUE`, etc. as well as several methods for performing color-related conversions, etc. For example,
  - `rgb(int red, int green, int blue)` - this method returns an integer representing the RGB color value specified in the parameters
  - `parseColor(String)` - this method takes a `String` parameter that contains either #AARRGGBB or #RRGGBB hex notation or a name of a color such as 'red', 'blue', 'green', 'black', 'white', 'gray', 'cyan', 'magenta', 'yellow', 'lightgray', 'darkgray'
- `AssetManager` - this class provides access to your application's assets, specifically, files containing font definition information.

Static Graphics in Two-Dimensions - Static Graphic Example #1

In this section, we create a small bitmap with a colored background and produce a single dashed line from the upper-left corner to the lower-right corner. We display the text *Static Graphic Example #1* centered at the top of the image. I placed a `Button` as well as an `ImageView` on the screen. Below is the code I used to generate the graph, shown below:

```java
//Create the graphic
public void createGraphic(View view) {

 //Main title to be displayed
 String sTitle = "Static Graphic Example #1";

 //Bitmap height and width
 int iBM_HEIGHT = 250;
 int iBM_WIDTH = 250;

 //Starting X and Y of Line
 float fX_BEG = 0;
 float fY_BEG = 0;

 //Ending X and Y of Line
 float fX_END = 250;
 float fY_END = 250;

 //Y-Coordinate of text
 float fY_TEXT = 25;

 //Text Size
 float fTextSize = 10;

 //Access the image view, imageView1, on the screen
 ImageView oIV = (ImageView) findViewById(R.id.imageView1);

 //Create a blank bitmap.
 Bitmap oBM = Bitmap.createBitmap(iBM_HEIGHT,
                                  iBM_WIDTH,
                                  Bitmap.Config.ARGB_8888);

 //Create a Canvas associating the bitmap oBM with it,
 Canvas oCV = new Canvas(oBM);

 //Set the background color of the Canvas
 oCV.drawARGB(255, 0, 0, 255);

 //Set up the dash effect
 DashPathEffect oDPE = new DashPathEffect(new float[] {5,1},0);

 //Create a Paint object for the line (red and dashed)
 Paint oPT_LINE = new Paint();
 oPT_LINE.setARGB(255, 255, 0, 0);
 oPT_LINE.setStrokeWidth(2);
 oPT_LINE.setStyle(Style.STROKE);
 oPT_LINE.setPathEffect(oDPE);

 //Add a line to the canvas using the Paint object
 oCV.drawLine(fX_BEG, fY_BEG, fX_END, fY_END, oPT_LINE);

 //Create a Paint object for the text (black and bold)
 Paint oPT_TEXT = new Paint(Paint.FAKE_BOLD_TEXT_FLAG);
 oPT_TEXT.setARGB(255, 255, 255, 255);
 oPT_TEXT.setTypeface(Typeface.SANS_SERIF);
 oPT_TEXT.setTextSize(fTextSize);
 oPT_TEXT.setColor(Color.BLACK);

 //Add the title to the canvas ensuring that the text is centered.
 float fTitleWidth = oPT_TEXT.measureText(sTitle);
 float fX_TEXT = ((float)iBM_WIDTH - fTitleWidth)/2;
```

```
oCV.drawText(sTitle, fX_TEXT, fY_TEXT, oPT_TEXT);

//Set the bitmap, oBM, as the image of imageView1.
oIV.setImageBitmap(oBM);

}
```

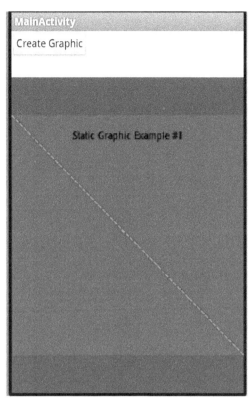

Despite what you see above, the image looks a lot nicer on the target device than it does on the emulator.

Now, if you are drawing a chart of, say, stock prices by date, you will no doubt want to have horizontal and vertical axes on your chart as well as, say, a copyright notice at the bottom of the chart. Rather than drawing all of this static information on each graph, you can create a Picture object that contains this static stuff. You can then further modify your chart with the appropriate data (stock prices and dates). According to the Android SDK: *A picture records drawing calls (via the canvas returned by beginRecording) and can then play them back (via picture.draw(canvas) or canvas.drawPicture). The picture's contents can also be written to a stream, and then later restored to a new picture (via writeToStream/createFromStream). For most content (esp. text, lines, rectangles), drawing a sequence from a picture can be faster than the equivalent API calls since the picture performs its playback without incurring any java-call overhead.*

Let's draw a few things on a `Picture` object and then create our graphic.

```
package com.example.andappe;

import android.os.Bundle;
import android.app.Activity;
import android.graphics.Bitmap;
import android.graphics.Canvas;
import android.graphics.Color;
import android.graphics.DashPathEffect;
import android.graphics.Paint;
```

```java
import android.graphics.Paint.Style;
import android.graphics.Picture;
import android.graphics.Typeface;
import android.view.View;
import android.widget.ImageView;

public class MainActivity extends Activity {

 @Override
 public void onCreate(Bundle savedInstanceState) {
  super.onCreate(savedInstanceState);
  setContentView(R.layout.activity_main);
 }

 //Create the graphic
 public void createGraphic(View view) {

  //Main title to be displayed
  String sTitle = "Static Graphic Example #1";

  //Bitmap height and width
  int iBM_HEIGHT = 250;
  int iBM_WIDTH = 250;

  //Create static picture (by calling createPicture and to be used later)
  Picture oPic = createPicture(iBM_HEIGHT,iBM_WIDTH);

  //Starting X and Y of Line
  float fX_BEG = 0;
  float fY_BEG = 0;

  //Ending X and Y of Line
  float fX_END = 250;
  float fY_END = 250;

  //Y-Coordinate of text
  float fY_TEXT = 25;

  //Text Size
  float fTextSize = 10;

  //Access the image view, imageView1, on the screen
  ImageView oIV = (ImageView) findViewById(R.id.imageView1);

  //Create a blank bitmap.
  Bitmap oBM = Bitmap.createBitmap(iBM_HEIGHT,
                                   iBM_WIDTH,
                                   Bitmap.Config.ARGB_8888);

  //Create a Canvas associating the bitmap oBM with it,
  Canvas oCV = new Canvas(oBM);

  //Add the picture to the canvas
  oCV.drawPicture(oPic);

  //Set the background color of the Canvas
  oCV.drawARGB(0, 0, 0, 255);

  //Set up the dash effect
  DashPathEffect oDPE = new DashPathEffect(new float[] {5,1},0);

  //Create a Paint object for the line (red and dashed)
  Paint oPT_LINE = new Paint();
  oPT_LINE.setARGB(255, 255, 0, 0);
  oPT_LINE.setStrokeWidth(1);
  oPT_LINE.setStyle(Style.STROKE);
  oPT_LINE.setPathEffect(oDPE);

  //Add a line to the canvas using the Paint object
  oCV.drawLine(fX_BEG, fY_BEG, fX_END, fY_END, oPT_LINE);
```

```
    //Create a Paint object for the text (black and bold)
    Paint oPT_TEXT = new Paint();
    oPT_TEXT.setARGB(255, 255, 255, 255);
    oPT_TEXT.setTypeface(Typeface.DEFAULT);
    oPT_TEXT.setTextSize(fTextSize);
    oPT_TEXT.setColor(Color.BLACK);

    //Add the title to the canvas ensuring that the text is centered.
    float fTitleWidth = oPT_TEXT.measureText(sTitle);
    float fX_TEXT = ((float)iBM_WIDTH - fTitleWidth)/2;
    oCV.drawText(sTitle, fX_TEXT, fY_TEXT, oPT_TEXT);

    //Set the bitmap, oBM, as the image of imageView1.
    oIV.setImageBitmap(oBM);
  }

 //Create the static picture
 private Picture createPicture(int pBM_HEIGHT,int pBM_WIDTH) {

   //Instantiate the blank picture
   Picture oPIC = new Picture();

   //Get the Canvas for the blank Picture
   Canvas oCAN = oPIC.beginRecording(pBM_WIDTH, pBM_HEIGHT);

   //Create a paint object for the horizontal and vertical axes
   Paint oPT = new Paint();
   oPT.setARGB(255, 0, 0, 0);
   oPT.setStrokeWidth(1);
   oPT.setStyle(Style.STROKE);

   //Set the background of the canvas to white
   oCAN.drawARGB(255, 255, 255, 255);

   //Draw the lines on the canvas
   oCAN.drawLine(0,
                 ((float) pBM_HEIGHT)/2,
                 (float) pBM_WIDTH,
                 ((float) pBM_HEIGHT)/2,
                 oPT);
   oCAN.drawLine(((float) pBM_WIDTH)/2,
                 0,
                 ((float) pBM_WIDTH)/2,
                 (float) pBM_HEIGHT,
                 oPT);

   //End the recording
   oPIC.endRecording();

   return(oPIC);

  }

}
```

As you can see above, the procedure `createPicture()` draws the two axes on the a canvas and the picture is returned. I add the `oCV.drawPicture(oPic)` code to add the picture directly to the canvas. One modification I did make was to make the graph transparent instead of opaque as in the example above (see `oCV.drawARGB(0, 0, 0, 255)`). This will allow the picture to show through.

Here is what this looks like on my Nook Color:

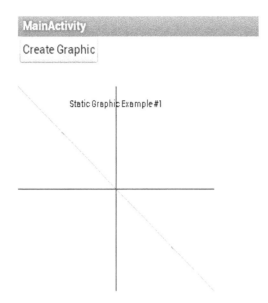

Usually axes have values on them such as the stock price values on the vertical axis and the dates on the horizontal axis. Now, you can easily place these values on the graph using one of the `drawText()` methods. But, notice that none of these methods allow you to specify an angle to draw the text at. One way around this is to use the `save()` and `restore()` methods of the `Canvas` object along with one of the `rotate()` methods. Here are the steps along with an explanation:

1. `save()` - this method saves the graphics state of the `Canvas`. This will allow you to fiddle with the `Canvas` without screwing up what you've already created.
2. `rotate()` - this method will allow you to rotate the canvas by a certain number of degrees. Positive values rotate clockwise, negative values rotate counterclockwise. There are two variants to the rotate method:
   a. `rotate(d)` - this method rotates around (0,0) by d degrees.
   b. `rotate(d,x,y)` - this method rotates around the point (x,y) by d degrees.
3. `drawText()` - this method will draw the text on the rotated canvas
4. `restore()` - this method will restore the state of the canvas prior to the rotation, but will keep any of the stuff you've already drawn on the canvas (it will not be wiped out)

Here is the code to do this:

```
//Save the state of the canvas
oCV.save();

//Rotate the canvas by 45 degrees around the origin of our axes
oCV.rotate(-45, ((float) iBM_WIDTH)/2, ((float) iBM_HEIGHT)/2);

//Draw some text just below the X-axis
String sXAxisText = "Jan2013";

//Modify the Paint object oPT_TEXT so that the text is drawn to the
// LEFT of the (x,y)-coordinate.
oPT_TEXT.setTextAlign(Paint.Align.RIGHT);

//Make the font slightly smaller for the axis text
oPT_TEXT.setTextSize(fTextSize - 2);
```

440

```
//Draw the text under the x-axis.
oCV.drawText(sXAxisText, ((float) iBM_WIDTH)/2 + 20, ((float) iBM_HEIGHT)/2 +
oPT_TEXT.measureText(sXAxisText), oPT_TEXT);

//Restore the state of the canvas
oCV.restore();
```

Note that I changed the paint object's text alignment attribute so that the text would appear to the left of the (x,y)-coordinate instead of the default. Note that the enumerator `Paint.Align` can be a bit confusing at first!!

Here is what this looks like:

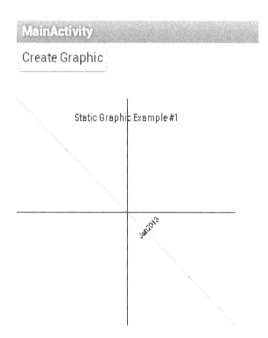

Although I shifted the coordinates of the horizontal text down and to the right, you can perform similar steps to the code above using the `translate()` method to shift things down a bit and THEN you can place the text on the graph. This prevents you from having to play with the parameters for the coordinates, but it's really six of one, half a dozen of the other.

Now, I'm none too happy with the default font, so I downloaded a free font called Jura (which is made up of the following four files: `Jura-Regular.ttf`, `Jura-Bold.ttf`, `Jura-Italic.ttf`, `Jura-BoldItalic.ttf`) and copied it to the `fonts` folder (which you may have to create) in the `assets` folder. In order to pull in that font, you use the `createFromAsset()` method of the `Typeface` class to create yourself a `Typeface` object for that font. At this point, you can use it as normal. Here is the relevant code:

```
//Bring in the Jura-Regular font
Typeface oTF_JuraRegular = Typeface.createFromAsset(getAssets(),
                                        "fonts/Jura-Regular.ttf");
oPT_TEXT.setTypeface(oTF_JuraRegular);
```

Another nice feature is to use the `Path` object to create closed path graphics such as circles, rectangles, arcs, lines, etc. Creation of rectangles, circles and arcs are

441

relatively easy, but creating lines using the `Path` object may be something of a new fish for some of you. In order to create a line, you must use the `moveto()` method to select the starting coordinate and then use the `lineTo()` or `rLineTo()` methods to draw a line to the coordinate passed as parameters to these methods. You continue this until you are done. You can using the `close()` method to close the path completing the circuit. For example, the following code...

```
//Create a Path object
Path oPath = new Path();
oPath.moveTo(250, 250);
oPath.lineTo(300, 200);
oPath.lineTo(300, 300);
oPath.close();

//Change the line color to blue and remove the dash effect
oPT_LINE.setColor(Color.BLUE);
oPT_LINE.setPathEffect(null);

//Draw the path on the canvas
oCV.drawPath(oPath, oPT_LINE);
```

...is responsible for the generating the triangle in the graph below:

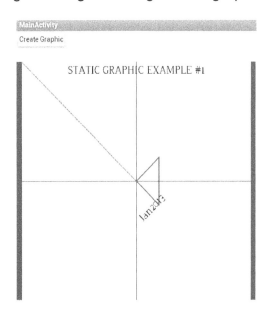

Tweened Animated Graphics in Two-Dimensions - An Overview

In this section, we describe two simple methods to create an animation, but not in the traditional sense. Here, by animated graphic we mean the translation, rotation, scaling, etc. of a `View` on the screen. The two methods available to you are *view animation* or *property animation* and perform *tweened animation*; that is, given a starting location of a `View` (say, a `Button`), an ending location, and the type of movement (or *interpolation*) you want the `Button` to perform (that is, start slow but gradually speed up, start fast but gradually slow down, constant speed, etc.), Android computes the frames *between* the starting and ending frames automatically. What you wind up with, in this example, is a `Button` that travels from one location to another on the screen.

While *view animation* and *property animation* are very similar there are differences:

1. As the name implies, you can only use *view animation* on a `View` or a subclass thereof.
2. When using *view animation*, the ending location of the `View` does not respond to events but the starting location still does. This is an issue and is solved when using *property animation*.
3. *View animation* is limited in the properties that can be animated: position, size, rotation and transparency.
4. *Property animation* is similar to *view animation* except that it is not limited to Views and can be used on your own classes to effectively animate anything regardless of whether it actually draws to the screen or not.
5. In both cases, you first use XML to specify the animation, and you use code to start the animation running. Both use the XML `<set>` tag along with a variety of child tags and attributes.
6. Deciding between the two: use the method that achieves the quickest and simplest results. If *view animation* works, then use that; otherwise, use *property animation*.

Note that you can ignore the XML file and define each *view animation* using the following view animation-related classes: `RotateAnimation`, `ScaleAnimation`, `TranslateAnimation`, `AlphaAnimation` and `AnimationSet` to hold the other four.

Now, both view animation and property animation make use of interpolators. An *interpolator* indicates what type of movement you would like your widget to show as the animation proceeds. Below is a list of interpolators available via "`@android:anim/`*name_of_interpolator*" (located in the `C:\android-sdk-windows\platforms\android-##\data\res\anim` folder):

1. `accelerate_decelerate_interpolator` - An interpolator whose rate of change starts and ends slowly but accelerates through the middle.
2. `accelerate_interpolator` - An interpolator whose rate of change starts out slowly and then accelerates.
3. `anticipate_interpolator` - An interpolator whose change starts backward then flings forward.
4. `anticipate_overshoot_interpolator` - An interpolator whose change starts backward, flings forward and overshoots the target value, then finally goes back to the final value.
5. `bounce_interpolator` - An interpolator whose change bounces at the end.
6. `cycle_interpolator` - An interpolator whose animation repeats for a specified number of cycles.
7. `decelerate_interpolator` - An interpolator whose rate of change starts out quickly and and then decelerates.
8. `linear_interpolator` - An interpolator whose rate of change is constant.
9. `overshoot_interpolator` - An interpolator whose change flings forward and overshoots the last value then comes back.

Each one of the interpolators has a corresponding class. For example, `bounce_interpolator` is related to the `BounceInterpolator` class, and so on. Also, if you wish to implement your own interpolator, please see the `TimeInterpolator` class.

Finally, both *view animation* and *property animation* are located in the `android.view.animation` package.

Tweened Animated Graphics in Two-Dimensions - View Animation

In this section, we describe *view animation*. As mentioned in the overview, view animation uses XML in an XML Resource file to describe the desired animation.

Here is the XML syntax for *view animations*:

```xml
<?xml version="1.0" encoding="utf-8"?>
<set xmlns:android="http://schemas.android.com/apk/res/android"
    android:interpolator="@[package:]anim/interpolator_resource"
    android:shareInterpolator=["true" | "false"] >
    <alpha
        android:fromAlpha="float"
        android:toAlpha="float" />
    <scale
        android:fromXScale="float"
        android:toXScale="float"
        android:fromYScale="float"
        android:toYScale="float"
        android:pivotX="float"
        android:pivotY="float" />
    <translate
        android:fromXDelta="float"
        android:toXDelta="float"
        android:fromYDelta="float"
        android:toYDelta="float" />
    <rotate
        android:fromDegrees="float"
        android:toDegrees="float"
        android:pivotX="float"
        android:pivotY="float" />
    <set>
        ...
    </set>
</set>
```

The following describes the XML tags available for view animation:

1. `<set>` - this tag contains one or more of the other tags and can be thought of as containing a *set of animation actions*. While not strictly necessary if you just want to perform, say, a rotation, you may want to use it just to be neat and tidy. Using this tag multiple times in one XML Resource file allows you to perform sequential and/or simultaneous actions; that is, moving and rotating, rotation and becoming opaque, etc.
   a. `android:shareInterpolator` - this attribute, when set to false, indicates that each animation within a `<set>` should use its own interpolator.
   b. `android:interpolator` - this indicates which interpolator you want to use. We talk about interpolators below.
2. `<rotate>` - this tag performs a rotation of the `View`.
   a. `android:duration` - amount of time (in milliseconds) for the animation to run

444

b. `android:fromDegrees` - rotation offset to apply at the start of the animation

c. `android:toDegrees` - rotation offset to apply at the end of the animation

d. `android:pivotX` - The X coordinate of the point about which the object is being rotated, specified as an absolute number where 0 is the left edge. This value can either be an absolute number if `pivotXType` is ABSOLUTE, or a percentage (where 1.0 is 100%) otherwise.

e. `android:pivotXtype` - Specifies how `pivotXValue` should be interpreted

   i. `Animation.ABSOLUTE` - The specified dimension is an absolute number of pixels.

   ii. `Animation.RELATIVE_TO_SELF` - The specified dimension holds a float and should be multiplied by the height or width of the object being animated.

   iii. `Animation.RELATIVE_TO_PARENT` - The specified dimension holds a float and should be multiplied by the height or width of the parent of the object being animated.

f. `android:pivotY` - The Y coordinate of the point about which the object is being rotated, specified as an absolute number where 0 is the top edge. This value can either be an absolute number if `pivotYType` is ABSOLUTE, or a percentage (where 1.0 is 100%) otherwise.

3. `<translate>` - this tag performs a translation, or movement from one position on the screen to another position

   a. `android:duration` - amount of time (in milliseconds) for the animation to run

   b. `android:fromXDelta` - change in X coordinate to apply at the start of the animation

   c. `android:toXDelta` - change in X coordinate to apply at the end of the animation

   d. `android:fromYDelta` - change in Y coordinate to apply at the start of the animation

   e. `android:toYDelta` - change in Y coordinate to apply at the end of the animation

4. `<scale>` - this tag makes the `View` larger or small

   a. `android:duration` - amount of time (in milliseconds) for the animation to run

   b. `android:fromXScale` - Horizontal scaling factor to apply at the start of the animation

   c. `android:toXScale` - Horizontal scaling factor to apply at the end of the animation

   d. `android:fromYScale` - Vertical scaling factor to apply at the start of the animation

   e. `android:toYScale` - Vertical scaling factor to apply at the end of the animation

   f. `android:pivotX` - the X coordinate of the point about which the object is being scaled, specified as an absolute number where 0 is the left edge. (This point remains fixed while the object changes size.)

g. `android:pivotY` - the Y coordinate of the point about which the object is being scaled, specified as an absolute number where 0 is the top edge. (This point remains fixed while the object changes size.)
5. `<alpha>` - this tag increases or decreases the transparency of the `View`.
   a. `android:duration` - amount of time (in milliseconds) for the animation to run
   b. `android:fromAlpha` - starting alpha value for the animation, where 1.0 means fully opaque and 0.0 means fully transparent.
   c. `android:toAlpha` - ending alpha value for the animation.

For example, let's move a `Button` from its starting position to an ending position while rotating it counter-clockwise and at the same time changing the alpha value slightly. Here is the XML file containing the *view animation* XML (called `myviewanimation.xml`):

```xml
<?xml version="1.0" encoding="utf-8"?>
<set xmlns:android="http://schemas.android.com/apk/res/android"
     android:shareInterpolator="false">

    <translate android:interpolator="@android:anim/overshoot_interpolator"
            android:toYDelta="500"
            android:duration="2000"/>
    <set>
     <rotate android:interpolator="@android:anim/linear_interpolator"
            android:fromDegrees="0"
            android:toDegrees="-5"
            android:pivotX="5%"
            android:pivotY="5%"
            android:duration="1000"/>
     <alpha android:fromAlpha="1.0"
            android:toAlpha="0.25"
            android:duration="1000"/>
    </set>

</set>
```

Take note above that those tags appearing within the `<set>` tag will occur simultaneously. That is, both `<rotate>` and `<alpha>` will occur simultaneously following the `<translate>`. Also, note that I have specified the `overshoot_interpolator` for the translation, whereas I specified the `linear_interpolator` for the rotation.

Here is the Java code to start the animation once the button is clicked:

```java
public class MainActivity extends Activity {

 @Override
 public void onCreate(Bundle savedInstanceState) {
  super.onCreate(savedInstanceState);
  setContentView(R.layout.activity_main);
 }

 public void StartViewAnimation(View view) {

  Button oBtn = (Button) findViewById(R.id.button1);
  Animation oAnim = AnimationUtils.loadAnimation(this,R.anim.myviewanimation);
  oBtn.startAnimation(oAnim);

 }
```

}

Note that the animation starts with the button at the top of the screen, then it proceeds down and to the right slowly fading away, as shown below:

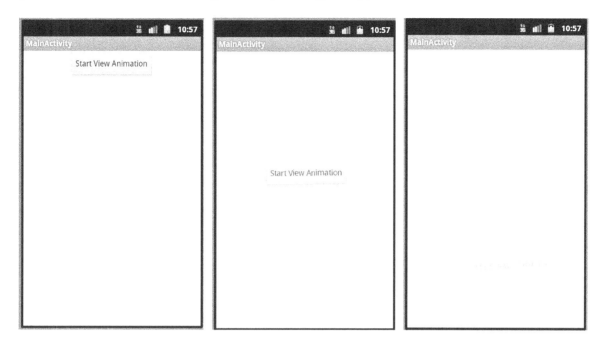

Note that if you attempt to push the button after the animation has started, the moving button does not respond to the onClick event. This is because the *image* of the button may be moving, but the *object* itself is still located at the top of the screen (even though it appears to be just a white background). For example, by clicking the location of the button at the top of the screen even after it has begun to move, the `onClick` event is triggered again. This is fixed in Android 3.0 and for Property Animation.

Tweened Animated Graphics in Two-Dimensions - Property Animation

In this section, we describe *property animation*. Property Animation is very similar to View Animation, but it allows you to modify properties other than just rotate, scale, transformation, alpha, etc. Property Animation also allows you to animate properties that are not necessarily shown on the screen. Since Property Animation and View Animation are so similar, we refer you to the Android documentation.

SurfaceView and the SurfaceHolder Interface

Drawing a static graphic, like the `Bitmap`, is fine, but if you need to have some interactivity with your graphic, or you would just like to use full-on animation for a video game, you should use the `SurfaceView` view. `SurfaceView`s are apparently better at handling animated graphics for things like video games. We don't go into too much on `SurfaceView` here.

Note that there is another view, `GLSurfaceView`, which is used with OpenGL and that whole mess. We won't be discussing that view here...or, hopefully, anywhere.

Note that you can use a `SurfaceView` in several different ways:

447

1. You can drag-and-drop a `SurfaceView` view from the Eclipse Advanced Palette onto the GUI and then access the `SurfaceView` in that manner.
2. You can have an empty GUI and create a class which extends `SurfaceView` and implements the `SurfaceHolder.Callback` interface. In the `onCreate()` method of your activity, pass in the instantiated class to the `setContentView()` method. This will force your surface to appear on the GUI.
3. Similar to #1, but you can use your own class in the XML file instead of the Android-provided `SurfaceView`, you use your own.

Below is an example of #2. First, the code for the `Activity`:

```
package com.example.andappf;

import android.os.Bundle;
import android.app.Activity;
import android.graphics.Canvas;
import android.graphics.DashPathEffect;
import android.graphics.Paint;
import android.graphics.Paint.Style;
import android.view.Menu;
import android.view.SurfaceHolder;
import android.view.SurfaceView;
import android.view.View;
import android.view.Window;
import android.view.WindowManager;
import android.widget.Toast;

public class MainActivity extends Activity {

  private MySurfaceView oSV;

  @Override
  public void onCreate(Bundle savedInstanceState) {
   super.onCreate(savedInstanceState);

   //Prevent the title from being shown and make the surface fullscreen.
   requestWindowFeature(Window.FEATURE_NO_TITLE);
   getWindow().setFlags(WindowManager.LayoutParams.FLAG_FULLSCREEN,
                    WindowManager.LayoutParams.FLAG_FULLSCREEN);

   //Access the SurfaceView
   oSV = new MySurfaceView(this);

   //Set the content view to the surface
   setContentView(oSV);

  }
}
```

Next, the class `MySurfaceView` that contains the class `MySurfaceView Thread`:

```
package com.example.andappf;

import android.content.Context;
import android.graphics.Bitmap;
import android.graphics.BitmapFactory;
import android.graphics.Canvas;
import android.graphics.Color;
import android.graphics.DashPathEffect;
```

```
import android.graphics.Paint;
import android.graphics.Paint.Style;
import android.util.AttributeSet;
import android.view.Surface;
import android.view.SurfaceHolder;
import android.view.SurfaceView;
import android.view.View;
import android.widget.Toast;

public class MySurfaceView extends SurfaceView implements SurfaceHolder.Callback
{

 private SurfaceHolder holder;
 private MySurfaceViewThread mySurfaceViewThread;
 private Bitmap oBM;
 private double RandX;
 private double RandY;

 MySurfaceView(Context context) {
  super(context);

  //Get the SurfaceHolder from oSV.
  holder=getHolder();

  //Add the callback
  holder.addCallback(this);

  //Instantiate the thread
  mySurfaceViewThread = new MySurfaceViewThread(holder,this);

  //Initialize the bitmap
  oBM = BitmapFactory.decodeResource(getResources(),
                             R.drawable.trafficlightgreen);
  oBM = Bitmap.createScaledBitmap(oBM, 100, 100, false);

 }

 protected void onDraw(Canvas canvas) {

  //Draw something on the canvas!
  canvas.drawColor(Color.GREEN);
  RandX = 500*Math.random();
  RandY = 500*Math.random();
  canvas.drawBitmap(oBM, (float) RandX,(float) RandY, null);

 }

 @Override
 public void surfaceCreated(SurfaceHolder holder) {

  mySurfaceViewThread.setRunnable(true);
  mySurfaceViewThread.start();

 }

 @Override
 public void surfaceDestroyed(SurfaceHolder holder) {

  boolean retry = true;
  mySurfaceViewThread.setRunnable(false);
  while(retry) {
   try {
    mySurfaceViewThread.join();
    retry=false;
   }
   catch (InterruptedException ex) {
    //nop
   }
  }
```

```
  mySurfaceViewThread=null;

}

@Override
public void surfaceChanged(SurfaceHolder holder,
                          int format,
                          int width,
                          int height) {
 //TODO
}

//-------------------------------------------------------------------------------
//-------------------------------------------------------------------------------
//-------------------------------------------------------------------------------

//MySurfaceViewThread Class
class MySurfaceViewThread extends Thread {

 private boolean run=false;
 private SurfaceHolder sh;
 private MySurfaceView sv;
 private Canvas canvas;

 //Constructor
 MySurfaceViewThread(SurfaceHolder _holder,MySurfaceView _sv) {
  super();
  sh=_holder;
  sv=_sv;
 }

 void setRunnable(boolean bRun) {

  run=bRun;

 }

 @Override
 public void run() {

  super.run();

  while (run) {
   canvas=null;

   //Lock the surface view's canvas.
   try {

    canvas = sh.lockCanvas(null);
    synchronized(sh) {
     sv.onDraw(canvas);
    }

   }
   finally {

    if (canvas != null) {
     //Unlock the canvas
     sh.unlockCanvasAndPost(canvas);
    }

   }

  }

 }

 public void onWindowResize(int w,int h) {
  //Deal with window resize!
 }
```

```
    }
  }
```

This class will draw a traffic light at random points on the surface:

A Comment about `WindowManager`

As shown in the code in the previous section, you can use the `WindowManager` class to get a flag to indicate full screen mode:

```
WindowManager.LayoutParams.FLAG_FULLSCREEN
```

But, you can also get the height and width of the device itself, as shown in the following:

```
//Get the width and height of the device
WindowManager wm = (WindowManager)
context.getSystemService(Context.WINDOW_SERVICE);
Display display = wm.getDefaultDisplay();
int iDeviceWidth = display.getWidth();
int iDeviceHeight = display.getHeight();
```

Armed with the device height and width, you can alter your graphics to fit the display.

A Comment on Infragistics Iguana Chart Widgets

In our published Android app, *equityYo Stock and Fund Database*, we made use of Infragistics' free charting widgets, Iguana Charts, for use with both the price and dividend displays. They are nice widgets and you should check them out if you need graphics in your app.

Chapter 24: Pinch! Zoom! Swipe! - Detecting Gestures

Overview

In this chapter, we look at how to handle various touch screen events such as the swipe (or fling) as well as pinch-and-zoom.

Note that, if your application needs it, you can define gestures specific to it. For example, if a user draws the letter Z on the touch screen while playing your game, maybe Zorro will appear to help your user out. The recognition of the letter Z gesture on the screen goes well beyond just a simple swipe or pinch-and-zoom maneuver.

There are various classes you can use to detect gestures:

1. `Gesture` - A gesture is a hand-drawn shape on a touch screen. It can have one or multiple strokes. Each stroke is a sequence of timed points. A user-defined gesture can be recognized by a `GestureLibrary`.
2. `GestureLibraries` - this class contains several helper methods to read in pre-defined gestures from a file or resource.
3. `GestureLibrary` - this class contains several methods used to add, remove, or otherwise manage gestures within a specific library. This class contains the `recognize()` method used to predict if the gesture "matches" one of those stored within the library.
4. `GestureOverlayView` - a transparent overlay for gesture input that can be placed on top of other widgets or contain other widgets.
5. `GesturePoint` - this class holds a timed point of a gesture stroke. Note that multiple points form a stroke. A timed point is an (x,y)-coordinate along with a long, called timestamp, holding the length of time for this point.
6. `GestureStore` - this class contains several methods used to add, remove and otherwise manage gestures. This class contains the `recognize()` method used to predict if a gesture "matches" one of those stored.
7. `GestureStroke` - a *gesture stroke* starts on a touch down and ends on a touch up. A *stroke* consists of a sequence of timed points. One or multiple strokes form a *gesture*.
8. `GestureUtils` - this class contains utility functions for gesture processing and analysis including the following:
    a. feature extraction - e.g., samplers and those for calculating bounding boxes and gesture path lengths
    b. geometric transformation - e.g., translation, rotation and scaling
    c. gesture similarity comparison - e.g., computing distances between gestures using Euclidean or Cosine distances.
9. `Prediction` - this class contains two fields:
    a. `name` - the name of the gesture
    b. `score` - the predicted score computed between the current gesture and the gesture in the library or store.

While the classes above are helpful if you plan to create a unique set of gestures used in your application ("Zorro! Save Me!"), you may not have to use them since the following are also available to make your life a lot simple. Note that the class `GestureDetector.SimpleOnGestureListener` listens for a fling.

1. `GestureDetector.OnGestureListener` - the listener that is used to notify when gestures occur. If you want to listen for all the different gestures then implement this interface.
2. `GestureDetector.OnDoubleTapListener` - the listener that is used to notify when a double-tap or a confirmed single-tap occur.
3. `GestureDetector.SimpleOnGestureListener` - this class is a convenience class to extend when you only want to listen for a subset of all of the gestures. This implements all of the methods in the `GestureDetector.OnGestureListener` class as well as `GestureDetector.OnDoubleTapListener`, but these do nothing and all return false. You can override these methods, if desired.
4. `ScaleGestureDetector` - detects transformation gestures involving more than one pointer (i.e., multi-touch or multiple fingers - at least we hope it's only fingers...tee-hee! - touching the screen at once) using the supplied MotionEvents. This can be used to determine pinch-and-zoom.

Finally, when you want much more control, you can use the `MotionEvent` class to report movement (mouse, pen, finger, trackball, etc.) events.

Detecting Flings

You can detect flings (i.e., swipes from right-to-left or left-to-right) by using similar code below. The following code was taken from the StackOverflow website: stackoverflow.com/questions/4952556/mygesturedetector-extends-simpleongesturelistener.

```
package com.example.andappe;

import android.os.Bundle;
import android.app.Activity;
import android.graphics.Bitmap;
import android.graphics.Canvas;
import android.graphics.Color;
import android.graphics.DashPathEffect;
import android.graphics.Paint;
import android.graphics.Paint.Style;
import android.graphics.Path;
import android.graphics.Picture;
import android.graphics.Typeface;
import android.view.GestureDetector;
import android.view.MotionEvent;
import android.view.View;
import android.widget.ImageView;
import android.widget.Toast;

public class MainActivity extends Activity {

 private static final int SWIPE_MIN_DISTANCE = 120;
 private static final int SWIPE_MAX_OFF_PATH = 250;
 private static final int SWIPE_THRESHOLD_VELOCITY = 200;
 private GestureDetector gestureDetector;
 public View.OnTouchListener gestureListener;

 @Override
 public void onCreate(Bundle savedInstanceState) {
```

453

```java
super.onCreate(savedInstanceState);
setContentView(R.layout.activity_main);

//Instantiate a new GestureDetector object setting the FlingDetector
// class as parameter
gestureDetector = new GestureDetector(new FlingDetector());

//Set up an OnTouchListener for this View.
gestureListener = new View.OnTouchListener() {
 public boolean onTouch(View v, MotionEvent event) {
  if (gestureDetector.onTouchEvent(event)) {
   return true;
  }
  return false;
 }
};
}

//Create the graphic
public void createGraphic(View view) {

 //Main title to be displayed
 String sTitle = "STATIC GRAPHIC EXAMPLE #1";

 //Bitmap height and width
 int iBM_HEIGHT = 500;
 int iBM_WIDTH = 500;

 //Create static picture to be used later
 Picture oPic = createPicture(iBM_HEIGHT,iBM_WIDTH);

 //Starting X and Y of Line
 float fX_BEG = 0;
 float fY_BEG = 0;

 //Ending X and Y of Line
 float fX_END = 250;
 float fY_END = 250;

 //Y-Coordinate of text
 float fY_TEXT = 25;

 //Text Size
 float fTextSize = 24;

 //Access the image view, imageView1, on the screen
 ImageView oIV = (ImageView) findViewById(R.id.imageView1);

 //Create a blank bitmap.
 Bitmap oBM = Bitmap.createBitmap(iBM_HEIGHT,
                                  iBM_WIDTH,
                                  Bitmap.Config.ARGB_8888);

 //Create a Canvas associating the bitmap oBM with it,
 Canvas oCV = new Canvas(oBM);

 //Add the picture to the canvas
 oCV.drawPicture(oPic);

 //Set the background color of the Canvas
 oCV.drawARGB(0, 0, 0, 255);

 //Set up the dash effect
 DashPathEffect oDPE = new DashPathEffect(new float[] {5,1},0);

 //Create a Paint object for the line (red and dashed)
 Paint oPT_LINE = new Paint();
 oPT_LINE.setARGB(255, 255, 0, 0);
 oPT_LINE.setStrokeWidth(2);
 oPT_LINE.setStyle(Style.STROKE);
```

454

```
    oPT_LINE.setPathEffect(oDPE);

  //Add a line to the canvas using the Paint object
  oCV.drawLine(fX_BEG, fY_BEG, fX_END, fY_END, oPT_LINE);

  //Create a Paint object for the text (black and bold)
  Paint oPT_TEXT = new Paint(/* Paint.FAKE_BOLD_TEXT_FLAG */);
  oPT_TEXT.setARGB(255, 255, 255, 255);

  //Bring in the Jura-Regular font
  Typeface oTF_JuraRegular = Typeface.createFromAsset(getAssets(),
                                             "fonts/Jura-Regular.ttf");
  oPT_TEXT.setTypeface(oTF_JuraRegular);
  oPT_TEXT.setTextSize(fTextSize);
  oPT_TEXT.setColor(Color.BLACK);

  //Add the title to the canvas ensuring that the text is centered.
  float fTitleWidth = oPT_TEXT.measureText(sTitle);
  float fX_TEXT = ((float)iBM_WIDTH - fTitleWidth)/2;
  oCV.drawText(sTitle, fX_TEXT, fY_TEXT, oPT_TEXT);

  //Save the state of the canvas
  oCV.save();

  //Rotate the canvas by 45 degrees around the origin of our axes
  oCV.rotate( -45, ((float) iBM_WIDTH)/2, ((float) iBM_HEIGHT)/2);

  //Draw some text just below the X-axis
  String sXAxisText = "Jan2013";

  //Modify the Paint object oPT_TEXT so that the text is drawn to the LEFT
  // of the (x,y)-coordinate.
  oPT_TEXT.setTextAlign(Paint.Align.RIGHT);

  //Make the font slightly smaller for the axis text
  oPT_TEXT.setTextSize(fTextSize - 1);

  //Draw the text under the x-axis.
  oCV.drawText(sXAxisText, ((float) iBM_WIDTH)/2 + 20,
                           ((float) iBM_HEIGHT)/2 +
                                  oPT_TEXT.measureText(sXAxisText), oPT_TEXT);

  //Restore the state of the canvas
  oCV.restore();

  //Create a Path object
  Path oPath = new Path();
  oPath.moveTo(250, 250);
  oPath.lineTo(300, 200);
  oPath.lineTo(300, 300);
  oPath.close();

  //Change the line color to blue and remove the dash effect
  oPT_LINE.setColor(Color.BLUE);
  oPT_LINE.setPathEffect(null);

  //Draw the path on the canvas
  oCV.drawPath(oPath, oPT_LINE);

  //Set the bitmap, oBM, as the image of imageView1.
  oIV.setImageBitmap(oBM);
}

//Create the static picture
private Picture createPicture(int pBM_HEIGHT,int pBM_WIDTH) {

  //Instantiate the blank picture
  Picture oPIC = new Picture();

  //Get the Canvas for the blank Picture
```

```
Canvas oCAN = oPIC.beginRecording(pBM_WIDTH, pBM_HEIGHT);

//Create a paint object for the horizontal and vertical axes
Paint oPT = new Paint();
oPT.setARGB(255, 0, 0, 0);
oPT.setStrokeWidth(1);
oPT.setStyle(Style.STROKE);

//Set the background of the canvas to white
oCAN.drawARGB(255, 255, 255, 255);

//Draw the lines on the canvas
oCAN.drawLine(0,
              ((float) pBM_HEIGHT)/2,
              (float) pBM_WIDTH,
              ((float) pBM_HEIGHT)/2,
              oPT);
oCAN.drawLine(((float) pBM_WIDTH)/2,
              0,
              ((float) pBM_WIDTH)/2,
              (float) pBM_HEIGHT, oPT);

//End the recording
oPIC.endRecording();

return(oPIC);

}

//Create a class to detect flings
class FlingDetector extends GestureDetector.SimpleOnGestureListener {

 //Implement the onFling method
 @Override
 public boolean onFling(MotionEvent e1,
                        MotionEvent e2,
                        float velocityX,
                        float velocityY) {

  try {

    if (Math.abs(e1.getY() - e2.getY()) > SWIPE_MAX_OFF_PATH) return false;

    if(e1.getX() - e2.getX() > SWIPE_MIN_DISTANCE
       && Math.abs(velocityX) > SWIPE_THRESHOLD_VELOCITY) {

     //Right to Left Swipe
     Toast toast = Toast.makeText(getApplicationContext(),
                                  "RIGHT-TO-LEFT SWIPE!",
                                  Toast.LENGTH_LONG);
     toast.show();
     return true;
    }
    else if (e2.getX() - e1.getX() > SWIPE_MIN_DISTANCE
             && Math.abs(velocityX) > SWIPE_THRESHOLD_VELOCITY) {

     //Left to Right Swipe
     Toast toast = Toast.makeText(getApplicationContext(),
                                  "LEFT-TO-RIGHT SWIPE!",
                                  Toast.LENGTH_LONG);
     toast.show();
     return true;
    }

  } catch (Exception e) {
    // do something wonderful!
  }

 return false;
 }
```

```
  }

  @Override
  public boolean onTouchEvent(MotionEvent event) {
   if (gestureDetector.onTouchEvent(event))
    return true;
   else
    return false;
  }

 }
```

Detecting Pinch-and-Zoom

You can detect pinch-and-zoom easily by using the `ScaleGestureDetector` class. This class contains the `getScaleFactor()` method which returns the ratio `getCurrentSpan()/getPreviousSpan()`.

Now, you can add the two lines of code below to the code in the previous section. Add these two lines to the class variables at the top of the program:

```
private ScaleGestureDetector scaleGestureDetector;
public View.OnTouchListener scaleGestureListener;
```

Within the `onCreate()` method, add the following lines:

```
//Instantiate the scaleGestureDetector
scaleGestureDetector = new ScaleGestureDetector(this,new ScaleListener());

//Set up an OnTouchListener for this View.
scaleGestureListener = new View.OnTouchListener() {
 public boolean onTouch(View v, MotionEvent event) {
  if (scaleGestureDetector.onTouchEvent(event)) {
   return true;
  }
  return false;
 }
};
```

Create another class that extends the following in order to handle the scale factor: `ScaleGestureDetector.SimpleOnScaleGestureListener`:

```
class ScaleListener extends ScaleGestureDetector.SimpleOnScaleGestureListener {

 @Override
 public void onScaleEnd(ScaleGestureDetector detector) {

  Toast toast1 = Toast.makeText(getApplicationContext(),
                                "HERE WE ARE!",
                                Toast.LENGTH_LONG);
  toast1.show();

  //Get the scale factor ratio
  float mScaleFactor = detector.getScaleFactor();

  if (mScaleFactor == 1.0f) {
   //No change
   Toast toast = Toast.makeText(getApplicationContext(),
                                "SCALE: NO CHANGE!",
                                Toast.LENGTH_LONG);
   toast.show();
  }
  else if (mScaleFactor > 1.0f) {
```

```
       //zoom indicated by fingers broadening
       Toast toast = Toast.makeText(getApplicationContext(),
                               "SCALE: ZOOM!",
                               Toast.LENGTH_LONG);
       toast.show();
      }
      else if (mScaleFactor < 1.0f) {
       //pinch indicated by fingers contracting
       Toast toast = Toast.makeText(getApplicationContext(),
                               "SCALE: PINCH!",
                               Toast.LENGTH_LONG);

       toast.show();
      }


     }


   }
```

You will have to modify the `onTouchEvent()` method:

```
@Override
public boolean onTouchEvent(MotionEvent event) {
 if (gestureDetector.onTouchEvent(event))
  return true;
 else if (scaleGestureDetector.onTouchEvent(event))
  return true;
 else
  return false;
}
```

Note that I am overriding the `onScaleEnd()` method in my class above rather than the `onScale()` method. The `onScale()` method is fired continuously and any code you have within it will be fired continuously as well. This may or may not be what you want depending on the purpose of your application.

Controlling the Scrolling of a TextView

While we're talking about detecting gestures on the screen, let's talk about controlling the display of text in a `TextView`. Normally, a `TextView` will display all of the text that you give to it. But, there may be times when you want to limit the number of lines of text and allow the user to scroll the `TextView` itself to see more text.

For example, in my Android app, equityYo, we do exactly this when displaying the stock's full summary description. Shown below is an image from the stock *Agilent Technologies* with its summary description displayed halfway in the middle. As you can see, the scroll bar on the right is about 50% the way down the `TextView`. If I allowed the `TextView` to display the entire description, it would take up a chunk of the entire display, so I opted to limit the number of rows displayed as well as allow the user to scroll the `TextView` itself to see more of the text.

A   **Last Price: $40.94**

Agilent Technologies Inc.

Chemical Analysis segment provides gas
chromatography systems, columns, and components;
gas chromatography mass spectrometry systems;
inductively coupled plasma mass spectrometry
instruments; atomic absorption instruments;
inductively coupled plasma optical emission
spectrometry instruments; molecular spectroscopy
instruments; software and data systems; and vacuum
pumps and measurement technologies. The
company s Diagnostics and Genomics segment offers
immunohistochemistry in situ hybridization

First, let's look at the XML for the `TextView`:

```
<TextView android:id="@+id/tvSTOCK_sInfo"
        android:padding="10.0px"
        android:background="@drawable/color7"
        android:fadeScrollbars="false"
        android:maxLines="10"
        android:scrollbars="vertical"
        android:scrollbarStyle="outsideOverlay"
        android:layout_height="wrap_content"
        android:layout_width="wrap_content"
        android:textStyle="italic"
        android:textAppearance="?android:attr/textAppearanceSmall"/>
```

Note that I am setting the number of lines to a maximum of 10 using the
`android:maxLines` attribute. Android will determine what a line means, so you
don't have to force in carriage returns/line feeds in your text. Note, also, that I
played with the `android:scrollbars` and `android:scrollbarStyle`
attributes to display only a vertical scrollbar. (There is no reason for a horizontal
scrollbar since the `TextView` wraps its text.)

Once you have the `TextView` set up, you need to programmatically control the
scrolling. This is easy to do, as shown in the code below. Note that the name of
my `TextView` is `StockInfoTextView`.

```
//Set the maximum number of lines that can be displayed
// (analogous to android:maxLines)
StockInfoTextView.setMaxLines(10);

//Set the movement method to ScrollingMovementMethod
StockInfoTextView.setMovementMethod(ScrollingMovementMethod.getInstance());

//You want to disallow intercept touch for this TextView
StockInfoTextView.setOnTouchListener(new View.OnTouchListener() {

 public boolean onTouch(View v, MotionEvent event)
 {
  v.getParent().requestDisallowInterceptTouchEvent(true);
  return false;
 }

});
```

Note that we can also programmatically set the maximum number of lines using the `setMaxLines()` method for the `TextView`.

Now, when you swipe up or down on a GUI interface, the display normally moves in accordance. This action occurs even if your finger is swiping across a `TextView` contained within the GUI. To prevent the entire GUI from moving and just allowing the `TextView` to scroll its contents, you have to tell the `TextView`'s parent to ignore touches, as shown above. The result is that when you swipe up or down within the `TextView`, its contents scrolls, and not the entire GUI.

Chapter 25: Detecting Device Rotation

Overview

In this chapter, we look at how to handle the rotation of the device; that is, from portrait to landscape and vice versa.

The Android Manifest and Device Orientation Changes

You'll recall that in Chapter 12, *The Android Manifest*, we discussed the `android:configChanges` attribute of the `<activity>` node. Normally, when the device's orientation changes, the activity is shutdown and restarted. If you specify `android:configChanges="orientation"` in the Android Manifest, then the `onConfigurationChanged()` method is called and the activity is not shutdown/restarted. Within `onConfigurationChanged()`, you can handle any orientation changes that you desire such as programmatically altering the layout you want shown.

Note that `onConfigurationChanged()` is an abstract method available in the interface `android.content.ComponentCallbacks` and you need to use the `implements` keyword on your class to use `onConfigurationChanged()`.

Here is my modification to my `AndroidManifest.xml` file for the main activity (see bold font below):

```
<manifest xmlns:android="http://schemas.android.com/apk/res/android"
    package="com.example.andappe"
    android:versionCode="1"
    android:versionName="1.0" >

    <uses-sdk
        android:minSdkVersion="10"
        android:targetSdkVersion="15" />

    <application
        android:icon="@drawable/ic_launcher"
        android:label="@string/app_name"
        android:theme="@style/AppTheme" >
        <activity
            android:name=".MainActivity"
            android:label="@string/title_activity_main"
            android:configChanges="orientation">
            <intent-filter>
                <action android:name="android.intent.action.MAIN" />
                <category android:name="android.intent.category.LAUNCHER" />
            </intent-filter>
        </activity>
    </application>

</manifest>
```

Now, I added the `implements` keyword to my `Activity`:

```
public class MainActivity extends Activity implements ComponentCallbacks {
```

Finally, I added the following code to the class:

```
//Handle orientation changes
@Override
public void onConfigurationChanged(Configuration newConfig) {
 super.onConfigurationChanged(newConfig);

 //Handle orientation changes
 if (newConfig.orientation == Configuration.ORIENTATION_LANDSCAPE) {
  //handle landscape orientation
 }
 else if (newConfig.orientation == Configuration.ORIENTATION_PORTRAIT) {
  //handle portrait orientation
 }

}
```

Now, whenever the device's orientation is changed, the method `onConfigurationChanged()` is called and the appropriate piece of code is executed based on whether the orientation is now landscape or portrait.

Take note that some authors suggest adding `keyboardHidden` to the `android:configChanges` attribute in the manifest, although I'm not quite sure why:

```
android:configChanges="orientation|keyboardHidden"
```

Note that some authors also suggest adding `screenSize` to the list as well:

```
android:configChanges="orientation|keyboardHidden|screenSize"
```

The Android Manifest and Preventing Orientation Changes

If you'd prefer that the orientation not change when the user rotates the device, you can add **one** of the following lines to the `<activity>` tag of the `AndroidManifest.xml` file to prevent orientation changes from occurring:

```
android:screenOrientation="landscape"
android:screenOrientation="portrait"
```

Another way to prevent orientation changes is to force your application into the orientation you desire by using the `setRequestedOrientation()` method of the `Activity` class:

```
setRequestedOrientation(ActivityInfo.SCREEN_ORIENTATION_PORTRAIT);
setRequestedOrientation(ActivityInfo.SCREEN_ORIENTATION_LANDSCAPE);
```

Note that in both cases above, the `onConfigurationChanged()` method will not be called since you are forcing a specific orientation up front.

Chapter 26: The `GridView` and `ExpandableHeightGridView`

Overview

In this chapter, we look at the `GridView` as well as the `ExpandableHeightGridView` class available via Neil Traft's response to a specific StackOverflow.com query (see stackoverflow.com/questions/4523609/grid-of-images-inside-scrollview/4536955#4536955).

The `GridView` Class

The `GridView` layout shows items in both a vertically and horizontally scrolling list (or "grid") which differs from a `ListView` which shows items vertically. Note that the intersection of a specific row with a specific column in the `GridView` - similar to a Microsoft Excel spreadsheet - is a *cell* (or *item*). Since the `GridView` class, unlike the `ListView` class, does **not** have an associated `android:entries=` attribute, cells must be added to the grid programmatically. The appearance of each cell is defined in an XML layout file located in the res\layout folder and is associated with the cells via the `LayoutInflator` class. Here are the usual steps to creating and populating a `GridView`:

1. Add a `GridView` view to your layout
2. Create an XML file (located in the res\layout folder) that defines the layout of each cell in the grid
3. Create a custom adapter subclassed from the `BaseAdapter` class which will be responsible for inflating the XML file defined in Step #2 above and filling in the appropriate text, image, etc.
4. Add code to the activity class (associated with the `GridView` in Step #1 above) that will instantiate the adapter class created in Step #3 and call the `setAdapter()` method for the `GridView` to populate it.

We go through each entry in turn below.

Step #1: Add a `GridView` view to the Layout

Using the Eclipse Graphical Layout, you can drag-and-drop a `GridView` view (located in the Composite section) to the GUI. Here is the XML that I used:

```
<RelativeLayout xmlns:android="http://schemas.android.com/apk/res/android"
                xmlns:tools="http://schemas.android.com/tools"
                android:layout_width="match_parent"
                android:layout_height="match_parent"
                tools:context=".GridViewActivity" >

 <GridView android:id="@+id/grid_id"
           android:layout_width="fill_parent"
           android:layout_height="wrap_content"
           android:numColumns="3" >
 </GridView>

</RelativeLayout>
```

Take note that you can set the number of columns up front using the `android:numColumns` attribute. Here I set it to 3.

Step #2: Define Each Cell's Layout

Based on your needs, define the layout of the cells. Note that this is generic for each cell. Here I define the cell to display an image as well as text directly below it:

```xml
<?xml version="1.0" encoding="utf-8"?>
<LinearLayout xmlns:android="http://schemas.android.com/apk/res/android"
            android:layout_width="wrap_content"
            android:layout_height="wrap_content"
            android:orientation="vertical" >

 <ImageView android:id="@+id/imgView_id"
            android:layout_width="wrap_content"
            android:layout_height="wrap_content"
            android:background="@drawable/ic_launcher"/>

 <TextView android:id="@+id/textView_id"
            android:layout_width="fill_parent"
            android:layout_height="wrap_content"
            android:gravity="center_horizontal" />

</LinearLayout>
```

It is this XML code which will be inflated within the adapter's `getView()` method.

Step #3: Create a Custom Adapter Subclassed from `BaseAdapter`

Based on the XML code defined for each cell (see Step #2 above), create a class subclassing the `BaseAdapter` class which overrides the `getView()` method. It is this method which inflates the XML defined in Step #2 as well as populates the entries such as the `ImageView` and the `TextView`. Here is the code we used:

```java
public class GridAdapter extends BaseAdapter {

 String[] textArray;
 Context contxt;

 public GridAdapter(String[] textArr, Context context) {

  textArray = textArr;
  contxt=context;
 }

 @Override
 public int getCount() {
  return textArray.length;
 }

 @Override
 public Object getItem(int arg0) {
  // TODO Auto-generated method stub
  return null;
 }

 @Override
 public long getItemId(int arg0) {
  // TODO Auto-generated method stub
  return 0;
 }
```

464

```
@Override
public View getView(int position, View convertView, ViewGroup parent) {

  //Create a new LayoutInflater
  LayoutInflater inflater = (LayoutInflater)
                       contxt.getSystemService(Context.LAYOUT_INFLATER_SERVICE);

  View gridView;
  gridView = null;
  convertView = null;// avoids recycling of grid view

  if (convertView == null) {
   gridView = new View(contxt);

    // inflating grid view item
    gridView = inflater.inflate(R.layout.grid_item, null);

    // set value into textview
    TextView textView = (TextView) gridView.findViewById(R.id.textView_id);
    textView.setText(textArray[position]);
  }

  return gridView;

 }

}
```

Step #4: Modify the Activity's Code

One place to populate the `GridView` is within the `onCreate()` method of your activity. For example, below we create an array as well as instantiate the `GridView` and populate it using the `setAdapter()` method:

```
public class MainActivity extends Activity {

 static final String[] numbers = new String[] { "one", "two", "three", "four",
    "five", "six","seven", "eight", "nine", "ten", "eleven", "twelve",
    "thirteen", "fourteen", "fifteen", "sixteen", "seventeen", "eighteen",
    "nineteen", "twenty", "twenty one" };

 GridView gridView;
 GridAdapter adapter;

 @Override
 public void onCreate(Bundle savedInstanceState) {
  super.onCreate(savedInstanceState);
  setContentView(R.layout.activity_main);

  gridView = (GridView) findViewById(R.id.grid_id);
  adapter = new  GridAdapter(numbers, this);
  gridView.setAdapter(adapter);
 }

}
```

Here is what this looks like when displayed on the device:

The `ExpandableHeightGridView` Class

Now, a `GridView` handles its own scrolling, so you don't have to put it in a `ScrollView`. In fact, Android prevents you from placing a `GridView` within a `ScrollView`. In my Android app, equityYo, I wanted my main screen (shown below, in part) to contain three individual GridViews each populated with specific items. Since there are many items, I needed scrolling to be enabled, but since you can't place `GridView`s within `ScrollView`s, I thought I was out of luck. However, I found a class created by Neil Traft that allows you to have multiple `GridView`s that scroll. This class is called `ExpandableHeightGridView` and is the focus of this section.

In equityYo, there are three separate sections entitled *Equity Statistics*, *External Websites* and *EquityYo! Information*. Within each section, there is a grid view

466

containing an image and text. In order to use this class, create a new Java source, called `ExpandableHeightGridView.java`, and place the following code within it:

```java
public class ExpandableHeightGridView extends GridView {

 boolean expanded = false;

 public ExpandableHeightGridView(Context context) {
  super(context);
 }

 public ExpandableHeightGridView(Context context, AttributeSet attrs) {
  super(context, attrs);
 }

 public ExpandableHeightGridView(Context context,
                                 AttributeSet attrs,
                                 int defStyle) {
  super(context, attrs, defStyle);
 }

 public boolean isExpanded() {
  return expanded;
 }

 @Override
 public void onMeasure(int widthMeasureSpec, int heightMeasureSpec) {
  // HACK! TAKE THAT ANDROID!
  if (isExpanded())
  {
   // Calculate entire height by providing a very large height hint.
   // But do not use the highest 2 bits of this integer; those are
   // reserved for the MeasureSpec mode.
   int expandSpec = MeasureSpec.makeMeasureSpec(Integer.MAX_VALUE >> 2,
                                                MeasureSpec.AT_MOST);
   super.onMeasure(widthMeasureSpec, expandSpec);

   ViewGroup.LayoutParams params = getLayoutParams();
   params.height = getMeasuredHeight();

  }
  else {
   super.onMeasure(widthMeasureSpec, heightMeasureSpec);
  }
 }

 public void setExpanded(boolean expanded) {
  this.expanded = expanded;
 }
}
```

Note that the `ExpandableHeightGridView` just extends the `GridView`.

Next, in my app, I created a class that will be used to hold all of the information for each cell (i.e., button) within each grid:

```java
private class cGridInfo {
 private String sGridLabel;
 private int iGridResourceImage;

 cGridInfo(int pPosition,String pLabel,int pResource) {
  sGridLabel=pLabel;
  iGridResourceImage=pResource;
 }
}
```

467

Next, I extended `BaseAdapter` to create `EquityYoGridAdapter` so that I can pass the instantiated class `cGridInfo` into it. Take note that, as usual, you modify the `getView()` code for your own purposes:

```
//Create an adapter used to fill in the grid.
private class EquityYoGridAdapter extends BaseAdapter {
 private Context context;
 private final cGridInfo[] GridInfo;

 EquityYoGridAdapter(Context pContext,cGridInfo[] pGridInfo) {
  context=pContext;
  GridInfo=pGridInfo;
 }

 public View getView(int position,View convertView,ViewGroup parent) {

  //Access the layout inflater system service.
  LayoutInflater inflater = (LayoutInflater)
                   context.getSystemService(Context.LAYOUT_INFLATER_SERVICE);

  View gridView;

  if (convertView == null) {

   //Create a new, empty view
   gridView = new View(context);

   //Set the empty view to the maingrid_contents layout
   gridView = inflater.inflate(R.layout.maingrid_contents, null);

   //Fill in the TextView based on the text located at position.
   TextView textView = (TextView) gridView.findViewById(R.id.grid_item_label);
   textView.setText(GridInfo[position].sGridLabel);

   //Fill in the ImageView based on the resource located at position.
   ImageView imageView = (ImageView) gridView.findViewById(R.id.grid_item_image);
   imageView.setImageResource(GridInfo[position].iGridResourceImage);

  } else {
   gridView = (View) convertView;
  }

  return gridView;
 }

 @Override
 public int getCount() {
  return GridInfo.length;
 }

 @Override
 public Object getItem(int position) {
  return null;
 }

 @Override
 public long getItemId(int position) {
  return 0;
 }

}
```

Note that you can just place both the `cGridInfo` and `EquityYoGridAdapter` classes within the `MainGridActivity` class for the activity instead of placing them within separate class files. Next, let's initialize the `cGridInfo` class:

```
ExpandableHeightGridView gridView1, //Statistics
                         gridView2, //External Websites
                         gridView3; //EquityYO! Users Guide, Video, etc.

//Populate the grid with the text and resource image number.
private cGridInfo GridInfo1[] = {
 new cGridInfo(0,"Stocks\n\n",R.drawable.dollar_currency_sign),
 new cGridInfo(1,"Closed-End\nFunds\n",R.drawable.euro_currency_sign),
 new cGridInfo(2,"Mutual\nFunds\n",R.drawable.sterling_pound_currency_sign),
 new cGridInfo(3,"Exchange\nTraded\nFunds",R.drawable.yen_currency_sign),
 new cGridInfo(4,"Market\nIndexes\n",R.drawable.chart)
};

private cGridInfo GridInfo2[] = {
 new cGridInfo(0,"Yahoo!\nFinance\nWebsite",R.drawable.world),
 new cGridInfo(1,"Google\nFinance\nWebsite",R.drawable.world),
 new cGridInfo(2,"NASDAQ\nWebsite\n",R.drawable.world),
 new cGridInfo(3,"NYSE\nWebsite\n    ",R.drawable.world),
 new cGridInfo(4,"SEC\nWebsite\n    ",R.drawable.world),
 new cGridInfo(6,"iShares\nWebsite\n          ",R.drawable.world),
 new cGridInfo(5,"CEF\nConnect\nWebsite",R.drawable.world)
};

private cGridInfo GridInfo3[] = {
 new cGridInfo(0,"EquityYO!\nUser's\nGuide",R.drawable.info),
 new cGridInfo(1,"EquityYO!\nManage\nPortfolio",R.drawable.briefcase),
 new cGridInfo(2,"EquityYO!\nSettings\n  ",R.drawable.settings),
 new cGridInfo(3,"EquityYO!\nMetadata\n  ",R.drawable.puzzle)
};
```

Finally, we set up each grid and associate an adapter to it:

```
//Access the grids.
gridView1 = (ExpandableHeightGridView) findViewById(R.id.maingrid1);
gridView2 = (ExpandableHeightGridView) findViewById(R.id.maingrid2);
gridView3 = (ExpandableHeightGridView) findViewById(R.id.maingrid3);

//Fill in the grid by using our class
gridView1.setAdapter(new EquityYoGridAdapter(this,GridInfo1));
gridView2.setAdapter(new EquityYoGridAdapter(this,GridInfo2));
gridView3.setAdapter(new EquityYoGridAdapter(this,GridInfo3));

//Turn setExpanded to true for all three grids.
gridView1.setExpanded(true);
gridView2.setExpanded(true);
gridView3.setExpanded(true);
```

Note that within the layout for the activity, three `ExpandableHeightGridView`s are placed at the appropriate places within the file. The code shown below is for `maingrid2`:

```
<com.sheepsqueezers.equityyo.ExpandableHeightGridView
    xmlns:android="http://schemas.android.com/apk/res/android"
    android:id="@+id/maingrid2"
    android:layout_width="fill_parent"
    android:layout_height="wrap_content"
    android:background="@drawable/color1"
    android:gravity="center_horizontal"
    android:horizontalSpacing="10dp"
    android:numColumns="3"
    android:stretchMode="columnWidth"
    android:verticalSpacing="10dp"
    android:padding="10dp"
    android:listSelector="@android:color/transparent" />
```

469

Note that no matter how many items you add to each grid, the entire screen will respond to scrolling. Very nice!

Chapter 27: Using Tabs in an Activity

Overview

In this chapter, we look into how to create tabs in an activity. We will show how to define the layout in XML as well as the code you must use to wire-up the tabs.

In order to use tabs, you must define an umbrella activity that will host the tabs as well as the activities to be displayed. This umbrella activity usually contains a `TabHost` as well as a `TabWidget` - which displays the tabs - and a `FrameLayout` - which displays the instantiated activity associated with the tab that was pressed.

Create the Umbrella Activity

For my Android app, equityYo, I created the following umbrella activity, called `activity_stocks.xml`:

```xml
<?xml version="1.0" encoding="utf-8"?>
<TabHost xmlns:android="http://schemas.android.com/apk/res/android"
        android:id="@android:id/tabhost"
        android:layout_width="fill_parent"
        android:layout_height="fill_parent">

    <LinearLayout android:orientation="vertical"
                android:layout_width="fill_parent"
                android:layout_height="fill_parent">

        <TabWidget android:id="@android:id/tabs"
                android:layout_width="fill_parent"
                android:layout_height="wrap_content" />

        <FrameLayout android:id="@android:id/tabcontent"
                android:layout_width="fill_parent"
                android:layout_height="fill_parent" />

    </LinearLayout>

</TabHost>
```

Note above that there is a `TabWidget`, called `tabs`, used to display the tabs, and a `FrameLayout`, called `tabcontent`, used to display the content associated with the pressed tab.

Create the Activity

Unlike other activities we've created in this book, we do not subclass the `Activity` class, but we subclass the `TabActivity` class. This will allow us to easily code the tabs. Here is some example code:

```java
public class StocksActivity extends TabActivity {

 @Override
 public void onCreate(Bundle savedInstanceState) {
  super.onCreate(savedInstanceState);
  setContentView(R.layout.activity_stocks);

  //Get the TabHost object
```

```
TabHost tabHost = getTabHost();

//Create the two tabs, one to hold the results of the Selector
// SlidingDrawer and the other to provide the details.
TabSpec tabspecStockSymbolList = tabHost.newTabSpec("Symbols");
TabSpec tabspecStockSymbolDetail = tabHost.newTabSpec("Details");

//Add text, icons and wire up the intents to the appropriate activities.
tabspecStockSymbolList.setIndicator("SYMBOLS",
                              getResources().getDrawable(R.drawable.pages));
Intent intentSymbolList = new Intent(this,StockSymbolListActivity.class);
tabspecStockSymbolList.setContent(intentSymbolList);

tabspecStockSymbolDetail.setIndicator("DETAILS",
                              getResources().getDrawable(R.drawable.page));
Intent intentSymbolDetail = new Intent(this,StockSymbolDetailActivity.class);
tabspecStockSymbolDetail.setContent(intentSymbolDetail);

//Add the tabs to the tab widget
tabHost.addTab(tabspecStockSymbolList);
tabHost.addTab(tabspecStockSymbolDetail);
tabHost.getTabWidget().setDividerDrawable(R.drawable.tabdivider);
tabHost.getTabWidget().setStripEnabled(true);
tabHost.getTabWidget().setLeftStripDrawable(R.drawable.tabstrip);
tabHost.getTabWidget().setRightStripDrawable(R.drawable.tabstrip);

//Initialize the colors for the tabs and set the padding a bit larger.
for(int i=0; i < tabHost.getTabWidget().getChildCount(); i++) {
 tabHost.getTabWidget().getChildAt(i).setBackgroundResource(
                                             R.drawable.tab_selector);
 tabHost.getTabWidget().getChildAt(i).setPadding(0, 0, 0, 0);
}

//Set the font color for the tabs.
View vwTabWidget;
TextView tvTabText;
for(int i=0; i < tabHost.getTabWidget().getChildCount(); i++) {
 vwTabWidget = tabHost.getTabWidget().getChildAt(i);
 tvTabText = (TextView) vwTabWidget.findViewById(android.R.id.title);
 tvTabText.setTextSize(12);
 tvTabText.setTypeface(null, Typeface.BOLD_ITALIC);
 if (i==0) {
  tvTabText.setTextColor(Color.parseColor("#FFFFFFFF"));
 }
 else if (i==1) {
  tvTabText.setTextColor(Color.parseColor("#FF212121"));
 }
}

//Set up a listener for the Details tab
getTabHost().setOnTabChangedListener(new OnTabChangeListener() {

 @Override
 public void onTabChanged(String tabId) {

  int i = getTabHost().getCurrentTab();
  if (i == 0) {
    //Current tab is the tab on the left (0).
    ( (TextView) ( (View) getTabHost().getTabWidget().getChildAt(0) )
                          .findViewById(android.R.id.title))
                          .setTextColor(Color.parseColor("#FFFFFFFF"));
    ( (TextView) ( (View) getTabHost().getTabWidget().getChildAt(1) )
                          .findViewById(android.R.id.title))
                          .setTextColor(Color.parseColor("#FF212121"));
  }
  else if (i == 1) {

   if (StocksActivity.oEquityYoSQLCursor != null) {

    if (StocksActivity.oEquityYoSQLCursor.getCount() > 0) {
```

```
                //Current tab is the tab on the right (1).
                ( (TextView) ( (View) getTabHost().getTabWidget().getChildAt(0) )
                                    .findViewById(android.R.id.title))
                                .setTextColor(Color.parseColor("#FF212121"));
                ( (TextView) ( (View) getTabHost().getTabWidget().getChildAt(1) )
                                    .findViewById(android.R.id.title))
                                .setTextColor(Color.parseColor("#FFFFFFFF"));

             }
             else {
              getTabHost().setCurrentTab(0);
              Toast.makeText(getApplicationContext(),
                        "Use the fly-out window to select desired data first.",
                        Toast.LENGTH_SHORT).show();
             }


           }
           else {
            getTabHost().setCurrentTab(0);
            Toast.makeText(getApplicationContext(),
                      "Use the fly-out window to select desired data first.",
                      Toast.LENGTH_SHORT).show();
           }
         }
        }
      });
   }
```

Take note of the intents in the code above. These are used to inflate the appropriate activity when a tab is clicked.

Take note that there can be display problems with the `TabWidget` as it is coded. Here is a work-around to be used instead of `TabWidget`. Create a blank Java class file called `cTabWidgetFix.java` and add the following code to it:

```
public class cTabWidgetFix extends TabWidget {

 private final View dummy;

 public cTabWidgetFix(Context context) {
  super(context);
  dummy = new View(context);
 }

 public cTabWidgetFix(Context context, AttributeSet attrs) {
  super(context, attrs);
  dummy = new View(context);
 }

 public cTabWidgetFix(Context context, AttributeSet attrs, int defStyle) {
  super(context, attrs, defStyle);
  dummy = new View(context);
 }

 @Override
 public View getChildTabViewAt(int i) {

  if (i < 0 || i >= getChildCount()) {
   return dummy;
  }

  return super.getChildTabViewAt(i);
 }

 @Override
```

```
public View getChildAt(int i) {

  if (i < 0 || i >= getChildCount()) {
   return dummy;
  }

  return super.getChildAt(i);
 }

}
```

Now, in the umbrella XML file, use the following code (modified for your package) instead of the `TabWidget` XML shown above:

```
<com.sheepsqueezers.equityyo.cTabWidgetFix
  xmlns:android="http://schemas.android.com/apk/res/android"
  android:id="@android:id/tabs"
  android:layout_width="fill_parent"
  android:layout_height="wrap_content" />
```

Chapter 28: Using the `SlidingDrawer`

Overview

In this chapter, we describe how to use a `SlidingDrawer` within an activity. This is a nice feature allowing an activity to slide out from the left, right, top or bottom of the screen. This feature is used within my Android app, equityYo, to allow the user to select subsetting criteria for stock symbols to be returned while allowing the user to view a `ListView` of those symbols. As you see below, the `SlidingDrawer` is displayed half-opened on the right, while you can see half of the `ListView` on the left. Along with the `SlidingDrawer`, you can define a drawable to be used as the handle for the `SlidingDrawer`. In the image below, the arrow pointing to the right is the handle.

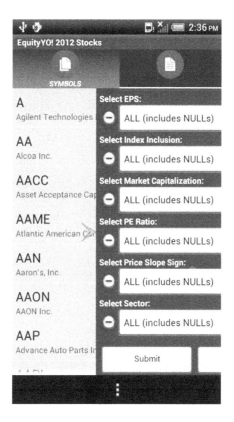

It may seem strange, but the XML definition of the `SlidingDrawer` is embedded in the same XML resource file as the definition of the `ListView` for the stock symbols. We explore this in the next section.

Defining the SlidingDrawer

In order to use a `SlidingDrawer`, you must define it within another XML resource layout file. One problem is deciding in which XML resource layout file you will be defining the `SlidingDrawer`. In my Android app, equityYo, since the user selects criteria used to populate the `ListView` of stock symbols, it made sense to me to place the `SlidingDrawer` in the same XML resource layout file that contained this `ListView`:

```
<RelativeLayout xmlns:android="http://schemas.android.com/apk/res/android"
                android:id="@+id/stock_symbol_list_layout"
```

```
                    android:layout_width="match_parent"
                    android:layout_height="match_parent"
                    android:gravity="center_vertical"
                    android:orientation="vertical"
                    android:background="@drawable/color4" >

    <ListView xmlns:android="http://schemas.android.com/apk/res/android"
              android:id="@+id/lvSymbols"
              android:layout_width="match_parent"
              android:layout_height="match_parent">
    </ListView>

    <SlidingDrawer android:id="@+id/SlidingDrawer"
                    android:layout_width="match_parent"
                    android:layout_height="match_parent"
                    android:content="@+id/contentLayout"
                    android:handle="@+id/slideButton"
                    android:orientation="horizontal"
                    android:padding="10dip" >

        <Button android:id="@+id/slideButton"
                android:layout_width="wrap_content"
                android:layout_height="wrap_content"
                android:background="@drawable/slidingdrawer_arrow_open3" >
        </Button>

        <ScrollView xmlns:android="http://schemas.android.com/apk/res/android"
                    android:id="@+id/contentLayout"
                    android:background="@drawable/color1"
                    android:layout_width="fill_parent"
                    android:layout_height="fill_parent" >

            <!-- Include the radio button group for the criteria selector  -->
            <include android:id="@+id/layout_criteria_selection"
                    layout="@layout/criteria_selection_long_stock" />

        </ScrollView>

    </SlidingDrawer>

</RelativeLayout>
```

Note that in the code above, within the `SlidingDrawer` XML, I define a `Button` to indicate the drawer handle (the arrow shown in the image above). Also, I include a `ScrollView` which will hold the selection criteria spinners (brought in using the `<include>`, discussed in the next chapter). If you don't have anything within `<SlidingDrawer>` and `</SlidingDrawer>`, you have a very boring display.

Setting Up Open/Close Listeners for the SlidingDrawer

Now, as mentioned above, a `Button` is used to display the handle for the `SlidingDrawer`. It's up to you to code the listeners for both the open and close events for the `SlidingDrawer` as well as changing the drawable for the `Button` (if desired). In my Android app, equityYo, a left-pointing arrow appears when the `SlidingDrawer` is closed, and a right-pointing arrow appears when the `SlidingDrawer` is opened. (Note that my `SlidingDrawer` opens from right to left and closes from left to right).

Here is the code I used (in the `onCreate()` method) to set up the listeners as well as the change in the handle:

476

```
slideButton = (Button) findViewById(R.id.slideButton); //Button
slidingDrawer = (SlidingDrawer) findViewById(R.id.SlidingDrawer); //SlidingDrawer

//Set up listeners for the opening and closing of the sliding drawer.
//These two listeners will change the drawer icon displayed.
slidingDrawer.setOnDrawerOpenListener(new OnDrawerOpenListener() {

 public void onDrawerOpened() {

   //change the button
   slideButton.setBackgroundResource(R.drawable.slidingdrawer_arrow_close3);

 }

});

slidingDrawer.setOnDrawerCloseListener(new OnDrawerCloseListener() {

 public void onDrawerClosed() {

   //change the button
   slideButton.setBackgroundResource(R.drawable.slidingdrawer_arrow_open3);

 }

});
```

Now, the opening and closing of the `SlidingDrawer` is handled for you, but you are responsible for setting and wiring up any views that you may want displayed within the `SlidingDrawer`.

Chapter 29: Using <include>

Overview

In this chapter, we take a look into the `<include>` XML tag and how to code with it. There are many comments about using `<include>` for things like footers to a display, but I find that it is much more flexible than that.

For example, in my Android app, equityYo, I use `<include>` to populate the `SlidingDrawer` layout based on the user's choice of selection criteria: Stats (Short), Stats(Long), LookUp (Symbol), Search (Name) and Search (Summary). In the image on the left, you see a series of radio buttons along the top of the `SlidingDrawer` as well as a list of spinners used to subsetting the data. In the image on the right, the user has clicked the Search (Name) radio button and the `SlidingDrawer` has a new display. All five of these radio buttons make use of the `<include>`. As a matter of fact, the radio buttons themselves are located in a separate XML resource file and are included at the appropriate location.

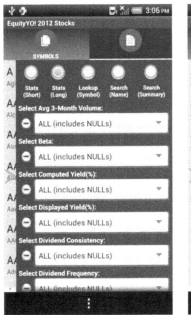 

For example, below is the default XML layout file associate with the Stats (Long) selection.

```
<?xml version="1.0" encoding="utf-8"?>
<LinearLayout xmlns:android="http://schemas.android.com/apk/res/android"
              xmlns:tools="http://schemas.android.com/tools"
              android:id="@+id/llLongList"
              android:layout_width="fill_parent"
              android:orientation="vertical"
              android:gravity="top|left"
              android:paddingTop="0dip"
              android:paddingLeft="5dip"
              android:paddingRight="5dip"
              android:paddingBottom="0dip"
              android:background="@drawable/color1"
              android:layout_height="wrap_content">
```

478

```xml
<!-- Include the radio button group for the criteria selector  -->
<include android:id="@+id/layout_criteria_selector"
        layout="@layout/criteria_selector" />

<TextView
    android:layout_width="wrap_content"
    android:layout_height="wrap_content"
    android:text="@string/sSTOCK_Average3MonthVolume"
    android:textColor="#FFFFFFFF"
    android:textStyle="bold" />

<LinearLayout xmlns:android="http://schemas.android.com/apk/res/android"
            android:layout_width="match_parent"
            android:layout_height="wrap_content"
            android:orientation="horizontal">
  <ImageView
    android:id="@+id/ivSTOCK_Average3MonthVolume"
    android:layout_width="wrap_content"
    android:layout_height="wrap_content"
    android:contentDescription="@null"
    android:layout_gravity="center_vertical|left"
    android:src="@drawable/sortorderselector" />
  <Spinner android:id="@+id/spinnerSTOCK_Average3MonthVolume"
        android:layout_width="match_parent"
        android:layout_height="wrap_content"
        android:entries="@array/aSTOCK_Average3MonthVolume"
        android:prompt="@string/sSTOCK_Average3MonthVolume" >
  </Spinner>
</LinearLayout>

<TextView
    android:layout_width="wrap_content"
    android:layout_height="wrap_content"
    android:text="@string/sSTOCK_Beta"
    android:textColor="#FFFFFFFF"
    android:textStyle="bold" />
<LinearLayout xmlns:android="http://schemas.android.com/apk/res/android"
            android:layout_width="match_parent"
            android:layout_height="wrap_content"
            android:orientation="horizontal">
  <ImageView
    android:id="@+id/ivSTOCK_Beta"
    android:layout_width="wrap_content"
    android:layout_height="wrap_content"
    android:contentDescription="@null"
    android:layout_gravity="center_vertical|left"
    android:src="@drawable/sortorderselector" />
  <Spinner android:id="@+id/spinnerSTOCK_Beta"
        android:layout_width="match_parent"
        android:layout_height="wrap_content"
        android:entries="@array/aSTOCK_Beta"
        android:prompt="@string/sSTOCK_Beta" >
  </Spinner>
</LinearLayout>

<TextView
    android:layout_width="wrap_content"
    android:layout_height="wrap_content"
    android:text="@string/sSTOCK_ComputedYield"
    android:textColor="#FFFFFFFF"
    android:textStyle="bold" />
<LinearLayout xmlns:android="http://schemas.android.com/apk/res/android"
            android:layout_width="match_parent"
            android:layout_height="wrap_content"
            android:orientation="horizontal">
  <ImageView
    android:id="@+id/ivSTOCK_ComputedYield"
    android:layout_width="wrap_content"
    android:layout_height="wrap_content"
    android:contentDescription="@null"
```

```xml
        android:layout_gravity="center_vertical|left"
        android:src="@drawable/sortorderselector" />
    <Spinner android:id="@+id/spinnerSTOCK_ComputedYield"
        android:layout_width="match_parent"
        android:layout_height="wrap_content"
        android:entries="@array/aSTOCK_ComputedYield"
        android:prompt="@string/sSTOCK_ComputedYield" >
    </Spinner>
</LinearLayout>

<TextView
    android:layout_width="wrap_content"
    android:layout_height="wrap_content"
    android:text="@string/sSTOCK_DisplayedYield"
    android:textColor="#FFFFFFFF"
    android:textStyle="bold" />
<LinearLayout xmlns:android="http://schemas.android.com/apk/res/android"
            android:layout_width="match_parent"
            android:layout_height="wrap_content"
            android:orientation="horizontal">
 <ImageView
    android:id="@+id/ivSTOCK_DisplayedYield"
    android:layout_width="wrap_content"
    android:layout_height="wrap_content"
    android:contentDescription="@null"
    android:layout_gravity="center_vertical|left"
    android:src="@drawable/sortorderselector" />
 <Spinner android:id="@+id/spinnerSTOCK_DisplayedYield"
        android:layout_width="match_parent"
        android:layout_height="wrap_content"
        android:entries="@array/aSTOCK_DisplayedYield"
        android:prompt="@string/sSTOCK_DisplayedYield" >
 </Spinner>
</LinearLayout>

<TextView
    android:layout_width="wrap_content"
    android:layout_height="wrap_content"
    android:text="@string/sSTOCK_DividendConsistency"
    android:textColor="#FFFFFFFF"
    android:textStyle="bold" />
<LinearLayout xmlns:android="http://schemas.android.com/apk/res/android"
            android:layout_width="match_parent"
            android:layout_height="wrap_content"
            android:orientation="horizontal">
 <ImageView
    android:id="@+id/ivSTOCK_DividendConsistency"
    android:layout_width="wrap_content"
    android:layout_height="wrap_content"
    android:contentDescription="@null"
    android:layout_gravity="center_vertical|left"
    android:src="@drawable/sortorderselector" />
 <Spinner android:id="@+id/spinnerSTOCK_DividendConsistency"
        android:layout_width="match_parent"
        android:layout_height="wrap_content"
        android:entries="@array/aSTOCK_DividendConsistency"
        android:prompt="@string/sSTOCK_DividendConsistency" >
 </Spinner>
</LinearLayout>

<TextView
    android:layout_width="wrap_content"
    android:layout_height="wrap_content"
    android:text="@string/sSTOCK_DividendFrequency"
    android:textColor="#FFFFFFFF"
    android:textStyle="bold" />
<LinearLayout xmlns:android="http://schemas.android.com/apk/res/android"
            android:layout_width="match_parent"
            android:layout_height="wrap_content"
            android:orientation="horizontal">
```

```xml
  <ImageView
    android:id="@+id/ivSTOCK_DividendFrequency"
    android:layout_width="wrap_content"
    android:layout_height="wrap_content"
    android:contentDescription="@null"
    android:layout_gravity="center_vertical|left"
    android:src="@drawable/sortorderselector" />
<Spinner android:id="@+id/spinnerSTOCK_DividendFrequency"
      android:layout_width="match_parent"
      android:layout_height="wrap_content"
      android:entries="@array/aSTOCK_DividendFrequency"
      android:prompt="@string/sSTOCK_DividendFrequency" >
</Spinner>
</LinearLayout>

<TextView
    android:layout_width="wrap_content"
    android:layout_height="wrap_content"
    android:text="@string/sSTOCK_EPS"
    android:textColor="#FFFFFFFF"
    android:textStyle="bold" />
<LinearLayout xmlns:android="http://schemas.android.com/apk/res/android"
            android:layout_width="match_parent"
            android:layout_height="wrap_content"
            android:orientation="horizontal">
  <ImageView
    android:id="@+id/ivSTOCK_EPS"
    android:layout_width="wrap_content"
    android:layout_height="wrap_content"
    android:contentDescription="@null"
    android:layout_gravity="center_vertical|left"
    android:src="@drawable/sortorderselector" />
<Spinner android:id="@+id/spinnerSTOCK_EPS"
      android:layout_width="match_parent"
      android:layout_height="wrap_content"
      android:entries="@array/aSTOCK_EPS"
      android:prompt="@string/sSTOCK_EPS" >
</Spinner>
</LinearLayout>

<TextView
    android:layout_width="wrap_content"
    android:layout_height="wrap_content"
    android:text="@string/sSTOCK_INDEXINCLUSION"
    android:textColor="#FFFFFFFF"
    android:textStyle="bold" />
<LinearLayout xmlns:android="http://schemas.android.com/apk/res/android"
            android:layout_width="match_parent"
            android:layout_height="wrap_content"
            android:orientation="horizontal">
  <ImageView
    android:id="@+id/ivSTOCK_INDEXINCLUSION"
    android:layout_width="wrap_content"
    android:layout_height="wrap_content"
    android:contentDescription="@null"
    android:layout_gravity="center_vertical|left"
    android:src="@drawable/sortorderselector" />
<Spinner android:id="@+id/spinnerSTOCK_INDEXINCLUSION"
      android:layout_width="match_parent"
      android:layout_height="wrap_content"
      android:entries="@array/aSTOCK_INDEXINCLUSION"
      android:prompt="@string/sSTOCK_INDEXINCLUSION" >
</Spinner>
</LinearLayout>

<TextView
    android:layout_width="wrap_content"
    android:layout_height="wrap_content"
    android:text="@string/sSTOCK_MktCapNetAssets"
    android:textColor="#FFFFFFFF"
```

```xml
                android:textStyle="bold" />
<LinearLayout xmlns:android="http://schemas.android.com/apk/res/android"
                android:layout_width="match_parent"
                android:layout_height="wrap_content"
                android:orientation="horizontal">
 <ImageView
    android:id="@+id/ivSTOCK_MktCapNetAssets"
    android:layout_width="wrap_content"
    android:layout_height="wrap_content"
    android:contentDescription="@null"
    android:layout_gravity="center_vertical|left"
    android:src="@drawable/sortorderselector" />
 <Spinner android:id="@+id/spinnerSTOCK_MktCapNetAssets"
      android:layout_width="match_parent"
      android:layout_height="wrap_content"
      android:entries="@array/aSTOCK_MktCapNetAssets"
      android:prompt="@string/sSTOCK_MktCapNetAssets" >
 </Spinner>
</LinearLayout>

<TextView
    android:layout_width="wrap_content"
    android:layout_height="wrap_content"
    android:text="@string/sSTOCK_PERatio"
    android:textColor="#FFFFFFFF"
    android:textStyle="bold" />
<LinearLayout xmlns:android="http://schemas.android.com/apk/res/android"
                android:layout_width="match_parent"
                android:layout_height="wrap_content"
                android:orientation="horizontal">
 <ImageView
    android:id="@+id/ivSTOCK_PERatio"
    android:layout_width="wrap_content"
    android:layout_height="wrap_content"
    android:contentDescription="@null"
    android:layout_gravity="center_vertical|left"
    android:src="@drawable/sortorderselector" />
 <Spinner android:id="@+id/spinnerSTOCK_PERatio"
      android:layout_width="match_parent"
      android:layout_height="wrap_content"
      android:entries="@array/aSTOCK_PERatio"
      android:prompt="@string/sSTOCK_PERatio" >
 </Spinner>
</LinearLayout>

<TextView
    android:layout_width="wrap_content"
    android:layout_height="wrap_content"
    android:text="@string/sSTOCK_PriceSlopeSign"
    android:textColor="#FFFFFFFF"
    android:textStyle="bold" />
 <LinearLayout xmlns:android="http://schemas.android.com/apk/res/android"
                android:layout_width="match_parent"
                android:layout_height="wrap_content"
                android:orientation="horizontal">
  <ImageView
    android:id="@+id/ivSTOCK_PriceSlopeSign"
    android:layout_width="wrap_content"
    android:layout_height="wrap_content"
    android:contentDescription="@null"
    android:layout_gravity="center_vertical|left"
    android:src="@drawable/sortorderselector" />
  <Spinner android:id="@+id/spinnerSTOCK_PriceSlopeSign"
      android:layout_width="match_parent"
      android:layout_height="wrap_content"
      android:entries="@array/aSTOCK_PriceSlopeSign"
      android:prompt="@string/sSTOCK_PriceSlopeSign" >
  </Spinner>
 </LinearLayout>
```

```
            <TextView
              android:layout_width="wrap_content"
              android:layout_height="wrap_content"
              android:text="@string/sSTOCK_Sector"
              android:textColor="#FFFFFFFF"
              android:textStyle="bold" />
            <LinearLayout xmlns:android="http://schemas.android.com/apk/res/android"
                          android:layout_width="match_parent"
                          android:layout_height="wrap_content"
                          android:orientation="horizontal">
          <ImageView
            android:id="@+id/ivSTOCK_Sector"
            android:layout_width="wrap_content"
            android:layout_height="wrap_content"
            android:contentDescription="@null"
            android:layout_gravity="center_vertical|left"
            android:src="@drawable/sortorderselector" />
          <Spinner android:id="@+id/spinnerSTOCK_Sector"
              android:layout_width="match_parent"
              android:layout_height="wrap_content"
              android:entries="@array/aSTOCK_Sector"
              android:prompt="@string/sSTOCK_Sector" >
          </Spinner>
          </LinearLayout>

    <!-- Include the submit/reset buttons  -->
    <include layout="@layout/submit_reset_buttons" />

</LinearLayout>
```

You'll note that both the radio buttons as well as the the Submit/Reset buttons are in separate XML resource files and are included using the `<include>`. For example, here is the XML for the radio buttons (located in `criteria_selector.xml`):

```
<?xml version="1.0" encoding="utf-8"?>
<LinearLayout xmlns:android="http://schemas.android.com/apk/res/android"
    android:layout_width="fill_parent"
    android:layout_height="wrap_content"
    android:orientation="horizontal"
    android:paddingBottom="10dip"
    android:paddingTop="0dip"
    android:layout_gravity="fill_horizontal">

 <RadioGroup
        android:id="@+id/rgCriteriaSelector"
        android:layout_width="fill_parent"
        android:layout_height="wrap_content"
        android:orientation="horizontal">

     <RadioButton
         android:id="@+id/rbSelectionShort"
         android:button="@null"
         android:background="@null"
         android:checked="false"
         android:drawableTop="@android:drawable/btn_radio"
         android:lines="2"
         android:text="Stats\n(Short)"
         android:textStyle="bold"
         android:textSize="12dip"
         android:textColor="#FFFFFFFF"
         android:layout_weight="1"
         android:gravity="center"
         android:tag="SHORT"/>

     <RadioButton
         android:id="@+id/rbSelectionLong"
```

```
        android:button="@null"
        android:background="@null"
        android:checked="true"
        android:drawableTop="@android:drawable/btn_radio"
        android:lines="2"
        android:text="Stats\n(Long)"
        android:textStyle="bold"
        android:textSize="12dip"
        android:textColor="#FFFFFFFF"
        android:layout_weight="1"
        android:gravity="center"
        android:tag="LONG" />

    <RadioButton
        android:id="@+id/rbSelectionSymbol"
        android:button="@null"
        android:background="@null"
        android:checked="false"
        android:drawableTop="@android:drawable/btn_radio"
        android:lines="2"
        android:text="Lookup\n(Symbol)"
        android:textStyle="bold"
        android:textSize="12dip"
        android:textColor="#FFFFFFFF"
        android:layout_weight="1"
        android:gravity="center"
        android:tag="SYMBOL"/>

    <RadioButton
        android:id="@+id/rbSelectionName"
        android:button="@null"
        android:background="@null"
        android:checked="false"
        android:drawableTop="@android:drawable/btn_radio"
        android:lines="2"
        android:text="Search\n(Name)"
        android:textStyle="bold"
        android:textSize="12dip"
        android:textColor="#FFFFFFFF"
        android:layout_weight="1"
        android:gravity="center"
        android:tag="NAME" />

    <RadioButton
        android:id="@+id/rbSelectionInfo"
        android:button="@null"
        android:background="@null"
        android:checked="false"
        android:drawableTop="@android:drawable/btn_radio"
        android:lines="2"
        android:text="Search\n(Summary)"
        android:textStyle="bold"
        android:textSize="12dip"
        android:textColor="#FFFFFFFF"
        android:layout_weight="1"
        android:gravity="center"
        android:tag="INFO" />
</RadioGroup>


</LinearLayout>
```

Take note of the attribute `android:tag=`. This will be used later on when we program with the `<include>` tag.

Also, take note of the attribute `android:layout_weight`. This is VERY useful to know! You can think of this attribute as a percentage distribution value for each view; that is, if all of the values are set to "1", then the distribution width of the views will be proportionally the same. For example, if you have five views all set with `android:layout_weight="1"`, then each view occupies 1/5 of the screen width. If all of the values are set to "1", except one is set to "2", then the view set to "2" will take up slightly more width than the rest of the views (2/6).

Using `<include>`

In order to use `<include>`, the file you are including must be a valid XML resource file that can stand on its own; that is, it must start with `<LinearLayout>` or other XML layout tag. To include a layout file, you use the `layout=` attribute specifying the layout located in the res\layout folder:

```
<include layout="@layout/submit_reset_buttons" />
```

The code above includes the layout located in the `submit_reset_buttons.xml` file which looks like this:

```xml
<?xml version="1.0" encoding="utf-8"?>
<LinearLayout xmlns:android="http://schemas.android.com/apk/res/android"
    android:layout_width="fill_parent"
    android:layout_height="wrap_content"
    android:gravity="center_vertical"
    android:orientation="horizontal"
    android:paddingTop="10dp">

  <Button android:id="@+id/btnFetch"
          android:layout_width="wrap_content"
          android:layout_height="wrap_content"
          android:layout_margin="2dp"
          android:layout_gravity="center_vertical|left"
          android:layout_weight="1.00"
          android:text="Submit"
          android:onClick="Fetch">
  </Button>
  <Button android:id="@+id/btnReset"
          android:layout_width="wrap_content"
          android:layout_height="wrap_content"
          android:layout_margin="2dp"
          android:layout_gravity="center_vertical|right"
          android:layout_weight="1.00"
          android:text="Reset"
          android:onClick="Reset">
  </Button>

</LinearLayout>
```

Coding with `<include>`

You can programmatically modify the layout specified on the `<include>` tag by adding the `android:id=` attribute. For example, the following `<include>` tag is used within the `SlidingDrawer` and it brings in the XML file `criteria_selection_long_stock.xml` which contains the long list of stats the user can subset by.

```
<include android:id="@+id/layout_criteria_selection"
         layout="@layout/criteria_selection_long_stock" />
```

When a user clicks on one of the other radio buttons (say, the short list of stats), we want the layout to change accordingly. Recall above that we used the `android:tag=` attribute on each of our five radio buttons (see the end of the Overview). In order to intercept the clicks of the RadioButtons, we have to set up an `onCheckedChangedListener` for the `RadioGroup` itself:

```
//Set up a listener for the radio group @+id/rgCriteriaSelector
RadioGroup oRGCS = (RadioGroup) findViewById(R.id.rgCriteriaSelector);

OnCheckedChangeListener listener = new RadioGroup.OnCheckedChangeListener() {
 public void onCheckedChanged(RadioGroup rGroup, int checkedId) {

  //Modify the sSelectionCriteria based on the radio button clicked.
  RadioButton checkedRadioButton = (RadioButton)rGroup.findViewById(checkedId);
  String sRBTag = checkedRadioButton.getTag().toString();
  sSelectionCriteria = sRBTag;
  symbolList.sSelectionCriteria = sSelectionCriteria;
  symbolList.onCheckedChanged(rGroup, checkedId);

 }

};
oRGCS.setOnCheckedChangeListener(listener);
```

Note that I have place the `onCheckedChanged()` method within the class associated with `symbolList`. You don't have to do that. The code that is called to modify the layout of the `SlidingDrawer` based on a click of a `RadioButton` is as follows:

```
@Override
public void onCheckedChanged(RadioGroup rGroup, int checkedId) {

 //Get Activity from the context.
 Activity oACT = (Activity) context;

 // This will get the radiobutton that has changed in its check state
 RadioButton checkedRadioButton = (RadioButton)rGroup.findViewById(checkedId);

 //Get the tag from the radio button
 String sRBTag = checkedRadioButton.getTag().toString();

 //Based on the tag, replace the current subsetting criteria
 //with the desired subsetting criteria.
 LayoutInflater inflater = oACT.getLayoutInflater();
 LinearLayout ll = (LinearLayout)
                        oACT.findViewById(R.id.layout_criteria_selection);

 if (sRBTag.contentEquals("SHORT")) {

  //Remove all of the views within the layout
  ll.removeAllViews();

   //Add in the views from the new layout.
   ll.addView(inflater.inflate(R.layout.criteria_selection_short_stock, null));

...and so on...
```

As you see above, we initially retrieve the `Activity` from the `context`. This will allow use the use the `findViewById()` method without tearing our hair out. This is very useful especially if you need to use `findViewById()` and have passed in an appropriate `context` to your class.

We then retrieve the particular `RadioButton` that was clicked and then pull in its tag to let us know which layout to replace the current layout with.

Next, we inflate the layout specified on the `<include>` tag with the id of `layout_criteria_selection`. By default, this is the long list of stats. This will then be emptied (using `removeAllViews`) and then populated with the appropriate layout (using `addView`):

```
//Remove all of the views within the layout
ll.removeAllViews();

//Add in the views from the new layout.
ll.addView(inflater.inflate(R.layout.criteria_selection_short_stock, null));
```

At this point, the currently displayed layout disappears and the desired new layout appears in its place.

Chapter 30: Introduction to Fragments

Overview

Throughout the course of the book, we have seen a fair amount of Android activities and views, been introduced to the `<include>` XML tag, created a `GridView` view component called `ExpandableHeightGridView`, and more. As far as we are concerned, life is good. What could possibly go wrong?

Take a look at the image below, the flight deck of an Airbus A380 (from Wikipedia).

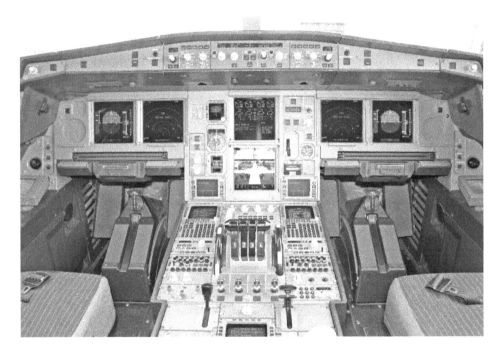

If looked at purely from a computer programming perspective, you have two choices: create one large computer program to handle all of the controls, or create separate code components for each of the controls allowing for communication between them.

If you decide to create a single monolithic computer program to handle all of the controls, good luck to you!

On the other hand, you can create individual code components, one for the primary flight display, one for the engine status display, one for the navigation display, and so on. Then, link up all of these individual components so that they communicate between themselves sharing important information.

Clearly, the second option would be best. But, I'm not telling you anything you don't already know. So, what about the following image of a key performance indicators (KPIs) dashboard from inetSoft being displayed on a tablet?

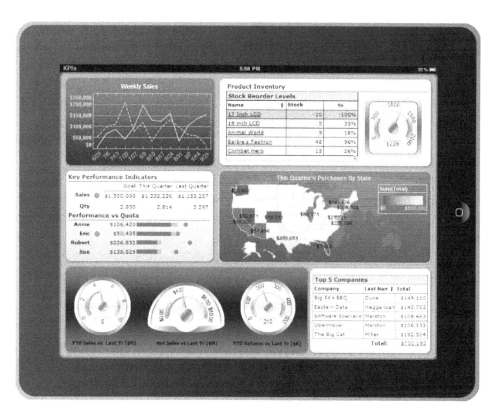

Would you approach the programming of the dashboard shown above in a monolithic way, or would you create one component for each of the individual displays? Clearly, the answer is the same as for the A380 flight deck controls: create individual components and allow them to communicate, if necessary.

But, up to now, we've seen that one display is equivalent to one activity. That is, the inflation of an activity takes up the entire screen whether it is a tablet or a smartphone. Sure, you can add as many views to an activity and have a crowded display, but views are not activities, they don't have the functionality of an activity, they don't have the lifecycle of an activity, and so on.

This is where fragments come in. A fragment can be considered as a sub-activity; that is, an activity within a parent activity and it is the job of each fragment to create its own view. You can have several fragments within the parent activity so that the display can be rather complex. You can even arrange your app to display its layout one way when in portrait mode and another way when in landscape mode.

Fragments, just like activities, have their own lifecycle, their own `onCreate()` method, their own `onPause()` method, their own `onDestroy()` method, and so on. Note that fragments have an additional method, `onCreateView()`, which is used to inflate the fragment's layout and is similar to using `onCreate()` to inflate an activity's layout. Needlesstosay, `onCreateView()` is extremely important!

Fragments, unlike activities, must be a part of a `ViewGroup`. You can add, replace, and remove fragments from a `ViewGroup` at will via code using the `FragmentManager` or you can use the `<fragment>` XML tag to add one or more fragments to a display. The act of adding, replacing or removing fragments happens within a fragment *transaction* and the change to the activity won't occur

489

until you *commit* the transaction. This is similar to updating data in a database table: the changes won't be seen until you issue a commit.

Since fragments have their own lifecycle and are mandated to be part of an activity, fragments are affected by the lifecycle of the containing activity itself. To put it another way, when an `Activity` is paused, all of the fragments contained within that `Activity` are paused; when an `Activity` is destroyed, all of the fragments contained within that `Activity` are destroyed; and so on.

Since you are allowed to programmatically add, replace and remove fragments within an activity, you can tell Android to place the old copy on the *back stack* before replacing it with the new fragment(s). This will allow the user of your application to press the back button to see the previous incarnation(s) of your display. You've probably see this type of action in apps such as the Twitter app.

According to the Android documentation:

> *Android introduced fragments in Android 3.0 (API level 11), primarily to support more dynamic and flexible UI designs on larger screens, such as tablets. Because a tablet's screen is much larger than that of a handset, there's more room to combine and interchange UI components. Fragments allow such designs without the need for you to manage complex changes to the view hierarchy. By dividing the layout of an activity into fragments, you become able to modify the activity's appearance at runtime and preserve those changes in a back stack that's managed by the activity.*

> *For example, a news application can use one fragment to show a list of articles on the left and another fragment to display an article on the right— both fragments appear in one activity, side by side, and each fragment has its own set of lifecycle callback methods and handle their own user input events. Thus, instead of using one activity to select an article and another activity to read the article, the user can select an article and read it all within the same activity, as illustrated in the tablet layout in the figure below.*

> *You should design each fragment as a modular and reusable activity component. That is, because each fragment defines its own layout and its own behavior with its own lifecycle callbacks, you can include one fragment in multiple activities, so you should design for reuse and avoid directly manipulating one fragment from another fragment. This is especially important because a modular fragment allows you to change your fragment combinations for different screen sizes. When designing your application to support both tablets and handsets, you can reuse your fragments in different layout configurations to optimize the user experience based on the available screen space. For example, on a handset, it might be necessary to separate fragments to provide a single-pane UI when more than one cannot fit within the same activity.*

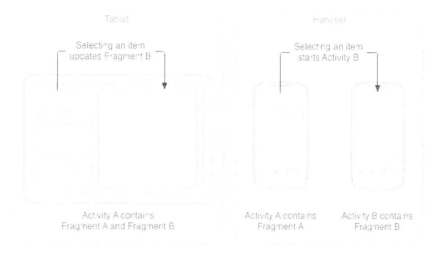

For example—to continue with the news application example—the application can embed two fragments in Activity A, when running on a tablet-sized device. However, on a handset-sized screen, there's not enough room for both fragments, so Activity A includes only the fragment for the list of articles, and when the user selects an article, it starts Activity B, which includes the second fragment to read the article. Thus, the application supports both tablets and handsets by reusing fragments in different combinations, as illustrated in the figure above.

Fragment Class and Android Support Libraries

As mentioned above in the quote from the Android documentation, fragments were introduced in Android 3.0 (API Level 11/Honeycomb). In order to support fragments in prior versions, you will need to include the appropriate Android Support Library depending on your requirements:

1. Using Fragments and Targeting Android 3.0 (API Level 11/Honeycomb) and higher - There is **no** need to include an Android Support Library since the `Fragment` class and related APIs are already included.
2. Using Fragments and Targeting Android 2.1 (API Level 7/Eclair) and higher - You will need to include the v7 Android Support Library (which itself depends on the v4 Android Support Library). There are several libraries under the v7 umbrella, but the one relevant to our discussion is the `v7 appcompat` library.
3. Using Fragments and Targeting Android 1.6 (API Level 4/Donut) and higher - You will need to include the v4 Android Support Library which features fragments, drawer layout, and more.
4. Not using Fragments - No need to include a support library (unless you need another bit of functionality contained within one of the support libraries).

In order to use the support libraries, you will need to download and install the support packages via the Android SDK Manager:

1. Start Eclipse.
2. Start the Android SDK Manager by clicking Window > Android SDK Manager.
3. In the Packages section of the Android SDK Manager dialog, scroll down until you see the folder labeled Extras. Expand this folder and ensure the checkbox to the left of the text *Android Support Library* is checked.

491

4. Click the *Install 1 package...* button to download and install the package.

Once downloaded and installed, these extras will be located - if you followed my setup instructions in Chapter 1, *Installing the Android SDK on Windows* - in `C:\androidSDK\sdk\extras\android\support`. There you will find folders for each support library version as well as sample code. Sweeeet!

In order to add a Support Library to your project, you need to add it to your application project. Rather than reproduce the Android instructions here, please see the following website for detailed instructions: `developer.android.com/tools/support-library/setup.html`.

Note that if you installed the Android SDK Bundle, the support libraries may already be installed and available for use when you set up a new project. Don't forget to import the appropriate class from the relevant support package. For example:

```
import android.support.v7.app.ActionBarActivity;
import android.support.v4.app.Fragment;
```

Fragments via the XML `<fragment>` Tag - Simple Example #1

You can include a fragment as part of your layout using the `<fragment>` XML tag, but be aware that you cannot use a fragment transaction via code to remove this type of fragment. With that said, you can code an empty layout such as a `RelativeLayout`, `FrameLayout`, `LinearLayout`, etc. and then subsequently add fragments via a fragment transaction to it. Note that adding fragments in this way will fill in the layout in the order in which you add the fragments based on the type of layout you're using. If you're using a horizontal layout, then the fragments are added horizontally from left to right. If you're using a vertical layout, then the fragments are added vertically from top to bottom.

For example, let's create a test project that uses the `<fragment>` XML tag within a layout file. The parent activity will contain a single button at the top as well as a fragment that contains a single textbox. When you create the new project, you will eventually arrive at the Blank Activity dialog box, as shown below. As you can see, there is an input box for your Fragment Layout Name and is filled in, by default, as `fragment_main`.

Now, the code generated based on the dialog box above is different than what I want to show you first. So, here's how I modified the code:

1. `activity_main.xml` - In the code below, I have included a `Button` as well as a `<fragment>` XML tag. Note that the `onClick()` method for the `Button` is called `PopulateFragment` which will change the `TextView` text within the fragment itself. Two comments about the `<fragment>` tag attributes:
   a. `tools:layout` - this indicates the layout to be displayed within the IDE GUI display and **not** necessarily what is displayed when the program actually runs. This is not strictly necessary.
   b. `android:name` - this indicates the **class** that will be used with the fragment. Despite this being an XML-only example, we can populate the fragment with its layout (`fragment_main.xml`), and that is done via code within the `onCreateView()` method of the class. As we shall see later in the chapter, this is not always necessary.

```
<LinearLayout xmlns:android="http://schemas.android.com/apk/res/android"
              xmlns:tools="http://schemas.android.com/tools"
              android:layout_width="match_parent"
              android:layout_height="match_parent"
              android:orientation="vertical">

    <Button
        android:id="@+id/button1"
        android:layout_width="fill_parent"
        android:layout_height="wrap_content"
        android:text="@string/popfragtext"
        android:onClick="PopulateFragment" />

    <fragment android:id="@+id/main_fragment"
              android:layout_width="fill_parent"
              android:layout_height="match_parent"
              android:layout_gravity="center_horizontal"
              tools:layout="@layout/fragment_main"
              android:name="com.example.fragmenttest1.FragmentControl"/>

</LinearLayout>
```

2. `fragment_main.xml` - Note that the code below contains the layout of the **fragment** and will be inflated in the `onCreateView()` method.

```
<RelativeLayout xmlns:android="http://schemas.android.com/apk/res/android"
                xmlns:tools="http://schemas.android.com/tools"
                android:layout_width="match_parent"
                android:layout_height="match_parent">

    <TextView
        android:id="@+id/textview_fragment"
        android:layout_width="fill_parent"
        android:layout_height="wrap_content"
        android:text="@string/hello_world"
        android:gravity="center_horizontal"
        android:textSize="30sp" />

</RelativeLayout>
```

3. `MainActivity.java` - As you know by now, this code is used to inflate the `activity_main.xml` layout. Note that this code contains the `onClick()` method `PopulateFragment()` which will change the fragment's text.

493

```
package com.example.fragmenttest1;

import java.util.Random;
import android.support.v7.app.ActionBarActivity;
import android.os.Bundle;
import android.view.View;
import android.widget.TextView;

public class MainActivity extends ActionBarActivity {

 @Override
 protected void onCreate(Bundle savedInstanceState) {
  super.onCreate(savedInstanceState);
  setContentView(R.layout.activity_main);
 }

 //Replaces the text in the fragment's textview.
 public void PopulateFragment(View view) {

  Random oRand = new Random();
  int iRandomInteger = oRand.nextInt(100);
  String sSomeText = "Now is the time..." +
                                Integer.toString(iRandomInteger);

  //Grab the id of the textbox
  TextView oTV = (TextView) findViewById(R.id.textview_fragment);

  //Change the text of the fragment's textbox
  oTV.setText(sSomeText);
 }

}
```

4. `FragmentControl.java` - This class, called `FragmentControl`, extends the `Fragment` class. This class overrides the `onCreateView()` method and returns a `View` object used to display the desired fragment. Take note that this class is also indicated in the `android:name` tag in the `<fragment>` XML tag in `activity_main.xml`.

```
package com.example.fragmenttest1;

import android.os.Bundle;
import android.support.v4.app.Fragment;
import android.view.LayoutInflater;
import android.view.View;
import android.view.ViewGroup;

public class FragmentControl extends Fragment {

 //Force fragment_main.xml to appear in the <fragment> of activity_main.xml.
 @Override
 public View onCreateView(LayoutInflater inflater,
                     ViewGroup container,
                     Bundle savedInstanceState) {

  //Create a View object from fragment_main
  View oFragmentMainView =
        inflater.inflate(R.layout.fragment_main,container,false);

  return oFragmentMainView;

 }

}
```

So, let's go through this in detail. The layout in `activity_main.xml`, as usual, is the initial layout displayed and contains a single button as well as a fragment. Take note that the `<fragment>` XML tag does **not** point to the layout `fragment_main.xml`, but instead points to a class used to inflate the display. Here, the XML attribute `android:name` refers to the class used to control the display of the fragment: `com.example.fragmenttest1.FragmentControl`. Now, it is the responsibility of the `FragmentControl` class to inflate the layout `fragment_main.xml` within its `onCreateView()` method. Before we see the code, a quick glance at the layout for `fragment_main.xml` reveals an unremarkable `TextView` that initially displays the text *Hello world!*...yawn!

Next, looking at the code in `MainActivity`, you will see the standard `onCreate()` method that inflates `activity_main.xml`.

Now, let's jump to the `FragmentControl` class. Recall that the `<fragment>` XML tag in `activity_main.xml` contains the `android:name` attribute which points to this class. As I've said, it is the responsibility of this class, similar to the `MainActivity` class, to inflate its fragment. As you can see in the code, you override the `onCreateView()` method which returns the `View` that you want the fragment to display. That is, the `<fragment>` XML in `activity_main.xml` can be thought of as being injected with the `View` returned from the `onCreateView()` method. Here, the layout in `fragment_main.xml` is what is being inflated and returned.

Now, once the fragment has been inflated, how do we update the `TextView` within it? You can do this in the normal manner: using `findViewById()` to point to the `TextView` and change the text using the `setText()` method:

```
Random oRand = new Random();
int iRandomInteger = oRand.nextInt(100);
String sSomeText = "Now is the time..." + Integer.toString(iRandomInteger);

//Grab the id of the textbox
TextView oTV = (TextView) findViewById(R.id.textview_fragment);

//Change the text of the fragment's textbox
oTV.setText(sSomeText);
```

Here is what the display initially looks like on my handheld device:

Hello world!

And here is what it looks like after clicking the *Populate Fragment Textbox* button:

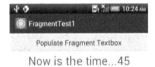

Now is the time...45

As mentioned above, you can add, remove or replace fragments using the `FragmentManager`. But, be aware that when using a static `<fragment>` XML tag in the layout, the original fragment can never actually be removed or replaced via code. For example, let's add the following code *to the end of* the `PopulateFragment()` method:

```
//Now, let's try to remove the fragment itself.

//Get access to the FragmentManager.
FragmentManager oFM = (FragmentManager) getSupportFragmentManager();

//Get access to our FragmentControl class.
FragmentControl oFC = (FragmentControl) oFM.findFragmentById(R.id.main_fragment);

//Begin a fragment transaction
FragmentTransaction oFT = oFM.beginTransaction();

//Attempt to remove our fragment.
oFT.remove(oFC);

//Commit the transaction.
oFT.commit();
```

The first thing we do is gain access to the `FragmentManager`, called `oFM`. Here, I am using `getSupportFragmentManager()` instead of `getFragment Manager()` because that is what is available within the Android Support Library.

Next, similar to using `findViewById()` to gain access to the underlying view object, we use `findFragmentById()` to gain access to the underlying fragment object, specifically the fragment associated with `main_fragment.xml`. Here, we call it `oFC`.

Next, we begin a fragment transaction using the `beginTransaction()` method of the `FragmentManager` object, `oFM`. At this point, we attempt to remove the fragment by calling the `remove()` method of the `FragmentTransaction` object, `oFT`, passing in the fragment object, `oFC`.

Finally, we commit the changes by issuing the `commit()` method of the `FragmentTransaction` object, `oFT`.

Now, despite my warnings about removing the fragment when it appears in XML using the `<fragment>` tag, you will not receive an error message and, based on our `PopulateFragment()` method, the `TextView`'s text will actually be replaced when the button is tapped. But, when you attempt to tap the button a second time, you will receive an error due to a `NullPointerException`, which is to be expected. Additionally, when you attempt to `replace()` the fragment with another fragment, you will still not replace the original XML `<fragment>`, but you will see two `TextView`s instead (shown below) one on top of the other.

Fragments via the XML `LinearLayout` Tag - Simple Example #2

Now, rather than using the `<fragment>` XML tag in our `activity_main.xml` layout, let's try a `LinearLayout` instead; that is, there will be no `<fragment>` XML tag in the layout, just an empty `LinearLayout`. This should allow us to add, remove and replace fragments within the `LinearLayout` without the trouble presented in Simple Example #1.

First, let's create a new project similar to the previous project, but in this case, let's add several additional layouts which will be inflated by fragments.

1. `activity_main.xml` - In the code below, I have included a `Button` as well as a `<LinearLayout>` tag. Note that the `onClick()` method for the `Button` is called `AddFragments` which will add the three fragments to the linear layout.

```xml
<LinearLayout xmlns:android="http://schemas.android.com/apk/res/android"
    xmlns:tools="http://schemas.android.com/tools"
    android:layout_width="fill_parent"
    android:layout_height="fill_parent"
    android:orientation="vertical">

 <Button
     android:id="@+id/button1"
     android:layout_width="fill_parent"
     android:layout_height="wrap_content"
     android:text="@string/popmainframe"
     android:onClick="AddFragments" />

 <LinearLayout
     android:id="@+id/mainframe"
     android:layout_width="fill_parent"
     android:layout_height="fill_parent"
     android:orientation="vertical"/>

</LinearLayout>
```

2. `fragment_textbox1.xml` - Note that this code contains a single `TextView`.

```xml
<LinearLayout xmlns:android="http://schemas.android.com/apk/res/android"
    xmlns:tools="http://schemas.android.com/tools"
    android:layout_width="wrap_content"
    android:layout_height="wrap_content"
    android:orientation="vertical">

  <TextView
     android:id="@+id/textview_fragment1"
     android:layout_width="wrap_content"
     android:layout_height="wrap_content"
     android:text="@string/textview_fragment1"
     android:textSize="20sp" />

</LinearLayout>
```

3. `fragment_textbox2.xml` - Note that this code contains a single `TextView`.

```xml
<LinearLayout xmlns:android="http://schemas.android.com/apk/res/android"
    xmlns:tools="http://schemas.android.com/tools"
    android:layout_width="wrap_content"
    android:layout_height="wrap_content"
    android:orientation="vertical">

  <TextView
     android:id="@+id/textview_fragment2"
     android:layout_width="wrap_content"
     android:layout_height="wrap_content"
     android:text="@string/textview_fragment2"
     android:textSize="20sp" />

</LinearLayout>
```

4. `fragment_textbox3.xml` - Note that this code contains a single `TextView`.

```xml
<LinearLayout xmlns:android="http://schemas.android.com/apk/res/android"
    xmlns:tools="http://schemas.android.com/tools"
      android:layout_width="wrap_content"
      android:layout_height="wrap_content"
      android:orientation="vertical">

  <TextView
      android:id="@+id/textview_fragment3"
      android:layout_width="wrap_content"
      android:layout_height="wrap_content"
      android:text="@string/textview_fragment3"
      android:textSize="20sp" />

</LinearLayout>
```

5. `MainActivity.java` - **Recall that this code is used to inflate the** `activity_main.xml` **layout. Note that this code contains the** `onClick()` **method** `AddFragments()` **which will add the three individual fragments to the** `LinearLayout` **defined in** `activity_main.xml`.

```java
package com.example.fragmenttest2;

import android.support.v4.app.FragmentManager;
import android.support.v4.app.FragmentTransaction;
import android.support.v7.app.ActionBarActivity;
import android.os.Bundle;
import android.view.View;

public class MainActivity extends ActionBarActivity {

 @Override
 protected void onCreate(Bundle savedInstanceState) {
     super.onCreate(savedInstanceState);
     setContentView(R.layout.activity_main);
 }

 //When user clicks the button, add the three fragments to the LinearLayout.
 public void AddFragments(View view) {

  //Create a new FragmentControlTextBox# classes
  FragmentControlTextBox1 oFC_TB1 = new FragmentControlTextBox1();
  FragmentControlTextBox2 oFC_TB2 = new FragmentControlTextBox2();
  FragmentControlTextBox3 oFC_TB3 = new FragmentControlTextBox3();

  //Get access to the FragmentManager.
  FragmentManager oFM = (FragmentManager) getSupportFragmentManager();

  //Begin a fragment transaction
  FragmentTransaction oFT = oFM.beginTransaction();

  //Add our new fragment
  oFT.add(R.id.mainframe,oFC_TB1);
  oFT.add(R.id.mainframe,oFC_TB2);
  oFT.add(R.id.mainframe,oFC_TB3);

  //Commit the change.
  oFT.commit();

  //Execute Pending Transactions
  oFM.executePendingTransactions();

 }
}
```

6. `FragmentControlTextBox1.java` - **This class, called** `FragmentControl TextBox1`, **extends the** `Fragment` **class. This class overrides the** `onCreate View()` **method which is used to display a desired** `View` **within the fragment.**

```java
package com.example.fragmenttest2;

import android.os.Bundle;
import android.support.v4.app.Fragment;
import android.view.LayoutInflater;
import android.view.View;
import android.view.ViewGroup;

public class FragmentControlTextBox1 extends Fragment {

  //Inflate fragment_textbox1.
  @Override
  public View onCreateView(LayoutInflater inflater,
                           ViewGroup container,
                           Bundle savedInstanceState) {

    //Create a View object from fragment_main
    View oFragmentMainView =
                inflater.inflate(R.layout.fragment_textbox1,container,false);

    return oFragmentMainView;
  }

}
```

7. `FragmentControlTextBox2.java` - **This class, called** `FragmentControl TextBox2`, **extends the** `Fragment` **class. This class overrides the** `onCreate View()` **method which is used to display a desired** `View` **within the fragment.**

```java
package com.example.fragmenttest2;

import android.os.Bundle;
import android.support.v4.app.Fragment;
import android.view.LayoutInflater;
import android.view.View;
import android.view.ViewGroup;

public class FragmentControlTextBox2 extends Fragment {

  //Inflate fragment_textbox1.
  @Override
  public View onCreateView(LayoutInflater inflater,
                           ViewGroup container,
                           Bundle savedInstanceState) {

    //Create a View object from fragment_main
    View oFragmentMainView =
                inflater.inflate(R.layout.fragment_textbox2,container,false);

    return oFragmentMainView;
  }

}
```

8. `FragmentControlTextBox3.java` - **This class, called** `FragmentControl TextBox3`, **extends the** `Fragment` **class. This class overrides the** `onCreate View()` **method which is used to display a desired** `View` **within the fragment.**

```java
package com.example.fragmenttest2;
```

500

```
import android.os.Bundle;
import android.support.v4.app.Fragment;
import android.view.LayoutInflater;
import android.view.View;
import android.view.ViewGroup;

public class FragmentControlTextBox3 extends Fragment {

  //Inflate fragment_textbox1.
  @Override
  public View onCreateView(LayoutInflater inflater,
                           ViewGroup container,
                           Bundle savedInstanceState) {

    //Create a View object from fragment_main
    View oFragmentMainView =
                  inflater.inflate(R.layout.fragment_textbox3,container,false);

    return oFragmentMainView;
  }

}
```

Here are the results of clicking the `Button`:

Recall that, in the previous example, the `android:name` attribute is used to specify the class responsible for controlling the fragment. Note that, in this example, we are **not** using the `android:name` attribute in the fragment layout because control of each fragment is handled in a different manner. This example is slightly different from the previous one, so let's go through it in detail.

There are three layouts (`fragment_textbox1`, `fragment_textbox2` and `fragment_textbox3`) one for each `TextView` to be added to the `LinearLayout`. We associate each one of these layouts with a class `FragmentControlTextBox1`, `FragmentControlTextBox2` and `Fragment ControlTextBox3`. These three classes override their `onCreateView()` methods and inflate the corresponding layout:

```
//Create a View object from fragment_main
View oFragmentMainView =
              inflater.inflate(R.layout.fragment_textbox3,container,false);
```

Now, in order to add these three fragments into the empty `LinearLayout`, we first instantiate the three fragment classes and then use the `add()` method to insert them into the `LinearLayout` in the order we want them to appear. In the code below, the `add()` method's first parameter indicates which layout to add to, and the second parameter indicates which instantiated fragment to add.

```
//Add our new fragment
oFT.add(R.id.mainframe,oFC_TB1);
oFT.add(R.id.mainframe,oFC_TB2);
oFT.add(R.id.mainframe,oFC_TB3);
```

When we issue a `commit()`, the fragments then appear one below the other in the vertical `LinearLayout`, as expected (see image above).

Fragments via the XML `LinearLayout` Tag - Simple Example #2.5

Let's modify Simple Example #2 above by adding code to store changes to a fragment so that the app user can see the previous fragment when the back button is tapped.

To accomplish this, just add a call to the method `addToBackStack(null)` on the `FragmentTransaction` object.

So, here is the modified `MainActivity` code:

```
public class MainActivity extends ActionBarActivity {

 @Override
 protected void onCreate(Bundle savedInstanceState) {
     super.onCreate(savedInstanceState);
     setContentView(R.layout.activity_main);
 }

 //When user clicks the button, add the three fragments to the LinearLayout.
 public void AddFragments(View view) {

  //Create a new FragmentControlTextBox# classes
  FragmentControlTextBox1 oFC_TB1 = new FragmentControlTextBox1();
  FragmentControlTextBox2 oFC_TB2 = new FragmentControlTextBox2();
  FragmentControlTextBox3 oFC_TB3 = new FragmentControlTextBox3();

  //Get access to the FragmentManager.
  FragmentManager oFM = (FragmentManager) getSupportFragmentManager();

  //Begin a fragment transaction
  FragmentTransaction oFT = oFM.beginTransaction();

  //Add our new fragment
  oFT.add(R.id.mainframe,oFC_TB1);
  oFT.add(R.id.mainframe,oFC_TB2);
  oFT.add(R.id.mainframe,oFC_TB3);

  //Store in back stack
  oFT.addToBackStack(null);

  //Commit the change.
  oFT.commit();

  //Execute Pending Transactions
  oFM.executePendingTransactions();
```

```
   }
 }
```

In Simple Example #2, when the user clicks the back button, he/she will drop out of the app. In this example, though, the user will see each previous incarnation of the fragments. For example, the image below shows the display when I clicked the button three times. Since we are not removing the previous fragments, just adding, they will continue to build up.

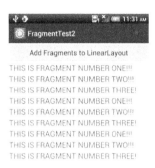

Note that three sets of three lines appear. When I hit the back button once, here is what you see:

And, when you hit the back button again, you will see this:

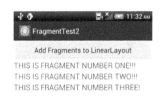

And, hitting the back button again, you will see this:

Finally, hitting the back button one last time drops you out of the app.

Note that you can add an animated transition between the movement from fragment to fragment using either the `setTransition()` or `setCustom Animations()` methods to define a transition on the `FragmentTransition` object.

The sole parameter for `setTransition()` takes on one of several constants such as `FragmentTransition.TRANSIT_FRAGMENT_FADE` (a subtle fade), `FragmentTransition.TRANSIT_FRAGMENT_OPEN` (a nice, but subtle, stretch effect), `FragmentTransition.TRANSIT_FRAGMENT_CLOSE` (a very subtle fade in/fade out effect), and so on. Unfortunately, I can't show you the effect of these, of course, so you'll have to try out the example. Here is how you add one of these animated transitions to the `FragmentTransition` object:

```
oFT.setTransition(FragmentTransaction.TRANSIT_FRAGMENT_OPEN);
```

Now, these effects are very subtle, and you may want a more *in your face* type of transition. In this case, you can use the `setCustomAnimations()` method. There are two overrides for this method:

1. `setCustomAnimation(enter-animation, exit-animation)` - this method allows you to specify an animation associated with the `add()` method (enter-animation) as well as the `remove()` method (exit-animation). Note that when hitting the back button, though, this method shows no animation.

2. `setCustomAnimation(enter-animation, exit-animation, popstack-enter-animation, popstack-exit-animation)` - this method is similar to the method above, but allows you to also specify animations for the popping of the fragment off the stack (when the back button is tapped).

Now, you can define your own animations as outlined in Chapter 23, *Graphics* or you can make use of several built-in animations:

1. `R.anim.abc_fade_in` - fade-in animation
2. `R.anim.abc_fade_out` - fade-out animation
3. `R.anim.abc_slide_in_bottom` - slide in from the bottom of the screen animation
4. `R.anim.abc_slide_in_top` - slide in from the top of the screen animation
5. `R.anim.abc_slide_out_bottom` - slide out towards the bottom of the screen animation
6. `R.anim.abc_slide_out_top` - slide out towards the top of the screen animation

For example, here is what `abc_slide_in_bottom.xml` contains:

```xml
<?xml version="1.0" encoding="utf-8"?>
<!-- Copyright (C) 2013 The Android Open Source Project

     Licensed under the Apache License, Version 2.0 (the "License");
     you may not use this file except in compliance with the License.
     You may obtain a copy of the License at

          http://www.apache.org/licenses/LICENSE-2.0

     Unless required by applicable law or agreed to in writing, software
     distributed under the License is distributed on an "AS IS" BASIS,
     WITHOUT WARRANTIES OR CONDITIONS OF ANY KIND, either express or implied.
     See the License for the specific language governing permissions and
     limitations under the License.
-->
<translate xmlns:android="http://schemas.android.com/apk/res/android"
        android:interpolator="@android:anim/decelerate_interpolator"
        android:fromYDelta="50%p" android:toYDelta="0"
        android:duration="@android:integer/config_mediumAnimTime"/>
```

Let me just say that fragment animation is SWEEEET!

Fragment Lifecycle

As mentioned, fragments can be thought of as sub-activites and, just like activities, they have their own lifecycle albeit it is tied to the parent activity's lifecycle. Recall that for activities we have methods such as `onCreate()`, `onPause()`, `onDestroy()`, and so on. For fragments, we have the same methods as well as a few more. Below is a list of relevant methods for fragments in the order in which they are called. Note that, just like for activities, you do not need to override all of the methods, but at the very least you should override `onCreateView()`:

1. `onAttach()` - this method is called when a fragment is first attached to its parent activity.
2. `onCreate()` - this method is called to do initial creation of a fragment. This is where you can pull any passed in arguments via a `Bundle`. We show examples of this below.
3. `onCreateView()` - this method is called to allow the fragment to instantiate its user interface view.
4. `onViewCreated()` - this method is called after `onCreateView()` has returned, but before any saved state has been restored in to the view.
5. `onActivityCreated()` - this method is called when the fragment's activity has been created and this fragment's view hierarchy instantiated.
6. `onStart()` - this method is called when the fragment is visible to the user. Note that this method is associated with the `onStart()` method of the containing `Activity`.
7. `onResume()` - this method is called when the fragment is visible to the user and is actively running. Note that this method is associated with the `onResume()` method of the containing `Activity`.
8. `onPause()` - this method is called when the fragment is no longer resumed. Note that this method is associated with the `onPause()` method of the containing `Activity`.
9. `onStop()` - this method is called when the fragment is no longer started. Note that this method is associated with the `onStop()` method of the containing `Activity`.
10. `onDestroyView()` - this method is called when the view previously created by `onCreateView()` has been detached from the fragment.
11. `onDestroy()` - this method is called when the fragment is no longer in use.
12. `onDetach()` - this method is called when the fragment is no longer attached to its activity.

Communication between Fragments

Recall at the top of the chapter, I showed you an image of the flight deck of an Airbus A380 and mentioned that the instruments should communicate between each other sharing important information such as whether the plane is about to crash or if the coffee has been made.

In fact, the instruments may not actually communicate with each other, but via a go-between; that is, if one instrument needs to send some information to another instrument, the first instrument may send information to a supervisor (coordinator, governor, etc.) which then forwards the information on to the second instrument. This is similar to how fragments communicate: fragments should never talk to each other, except through the containing activity acting as the supervisor. This is recommended because fragments are supposed to be modular (self-contained) components similar to the instruments in an aircraft. For example, if one of your fragments allows for the selection of a stock market symbol, once the user has clicked, say, a `Spinner` in the fragment, the fragment can then tell the containing activity that there has been a change in the symbol and that all fragments relying on this information should be sent an update request with the new symbol. This will allow each fragment to pull the appropriate data and update its own display. One way to allow this direction of communication to occur is to define an `interface` within each fragment and have the containing `Activity` implement the interface's method(s).

Another direction of communication is from containing activity to a particular fragment; that is, based on an action occurring in the containing activity (e.g., a user tapped a button), the containing activity can execute a method within one or more fragments. For example, say the containing activity has a `ListView`. Once the user clicks an item, the activity can then tell each fragment to update itself based on the item selected. One way to allow this direction of communication is to allow the parent `Activity` to gain access to one or more `public` methods within each fragment.

Recall that when using `startActivity()` we were able to pass in a `Bundle` through an `Intent` as the parameter to share important information with the activity. This is true, as well, for fragments except that you only need to pass a `Bundle` object as the parameter of the `setArguments()` method. Note that this method should be called as soon as you create the fragment itself rather than waiting until the fragment is displayed because by that time it's too late for your fragment to get the data in the `Bundle` and act on it.

To sum up the communication methods:

1. Fragment-to-Fragment - this is a no-no. Fragments should never communicate with each other. So there!
2. Fragment-to-Activity - create an `interface` in the fragment which is then implemented in the activity. (Another way, although it seems it's frowned upon, is to access the parent `Activity` from within the fragment and then execute a method in parent `Activity`. We show an example of this when we talk about the `AlertDialog.Builder` class later on in the chapter.)
3. Activity-to-Fragment - the activity executes one or more `public` methods within the fragment.
4. Passing Data to Fragment - use the `setArguments()` method to pass in a `Bundle` containing the appropriate data. Note that you should retrieve the `Bundle` arguments within the fragment's `onCreate()` method.

EquityYo! and Fragments - Complex Example #1

Let's create an extended example by taking my app *EquityYo!* and re-work it, in part, using fragments. Now, I won't include all of the functionality in *EquityYo!*, but enough to show you a more detailed example of fragments.

Recall that the original *EquityYo!* app is made up of five activities: Stocks, Closed-End Funds, Mutual Funds, Exchange Traded Funds and Market Indexes. Each

`Activity` is started by clicking one of the buttons on the home screen, as shown below in the section labeled EQUITY STATISTICS:

But, is that the best use of layout? Below is a mock-up of what I'd like the second attempt to look like. In the example below, we will concentrate solely on stocks and ignore mutual funds, closed-end funds and exchange traded funds. Naturally, we will make use of fragments. Here is a mock-up of what I'd like (hope, desire, dream) to see as the final result:

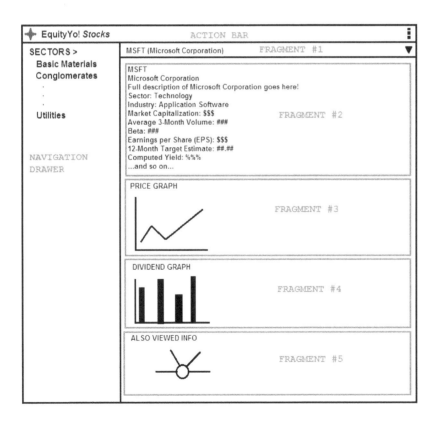

As you see, we have an `ActionBar` at the top used to display the app icon, the app title, the menu button, and so on. On the left, we have a `DrawerLayout`, which displays a choice of stock sectors such as Basic Materials, Conglomerates, and so on. The `DrawerLayout` slides out from the left allowing you to select a sector, and then slides back to make the screen fully available for the rest of the information (shown to the right in the mock-up above). (Note that the `DrawerLayout` class is similar to the `SlidingDrawer` class, so we won't go through it in detail. Please see the Android document *Creating a Navigation Drawer* for more information.) To the right, we have several fragments: one for a `Spinner` displaying a list of stocks associated with the selected sector (by default, all stocks appear when the app first starts); one containing several `TextView`s showing information related to a stock such as the symbol, name, description, earnings per share, and so on; a price graph; a dividend graph; and an image displaying those stocks also viewed by Yahoo! Finance users.

Now, all of the fragments will be stored within a vertical `LinearLayout`, just like the earlier examples, located on the right side of the mock-up. Each fragment will be added when a sector is selected in the sector `Spinner`. Each fragment will be updated when the user selects a new stock from the Fragment #1 `Spinner`.

Recall our talk about communication between fragments. In the mock up above, when the user selects a different stock in the `Spinner` located in Fragment #1, the fragment communicates to the parent `Activity`. The parent `Activity` will then ask each fragment to update its own view to show information for the selected stock. Note that the first method of communication is from fragment to parent via an `interface`, and the second method of communication is from parent to fragment via `public` methods. Note that the `Spinner` does not have to be in a fragment on its own, I am doing it that way to show you these communication methods.

Next, when the user selects a different sector in the parent `Activity`, the `Spinner` in Fragment #1 will be updated to contain the sector-specific stocks. The first stock entry for that sector will be used to update the remaining fragments. Note that this method of communication will be from parent `Activity` to the fragments using the `public` methods within each fragment.

Note that I will be using the SQLite database `EQUITY_DATABASE.db3` used with the original EquityYo! app, so I don't have to worry about data. Now, in order to work with the database, I will be again using readyState Software's `SQLiteAssetHelper` Class. This requires that the database be zipped and stored in the `assets/databases` folder in the project (although the newer version of the software does not enforce zipping).

In order to create the price and dividend graphs, I will be using Infragistics' Iguana UI charts I used in the original app.

Finally, in order to create the Also Viewed image, I will be using Android's built-in graphics functionality as explained in Chapter 23, *Graphics*.

1. `activity_main.xml` - this layout is used to define the navigation drawer (`DrawerLayout`), the `ListView` used to display the sectors, and the `LinearLayout` used to house the fragments. Note that we have a `ScrollView` surrounding the `LinearLayout` in order to allow the user to scroll the window to see all of the fragments.

```xml
<android.support.v4.widget.DrawerLayout
    xmlns:android="http://schemas.android.com/apk/res/android"
    xmlns:tools="http://schemas.android.com/tools"
    android:id="@+id/drawer_layout"
    android:layout_width="match_parent"
    android:layout_height="match_parent">

  <ScrollView xmlns:android="http://schemas.android.com/apk/res/android"
            android:id="@+id/svFragments"
            android:layout_width="fill_parent"
            android:layout_height="fill_parent"
            android:scrollbarStyle="outsideOverlay">
    <LinearLayout
        android:id="@+id/mainframe"
        android:layout_width="match_parent"
        android:layout_height="match_parent"
        android:orientation="vertical" />
  </ScrollView>

  <ListView
      android:id="@+id/sector_drawer"
      android:layout_width="240dp"
      android:layout_height="match_parent"
      android:layout_gravity="left"
      android:choiceMode="singleChoice"
      android:dividerHeight="0dp"
      android:background="#FFFFFF"
      android:listSelector="#A3BA42" />

</android.support.v4.widget.DrawerLayout>
```

2. `fragment1_spinner.xml` - this fragment layout is used to hold a `Spinner` which will display the list of stocks for the selected sector.

```xml
<?xml version="1.0" encoding="utf-8"?>
<LinearLayout xmlns:android="http://schemas.android.com/apk/res/android"
    xmlns:tools="http://schemas.android.com/tools"
    android:layout_width="fill_parent"
    android:layout_height="wrap_content"
    android:orientation="vertical">

    <Spinner android:id="@+id/idfragment1_spinner"
            android:layout_width="fill_parent"
            android:layout_height="wrap_content"
            android:prompt="@string/prmpt"/>

</LinearLayout>
```

3. `fragment2_details.xml` - this fragment layout is used to hold several `TextView`s displaying the stock symbol, the name of the company, and so on.

```xml
<?xml version="1.0" encoding="utf-8"?>
<LinearLayout xmlns:android="http://schemas.android.com/apk/res/android"
    xmlns:tools="http://schemas.android.com/tools"
    android:layout_width="fill_parent"
    android:layout_height="wrap_content"
    android:orientation="vertical"
    android:id="@+id/llstock_symbol_detail_layout">
```

```xml
    <RelativeLayout android:padding="5.0px" android:layout_width="fill_parent"
android:layout_height="wrap_content">
    <TextView android:id="@+id/tvSTOCK_Symbol"
android:layout_alignParentLeft="true" android:gravity="left"  android:padding="10.0px"
android:layout_height="wrap_content" android:layout_width="match_parent"
android:textStyle="bold" android:textAppearance="?android:attr/textAppearanceLarge"/>
    <TextView android:id="@+id/tvSTOCK_MaxMonthPriceNAV"
android:layout_alignParentRight="true" android:gravity="right" android:padding="10.0px"
android:layout_height="wrap_content" android:layout_width="match_parent"
android:textStyle="bold" android:textAppearance="?android:attr/textAppearanceLarge"/>
    </RelativeLayout>

    <TextView android:id="@+id/tvSTOCK_sName" android:background="@drawable/color5"
android:paddingTop="2.0px" android:paddingLeft="10.0px" android:paddingRight="10.0px"
android:paddingBottom="10.0px" android:layout_height="wrap_content"
android:layout_width="fill_parent" android:textStyle="bold"/>
    <TextView android:id="@+id/tvSTOCK_sInfo" android:padding="10.0px"
android:background="@drawable/color7" android:fadeScrollbars="false"
android:maxLines="10" android:scrollbars="vertical"
android:scrollbarStyle="outsideOverlay" android:layout_height="wrap_content"
android:layout_width="wrap_content" android:textStyle="italic"
android:textAppearance="?android:attr/textAppearanceSmall"/>
    <TextView android:id="@+id/tvSTOCK_Sector" android:textStyle="bold"
android:background="@drawable/color5" android:padding="10.0px"
android:layout_height="wrap_content" android:layout_width="fill_parent"/>
    <TextView android:id="@+id/tvSTOCK_Industry" android:textStyle="bold"
android:background="@drawable/color5" android:padding="10.0px"
android:layout_height="wrap_content" android:layout_width="fill_parent"/>
    <TextView android:id="@+id/tvSTOCK_sMktCapNetAssets" android:textStyle="bold"
android:background="@drawable/color5" android:padding="10.0px"
android:layout_height="wrap_content" android:layout_width="fill_parent" />
    <TextView android:id="@+id/tvSTOCK_sAverage3MonthVolume" android:textStyle="bold"
android:background="@drawable/color5" android:padding="10.0px"
android:layout_height="wrap_content" android:layout_width="fill_parent" />
    <TextView android:id="@+id/tvSTOCK_sBeta" android:textStyle="bold"
android:background="@drawable/color5" android:padding="10.0px"
android:layout_height="wrap_content" android:layout_width="fill_parent" />
    <TextView android:id="@+id/tvSTOCK_sEPS" android:textStyle="bold"
android:background="@drawable/color5" android:padding="10.0px"
android:layout_height="wrap_content" android:layout_width="fill_parent" />
    <TextView android:id="@+id/tvSTOCK_sPERatio" android:textStyle="bold"
android:background="@drawable/color5" android:padding="10.0px"
android:layout_height="wrap_content" android:layout_width="fill_parent" />
    <TextView android:id="@+id/tvSTOCK_sTargetEstimate" android:textStyle="bold"
android:background="@drawable/color5" android:padding="10.0px"
android:layout_height="wrap_content" android:layout_width="fill_parent" />
    <TextView android:id="@+id/tvSTOCK_PriceGain" android:textStyle="bold"
android:background="@drawable/color5" android:padding="10.0px"
android:layout_height="wrap_content" android:layout_width="fill_parent" />
    <TextView android:id="@+id/tvSTOCK_ComputedYield" android:textStyle="bold"
android:background="@drawable/color5" android:padding="10.0px"
android:layout_height="wrap_content" android:layout_width="fill_parent" />
    <TextView android:id="@+id/tvSTOCK_ComputedDividend" android:textStyle="bold"
android:background="@drawable/color5" android:padding="10.0px"
android:layout_height="wrap_content" android:layout_width="fill_parent" />
    <TextView android:id="@+id/tvSTOCK_sDisplayedYield" android:textStyle="bold"
android:background="@drawable/color5" android:padding="10.0px"
android:layout_height="wrap_content" android:layout_width="fill_parent" />
    <TextView android:id="@+id/tvSTOCK_sDisplayedDividend" android:textStyle="bold"
android:background="@drawable/color5" android:padding="10.0px"
android:layout_height="wrap_content" android:layout_width="fill_parent" />
    <TextView android:id="@+id/tvSTOCK_DividendFrequency" android:textStyle="bold"
android:background="@drawable/color5" android:padding="10.0px"
android:layout_height="wrap_content" android:layout_width="fill_parent" />
    <TextView android:id="@+id/tvSTOCK_DividendConsistency" android:textStyle="bold"
android:background="@drawable/color5" android:padding="10.0px"
android:layout_height="wrap_content" android:layout_width="fill_parent" />
```

```
        <TextView android:id="@+id/tvSTOCK_DivGain" android:textStyle="bold"
    android:background="@drawable/color5" android:padding="10.0px"
    android:layout_height="wrap_content" android:layout_width="fill_parent" />

    </LinearLayout>
```

4. `fragment3_price.xml` - this fragment layout will display the stock's historical prices using Infragistic's Iguana UI Charts.

```
<?xml version="1.0" encoding="utf-8" ?>
<LinearLayout xmlns:android="http://schemas.android.com/apk/res/android"
    xmlns:tools="http://schemas.android.com/tools"
    android:layout_width="fill_parent"
    android:layout_height="wrap_content"
    android:orientation="vertical"
    android:id="@+id/llPriceChart">

    <TextView android:text="PRICE INFORMATION:"
        android:textSize="15sp"
        android:textStyle="bold"
        android:padding="10.0px"
        android:layout_height="wrap_content"
        android:layout_width="fill_parent" />
    <com.iguanaui.controls.DataChart android:id="@+id/igPriceChart"
        android:contentDescription="@null"
        android:layout_width="fill_parent"
        android:layout_height="wrap_content" />

    </LinearLayout>
```

5. `fragment4_dividend.xml` - this fragment layout will display the stock's historical dividends using Infragistic's Iguana UI Charts.

```
<?xml version="1.0" encoding="utf-8" ?>
<LinearLayout xmlns:android="http://schemas.android.com/apk/res/android"
    xmlns:tools="http://schemas.android.com/tools"
    android:layout_width="fill_parent"
    android:layout_height="wrap_content"
    android:orientation="vertical"
    android:id="@+id/llDivChart">

    <TextView android:text="DIVIDEND INFORMATION:"
        android:textSize="15sp"
        android:textStyle="bold"
        android:padding="10.0px"
        android:layout_height="wrap_content"
        android:layout_width="fill_parent" />
    <com.iguanaui.controls.DataChart android:id="@+id/igDivChart"
        android:contentDescription="@null"
        android:layout_width="fill_parent"
        android:layout_height="wrap_content" />

    </LinearLayout>
```

6. `fragment5_alsoviewed.xml` - this fragment layout will display the Also Viewed information as an image.

```
<?xml version="1.0" encoding="utf-8" ?>
<LinearLayout xmlns:android="http://schemas.android.com/apk/res/android"
    xmlns:tools="http://schemas.android.com/tools"
    android:layout_width="fill_parent"
    android:layout_height="wrap_content"
    android:orientation="vertical"
    android:id="@+id/llAlsoViewed">
```

```
        <TextView android:text="ALSO VIEWED INFORMATION:"
            android:textSize="15sp"
            android:textStyle="bold"
            android:padding="10.0px"
            android:layout_height="wrap_content"
            android:layout_width="fill_parent"/>
        <ImageView android:id="@+id/igAVImageView"
            android:contentDescription="@null"
            android:layout_width="fill_parent"
            android:layout_height="wrap_content"
            android:gravity="center_horizontal" />

    </LinearLayout>
```

7. `arrays.xml` - this XML file contains the sector names, default stock symbols for each sector, and the sector keys associated with the `SectorKey` column in the database.

```
<resources xmlns:android="http://schemas.android.com/apk/res/android">
 <string-array name="sectors">
  <item name="S0">All Sectors</item>
  <item name="S3">Basic Materials</item>
  <item name="S4">Conglomerates</item>
  <item name="S5">Consumer Goods</item>
  <item name="S6">Financial</item>
  <item name="S7">Healthcare</item>
  <item name="S8">Industrial Goods</item>
  <item name="S9">Services</item>
  <item name="S10">Technology</item>
  <item name="S11">Utilities</item>
  </string-array>
 <string-array name="sectordefaultsymbol">
  <item name="S0">A</item>
  <item name="S3">AA</item>
  <item name="S4">ANDA</item>
  <item name="S5">ACAT</item>
  <item name="S6">AACC</item>
  <item name="S7">ABAX</item>
  <item name="S8">AAON</item>
  <item name="S9">AAN</item>
  <item name="S10">A</item>
  <item name="S11">ADGE</item>
  </string-array>
 <string-array name="sectorkeys">
  <item name="0">0</item>
  <item name="3">3</item>
  <item name="4">4</item>
  <item name="5">5</item>
  <item name="6">6</item>
  <item name="7">7</item>
  <item name="8">8</item>
  <item name="9">9</item>
  <item name="10">10</item>
  <item name="11">11</item>
  </string-array>
</resources>
```

8. `strings.xml` - this XML file contains strings used throughout the program.

```
<?xml version="1.0" encoding="utf-8"?>
<resources>

    <string name="app_name">EquityYoStocks</string>
    <string name="menu_settings">Settings</string>
    <string name="menu_usersguide">User&amp;s Guide</string>
    <string name="menu_portfolio">Portfolio</string>
```

```
        <string name="title_activity_users_guide">equityYO! User\'s Guide</string>
        <string name="prmpt">Stock Symbols</string>

</resources>
```

9. `menu.xml` - this XML file contains the menus displayed on the `ActionBar`. Note that the menu item `mSearch` is not implemented in the code below, but will be in the next example.

```xml
<menu xmlns:android="http://schemas.android.com/apk/res/android"
    xmlns:app="http://schemas.android.com/apk/res-auto"
    xmlns:tools="http://schemas.android.com/tools"
    tools:context="com.example.equityyostocks.MainActivity" >

    <item
        android:id="@+id/mUsersGuide"
        android:orderInCategory="100"
        android:title="User's Guide"
        />
    <item
        android:id="@+id/mManagePorfolio"
        android:orderInCategory="200"
        android:title="Portfolio"
        />
    <item
        android:id="@+id/mSettings"
        android:orderInCategory="300"
        android:title="Settings"
        />
    <item
        android:id="@+id/mSearch"
        android:orderInCategory="400"
        android:title="Search"
        />

</menu>
```

10. `MainActivity.java` - this is the main activity code used to inflate `activity_main.xml`, populate the `Spinners` and display the fragments.

```java
package com.example.equityyostocks;

import android.support.v7.app.ActionBarActivity;
import android.support.v4.app.FragmentManager;
import android.support.v4.app.FragmentTransaction;
import android.content.Context;
import android.content.Intent;
import android.graphics.Color;
import android.os.Bundle;
import android.view.Display;
import android.view.LayoutInflater;
import android.view.Menu;
import android.view.MenuInflater;
import android.view.MenuItem;
import android.view.View;
import android.view.ViewGroup;
import android.view.WindowManager;
import android.support.v4.widget.DrawerLayout;
import android.widget.AdapterView;
import android.widget.ArrayAdapter;
import android.widget.ListView;
import android.widget.ScrollView;
import android.widget.TextView;
import android.widget.Toast;

public class MainActivity extends ActionBarActivity implements
```

```
                    Fragment1SpinnerControl.OnFragment1SpinnerChangedListener {
   ListView oSectorListView;
   Fragment1SpinnerControl oF1C_SP;
   Fragment2DetailsControl oF2C_DE;
   Fragment3PriceChartControl oF3C_PC;
   Fragment4DividendChartControl oF4C_DC;
   Fragment5AlsoViewedImageControl oF5C_AC;
   FragmentManager oFM;
   FragmentTransaction oFT;
   DrawerLayout oSectorDrawerLayout;
   View viewSectorOLD;
   Boolean bFirstTimeThrough = true;
   ScrollView oScrollView;
   int iDeviceWidth,iDeviceHeight;

   @Override
   protected void onCreate(Bundle savedInstanceState) {
    super.onCreate(savedInstanceState);
    setContentView(R.layout.activity_main);

    //Access the DrawerLayout object.
    oSectorDrawerLayout = (DrawerLayout) findViewById(R.id.drawer_layout);

    //Access the ScrollView object.
    oScrollView = (ScrollView) findViewById(R.id.svFragments);

    //Access the sector ListView object.
    oSectorListView = (ListView) findViewById(R.id.sector_drawer);

    //Place the sector names in an array.
    String[] aSectorNames = getResources().getStringArray(R.array.sectors);

    //Rig up a custom ArrayAdapter to the list of sector names in the array.
    CustomArrayAdapter adapter = new CustomArrayAdapter(this,
                                         android.R.layout.simple_list_item_1,
                                         aSectorNames);

    //Associate the adapter with the sector ListView.
    oSectorListView.setAdapter(adapter);

    //Access the FragmentManager.
    oFM = (FragmentManager) getSupportFragmentManager();

    //Get the width and height of the device
    WindowManager wm = (WindowManager) getSystemService(Context.WINDOW_SERVICE);
    Display display = wm.getDefaultDisplay();
    iDeviceWidth = display.getWidth();
    iDeviceHeight = display.getHeight();

    //Load the five fragments into the mainframe.
    initialLoadFragments();

    //Open the drawer containing the sectors.
    oSectorDrawerLayout.openDrawer(oSectorListView);

    //Set up a listener for the click of the NavigationDrawer.
    SectorDrawerItemClickListener sectorDrawerListener =
                                  new SectorDrawerItemClickListener();
    oSectorListView.setOnItemClickListener(sectorDrawerListener);

   }

   //Override the onRestart method.
   @Override
   protected void onRestart() {
    super.onRestart();

    //Re-init the boolean variable bFirstTimeThrough to true.
    bFirstTimeThrough=true;
```

```
//Remove the fragments.
oFT = oFM.beginTransaction();
oFT.remove(oF5C_AC);
oFT.remove(oF4C_DC);
oFT.remove(oF3C_PC);
oFT.remove(oF2C_DE);
oFT.remove(oF1C_SP);
oFT.commitAllowingStateLoss();
oFM.executePendingTransactions();

//Re-initialize the sector ListView
oSectorListView = (ListView) findViewById(R.id.sector_drawer);
String[] aSectorNames = getResources().getStringArray(R.array.sectors);
CustomArrayAdapter adapter = new CustomArrayAdapter(this,
                                 android.R.layout.simple_list_item_1,
                                 aSectorNames);
oSectorListView.setAdapter(adapter);

//Re-initialize the fragments
initialLoadFragments();

//Move the ScrollView up to the top.
oScrollView.scrollTo(0, 0);

}

//Populate the menu on the ActionBar (will show three vertical dots)
@Override
public boolean onCreateOptionsMenu(Menu menu) {

 MenuInflater inflater = getMenuInflater();
 inflater.inflate(R.menu.main, menu);

 return true;

}

//Handle the menu item clicks.
@Override
public boolean onOptionsItemSelected(MenuItem item) {

 switch (item.getItemId()) {

  case R.id.mUsersGuide:
   Intent intent = new Intent(MainActivity.this,UsersGuideActivity.class);
   startActivity(intent);
  return true;

  case R.id.mManagePorfolio:
   Toast.makeText(getApplicationContext(),
                 "This feature is not implemented.",
                 Toast.LENGTH_SHORT).show();
  return true;

  case R.id.mSettings:
   Toast.makeText(getApplicationContext(),
                 "This feature is not implemented.",
                 Toast.LENGTH_SHORT).show();
  return true;

  default:
  return super.onOptionsItemSelected(item);
 }

}

//Method to load the fragments initially.
private void initialLoadFragments() {
```

```
//Instantiate the five fragments.
oF1C_SP = new Fragment1SpinnerControl(); //Fragment #1: Spinner
oF2C_DE = new Fragment2DetailsControl(); //Fragment #2: Details
oF3C_PC = new Fragment3PriceChartControl(); //Fragment #3: Price Chart
oF4C_DC = new Fragment4DividendChartControl(); //Fragment #4: Dividend Chart
oF5C_AC = new Fragment5AlsoViewedImageControl(); //Fragment #5: AV Image

//Set up a Bundle for use with the five fragment objects.
Bundle oBundleArgs = new Bundle();

//Populate oBundleArgs for use with the fragments.
oBundleArgs.putString("SECTORKEY", "0");
oBundleArgs.putString("SYMBOL", "A");
oBundleArgs.putInt("WIDTH", iDeviceWidth);
oBundleArgs.putInt("HEIGHT", iDeviceHeight);

//Fragment #1: Spinner
oF1C_SP.setArguments(oBundleArgs);

//Fragment #2: Details
oF2C_DE.setArguments(oBundleArgs);

//Fragment #3: Price Chart
oF3C_PC.setArguments(oBundleArgs);

//Fragment #4: Dividend Chart
oF4C_DC.setArguments(oBundleArgs);

//Fragment #5: Also Viewed Image
oF5C_AC.setArguments(oBundleArgs);


//Begin a fragment transaction
oFT = oFM.beginTransaction();

//Add in the fragments
oFT.add(R.id.mainframe,oF1C_SP);
oFT.add(R.id.mainframe,oF2C_DE);
oFT.add(R.id.mainframe,oF3C_PC);
oFT.add(R.id.mainframe,oF4C_DC);
oFT.add(R.id.mainframe,oF5C_AC);

//Commit the change.
oFT.commitAllowingStateLoss();

//Execute Pending Transactions
oFM.executePendingTransactions();

}

//Create a class to handle clicks for the Sector Drawer.
private class SectorDrawerItemClickListener implements
                                ListView.OnItemClickListener {

@Override
public void onItemClick(AdapterView<?> adapter,
                    View view,
                    int position,
                    long id) {

  //Highlight the clicked sector
  highlightSector(view,position);

  //Update the Spinner with the new sector key.
  updateSpinner(position);

  //Update fragment #2 (Details)
  updateDetails(position);

  //Update fragment #3 (Price Chart)
```

```java
   updatePriceChart(position);

   //Update fragment #4 (Dividend Chart)
   updateDividendChart(position);

   //Update fragment #5 (Also Viewed Image)
   updateAlsoViewedImage(position);

   //Move ScrollView to top
   oScrollView.scrollTo(0, 0);

   //Close the drawer
   oSectorDrawerLayout.closeDrawer(oSectorListView);

}

//Highlight the appropriate sector when it is clicked
private void highlightSector(View view,int iPosition) {

   //Change the background color from green to white for the old position
   if (viewSectorOLD != null) {
    viewSectorOLD.setBackgroundColor(Color.rgb(255, 255, 255));
   }

   //Change the background color from white to green.
   view.setBackgroundColor(Color.rgb(163, 186, 66));

   //Swap views
   viewSectorOLD = view;

}

//Update the spinner with the set of stocks for the newly selected sector.
private void updateSpinner(int iPosition) {

   //Create an array from the sectorkeys array
   String[] sArray = getResources().getStringArray(R.array.sectorkeys);

   //String to hold this sectorkey
   String sThisSectorKey = sArray[iPosition];

   //Update the spinner in Fragement #1.
   oF1C_SP.populateSpinner(sThisSectorKey);

}

//Update the details fragment with the default stock for this sector.
private void updateDetails(int iPosition) {

   //Create an array from the sectordefaultsymbol array
   String[] sArray =
             getResources().getStringArray(R.array.sectordefaultsymbol);

   //String to hold this sectorkey's default stock
   String sThisSectorKeyDefaultStock = sArray[iPosition];

   //Update the spinner in Fragment #1.
   oF2C_DE.populateDetails(sThisSectorKeyDefaultStock);

}

//Update the Price Chart fragment with the default stock for this sector.
private void updatePriceChart(int iPosition) {

   //Create an array from the sectordefaultsymbol array
   String[] sArray =
             getResources().getStringArray(R.array.sectordefaultsymbol);

   //String to hold this sectorkey's default stock
   String sThisSectorKeyDefaultStock = sArray[iPosition];
```

```
    //Update the price chart in Fragment #3.
    oF3C_PC.populatePriceChart(sThisSectorKeyDefaultStock);

  }

  //Update the Price Chart fragment with the default stock for this sector.
  private void updateDividendChart(int iPosition) {

    //Create an array from the sectordefaultsymbol array
    String[] sArray =
            getResources().getStringArray(R.array.sectordefaultsymbol);

    //String to hold this sectorkey's default stock
    String sThisSectorKeyDefaultStock = sArray[iPosition];

    //Update the price chart in Fragment #3.
    oF4C_DC.populateDividendChart(sThisSectorKeyDefaultStock);

  }

  //Update the Price Chart fragment with the default stock for this sector.
  private void updateAlsoViewedImage(int iPosition) {

    //Create an array from the sectordefaultsymbol array
    String[] sArray =
            getResources().getStringArray(R.array.sectordefaultsymbol);

    //String to hold this sectorkey's default stock
    String sThisSectorKeyDefaultStock = sArray[iPosition];

    //Update the price chart in Fragment #3.
    oF5C_AC.generateAlsoViewedImage(sThisSectorKeyDefaultStock,
                                    iDeviceWidth,iDeviceWidth);

  }

}

//Create a CustomArrayAdapter in order to highlight the first ListView entry.
private class CustomArrayAdapter extends ArrayAdapter<String> {

 private String[] sArray;
 private Context context;

 public CustomArrayAdapter(Context context,
                           int textViewResourceId,
                           String[] objects) {
  super(context, textViewResourceId, objects);
  this.sArray = objects;
  this.context = context;
 }

 public int getCount() {
  return sArray.length;
 }

 @Override
 public String getItem(int position) {
  return sArray[position];
 }

 @Override
 public View getView(int position, View convertView, ViewGroup parent) {

  View view = convertView;

  //If convertView is null, inflate it with mytextview.
  if (view == null) {
   LayoutInflater inflater = (LayoutInflater)
```

```java
            context.getSystemService(Context.LAYOUT_INFLATER_SERVICE);
   //Inflate the layout.
   view = inflater.inflate(android.R.layout.simple_list_item_1, null);
  }

  //Get the current item based on the position passed in
  String sItem = sArray[position];

  //Create a variable to point to our TextView tvSS.
  TextView oTVSS = (TextView) view.findViewById(android.R.id.text1);

  //Set the text to whatever you want in mytextview
  oTVSS.setText(sItem);

  //Set the background
  if (bFirstTimeThrough && position==0) {
   view.setBackgroundColor(Color.rgb(163, 186, 66));
   viewSectorOLD = view;
  }
  else {
   view.setBackgroundColor(Color.rgb(255, 255, 255));
  }

  if (bFirstTimeThrough) {
   bFirstTimeThrough=false;
  }

  return view;
 }

}

//Called when the user changes the Fragment #1 spinner.
@Override
public void OnFragment1SpinnerChanged(String sSymbol) {

 oF2C_DE.populateDetails(sSymbol);
 oF3C_PC.populatePriceChart(sSymbol);
 oF4C_DC.populateDividendChart(sSymbol);
 oF5C_AC.generateAlsoViewedImage(sSymbol,iDeviceWidth,iDeviceWidth);

 }

}
```

11. `EquityYoDatabaseAccess.java` - this code extends the class `SQLiteAssetHelper` and is used throughout the program to access the database.

```java
package com.example.equityyostocks;

import android.content.Context;
import com.readystatesoftware.sqliteasset.SQLiteAssetHelper;

public class EquityYoDatabaseAccess extends SQLiteAssetHelper {

 private static final String DATABASE_NAME = "EQUITY_DATABASE";
 private static final int DATABASE_VERSION = 1;

 public EquityYoDatabaseAccess(Context context) {
  super(context, DATABASE_NAME, null, DATABASE_VERSION);

  //Force any new database to overwrite an existing database.
  setForcedUpgradeVersion(DATABASE_VERSION);

  //Close the database once it has been installed.
  //I will open the database again later.
  close();
```

```
    }

  }
```

12. `Fragment1SpinnerControl.java` - this code extends `Fragment` and is used to populate the `Spinner` located within Fragment #1.

```java
package com.example.equityyostocks;

import android.app.Activity;
import android.database.Cursor;
import android.database.sqlite.SQLiteDatabase;
import android.os.Bundle;
import android.support.v4.app.Fragment;
import android.support.v4.widget.SimpleCursorAdapter;
import android.widget.AdapterView;
import android.widget.Spinner;
import android.widget.AdapterView.OnItemSelectedListener;
import android.widget.TextView;
import android.util.Log;
import android.view.LayoutInflater;
import android.view.View;
import android.view.ViewGroup;

public class Fragment1SpinnerControl extends Fragment {

  String sSectorKey = "0"; //By default, the sector key is zero.
  View oFragment1Spinner;
  OnFragment1SpinnerChangedListener mCallback;

  //Interface to alert the parent of a change in the Fragment 1 spinner.
  public interface OnFragment1SpinnerChangedListener {
   public void OnFragment1SpinnerChanged(String sSymbol);
  }

  //Pull the arguments from Bundle.
  @Override
  public void onCreate(Bundle savedInstanceState) {
   super.onCreate(savedInstanceState);
   sSectorKey = getArguments() != null ?
                                  getArguments().getString("SECTORKEY")
                                  : "0";
  }

  //Display Fragment #1.
  @Override
  public View onCreateView(LayoutInflater inflater,
                           ViewGroup container,
                           Bundle savedInstanceState) {

   //Create a View object from fragment1_spinner
   oFragment1Spinner =
               inflater.inflate(R.layout.fragment1_spinner,container,false);

   //Add the list of stocks to the spinner in this fragment
   populateSpinner(sSectorKey);

   return oFragment1Spinner;
  }

  //Hook up mCallback to the activity
  @Override
  public void onAttach(Activity activity) {
   super.onAttach(activity);
   mCallback = (OnFragment1SpinnerChangedListener) activity;
  }

  //Populate Fragment #1 Spinner with appropriate data based on sector.
```

```java
 public void populateSpinner(String sSectorKey) {

   EquityYoDatabaseAccess equityYoDB = new
                 EquityYoDatabaseAccess(getActivity().getApplicationContext());
   SQLiteDatabase dbEquityYoDB = equityYoDB.getReadableDatabase();
   String sSQLClause;

   //Set up the SQL clause based on the iSectorKey
   if (sSectorKey.equals("0")) {
    sSQLClause="SELECT DISTINCT _id,Symbol || '/' || sName AS SYMBOL_SNAME FROM
EquityYoSymbolMaster WHERE Type='S' AND SectorKey IS NOT NULL AND IndustryKey
IS NOT NULL ORDER BY 2";
   }
   else {
    sSQLClause="SELECT DISTINCT _id,Symbol || '/' || sName AS SYMBOL_SNAME FROM
EquityYoSymbolMaster WHERE Type='S' AND SectorKey IS NOT NULL AND IndustryKey
IS NOT NULL AND SectorKey=" + sSectorKey + " ORDER BY 2";
   }

   //Obtain a cursor for the query.
   Cursor oCSR = dbEquityYoDB.rawQuery(sSQLClause, null);

   //Attach the cursor to the Fragment #1 Spinner.

   //Instantiate the Spinner as an object
   Spinner oSP = (Spinner)
                   oFragment1Spinner.findViewById(R.id.idfragment1_spinner);

   //Create a new instance of GenericSpinnerListener for the Spinner.
   oSP.setOnItemSelectedListener(new cGenericSpinnerListener());

   //Set up a cursor adapter for the ListView using oCSR
   SimpleCursorAdapter adapter =
             new SimpleCursorAdapter(oFragment1Spinner.getContext(),
                                     android.R.layout.simple_spinner_item,
                                     oCSR,
                                     new String[] {"SYMBOL_SNAME"},
                                     new int[] {android.R.id.text1},0);

   //Indicate which layout to use when the drop-down arrow is clicked.
   adapter.setDropDownViewResource(
                           android.R.layout.simple_spinner_dropdown_item);

   //Assign adapter as the adapter to the spinner.
   oSP.setAdapter(adapter);

   return;
 }

 //*-----------------------------------------------------------------*
 //* Name: cGenericSpinnerListener                                   *
 //* Type: Class                                                     *
 //* Purpose: This class implements the OnItemSelectedListener in order to *
 //*          to create a generic listener for the spinners that appear in *
 //*          the SlidingDrawer.                                      *
 //*-----------------------------------------------------------------*
 private class cGenericSpinnerListener implements OnItemSelectedListener {

  private boolean isFirstTimeThru = true;

  // The onItemSelected method is triggered when a user changes the
  // selected item in a spinner.
  @Override
  public void onItemSelected(AdapterView<?> parent,
                             View view,
                             int position,
                             long id) {

   if (isFirstTimeThru) {
```

```
      isFirstTimeThru = false;

    } else {

      //Based on the new symbol, tell the parent Activity to update
      // fragments 2, 3, 4, and 5.
      String sSpinnerText = (String) ((TextView) view).getText();
      String sSymbol = sSpinnerText.substring(0, sSpinnerText.indexOf("/"));

      mCallback.OnFragment1SpinnerChanged(sSymbol);

    }

  }

  @Override
  public void onNothingSelected(AdapterView<?> parent) {
    // NOP
  }

  } //end of private class GenericSpinnerListener

}
```

13. `Fragment2DetailsControl.java` - this code extends `Fragment` and is
    used to fill in the `TextView`s within Fragment #2.

```
package com.example.equityyostocks;

import java.text.DecimalFormat;

import android.database.Cursor;
import android.database.sqlite.SQLiteDatabase;
import android.os.Bundle;
import android.support.v4.app.Fragment;
import android.text.method.ScrollingMovementMethod;
import android.util.Log;
import android.view.LayoutInflater;
import android.view.MotionEvent;
import android.view.View;
import android.view.ViewGroup;
import android.widget.TextView;

public class Fragment2DetailsControl extends Fragment {

  String sSymbol = "A"; //By default, the symbol for sector zero is A.
  View oFragment2Details;
  int[] aiTextViewIDs = new int[] {
    R.id.tvSTOCK_Symbol,
    R.id.tvSTOCK_MaxMonthPriceNAV,
    R.id.tvSTOCK_sName,
    R.id.tvSTOCK_sInfo,
    R.id.tvSTOCK_Sector,
    R.id.tvSTOCK_Industry,
    R.id.tvSTOCK_sMktCapNetAssets,
    R.id.tvSTOCK_sAverage3MonthVolume,
    R.id.tvSTOCK_sBeta,
    R.id.tvSTOCK_sEPS,
    R.id.tvSTOCK_sPERatio,
    R.id.tvSTOCK_sTargetEstimate,
    R.id.tvSTOCK_PriceGain,
    R.id.tvSTOCK_ComputedYield,
    R.id.tvSTOCK_ComputedDividend,
    R.id.tvSTOCK_sDisplayedYield,
    R.id.tvSTOCK_sDisplayedDividend,
    R.id.tvSTOCK_DividendFrequency,
    R.id.tvSTOCK_DividendConsistency,
    R.id.tvSTOCK_DivGain
```

```java
      };

String[] asDetailColumnNames = new String[] {
  "Symbol",
  "MaxMonthPriceNAV",
  "sName",
  "sInfo",
  "Sector",
  "Industry",
  "sMktCapNetAssets",
  "sAverage3MonthVolume",
  "sBeta",
  "sEPS",
  "sPERatio",
  "sTargetEstimate",
  "YearlyGrowth",
  "ComputedYield",
  "ComputedDividend",
  "sDisplayedYield",
  "sDisplayedDividend",
  "DividendFrequency",
  "DividendConsistency",
  "YearlyDivCapGain"
  };

String[] asDetailColumnLabels = new String[] {
  "Symbol: ",
  "Last Price: $",
  "Company Name: ",
  "Description: ",
  "Sector: ",
  "Industry: ",
  "Market Capitalization: ",
  "Average 3-Month Volume: ",
  "Beta: ",
  "Earnings Per Share(EPS): ",
  "Price/Earnings (PE) Ratio: ",
  "12-Month Target Estimate: ",
  "$10,000 Growth (due to Price): $ ",
  "Computed Yield: ",
  "Computed Dividend: ",
  "Displayed Yield: ",
  "Displayed Dividend: ",
  "Dividend Frequency: ",
  "Dividend Consistency: ",
  "$10,000 Growth (due to Div/CapGain): $"
  };

//Pull the arguments from the Bundle.
@Override
public void onCreate(Bundle savedInstanceState) {
 super.onCreate(savedInstanceState);
 sSymbol = getArguments() != null ? getArguments().getString("SYMBOL") : "A";
}

//Display the fragment.
@Override
public View onCreateView(LayoutInflater inflater,
                         ViewGroup container,
                         Bundle savedInstanceState) {

 //Create a View object from fragment2_details
 oFragment2Details =
         inflater.inflate(R.layout.fragment2_details,container,false);

 //Add the list of stocks to the spinner in this fragment
 populateDetails(sSymbol);

 return oFragment2Details;
}
```

```java
  //Populate Fragment #2.
public void populateDetails(String sSymbol) {

  EquityYoDatabaseAccess equityYoDB = new
            EquityYoDatabaseAccess(getActivity().getApplicationContext());
  SQLiteDatabase dbEquityYoDB = equityYoDB.getReadableDatabase();
  String sSQLClause;
  int iColumnIndex;
  String sColumnValue="";
  TextView aTextView;
  String sColumnLabel="";

  //Set up the SQL clause based on the iSectorKey
  sSQLClause="SELECT * FROM vwEquityYoSymbolMasterSTOCKS WHERE Symbol=" +
                                        '"' + sSymbol + '"';

  //Obtain a cursor for the query.
  Cursor oCSR = dbEquityYoDB.rawQuery(sSQLClause, null);
  oCSR.moveToFirst();

  //Only one line will come in from the database.
  //Match up each textview with its corresponding data from the cursor.
  //Loop around filling in the TextViews.
  for(int i=0;i<aiTextViewIDs.length;i++) {

   //Get the index of the column based on its column name
   iColumnIndex = oCSR.getColumnIndex(asDetailColumnNames[i]);

   //Get the column label
   sColumnLabel = asDetailColumnLabels[i];

   //Set the column text to the corresponding cursor entry.
   if (asDetailColumnNames[i] == "DividendFrequency") {

       sColumnValue = oCSR.isNull(iColumnIndex) ? "-" :
                        Integer.toString(oCSR.getInt(iColumnIndex));

   }
   else if (asDetailColumnNames[i] == "sDisplayedDividend" ||
           asDetailColumnNames[i] == "sDisplayedYield") {

    sColumnValue = oCSR.isNull(iColumnIndex) ? "-" :
                      oCSR.getString(iColumnIndex);

   }
   else if (asDetailColumnNames[i] == "ComputedDividend") {

    if (!oCSR.isNull(iColumnIndex)) {

      //Get the data from the cursor based on the column index
      float fComputedDividend = oCSR.getFloat(iColumnIndex);

      //Set up a DecimalFormat
      DecimalFormat oNF = new DecimalFormat("#,###.##");
      sColumnValue = oNF.format(fComputedDividend);

    } else {

      sColumnValue = "-";

    }
   }
   else if (asDetailColumnNames[i] == "ComputedYield") {

    if (!oCSR.isNull(iColumnIndex)) {

      //Get the data from the cursor based on the column index
      float fComputedYield = oCSR.getFloat(iColumnIndex);
```

525

```
   //Set up a DecimalFormat
   DecimalFormat oNF = new DecimalFormat("#,###.##");
   sColumnValue = oNF.format(fComputedYield)  + "%";

  } else {

   sColumnValue = "-";

  }

 }
 else if (asDetailColumnNames[i] == "MaxMonthPriceNAV") {

  if (!oCSR.isNull(iColumnIndex)) {

   //Get the data from the cursor based on the column index
   float fMaxMonthPriceNAV = oCSR.getFloat(iColumnIndex);

   //Set up a DecimalFormat
   DecimalFormat oNF = new DecimalFormat("#,###,###.00");
   sColumnValue = oNF.format(fMaxMonthPriceNAV) ;

  } else {

   sColumnValue = "-";

  }

 }
 else if (asDetailColumnNames[i] == "YearlyDivCapGain") {

  if (!oCSR.isNull(iColumnIndex)) {

   //Get the data from the cursor based on the column index
   float fYearlyDivCapGain = oCSR.getFloat(iColumnIndex);

   //Set up a DecimalFormat
   DecimalFormat oNF = new DecimalFormat("#,###,###.00");
   sColumnValue = oNF.format(fYearlyDivCapGain);

  } else {

   sColumnValue = "-";

  }

 }
 else if (asDetailColumnNames[i] == "YearlyGrowth") {

  if (!oCSR.isNull(iColumnIndex)) {

   //Get the data from the cursor based on the column index
   float fYearlyGrowth = oCSR.getFloat(iColumnIndex);

   //Set up a DecimalFormat
   DecimalFormat oNF = new DecimalFormat("#,###,###.00");
   sColumnValue = oNF.format(fYearlyGrowth);

  } else {

   sColumnValue = "-";

  }

 }
 else if (asDetailColumnNames[i] == "DividendConsistency" ||
          asDetailColumnNames[i] == "Sector" ||
          asDetailColumnNames[i] == "Industry") {

  //Get the data from the cursor based on the column index
```

```
                sColumnValue = oCSR.isNull(iColumnIndex) ? "-" :
                               oCSR.getString(iColumnIndex);

         }
         else if (asDetailColumnNames[i] == "Symbol" ||
                  asDetailColumnNames[i] == "sName") {

           //Get the data from the cursor based on the column index
           sColumnValue = oCSR.getString(iColumnIndex);

         }
         else if (asDetailColumnNames[i] == "sInfo") {

           //Get the data from the cursor based on the column index
           sColumnValue = oCSR.isNull(iColumnIndex) ? "-" :
                               oCSR.getString(iColumnIndex);

           //Move the sInfo TextView back to the top.
           TextView oTV = (TextView)
                          oFragment2Details.findViewById(R.id.tvSTOCK_sInfo);
           oTV.setMaxLines(10);
           oTV.setMovementMethod(ScrollingMovementMethod.getInstance());
           oTV.setOnTouchListener(new View.OnTouchListener() {

             @Override
             public boolean onTouch(View v, MotionEvent event)
             {
              v.getParent().requestDisallowInterceptTouchEvent(true);
              return false;
             }

           });
           oTV.scrollTo(0, 0);

         }
         else if (asDetailColumnNames[i] == "sMktCapNetAssets") {

           sColumnValue = oCSR.isNull(iColumnIndex) ? "-" :
                               oCSR.getString(iColumnIndex);

         }
         else if (asDetailColumnNames[i] == "sAverage3MonthVolume") {

           sColumnValue = oCSR.isNull(iColumnIndex) ? "-" :
                               oCSR.getString(iColumnIndex);

         }
         else if (asDetailColumnNames[i] == "sBeta" ||
                  asDetailColumnNames[i] == "sEPS" ||
                  asDetailColumnNames[i] == "sPERatio" ||
                  asDetailColumnNames[i] == "sTargetEstimate") {

           sColumnValue = oCSR.isNull(iColumnIndex) ? "-" :
                               oCSR.getString(iColumnIndex);

         }
         else {
           sColumnValue = oCSR.isNull(iColumnIndex) ? "-" :
                               oCSR.getString(iColumnIndex);
         }

         //Create pointer to object TextView for this iteration
         aTextView = (TextView) oFragment2Details.findViewById(aiTextViewIDs[i]);

         //Set the text
         aTextView.setText(sColumnLabel + sColumnValue);

       }

    return;
```

527

```
    }

  }
```

14. `Fragment3PriceChartControl.java` - this code extends `Fragment` and
   is used to fill in the Infragistic's Iguana UI Chart with price data within Fragment
   #3.

```java
package com.example.equityyostocks;

import android.database.Cursor;
import android.database.sqlite.SQLiteDatabase;
import android.graphics.Color;
import android.os.Bundle;
import android.support.v4.app.Fragment;
import android.view.LayoutInflater;
import android.view.View;
import android.view.ViewGroup;
import java.text.NumberFormat;
import java.util.ArrayList;
import java.util.List;
import com.iguanaui.controls.DataChart;
import com.iguanaui.controls.Series;
import com.iguanaui.controls.axes.CategoryAxis;
import com.iguanaui.controls.axes.CategoryXAxis;
import com.iguanaui.controls.axes.NumericAxis;
import com.iguanaui.controls.axes.NumericYAxis;
import com.iguanaui.controls.valuecategory.AreaSeries;
import com.iguanaui.controls.valuecategory.ColumnSeries;
import com.iguanaui.controls.valuecategory.ValueCategorySeries;
import com.iguanaui.graphics.SolidColorBrush;

public class Fragment3PriceChartControl extends Fragment {

  String sSymbol = "A"; //By default, the symbol for sector zero is A.
  View oFragment3PriceChart;
  DataChart igPriceChart,igDivChart;
  cEquityYoIguanaPriceCharts PriceChart,DivChart;

  //Pull the arguments from the Bundle.
  @Override
  public void onCreate(Bundle savedInstanceState) {
   super.onCreate(savedInstanceState);
   sSymbol = getArguments() != null ? getArguments().getString("SYMBOL") : "A";
  }

  //Display the price chart.
  @Override
  public View onCreateView(LayoutInflater inflater,
                           ViewGroup container,
                           Bundle savedInstanceState) {

  //Create a View object from fragment3_price
  oFragment3PriceChart =
           inflater.inflate(R.layout.fragment3_price,container,false);

  //Set up the price chart.
  igPriceChart = (DataChart)
                    oFragment3PriceChart.findViewById(R.id.igPriceChart);
  PriceChart = new cEquityYoIguanaPriceCharts("P",igPriceChart);

  //Add the list of stocks to the spinner in this fragment
  populatePriceChart(sSymbol);

  return oFragment3PriceChart;
  }

  //Populate the chart with the data for the requested symbol.
```

528

```
public void populatePriceChart(String sSymbol) {

 //Update the price chart with the data for this symbol.
 PriceChart.UpdatePriceChart(sSymbol, igPriceChart);

}

//Class to handle the price charts.
public class cEquityYoIguanaPriceCharts {

 //Set up a number format
 final NumberFormat numberFormat = NumberFormat.getInstance();
 private List<String> categories;
 private List<Float> column1;
 private ValueCategorySeries series;
 private CategoryXAxis categoryAxis;
 private NumericYAxis valueAxis;

 EquityYoDatabaseAccess equityYoDB = new
            EquityYoDatabaseAccess(getActivity().getApplicationContext());
 SQLiteDatabase dbEquityYoDB = equityYoDB.getReadableDatabase();
 String sSQLClause;

 //Constructor
 public cEquityYoIguanaPriceCharts(String pWhichData,DataChart igChart) {

  categoryAxis = new CategoryXAxis();
  valueAxis = new NumericYAxis();

  categoryAxis.setLabelBrush(new SolidColorBrush(Color.BLACK));
  valueAxis.setLabelBrush(new SolidColorBrush(Color.BLACK));

  categories = new ArrayList<String>();
  categories.add("1");
  categories.add("2");
  categories.add("3");
  categories.add("4");
  categories.add("5");
  categories.add("6");
  categories.add("7");
  categories.add("8");
  categories.add("9");
  categories.add("10");
  categories.add("11");
  categories.add("12");

  column1 = new ArrayList<Float>();
  column1.add(0.0f);
  column1.add(0.0f);
  column1.add(0.0f);
  column1.add(0.0f);
  column1.add(0.0f);
  column1.add(0.0f);
  column1.add(0.0f);
  column1.add(0.0f);
  column1.add(0.0f);
  column1.add(0.0f);
  column1.add(0.0f);
  column1.add(0.0f);

  //Create the X-Axis categories
  categoryAxis.setDataSource(categories);
  categoryAxis.setLabelFormatter(new CategoryAxis.LabelFormatter() {

   @Override
   public String format(CategoryAxis axis, Object item) {

    String sItem = item.toString();
    String sResult = "W";
```

```java
      if (sItem.contentEquals("1")) sResult="J";
      if (sItem.contentEquals("2")) sResult="F";
      if (sItem.contentEquals("3")) sResult="M";
      if (sItem.contentEquals("4")) sResult="A";
      if (sItem.contentEquals("5")) sResult="M";
      if (sItem.contentEquals("6")) sResult="J";
      if (sItem.contentEquals("7")) sResult="J";
      if (sItem.contentEquals("8")) sResult="A";
      if (sItem.contentEquals("9")) sResult="S";
      if (sItem.contentEquals("10")) sResult="O";
      if (sItem.contentEquals("11")) sResult="N";
      if (sItem.contentEquals("12")) sResult="D";

    return sResult;
   }

 });
 igChart.scales().add(categoryAxis);

 //Create the Y-Axis
 valueAxis.setMinimumValue(valueAxis.getMinimumValue());
 valueAxis.setMaximumValue(valueAxis.getMaximumValue());
 valueAxis.setLabelFormatter(new NumericAxis.LabelFormatter() {

  @Override
  public String format(NumericAxis axis, float item, int precision) {

    if (precision != numberFormat.getMinimumFractionDigits()) {
     numberFormat.setMinimumFractionDigits(precision);
     numberFormat.setMaximumFractionDigits(precision);
    }

    return numberFormat.format(item);
   }

 });
 igChart.scales().add(valueAxis);

 if (pWhichData == "P") {

  series = new AreaSeries();

 }
 else if (pWhichData == "D") {

  series = new ColumnSeries();

 }

 series.setCategoryAxis(categoryAxis);
 series.setValueAxis(valueAxis);
 series.setValueMember("");
 series.setDataSource(column1);
 igChart.series().add(series);

}

//Update the chart
public void UpdatePriceChart(String sSymbol,DataChart igChart) {

 int iMonth;
 float fDiv,fPrice;
 EquityYoDatabaseAccess equityYoDB = new
           EquityYoDatabaseAccess(getActivity().getApplicationContext());
 SQLiteDatabase dbEquityYoDB = equityYoDB.getReadableDatabase();
 String sSQLClause;
 String sWhichData = "P";
 String sType="S";

 if (sWhichData=="P") {
```

```java
        //Query the database table EquityYoPriceData.
        sSQLClause = "SELECT Month,CAST(TOTAL(Price) AS REAL) AS Price FROM
(SELECT Month,Price FROM EquityYoPriceData WHERE Type=? AND Symbol=? UNION ALL
SELECT Month,0 AS Price FROM EquityYoDateData) GROUP BY Month ORDER BY Month";

        //Execute the query
        Cursor oCsr = dbEquityYoDB.rawQuery(sSQLClause,
                                            new String[] {sType,sSymbol});
        oCsr.moveToFirst();

        //Pull in the indices for the month and price to be used below.
        int iMonthIndex = oCsr.getColumnIndex("Month");
        int iPriceIndex = oCsr.getColumnIndex("Price");

        //Fill in categories and column1 based on the Month and Price data.
        if (oCsr.getCount()>0) {
         while (oCsr.moveToNext()) {

          //Pull the month and format it to a character string.
          iMonth = oCsr.getInt(iMonthIndex);

          //Pull the price.
          fPrice = oCsr.getFloat(iPriceIndex);

          //Fill in the arrays
          categories.set(iMonth-1,Integer.toString(iMonth));
          column1.set(iMonth-1,fPrice);

         }
        }

        //Close the cursor.
        oCsr.close();

        valueAxis.setMinimumValue(0.90f * valueAxis.getMinimumValue());
        valueAxis.setMaximumValue(1.10f * valueAxis.getMaximumValue());

        series.setDataSource(null);
        series.setDataSource(column1);
        for (Series s: igChart.series()) {
         s.notifyDataReset();
        }
        series.notifyDataUpdate(0, 12);

      }

    }

  }

}
```

15. `Fragment4DividendChartControl.java` - this code extends `Fragment` and is used to fill in the Infragistic's Iguana UI Chart with dividend data within Fragment #4.

```java
package com.example.equityyostocks;

import android.database.Cursor;
import android.database.sqlite.SQLiteDatabase;
import android.graphics.Color;
import android.os.Bundle;
import android.support.v4.app.Fragment;
import android.view.LayoutInflater;
import android.view.View;
import android.view.ViewGroup;
import java.text.NumberFormat;
```

531

```java
import java.util.ArrayList;
import java.util.List;
import com.iguanaui.controls.DataChart;
import com.iguanaui.controls.Series;
import com.iguanaui.controls.axes.CategoryAxis;
import com.iguanaui.controls.axes.CategoryXAxis;
import com.iguanaui.controls.axes.NumericAxis;
import com.iguanaui.controls.axes.NumericYAxis;
import com.iguanaui.controls.valuecategory.AreaSeries;
import com.iguanaui.controls.valuecategory.ColumnSeries;
import com.iguanaui.controls.valuecategory.ValueCategorySeries;
import com.iguanaui.graphics.SolidColorBrush;

public class Fragment4DividendChartControl extends Fragment {

  String sSymbol = "A"; //By default, the symbol for sector zero is A.
  View oFragment4DividendChart;
  DataChart igDivChart;
  cEquityYoIguanaDividendCharts DivChart;

  //Pull the arguments from the Bundle.
  @Override
  public void onCreate(Bundle savedInstanceState) {
   super.onCreate(savedInstanceState);
   sSymbol = getArguments() != null ? getArguments().getString("SYMBOL") : "A";
  }

  //Display the fragment.
  @Override
  public View onCreateView(LayoutInflater inflater,
                           ViewGroup container,
                           Bundle savedInstanceState) {

   //Create a View object from fragment4_dividend
   oFragment4DividendChart =
           inflater.inflate(R.layout.fragment4_dividend,container,false);

   //Set up the price chart.
   igDivChart = (DataChart)
                oFragment4DividendChart.findViewById(R.id.igDivChart);
   DivChart = new cEquityYoIguanaDividendCharts("D",igDivChart);

   //Add the list of stocks to the spinner in this fragment
   populateDividendChart(sSymbol);

   return oFragment4DividendChart;
  }

  //Populate the chart with the data for the requested symbol.
  public void populateDividendChart(String sSymbol) {

   DivChart.UpdateDivChart(sSymbol, igDivChart);

  }

  //Class to handle the price charts.
  public class cEquityYoIguanaDividendCharts {

   //Set up a number format
   final NumberFormat numberFormat = NumberFormat.getInstance();
   private List<String> categories;
   private List<Float> column1;
   private ValueCategorySeries series;
   private CategoryXAxis categoryAxis;
   private NumericYAxis valueAxis;

   EquityYoDatabaseAccess equityYoDB = new
           EquityYoDatabaseAccess(getActivity().getApplicationContext());
   SQLiteDatabase dbEquityYoDB = equityYoDB.getReadableDatabase();
   String sSQLClause;
```

532

```java
//Constructor
public cEquityYoIguanaDividendCharts(String pWhichData,DataChart igChart) {

    categoryAxis = new CategoryXAxis();
    valueAxis = new NumericYAxis();

    categoryAxis.setLabelBrush(new SolidColorBrush(Color.BLACK));
    valueAxis.setLabelBrush(new SolidColorBrush(Color.BLACK));

    categories = new ArrayList<String>();
    categories.add("1");
    categories.add("2");
    categories.add("3");
    categories.add("4");
    categories.add("5");
    categories.add("6");
    categories.add("7");
    categories.add("8");
    categories.add("9");
    categories.add("10");
    categories.add("11");
    categories.add("12");

    column1 = new ArrayList<Float>();
    column1.add(0.0f);
    column1.add(0.0f);
    column1.add(0.0f);
    column1.add(0.0f);
    column1.add(0.0f);
    column1.add(0.0f);
    column1.add(0.0f);
    column1.add(0.0f);
    column1.add(0.0f);
    column1.add(0.0f);
    column1.add(0.0f);
    column1.add(0.0f);

    //Create the X-Axis categories
    categoryAxis.setDataSource(categories);
    categoryAxis.setLabelFormatter(new CategoryAxis.LabelFormatter() {

        @Override
        public String format(CategoryAxis axis, Object item) {

            String sItem = item.toString();
            String sResult = "W";

            if (sItem.contentEquals("1")) sResult="J";
            if (sItem.contentEquals("2")) sResult="F";
            if (sItem.contentEquals("3")) sResult="M";
            if (sItem.contentEquals("4")) sResult="A";
            if (sItem.contentEquals("5")) sResult="M";
            if (sItem.contentEquals("6")) sResult="J";
            if (sItem.contentEquals("7")) sResult="J";
            if (sItem.contentEquals("8")) sResult="A";
            if (sItem.contentEquals("9")) sResult="S";
            if (sItem.contentEquals("10")) sResult="O";
            if (sItem.contentEquals("11")) sResult="N";
            if (sItem.contentEquals("12")) sResult="D";

            return sResult;
        }

    });
    igChart.scales().add(categoryAxis);

    //Create the Y-Axis
    valueAxis.setMinimumValue(valueAxis.getMinimumValue());
    valueAxis.setMaximumValue(valueAxis.getMaximumValue());
```

```java
    valueAxis.setLabelFormatter(new NumericAxis.LabelFormatter() {

     @Override
     public String format(NumericAxis axis, float item, int precision) {

      if (precision != numberFormat.getMinimumFractionDigits()) {
       numberFormat.setMinimumFractionDigits(precision);
       numberFormat.setMaximumFractionDigits(precision);
      }

      return numberFormat.format(item);
     }

    });
    igChart.scales().add(valueAxis);

    if (pWhichData == "P") {

     series = new AreaSeries();

    }
    else if (pWhichData == "D") {

     series = new ColumnSeries();

    }

    series.setCategoryAxis(categoryAxis);
    series.setValueAxis(valueAxis);
    series.setValueMember("");
    series.setDataSource(column1);
    igChart.series().add(series);

   }

  //Update the chart
  public void UpdateDivChart(String sSymbol,DataChart igChart) {

   int iMonth;
   float fDiv,fPrice;
   EquityYoDatabaseAccess equityYoDB = new
        EquityYoDatabaseAccess(getActivity().getApplicationContext());
   SQLiteDatabase dbEquityYoDB = equityYoDB.getReadableDatabase();
   String sSQLClause;
   String sWhichData = "D";
   String sType="S";

   if (sWhichData=="D") {

    //Query the database table EquityYoPriceData.
    sSQLClause = "SELECT Month,CAST(TOTAL(Dividend) AS REAL) AS Dividend FROM
(SELECT Month,Dividend FROM EquityYoDividendData WHERE Type=? AND Symbol=?
UNION ALL SELECT Month,0 AS Dividend FROM EquityYoDateData) GROUP BY Month
ORDER BY Month";

    //Execute the query
    Cursor oCsr = dbEquityYoDB.rawQuery(sSQLClause,
                                  new String[] {sType,sSymbol});
    oCsr.moveToFirst();

    //Pull in the indices for the month and price to be used below.
    int iMonthIndex = oCsr.getColumnIndex("Month");
    int iDivIndex = oCsr.getColumnIndex("Dividend");

    //Fill in categories and column1 based on the Month and Price data.
    if (oCsr.getCount()>0) {
     while (oCsr.moveToNext()) {

      //Pull the month and format it to a character string.
      iMonth = oCsr.getInt(iMonthIndex);
```
534

```
        //Pull the price.
        fDiv = oCsr.getFloat(iDivIndex);

        //Fill in the arrays
        categories.set(iMonth-1,Integer.toString(iMonth));
        column1.set(iMonth-1,fDiv);

      }
    }
    else {
     for(int i=0;i<12;i++) {

       categories.set(i,Integer.toString(i+1));
       column1.set(i,0.0f);

     }
    }

    //Close the cursor.
    oCsr.close();

    valueAxis.setMinimumValue(0.00f);
    valueAxis.setMaximumValue(1.10f * valueAxis.getMaximumValue());

    series.setDataSource(null);
    series.setDataSource(column1);
    for (Series s: igChart.series()) {
     s.notifyDataReset();
    }
    series.notifyDataUpdate(0, 12);

   }

  }

 }

}
```

16. `Fragment5AlsoViewedImageControl.java` - this code extends `Fragment` and is used to generate the Also Viewed image within Fragment #5.

```
package com.example.equityyostocks;

import android.graphics.Bitmap;
import android.graphics.Canvas;
import android.graphics.Color;
import android.graphics.Paint;
import android.graphics.Paint.Style;
import android.graphics.Rect;
import android.graphics.RectF;
import android.graphics.Typeface;
import android.view.LayoutInflater;
import android.view.View;
import android.view.ViewGroup;
import android.widget.ImageView;
import android.os.Bundle;
import android.support.v4.app.Fragment;
import android.util.FloatMath;
import android.database.Cursor;
import android.database.sqlite.SQLiteDatabase;

public class Fragment5AlsoViewedImageControl extends Fragment {

 String sSymbol = "A"; //By default, the symbol for sector zero is A.
 View oFragment5AlsoViewedImage;
 private cAlsoViewed AlsoViewed;
```

535

```java
 private ImageView igAVImageView;
 int iAlsoViewedMeasuredHeight=0;
 int iAlsoViewedMeasuredWidth=0;
 String sPV;

 //Pull the arguments from the Bundle.
 @Override
 public void onCreate(Bundle savedInstanceState) {
  super.onCreate(savedInstanceState);
  sSymbol = getArguments() != null ? getArguments().getString("SYMBOL") : "A";
  iAlsoViewedMeasuredHeight = getArguments() != null ?
                                      getArguments().getInt("HEIGHT") : 0;
  iAlsoViewedMeasuredWidth = getArguments() != null ?
                                      getArguments().getInt("WIDTH") : 0;
 }

 //Display the fragment.
 @Override
 public View onCreateView(LayoutInflater inflater,
                          ViewGroup container,
                          Bundle savedInstanceState) {

  //Create a View object from fragment5_alsoviewed
  oFragment5AlsoViewedImage =
              inflater.inflate(R.layout.fragment5_alsoviewed,container,false);

  igAVImageView = (ImageView)
              oFragment5AlsoViewedImage.findViewById(R.id.igAVImageView);
  AlsoViewed = new cAlsoViewed(igAVImageView);

  //Generate the image first time round.
  generateAlsoViewedImage(sSymbol,
                          iAlsoViewedMeasuredWidth,
                          iAlsoViewedMeasuredWidth);

  return oFragment5AlsoViewedImage;
 }

 //Generate the Also Viewed image.
 public void generateAlsoViewedImage(String sSymbol,int piHeight,int piWidth)
 {

  AlsoViewed.UpdateAlsoViewedImage(sSymbol, piHeight, piWidth);

 }

 //Class to handle generating the AlsoViewed bitmap image.
 public class cAlsoViewed {

  //String sSymbol = "";
  String sPV = "-";
  ImageView oAVIV = null;

  EquityYoDatabaseAccess equityYoDB = new
              EquityYoDatabaseAccess(getActivity().getApplicationContext());
  SQLiteDatabase dbEquityYoDB = equityYoDB.getReadableDatabase();
  String sSQLClause;

  public cAlsoViewed(ImageView poAVImageView) {

   oAVIV = poAVImageView;

  }

  public void UpdateAlsoViewedImage(String psSymbol,int piHeight,int piWidth)
 {

   sSymbol = psSymbol;
   iAlsoViewedMeasuredHeight = piHeight;
   iAlsoViewedMeasuredWidth = piWidth;
```

536

```
    //Pull the PV column from the database.
    sSQLClause = "SELECT sPV FROM vwEquityYoSymbolMasterSTOCKS WHERE sPV IS NOT
NULL AND SYMBOL='" + sSymbol + "'";

    //Execute the query
    Cursor oCSR = dbEquityYoDB.rawQuery(sSQLClause, null);
    oCSR.moveToFirst();
    int iColumnIndex = oCSR.getColumnIndex("sPV");
    if (oCSR.getCount() > 0) {
     sPV = (oCSR.isNull(iColumnIndex) ? "-" : oCSR.getString(iColumnIndex));
    }
    else {
     sPV="-";
    }

    Rect oSymbolRect = new Rect();
    Rect oTextRect = new Rect();

    //Update the imageview's height.
    oAVIV.setMinimumHeight(iAlsoViewedMeasuredHeight);

    //Create a blank bitmap.
    Bitmap oBM = Bitmap.createBitmap(iAlsoViewedMeasuredHeight,
                                     iAlsoViewedMeasuredWidth,
                                     Bitmap.Config.ARGB_8888);

    //Create a Canvas associating the bitmap oBM with it,
    Canvas oCanvas = new Canvas(oBM);

    //Paint to canvas oCanvas.
    oCanvas.drawARGB(255, 255, 255, 255);

    //Create a Paint object for the line
    Paint oPT_LINE = new Paint(Paint.DITHER_FLAG | Paint.ANTI_ALIAS_FLAG);
    oPT_LINE.setARGB(255, 255, 255, 255);
    oPT_LINE.setStrokeWidth(3);
    oPT_LINE.setColor(Color.BLACK);
    oPT_LINE.setStyle(Style.STROKE);

    //Create a Paint object for the dot
    Paint oPT_DOT = new Paint(Paint.DITHER_FLAG | Paint.ANTI_ALIAS_FLAG);
    oPT_DOT.setARGB(255, 255, 255, 255);
    oPT_DOT.setStrokeWidth(3);
    oPT_DOT.setColor(Color.BLACK);
    oPT_DOT.setStyle(Style.FILL_AND_STROKE);

    //Create a Paint object for the text (black and bold)
    Paint oPT_TEXT = new Paint(Paint.DITHER_FLAG | Paint.ANTI_ALIAS_FLAG);
    oPT_TEXT.setARGB(255, 255, 255, 255);
    oPT_TEXT.setTypeface(Typeface.DEFAULT_BOLD);
    oPT_TEXT.setTextSize(24);
    oPT_TEXT.setColor(Color.BLACK);
    oPT_TEXT.setTextAlign(Paint.Align.CENTER);

    //Determine the center of the canvas
    int iCanvasHeight = oCanvas.getHeight();
    int iCanvasWidth = oCanvas.getWidth();
    float fCanvasHeight_CENTER = ( ((float) iCanvasHeight) / 2.0f);
    float fCanvasWidth_CENTER = ( ((float) iCanvasWidth) / 2.0f);

    if (sPV.contentEquals("-")) {

     //Determine the bounding box for the text sSymbol.
     oPT_TEXT.getTextBounds("NO DATA AVAILABLE",
                            0,
                            "NO DATA AVAILABLE".length(),
                            oSymbolRect);

     //Place the sSymbol on the canvas.
```

```
        oCanvas.drawText("NO DATA AVAILABLE",
                          fCanvasWidth_CENTER,
                          fCanvasHeight_CENTER + (oSymbolRect.height())/2,
                          oPT_TEXT);

  //Place a line around the perimeter of the bitmap
  oCanvas.drawRoundRect(new RectF(0f,0f,(float) piWidth,(float) piHeight),
                        20.0f, 20.0f, oPT_LINE);

} else {

  //Place a line around the perimeter of the bitmap
  oCanvas.drawRoundRect(new RectF(0f,0f,(float) piWidth,(float) piHeight),
                        20.0f, 20.0f, oPT_LINE);

  //Determine the bounding box for the text sSymbol.
  oPT_TEXT.getTextBounds(sSymbol, 0, sSymbol.length(), oSymbolRect);

  //Place the sSymbol on the canvas.
  oCanvas.drawText(sSymbol,
                   fCanvasWidth_CENTER,
                   fCanvasHeight_CENTER + (oSymbolRect.height())/2,
                   oPT_TEXT);

  //Parse sPV in to an array.
  String[] aPV = sPV.split((";"));

  //Determine the number of entries in aPV
  int iNbrPV = aPV.length;

  //Determine the number of degrees we will place each entry
  // in aPV on the SurfaceView.
  float fDegrees = 360f / (float)iNbrPV;

  //Determine the width of the text WWWWW.
  Rect oWWWWWRect = new Rect();
  oPT_TEXT.getTextBounds("WWWWW", 0, "WWWWW".length(), oWWWWWRect);
  float fWWWWWWidth = (float) (Math.abs(oWWWWWRect.width()));

  //Compute the x-coordinate from the right side based on WWWWW
  // (assumes the translate() has occurred!)
  float fXCoord = fCanvasWidth_CENTER - fWWWWWWidth;

  //Draw each entry in sPV in turn on the surface starting at
  // zero degrees and working clockwise fDegrees.
  oCanvas.save();
  oCanvas.translate(fCanvasWidth_CENTER, fCanvasHeight_CENTER);

  //Place a circle around the sSymbol
  oCanvas.drawCircle(0, 0, fWWWWWWidth/2f, oPT_LINE);
  float fThisX;
  float fThisY;
  for(int i=0;i<iNbrPV;i++) {

   //Re-initialize variables
   fThisX=0;
   fThisY=0;
   oTextRect.setEmpty();

   //Get the symbol for this iteration
   String sThisSymbol = aPV[i];

   //Based on i, determine the degrees to place it at.
   float fThisDegrees = fDegrees * ( (float) i );
   float fThisRadians = (float) Math.toRadians(fThisDegrees);

   //Rotate the canvas
   fThisX = (float) (fXCoord * FloatMath.cos(fThisRadians));
   fThisY = (float) (fXCoord * FloatMath.sin(fThisRadians));
```

538

```
            //Get the bounds of the this iteration's symbol
            oPT_TEXT.getTextBounds(sThisSymbol, 0, sThisSymbol.length(), oTextRect);

            //Draw a line from the origin (0,0) to the center of this
            // iteration's symbol.
            float fThisXOrigin = (float) (fWWWWWWidth/2f *
                                                FloatMath.cos(fThisRadians));
            float fThisYOrigin = (float) (fWWWWWWidth/2f *
                                                FloatMath.sin(fThisRadians));
            float fThisXEnd = (float) (0.90f * fXCoord *
                                                FloatMath.cos(fThisRadians));
            float fThisYEnd = (float) (0.90f * fXCoord *
                                                FloatMath.sin(fThisRadians));

            //Draw a line from the sSymbol to this iteration's symbol.
            oCanvas.drawLine(fThisXOrigin,
                            fThisYOrigin,
                            fThisXEnd,
                            fThisYEnd,
                            oPT_LINE);

            //Draw a small filled circle at the (fThisXOrigin,fThisYOrigin)
            oCanvas.drawCircle(fThisXOrigin, fThisYOrigin, 4f, oPT_DOT);

            //Place the sSymbol on the canvas.
            if (fThisDegrees == 0f) {
             oPT_TEXT.setTextAlign(Paint.Align.LEFT);
             oCanvas.drawText(sThisSymbol,
                            fThisX,
                            fThisY + (oTextRect.height()/2),
                            oPT_TEXT);
            } else if (fThisDegrees == 180f ) {
             oPT_TEXT.setTextAlign(Paint.Align.RIGHT);
             oCanvas.drawText(sThisSymbol,
                            fThisX,
                            fThisY + (oTextRect.height()/2),
                            oPT_TEXT);
            } else if (fThisDegrees > 0f && fThisDegrees < 180f ) {
             oPT_TEXT.setTextAlign(Paint.Align.CENTER);
             oCanvas.drawText(sThisSymbol,
                            fThisX,
                            fThisY + (oTextRect.height()/2),
                            oPT_TEXT);
            } else if (fThisDegrees > 180f && fThisDegrees < 360f ) {
             oPT_TEXT.setTextAlign(Paint.Align.CENTER);
             oCanvas.drawText(sThisSymbol,
                            fThisX,
                            fThisY + (oTextRect.height()/2),
                            oPT_TEXT);
            } else {
             oPT_TEXT.setTextAlign(Paint.Align.CENTER);
             oCanvas.drawText(sThisSymbol, fThisX, fThisY, oPT_TEXT);
            }

          }
         oCanvas.restore();

        }

     //Set the bitmap, oBM, as the image of imageView1.
     oAVIV.setImageBitmap(oBM);

    }
  }

}
```

Let's go through the fragment-related code. In the `onCreate()` method of `MainActivity.java`, I initialize the global variable `oFM` to the `FragmentManager` using the `getSupportFragmentManager()` method. (Note that if you are not using the Support Library, you can use `getFragmentManager()` instead.) I then call `initialLoadFragments()` to instantiate the five fragments like so:

```
//Instantiate the five fragments.
oF1C_SP = new Fragment1SpinnerControl(); //Fragment #1: Spinner
oF2C_DE = new Fragment2DetailsControl(); //Fragment #2: Details
oF3C_PC = new Fragment3PriceChartControl(); //Fragment #3: Price Chart
oF4C_DC = new Fragment4DividendChartControl(); //Fragment #4: Dividend Chart
oF5C_AC = new Fragment5AlsoViewedImageControl(); //Fragment #5: Also Viewed Image
```

Next, I create a `Bundle` and fill each fragment in with the appropriate arguments, usually the stock symbol (e.g., MSFT for Microsoft) and other information:

```
//Set up a Bundle for use with the five fragment objects.
Bundle oBundleArgs = new Bundle();

//Populate oBundleArgs for use with the fragments.
oBundleArgs.putString("SECTORKEY", "0");
oBundleArgs.putString("SYMBOL", "A");
oBundleArgs.putInt("WIDTH", iDeviceWidth);
oBundleArgs.putInt("HEIGHT", iDeviceHeight);

//Fragment #1: Spinner
oF1C_SP.setArguments(oBundleArgs);
...and so on...
```

Next, I begin a transaction and add each fragment in turn into it using the `add()` method. I then commit the transactions using the `commit()` or `commitAllowingStateLoss()` methods. Finally, although not necessary, you can force the transactions to occur immediately by issuing `executePending Transactions()`. Note that I add in the fragments in the order I want them to appear, top to bottom, in my vertical `LinearLayout`.

```
//Begin a fragment transaction
oFT = oFM.beginTransaction();

//Add in the fragments
oFT.add(R.id.mainframe,oF1C_SP);
oFT.add(R.id.mainframe,oF2C_DE);
oFT.add(R.id.mainframe,oF3C_PC);
oFT.add(R.id.mainframe,oF4C_DC);
oFT.add(R.id.mainframe,oF5C_AC);

//Commit the change.
oFT.commitAllowingStateLoss();

//Execute Pending Transactions
oFM.executePendingTransactions();
```

Now, usually you want to use `commit()` instead of `commitAllowing StateLoss()`, but here are some important comments from the Android documentation:

1. `commit()` - *Schedules a commit of this transaction. The commit does not happen immediately; it will be scheduled as work on the main thread to be done*

the next time that thread is ready. A transaction can only be committed with this method prior to its containing activity saving its state. If the commit is attempted after that point, an exception will be thrown. This is because the state after the commit can be lost if the activity needs to be restored from its state. See `commitAllowingStateLoss()` *for situations where it may be okay to lose the commit.*

2. `commitAllowingStateLoss()` - *Like* `commit()` *but allows the commit to be executed after an activity's state is saved. This is dangerous because the commit can be lost if the activity needs to later be restored from its state, so this should only be used for cases where it is okay for the UI state to change unexpectedly on the user.*

In the example, I use `commitAllowingStateLoss()` because I received the error message *Can not perform this action after onSaveInstanceState* when using `commit()` instead. Please see the following StackOverflow page for more information and suggestions for alternate approaches:

`http://stackoverflow.com/questions/7575921/illegalstateexcept`
`ion-can-not-perform-this-action-after-onsaveinstancestate-h.`

Now, after the `Bundle` is attached to each fragment object, its `onCreate()` method is called so that you can unload the `Bundle`:

```
//Pull the arguments from the Bundle.
@Override
public void onCreate(Bundle savedInstanceState) {
 super.onCreate(savedInstanceState);
 sSectorKey = getArguments() != null ? getArguments().getString("SECTORKEY")
                                     : "0";
}
```

Next, the fragment's `onCreateView()` will be called whereupon you can create its view based on the arguments passed in via the `Bundle`. In fact, I keep each fragment's `onCreateView()` method simple, usually inflating the fragment (here, `fragment1_spinner.xml`) and then populating the fragment (below, the `Spinner` containing the list of sector-specific stock symbols).

```
@Override
public View onCreateView(LayoutInflater inflater,
                         ViewGroup container,
                         Bundle savedInstanceState) {

 //Create a View object from fragment1_spinner
 oFragment1Spinner =
         inflater.inflate(R.layout.fragment1_spinner,container,false);

 //Add the list of stocks to the spinner in this fragment
 populateSpinner(sSectorKey);

 return oFragment1Spinner;
}
```

Now, the code for the remaining fragments is about the same, so I won't go through them, so please peruse the code above.

Recall above that I described how fragments communicate. First, let's see how a change in the Fragment #1 `Spinner` alerts the parent `Activity` which then updates Fragment #2, Fragment #3, Fragment #4 and Fragment #5. Within `Fragment1SpinnerControl.java`, I created an `interface` along with a global variable to that `interface`:

```
OnFragment1SpinnerChangedListener mCallback;

//Interface used to alert the parent Activity of change in Fragment #1 Spinner.
public interface OnFragment1SpinnerChangedListener {
 public void OnFragment1SpinnerChanged(String sSymbol);
}
```

Notice that the name of the function that will be called is `OnFragment1Spinner Changed()`. Further below in the code, I hook up this listener to the parent `Activity` by overriding the `onAttach()` method, as shown below:

```
//Hook up mCallback to the activity
@Override
public void onAttach(Activity activity) {
 super.onAttach(activity);
 mCallback = (OnFragment1SpinnerChangedListener) activity;
}
```

Next, we have to call `OnFragment1SpinnerChanged()` somehow and this occurs whenever the user selects a new stock from the Fragment #1 `Spinner`. In this case, I created my own class that implements `OnItemSelectedListener`. First, here is how I link the Fragment #1 `Spinner` with my new class:

```
//Create a new instance of GenericSpinnerListener for the Spinner.
oSP.setOnItemSelectedListener(new cGenericSpinnerListener());
```

The class `cGenericSpinnerListener` is below:

```
private class cGenericSpinnerListener implements OnItemSelectedListener {

 private boolean isFirstTimeThru = true;

 // The onItemSelected method is triggered when a user changes the
 // selected item in a spinner.
 @Override
 public void onItemSelected(AdapterView<?> parent,
                            View view,
                            int position,
                            long id) {

  if (isFirstTimeThru) {

   isFirstTimeThru = false;

  } else {

   //Based on the new stock symbol, tell the parent Activity to
   // update fragments 2, 3, 4, and 5.
   String sSpinnerText = (String) ((TextView) view).getText();
   String sSymbol = sSpinnerText.substring(0, sSpinnerText.indexOf("/"));
   mCallback.OnFragment1SpinnerChanged(sSymbol);

  }

 }
```

```
@Override
public void onNothingSelected(AdapterView<?> parent) {
  // NOP
 }

} //end of private class GenericSpinnerListener
```

Take note that it is the code `mCallback.OnFragment1SpinnerChanged` `(sSymbol);` which actually calls the corresponding code implemented in the parent `Activity`. Let's talk about that now. Within `MainActivity.java`, we implement the `interface` as shown below:

```
public class MainActivity extends ActionBarActivity
         implements Fragment1SpinnerControl.OnFragment1SpinnerChangedListener {
```

Next, we implement the method `onFragment1SpinnerChanged()` somewhere within `MainActivity.java`:

```
//Called when the user changes the Fragment #1 spinner.
@Override
public void OnFragment1SpinnerChanged(String sSymbol) {

 oF2C_DE.populateDetails(sSymbol);
 oF3C_PC.populatePriceChart(sSymbol);
 oF4C_DC.populateDividendChart(sSymbol);
 oF5C_AC.generateAlsoViewedImage(sSymbol,iDeviceWidth,iDeviceWidth);

}
```

Notice that I just call the appropriate `public` methods within each fragment in turn.

The other method of communication is from `Activity` to `Fragment` and is illustrated above by calling the `public` methods `populateDetails()`, `populatePriceChart()`, etc.

In order to ensure that the app functions when the user leaves the app and then goes back into the app, I created an override to the `onRestart()` method of `MainActivity.java`. In this case, I just wanted the app to re-initialize to the way it looks when it is first started. Here is my `onRestart()` method:

```
//Override the onRestart method.
@Override
protected void onRestart() {
 super.onRestart();

 //Re-init the boolean variable bFirstTimeThrough to true.
 bFirstTimeThrough=true;

 //Remove the fragments.
 oFT = oFM.beginTransaction();
 oFT.remove(oF5C_AC);
 oFT.remove(oF4C_DC);
 oFT.remove(oF3C_PC);
 oFT.remove(oF2C_DE);
 oFT.remove(oF1C_SP);
 oFT.commitAllowingStateLoss();
 oFM.executePendingTransactions();
```

```
//Re-initialize the sector ListView
oSectorListView = (ListView) findViewById(R.id.sector_drawer);
String[] aSectorNames = getResources().getStringArray(R.array.sectors);
CustomArrayAdapter adapter = new CustomArrayAdapter(this,
                                     android.R.layout.simple_list_item_1,
                                     aSectorNames);
oSectorListView.setAdapter(adapter);

//Re-initialize the fragments
initialLoadFragments();

//Move the ScrollView up to the top.
oScrollView.scrollTo(0, 0);

}
```

Note that I remove the fragments in the **reverse** order I added them which may seem strange. When I attempted to remove them in the opposite order (oF1C_SP first, oF5C_AC last), and then subsequently add them in the correct order shown in the `initialLoadFragments()` method, the fragments displayed in the *opposite* order with Fragment #5 appearing at the top of the LinearLayout and Fragment #1 appearing at the bottom of the LinearLayout. Yikes! To correct this, I reversed the order I removed them (as shown above) and the fragments appeared in the correct order when the onRestart() method executed. So, the takeaway is that if your fragments are appearing in the wrong order, check the order of the remove() methods and see if switching the order around helps.

Some additional comments:

1. I created a CustomArrayAdapter class derived from ArrayAdapter in order to set the *All Sectors* item in the sector Spinner to have a green background color. Attempts to do this using code such as getChildAt().setBackgroundColor(), getFirstVisible Position() along with setBackgroundColor(), performItemClick() to fake an item click, and so on did not work. The only thing that did work was overriding the getView() method in the custom class.
2. I did not show the code associated with the menu click that displays the user guide. Similar code will be found in Chapter 31, *Working with WebView and WebViewClient*.
3. Note that rather than continually removing a fragment and then adding it back in, I just updated the View within the fragment. I think this is a better way to update fragments, but your app requirements may be different from my example.
4. Note that I did not use addToBackStack() within my app, since I did not want the user to hit the back button to go back, but rather click the Fragment #1 Spinner instead. Again, your app requirements may be different from my example. Please see Simple Example #2.5 for more on addToBackStack().
5. Another nice use of fragments is to control what happens when the device changes from portrait to landscape mode or vice versa. Since an example of this appears in the Android documentation on Fragments (see *Building a Flexible UI* on the Android Developers website) as well as on several other websites, I won't repeat it here.

Fragment Subclasses (`DialogFragment`, `ListFragment`, `PreferenceFragment`)

There are several subclasses of `Fragment` available to use and we go through some of them in this section. Take note that the three subclasses were added in API Level 11 (Honeycomb 3.0).

1. `DialogFragment` - this is a fragment that displays a dialog window floating on top of the parent `Activity`. For example, the Amazon app occasionally displays the following dialog which may be implemented as a `DialogFragment` (or an `AlertDialog`, which we explain below):

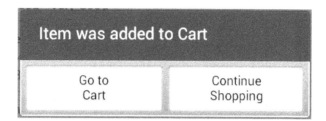

2. `ListFragment` - According to the Android documentation, this is *a fragment that displays a list of items by binding to a data source such as an array or Cursor, and exposes event handlers when the user selects an item. ListFragment hosts a ListView object that can be bound to different data sources, typically either an array or a Cursor holding query results.*

3. `PreferenceFragment` - this class is used *to show a hierarchy of* `Preference` *objects as lists. These preferences will automatically save to* `SharedPreferences` *as the user interacts with them.* This is similar to `PreferenceActivity` we described in Chapter 14, *Saving State: Bundle, SharedPreference and PreferenceActivity.* We won't talk about `PreferenceFragment` in this book, so please see the Android documentation for more about it.

EquityYo! and Fragments - Complex Example #2

Let's extend Complex Example #1 to include a search feature which will be displayed when the user clicks the menu item *Search* on the `ActionBar`. This will bring up a fragment that will allow you to search the company name and display the results in a `ListFragment` which is similar to `ListActivity`. The search results will be added to the back stack using `addToBackStack()` along with an animation which slides in and out from the right side. Here is what the search activity looks like when its `ListFragment` is filled in based on the search criteria "BIO":

Note that if the user searches several times, several fragments are built up due to the `addToBackStack()` method. Hitting the back button reveals the previous search request.

Now, when the user's search criteria is blank, a dialog will be displayed asking the user if he wants to search again or close the search activity. To display this, we subclass the `DialogFragment` class and use the `AlertDialog.Builder` class to easily create a two-button alert. Here is what our alert will look like:

When the user clicks on the *Search Again* button, the dialog itself closes. When the user clicks on the *Go Home* button, the search activity will be closed (`finished()`) and the user will see the main screen. We won't describe the `DialogFragment` class per se since `AlertDialog`, which is a subclass of `DialogFragment`, is sweeeeeet!

First, let's see the code and then we'll explain it further below.

1. `activity_search.xml` - this layout describes what the search `Activity` will look like. In this case, an `EditText`, a `Button` and a `LinearLayout` used to hold the `ListFragment` containing the search results.

```xml
<?xml version="1.0" encoding="utf-8"?>
<LinearLayout xmlns:android="http://schemas.android.com/apk/res/android"
    android:layout_width="match_parent"
    android:layout_height="match_parent"
    android:orientation="vertical" >

    <LinearLayout
        android:layout_width="match_parent"
        android:layout_height="wrap_content"
        android:orientation="horizontal" >

        <EditText
            android:id="@+id/etSearchText"
            android:layout_width="wrap_content"
            android:layout_height="wrap_content"
            android:text="bio"
            android:textSize="15sp"
            android:layout_weight="4"/>

        <Button
            android:id="@+id/button1"
            style="?android:attr/buttonStyleSmall"
            android:layout_width="wrap_content"
            android:layout_height="32dp"
            android:text="GO!"
            android:onClick="SearchDatabase"/>

    </LinearLayout>

    <LinearLayout
        android:id="@+id/searchframe"
        android:layout_width="fill_parent"
        android:layout_height="fill_parent"
        android:orientation="vertical" />

</LinearLayout>
```

2. `fragment_search.xml` - this layout describes what the search `Fragment` will look like. In this case, a `ListView` and a `TextView`. Note that the `ListView` must have its `android:id` set to `@android:id/list`. The `TextView` is used to display the text *NO DATA FOUND!* when no results are returned from the search. Note that this is automatic if you set the `TextView`'s `android:id` to `@android:id/empty`.

```xml
<?xml version="1.0" encoding="utf-8"?>
<LinearLayout xmlns:android="http://schemas.android.com/apk/res/android"
    android:layout_width="fill_parent"
    android:layout_height="fill_parent"
    android:orientation="vertical" >

    <ListView
        android:id="@android:id/list"
        android:layout_width="fill_parent"
        android:layout_height="match_parent"
        android:drawSelectorOnTop="false" >

    </ListView>

    <TextView
        android:id="@android:id/empty"
        android:layout_width="fill_parent"
        android:layout_height="match_parent"
```

```
                android:text="NO DATA FOUND!!" />

    </LinearLayout>
```

3. `MainActivity.java` - the only addition to this class is the handling of the click event for the menu item *Search*. In this case, we just inflate the `SearchActivity`.

```
case R.id.mSearch:
  Intent intentSearch = new Intent(MainActivity.this,SearchActivity.class);
  startActivity(intentSearch);
return true;
```

4. `SearchActivity.java` - this is the class that inflates the `activity_search.xml` layout file. Don't forget to add this to the `AndroidManifest.xml` file!

```
package com.example.equityyostocks;

import android.support.v7.app.ActionBarActivity;
import android.support.v4.app.FragmentManager;
import android.support.v4.app.FragmentTransaction;
import android.os.Bundle;
import android.view.View;
import android.widget.EditText;

public class SearchActivity extends ActionBarActivity {

  FragmentManager oFM;
  FragmentTransaction oFT;
  FragmentSearch oFC_SE;
  FragmentSearch oFC_SE_OLD=null;

  @Override
   protected void onCreate(Bundle savedInstanceState) {
     super.onCreate(savedInstanceState);
     setContentView(R.layout.activity_search);

     //Access the FragmentManager.
     oFM = (FragmentManager) getSupportFragmentManager();

  }

  //Handle the onClick event for the Go! button!
  public void SearchDatabase(View view) {

    //Set up a Bundle for use with the search fragment.
    Bundle oBundleArgs = new Bundle();

    //Pull the text in the TextView tvSearchText
    EditText oET = (EditText) findViewById(R.id.etSearchText);
    String sSearchText = oET.getText().toString().toUpperCase();

    //Add the text to the Bundle
    oBundleArgs.putString("SEARCHTEXT", sSearchText);

    //Begin a fragment transaction
    oFT = oFM.beginTransaction();

    //Add a custom animation
    oFT.setCustomAnimations(R.anim.my_slide_in_from_right,
                            R.anim.my_slide_out_to_right);

    //Instantiate the search fragment.
    oFC_SE = new FragmentSearch();
```

```
  //Add the Bundle to oFC_SE
  oFC_SE.setArguments(oBundleArgs);

  //Remove previous fragment, if it exists.
  if (oFC_SE_OLD != null) {
   oFT.remove(oFC_SE_OLD);
   oFC_SE_OLD=oFC_SE;
   oFT.addToBackStack(null);
  }
  else if (oFC_SE_OLD == null) {
   oFC_SE_OLD=oFC_SE;
  }

  //Add in the fragments
  oFT.add(R.id.searchframe,oFC_SE);

  //Commit the change.
  oFT.commit();

  //Execute Pending Transactions
  oFM.executePendingTransactions();

 }


 //Close the SearchActivity.
 public void CloseSearchActivity() {
  this.finish();
 }

}
```

5. `FragmentSearch.java` - this class handles searching the database based on the search criteria in the `EditText` as well as populating the `ListFragment` with results.

```
package com.example.equityyostocks;

import android.view.LayoutInflater;
import android.view.View;
import android.view.ViewGroup;
import android.os.Bundle;
import android.support.v4.app.DialogFragment;
import android.support.v4.app.ListFragment;
import android.support.v4.widget.SimpleCursorAdapter;
import android.app.AlertDialog;
import android.app.Dialog;
import android.content.Context;
import android.content.DialogInterface;
import android.database.Cursor;
import android.database.sqlite.SQLiteDatabase;

public class FragmentSearch extends ListFragment {

 View oFragmentSearch;
 String sSearchText="-";

 //Pull the arguments from the setArguments Bundle.
 @Override
 public void onCreate(Bundle savedInstanceState) {
  super.onCreate(savedInstanceState);

  sSearchText = getArguments() != null ?
                    getArguments().getString("SEARCHTEXT") : "-";

  if (sSearchText.length() == 0) {
```

549

```
  sSearchText="-";
 }

}

//Display the fragment_search fragment and populate it.
@Override
public View onCreateView(LayoutInflater inflater,
                         ViewGroup container,
                         Bundle savedInstanceState) {

  //Create a View object from fragment_main
  oFragmentSearch = inflater.inflate(R.layout.fragment_search,
                                     container,
                                     false);

  //Populate the ListView based on the search criteria.
  SimpleCursorAdapter adapter=populateListView(sSearchText);

  //Set the list adapter here.
  setListAdapter(adapter);

  return oFragmentSearch;
}

//Populate the ListFragment by providing the appropriate adapter.
public SimpleCursorAdapter populateListView(String sSearchText) {

  EquityYoDatabaseAccess equityYoDB = new
            EquityYoDatabaseAccess(getActivity().getApplicationContext());
  SQLiteDatabase dbEquityYoDB = equityYoDB.getReadableDatabase();
  String sSQLClause="";
  SimpleCursorAdapter adapter;

  //Set up the SQL clause based on the iSectorKey
  if (sSearchText.equals("-") || sSearchText.trim().length() == 0) {


    //Display a alert indicating that no usable search criteria was entered.
    DialogFragment oAlertNoDataFragment =
                   FragmentAlertSearchCriteriaControl.newInstance();
    oAlertNoDataFragment.show(getFragmentManager(), "dialog");


    //Set the adapter to null.
    adapter=null;
  }
  else {
    sSQLClause="SELECT _id,Symbol || '/' || sName AS SYMBOL_SNAME FROM
vwEquityYoSymbolMasterSTOCKS WHERE sName LIKE '%" + sSearchText + "%' ORDER BY
1";

    //Obtain a cursor for the query.
    Cursor oCSR = dbEquityYoDB.rawQuery(sSQLClause, null);
    oCSR.moveToFirst();

    //Set up a cursor adapter for the ListView using oCSR
    adapter = new SimpleCursorAdapter(oFragmentSearch.getContext(),
                 android.R.layout.simple_list_item_1,
                 oCSR,
                 new String[] {"SYMBOL_SNAME"},
                 new int[] {android.R.id.text1},0);

  }

  return adapter;
}

//Class to handle the no search results alert.
```
550

```java
public static class FragmentAlertSearchCriteriaControl extends DialogFragment
{

  public static FragmentAlertSearchCriteriaControl newInstance() {
   FragmentAlertSearchCriteriaControl oAlert = new
                                    FragmentAlertSearchCriteriaControl();
      return oAlert;
  }

  @Override
  public Dialog onCreateDialog(Bundle savedInstanceState) {

   //Set up several string variables.
   String sTitle = "Enter in your search criteria!";
   String sSearchAgain = "Search Again";
   String sGoHome = "Go Home";

   //Create an Alert Dialog object via the Builder.
   AlertDialog.Builder oADB = new AlertDialog.Builder(getActivity());

   //Set the title of the AlertDialog
   oADB.setTitle(sTitle);

   //Set the icon to the app icon.
   oADB.setIcon(R.drawable.ic_launcher);

   //Create a listener associated with the Search Again click.
   DialogInterface.OnClickListener onClickSearchAgainListener = new
                                    DialogInterface.OnClickListener() {

    //Close the dialog box itself when user clicks Search Again.
    @Override
    public void onClick(DialogInterface dialog, int whichButton) {
     dialog.cancel(); //Close this dialog box
    }

   };

   //Associate the setNegativeButton with the listener above.
   oADB.setNegativeButton(sSearchAgain, onClickSearchAgainListener);

   //Create a listener associated with the Go Home click.
   DialogInterface.OnClickListener onClickGoHomeListener = new
                                    DialogInterface.OnClickListener() {

    //Close the SearcActivity when user clicks Go Home.
    @Override
    public void onClick(DialogInterface dialog, int whichButton) {
     ((SearchActivity)getActivity()).CloseSearchActivity();
    }

   };

   //Associate the setNegativeButton with the listener above.
   oADB.setPositiveButton(sGoHome, onClickGoHomeListener);

   //Create the AlertDialog and return it.
   return oADB.create();

  }

 }

}
```

Now, when a user clicks on the *Search* menu item on the `ActionBar`, `SearchActivity` is called via `startActivity()` which then inflates `activity_search.xml` displaying the `EditText` as well as the Go! `Button`.

Note that the `onClick` event for the Go! button is wired up to the `SearchDatabase` method within the `SearchActivity` class. Similar to Extended Example #1, `SearchActivity` instantiates the `FragmentManager`, `FragmentTranaction` as well as a `Bundle` to hold the user's search criteria. Here is the code within `SearchDatabase`:

```
//Set up a Bundle for use with the search fragment.
Bundle oBundleArgs = new Bundle();

//Pull the text in the TextView tvSearchText
EditText oET = (EditText) findViewById(R.id.etSearchText);
String sSearchText = oET.getText().toString().toUpperCase();

//Add the text to the Bundle
oBundleArgs.putString("SEARCHTEXT", sSearchText);

//Begin a fragment transaction
oFT = oFM.beginTransaction();

//Add a custom animation
oFT.setCustomAnimations(R.anim.my_slide_in_from_right,
                        R.anim.my_slide_out_to_right);

//Instantiate the search fragment.
oFC_SE = new FragmentSearch();

//Add the Bundle to oFC_SE
oFC_SE.setArguments(oBundleArgs);

//Remove previous fragment, if it exists.
if (oFC_SE_OLD != null) {
 oFT.remove(oFC_SE_OLD);
 oFC_SE_OLD=oFC_SE;
 oFT.addToBackStack(null);
}
else if (oFC_SE_OLD == null) {
 oFC_SE_OLD=oFC_SE;
}

//Add in the fragments
oFT.add(R.id.searchframe,oFC_SE);

//Commit the change.
oFT.commit();

//Execute Pending Transactions
oFM.executePendingTransactions();
```

Note that we instantiate the `FragmentSearch` class, create a `Bundle`, and place the search criteria into it. Next, we begin a transaction, set two custom animations to it, add the fragment into the `LinearLayout searchframe`, and then `commit()` the transaction. Note that I am saving the old fragment so that I can remove it from the fragment if the user performs another search. Also, I am conditionally calling `addToBackStack()` in order to avoid saving the blank search fragment to the back stack. This will prevent the user from seeing a blank screen while hitting the back button.

So, let's take a look at the `FragmentSearch` class. Take note that this class extends the `ListFragment` class. Similar to the fragments in Extended Example #1, I pull out the search criteria argument within the `onCreate()` method. In the `onCreateView()` method, I inflate the fragment containing the `ListView` (`fragment_search.xml`), populate the `ListView` by calling the `populateListView()` method, and set the adapter of the `ListView` using `setListAdapter()`. Take note that when using `ListActivity` you use `setAdapter()` and when using `ListFragment` you use `setListAdapter()`.

Note that the `populateListView()` method returns a `SimpleCursorAdapter` based on the cursor used to query the database.

Now, if the user enters no search criteria, an `AlertDialog` is displayed by calling the following code:

```
//Display a DialogFragment indicating that no usable search criteria was entered.
DialogFragment oAlertNoDataFragment =
                            FragmentAlertSearchCriteriaControl.newInstance();
oAlertNoDataFragment.show(getFragmentManager(), "dialog");
```

The class `FragmentAlertSearchCriteriaControl`, besides being a very long class name, is also responsible for setting up the alert dialog. Note that the `show()` method, similar to displaying a `Toast`, must be used to display the alert dialog. Be aware that the `FragmentAlertSearchCriteriaControl` is located within the `FragmentSearch` class and not `MainActivity`!

In order to create an `AlertDialog`, we use the `AlertDialog.Builder` class. We start off by instantiating an `AlertDialog.Builder` object:

```
//Create an Alert Dialog object via the Builder.
AlertDialog.Builder oADB = new AlertDialog.Builder(getActivity());
```

Next, I create three text strings used to hold the title text, the Search Again text, and the Go Home text:

```
String sTitle = "Enter in your search criteria!";
String sSearchAgain = "Search Again";
String sGoHome = "Go Home";
```

Next, I set the title as well as the icon displayed when the `AlertDialog` is displayed. Note that I am using the icon associated with the app itself.

```
//Set the title of the AlertDialog
oADB.setTitle(sTitle);

//Set the icon to the app icon.
oADB.setIcon(R.drawable.ic_launcher);
```

Now, the `AlertDialog` allows for several buttons (termed positive, neutral, and negative) as well as a list of single or multiple choices items. Note that you can also use the `setView()` method to display your own homemade `View`. In our example, we display two buttons, one to display *Search Again* and the other to display *Go Home*. The *Search Again* button's click event is handled via the `setNegativeButton()` method and the *Go Home* button's click event is set via the `setPositiveButton()` method. (Note that the order the buttons display is negative on the left, neutral in the center, and positive on the right.) In order to use these methods, you need to code two listeners, one for *Search Again* and one for

Go Home. Here is the code to create the listeners as well as wire up the click events:

```
//Create a listener associated with the Search Again click.
DialogInterface.OnClickListener onClickSearchAgainListener = new
                                       DialogInterface.OnClickListener() {

 //Close the dialog box itself when user clicks Search Again.
 @Override
 public void onClick(DialogInterface dialog, int whichButton) {
  dialog.cancel(); //Close this dialog box
 }

};

//Associate the setNegativeButton with the listener above.
oADB.setNegativeButton(sSearchAgain, onClickSearchAgainListener);

//Create a listener associated with the Go Home click.
DialogInterface.OnClickListener onClickGoHomeListener = new
                                       DialogInterface.OnClickListener() {

 //Close the SearcActivity when user clicks Go Home.
 @Override
 public void onClick(DialogInterface dialog, int whichButton) {
   ((SearchActivity)getActivity()).CloseSearchActivity();
 }

};

//Associate the setNegativeButton with the listener above.
ADB.setPositiveButton(sGoHome, onClickGoHomeListener);
```

Take note the when the user clicks *Search Again*, the `dialog.cancel()` method is called dismissing the `AlertDialog` and allowing the user to search the database again. Also, note that when the user clicks *Go Home*, the `CloseSearchActivity()` method, located in the parent activity (i.e., `SearchActivity`), is called dismissing the `AlertDialog` as well as closing the `SearchActivity`. Here is what `CloseSearchActivity()` contains:

```
//Close the SearchActivity.
public void CloseSearchActivity() {
 this.finish();
}
```

Summary

In this chapter, we learned a little bit about fragments. While this chapter is definitely not the last word on fragments, I hope that I've given you enough information to start using fragments in your apps.

Chapter 31: Working with `WebView` and `WebViewClient`

Overview

In this chapter, we describe both the `WebView` and the `WebViewClient` widgets, both of which are responsible for displaying a web page. In our Android app, equityYo, we use a `WebView` to easily display the onboard User's Guide:

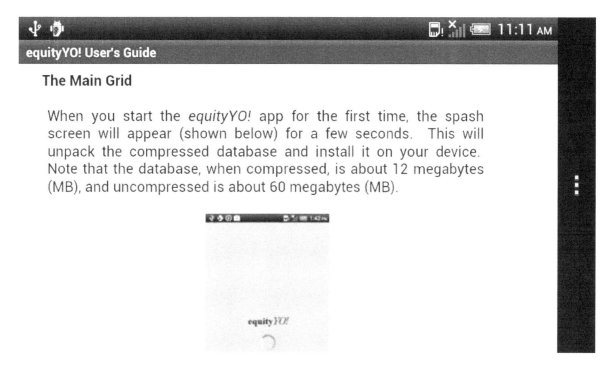

We also modify the corresponding `WebViewClient` to display a progress bar while the webpage is being loaded into the browser (if you can't tell by now, I have a tendency to blather on a bit...same with the User's Guide!).

There are two steps to perform to display a webpage using the `WebView` widget:

1. Drag-and-drop the `WebView` widget to your GUI. This widget is located in the Composite section in the Palette on the Graphical Layout within Eclipse.
2. Wire up the `WebView` and `WebViewClient` within the `onCreate()` method of the corresponding activity.

We discuss each of these in turn below.

Step #1 - Add the `WebView` to the GUI

This is easy to do: drag-and-drop the `WebView` widget to your GUI. This widget is located in the Composite section in the Palette on the Graphical Layout within Eclipse. Alternately, you can just code the XML yourself:

```
<RelativeLayout xmlns:android="http://schemas.android.com/apk/res/android"
                xmlns:tools="http://schemas.android.com/tools"
                android:layout_width="match_parent"
                android:layout_height="match_parent" >

    <WebView
```

```
            android:id="@+id/webViewUsersGuide"
            android:layout_width="fill_parent"
            android:layout_height="fill_parent"
            android:layout_alignParentLeft="true"
            android:layout_alignParentTop="true" />

</RelativeLayout>
```

Step #2 - Wire up the `WebView` and the `WebViewClient`

The next step is to code the `WebView` and the `WebViewClient` within the `onCreate()` method, or a method of your choosing:

```
public class UsersGuideActivity extends Activity {

 private WebView oWVMD;
 private ProgressDialog progressDialog;

 @Override
 public void onCreate(Bundle savedInstanceState) {
  super.onCreate(savedInstanceState);
  setContentView(R.layout.activity_users_guide);

  progressDialog = ProgressDialog.show(this, "Loading", "...one moment...");
  oWVMD = (WebView) findViewById(R.id.webViewUsersGuide);

  //Display a progress dialog while the webpage is being loaded into the browser.
  oWVMD.setWebViewClient(new WebViewClient() {

   @Override
   public boolean shouldOverrideUrlLoading(WebView view, String url) {
    super.shouldOverrideUrlLoading(view, url);
    oWVMD.loadUrl(url);
    return true;
   }

   @Override
   public void onPageFinished(WebView view, String url) {
    super.onPageFinished(view, url);
    if (progressDialog.isShowing()) {
     progressDialog.dismiss();
    }
   }

  });
  oWVMD.loadUrl("file:///android_asset/eyug.html");
 }

}
```

Note that we gain the `WebView` object from the `findViewById()` method. We then modify the `WebViewClient` to load the webpage and dismiss the progress dialog once the loading is complete.

Note that you still need to execute the `loadUrl()` method to start loading the `WebView`. As you see above, I am loading the onboard User's Guide for equityYO (`eyug.html`) using the `file://` scheme, but you can just as easily use `http://`.

One comment about the URL within the `loadUrl()` method above: you can place any additional asset, such as an HTML file or text file, within the \assets folder in

556

Eclipse for your app and you can use `file:///android_asset/`*name-of-your-file* to access it.

Chapter 32: Styles and Themes

Overview

In this chapter, we discuss styles and themes. For those familiar with cascading style sheets in HTML, you'll immediately see a correspondence.

Each view has several properties allowing you to modify a stylistic aspect of it. For example, the `TextView` view has the `android:textSize` property allowing you to alter the size of the text being displayed. We've worked with this property before several times. Each view's stylistic properties are listed in the XML section of the documentation.

A collection of properties used to modify the stylistic aspect of a **view** is called a *style*. A collection of properties used to modify the stylistic aspect of a specific **activity** or an entire **application** is called a *theme*. Clearly, styles and themes are two sides of the same coin. When you apply a theme to an application, it applies across all views and activities.

You can give names to your styles/themes and refer to them using either the `style=` attribute within the XML for views, or the `android:theme=` attribute within the manifest for an activity (within the `<activity>` tag) or the application (within the `<application>` tag).

Besides creating your own styles and themes, the Android SDK comes with its own styles and themes you can use. These are called *platform styles* and *platform themes*. I've placed a copy of both `styles.xml` and `themes.xml` in the appendix so you can peruse them.

Creating Your Own Style

In order to create your own style, gather all of the properties you want to apply to the view and place them in a resource file called `styles.xml` in the `res/values` folder in Project Explorer. Similar to other resource files we've worked with, `styles.xml` contains one or more `<style>` tags containing `<item>` tags associated with each property you want to modify. For example,

```xml
<resources>
 <style name="mystyle">
   <item name="android:layout_width">wrap_content</item>
   <item name="android:layout_height">fill_parent</item>
   <item name="android:textSize">25sp</item>
 </style>
</resources>
```

Here we create a style called `mystyle` containing several properties, one `<item>` tag for each one. The property is entered in the `name=` attribute. The value we want to set each property to is entered as the value of the `<item>` tag. To apply this style to your view, use the `style=` attribute for the view itself:

```xml
<TextView style="@style/mystyle"
          android:text="Hello World!" />
```

Note that the @-sign indicates a reference to a previously defined resource. Here `@style/mystyle` indicates to the Android system to look for a `<style>` tag with a `name=` attribute of `mystyle` which just happens to appear in our XML file `styles.xml`.

Modifying a Previously Defined Style of Yours

Once you create a style, you can use it as the base for your other styles. To do this, you add the name of your original style followed by a period followed by the name of the modified style. For example,

```
<resources>
 <style name="mystyle">
   <item name="android:layout_width">wrap_content</item>
   <item name="android:layout_height">fill_parent</item>
   <item name="android:textSize">25sp</item>
 </style>
 <style name="mystyle.puny">
   <item name="android:textSize">3sp</item>
 </style>
</resources>
```

Here we create a new style, called `mystyle.puny`, based on `mystyle`. The way we know that `mystyle.puny` is based on `mystyle` is because we specify the name of the original style followed by a period followed by an additional name. You can refer to this new style in the normal manner: `@style/mystyle.puny`.

Modifying an Android-Defined Style

Unlike styles of your own, in order to modify Android-defined styles, you need to use the `parent=` attribute. Now, if you look in Appendix E (in a file located on my website `www.sheepsqueezers.com`), you will see the following Android-defined style called `TextAppearance`:

```
<style name="TextAppearance">
  <item name="android:textColor">?textColorPrimary</item>
  <item name="android:textColorHighlight">?textColorHighlight</item>
  <item name="android:textColorHint">?textColorHint</item>
  <item name="android:textColorLink">?textColorLink</item>
  <item name="android:textSize">16sp</item>
  <item name="android:textStyle">normal</item>
</style>
```

If you wish to create your own style based on this Android-provided style, you can do something like the following:

```
<resources>
 <style name="mystyle">
   <item name="android:layout_width">wrap_content</item>
   <item name="android:layout_height">fill_parent</item>
   <item name="android:textSize">25sp</item>
 </style>
 <style name="mystyle.puny">
   <item name="android:textSize">3sp</item>
 </style>
 <style name="myTextAppearance" parent="@android:style/TextAppearance">
   <item name="android:textSize">14sp</item>
```

```
  </style>
 </resources>
```

Again, the @-sign means to pull in the Android-defined style called `TextAppearance`. So, this means that you do not have to live with Android's styles and can change them very easily.

As the previous section showed, you do not need to use the `parent=` attribute when defining new styles based on your own styles, just use the dot notation instead.

A Question about the Question Mark (?)

You probably noticed the use of the question mark (?) in the XML for the Android-defined style `TextAppearance` above. Unlike the @-sign which indicates an *item* within a resource file, the question mark indicates the *value* of the item. That is, if you like the `textSize` you've previously defined, you can refer to its value using the question mark. For example,

```
<resources>
 <style name="mystyle">
   <item name="myFavoriteTextSize">25sp</item>
   <item name="android:layout_width">wrap_content</item>
   <item name="android:layout_height">fill_parent</item>
   <item name="android:textSize">?myFavoriteTextSize</item>
 </style>
 <style name="mystyle.puny">
   <item name="android:textSize">3sp</item>
 </style>
 <style name="myTextAppearance" parent="@android:style/TextAppearance">
   <item name="android:textSize">14sp</item>
 </style>
 <style name="mystyle.huge">
   <item name="android:textSize">?myFavoriteTextSize</item>
 </style>
</resources>
```

In the `mystyle` style, I defined a completely new attribute called `myFavoriteTextSize` and set it to `25sp`. Then, below, I pull in its *value* by referring to it as `?myFavoriteTextSize`.

Now, you can do that for Android-provided items as well, but you will have to provide the package name in order to do that. You can find a full list of styles in the `attrs.xml` file (which is way too big to reproduce in the appendix!) and use those values in your styles:

```
<style name="mystyle.huge">
 <item name="android:textSize">?android:attr/windowTitleSize</item>
</style>
```

Applying Styles to Activities and/or Applications: Themes

Now, you can bring together all of your properties and their values and place them in one style called, say, `MyTheme`. In order to apply this theme to an activity, within the manifest, place the `android:theme=` attribute on the `<activity>` tag:

```
<activity android:theme="@style/MyTheme"> ...
```

To apply your theme across an entire application, do a similar thing to the `<application>` tag:

```
<application android:theme="@style/MyTheme"> ...
```

Now, you can still refer to Android-defined themes and styles by using the `@android:style/style-name` syntax:

```
<activity android:theme="@android:style/Theme.Dialog"> ...
```

where `Theme.Dialog` is defined as follows:

```
<style name="Theme.Dialog">
 <item name="android:windowFrame">@null</item>
 <item name="android:windowTitleStyle">@android:style/DialogWindowTitle</item>
 <item name="android:windowBackground">@android:drawable/panel_background</item>
 <item name="android:windowIsFloating">true</item>
 <item name="android:windowContentOverlay">@null</item>
 <item name="android:windowAnimationStyle">@android:style/Animation.Dialog</item>
 <item name="android:windowSoftInputMode">stateUnspecified|adjustPan</item>
 <item name="android:windowCloseOnTouchOutside">
   @bool/config_closeDialogWhenTouchOutside
 </item>
 <item name="android:windowActionModeOverlay">true</item>
 <item name="android:colorBackgroundCacheHint">@null</item>
 <item name="textAppearance">@android:style/TextAppearance</item>
 <item name="textAppearanceInverse">@android:style/TextAppearance.Inverse</item>
 <item name="textColorPrimary">@android:color/primary_text_dark</item>
 <item name="textColorSecondary">@android:color/secondary_text_dark</item>
 <item name="textColorTertiary">@android:color/tertiary_text_dark</item>
 <item name="textColorPrimaryInverse">@android:color/primary_text_light</item>
 <item name="textColorSecondaryInverse">@android:color/secondary_text_light</item>
 <item name="textColorTertiaryInverse">@android:color/tertiary_text_light</item>
 <item name="textColorPrimaryDisableOnly">
   @android:color/primary_text_dark_disable_only
 </item>
 <item name="textColorPrimaryInverseDisableOnly">
   @android:color/primary_text_light_disable_only
 </item>
 <item name="textColorPrimaryNoDisable">@android:color/primary_text_dark_nodisable</item>
 <item name="textColorSecondaryNoDisable">
   @android:color/secondary_text_dark_nodisable
 </item>
 <item name="textColorPrimaryInverseNoDisable">
   @android:color/primary_text_light_nodisable
 </item>
 <item name="textColorSecondaryInverseNoDisable">
   @android:color/secondary_text_light_nodisable
 </item>
 <item name="textColorHint">@android:color/hint_foreground_dark</item>
 <item name="textColorHintInverse">@android:color/hint_foreground_light</item>
 <item name="textColorSearchUrl">@android:color/search_url_text</item>
 <item name="textAppearanceLarge">@android:style/TextAppearance.Large</item>
 <item name="textAppearanceMedium">@android:style/TextAppearance.Medium</item>
 <item name="textAppearanceSmall">@android:style/TextAppearance.Small</item>
 <item name="textAppearanceLargeInverse">@android:style/TextAppearance.Large.Inverse</item>
 <item name="textAppearanceMediumInverse">
   @android:style/TextAppearance.Medium.Inverse
 </item>
 <item name="textAppearanceSmallInverse">@android:style/TextAppearance.Small.Inverse</item>
 <item name="listPreferredItemPaddingLeft">10dip</item>
 <item name="listPreferredItemPaddingRight">10dip</item>
</style>
```

Note that when you create a new Android project in Eclipse, the default theme is called `AppTheme` which parents the `android:Theme.Light` theme in the `styles.xml` file:

```
<resources>

 <style name="AppTheme" parent="android:Theme.Light" />

</resources>
```

Now, in the `AndroidManifest.xml` file, you will see `AppTheme` referred to as the theme across the entire application:

```
<manifest xmlns:android="http://schemas.android.com/apk/res/android"
    package="com.example.andapp2"
    android:versionCode="1"
    android:versionName="1.0" >

    <uses-sdk
        android:minSdkVersion="8"
        android:targetSdkVersion="15" />

    <uses-permission
        android:name="com.example.andapp1.provider.permission.READ_PROVIDER"/>

    <application
        android:icon="@drawable/ic_launcher"
        android:label="@string/app_name"
        android:theme="@style/AppTheme" >
        <activity
            android:name=".MainActivity"
            android:label="@string/title_activity_main" >
            <intent-filter>
                <action android:name="android.intent.action.MAIN" />
                <category android:name="android.intent.category.LAUNCHER" />
            </intent-filter>
        </activity>
    </application>

</manifest>
```

When I changed `AppTheme` to `android:Theme` here is what our expandable list from the previous chapter looks like:

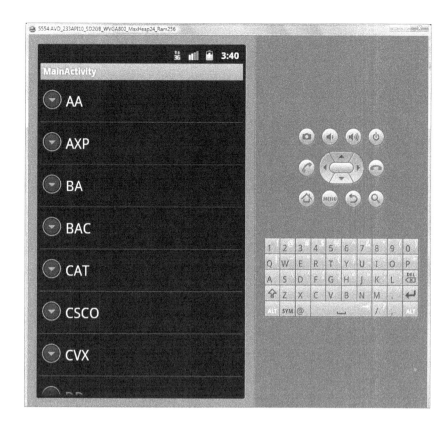

As you see, instead of a light background with dark colored text, we have a dark background with light colored text.

Applying Style Changes to Android-Provided Layouts

When you create your own activity's layout and drag-and-drop your views to the user-interface, you have complete control over your styles for each view within your layout. This means that you can change the properties whenever you want. This is not the case when using Android-provided layouts such as `simple_list_item_1`, `simple_expandable_list_item_1`, etc. These layouts seem to take control of the properties even if you modify the XML for the `ListView` widget in the layout yourself by adding additional properties. With that said, you can modify these properties in code. For example, in our example of the simple list item in the previous chapter, I decided that I want the divider line to be red instead of grey. Here is the code to do that:

```
//Get reference to the ListView
ListView oLV = (ListView) findViewById(android.R.id.list);

//Create a new ColorDrawable to represent our color.
ColorDrawable oRedAlert = new
        ColorDrawable(this.getResources().getColor(R.color.red_alert));

//Set the color of the ListView's divider to our color red_alert.
oLV.setDivider(oRedAlert);

//Since a color does not have an "intrinsic" height, unlike an image,
//you must set the height of the divider to 3 pixels.
oLV.setDividerHeight(3);
```

In the XML file `colors.xml`, I define the color `red_alert`:

```
<resources>
    <color name="red_alert">#FF0000</color>
</resources>
```

Here is what this looks like:

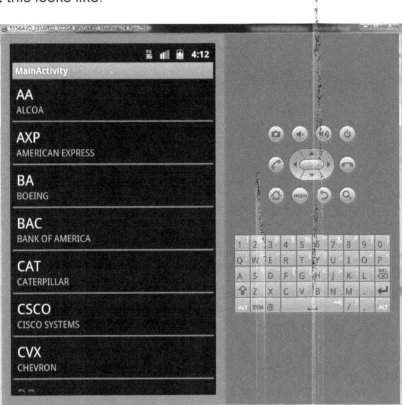

It is very important to note that the code above *must* follow the `setListAdapter()` method or it will not work!

Also, as a reminder, the following will **not** work when using Android-provided layouts (see the emboldened code below):

```
<LinearLayout xmlns:android="http://schemas.android.com/apk/res/android"
            android:layout_width="fill_parent"
            android:layout_height="fill_parent"
            android:orientation="vertical">

  <ListView android:layout_width="fill_parent"
          android:layout_height="fill_parent"
          android:divider="#FF0000"
          android:dividerHeight="3dp"
          android:id="@android:id/list">
  </ListView>

</LinearLayout>
```

But, if you add **your own** `ListView` to the layout, rather than using an Android-provided layout (provided by subclassing the `ListActivity` class), you can change the properties in the XML directly:

```
  <ListView android:layout_width="fill_parent"
          android:layout_height="fill_parent"
          android:divider="#FF0000"
          android:dividerHeight="3dp"
          android:entries="@array/list_entries"
```

564

```
                android:id="@+id/mylist">
    </ListView>
```

Summary

In this chapter, we learned about styles and themes and how they can be applied to views, activities or an entire application.

Chapter 33: Distributing Your Android Application

Overview

In this chapter, we take a breather from all of the coding to learn how to prepare our application for publication to Google's Android market, known as Google Play (play.google.com). Google Play is just one of several places you can peddle your wares. For example, Amazon has its own app store called the Amazon AppStore for Android.

If you are planning to sell your application, you must provide them with a bank checking account along with your tax identification number. In the United States, it's the Social Security Number (SSN). Outside the United States, you will have to provide your own country's tax identification number (for example, in the United Kingdom, it's the National Insurance Number).

Even if you aren't planning to sell your application, you will need to sign up with the appropriate marketplace to upload your app. We describe this in detail later on in the chapter.

Signing Your Application

Before you upload your application to any marketplace, you have to prepare it for publication. This entails signing your application; that is, creating a certificate that will be used to uniquely identify your application throughout its lifetime. Whenever you upload a new version of your application to the marketplace, it is this certificate that allows users of your app to feel secure that the update comes from you and not someone bent on evil and world domination.

Note that when you are developing an application, Eclipse automatically generates a *debugging certificate* that expires in short order unlike a *production certificate* generated for the publication of your application, which can be set to expire many decades from now. By default, the debugging certificate is called `debug.keystore` and, for Windows, is located in the `.android` folder of your personal user account (for me, it's `C:\Users\Scott\.android`).

There are two ways to generate a production certificate:

1. Using the command line program `keytool.exe` at the Windows command prompt. (I have placed the output of `keytool -help` in Appendix F in the external file located on my website www.sheepsqueezers.com).
2. Using the Create new keystore option when exporting your application.

To use `keytool`, follow these instructions:

1. Open up a Windows Command Prompt (Start...Run...`cmd.exe`...OK).
2. Enter the following code *on one line*:

```
keytool -genkeypair -v -keystore com_example_andapp1.keystore
        -alias com_example_andapp1 -keyalg RSA -keysize 2048 -validity 10000
```

Note that `com_example_andapp1.keystore` is the name of the file `keytool` will generate containing your private key and can be any name. The alias can be the same name without the `.keystore` extension. The validity option indicates the number of days that the certificate will be valid. Note that this number must be large enough to exceed the year 2033 which is a requirement of the Android marketplace. Here, I've set it to be 10000 days or about 27 years. Since these notes were written in 2012, adding 27 to 2012 yields the year 2039 which is greater than 2033. Woo-hoo!

3. Next, answer the questions as they are posed at the command line:
   a. `Enter keystore password` - Enter the password for the keystore (don't forget it!!)
   b. `What is your first and last name?` - Enter your first and last name
   c. `What is the name of your organizational unit?` - Since our application's package is `com.example.andapp1`, we would enter in `example.com`. Do the same for your organizational unit.
   d. `What is the name of your organization?` - Since our application's package is `com.example.andapp1`, we would enter in `example`. Do the same for your organization.
   e. `What is the name of your City or Locality?` - Enter the name of your city or locality.
   f. `What is the name of your State or Province?` - Enter the name of your two-letter state code or province.
   g. `What is the two-letter country code for this unit?` - Enter the two-letter country code such as `us` for United State, `uk` for United Kingdom, and so on.
   h. You will be shown the information above and asked if it is correct. Enter yes and hit the Enter key if it is correct.
   i. At this point, the software will generate the certificate and you will be asked to enter a key password. Hit the Enter key if you want the password to be the same as in Step 3a.
4. At this point, the file `com_example_andapp1.keystore` has been generated on disk. **SAVE THIS FILE TO A SAFE PLACE!! LOSING IT WILL CAUSE YOU UNTOLD AMOUNTS OF TROUBLE AND YOU'LL DEVELOP A CASE OF WHOOPING COUGH!! SAVE BOTH OF YOUR PASSWORDS AS WELL!!**
5. If you wish to see what `keytool` generated, you can use the `list` option from the command line:

```
keytool -list -keystore com_example_andapp1.keystore

C:\Users\Scott\.android>keytool -list -keystore com_example_andapp1.keystore
Enter keystore password:

Keystore type: JKS
Keystore provider: SUN

Your keystore contains 1 entry

com_example_andapp1, Oct 24, 2012, PrivateKeyEntry,
Certificate fingerprint (MD5): 86:F2:99:2D:28:31:BC:3F:1D:8F:19:7F:86:4E:D7:99
```

Make sure that you make several copies of the certificate file. If you lose it, you will never be able to update the application. You may want to consider a **secure** web service that allows you to upload files from your computer to the cloud. DVDs, CDs, flash drives and external drives are **all** good options (and I do mean ALL).

Now that the certificate has been generated, we will use it during the export process for your application.

Exporting Your Application

In order to publish your application, you have to run the Export tool from within Eclipse to generate the signed Android Package, or .apk, file which is then uploaded to the marketplace. To create the .apk, follow these instructions:

1. Within Eclipse, right-click on the name of the application within Project Explorer and click on the Export... popup menu item.
2. From the Select export destination dialog box, expand the Android folder, click on Export Android Application, and click on Next.

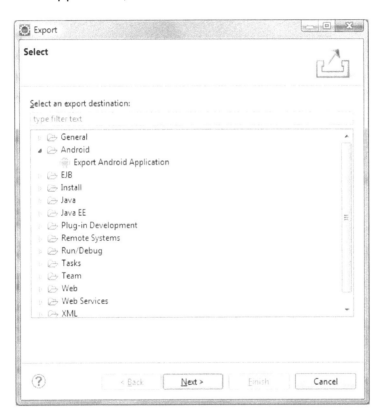

3. The Project Checks dialog box will appear. This dialog box will check if there are any errors in your project. If none is found, the text *No errors found. Click Next.* will appear. Click Next.

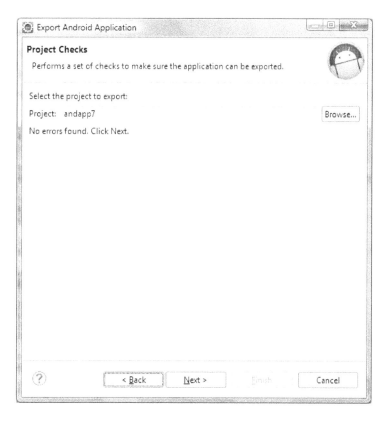

4. The Keystore Selection dialog box will appear. There are two options you can choose:
   a. If you have generated a keystore using `keytool.exe` as described above, ensure that the radio button to the left of the text *Use existing keystore* is checked. Click the Browse... button and locate the appropriate keystore. Fill in the password you set for your keystore and click Next.

b. If you have not generated a keystore, ensure that the radio button to the left of the text *Create new keystore* is checked. Since we already generated a keystore in the previous section, we will not outline this path. Follow the instructions if you do use this path.

5. When the Key Alias Selection dialog box appears, select the alias from the drop-down box and enter in the associated password. Click the Next button. As for Step 4b, click the *Create new key* radio button and follow the instructions.

6. When the Destination and key/certificate checks dialog box appears, enter the location and file name of the outgoing .apk file. Click Finish. See below and take note of the comments!

7. Once complete, the dialog box disappears indicating your `.apk` file has been generated and signed. Congratulations!!

Signing Up with Google Play

In this section, we show you in detail how to sign up with Google Play. You must have a Google E-Mail account to sign up with Google Play. If you don't have one, navigate your browser to Google and sign up for an email address.

To sign up with Google Play (including the $25.00 registration fee), follow these instructions:

1. Open your browser and naviagate to http://market.android.com/publish/signup
2. Sign in with your Google E-Mail username and password
3. Once signed in, you will be asked to perform three tasks. First, create a developer profile. Second, agree to the Developer Distribution Agreement; and, third, pay a $25.00 registration fee (or hand over your first born child). You will be asked to fill out the following information:
    a. Developer Name - this will appear to users under the name of your application
    b. Email Address - this is your Gmail e-mail address
    c. Website URL - this is the URL of your website
    d. Phone Number - this is your phone number including the plus-sign and country code.
    e. Email Updates - check the checkbox if you would like to receive email updates.
4. Click the Continue link
5. When the *Developer Distribution Agreement* is shown (see Appendix G), read it, click the checkbox to the left of the text *I agree and I am willing to associate*

571

my account registration with the Developer Distribution Agreement., and click the *I agree, Continue* link.

6. The next screen will ask you to pay a $25.00 registration fee. Click the Continue link to move on to the payment screen.
7. Review your order of $25.00 for your Developer Registration Fee. If you don't have a credit card associated with your Google account (which is very likely if you just signed up with one), then scroll down and fill in the credit card information section. Click Agree and Continue.
8. You will be sent to the Place Order Now page where you can review your payment of $25.00 for the Developer Registration Fee. In the Email Preferences section, check *Send me Google Wallet special offers, market research and newsletters*, *Keep my email address confidential* and *I want to receive promotional email from Google*. If everything is in order, click the Place Order Now button.
9. At this point, you have completed sign-up with Google Play and paid the registration fee. Woo-hoo! Click on the *Google Play Developer Site* link to go to the Android Developer Console. This page displays two very important things:
    a. The **Upload Application** button on the bottom right which allows you to upload an application
    b. The Setup Merchant Account link at the bottom which will allow you to sell your applications. To do this, you will need your bank account information as well as a Tax ID.

Uploading an Application to Google Play

After successfully signing up with Google Play and paying the $25.00 registration fee, as described in the previous section, you are now able to upload your application. Follow these instructions:

1. Log into the Android Developer Console by navigating your browser to https://play.google.com/apps/publish and signing in with your Gmail account information.
2. Ensure that you have signed and exported your application. Take note of its name and location on your hard-drive. Also, ensure that you are not using `com.example.` as the start of your package name; otherwise, Google Play will not allow it to be uploaded!
3. Click the Upload Application button.
4. When the Upload new APK screen appears, click the Browse button to locate your application's .apk file, then click the Upload button. Take note that if your application exceeds 50MB in size, you can add an expansion file. Click Add file and follow the instructions, if necessary.

Required: Select your application's APK

ott\.android\andapp7.apk [Browse...]   [Upload]

Optional: Add an expansion file
If your app exceeds the 50MB APK limit, you can add expansion files. Learn more

Add file

Close

5. After the upload is complete, you are sent to the Edit Application page. Fill out the information as required on the Product Detail tab:
   a. Screenshots - add at least two screen shots of your application. Image sizes are limited to 320 x 480, 480 x 800, 480 x 854, 1280 x 720, 1280 x 800, 24 bit PNG or JPEG (no alpha). Ensure these images are full bleed (that is, the image extends to the full size of the image dimensions) and that there is no border in the artwork. You may upload screenshots in landscape orientation. The thumbnails will appear to be rotated, but the actual images and their orientations will be preserved. Click on the Browse button to locate the image and then click on the Upload button to upload the image.
   b. High Resolution Application Icon - upload a hi-res application icon with a size of 512 x 512, 32 bit PNG or JPEG and a maximum file size of 1024 KB
   c. Promotional Graphic (optional) - add a promotional graphic with a size of 180w x 120h at 24 bits, PNG or JPEG (no alpha) and no border in art.
   d. Feature Graphic (optional) - add a feature graphic with a size of 1024 x 500 at 24 bit PNG or JPEG (no alpha). It will be downsized to mini or micro.
   e. Promotional Video (optional) - add a YouTube URL to your promotional video.
   f. Privacy Policy - either add a URL to your privacy policy or check *Not submitting a privacy policy URL at this time*.
   g. Marketing Opt-Out - check this box if you do not want Google to promote your application except in Google Play and in any Google-owned online or mobile properties. Understand that any changes to this preference may take sixty days to take effect.
   h. Language - add a language for your application
   i. Title - add a title for your application (30 characters maximum)
   j. Description - add a description for your application (4000 characters maximum)
   k. Recent Changes - add a description of recent changes to your application. This is pertinent when uploading an update to your application. (500 characters maximum)
   l. Promo Text - add promotional text (80 characters maximum)
   m. Application Type and Category - select a type of Applications or Games from the drop-down depending on the type of application you are uploading, then select an appropriate category for your application.
   n. Copy Protection - select Off. (This feature is deprecated.)
   o. Content Rating - select the appropriate content rating (High Maturity, Medium Maturity, Low Maturity, Everyone).

573

p. Pricing - Defaults to Free. Set up a Merchant Account at Google Checkout to charge for your product.

q. All Countries - select this checkbox if you would like your application to be available everywhere; otherwise, select the appropriate countries.

r. Supported Devices - this is automatically detected based on your Android Manifest

s. Under Contact Information, fill in your website, email address and phone number as contact information. The phone number is optional.

t. Enable Google Cloud Messaging Stats - Google Cloud Messaging (GCM) is a service that helps you to send data from your servers to your applications. Link your GCM sender ID with the app to enable stats. You can add up to three GCM sender IDs by providing a GCM API Key or C2DM Client Login Token.

u. Under Consent, ensure that both *This application meets Android Content Guidelines* and *I acknowledge that my software application may be subject to United States export laws, regardless of my location or nationality. I agree that I have complied with all such laws, including any requirements for software with encryption functions. I hereby certify that my application is authorized for export from the United States under these laws.* are checked.

6. On the APK Files tab, ensure that the correct file(s) are listed.

7. Click on the Publish button to publish your application to the Google Play market.

Now, if you've subsequently updated your app and want to upload the new version to the market, you must modify the `AndroidManifest.xml`'s `android:versionCode` and `android:versionName` attributes first; otherwise, Google Play will reject your update thinking it's the original version. Also, if you are using ReadyState's `SQLiteAssetHelper` class (as described in *Chapter 15, Working with the SQLite Database*), don't forget to update the `DATABASE_VERSION` attribute in order to have your latest database loaded onto the device assuming you are calling the `setForcedUpgradeVersion(DATABASE_VERSION);` method.

Making Money Selling Your Applications on Google Play

After successfully uploading your application to Google Play and setting the price of your application to something other than free (see Step 5p in the previous section), you may wonder how you will be paid. You need to set up a Merchant Account in order for any sales to be recorded and, in the United States, a 1099 Form to be issued to you at the end of the year for tax purposes. To set up a Merchant Account, navigate your browser to the Google Play Developer Site and click on the Setup Merchant Account link at the bottom of the page. You will need to have a checking account number as well as your Social Security Number (SSN) in order to set up the merchant account. Once completed, each time someone downloads your application, you will receive that amount in your checking account.

Note that you may want to set up a checking account that is completely separate from your normal accounts, such as your day-to-day savings and checking accounts. This is just paranoia on my part, but better to be safe than sorry. I don't necessarily mean that you have to open up a new account at a completely separate bank, but just a new account number at your current bank will probably suffice.

Finally, be aware that when you charge for applications, the number of downloads drops drastically. People love free! However, if you have a killer app, then go forth and charge for it! If you decide to leave your application free, then there are several other ways to monetize your efforts. For example, you can display Google ads in your app, or you can have a series of links to, say, Amazon that if clicked on and purchased you will receive a portion of the sales charge. Think about it.

Summary

In this chapter, we learned about how to deploy our application as well as monetize your efforts. All of your hard work can really pay off, but don't get your hopes up too much. ☺

www.ingramcontent.com/pod-product-compliance
Lightning Source LLC
Chambersburg PA
CBHW080131060326
40689CB00018B/3747

separate bank, but just a new account number at your current bank will probably suffice.

Finally, be aware that when you charge for applications, the number of downloads drops drastically. People love free! However, if you have a killer app, then go forth and charge for it! If you decide to leave your application free, then there are several other ways to monetize your efforts. For example, you can display Google ads in your app, or you can have a series of links to, say, Amazon that if clicked on and purchased you will receive a portion of the sales charge. Think about it.

Summary

In this chapter, we learned about how to deploy our application as well as monetize your efforts. All of your hard work can really pay off, but don't get your hopes up too much. ☺

www.ingramcontent.com/pod-product-compliance
Lightning Source LLC
Chambersburg PA
CBHW080131060326
40689CB00018B/3747